Nineteenth-Century Music

California Studies in 19th Century Music
JOSEPH KERMAN, *General Editor*

CARL DAHLHAUS

Nineteenth-Century Music

English translation by J. Bradford Robinson

University of California Press / *Berkeley, Los Angeles*

The publisher wishes to acknowledge with gratitude
the gift from Gordon P. Getty and Ann G. Getty
in support of this book.

Translated from the German *Die Musik des 19.
Jahrhunderts* (Neues Handbuch der Musikwissenschaft,
Volume 6), Akademische Verlagsgesellschaft
Athenaion, Wiesbaden, 1980. German publication
in collaboration with Laaber-Verlag Dr. Henning
Müller-Buscher, Laaber.

University of California Press
Berkeley and Los Angeles, California
© 1989 by
The Regents of the University of California
Printed in the United States of America
1 2 3 4 5 6 7 8 9

Library of Congress Cataloging-in-Publication Data

Dahlhaus, Carl, 1928–
    [Musik des 19. Jahrhunderts. English]
    Nineteenth-century music / Carl Dahlhaus ; English
translation by J. Bradford Robinson.
        p. cm.—(California studies in 19th century music ; 5)
    Translation of: Die Musik des 19. Jahrhunderts.
    Includes bibliographies and index.
    ISBN 0-520-05291-9
    1. Music—19th century—History and criticism.   I. Title.
II. Series.
ML196.D2513 1989
780′.903′4—dc19   88-15472

Contents

List of Illustrations

CHAPTER ONE

Introduction

The Nineteenth Century as Past and Present

As a period in music history, the nineteenth century extends from Beethoven's late works, Rossini's operas, and Schubert's lieder to Schönberg's "emancipation of dissonance" and the complementary rejection of "modernism" brought about by Richard Strauss in *Der Rosenkavalier*. The fact that this period fits comfortably within the years 1814 and 1914—years whose significance derives in the main from political history—is neither a meaningless accident nor a correspondence that invites profound historiosophical conclusions. Heinrich Heine felt that Rossini's operas embodied the spirit of the Restoration, and it is a journalistic cliché that Schönberg's assault on musical tradition in his post-1908 atonal works prefigured the crumbling of sociopolitical traditions in our own age of world wars. We, however, can accept both of these claims and nevertheless maintain that it is methodologically questionable to make political and social history the main pillars of music historiography. "Relative autonomy"—which even Marxists concede a place in the "superstructure"—enables us to emphasize connections within music history itself. As a result, the problem we face when we write music history resides not in finding musical documents to illustrate social structures and processes, but rather in establishing a relation between the aesthetic and the historical substance of works of music. Nor need we enter the debate as to which arbiters are final or imperative when we link the history of composition with intellectual history on the one hand, and with social and economic history on the other. All we need to do is to sketch, without going back to first causes, the contextual system that joins the structures and processes of these three branches of history.

Accordingly, we should not belabor the point that "watershed years" in music history and political history seem to coincide. By the same token, however, music historians have obviously failed to reach a satisfactory consensus about the divisions within music history itself. Some, like Georg Knepler, feel that the "eighteenth century" ended in 1789 with the French Revolution, like a musical ancien régime. Others, such as Guido Adler, see a Viennese Classic period extending to 1812 as apart from a "nineteenth century" that may be termed an age of "romanticism." Still others, among them Thrasybulos Georgiades and Friedrich Blume, extend the Viennese Classic period far enough into the nineteenth century to encompass Beethoven's late works and Schubert's entire oeuvre, thereby postponing the "watershed year" to 1830 and Berlioz's *Symphonie fantastique,* whose origins can then be linked to the July Revolution of that year in Paris. Yet all of these claims are equally suspect.

If the beginning of this age which, metaphorically if not chronologically, we call the "nineteenth century" is contested, so is its end. We might take 1889, the year of Strauss's *Don Juan* and Mahler's First Symphony, as a music-historical juncture coinciding with a similar break in political history whose significance has been underscored by the English historian Geoffrey Barraclough. Nor would it be farfetched to maintain that the "modernist period," as Hermann Bahr called the years following 1889, includes expressionism, and thus did not end until the outset of the "twenties"—or, more specifically, in 1924.

All the same, it need not be taken as a sign of desperation—a compulsion to draw some sort of boundary, even with a nagging conscience—when the author of a book on the "nineteenth century" in social, intellectual, and compositional history chooses to single out the years 1814 and 1914 as historical junctures. On the contrary, any historian interested in establishing connections will naturally gravitate toward the emergence and crystallization of the new rather than the demise and disintegration of the old, which always follows after a certain time lag. Nor can it be denied that Beethoven and Rossini—the musical duumvirate of 1814—cast their shadows over the "nineteenth century," just as Schönberg's *Erwartung* (1909) and Stravinsky's *Le sacre du printemps* (1913) mark the advent of the "twentieth century," when avant-gardism became the criterion for winnowing the essential from the inessential in music.

Justified as we may be in treating the "nineteenth century" as the period between the Viennese Classics and modern music, we fall into difficulties the moment we shift from the chronological to the stylistic aspect of this concept. Namely, it forces us to consign to the "nineteenth century" the late works of Strauss and Pfitzner, which were written during the age of modern music. It is not immediately apparent from works such as Pfitzner's C#-minor Quartet (1925) or Strauss's *Capriccio* (1942) that historical noncontemporaneity must necessarily betoken a divergent aesthetic. Nor, for the moment, is there any way of telling when the tradition undermined by Schönberg's emancipation of dissonance became irrevocably hollow and devoid of aesthetic meaning. To put it paradoxically, the end of the "nineteenth century" in music is impossible to date.

Any history of music that attempts to reconstruct part of the past as a structural, aesthetic, and social reality, rather than merely collecting major works in an imaginary museum, must deal not only with the history of composition but with the history of reception as well. Mahler's symphonies are no less a phenomenon of the turn of the century than of the 1960s and 1970s, and it would distort their place in music history if we neglected to analyze the overlap between postserial music and the Mahler renaissance. However blurred the question of what caused what, there is no denying that the Mahler wave, the interest in collage techniques, the discovery of Ives, and a parodistic bent toward the popular are all interlinked. The compositional currents of an age shed light on the way it interprets past music, and vice versa.

Thus, the subsequent history of nineteenth-century works is part of music history. Conversely, it is no less true that our view of the past is conditioned by a present whose everyday concert and operatic life comprises, in part, an uneasy and largely unarguable selection and interpretation of nineteenth-century music. The only way the historian can discover the past—meaning the musical legacy from the period between the Viennese Classics and modern music—is through the mediation of the present in which it manifests itself. A historical trait may gradually disengage itself from the aesthetic presence of past music, but it cannot rudely brush that presence aside.

Music historiography is incapable of reconstructing the way things really were. But neither should it be content merely to retrace the dim outlines left on the present by the past. The former is impossible, the latter inadequate. If, undaunted by the realization that past and present merge, we were to attempt a straightforward reconstruction of the past, we would already find ourselves in a quandary when trying to select the works that "belong to history." True, given sufficient data, we can objectively depict and analyze the reception history of works. However, the historical vantage point we select in order to draw our findings from the process of reception—that is, whether or not a work "belongs to history"—remains fundamentally arbitrary. No criterion has yet been discovered which would enable us to argue conclusively that the consensus of the German educated classes of 1830, rather than those of 1910 or 1960, is decisive for a historical assessment of Louis Spohr's *Faust* (1816) or *Jessonda* (1823). Historians with antiquarian proclivities will inevitably tend to emphasize contemporary judgments without realizing that this is no less "metaphysical" than the common, if tacit, practice of deciding whether a work does or does not belong to history by seeing whether it has or has not survived in the present-day repertoire. Strictly speaking, all we can conclude "empirically" is that opinions, assessments, and repertoires have changed.

Indeed, rather than adopting principles and pursuing them to first causes and ultimate consequences, historians are almost always eclectic. They place stress variously on the prestige a work enjoyed among contemporary listeners, on the accumulation of later judgments that make up a "tradition," on the influence it had on later works, its steadfastness in remaining in the repertoire, and finally its documentary value to the history of culture and its rating by the aesthetic and compositional standards that happen to apply today. Obviously, the eclectic approach is fraught with difficulties and contradictions; for the moment, however, it is all we have.

The history of nineteenth-century music presents itself as a panorama. If we proceed from today's opera, concert, and recording repertoire, this panorama bears scant resemblance to the picture which a contemporary living in Paris, Vienna, or Leipzig might have formed around 1830 or 1870. Nor is there an a priori way of determining whether the substance of the music has thereby been made recognizable or altered beyond recognition. At all events, reception history and aesthetic judgment inextricably intertwine. The French *opéra comique* of the Restoration period and the July Monarchy, the mainstay of the opera repertoire for over a century, has vanished in recent decades without so much as a raised eyebrow from critical observers, while the Italian opera seria of the same period, long presumed dead in every land but Italy, has witnessed an unexpected up-surge of popularity. These are among the caprices of reception history which clearly illustrate its tight-knit skein of aesthetic, compositional, and institutional factors. In today's opera system, singers are interchangeable across the globe; the repertoires of the stage and the recording industry interact with far-reaching consequences; and opera productions favor mammoth tableaux over fine-honed dialogue. This has removed the conditions of existence for *opéra comique*, which thrives on spoken dialogue, while opera seria, where singing counts for every-thing, has by grace of the system been given a hitherto unpredicted new lease on life.

However, these "extrinsic" motives bearing the imprint of our "technologi-cal age" are closely linked to alterations in aesthetic interests, which in turn har-bor consequences for the writing of history. It would, of course, be absurd to measure *opéra comique* against opera seria, or vice versa. However, there is no need to stress that audiences both inside and outside Italy have rediscovered the art of broad cantabile melody as "great," rather than merely "agreeable," at the same time that their fondness for terse song forms, whether sentimental or tren-chant, has receded. This fact is doubtless symptomatic of a change in musical consciousness which goes to the root of music historiography, all twisted compar-isons of unlike genres aside. The restoration of cantabile as a "central" category rather than one associated with "peripheral," "middlebrow," or "lowbrow" music means that all histories that lopsidedly took their aesthetic and compositional starting point from the "ideal types" of symphonic development, the (varied) strophic lied, and musicodramatical dialogue—that is, from Beethoven, Schu-bert, and Wagner—will have to be adjusted accordingly. The Italian notion of melody, once derided by Schumann as the "battle cry of the dilettantes," must be restored its historical rights if we wish to comprehend the musical poetics of Chopin and Liszt, of Meyerbeer and Berlioz—poetics that are unthinkable with-out the influence of Bellini. In other words, it may have been coincidence that, for reasons partly technological and institutional, musical "fashion" has re-claimed early nineteenth-century opera seria. But this coincidence gives us an opportunity which we should seize upon to expand our knowledge and revitalize our views of a formerly semidefunct category that, though familiar in the ab-stract, was long incapable of being experienced at first hand.

On the other hand, no historian who has adopted earlier views of *opéra com-ique* need feel daunted by its neglect in the current repertoire. If there is prog-ress in historiography, it rests on the dual possibility of retaining former insights even after their inner affinity to their objects has faded, and of gaining new insights that were closed to past generations from lack of an aesthetic relation to a period or genre. The self-aware historian is sustained by the—perhaps presumptuous—conviction that we can make use of the experiences of our own day without sharing its blind spots.

One of the far-reaching changes to which nineteenth-century music has been subjected by its reception in twentieth-century concert halls and opera houses is a shift in the system of genres considered representative: an era that seems in retrospect to have been an age of opera and instrumental music was, at the time when it was "the present," dominated by nontheatrical vocal genres from the lied to the cantata to the oratorio. This displacement of emphasis has forced once enormously prolific traditions into the background, not only of the repertoire but also of our historical awareness. The causes for this are both institutional and, in conjunction with this institutional factor, aesthetic.

From the beginning of the nineteenth century, nontheatrical vocal music was sustained largely by choral societies. These societies had by no means decreased in number by the end of the century—indeed, their number has probably increased in our own—but their significance and standing in present-day music culture has constantly declined. In the nineteenth century it was the bourgeois establishment that took the lead in this movement, whereas in recent decades choirs have been formed almost exclusively by students. Moreover, unlike the unforeseen spread of classical and romantic instrumental music in our century, the proportion of vocal music in our concert repertoire has declined so drastically that we might almost speak of a "collapse." Finally, the literary element in music culture—without which nineteenth-century vocal music would be inconceivable—has continuously receded in importance. In a word, the nineteenth-century tendency to view instrumental works as vocal music by supplying them with an imaginary text has given way to an opposite inclination to listen to vocal music instrumentally and ignore the text. (One of the earliest documents evincing this change is Arnold Schönberg's essay of 1911, "Das Verhältnis zum Text.")

For the moment, the institution of the lieder recital seems to be fully intact. However, it has long lacked its former basis in domestic song. This basis made the lied more accessible, even if it may also have restricted the repertoire by creating a circle of mutual dependencies between amateur and professional music-making, with the former being patterned after the latter and the latter propped up by the former.

Neglect of the text is a key feature of music aesthetics as practiced in our century, but its impact has been less severe and devastating in opera than in nontheatrical vocal music. Originally, opera librettos were read during the performance; later they served as preparatory reading for a performance, a role ultimately taken over by the opera guide or a quick glance at a plot summary a few minutes before the curtain goes up. Today, productions focus on striking tableaux instead of dialogue, thereby compensating for our lack of familiarity with the text: the literary has been supplanted, if not totally, by the scenic. Lieder and

Fig. 1 Gustav Philipp Zwinger: *Abendmusik im Freien,* 1807. Here chamber music—a trio for flute, violin, and guitar—takes the form of a garden concert, thereby illustrating the divertimento character of the genre. This transplantation of domestic music-making to an outdoor setting is also linked with the fondness of the romantic-classical age for masking art works as creations of nature, and for seeking pictorial backdrops appropriate to its interpretation of art as "second nature." (Nuremberg, Stadtbibliothek.)

oratorios, however, whose texts pass unnoticed or are even deliberately ignored, resemble a language whose meaning, at least in nineteenth-century terms, has largely fallen into obscurity. When we reduce vocal pieces to absolute music by listening to them "instrumentally"—thereby creating expectations regarding their thematic material, motivic elaboration, and formal articulation—we subject them to an aesthetic for which they were not intended and against which they most often fall short. Originally, in the nineteenth century, vocal music was in equal measure part of the literary and the musical culture of the educated classes, the "carrier strata" for culture; and these classes only gradually, under the influence of Beethoven's symphonies and string quartets, accustomed themselves to the notion that music by itself, without an explanatory and justifying text, might exercise an educational and cultural function comparable to literature. (No one in the nineteenth century could have foreseen that classical music would increase its audience a hundredfold while the readership for classical literature constantly shrank. Indeed, this would have been viewed as a symptom of decline.) Music was more a vehicle for the text than vice versa; in any event, the text was not an "extramusical ingredient" so much as part of "music itself," which, in accordance with the teachings of antiquity, was thought to consist not only of *harmonia* and *rhythmos* but also of *logos,* language. (The gradual establishment of the idea of absolute music in opposition to this view is one of the key historical processes in the music of the nineteenth century.)

Thus, not only does the historian of nineteenth-century music need to view his period as belonging to the past in the same or at least a similar way as the *trecento* or the Baroque, it is also impossible for him to ignore the presence of nineteenth-century music in today's concert and operatic repertoires. This strangely paradoxical relation forces him to intersperse his picture of past music with reflections from aesthetics and reception history, thereby turning some of the difficulties of writing history into topics in their own right. Unless we want to see works interpreted aesthetically as art or historically as documents, with no connection between the two, we must go beyond a simplistic dichotomy between past meaning and present meaning, as this would lead to exactly what we wish to avoid: a dichotomy between the artistic and the documentary value of works. Instead, we should bear in mind that historicality is just as much a factor in the way we hear music as aesthetic survival is part of belonging to history. A sharp cleavage between the history and the philosophy of art—that is, an art history which collapses works of music into documents or mere illustrations of a style, idea, or milieu, and an art philosophy that extracts artifacts from history in order to place them in an imaginary museum—gains the methodological advantage of clearly separating these disciplines, but only at the price of sweeping crucial problems of music historiography into the gap between history and aesthetics rather than solving them. A *history* of art which is not at the same time a history of *art*—that is, one that bypasses aesthetic interpretation in favor of documentary interpretation, or vice versa—falls wide of the goals of any music history with a claim to be more than a collage pieced together from composers' biographies, concert guides, and cultural-historical panoramas.

To divide a century by turning points coinciding with epoch-making events in political history is not to imply that music history merely reflects extramusical occurrences and chains of events. The question whether, and if so with what implications, we may speak of a connection between the July Revolution, the "demise of the age of art" proclaimed by Heine, the musical consequences of the deaths of Beethoven and Schubert, and the simultaneous and dramatic appearance of Chopin and Liszt, Berlioz and Meyerbeer, and Schumann and Mendelssohn, must remain open for the time being. However obscure this leaves the ultimate meaning of our concept of "watershed year," that is, one with a striking density of events, we are nevertheless unable to dispel the impression that 1830 was a watershed year in the history of music.

If the elements constituting a watershed year seem at first to stand disjointly side by side, the same applied to the works, events, and institutions that make up our picture of a period bound, say, by the years 1814 and 1830. To claim that Beethoven's retreat to the esoteric following the Congress of Vienna, and Rossini's triumph through the whole of Europe, stand in a sort of "complementary" relation to each other is, at first, meaningless. Nor is it at all conceivable how both Beethoven's late works and Rossini's operas relate to the romantic aesthetic of music, which began at the same time to take hold as a mode of musical cognition and perception. If we nevertheless attempt to turn this apparently accidental hodgepodge into a distinct configuration, we should do so not by trying to un-earth a common root for these phenomena—this would be mere fabrication—but rather by outlining a nexus into which these at first disparate occurrences, under the pressure of "contemporaneity," gradually coalesced. The debate whether Beethoven was a romantic composer will remain just as undecided as the controversy over the extent to which romanticism represents a spiritual efflu-vium permeating a large number of works, events, and trends in the period. What can be reconstructed, however, is the process whereby Beethoven's formal principles, Rossini's notion of melody, and the romantic aesthetic of music inter-twined in a way that, however obscure and distorted at times, nevertheless left an imprint on the entire century.

The Twin Styles

Raphael Georg Kiesewetter, a connoisseur of early music whom one could scarcely accuse of being brainlessly susceptible to the "Rossini craze," referred in his *Geschichte der europäisch-abendländischen oder unserer heutigen Musik* of 1834 to his own age as the "era of Beethoven and Rossini." As jarring as this combination may at first seem, we could find worse criteria for judging any music history that attempts to reconstruct the past in its own terms than to see whether it was able to find a vantage point that illuminates the reasons for Kiesewetter's claim.

No one denies that Italian opera of the nineteenth century represents a musical culture in its own aesthetic right and should not be measured against a concept of music drawn from Beethoven's symphonies or Wagner's music dra-mas. Still, this simple fact is seldom respected or pursued to ultimate conclusions. Apart from Italians, those who concede that Rossini's music is a product of ge-nius "in its fashion" almost always add the caveat that the "fashion" it represents merits an inferior rung in the musical hierarchy. In the final analysis, as a whole if not in detail, we measure Rossini with the wrong yardstick. And when we then speak of an "era of Beethoven and Rossini" we are referring more to their role in cultural history than to their importance in the history of music.

The difference between these "twin musical cultures" which Beethoven and Rossini stand for in Kiesewetter's thoroughly representative portrayal points to nothing less than a far-reaching rift in the concept of music, a rift that constitutes one of the fundamental musical facts of the nineteenth century. This distinction between opera and instrumental music—characteristically condensed by Verdi into a distinction between Italian opera and German instrumental music—was a major, if not the decisive, factor in the resultant duality of styles. The virtuosity of Paganini and Liszt was nourished on Rossini's notion of music, Wagner's mu-sic dramas on the aesthetic premises of Beethoven; and in order to underscore the significance and the historical import of this aesthetic dichotomy, we might speak of the former as an instrumental variant of operatic virtuosity and the

Fig. 2 Gédéon: *Il maestro Verdi.* Following the success of *Rigoletto, Il trovatore,* and *La traviata,* Verdi traveled to Paris in the hope of adding a cosmopolitan dimension to his reputation as a national composer by turning from opera seria to French grand opera. Among the educated classes, particularly in Germany but also in France, he encountered ambivalent feelings of mingled enthusiasm and repugnance. The praise granted him as a "man of the theater" was mixed with a note of condescension for a musical dramatist who thought nothing of turning to world literature (here Schiller's *Don Carlos*) but was at root a "hurdy-gurdy man" whose tunes were equally irresistible when performed in the street. (Frankfurt am Main, Stadt- und Universitätsbibliothek, Music and Theater Collection.)

latter as an operatic variant of Beethoven's symphonic style—distinctions fully in accord with both Wagner's and Verdi's understanding of history.

Beethoven, virtually in one fell swoop, claimed for music the strong concept of art, without which music would be unable to stand on a par with literature and the visual arts; Rossini, however, preserving in the nineteenth century a residue of the eighteenth-century spirit, was completely oblivious of this concept. Beethoven's symphonies represent inviolable musical "texts" whose meaning is to be deciphered with "exegetical" interpretations; a Rossini score, on the other hand, is a mere recipe for a performance, and it is the performance which forms the crucial aesthetic arbiter as the realization of a draft rather than an exegesis of a text. Rossini's musical thought hinged on the performance as an event, not on the work as a text passed down and from time to time given acoustical "explications"; and a score could be adapted to the changing conditions governing various theaters without violating its meaning. (Strictly speaking, there is no "authentic," "firsthand," or "final" version of a Rossini opera, a version from which others "deviated" under the force of circumstances. Instead, all we have is a series of instances standing side by side as equivalent realizations of a mutable conception, like a set of variations without a theme.) Thus, Rossini's docile attitude toward his singers was not evidence of aesthetic spinelessness, of a willingness to sacrifice the "authenticity" of his "text" to the "effect" of a performance, but rather a direct consequence of the view that the reality of music resides in its performance.

Anyone who adopts the premises of modern communication theory—the notion that music manifests itself in the interplay of written score, interpretation, and reception—will doubtless consider Rossini's concept of music "realistic." (That there were power struggles and attempts at subjugation among composers, singers, and audiences does not alter the presupposition that the sole point of reference among all these efforts was not an abstract idea of hegemony so much as the concrete, and hence ever-changing, circumstances of the individual performance.) Conversely, the categories that gradually took hold in the nineteenth-century reception of Beethoven seem symptomatic and indicative of a claim so unusual as to be almost defiant: however complete their domination of later music historiography, these categories more or less suspend the general rule in music history. That a composer who did not care a whit about Ignaz Schuppanzigh's "wretched fiddle," as Beethoven called it, could successfully demand that performances be a function of the text, rather than vice versa, can only have astonished early-nineteenth-century contemporaries; and even though this view is now taken for granted among the artistically well educated, historians ought to receive it in its original spirit. The new insight that Beethoven thrust upon the aesthetic consciousness of his age was that a musical text, like a literary or a philosophical text, harbors a meaning which is made manifest but not entirely subsumed in its acoustic presentation—that a musical creation can exist as an "art work of ideas" transcending its various interpretations.

One of the oddest facts in the early reception of Beethoven is a type of failure that was apparently new to the history of music. To say of one of the post–Op. 59 string quartets that, like some Rossini operas, its first performance was a "fiasco" would be a wrongheaded and inappropriate choice of terms, one that conceals the element of innovation that Beethoven introduced as a potential musical effect. Audiences were astonished, believing themselves at times to be victims of a weird or raucous joke, and at all events feeling that they understood little or nothing of what happened in Beethoven's work, even though they were supposed to understand it all. But even those who were disappointed felt basically that the acoustic phenomenon whose sense they were unable to grasp nevertheless harbored a meaning which, with sufficient effort, could be made intelligible. And the extent to which Beethoven's music was comprehended by his contemporaries was at least as essential to music history as the degree to which listeners realized in the first place that his music was capable of being "understood" like a work of literature or philosophy. The thought that music can be destined to be "understood" had probably arisen a few decades earlier, around 1800; but only in connection with the reception of Beethoven did it have a signi-

ficant impact on music history—a significance which then grew steadily throughout the nineteenth and twentieth centuries. There was nothing to "understand"
about the magic that emanated from Rossini's music; the emotions that
Beethoven's works engendered, however, were mingled with a challenge to decipher, in patient exertion, the meaning of what had taken place in the music.

The interpretation of Beethoven kindled a dispute between the "formalists," who sought to understand his music primarily by means of structural analysis, inching forward to the indwelling formal principle of a work, and the "content aestheticians," who attempted the same thing by discovering a "hidden
program." Unlike most controversies, these views at least have an underlying
premise in common—namely, that Beethoven's music conceals an "idea" which
must be grasped in order to do the work aesthetic justice. (A structural analysis
of Rossini's music which likewise searched for an underlying formal idea would
be no less superfluous and doomed to failure than a content analysis which
sought footholds outside broadly defined dramatic actions or effects.) To un-
earth a constellation of a few notes from which all the structures in a movement
by Beethoven supposedly derive, and to search for a subject or "poetic idea"
whose depiction or expression imparts sense and coherence to a piece of instrumental music: both are consequences of the belief that before one can come to
grips aesthetically with a work by Beethoven one must penetrate to a "second
level" of the music. Analysis and hermeneutics—or rather the "analytic principle" and the "hermeneutic principle"—arose in music history (or at least attained historical significance) simultaneously as opposite ways of unraveling the
difficulties posed by the reception of Beethoven. It is no coincidence that virtually all analytic methods of the nineteenth and twentieth centuries, from Adolf
Bernhard Marx's to Hugo Riemann's, from Heinrich Schenker's to Rudolf
Réti's, took their examples primarily from Beethoven. By the same token, the
hermeneutics of music—meaning the attempt to supply a unified context (in
extreme cases a narrative) for elements thought to depict emotions, characters,
or subjects in a piece of music—have again and again, from Schumann and
Wagner to Hermann Kretzschmar and Arnold Schering, taken as their starting
point the interpretation of Beethoven.

For the esoteric but historically influential listeners who took their notion of
music from Beethoven's oeuvre, any music such as Rossini's, which calls neither
for formal analysis nor for an interpretation of contents where these methods
could find a foothold, was suspected of being empty and meaningless, nothing
more than a momentary diversion. Even German criticism of Verdi in the latter
half of the century, whether laudatory or pejorative, had a deprecatory undertone for the "hurdy-gurdy man" regardless of the opinion of the work in question. Indeed, the arrogance encountered by Verdi as late as the 1920s was, at
root, worse than the sometimes spiteful polemics heaped on Wagner. (Like analysis and hermeneutics, music criticism—meaning specifically "higher criticism"
rather than mere reviews and grade-point assignments—was likewise one of the

ways of confronting music which found more congenial objects in Beethoven or Wagner than in Rossini or Verdi.)

Categories such as "overriding formal concept," theme, and thematic-motivic manipulation, on the one hand, and "stage emotion," melody, and melodic continuation, on the other, represent initial halting attempts to grasp, in grossly simplified form, the differences between these twin "cultures of music" in aesthetic and compositional terms which do not harbor built-in terminological prejudices. The categories must be defined narrowly enough to seem capable of illuminating the specific qualities in the musical thought of these two opposing nineteenth-century "factions." If Schumann could speak of melody as the "battle cry of the dilettantes," our primary task in discussing stylistic dualism is to obtain a firm grasp precisely of the rough, colloquial notion of melody as experienced by the audiences, not the sophisticated notion given by music theory.

The Gb-major Cavatina from Act 4 of Meyerbeer's *Les Huguenots* (1836) is one of those musical ideas in which audiences favoring the Franco-Italian opera of the nineteenth century saw their inborn dream of "melody" fulfilled (Ex. 1). Despite its brevity, a quality it shares with Beethoven's themes, it is thoroughly appropriate to call Meyerbeer's idea a theme: the four measures into which the musical substance has been compressed are self-sufficient, neither requiring a continuation nor even compelling development. The only expectation aroused by this idea is that it be repeated.

Example 1

The melody stands out in the duet as an isolated, self-contained entity. In this respect, as in its urge toward repetition, it likewise reflects the situation on stage. Amidst the tragic and horrifying proceedings whose machinery has now been set relentlessly in motion, Raoul and Valentine confess a love that is granted them only for a single instant—the instant compassed in music by the Gb-major Cavatina. The Cavatina's melodic gesture maintains its urgent eloquence without once overstepping the bounds of beautiful cantabile—beauty as expressible in song. But if the melodic idea expresses an isolated moment, its almost obsessive repetition and imitation convey an urge to cling against all odds to an instant destined to pass. (That Meyerbeer has made convincing dramaturgical use of a melodic technique shared by popular-song writers—the technique of focusing on a single idea and repeating it ad infinitum—is one of the factors that contribute to the aesthetic distinction of the Gb-major Cavatina.)

The idea is couched in a da capo form (A^1 B A^2), with the A^1 section being divided into a^1 a^2 b a^1. This form functions as an arrangement that imparts meaning to the ceaseless recurrence of the principal idea and vindicates it with interpolations that serve the purposes of interruption and preparation. The idea itself is the quintessence of *bel canto,* its cantabile being expressive and its expression being captured in song. Thus, the six measures of the *b* phrase form not only a declamatory foil but also an urgent transition to the return of the principal idea. The eighteen measures of section *B*—a diluted, less expressive, less cantabile variant of the principal idea in rapt, stammering declamation—merely form the backdrop for a recapitulation that seems to unleash a flood of repressed emotion. The meaning of the form, then, resides not in the development of theme but in the presentation of melody. Unlike thematic ideas, the aim of a melodic idea does not lie in the consequences to be drawn from it, thereby revealing its potential; instead, the interpolations that interrupt the actual melody merely function as vehicles to present that melody in a new light. With regard to the Cavatina's dramaturgical function, one might also use Stockhausen's term and speak of a musical *Momentform*: the isolated moment does not point to a larger context through which it receives its meaning; instead, the proceedings are, in a manner of speaking, compacted into the moment, which in its isolation represents the actual musical event. This is not to say that the context is irrelevant or a mere prop, as in a potpourri; but it is not a unified whole into which the particular slips into place so much as a backdrop from which the particular stands out.

Yet the Gb-major Cavatina, if its effect is to be comprehensible, must be related to the overall proceedings within the duet. In a formal-functional sense, it is, to use the Italian terminology, the cantabile to a cabaletta, that is, to a concluding section in quick tempo motivated dramaturgically by an intervening event, the tolling of the alarm bell on St. Bartholomew's Eve. Further, the Cavatina is preceded by an Allegro Maestoso and an Allegretto Moderato, and the contrasting rhythmic patterns of the duet's four sections produce a sense of logical succession, undergirding the form in the same manner as the combination of movements in a sonata. Finally, the duet as a whole falls under the shadow of the "Benediction of the Swords"—the gloomy, grandiose ensemble that immediately precedes it.

Thus, we have a dichotomy between a music culture which saw the essence of music in opera—more specifically in Italo-French opera—and the German classical tradition which, Mozart notwithstanding, stood for instrumental music in the European consciousness. This dichotomy extended to the very roots of the nineteenth-century concept of music, far transcending differences of genre or national style. And however fruitless it would be to compare Meyerbeer's Gb-major Cavatina with a sonata movement by Beethoven, it is crucial to get to the bottom of their dissimilarity if we wish to reveal the depth of the chasm separating these "twin cultures of music."

The D-minor Sonata, Op. 31, No. 2 (1801–2)—which Beethoven, in a cryptic comment to Anton Schindler, linked with Shakespeare's *The Tempest*—is one of the works in which the composer, around 1802, struck out on what he called a "new path." It is no coincidence that its first movement has been the object of countless analyses and has always been considered a paradigm of Beethoven's concept of form, a creation whose very irregularities illuminate the central problems of an art that is by nature "problematical." The movement opens in the manner of an improvised prelude (Ex. 2): neither the broken sixth chord in slow tempo nor the "reptilian" allegro figure—as Hugo Riemann called it—are thematic in character. The underlying musical gesture is that of an introduction. Yet, not even when the broken triad crystallizes into the terse theme of measures 21 to 41 are we justified in classifying it by the letter of the theory of musical form as an exposition of the theme, since the passage, instead of remaining in a single tonality, modulates to the second theme and thereby takes on the appearance of an episode, a developing variation of the pattern in measures 21 to 24 (Ex. 3). This rough sketch of the problem to be tackled by formal analysis is enough to illustrate the dichotomy between sonata technique as revealed by Beethoven on his "new path" and the categories that underlie French or Italian opera. By the criteria of Italo-French music, Beethoven's D-minor Sonata does not have the slightest claim to a musical idea worthy of the name. What his work is based on is not a thematic—much less melodic—"inspiration" so much as a formal concept: the arpeggiated triad, at first vague and inconspicuous, gains its significance by creating a functional context between the opening of the movement and its crystallization in measure 21—a context that thwarts and negates the received categories of sonata form. The opening, seemingly an introduction, can be viewed in retrospect as an exposition, since it is set in a single key and constitutes an initial, if rudimentary, instance of the thematic substance. Conversely, when the arpeggiated chord coalesces into a terse theme with the character of an exposition, it eventually proves to be a transitional modulatory passage. However, even after this second interpretation of the formal design has, in a manner of speaking, been superimposed on the first, it by no means becomes the "correct" one. The formal concept resides, not in a trick which the listener sees through, but rather in an ambiguity which he must bear in mind as an aesthetic principle in its own right: the contradiction between gesture and tonality in the

Example 2

Example 3

exposition shows not that the work lacks form but what that form means. In other words, musical form as manifest in Beethoven's Op. 31, No. 2, is reflective: in order to be comprehensible, it presupposes an awareness of the pattern from which it deviates, and through this deviation draws attention to a change in the central category of instrumental music—the concept of theme. The "theme" is both an improvisatory introduction and a transitional pattern; instead of being presented in a standard exposition, it dissolves into an *ante quem* and a *post quem*: measure 1 is "not yet" and measure 21 is "no longer" the "actual" exposition, which in Op. 31, No. 2, does not exist. Nowhere does the thematic material take on a basic form; instead, it manifests itself in changing guises according to its location in the formal process, like variations without an explicit theme.

Seen in this light, the formal concept behind the D-minor Sonata, which is thoroughly typical of its kind, has two "levels." In the "surface structure," an improvisatory opening is offset by a modulating episode containing thematic material. This in turn is sustained by a "deep structure" where, on close hearing, the broken triads of measure 1 and measures 21 and 22 are seen to interlink. This interconnection is indispensable, since without it we could not notice that the traditional concept of theme has been split into its tonal and gestural components—a split which in turn is essential if we are to understand the movement as a variant of sonata form, and hence to perceive its form at all.

Furthermore, the form of the music is, in the strong sense of the word, "processual": the theme is not so much the object of a musical discourse as a mere substrate of a process which imparts meaning to the music by providing that substrate with formal functions. In contrast, the formal design of a work such as Meyerbeer's G♭-major Cavatina is simply a showcase for the musical idea, whose meaning is self-contained. In a word, one musical culture which sees the essence of music in melody—the "inspiration"—confronts another dominated by the role of function—the idea that the crucial aesthetic factor is not the initial substrate but rather its subsequent development. This is not to say that for melodic substance to be a means to an end—the form—it must be as unassuming as it is in Beethoven's Op. 31, No. 2. But it does mean that the melody may be spare and inchoate without necessarily dulling the rigor of the musical process, the realization of a formal idea. If one extreme of music is the melodic "inspiration," limited to a few measures and with the form functioning merely as an arrangement, the other would seem to be the almost disembodied formal process emerging from a void.

Music and Romanticism

In everyday language—the language that matters most for the history of ideas—the concept of romantic music or musical romanticism is connected with a stereotype notion which, misleading as it may be, we cannot simply ignore, since it is so deeply ingrained as to be virtually ineradicable. According to this notion, musical romanticism, meaning a self-contained era extending from the Classic period to the modern music of our century, is distinguished from classicism by a tendency toward formal disintegration, and from modern music by its direct expressivity, which then turned abstract in expressionism. "Romanticism" is a term used to denote an entire era, a portmanteau word covering all important composers from Schubert to Mahler, and the unimportant ones as well. This is a bad blunder: a category taken from the history of ideas but lacking sufficient focus to be useful for historiography has been hewn into a rough-and-ready label simply because our underdeveloped historical awareness balks at the thought that the nineteenth century, like most other periods, was inwardly divided, and hence the search for a single valid name for it is doomed to failure. Neither Verdi nor Bizet nor Mussorgsky were romantics; and while we are justified in calling Bellini and Donizetti romantics, this tells us little about them.

If romanticism in nineteenth-century music is a mere subcurrent used to characterize the age in its entirety, referring to romantic music as "emotional art" is a clichéd half-truth which, however valid from the standpoint of reception history, is vague as far as compositional technique is concerned. That romantic music, like that of *Empfindsamkeit* and the *Sturm und Drang*, presupposes a mode of perception once described by Wilhelm Heinrich Wackenroder as "utter submersion of the spirit in the surging torrent of feelings" is a fundamental fact for the reception history of the era, one which an aesthetic rationale based on the logic of musical forms is almost powerless to oppose. Yet ever since the writing of Goethe's *Werther* became a paradigm for the production of art, no one has seriously denied that exaltation requires detachment, analysis, and calculation before it can bring forth a work of art. Edgar Allan Poe's *Philosophy of Composition* (1846) is not only a foretaste of modernism but also a document of the romantic age; and Diderot's phrase "Ce n'est pas son [the artist's] coeur, c'est sa tête qui fait tout" may contradict the exoteric aesthetic which romantics offered to their audiences, but it is thoroughly compatible with the esoteric poetics they in fact followed. Thus, it seems as though the varying emphasis placed on "rationality" or on "emotionality" (with creation being rational and response emotional) was grounded less in inherent contrasts between the periods than in a "tactical" distinction as to whether the "public" aesthetic centered primarily on the production or on the reception of art—a distinction which in turn requires a sociohistorical explanation of its own.

The difficulties we face when we try to formulate a valid, nonstereotyped definition of musical romanticism stem, it seems, from a paradox: although the musical notion of romanticism derives from literature, there are no literary parallels for some of the basic traits that distinguish nineteenth-century music culture from that of the eighteenth century—above all for the profound changes in its relation to past music. (The concept of classicism, though new to music, was a millennia-old legacy in literature.) Rigorous champions of the separation of disciplines may demand for music an autonomous concept of romanticism, but this is merely an abstract methodological axiom which would ride roughshod over

Fig. 3 Franz Gerhard von Kügelgen: *Duett im Freien.* The combination of flute and harp, as in Mozart's C-major Concerto K299 (1788), was the acoustical ideal of the age of sensitivity, or *Empfindsamkeit,* whose spirit survived as a cultural undercurrent in the romantic era, partly in the *Biedermeier* style. Features considered in the popular imagination to be "romantic" not infrequently prove to derive from the legacy of the eighteenth century, an age when, in bourgeois culture, "sentimental" music formed a foil and counterweight to the rationalism of social practice. Music was meant to unite mankind in a "bond of sympathy," and a premium was placed on a soft, quivering tone, thought to embody the *Seelenlaut,* or "sound of the soul," which Jean-Jacques Rousseau and Johann Gottfried Herder lauded as the source of all music. (Dresden, Staatliche Kunstsammlungen, Engraving Collection.)

historical reality, one of whose key features is precisely that the romantic ideal in music is rooted in literature. Unless we digress into literary history, we stand no chance of explaining in what way both Mendelssohn and Berlioz were romantics, or why Verdi, though not a romantic, was nevertheless connected with Italian romanticism.

In 1804, in his novel *Oberman,* Sénancour drew a distinction between the "romanesque," which he disparaged, and the "romantic," which he praised to the hilt. "Le romanesque," he wrote, "séduit les imaginations vives et fleuries, le romantique suffit seul aux âmes profondes, à la véritable sensibilité." The romanesque retained those characteristics that derive from the etymological history of this term: it referred to non-Latin ("romance") writings which, unlike elevated literature with its rigid standards and claims to truth, tended to divagate into the unbridled and fantastical, not to say mendacious, and hence were considered a base genre. By separating the romantic from the romanesque—and this precisely in a novel, or *roman,* the genre opposed to the standardized classic drama—Sénancour ennobled the term so as to make it seem antithetical to, but on a par with, the classical, elevating this once despised genre by discovering sublimity and profundity in the "unbridled and fantastical." (The vernacular romanesque was left behind as a trivial residue far beneath the sphere of the romantic.) This terminological distinction, which made history in the aesthetics of literature, also has significance for music history in that it enables us, in our discussion of music and romanticism, to ignore the genre of singspiel, which was called "romantic" around 1800 simply because fairy-tale fantasies luxuriated in its plots.

E. T. A. Hoffmann, a major contributor to the notion of romanticism in music, likewise had a normative concept in mind when, in a review of Beethoven's Fifth Symphony in 1810, he lauded the instrumental music of Haydn, Mozart, and Beethoven as "genuinely romantic." Hoffmann's underlying idea derives from Ludwig Tieck's *Phantasien über die Kunst* (1799)—namely, that once music is freed from having to depict "finite," distinct emotions it becomes the expression of "infinite yearning," and that this indefinite quality is superior to the exactness of vocal music, rather than inferior, as was believed during the Enlightenment. If the eighteenth century suspected instrumental music of being empty if agreeable noise, the romantics saw in it a sublime language of sounds whose obscure ciphers were richer, not poorer, than the precise concepts of verbal language.

If, then, the separation between a sublime and a demotic concept of romanticism was part of the aesthetic program of romanticism itself, our understanding has nevertheless been clouded by countless terminological confusions arising from the contorted relation in literary history between French and German romanticism, a relation which was in turn mirrored in music history. (English romanticism was represented in music solely by John Field—in other words, poorly—but left its mark on the history of opera librettos and program music through the literary influence of Scott and Byron.)

Literary historians customarily date the beginnings of French romanticism, not around 1800 with Chateaubriand's *René* (1802) and Sénancour's *Oberman* (1804), but rather around 1830 with the scandal surrounding Victor Hugo's *Hernani* (1830) and the preface to *Cromwell* (1827). Not only does this obviously reflect an attempt to find a spectacular event to mark the bounds of an era and a manifesto to provide handy catchwords, it also results from the preconceived notion that romanticism cannot truly emerge as the rival of classicism until it has conquered the most prestigious of literary genres, the drama. However, this argument is not at all airtight, and we are thoroughly justified in maintaining that the historically crucial point was not the éclat associated with a break in this traditionally prestigious genre so much as the inconspicuous emergence of the new accompanied by a shift of hegemony among the genres.

For music history, the fact that literary historians stressed the *Hernani* scandal in the same way that political historians emphasized military battles had an important consequence: the proclamation of Berlioz's *Symphonie fantastique* (1830) as the watershed work of French romanticism, a proclamation vindicated by the stature of the work itself. Moreover, historians concerned with parallels between politics and culture could feel all the more satisfied with this date, since it coincided with the 1830 revolutions. (A historian who decided to add Meyerbeer's *Robert le diable* of 1831 to the *Symphonie fantastique* as the beginning of French romanticism could always point to Wagner's 1851 treatise *Oper und Drama* for corroboration.)

In contrast, Edward Dent's striking suggestion, in *The Rise of Romantic Opera* (1976), that romantic opera originated in works such as Cherubini's *Lodoïska* (1791) and Le Sueur's *La caverne* (1793) is startling at first, since it rubs against our habitual patterns of thought. Nevertheless, it is thoroughly plausible in the context of the literary and intellectual history of European romanticism, particularly since it allows us to date French romanticism back to the late eighteenth century when, after all, the German variant originated, not to mention the even earlier English version. The choice of subjects in the aforementioned works, as well as their elevated style and musical devices—Le Sueur's *La caverne* seems almost provocatively anticlassical in this respect—justify the term "romantic opera."

However, once we adopt Dent's views on French revolutionary opera and E. T. A. Hoffmann's thesis that the symphonies of Haydn, Mozart, and Beethoven manifest the "romantic" essence of modern instrumental music, we are forced to conclude that musical romanticism arose around 1790 independently in French opera, in Viennese instrumental music (as perceived by the generation of Wackenroder, Tieck, and Hoffmann), and in the north German music aesthetic which put the "zeitgeist" into words. The simultaneous existence of classicism and romanticism may disturb historians who, to use Ernst Bloch's phrase, want historical periods to "march in single file." Yet it is familiar from German literature of the 1790s, and alerts us to a fact that deserves to be underscored—namely, that Viennese classical music is not representative of European music of the time, but was simply one "culture of music" that tolerated the coexistence of other, nonclassical cultures.

One might object that E. T. A. Hoffmann's picture of classical instrumental music is a "romanticization" far afield from Haydn's and Beethoven's own aesthetic. This objection carries some force and should not simply be cast aside. However, once we recall that, in Europe as a whole at that time, Goethe's writings were considered "romantic," and for that very reason made literary history, we can sense at least the possibility, though not the necessity, of placing a stronger emphasis on reception history than happens when we reconstruct intellectual history—and the concept of romanticism is comprehensible only as part of intellectual history—almost entirely from the history of composition. And the fact that the "zeitgeist" of the years around 1800 took the form of an aesthetic of reception at odds with the production aesthetic of the classical symphony loses its paradoxical aura if we bear in mind that we can believe in the existence and influence of the "zeitgeist" without necessarily conceding it a position at the roots of an era. In other words, to sense the existence of a "zeitgeist" is not to say that its whereabouts must necessarily constitute the cornerstones of an age.

If many literary historians doubt whether we can speak of a French romanticism at the outset of the century, terminology also became confused by the habit among scholars of referring to the post-1830 German parallel to French romanticism as *Junges Deutschland* ("Young Germany") and contrasting it with German romanticism—a view that does grave injustice to Heine. At the same time, all musical phenomena or musicoaesthetic doctrines bearing an affinity to the pre-1848 "Young German" spirit— be they Schumann's or Wagner's—were lumped under the heading of romanticism with no mention of the ambivalence in terminology.

These vacillations in nomenclature apparently harbor political implications. Ever since the proclamations of Victor Hugo, the notion of political romanticism has been associated in France with revolutionary liberalism, whereas in Germany it is linked with restoration. And it was primarily for political reasons that "Young German" liberals parted company with romanticism, distrusting its preoccupation with the Middle Ages and the early Teutonic. Still, in reality the situation was more complicated than these threadbare terminological links—which in turn made history—imply. Some French romantics (Chateaubriand) switched from royalism to liberalism while some Germans (Friedrich Schlegel) took the exact opposite path—a fact as irrefutable as it is easily explained by political developments from the Revolution, Empire, and Restoration to the July Monarchy. In any event, simple correlations between romanticism and politics are not to be found. It is revealing that in music history, where political consequences have less of an impact, the relation between German romanticism, French romanticism, and "Young Germany" that so exercises literary historians is not a problem at all: the picture of musical romanticism conjured up by the names of Schumann, Chopin, Berlioz, Liszt, and Wagner remains intact.

Fig. 4 *Ossians Gesänge.* Around 1800 Ossian, the mythical bard of Celtic legend and heroic verse, was considered to be the "Nordic Homer." The fact that the authenticity of this Gaelic poetry, supposedly based on the "translation" of Ossian's *Fingal* by James MacPherson (1762), was contested from the very outset did nothing to diminish the enthusiasm of its readers, as is documented in its most celebrated form by Goethe's *Werther.* From the standpoint of music history, the Ossian craze was one of the literary preconditions for the "romantic tone" in *opéra comique* and the lied. In addition to countless ballads and several cantatas, Ossian provided the material for operas in Denmark (Aemilius Kunzen's *Ossians Harfe,* 1799), England (Busby's *Comala,* 1800), France (Jean-François Le Sueur's *Ossian* of 1804, Etienne Nicolas Méhul's *Uthal* of 1806, and Johann Georg Kastner's *La mort d'Oscar* of 1833), Italy (Pavesi's *Fingallo e Comala,* 1805), and Germany (Peter von Winter's *Colmal,* 1809). Here, on the title page of *Ossians Gesänge,* the maid listening to the bard is probably not intended to represent a character from his works, such as Malvina or Oina-Morul, but rather allegorizes the ideal readership that flocked by the thousands to MacPherson's forgeries (the proof had to wait until 1895) during the age of *Empfindsamkeit.* (Vienna, Gesellschaft der Musikfreunde.)

Yet it is precisely this close association between romanticism and the liberal-patriotic currents of the times that explains in part how Verdi, as a representative of the *Risorgimento,* could be placed in the vicinity of Italian romanticism as expressed in literature by Manzoni and Leopardi. And the librettos on which Verdi, like Donizetti, based his work combine political romanticism with literary romanticism insofar as the literary sources they plundered were written either by romantics, such as Scott and Hugo, or by others, like Shakespeare and Schiller, who were so classified at the time. (It was characteristic of romanticism as a whole, and not merely in opera librettos, to take its inspiration less from contemporary manifestations in other languages than from earlier, in fact nonromantic authors, such as Dante, Shakespeare, Milton, Goethe, or Calderon, who were then recast in a romantic spirit. Basic premises of romanticism of one nation were discovered in the protoromanticism of other nations. This explains why we should not flinch at applying the customary term "romanticism" to the "Slavic renaissance" of the nineteenth century—where a sense of kinship among the Slavic peoples was united with an urge to national liberation and a fondness for folk art as an assurance of their collective identity—even though this movement was inspired in large part by the eighteenth-century German philosopher Herder. Coarsely put, over wide areas "romanticism" was less a category of origin than one of reception.)

Romanticism is ordinarily considered, and terminologically construed, as the opposite of classicism. This often hides the underlying significance of a fact without which music history of the last century and a half would be incomprehensible: the fact that it was in the nineteenth century that a concept of musical classicism emerged in the first place, and that a selection of past works established itself in the opera house and concert hall as a "repertoire." What was fundamentally new about nineteenth-century music culture was the overpowering presence of earlier music, a presence that has apparently become irrevocable in our century. (This is not to say that in earlier centuries music was produced solely for immediate consumption; however, the survival of the Notre Dame repertoire into the fourteenth century, the Josquin renaissance in the mid-sixteenth century, and the hundred-year life-span of Lully's *tragédie lyrique* in no way weaken our claim that the relation to past music changed radically around 1800.)

In music, unlike literature, classicism was not challenged by romanticism; indeed, not until romanticism did classicism come into existence in the first place—into a supportive or an oppressive presence against which new music had to assert itself. Unlike literature, where there had been a canon of *classici auctores* for centuries or even millennia, it was not until the nineteenth century that music received a canon of composers considered exemplary in particular genres: Palestrina for Catholic church music and Bach for its Protestant counterpart, Handel for the oratorio and Gluck for musical tragedy, Mozart for opera buffa and Haydn for the string quartet, Beethoven for the symphony and Schubert for the lied. (Sometimes we hear Schubert referred to as a "classical" composer, but

Figs. 5 and 6 *Above*: Franz Weigl: *Erlkönig*. Engraving for the second edition of Schubert's lied, published by Diabelli & Co. (Vienna, Gesellschaft der Musikfreunde.) *Below*: Moritz von Schwind: *Erlkönig*. In Diabelli's edition, the Erl King appears as a fairy-tale creation in the midst of a genre painting, whereas for Moritz von Schwind he is a fearsome hallucination recalling the paintings of Füssli. The urgent dynamism of Schubert's lied, rushing headlong to its climax, is nonexistent in the Diabelli illustration but dominates Schwind's painting to such an extent that the figures and objects have become mere functions of motion. (Munich, Schack-Galerie.)

the process of canonization stopped short of the lyrical piano pieces of Schumann and Chopin, Wagner's music drama, and Liszt's symphonic poems.) True, emphases were variously distributed within the canon: the "New German School" revered Bach and disparaged Handel, and reverence for Haydn was mingled with condescension. However, this little alters the fundamental fact that it was the presence of an imaginary museum of classical works that formed a counterweight to the quest for innovation in the nineteenth century.

In short, we have no cause to speak of a profound opposition to the past in musical romanticism, which Friedrich Blume, with some justification, united with classicism to form a classical-romantic age. We cannot even speak of it in the case of Berlioz (our star witness for a break with tradition in French music), for the point is not that Berlioz regarded Bach and Handel with contempt but rather that he unconditionally lionized Gluck and Beethoven. In an age when a classical canon was only gradually beginning to take shape, to disagree about the choice of works was not to reject the notion of classicism out of hand. Instead, Berlioz's veneration of Gluck and Beethoven was part of the historical process that accorded classical significance to certain parts of the musical past. (In the nineteenth century it was no sign of inconsistency for a composer like Berlioz to show ostentatious contempt for traditional rules and pious reverence for the classical composers from whom he took his bearings.)

However, it was precisely this overwhelming presence of earlier music which made the nineteenth century's relation to it problematical. Before 1800 relations to the past had been regulated by a pattern of one generation being supplanted by another; thereafter this pattern failed, though without casting avant-gardism and historicism into unrelated spheres, as has happened in our century. The shadow of Beethoven rested on the symphony throughout the entire age, and the symphonies of Bruckner and Brahms were less successors to Schubert and Schumann than "immediate offshoots" of Beethoven.

Berlioz and Mendelssohn drew opposite conclusions from the legacy of Beethoven, and it is precisely these glaring extremes that point to a problematical—not staid but troubled—relation to the past. Mendelssohn's restraint and Berlioz's daring may both be viewed as forms of reaction sharing a common premise in the realization that Beethoven's oeuvre, as an overt or covert point of reference, was likely to coexist with or even outlive their own rather than being superseded. (A similar development took place in opera after Wagner as Wagnerians who wished to be more than mere epigones sought either, like Strauss, to take to extremes the "psychological counterpoint" of the leitmotiv system or, like Humperdinck, to seek refuge in fairy-tale opera, following the example of the first act of *Siegfried*.)

This at once close and problematical relation to the musical past—a past that entered current musical culture in the form of a standing repertoire—was apparently linked with the emergence in the nineteenth century of a strange jumble of trends, toward intimacy, monumentality, and virtuosity. These trends cannot be derived from a common root in spiritual or material circumstances of the time, but become intelligible only when viewed as alternatives to, or perhaps as escapes from, the legacy of classicism. (We learn little about their historical origins or significance if we are content, like Alfred Einstein, to describe them merely as characteristic contradictions of an age riddled with contrasts—a claim that might equally be made of the Baroque period.) The post-Schubert German lied, the lyrical piano pieces of Schumann and Chopin, and the grand operas of Meyerbeer and Halévy—all genres that can be called without exaggeration the musical hallmarks of the first half of the century—originated or gained their significance either by being former subspecies of the classical legacy which, like the operatic ensemble, were taken to extremes, or peripheral forms, like the lied or piano bagatelle, which were elevated to a central position. It is as though the overpowering presence of the classical legacy gradually depleted the center of the formal inheritance and forced composers to seek novelty in the outskirts. Whatever the case, the attempt to outdo the past in monumentality or sophistication presupposed the continued existence of a repertoire documenting the dignity of a moderate, nonextremist style in works that had attained classical status.

Countless attempts have been made to define the nature of romanticism, most of them proceeding from the none too obvious, unreflected premise that any coherent but unsystematic complex of historical ideals must be derivable from a single nucleus to which it owes its substance and vitality. However, any historian who, without denying its obvious impact, views the "zeitgeist" as a surface structure rather than a deep structure will naturally tend to a more complex hypothesis—namely, to the heuristic assumption that a collective term such as "romanticism" will contain some ideas that derive from a common root, others that merged from different sources, and still others that only came into casual contact with each other. And while the web they form is loose in some places and tight-knit in others, it nonetheless deserves the appellation of a collective name without necessarily being reconstructable from an underlying structure or substance from which all of its elements derive.

Thus, only within certain limits is it possible to reduce romanticism to a single essence without narrowing the subject or doing it methodological violence. Nevertheless, there is no overlooking the close connection between exoticism, historicism, and folklorism—all features as characteristic of nineteenth-century music as they are of the literature and painting of the time. (The heightened national awareness in the nineteenth century sometimes distracted observers from noting a basic similarity between "folklorism"—the effort to seek substance in one's own folk music for the expression of national identity—and exoticism, which usually fell into the category of the picturesque.) Whether the bourgeois educated classes—the "carrier strata" of musical romanticism—chose to overstep social bounds to folk music, historical bounds to early music, or geographical and ethnic bounds to oriental music, the motivation was always the same: an urge to "disinhibit," to remove the barriers posed by classical rules of style. There was an irresistible attraction to what seemed different or remote. This explains why Viktor Klemperer, following Fritz Strich's initiative, could view the process of continual "disinhibition"—rather than any state attained by that process—as the crucial defining trait of romanticism. (Another side of "disinhibition" is the nineteenth century's sympathy for dark, schizoid, melancholy, or exalted mental states, one of the most striking features of an age that looked upon good health virtually as a symptom of banality.) All the same, we must abandon our hope of capturing "Romanticism" (writ large) in a single concept. The desire to describe historical complexes as systems is a misguided ambition felt by historians who have let themselves be intimidated by a notion of science and scholarship which stands at odds with history.

Tradition and Restoration

Each age has a characteristic relation to the past. This relation depends on the extent to which it takes traditions more or less tacitly for granted, and on the ways it receives the legacy of still earlier ages. Whether composers take their bearings from general rules of composition, generic conventions, or individual works is just as much subject to the vicissitudes of time as the system of aesthetic categories which guides them as they assimilate earlier traditions.

Unlike our own century, the nineteenth century seldom spoke of tradition. The transition to romanticism was apparently not seen as a musical revolution to be held in check by invoking "cherished values," that is, by formulating a strong concept of tradition. Neither around 1815 nor around 1830 can we sense a break in the underlying principles of composition, as had happened around 1730, despite the almost unimaginably deep chasm that Thrasybulos Georgiades claimed to see between Beethoven and Berlioz. Nor did classical music ever become "early music," even though the time span from the beginning to the end of the nineteenth century is greater than that separating Mozart and Beethoven from Bach and Handel. In contrast to the break of 1730, posterity has never severed the connection between classical and romantic music; no restoration comparable to Mendelssohn's rediscovery of the *St. Matthew Passion* has been necessary.

If there was no break in tradition to separate the eighteenth from the nineteenth century, the years around 1800 nevertheless witnessed a profound change in the ways in which past music was received. Ever since the seventeenth century there had existed a stylistic duality between a *prima prattica*, preserved in the teaching of counterpoint, and a *seconda prattica*, which predominated in ordinary music life. This duality led to a crisis in the teaching of musical craftsmanship, a crisis for which Beethoven's declaration of the inviolability of the figured bass gives evidence all the more ample for being contradicted by his music. We must not let our knowledge that sixteenth-century compositional rules survived intact into the nineteenth century deceive us into thinking they had suffered no loss of substance. The instruction that was meant to make professional composers superior to dilettantes resembled exercises in a dead language, the easy codifiability of which is obtained only at the price of its irrelevance. That composers learned the Palestrina style in order to write operas later is a paradox somewhat blunted, but not resolved, by the observation that some Italian opera composers also functioned as church music directors (especially considering that the sacred works of, say, Zingarelli scarcely accord with what he must have taught as director of the Naples Conservatory). Nor does it help much to object, as was doubtless the case, that music theory involved more than strict counterpoint. As Arnold Schönberg rightly remarked, precisely what was not taught in harmony was how to write meaningful chord progressions not bound to a given voice; melody was taught from aesthetic rationalizations and a few compositional platitudes, insofar as it was not simply pronounced a self-contradiction; and the doctrine of form that arose in the late eighteenth century never went beyond a few schemata, which forever prevented it from becoming the fitting way to teach composition in an age whose formal aesthetic was based on the exact opposite notion—namely, that form resulted uniquely from the individuality of its underlying thematic material.

This crisis in the teaching of musical craftsmanship explains the strangely fractured, insecure relation toward the composer's métier shown by Schubert when he decided as late as 1828 to take lessons from Simon Sechter, or by Schumann in his somewhat recherché Bach studies, or by Wagner in his resentment, mingled with envy, toward Mendelssohn, who always seemed to know how to compose. Yet the cries of dilettantism invariably raised in the nineteenth century when one composer disapproved of the path taken by another are virtually devoid of meaning and substance; given the lack of criteria, they are no less irrational than the accusations of kitsch which post-1900 avant-gardists hurled at earlier composers in an attempt to relegate them to a distant and forgotten past.

Another factor contributed to this crisis. The notion of a classical model—the *exemplum classicum* on which a composer could and ought to take his bearings—necessarily assumed a different function in an age premised on the aesthetic of originality. Of course, the teaching of abstract compositional rules was always supplemented by the study of models. But Bach's zeal when he copied pieces by Froberger was different in kind from Wagner's enthusiasm when he wrote out Beethoven's Ninth Symphony (1822–24). Bach looked upon Froberger's devices as paradigms that gave him a "strong foretaste of composition," as he put it in the preface to his *Inventions* of 1720 to 1723 (themselves expressly conceived as models for composition). The Ninth Symphony, on the other hand, is an object of imitation only insofar as Wagner learned from Beethoven how to be inimitable. In the language of eighteenth-century aestheticians, *imitatio* was replaced and superseded by *aemulatio*.

It may have seemed as though there was an unbridgeable gulf separating, on the one hand, general rules of composition, which pass unchallenged precisely because they merely brushed the periphery of musical reality, and on the other, the uncontested aesthetic postulate that all music must be original to be authentic. However, in many traditions this gulf was narrowed by generic norms or conventions. In Italian opera around 1800, Rossini oriented himself less on particular works by Paisiello or Cimarosa than on the stylistic hallmarks of opera seria or opera buffa as a whole, though in his case with a tendency to incorporate buffa techniques into serious opera. True, he at first hesitated to write a second setting of *Il barbiere di Siviglia* (1816) following Paisiello's of 1782, but he soon overcame his qualms, as did Verdi later when confronted with Rossini's own *Otello* (1816). Both elements are equally characteristic: the double composition may no longer have been taken for granted, as it was in the eighteenth century, but neither was it the impossibility that it became with the formation of a fixed repertoire. Tradition stood midway between propagating genres, with individual works merely serving as links in a chain, and singling out works to survive their own time as repertoire pieces, not by representing a genre but by expressing a claim to uniqueness. Earlier tradition might be said to have "passed through" works, which manifest some but not all of the substance being handed down—the generic norm—whereas more recent tradition "consists" of works which themselves, rather than generic norms, constitute the substance handed down.

In Italian opera, then, generic norms formed a tradition which sustained the production of new works designed to last no longer than a season; as such it required no special reflection on its relation to the past. At the other end of the spectrum, however, in the string quartet, we encounter the exact opposite phenomenon: the formal principle governing the evolution of this genre, although likewise remarkably stable, shows a level of self-reflection that actually undercuts the purpose of tradition to ensure intelligibility. That the almost rampant string-quartet production of the late eighteenth century collapsed to a meager residuum around 1820; that the proclaimed champion of chamber music, Johannes Brahms, managed to write so few string quartets—these facts obviously imply that Beethoven had brought this genre to the stage where composers were acutely aware of its inherent problems, a stage where the stability of generic norms was less a stimulus than an obstacle to the genre's proliferation. It had become virtually impossible to strike the precarious and mutually conditioned balance between subjectivity of expression—as in late Beethoven—and rigorous objectivity of form; composers saw almost no escape from the trap of succumbing either to musical academicism or to programmatic confessions, that is, falling short of the aesthetic standards of this genre from opposite directions. After Beethoven, string quartets resembled fossil specimens of an extinct genre, despite a few isolated works by composers who either, like Brahms, attempted squarely to face the dilemma posed by Beethoven or, like Smetana, avoided it by lopsidedly favoring subjectivity. (The restoration of the string quartet in our century is one of the strangest chapters of music history.)

If living tradition resembles an unbreakable chain, restoration, as the word is generally understood, means re-creating a lost past following a break in continuity. Despite all efforts to make the reconstituted tradition appear natural, traces of the original break will always remain. The attempt to recapture lost

Fig. 7   Gottlieb Schick: *David vor Saul.* Along with the Orpheus legend, the story of
David playing his harp and thereby curing Saul of his melancholy is one of those age-old
musical myths which managed to maintain its time-honored position in the nineteenth-
century imagination. This pictorial representation of the biblical narrative is not simply
a historical painting unrelated to the nineteenth-century "zeitgeist." Music, according
to the aesthetic axioms of positivism, the reigning popular philosophy of the mid-nineteenth century, was "different," and in the midst of its mania for progress the nineteenth
century discovered Schopenhauer, the creator of both a philosophy of melancholy and a
metaphysic of music. (Stuttgart, Staatsgalerie.)

"substantiality" by means of reflection is intrinsically self-contradictory, and
turns even superficially successful restoration into a task which, strictly speaking,
thwarts itself.

The nineteenth-century Palestrina renaissance, intended as an attempt to
reconstitute "established truths" in church music, gives clear and even musically
palpable evidence of the "sentimental" element that clings to the second life of
music reclaimed from the past. In the nineteenth century, *a cappella* music was
sung at excessively slow tempos. This was not merely a result of misreading the
piously preserved original notation, that is, mistakenly equating the original note
values with current ones. Rather, the "seraphic aura" conveyed by this half-

deliberate expansion in time scale contained, whether or not composers were aware of it, a note of "longing," which expressed a sense of the historical distance separating the present from the age of "true" church music. In a manner of speaking, the restoration, trapped in Schiller's dialectic between the naive and the sentimental, went halfway to canceling itself out. The tone which this attempted reconstitution imposed on musical performance gave involuntary proof that the restoration was more self-conscious than successful. And this same note of "longing" as expressed in the exploded time scale also found its way into composers' attempts to recapture the aesthetic of sixteenth-century ecclesiastical modes. Modes change character radically when heard in the context of major and minor tonality—and in the nineteenth century there was no other way to hear them. They automatically seem to deviate from the norm of major and minor, forming expressive or picturesque variants. In the sixteenth century there was no such thing as a "Dorian sixth" forming the "characteristic scalar degree" that distinguished Dorian from minor (in its original form the second or third degrees were no less characteristic of the mode than the sixth). When considered a variant, however, the "characteristic degree" does indeed become an expressive element, but one which the ecclesiastical mode only acquired in the nineteenth century. And the fact that modes were felt to be deviations is the "compositional correlate" to the sentimental trait which gave the reconstituted Palestrina style its romantic tinge.

One of the received truths of our time is that Bach's music, like Palestrina's, was "romanticized" in the nineteenth century. This cliché is ceaselessly invoked for polemical ends to separate trends characteristic of our own century (i.e., the attempts to reconstruct Baroque performance practice, to take Bach's documented Lutheranism at its own word, and to restore his cantatas to a place in the liturgy) from contrary tendencies in the nineteenth century, such as the expressive, agogic performance style, Schleiermacher's "religion of feeling," and the fluid boundaries between church and concert hall. The disputes that this has provoked are very much with us today: Is the forced restraint of current Bach performances no less a reflection of a latter-day style (*Neue Sachlichkeit*) than was romanticization? Should we concede equal historical authenticity to the nineteenth-century religion of feeling as compared with the dialectic theology of our own century? Does the claim that art can preserve the substance of religion deserve serious consideration from theologians instead of being contemptuously cast aside? Whatever the outcome of these disputes, we can nevertheless say that it would be one-sided to characterize the reception of Bach by emphasizing solely those nineteenth-century characteristics which prompted objections from the twentieth.

The rediscovery—actually a first discovery—of the *St. Matthew Passion* gave as it were musical validity to a Gothic ideal which had become an *idée fixe* in German aesthetics ever since Goethe's paean to the Strasbourg Minster—namely, that an overall impression of sublimity and monumentality can result from extreme refinement of detail. (Adolf Bernhard Marx wrote of the opening chorus of the *St. Matthew Passion*: "This overly ornate art is as simple in its overall effect as the Strasbourg Minster which Goethe taught us to see.") However, this ideal impression conveyed by the *St. Matthew Passion* should not blind us to the fact that, in terms of musical performance, Bach reception in the nineteenth century involved instrumental music and not, or not primarily, vocal music. To put it more strongly, the familiarity of musicians with the *Well-Tempered Clavier* (1722) combined with the aura of holiness surrounding the *St. Matthew Passion* to form the substance of a Bach renaissance which, in countless variants and ramifications, formed one of the central processes in the history of nineteenth-century music.

This emphasis which performers placed on Bach's instrumental music is an obvious upshot of an unlikely but profound aesthetic reinterpretation whose impact on music history can scarcely be overestimated. Not only did this reinterpretation transmute Bach's works into autonomous, absolute music, it elevated them virtually into the model and paradigm of "pure instrumental music," which the romantics considered the essence of music per se. By romanticizing Bach the romantics could reassure themselves of the musical reality of an otherwise imaginary aesthetic ideal. Rahel, whose sense of the zeitgeist was almost infallible, wrote in 1829 to Varnhagen von Ense that Bach is "invariably sublime, and entertaining, whenever he obeys the dictates of his inspiration, not however when he puts music to words and texts," for it is "evident that vocal music is not, and cannot be, as pure, as lofty, as heavenward as instrumental music." An annoyance with Bach's cantata texts was sharply expressed by composers as early as Zelter, and it combined with E. T. A. Hoffmann's aesthetic of "pure instrumental music" to form a view of Bach which was fundamental to the nineteenth century. This view was upheld by the notion of absolute music—namely, that by ridding itself of texts and the expression of definite emotions music does not degenerate into preliterate vagueness, as was believed in the eighteenth century, but rather transcends language to become a prefiguration of the infinite and absolute.

On the other hand, it was in the nineteenth century that Bach—in vague accord with his intentions in writing his musical primer *Die Kunst der Fuge* (1749–50)—became a "composer's composer." The proof of this lies less in the fugues that Mendelssohn and Schumann wrote and published than in the influence of Bach which can be sensed even in composers like Chopin and Wagner, who shunned public displays of this sort. Bach's influence emerged from an idea that was central to nineteenth-century musical thought: the idea that expressivity and counterpoint need not be mutually exclusive, but may complement each other, or even bring each other into being. Where arbiters of the public aesthetic thought they saw a clash of opposites, composers practiced a dialectic for which they found a prototype in Bach. The main thing which the nineteenth century owed to Bach's music was the insight that fugues can be character pieces and that character pieces can be fugues—that is, that the strict style does not have to produce musical fossils, and a wealth of expression does not have to be lawless.

Just as Hegel spoke of a "second nature," we might speak of a "second tradition" to indicate the type of tradition which Bach's music, first as an object of restoration, gradually entered in the nineteenth century. The earliest composers whose musical output became a permanent part of the repertoires, with no break in continuity, were Gluck, Haydn, and Mozart. Gluck's *Iphigénie en Tauride* (1767), Mozart's *Don Giovanni* (1787) and *Die Zauberflöte* (1791), as well as several of Haydn's London symphonies (1791–95), figured among the key works in the historical process which gave rise in the first place to our modern notion of the operatic and concert repertoires.

Yet by mid-century, to a certain extent as a counterweight to Bach's increasing fame, a crisis reared its head in the nineteenth century's relation to pre-Beethoven classic composers. Like Handel, though with an opposite constellation of adherents and detractors, Gluck had always been a controversial composer. This was evidently because the substance of his music is less easily separated from its dramatic side than is the case with Mozart, but also because this dramatic side was in turn dependent on developments in the theater, which is apparently more susceptible than musical performance practice to influences from a wavering zeitgeist.

Haydn's music, which "betrays not the slightest trace of weariness with life," was compared by Schumann in 1836 to the music of a "pathological" age imbued with a Byronic spirit, and was recommended, so to speak, as an antidote. However, this praise is double-edged, and the barb became apparent when Schumann, in 1841, wrote that Haydn, though still venerated, "was no longer of profound interest for the present day." To an age before the 1848 revolutions—an age either portrayed in the raucous literature of "Young Germany" or withdrawn into idyllic resignation—any music marked by the rationalism of the eighteenth century, at once circumspect and recklessly cheerful, could only seem obsolete for the poverty of its expressive range.

The history of Mozart reception in the nineteenth century shows a sharp discontinuity quite unlike the continuity with which the Beethoven myth was handed down. It provides drastic proof that the concepts of classic and romantic did not necessarily have to refer to opposites, and that the varying configurations they bore to each other exercised a strong influence on the aesthetic perception of the object in question: Mozart's music. In sharp contrast to the catastrophe that silently befell him in the 1780s, Mozart's fame began to spread in the 1790s, for reasons that seemed to coincide by accident rather than emerge from a common source. The triumph of *Die Zauberflöte* with a heterogeneous audience was no less crucial than the at first esoteric reception given to *Don Giovanni* in literary romantic circles, or than the increasingly urgent need, in the wake of the post-1800 military and political setbacks, to find a specifically German classical music to place alongside its classical literature. (Viennese classicism is, at least in part, a reflection of the Weimar classics.) E. T. A. Hoffmann was convinced that Mozart was both a classic and a romantic in equal measure; he found "pure romantic essence" in the late symphonies and above all in the figure of Don Giovanni, who from Hoffmann to Kierkegaard was viewed as "Don Juan," a recasting (brought about by music) of a buffo character into a mythical figure fully as demonic as Goethe's Faust, as was amply illustrated by Lenau's Don Juan epic. As Hoffmann remarked, "Only a deeply romantic spirit will be able fully to recognize the profound romanticism in Mozart." Even the otherwise sober Rochlitz spoke of Mozart in terms usually reserved for Beethoven: "In the realm of grandeur, of turmoil—there is his native soil! and there too he tarried with zest unmistakable, in a land whose everlasting tempests and earthquakes must needs have sealed his early doom." This romantic stylization of Mozart gave way to a classical stylization: Schumann was capable of hearing even in such works as the G-minor Symphony (1788) nothing but "cheerfulness, placidity, grace—hallmarks of the art of Antiquity." This might be understandable as an expression of "sentimental" longing in a composer who needed to find a foil to his own psyche, but it is almost incredible that Schumann's view of Mozart, as canonized in the 1850s by Otto Jahn's Mozart biography, could represent the composer for nearly a century, even when we consider that this was the century of Richard Wagner. It seems as though the reception of Mozart was governed less by listening to his music than by an abstract notion of musical classicism—a notion based on Winckelmann's dictum but long worn thin and divested of its original paradoxical barb. Listeners were less willing to pay attention to what really happened in the music than to cling to ideas that partially concealed the very reality they were meant to illuminate.

The more the image of Mozart faded in the nineteenth century, the more garish became its picture of Beethoven. This led ultimately to the antihistorical construct of Mozart and Beethoven as opposites, a construct derived typologically from the alleged opposition of Raphael and Michelangelo and encompassing not merely their music but their biographies as well. A history of the Beethoven myth would be tantamount to an intellectual history of the nineteenth century; yet, a few first steps aside, this history has yet to be written. To Schumann, Beethoven was a "disorderly and troubled" genius; to Bettina Brentano, a revolutionary who caused an embarrassing scene at Teplitz; to E. T. A. Hoffmann, a "sorcerer and priest" of music. And for the moment we have no way of knowing whether the nineteenth-century picture of Beethoven the man was primarily responsible for deciding which of his works were to be considered representative and characteristic, or, conversely, whether a selection based on aesthetic considerations (but condemning to oblivion all his works in the divertimento tradition) determined the way his music was heard and his biography written, in the same way that Otto Jahn based his Mozart biography (which, incidentally, emerged from preliminary work on a biography of Beethoven) from preconceived notions as to the spirit of Mozart's music.

There is a widespread view that Beethoven's music was reinterpreted in the nineteenth century from absolute to programmatic music and "romanticized" by misconstruing his reflected form as fragmented. This is one of those prejudices which seem ineradicable, not because they are completely harebrained but because they are so distorted that it is cumbersome to correct them. The notion of absolute music which romanticism allegedly abandoned is itself a product of romanticism. It originated with Ludwig Tieck and E. T. A. Hoffmann and says that we must distinguish between instrumental music that is programmatic (i.e., recounts a subject) or characteristic (i.e., depicts emotions and characters), and a "poetic" instrumental music that abandons clearly defined subjects, characters, and emotions in order to become a language capable of portending the "infinite." To question the legitimacy or illegitimacy of E. T. A. Hoffmann's "romanticization" of Beethoven, we would have to ask to what extent Beethoven's instrumental music essentially depicts emotions, characters, and subjects, or projects an "endless longing" transcending the limits of the finite. Whatever the case, the difference between absolute and programmatic music was not the decisive factor in the process of "romanticization": any piece of absolute music with a semblance of the transcendental is just as "romantic" as a piece of programmatic music infused with the same spirit but devoid of "prosaic" details.

The notion corresponding to the thesis that Beethoven's music was "romanticized" by being made "literary" is that the nineteenth century misconstrued his formal procedures, taking his "quasi una fantasia" principle to mean a lack of form warranted by the variety of the contents. This notion is one-sided: the key distinction in the nineteenth century's relation to Beethoven is not to be found between "strict" and "broken" form but rather between "problematical" form, on the one hand, and the unhappy alternatives of "schematic" and "disintegrated" form on the other. Beethoven's formal designs are individual and unique in the sense that they represent solutions to specific formal problems, no two of which are ever alike; and as August Halm recognized, their thematic material is a function of the form. By the same token, however, the individuality and artistic value of a romantic work hinged on its thematic or motivic material and its poetic

Fig. 8 Felix Mendelssohn-Bartholdy: *Die Thomasschule und -kirche in Leipzig.* Mendelssohn's rediscovery of the *St. Matthew Passion* in 1829 was actually its discovery, for there is no evidence that Bach's contemporaries had ever recognized its significance. To Mendelssohn, however, Bach's former place of employment was not an admonitory memorial to his undignified and oppressive working conditions so much as a site of pious veneration. The park in the foreground shows the Bach monument donated by Mendelssohn in 1840. (Berlin, Staatsbibliothek Preußischer Kulturbesitz, Mendelssohn Archives.)

significance. This enabled romantic composers to keep their forms either schematic (since form was incidental) or disintegrated (by adapting them to poetic content in the guise of a tangible subject). Thus, to say that the romantics misconstrued Beethoven's form is to make two contradictory claims at once: that they regarded his forms as "disintegrated" rather than as individual, nonrhapsodic solutions to formal problems, and that they codified his clear-cut but idiosyncratic forms into textbook diagrams. (The doctrine of musical forms devised by Adolf Bernhard Marx is a codification of the forms in Beethoven's music.)

Nationalism and Universality

Viennese classicism is lauded for its universality, a universality that offsets the sense of disintegration, of divergent particularist trends, conveyed by nineteenth-century music. Though an inner coherence still reigned in the eighteenth century, whether in the Baroque or Classic periods, it apparently broke down in the age of political and industrial revolutions. Still, before the concept of the universal can be useful as a historiographical category, we must first analyze it into the heterogeneous parts from which it originated.

It is patently wrong to claim of nineteenth-century composers, whether of light or of serious music, that they abandoned or broke the traditional universal codex of rules that governed compositional technique. As far as the elements and principles of composition are concerned, Friedrich Blume was not unjustified in speaking of a classical-romantic age—an age that formed a self-contained entity distinct from the Baroque on the one hand, and from modern music on the other. Like the twelfth century, and most unlike the twentieth, the composer's métier in the nineteenth century was bound by seemingly incontrovertible laws, which, however, were not sufficient to justify a work's claim to artistic status. If a composer such as Mussorgsky broke these laws, he invited others to doctor his works with the purpose of salvaging their substance by ironing out the "dilettantism" of their technique. Yet the accusations of dilettantism that were raised time and time again in the nineteenth century—against Weber no less than Berlioz and Wagner—are not a sign that the tradition of musical craftsmanship had broken down; on the contrary, that sign came in the twentieth century when these accusations ceased.

Thus, in its basic features, compositional technique remained universal until Debussy's inconspicuous and Schönberg's spectacular musical revolutions. Yet the notion of universal music includes a utopian view of society, which, perhaps under the pressure of a "reality principle" introduced into art from politics, gradually seemed to wither in the nineteenth century. Works such as Mozart's *Die Zauberflöte* (1791) and Haydn's *Die Schöpfung* (1793) transcend the distinction between popular and esoteric music, and this fact is a hallmark of an age that stands out as a moment of blissful reconciliation in a history of schisms and conflicts. Moreover, the audience for whom Beethoven wrote his symphonies was nothing less than "humanity," in the dual sense of an all-embracing throng and a substance which, however buried in convention, was common to all people. In contrast, the nineteenth century, as a result both of the cult of genius and of the industrialization of popular music, witnessed an increasing rift between "highbrow" and "lowbrow" music until, in our century, music reached a state of alienation which Theodor W. Adorno could portray as a rift between avant-gardism and kitsch. Still, this outline of the ineluctable deterioration of postclassical music is too crude to be unconditionally valid. First of all, the balance or merging of opposites in *Die Zauberflöte* represents an exception to the general rule, even in the age of classicism; before the nineteenth century, too, there existed a "lowbrow" music which was "ostracized," although this music, being unwritten, must remain beyond the historian's grasp. Second, our habit of despising nineteenth- and twentieth-century popular music as "trivial" while praising the "genuine folk music" of earlier times should not blind us to the fact that popular music of high quality was written in the nineteenth century, too, and conversely that earlier folk music was riddled with trivialities, which remained unexpunged until subjected to the selection criteria of idealistic collectors. The notion that there was a social universality to the music of the classical period is a pipe dream nourished by the impetus of a still unspent revolution, an idealized vision of folk music, and an underestimation of the stylistic and social distances separating popular and art music.

But to claim of Viennese classicism that it was stylistically universal is to say not only that it bridged the gap between "highbrow" and "lowbrow" style, but also that it rose above the boundaries of nations and genres. The ease with which the stylistic devices of Haydn, Mozart, and even Beethoven were able to infuse all musical genres—from the opera and the oratorio to the mass, from the symphony and the divertimento to the piano sonata—gave way in the nineteenth century to a trend toward specialization, making it impossible for us to imagine Chopin as a symphonist, Wagner as a composer of string quartets, or Bruckner as a writer of song cycles. Yet, however tantalizing in its simplicity, this conflict of eras begins to falter once we take the historically untenable step of equating Viennese classicism with the classic age in Europe as a whole. Meyerbeer had already been preceded by Spontini as a composer exclusively of operas, and Clementi was no less a specialist in piano music than Chopin. Mozart's universality is an exception and must not obscure the fact that contemporaries of the Viennese Classics saw an opposition between Italian opera and German instrumental music which made them view music as a divided culture. Moreover, some differences between genres paled in the nineteenth century while others became more pronounced. This has dulled our awareness of subtle distinctions in the arsenal of stylistic devices, such as the difference between a concert sonata and one intended for private use, between an overture and a movement in a symphony, or between a singspiel with dialogue and a through-composed opera.

The idea of universality—a legacy of the classic period—and the national character which nineteenth-century composers tried to instill into music, particularly in the opera, were never viewed as opposites. Nationalism was seen as a means, not a hindrance, to universality. Nor was a strong national tint—from Weber and Chopin to Mussorgsky—necessarily an obstacle to international recognition; indeed, it was almost always the vehicle. Interest in music expressing other nationalities was conditioned in part by contemporary events in literature and politics, such as the appearance of Madame de Staël's book *De l'Allemagne* (1813), the Polish revolution of 1830, or the reception of Russian novels. By no means was it restricted to a mere liking for the strange and picturesque.

Thus, the degree to which a composer's fame was international was not in proportion to the cosmopolitanism of his music. But neither was a cosmopolitan outlook, as we find for example in Meyerbeer, a hindrance to the emergence and spread of his success. The dialectics of nationalism and universality in music cannot be captured in a simple formula. The notions of human commonality, cosmopolitanism, nationalism, and individualism all impinged on music aesthetics in the nineteenth century, and it is precisely because nineteenth-century thought went around and around these anthropological categories that the relations between them are so tangled.

One of the characteristic claims of the nineteenth century is that for individuality to be truly original it must be rooted in the "national spirit." Paradoxical as this proposition may seem in retrospect, it was taken as a matter of course at the time. A composer was expected to be original, to bring forth the new in a manner which, at the same time, manifested the "origins" of his existence. In Schumann's aesthetic, this originality was opposed, on the one hand, by epigonism and, on the other, by the musical *juste milieu,* meaning a cosmopolitan mixture of elements from various national styles. However, it is a prejudice to equate lack of an unambiguous national stamp with eclecticism: Meyerbeer's music—the target of Schumann's criticism—is not without its "individual tone," and there is no justification in principle for regarding the "mixed *goût*" of Gluck and Mozart as a less solid foundation for originality than an unalloyed national style, which in any case even Weber's *Der Freischütz* (1821) reveals to be an illusion.

If, as one of the characteristic prejudices of the day, nationalism was expected to nourish composers lest they degenerate into eclecticism, composers were nevertheless expected not to remain trapped by their dependence on a national identity. Schumann, in an 1836 review, may have praised Chopin's "strong, original nationality," but he added, "The minor interest attaching to the patch of earth on which he was born was destined to be sacrificed to the Universal [*weltbürgerlich*]; and true enough, his recent works have shed their excessively specific Sarmatic physiognomy." In other words, Schumann did not regard the national and the universal as opposites or as mutually exclusive (by *weltbürgerlich* he meant universal, as opposed to the cosmopolitanism of the *juste milieu* that he abhorred in Meyerbeer). True, he wanted the national to be subsumed in the universal, or *weltbürgerlich,* rather than to flaunt its own limitations and narrowness ("minor interest"); but it was not meant to disappear altogether. The national per se is thoroughly compatible with the *weltbürgerlich,* and Schumann was mirroring the general view of his times in wishing to "sacrifice," not the national per se to the universal, but rather that narrow brand of nationalism which immures itself in fear or arrogance.

Still, the relation between individuality and nationality is not nearly as straightforward as those would have us believe who hold that a composer's originality hinges on his national heritage, his dowry from the "national spirit." Hence, despite the ingrained nineteenth-century habit of accepting the "primacy" of the "national spirit," we cannot say to what extent the individuality of a composer determines, or is determined by, the musical substance of his nation. Did Chopin and Smetana lay bare the essence of Polish and Czech music and capture it in art? Or were the hallmarks of their music declared national property by general acclaim?

Nationalistic music, it seems, invariably emerges as an expression of a politically motivated need, which tends to appear when national independence is being sought, denied, or jeopardized rather than attained or consolidated. Cynics might remark that those who look to music for additional reassurance of their own national identity will always find what they need: any high-quality music written in an emerging nation will be taken as national music simply because it meets the nation's need for a common musical property.

Attempts were also made in the nineteenth century, with far more failures than successes, to give art music a nationalist slant by seeking recourse in folk music. These attempts were precarious in two respects. First, folk music (Bartók would say peasant music) is more regional and social than national in its definition and localization; and the repertoire of wandering folk musicians stood outside nationality altogether, being pieced together from international sources. Second, it turned out time and time again that merely to cite folk music—that is, to deck out the imported stylistic models of the opera seria or *opéra comique* with folk melodies—was never sufficient to establish an authentic national style in which a nation could recognize itself. As Boris Asaf'ev would put it, it is not citation but "intonation" that constitutes national character in music—albeit his term "intonation" captures the problem in a single word, but not the solution.

Finally, despite countless efforts to do so, it is still difficult to grasp the musical substance of a national style using tangible criteria. The open fifths of a bagpipe drone, the Lydian fourth, a rhythmic-agogic pattern—how often have these been claimed as attributes of Polish music only to appear Scandinavian in other contexts. Yet this is the least of our difficulties: it is a cornerstone of any hermeneutical study with pretenses to being more than a collection of musical statistics that musical character resides not in a single feature but in a configuration of features. Greater difficulties lie in the fact that the national element in music, no less than its poetic and programmatic content, is apparently one of those qualities which exist aesthetically but accrue to an object over a period of time—through a confused web of events, circumstances, decisions, and intentions—rather than being arbitrarily given. The extreme instance of national music, the national anthem, shows unmistakably that the national aspect of music is not a property attached to a musical creation from its origins but one which emerges in a historical process.

In sum, a historical analysis of national character in music faces several difficulties: uncertainty regarding the imprint of the individual in the national; extrinsic motivation due to political necessity; and the negligible effect of adopting folk music. This may tempt us to avoid these difficulties by defining national music in reference to its function rather than its substance. This change in logical status entails nothing less than jettisoning Herder's and Hegel's thesis of the "national spirit" as a hidden agent in history, and seeking the national side of music, not just in its ethnic and melodic-rhythmic substance, but to a greater extent in a historical function in which aesthetic and political elements merge.

As the example of Lully shows, one need not be French to found a musical style capable of being regarded as the quintessence of French music for more than a century. And that the Spanish element in Glinka is considered less "authentic" than his Russian side is a prejudice originating solely in the nationality of the composer rather than in tangible musical facts. There is no difference in kind between Lully's "Frenchness" and Glinka's "Spanishness" which would enable us to distinguish between an authentic and an inauthentic style according to aesthetic and compositional criteria. All we can speak of is a difference in historical function—namely, that Lully was accepted by the French, and Glinka rejected by the Spanish, as a "national composer" whose music reflected the nation and confirmed its national identity. Further, this acceptance took place under the aegis of the "national spirit" hypothesis, which was unknown in the seventeenth and eighteenth centuries and did not become a motivating factor in history until the nineteenth. The nationality of a composer, though irrelevant in the case of Lully, became with Glinka the touchstone of "authenticity" in national music. Any national music that did not come "from within" and thrive on "ethnic substance" was categorized as "exotic."

Once we ignore nineteenth-century prejudice and insist that nationalism in music must be understood primarily in terms of its historical function, one seemingly intractable problem virtually solves itself: the problem of how to do justice to the profound historical changes undergone by a concept such as "German music." Around 1800 Bach's music, with its amalgam of pensiveness, caprice, and pedantry, was regarded as a sort of acoustical form of Gothic art. Its "Germanness" is a completely different quality from the "Germanness" of classical instrumental music, which persons of culture throughout Europe saw as the counterpart to Italian opera, or from the "Germanness" of *Der Freischütz*, whose romantic national character was appreciated no less in Paris, albeit under the rubric of the strange and picturesque, than in Berlin. There is little sense in trying to detect a "substantive" unity in the "Germanness" of Bach, Haydn, and Weber, at least not in a discussion where priority is to be given to musical arguments. Nor do we have to unravel all the separate political, social, aesthetic, and compositional conditions and motives that make up a concept such as "German music" at a given point in history in order to maintain, in general, that it is an analysis of this sort—and not the quest for an immutable ethnomusical component—that should guide any historian who wishes to use historical rather than mythical categories in order to come to grips with the phenomenon of musical nationalism.

In addition to the various meanings attached to terms such as "German" or "French" music, the onset of the nineteenth century also witnessed a gradual change in the aesthetic status of musical nationalism. In the seventeenth and eighteenth centuries the "French style" established by Lully was generally available to all composers, regardless of their ethnic origins; even German or Italian composers could adopt it without being accused of lacking "authenticity." Composers chose between the French or the Italian "manner" just as they chose between a bucolic or an elegiac tone; nothing was said of an ethnic substance that imparted national character to a piece of music from within. No matter how violent the arguments as to the alleged superiority of the French or the Italian style, the fact remains that Gluck first chose one and then the other without being a Frenchman or an Italian at all. His nationality was beside the point.

This situation changed in the nineteenth century. Nationalism in music began to be seen not just as a stylistic option but as a heritage of the "national spirit." Herder's "national spirit" hypothesis coincided with a political nationalism that arose in the age of revolution, and the characteristic thought behind this nationalism was that, in a conflict of loyalties, a citizen owed his primary allegiance, not to his creed, class, or dynasty, but to his nation. Anthropological and political motives united with the notion of aesthetic originality, which had burst on the scene in the late eighteenth century with the *Sturm und Drang,* to form a complex of ideas in which the concepts of originality, nationality, and authenticity merged. We have already seen how Schumann, without chauvinism, could only envision "original" or "unspoiled" music as rooted in a national culture; composers lacking "original nationality" were condemned to eclecticism.

No historian who is aware of the sharp difference between the earlier and the more recent concepts of musical nationalism—that is, the difference between a national "manner" and the musical expression of a "national spirit"—is compelled to decide in favor of one view or the other. And the rules of historiographical method prohibit him from using the principles of one century to criticize those of another. On the other hand, to adopt nineteenth-century assumptions with respect to that century and only that century—that is, to adopt the "national spirit" hypothesis as a heuristic tool—would mean dispensing with historical explanation altogether, since, as we have seen, these explanations point to paths that only open up when we abandon the "national spirit" hypothesis. Our only choice, therefore, is to concede wholeheartedly that the belief in the reality of a "national spirit" was an active force in history, but not to take it as our final arbiter. The fact that nationalism was viewed as an ethnomusical substance rather than an interchangeable style can itself form a strand in a historical analysis. That Glinka's "Spanish tone" was considered "inauthentic" and de Falla's "authentic" is revealing precisely because the difference between them is so difficult to capture in pure musical terms. On the one hand, this decision was politically motivated: Spain needed a national cultural identity following the setbacks of 1898; on the other hand, it was rooted in the preconception that national musics possess an ethnic substance—a preconception which the historian is free to accept or reject, but one he has to take seriously, since it made history.

Furthermore, any aesthetic that refuses to be limited to the obvious will proceed from the premise that features suspected by rigorous champions of the written musical text of being ideological additives may in fact be fully to the point—that is, they may form part of the work as an aesthetic object, just as it was constituted in the minds of listeners for decades. Music does not stop at its underlying acoustical substrate; it is the outgrowth of a process of categorical formation, and the categories that take a formative part in musical perception are just as aesthetically "real" when they owe their impact less to a solid foothold in the musical material than to associations accumulated over the years. The same anthem can be "characteristically Prussian" in Prussia and "characteristically English" in England. And the complex of mazurka rhythm, bagpipe drone, and Lydian fourth can leave a "specifically Polish" impression on the musical imagination through the Chopin tradition whether or not it recurs in the folk musics of other nations. As little heed as the critical historian should pay to the ethnic substance of national musics as a final arbiter, the way we hear specifically national qualities will remain forever untouched by the attempted reductionism of history.

The Music Culture of the Bourgeoisie

It is now commonplace to say of nineteenth-century music culture that, notwithstanding institutions such as the court theater and court orchestra, it belonged basically to the middle class, or bourgeoisie. This claim is almost beyond contesting; yet its significance is not absolutely clear, as it seems to hover between different if interlocking meanings. "Bourgeois" can refer to a large part of the institutional framework that sustained music culture, or to what Levin Schücking called the "taste-bearing stratum" (*Geschmacksträgerschicht*) whose judgments on music of distinction were definitive, or finally to the social character of the principles or conceptions upon which the central genres of music were based. (It need hardly be mentioned that any outline of the sociology of music which resorts to categories such as "music of distinction" or "central genre of music" and finds the hallmarks of the age in the concert hall, the educated classes, and genres such as the symphony and string quartet, is not being sociographically neutral but is using aesthetic criteria to construe music history as a history of art music.)

For centuries composers and performers came from the middle class, apart from a few aristocrats and plebeians who formed the exception. However, we should not conclude from this that, despite the supremacy of the aristocracy, music culture had always borne the imprint of the bourgeoisie, in accordance

Fig. 9 Adolph von Menzel: *Die Familie Menzel am Flügel*, 1851. Piano duets have unjustly fallen into disrepute in our century. In the nineteenth century, however, they formed a cornerstone of bourgeois music culture, allowing one to become familiar with the key works of chamber music and the symphonic literature by playing them at home. Arrangements are important documents on how music was received at the time. If music culture in our century, parceled out between the concert hall, radio station, and gramophone recording, has become by and large a culture of the "lonely crowd" (to use David Riesman's phrase), nineteenth-century music culture was part of a mode of life in which education and conviviality each served as the goal of the other. (East Berlin, Staatliche Museen, Nationalgalerie.)

with the master-slave dialectic. As late as the early nineteenth century musicians in noble households were considered part of the higher retinue, alongside the major domo, the steward, and the surgeon, and though this was by no means degrading, it may have been difficult to endure for any number of reasons (musicians were no different from other citizens in regarding class supremacy as oppressive). When music took the form of chamber music in which noble dilettantes could participate, it functioned as a domain where class distinctions could momentarily be suspended. Still, this only made the contrast all the more noticeable, and in Beethoven we have the striking instance of a musician whose sense of artistic superiority to the bourgeoisie gave rise to a claim to stand above them as an individual. Admittedly, a musician who had to play for money was in a position faintly reminiscent of that of the court minstrel, and his social standing toward the grand bourgeoisie was almost as precarious as his stance toward the aristocracy, which in the nineteenth century occasionally accepted a musician—notably Liszt—virtually as one of its own. (In England, a musician who played at private concerts was given the option of accepting payment or of being treated as a gentleman belonging to "Society"—in other words, as an amateur instead of a professional.) In short, we must distinguish between the emancipation of the bourgeoisie, which also liberated musicians insofar as they were, or wished to be, considered part of it, and its integration into the grand bourgeoisie of merchants, civil servants, and academics, an integration that was not complete until our century.

It is thoroughly justifiable to use the term "bourgeois" for a music culture in which middle-class citizens disparaged the professional musician socially but nevertheless played string quartets, sang in choral societies, and performed in amateur orchestras. Yet we should not forget that there were also noblemen, even their royal majesties in Vienna and Berlin, who played in string quartets, and that aristocrats were at times not averse to joining a choral society or an amateur orchestra. The social character of concert and chamber music was not conditioned by a bourgeoisie that clearly separated itself from the nobility. Rather, it was characterized by a tendency to use the musical dialogue—as Goethe regarded string quartet playing—as a means, if not to eliminate class distinctions, at least to forget them for a while. (In this respect the musical dialogue resembled eighteenth-century salon conversation, where a plebeian like d'Alembert could feel on a par with aristocrats; string quartet playing was, as Ernst Bloch would put it, "utopian" in the sense that it offered an "aesthetic prefiguration" of social relations directed toward more humane ends.)

In chamber music, then, it was the spirit of conversation—under the aegis of humane education—which suspended class distinctions, at least until countermanded. In the opera, however, a sharp opposition of classes was manifest visually in a distinction between the loges, reserved for the nobility, and the stalls, which were filled by the bourgeoisie and an admixture of plebeians. Hence, the audience was divided. This raises the question of who formed the "taste-bearing stratum"—that is, which class set the fashion in a particular musical or musico-theatrical genre at one or another time, thereby dictating the aesthetic verdict which was then accepted as public opinion.

In the eighteenth century the genre of pomp and ostentation was the opera seria, with its international system of court theaters extending from Naples to St. Petersburg and from Vienna to London. Here court society unquestionably represented the decisive arbiter, no matter how large the bourgeois audience that flocked into the standing-room stalls, particularly since, outside Italy, they were unlikely to understand the language of the libretti. (This last point is not incidental: the view that a Metastasio text was nothing but a vehicle for the music is a myth fabricated by polemicists who wished to disparage the drama of intrigue and affects from the vantage point of the drama of ideas and characters.) The opera seria audience, though it paid for its tickets, bore features which Jürgen Habermas ascribes to a type known as the "prestige public," a type most likely to be found at court festivities surrounded by a gaping throng. A performance did not simply present an opera to *la cour et la ville*—that is, to a mixed audience from court society and the bourgeoisie. It also displayed court society for the benefit of the bourgeois in the stalls, accompanied by an opera designed to reflect artistically the social splendor of the court.

In early nineteenth-century Vienna, Italian opera was sometimes performed in the original language during the Italian season at the court opera, and at other times in German translation on other stages; sometimes the same work was played in both versions in a single year. However, as the language and the venue changed, so did the "taste-bearing stratum," although the constitution of the audience in the stalls probably changed little from theater to theater. In these circumstances the aesthetic criteria, or at least some of them, were switched: it apparently depended on the nature of the "taste-bearing stratum"—aristocratic or bourgeois—whether the decisive factor lay in the nobility of a singer's voice and stage postures, or in the passion, alternating with touching simplicity,

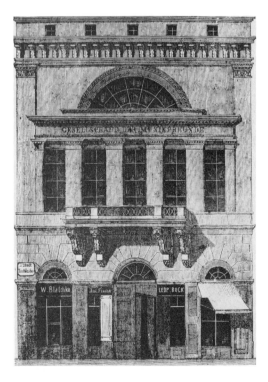

Fig. 10 The Gesellschaft der Musikfreunde in Vienna: Golden Hall of the Old Conservatory. The custom of decking out concert halls with temple façades became a matter of course in the nineteenth century, so that ultimately the claims advanced by this architectural symbolism on behalf of the symphony and the bourgeois concert no longer appeared as strange and haughty as they in fact were. In an architectonic system that allowed museums to be Egyptianesque, theaters Greek, and churches Gothic (apart from court churches, which sometimes partook of the style of Renaissance or Baroque palaces), concert-house architecture expressed a "religion of art" in which Christian images shaded into intimations of Antiquity. (Vienna, Österreichische Nationalbibliothek.)

of his acting and singing style. (In opera, the work as represented in the score is merely the substrate of a theatrical event which, to a large extent, results from the interaction between performance and reception.)

The ascendancy of the bourgeoisie in nineteenth-century opera seria has never been examined with the thoroughness necessary to clarify a complex process in which socioeconomic, sociopsychological, aesthetic, and compositional elements merged. For the moment it is unclear to what extent the status of the court theater and its business side influenced which works were performed, how audiences were constituted, and how they formed their opinions. Equally unclear is the sociopsychological process that caused the bourgeoisie to adopt the aristocratic view of opera seria as a prestige art and a means of self-presentation, and conversely the aristocracy to take over the bourgeois "religion of art" and to abandon, or at least suppress, if hesitantly and incompletely, its hereditary conception of musicotheatrical divertissements. (We might ask whether the Jockey Club, which precipitated the scandal at the Paris performance of *Tannhäuser*, was made up of philistines with no idea what they were doing, or of adherents of an earlier aristocratic conception of art who balked at what they regarded as the lower-class presumption of Wagner's overbearing artistic claims.) It is also unclear to what extent we can speak of the social character of musical forms, that is, of a bourgeois tendency to favor ensembles over arias, and scenas over recitative.

The bourgeois ascendancy in opera seria is revealed most strikingly in its libretti. The ancient myths and histories in which court society had enjoyed projecting itself gave way to "romantic" subjects from the novels of Scott or the plays of Shakespeare and Victor Hugo. This suppression, already noticeable in Rossini well before Bellini and Donizetti, shows unmistakably that from a literary standpoint nineteenth-century opera seria, even when performed in court theaters, was primarily aimed at the bourgeois audience in the stalls as its "taste-bearing stratum."

In music histories today, at least in the popular ones, we are still likely to read that the opera buffa, unlike the opera seria, was from the outset a bourgeois genre through and through, one in which the bourgeoisie recognized and confirmed its own identity. This is one of those gross simplifications which, without being dead wrong, hide important aesthetic and sociopsychological distinctions. Ever since Antiquity theatrical genres had been governed by a rule of social standing: tragedies are set among kings and potentates, comedies among ordinary citizens. However, this does not mean that the vantage point from which audiences viewed the bourgeoisie was itself bourgeois. (The distinction between subject matter and social character is utterly unrecognizable in the third dramatic genre, the pastorale.) Indeed, it was more often an aristocratic pose, mingled with condescension and scornful detachment, to turn the everyday life of the bourgeoisie exclusively into an object of comedy. The first unambiguously bourgeois genre was the sentimental *comédie larmoyante*, which aristocratic audiences must have found insufferable, and the emancipation of the bourgeoisie in the theater became complete with the bourgeois tragedy of the eighteenth century. Here the bourgeoisie raised claims to the dignity of tragedy, which had earlier been a privilege of the aristocracy.

In opera, from Piccinni's *La buona figliuola* of 1760 (based on Richardson's novel *Pamela*) to Rossini's *La gazza ladra* (1817), the *comédie larmoyante,* or "tearful comedy," formed a subspecies of opera buffa in which the bourgeoisie, so to speak, clasped itself with sentimental panache in its own arms. If the parodistic opera buffa shows the aggressive side of bourgeois emancipation, in that it aimed a polemical barb at opera seria as a nobleman's art, the *comédie larmoyante* represents a form of self-contemplation. Yet, for some as yet unknown reason, opera remained aloof from the most striking expression of the bourgeoisie in the

Fig. 11   Concert in the Hanover Square Concert Rooms, 1843. The modern arrangement of the orchestra, introduced by Mendelssohn at the Leipzig Gewandhaus in 1835, places the musicians in a semicircle about the conductor, who stands at the front of the platform with his back to the audience. As late as 1843, however, a different arrangement was practiced in London, where the conductor stood in the midst of the musicians facing the audience. The reason for this seemingly absurd practice, like the placement of the double basses in the foreground (a holdover from the age of the basso continuo), lies in the tradition of the eighteenth century when the conductor, seated amidst the other musicians as a *primus inter pares,* also functioned as harpsichordist or first violinist. (Hamburg, Staats- und Universitätsbibliothek.)

theater, the bourgeois tragedy. The most we can point to by way of bourgeois tragedy, since it shows bourgeois figures ensnared in tragic circumstances, is the "rescue opera" exemplified by Beethoven's *Fidelio* (1804–5; third version, 1814) —that is, to the operatic genre that emerged from the French Revolution. (As in eighteenth-century opera seria, which likewise permitted a *lieto fine,* it is immaterial whether the plot has a happy or an unhappy ending.) Nonetheless, it would seem that the bourgeois tragedy, as represented in its most basic form by Lessing's *Emilia Galotti* (1772) or the dramas of the *Sturm und Drang,* was ignored by eighteenth- and early-nineteenth-century librettists. And when Verdi finally adopted the plot structure of the bourgeois tragedy in *La traviata* (1853), the heroine was no longer a victim of the aristocracy, like Emilia Galotti, but rather a demimondaine ruined by the bourgeoisie.

Another bourgeois phenomenon in nineteenth-century music culture was the untold number of amateur choruses: the singing academies, *Liedertafeln,* and *Liederkränze* that formed an increasingly dense web of musical societies mingling companionship and music in equal measure. If the London Handel Festivals from 1784 or Johann Adam Hiller's Berlin performance of *The Messiah* in 1786 were merely outstanding isolated events, choral singing in nineteenth-century Germany, England, and even France reached the proportions of a mass movement (whose sociopsychological roots, however, have largely remained unstudied). The political implications of this movement are unmistakable: it originated in the spirit of the French Revolution (in 1795 the National Convention proposed celebrating national holidays with *choeurs universels*), and the memory of the Revolution was kept alive by the democratic and nationalist sentiments that typically arose in amateur choruses, especially in men's choral societies, which for that reason were prohibited in Austria during the Restoration. In Hans Georg Nägeli, a pupil of Pestalozzi's and a founder of the *Liederkranz* movement, democratic fervor was sustained by assumptions of a pedagogical and philanthropic nature, namely, by the conception of popular education, which arose in the eighteenth century and became institutionalized in the nineteenth:

> Take hordes of people, take them by hundreds, by thousands, bring them into human interaction, an interaction where each is at liberty to express his personality in feelings and words, where he receives at the same time like-minded impressions from all the others, where he becomes aware in the most intuitive and multifarious way possible of his human self-sufficiency and camaraderie, where he radiates and breathes love, instantly, with every breath—and can this be anything other than choral singing? . . . The artistic essence of music is democratic in the exercise of its nature.

But as deeply as the amateur choral movement affected the social history of music, its position in the evolution of music as art remained dubious. And this development deserves special emphasis, since the nineteenth century was not just a bourgeois era but also an era of artistic autonomy. The Berlin Liedertafel, founded by Zelter as an exclusive society in 1809, may have required of its twenty-four members that they be poets, composers, or singers, but it was not without reason that the expression "Liedertafel style" came to signify shallow, sanctimonious music in which the "noble simplicity" still preserved by Friedrich Silcher gradually degenerated into kitsch. The modern repertoire of the singing academies and oratorio choirs, from Friedrich Schneider's *Weltgericht* (1819) to Max Bruch's *Gustav Adolf* (1898), when not imperiled by the near proximity of Handel's and Bach's works, was likewise made dubious by the glaring disproportion between the societies' institutional prerequisites and the composers' aesthetic intentions. By writing for amateur singers with a deep and well-rounded knowledge of literature and music, but with limited musical capabilities, composers were forced to take up a choral style which had to preserve simplicity without the slightest sacrifice of artistic pretense. Oratorio composers set out to create a "noble simplicity" at the "pinnacle of culture of the day," which under the compositional preconditions of the nineteenth century was virtually a paradox, realizable at best in the "sublime style." This kept them trapped in the Handelian tradition and prevented them from drawing far-reaching compositional consequences from the enthusiasm for Bach unleashed by the rediscovery of the *St. Matthew Passion*.

There is no end in sight to the dispute as to whether the educational function, the democratic component, and the patriotic utility that Philipp Spitta found so praiseworthy in men's choruses are enough to offset and consign to oblivion the aesthetic shortcomings of this music. This is because its apologists and detractors proceed from different conceptions of music. For the critics of this now dubious genre, "music" means compositional technique, the weaknesses of which are only too obvious. Its advocates stress the overall interaction of music and companionship, a process that includes political or, in the case of oratorio, religious factors as essential characteristics, and in which the composition is merely a substrate rather than the "main issue."

Hence, to measure nineteenth-century music as a whole against a conception of art drawn from classical instrumental music is to distort the historical significance of large parts of the vocal traditions of the era. The oratorio has no less claim to an undisputed aesthetic position as a genre in the grand style than opera seria and the symphony. Yet even though the oratorios of the age have disappeared from the twentieth-century repertoire, with the exception of Mendelssohn's *St. Paul* (1832–36) and *Elijah* (1845–46), we should not let this fact prevent us from doing historical justice to music whose "extramusical" educational elements—whether religious, nationalist, or literary—are part of its substance and cannot be extracted from it in order to form a "purely musical" opinion. Dead as these works may be as musical artifacts, they still remain valuable documents of cultural history.

If choral music has been eclipsed aesthetically despite its enormous significance to social history, the concert life that emerged in the eighteenth century from prototypes such as the *collegium musicum* has always been regarded as the representative institution of bourgeois musical culture. Public concerts are open to all, for a fee, and are also the object of descriptions and reviews in the central public medium of the bourgeoisie, the press. It was here that the emancipated bourgeoisie confirmed in its own eyes its status as the "taste-bearing stratum" in music.

The spirit of the bourgeoisie, then, found its musical manifestation in the public concert. However, this is not to say that the music culture of the age was bourgeois in its entirety. It would be a gross exaggeration to think of private aristocratic concerts as mere relics which survived the earlier notion of chamber music as a nonpublic form of concert. No less a composer than Beethoven established his fame in private concerts where admission was allowed only by invitation, rather than for a fee with no regard to personal standing. Even as late as the mid-nineteenth century, we can still be in doubt whether it was the public or the private concert—the bourgeois or the aristocratic—that formed the decisive arbiter in the making of aesthetic judgments and musicohistorical decisions. (We are probably still justified in calling private concerts aristocratic during the July Monarchy, when a parvenu nobility of bankers vied with the old Napoleonic and Bourbon nobility.) A glance at the biographies of Spohr, Moscheles, Chopin, or Liszt will suffice to assess the historical significance of the private concert, the form in which the earlier music culture of the nobility survived into the nineteenth century. (In pre-1848 Vienna audiences were also allowed to attend domestic bourgeois performances of *Hausmusik,* the principal difference being that, in an aristocratic private concert, professional musicians played for a fee. It was possible to refuse the fee, as did Mendelssohn or, later, Joseph Joachim, in order to appear as a gentleman rather than as a musical employee. However, this conveyed the impression of a *Hausmusik* performance among amateurs, for no matter how well or ill a gentleman played he was always considered an amateur. Artistic status was concealed by social standing.)

The importance to music history of the private concert only began to recede in the late nineteenth century. Yet scholarly and popular writings on music almost invariably overlook or belittle its importance. This is probably explained, for one, by an unconscious prejudice on the part of bourgeois historians against aristocratic traditions; for another, by the habit of searching the past for a prehistory of the present, a present whose musical culture is marked by the public concert; and finally by an inherent lack of documents. Public concerts were regularly reported in journals and newspapers, private concerts only rarely. Still, no historian would maintain that the best-documented parts of music history are a fortiori the most significant. To write a history of the private concert would be an act of historical justice which should not be difficult in an age that sees itself as the end of the bourgeois era.

The bourgeois concert consisting of an overture, a solo concerto, and a symphony emerged around the middle of the nineteenth century and seems classical in retrospect because it predominated for an entire century. Yet by the criteria of

Fig. 12 Friedrich August Bruckner (after a French drawing): *Sologesang mit Harmonium,* 1848. Given the number of songs which placed no inconsiderable emphasis on sentimental *religioso,* it is hardly surprising that, besides the piano, the harmonium (or *orgue expressif*) was likewise considered suitable for accompanying the solo voice. In an age in which Louis James Alfred Lefébure-Wély, the composer of *Les cloches du monastère,* was organist at the Madeleine in Paris, domestic and salon music, whether vocal or instrumental, did not hesitate an instant to incorporate religious motifs into their repertoire of musical clichés. (Kassel, Bärenreiter Bildarchiv.)

social history it does not represent the bourgeoisie per se, but simply reveals the ascendance of the aesthetic demands of a social stratum known as the *Bildungsbürgertum,* the "educated" or "cultured" classes. (This stratum is sometimes referred to sardonically as the "educated and propertied classes," and while there is a modicum of truth to this formula, it stands in the way of a just historical appraisal, which must always be morally just as well.) The emphasis fell on the educative and edifying function of music, and of autonomous music in particular. Education—*Bildung*—meant gaining an inner detachment from the "realm of necessity," as the bourgeoisie regarded their everyday existence, and one of the paths to education, in the still untarnished sense of the term as used by Humboldt and Hegel, was aesthetic contemplation, the selfless immersion in a type of music held by the romantics to manifest "another world." Music was meant not merely to be "enjoyed" but to be "understood." And in order to fulfill its educative function it forced audiences to listen silently, a mode of behavior which only after a long and tedious process gained ascendancy over the earlier habit of using music as a stimulus to conversation, at least in those moments when the emotions were not being touched.

Thus, it was the need to understand autonomous, nonfunctional music that made listeners silently retrace the act of composition in their minds. In terms of performance practice, this meant that a work contained its own meaning and had to be presented whole and intact, since, according to the classical aesthetic proclaimed as early as 1780 by Karl Philipp Moritz, the autonomous work is a self-sufficient entity. In earlier times symphonies were torn apart and played with one movement at the beginning of a concert and another at the end, with virtuoso pieces and opera excerpts sandwiched in between. This custom was abandoned; more accurately, the light concert, which could easily accommodate a movement from a symphony, split off from the symphony concert, where the integrity of the works was preserved. In other words, the standard mid-century concert program consisting of an overture, a solo concerto, and a symphony; the strong conception of musical works which prohibited their dismemberment; and aesthetic contemplation as a mode of behavior which allowed music to serve an educative function approximating that of literature—all were part and parcel of one and the same process, and all were associated with the bourgeois educated classes. This process gave rise to a concert aesthetic which, in the first half of the nineteenth century, gradually supplanted the earlier practice of cobbling together musical programs from heterogeneous parts to attain an effect where entertainment shaded into emotion and back again. And if we understand institution to mean, not simply an organization, but a crystallization of social facilities, modes of behavior, and categories of judgment, then the concert as an institution includes aesthetic and sociopsychological levels as well, and becomes a representative instance of bourgeois music culture in the nineteenth century.

Bibliographic References

Abraham, Gerald. *A Hundred Years of Music*. 4th ed. London: Duckworth, 1974.

Adler, Guido. "Der Wiener klassischer Stil." In *Handbuch der Musikgeschichte*, edited by Guido Adler. 2d rev. ed. Berlin-Wilmersdorf: H. Keller, 1930.

Adorno, Theodor Wiesengrund. *Einleitung in die Musiksoziologie*. Frankfurt am Main: Suhrkamp, 1962. Eng. trans. by E. B. Ashton as *Introduction to the Sociology of Music*. New York: Continuum, 1988.

Asaf'ev, Boris. *Muzykal'naja forma kak process*. Leningrad: Gos. muzykal'noe izd-vo, 1963. Eng. trans. as *Musical Form as a Process*. Ph.D. Diss., Ohio State University, 1977. Ann Arbor, Mich.: University Microfilms, 1978.

Barraclough, Geoffrey. *An Introduction to Contemporary History*. London: C. A. Watts, 1964.

Becking, Gustav. *Der musikalische Rhythmus als Erkenntnisquelle*. Augsburg: B. Filser, 1928.

———. "Zur musikalischen Romantik." *Deutsche Vierteljahrschrift für Literaturwissenschaft und Geistesgeschichte* 2 (1924).

Blume, Friedrich. "Romantik." In *Musik in Geschichte und Gegenwart*, vol. 11. Kassel: Bärenreiter, 1963. Eng. trans. in Blume, Friedrich. *Classic and Romantic Music*. London: Faber & Faber, 1972.

Bücken, Ernst. *Die Musik des 19. Jahrhunderts*. Wildpark-Potsdam: Akademische Verlagsgesellschaft Athenaion, 1929.

Carse, Adam. *The Orchestra from Beethoven to Berlioz*. Cambridge: W. Heffer, 1948.

Dahlhaus, Carl. "Zur Problematik der musikalischen Gattungen im 19. Jahrhundert." In *Gattungen der Musik*, edited by Wulf Arlt. Vol. 1. Berne and Munich: Francke, 1973.

Dent, Edward. *The Rise of Romantic Opera*. Edited by Winton Dean. Cambridge: Cambridge University Press, 1976.

Edler, Arnfried. *Studien zur Auffassung antiker Musikrhythmen im 19. Jahrhundert*. Kassel: Bärenreiter, 1970.

Einstein, Alfred. *Music in the Romantic Era.* New York: W. W. Norton, 1947.

Engel, Hans. *Musik und Gesellschaft. Bausteine zu einer Musiksoziologie.* Berlin: M. Hesse, 1960.

Erpf, Hermann Robert. *Studien zur Harmonie- und Klangtechnik der neueren Musik.* Leipzig: Breitkopf & Härtel, 1927. 2d ed. Leipzig: Breitkopf & Härtel, 1969.

Georgiades, Thrasybulos. *Musik und Sprache.* Heidelberg: Springer, 1954. Eng. trans. as *Music and Language.* Cambridge: Cambridge University Press, 1983.

Grout, Donald. *A Short History of Opera.* New York: W. W. Norton, 1947. 2d ed. New York: Norton, 1965.

Habermas, Jürgen. *Strukturwandel der Öffentlichkeit.* Neuwied: H. Luchterhand, 1962.

Halm, August. *Von zwei Kulturen der Musik.* Munich: Georg Müller, 1913. 3d ed. Stuttgart: Klett, 1947.

Hauser, Arnold. *Sozialgeschichte der Kunst und Literatur.* 2 vols. 2d ed. Munich: Beck, 1958. Eng. trans. as *The Social History of Art and Literature.* London: Routledge & Kegan Paul, 1951.

Jahn, Otto. *W. A. Mozart.* 4 vols. Leipzig: Breitkopf & Härtel, 1856–59.

Klemperer, Viktor. "Romantik und französische Romantik." In *Begriffsbestimmung der Romantik,* edited by Helmut Prang. Darmstadt: Wissenschaftliche Buchgesellschaft, 1968.

Knepler, Georg. *Musikgeschichte des 19. Jahrhunderts.* Berlin: Henschelverlag, 1961.

———. *Geschichte als Weg zum Musikverständnis.* Leipzig: P. Reclam, 1977. 2d ed. Leipzig: P. Reclam, 1982.

Kretzschmar, Hermann. *Führer durch den Konzertsaal.* Leipzig: Liebeskind, 1887–90.

Kurth, Ernst. *Romantische Harmonik und ihre Krise in Wagners "Tristan."* Berne und Leipzig: P. Haupt, 1920. 3d ed. Berlin: M. Hesse, 1923.

Lissa, Zofia. "Über die nationalen Stile," *Beiträge zur Musikwissenschaft* 6 (1964): 187–214.

Loewenberg, Alfred. *Annals of Opera.* Cambridge: W. Heffer, 1943. 2d ed. Geneva: Societas Bibliographica, 1955.

Longyear, Roy M. *Nineteenth Century Romanticism in Music.* Englewood Cliffs, N.J.: Prentice-Hall, 1969. 2d ed. Englewood Cliffs, N.J.: Prentice-Hall, 1973.

Marothy, Janos. *Music and the Bourgeois—Music and the Proletarian.* Budapest: Akademiai Kiado, 1974.

Marx, Adolf Bernhard. *Die Musik des 19. Jahrhunderts und ihre Pflege. Methode der Musik.* Leipzig: Breitkopf & Härtel, 1855. 2d ed. Leipzig: Breitkopf & Härtel, 1873. Eng. trans. as *The Music of the Nineteenth Century and Its Culture: Method of Musical Instruction.* London: R. Cocks, 1854.

Mendel, Hermann. *Musikalisches Conversations-Lexikon.* 11 vols. Berlin: L. Heimann; New York: J. Schuberth, 1870–79. Vols. 7–11 edited by August Reissmann.

Nineteenth Century Music. Berkeley and Los Angeles: University of California Press, 1971–.

Reichert, Georg, and Just, Martin, eds. *Die Musik von 1830 bis 1914. Bericht über den internationalen musikwissenschaftlichen Kongreß Kassel 1962.* Kassel and Basle: Bärenreiter, 1963.

Réti, Rudolf. *The Thematic Process in Music.* New York: Macmillan, 1951.

Riemann, Hugo. *Geschichte der Musik seit Beethoven (1800–1900).* Berlin and Stuttgart: W. Spemann, 1901.

Salmen, Walter. *Haus- und Kammermusik zwischen 1600 und 1900.* Musikgeschichte in Bildern. Edited by Heinrich Besseler and Max Schneider, Vol. 4, no. 3. Leipzig: Deutscher Verlag für Musik, 1969.

Schenker, Heinrich. *Die letzten fünf Sonaten Beethovens.* Vienna: Universal Edition, 1913–21.

Schering, Arnold. *Beethoven und die Dichtung.* Berlin: Junker & Dünnhaupt, 1936.

Schilling, Gustav. *Encyclopädie der gesamten musikalischen Wissenschaften oder Universal-Lexikon der Tonkunst.* 6 vols. Stuttgart: F. H. Köhler, 1835–37.

Schreiber, Ottmar. *Orchester und Orchesterpraxis in Deutschland zwischen 1780 und 1850.* Berlin: Junker & Dünnhaupt, 1938.

Schücking, Levin Ludwig. *Soziologie der literarischen Geschmacksbildung.* 3d rev. ed. Berne and Munich: Francke, 1961. Eng. trans. as *The Sociology of Literary Taste.* London: Routledge & Kegan Paul, 1950.

Schwab, Heinrich W. *Konzert. Öffentliche Musikdarbietung vom 17. bis 19. Jahrhundert.* Musikgeschichte in Bildern. Edited by Heinrich Besseler and Max Schneider. Vol. 4, no. 2. Leipzig: Deutscher Verlag für Musik, 1971.

Spitta, Philipp. "Der deutsche Männergesang." In *Musikalische Aufsätze.* Berlin: Gebrüder Paetel, 1894.

Strich, Fritz. "Die Romantik als europäische Bewegung." In *Festschrift für Heinrich Wölfflin.* Munich: Hugo Schmidt, 1924.

———. *Studien zur Musikgeschichte des 19. Jahrhunderts.* Regensburg: G. Bosse, 1965–.

Tovey, Donald Francis. *Essays in Musical Analysis.* London: Oxford University Press, 1935–44.

Wiora, Walter. "Die Musik im Weltbild der deutschen Romantik." In *Beiträge zur Geschichte der Musikanschauung im 19. Jahrhundert.* Studien zur Musikgeschichte des 19. Jahrhunderts, vol. 1. Edited by Walter Salmen. Regensburg: G. Bosse, 1965.

Wolff, Hellmuth Christian. *Oper, Szene und Darstellung von 1600 bis 1900.* Musikgeschichte in Bildern. Edited by Heinrich Besseler and Max Schneider. Vol. 4, no. 1. Leipzig: Deutscher Verlag für Musik, 1968.

CHAPTER TWO

1814-1830

The premise underlying our choice of period is that, though not obligatory, it is at least expedient to extract from the continuum of history a "nineteenth century" extending from the Congress of Vienna to the outbreak of the First World War. This premise encourages us to divide the century into subperiods or evolutionary stages bounded by dates such as 1830 and 1848 which are regarded as turning points in political history. Yet it is not absolutely clear just what chronological and substantive relations obtain at all between so-called epoch-making events and the profound sociohistorical changes that constitute the actual object of written history, changes of which these events are merely the visible expression.

For the moment, the connection between structural history and the history of events is hopelessly confused, even within political and social history, both of which lay claim to being "general history," as though cultural history were nothing but an afterthought. As a result, the significance of epoch-making years in music history remains as obscure as their existence is undeniable. Obviously, the years immediately surrounding 1814 and 1830 witnessed an accumulation of events so striking that we are fully justified in calling these two dates turning points in music history without arousing suspicions that we have tendentiously selected our facts. We need only recall Beethoven's transition to the late period after 1814, Rossini's breakthrough with *Tancredi* and *L'italiana in Algeri* (both of 1813), and Schubert's establishment of the lied as a central genre in romantic music with full claim to artistic status (*Gretchen am Spinnrade*, 1814). As for 1830, we could mention—following Beethoven's and Schubert's deaths and Rossini's self-imposed silence—the founding of grand opera by Meyerbeer (*Robert le diable*, 1831), the emergence of a French strain of musical romanticism with Berlioz's *Symphonie fantastique* (1830), Bellini's breakthrough with *La straniera* (1829), the confrontation in Milan between Bellini's *La sonnambula* (1831) and Donizetti's *Anna Bolena* (1830), Mendelssohn's rediscovery of the *St. Matthew Passion* in 1829 (his overture to *A Midsummer Night's Dream* had already appeared in 1826), Chopin's removal to Paris in 1830, and Schumann's Abegg Variations of the same year. To the latter we could also add Schumann's 1831 essay on Chopin, a musicoaesthetic Opus 1 of "epoch-making" importance to the history of criticism.

The mere fact that important events accumulate in certain years is sufficient, pragmatically, to vindicate our subdivision of nineteenth-century music history. As purely descriptive historians we are not obliged to tackle the historiosophical import of this accumulation of music-historical occurrences in or about 1814 and 1830 and their coincidence with turning points in political history. Nor would it even undermine the legitimacy of our choice—provided we raise no metaphysical claims for it—to maintain in a spirit of rigorous skepticism that any correspondence between music and politics at this time is purely accidental.

On the other hand, there are historians who allow ample room for accident in history without wishing a priori to forego reconstructing a context that defines a period from within. And these historians will be tempted to speak, with Heinrich Heine, of a "spirit of the Restoration period," a spirit which was embodied by Rossini and which caused Beethoven to withdraw to the hermeticism of his late works. After decades of Napoleonic wars Europe clearly felt a deep-seated need for peace, and we can at least sense this need, albeit in various guises, in the music of the time, whether in Rossini's nonchalance, in the curious amalgam of cantabile and abstraction which, in Beethoven's late works, supplanted the heroic stance of his middle period, or in the note of resignation that recurs time and time again in Schubert. (Melancholy and renunciation are not likely to spread in times endangered by revolution and war.)

Yet, if the "zeitgeist" can be felt most closely in the moods it engenders, the changes in intellectual history which affect the history of music almost invariably resist categorization into clearly datable periods. We stand little chance of determining when the notion of "organic development" entered our awareness of musical form: in music theory it happened sometime between Heinrich Christoph Koch and Adolf Bernhard Marx, but theory is merely a reflection of events rather than the event itself. Nor can we establish the exact moment when Herder's idea of "national spirit"—an idea which, at least in its later stages, united a social, political, and historical conception of "nationhood"—began to exercise its influence. All we know is that at some time between the eighteenth and the nineteenth century—in Germany between Gluck and Weber—a fundamental change took place in the meaning of "national style" in music.

One of the platitudes of history, particularly of the Marxist variety, is that romanticism belongs to the Restoration period, and indeed represents a form of restoration. This view raises questions regarding its chronology and substance, in the latter case because it posits an intrinsic affinity between political and intellectual history which, though plausible at first glance, derives in a strict sense from nothing more substantial than Friedrich Schlegel's conversion to Metternich and Eichendorff's inborn conservatism. (The claim that the Gothic revival was linked with "reactionary" tendencies proves flawed the moment we understand "reactionary" to mean a political stance in favor of royalism and opposed to national sovereignty.) But the most cursory glance will show that chronologically, too, it is no easy matter to pinpoint the romantic period. First

Fig. 13   Contemporary engraving of the Congress of Vienna. In the post-1814 Restoration period, following the upheavals of the Napoleonic wars, there arose a desire for calm and repose, which, however, in the wake of political oppression, gradually took on the character of a tomb-like silence. The spreading aura of resignation also left its mark on music, the "times as captured in notes," whether in Beethoven's withdrawal to the esoteric, Schubert's abrupt changes from rapture to melancholy, or Rossini's cheerful cynicism, with its covert tendency toward the chaotic. (Vienna, Österreichische National-bibliothek.)

of all, early German romanticism dates back to the 1790s with Wackenroder's and Tieck's metaphysic of instrumental music—a metaphysic that laid the foundations of nineteenth-century music aesthetics and, as passed down by Schopenhauer from Tieck and by Wagner from Schopenhauer, reigned virtually unchallenged even in the decades of fin-de-siècle modernism. French romanticism, on the other hand, whose advent in music is supposedly attested by the *Symphonie fantastique,* is a phenomenon of the 1830s (unless, following Edward Dent's suggestion, we espy the "rise of French romantic opera" in a few revolutionary operas of the 1790s and then bridge the resultant time lag to French romantic literature by considering, as we probably should, the novels of Chateaubriand and Sénancour as romantic). The only evidence that remains is the fact that Schubert's and Weber's works were contemporary with the Heidelberg Romantics and the Restoration period (we might also mention Scott's *Waverley* novels, which began to appear in 1814). All told, it is doubtful whether this evidence is sufficient to proclaim romanticism in all seriousness as a correlate to the Restoration in the history of music and ideas. It looks as though this old historiographical saw will have to be abandoned.

However closely the major works and characteristic aesthetic views of early-nineteenth-century music may have been connected with the ideals of romanticism, the impact of the Restoration was weak and diffuse, if we take "restoration" in the narrow and more precise sense to mean tangible royalist and clericalist tendencies rather than simply a "zeitgeist" representing a need for peace and resignation. Admittedly, the oratorios of Le Sueur, by invoking the spirit of the Middle Ages, sought to give musical expression to a royalist attitude that honored Napoleon in 1804 and Charles X in 1824; and the musical side of the "Prussian Agenda" (*Kirchenagende für die Hof- und Domkirche in Berlin*) promulgated in 1822 by Friedrich Wilhelm III was taken up in part by the Russian-flavored Palestrina style of Dmitri Bortnyansky. But we are hard pressed to identify any musical consequences caused by the reinstatement of the first and second estates to their former privileges. In the first half of the nineteenth century the churches drifted toward sclerotic orthodoxy, hoping to regain in political power what they had lost in spiritual influence; this helps to explain how their institutional hegemony during the Restoration could nevertheless remain virtually irrelevant in the domain of art, where nothing is attainable by decree. The courts, for their part, found themselves gradually restricted to formal patronage, a role which republican governments could take over virtually intact following successful revolutions. To be sure, throughout the century there were court musicians whose social prestige should not be underestimated: witness court conductors from Weber and Wagner to Mahler and Strauss. However, following the disintegration of the international system of Italian court opera and the decline of ostentatious ceremonial church music (a Baroque holdover amidst the Classic period), court music was no longer a deciding factor in musical style. The musical traditions that toppled during the Revolution proved impossible to revive during the Restoration.

Rossini and the Restoration

From a musical standpoint, the nineteenth century was just as much the age of Beethoven and Rossini during its first half as it was dominated by Wagner and Verdi in the second. Yet, however violent the arguments alternately imputing and denying Wagner's influence on Verdi, music historians have remained curiously silent about the simultaneous appearance of Rossini's output and Beethoven's late works, a fact whose inherent unlikelihood has made it one of the riddles of history.

It is, of course, pointless and futile to pronounce verdicts on the relative dignity of the symphony and opera buffa as genres in order to cast the composer of *Il barbiere di Siviglia* as a prankster alongside the titanic author of the Ninth

Symphony: the most cursory reflection devoid of national prejudice will suffice to show that these verdicts are nonhistorical. First of all, like his musical forebears Paisiello and Cimarosa, Rossini was not merely a *buffonist* but at least in equal measure a composer of opera seria: the Rossini renaissance in recent years has consisted largely in the rediscovery of him as a seria composer whose *Maometto II* (1820), *Otello* (1816), and *Mosè in Egitto* (1818) undeservedly disappeared in the shadow cast by the enormous popularity of *Il barbiere* (1816). Moreover, according to contemporary opinion (which no historian can afford to dismiss out of hand), Italian opera, whether seria, semiseria, or buffa, ranked aesthetically alongside German instrumental music—the symphony and the string quartet—as the leading musical genre of its age. In its day, Mozart's operas notwithstanding, Viennese classicism was considered primarily a form of instrumental music and represented not musical culture in its entirety but merely one culture among many. Finally, in the case of Mozart, who was admired equally by both Rossini and Beethoven, the symphony and opera buffa stand aesthetically on an equal footing. This leads us to ask how it came about that a few decades later this common legacy could give rise to consequences so wildly antithetical that, by the end of the century, writers who clung to the notion of a "German century in music" found it no less absurd to compare Beethoven and Rossini than to compare Wagner and Offenbach.

If Rossini, in a letter of 1854 to Count Fay, could refer to himself as the "last of the classics," Beethoven's name was already being linked with Haydn and Mozart in the early part of the century by contemporaries such as Reichardt and E. T. A. Hoffmann. And if there is any intrinsic similarity between Beethoven and Rossini that makes their contemporaneity less of a riddle, we are likely to find it in the way that these two composers, who could be lionized as the "last of the classics" and yet stood as the founders of two "musical cultures" dominating the entire century, confronted their common tradition. One aspect arising from their moment in history and held by both composers in common was the degree of reflection in their compositional methods and in their attitude to musical material. It seems as though an immediate relation to music was as impossible in the postrevolutionary period as it was natural around 1800. In a word, both Rossini and Beethoven (in his later years) wrote music about music: music at one remove. To a certain extent, music-making was no longer a natural and self-evident endeavor, neither for Beethoven and Rossini nor, later, for Berlioz, Wagner, or Verdi, all of whom underwent years of crisis. And however dissimilar the psychological motivation of Beethoven's withdrawal around 1816 and Rossini's around 1829, the very fact that a composer could feel alienated from the musical expression that constituted his raison d'être was a new and unusual phenomenon, one that arose first in Beethoven and Rossini only to recur throughout the nineteenth century, specifically in composers of stature. Rossini may have regarded the spirit, or perhaps distemper, of the Restoration with unprotesting nonchalance while Beethoven adopted a bristling critical stance; but this does not alter the fact that both partook of a zeitgeist that called for resigned detachment from their surroundings, a detachment of cheerful skepticism or melancholy self-absorption that set them apart from other people and things.

We often read of the playfulness of Rossini's works and the irony in his musical diction. This vague, pat formula takes on clearer focus when we view it as an attempt to capture in words a sense of ambivalence, a feeling that Rossini distanced himself from the music he wrote in a manner that itself became part of his music. We sense a fracture or rift in his work which conveys the impression that we are dealing with music about music. This aesthetic phenomenon can be accounted for technically as an upending of the customary hierarchy among the parameters or dimensions of musical composition.

The crucial element in Rossini's music and its effect is not the substance it is based on so much as the whirligig frenzy it is drawn into. As later in Labiche's farces, which the stage director Peter Stein has interpreted as fragments of a pathology of the nineteenth century, flimsy incidents and motives give rise gradually and unpredictably to a furious tumult that increasingly, for all its giddy humor, takes on the character of a catastrophe only to dissolve abruptly into eerie nothingness.

Those of us who grew up with and are unable to escape the categories of the German musical tradition from Bach to Schönberg would have to say that, in Rossini's music, the relation between his musical ideas and their formal presentation is disturbed and out of joint: motives that are often rudimentary or even tawdry are whisked pell-mell into juggernaut crescendos. However, if we wish to do justice aesthetically and historically to Rossini's technique, we will have to discard the categories of idea and presentation (which tacitly presuppose the superiority of the former to the latter) and instead substitute the more appropriate concepts of substrate and realization.

Rossini not infrequently gives precedence to rhythm over themes, to instrumentation and coloratura over melodic contour, to intensified repetition over motivic manipulation. In doing so he stood the hierarchy of musical parameters on its head. Once his audiences had recovered from their initial puzzlement, as reflected in their (soon forgotten) rejection of *Il barbiere di Siviglia* at its premiere, they found that this technique made perfect sense. Aestheticians, however, continued to voice displeasure, seeing in Rossini's inversion of musical values nothing but "effects without causes," as though it went without saying that instrumentation, coloratura, and repetition had to be "grounded" in an overriding edifice of melody.

To measure Rossini's melody with Mozart as its yardstick is to lead ourselves astray. When we try to extract an underlying melody from the coloratura, we sometimes arrive at nothing even remotely resembling a musical idea. We should not view this as a technical or artistic shortcoming on Rossini's part so much as an indication that, in Rossini's case, the premise that the substance of music resides in its melodic contour, with coloratura a mere adjunct or paraphrase, will often lead us nowhere. With respect both to its structure and to its expression, the external trappings of Rossini's music prove to be its essence, an essence that lies on the surface rather than being concealed beneath it.

The substrate of Rossini's melodies and harmonies, then, is trivial; his rhythms have a sharpness of focus that emphasizes the banal; his formal designs are guilelessly simplistic; his relentless and rigorous crescendos whip rudimentary themes into a cyclonic frenzy. Yet all these factors complement one another, forming an aesthetic and compositional unity in which cleverness and primitivity merge in such a way that each element thrives on the other rather than undercutting its effect. It is precisely because the "substance" of his melody remains undeveloped that his sharply focused rhythms can assume the main musical burden; it is precisely because his themes are limited to motivic gestures which are boldly stated without seeming in any way significant, that his technique of unrelenting, almost obsessive repetition can generate a manic intoxication without devolving into monotony. The "shortcomings" of Rossini's music are the cornerstone of its "effect."

"Rossini's music," wrote Heine in 1837, comparing Rossini with Meyerbeer, the musical embodiment of the July Monarchy, "was more appropriate to the Restoration period when, now that the mighty battles were over and lost, a dulled and apathetic populace was forced to forget its great common causes, and the sentiments of self-interest could be restored to their legitimate rights." (The word "legitimate" causes Heine's sympathy for "self-interest" to cancel out his antipathy toward the Restoration.) These "sentiments of self-interest," he continues, the "individual joys and sufferings of humanity: love and hatred, tenderness and yearning, jealousy and sulking," find their musical expression in melody. "Hence it is fully in keeping with Rossini's music that melody should prevail: melody, ever the immediate expression of feeling in isolation."

Rossini's melody captivated an entire age, not excluding such abstract thinkers as Hegel. In *Oper und Drama,* Wagner denounced it as "narrow melody"— that is, melody which inevitably breaks off after a few bars instead of being prolonged into the infinite, like Beethoven's. This preconception—that Rossini cobbled his melodies together from unrelated momentary effects—became even more deeply ingrained as the polemics of his detractors were met by unsatisfactory arguments on the part of his adherents, who remained prisoners of their time. In the literature on Rossini we find scarcely a word about musical form, as though there were nothing to say about the thread that holds his musical thoughts together. Secretly, it would seem, people are convinced that Rossini's music is a sort of potpourri, a term of disparagement that begs the question of what distinguishes a good potpourri from a bad one.

Even concert audiences who are incapable of following sonata-allegro form will concede that the form demands a particular mode of listening. The same does not apply to opera, least of all to Italian opera, where listeners roundly reject the thought that they should listen in terms of form. In fact, it is especially urgent that they do so, for Rossini's operas—despite Wagner's claim to the con-

Fig. 14 The Act 2 finale from Rossini's *Assedio di Corinto*. This is one of those large-scale tableaux with chorus and ensemble which formed the backbone of opera seria during its transition to grand opera. Here an amorous intrigue, patterned after the eighteenth-century Metastasian opera, is combined with a state action manifesting the political tenor of the early nineteenth century on the operatic stage. Maometto II, the Turkish conqueror of Corinth, commands the city to be razed because of unrequited love. (Vienna, Österreichische Nationalbibliothek.)

trary, which so profoundly influenced their later reception—consist over long periods, if not throughout, of "large-scale forms."

The terzetto "Destin terribile" from Act 1 of Rossini's opera seria *L'assedio di Corinto*—the 1826 French version, retranslated into Italian, of *Maometto II* (1820)—appears as a complex of no fewer than five sections whose combination is justified both musically and dramaturgically. The opening scena, an accompanied recitative, quotes a reminiscence motive from the introduction which later occurs in the scena of the finale, thus bracketing the entire act. The first arioso section, marked "adagio non troppo," begins hesitantly, its melody broken by rests. This jagged, rhapsodic opening is thoroughly typical of Rossini, who prefers to have his cantabile emerge from exclamations rather than presenting it directly in sharp contrast to the recitative. In "Destin terribile" these exclamations express the characters' perplexity at the tragic course of events. The cantabile itself, the central slow section ("Oh ciel"), consists of three strophes with an increasing number of voices. And as in every successful fugue, it is the relation between the principal and secondary voices in the second and third entrances that brings the form to life. The fact that the secondary voice (by no means secondary in importance) is made up of scraps of expressive melody should not deter us from speaking of "cantabile counterpoint": expressive declamation is one of the elements that constitute bel canto in the full sense of the term, and it is the interaction—that is, a contrapuntal relation—between sustained cantabile and dramatic exclamation that represents the fullest realization of melody as Rossini imagined it. Thus, to claim that operatic melody attained its most perfect form in the ensemble rather than in the aria is not merely to coin a paradox but, at least in Rossini's case, to put our finger on a very real trend.

The fourth section of the terzetto is a scena with choral declamation whose musicodramatic function is to provide psychological motivation for switching to the quick tempo of the cabaletta. (Hence, it is the librettist's job to create a disturbance on stage without changing the persons doing the singing.) The concluding cabaletta ("La data fè rammento") is one of Rossini's crescendo forms. These forms invariably follow a single pattern: an initial musical idea, which may have a closed periodic structure, is followed by a second, which must remain syntactically open-ended to allow for ostinato repetitions; and these repetitions draw the second idea into an ineluctable crescendo, which ultimately, in a third idea, discharges into a wild frenzy. This dynamic pattern was at least as important as Rossini's melody in establishing his fame; it is effective regardless of whether, as in the terzetto, it has a binary form (*ABCABC*) without modulation or a ternary form with modulation—that is, with a rudimentary "development" section and a transposition of the second theme from dominant to tonic. For Rossini, sonata-allegro form was incidental, just one schema among others which offers little or no basis for understanding his music. The substance of his form resides in its pattern of dynamics.

Although it adheres to a basic pattern, the five-part structure of the terzetto proves to be motivated by the psychology of the drama (or, conversely, the librettist drew on a formal musical pattern to which he then tried to give an intrinsic psychological and dramatic justification). A dramatic conflict (I) gives rise to hushed perplexity (II), which then dissolves into a cantabile (III) representing an outpouring of pent-up emotion. A second disturbance on stage (IV) changes the situation, whether outwardly or psychologically, and justifies the transition to a madcap cabaletta (V). It should be obvious that this five-part design has its own logic: the plausibility of the music—which thrives on traditional elements such as the opposition of slow and fast and a regular alternation of recitative and arioso—dovetails with the plausibility of the drama. And anyone who views the cantabile and cabaletta sections as isolated "numbers," thereby relegating the intermediate scena to the role of a caesura interrupting the melodic flow with a bit of "drama," has understood little or nothing of a type of form that is thoroughly deserving of the term "large-scale" and that derives its meaning from the juxtaposition of cantabile and cabaletta, a juxtaposition as compelling musically as it is motivated dramatically.

The relation between opera seria and opera buffa is, in Rossini's case, ambivalent. *Il barbiere di Siviglia* may have established the composer's subsequent fame, but this fact is offset by the contrary fact that from 1813 to 1829 the focus of his composition gradually shifted from opera buffa to opera seria. (His last comic opera, *La gazza ladra* of 1817, is a musical *comédie larmoyante*.) And if Rossini marks an end in the history of the opera buffa—Donizetti's *Don Pasquale* of 1843 is a "straggler," and Verdi's *Un giorno di regno* of 1840, his sole comic opera before *Falstaff*, was a fiasco—he nevertheless marks a new beginning in the evolution of the opera seria, which by 1810 had fallen into rigidity and decline. This new beginning was to prove viable for an entire century, to the time of Puccini.

The choice of subject matter seems to have played only a minor part in the renaissance of opera seria. Rossini did not bother with local color until *Guillaume Tell* in 1829, and wrote his works in lofty disregard of any distinctions between "classical" and "romantic" subjects. Still, it is noteworthy that a composer who could apostrophize himself as "the last of the classics" nearly always avoided "classical" subject matter from ancient history and myth when writing his serious operas (among his later works, *Semiramide* of 1823 forms the exception). Instead, he tended toward subjects from what the early nineteenth century regarded as "romantic" literature: *Tancredi* (1813) after Ariosto, *Otello* (1816) after Shakespeare, *Armida* (1817) after Tasso, *La donna del lago* (1819) after Scott, *Bianca e Falliero* (1819) after Manzoni. (His plans to set *Faust* were later abandoned, but it is nonetheless remarkable that he even contemplated doing it.)

Even more confused than the "extrinsic" relation between opera buffa and opera seria (i.e., in the history of their origins and subsequent reception) is the "intrinsic" relation between them from the standpoint of intellectual history and the history of composition. The most obvious feature that separated Rossini's buffo style from the tradition represented by Paisiello and Cimarosa—whether in straightforward buffo farces (*L'italiana in Algeri*), in comic operas with *parti serie* (*Il barbiere di Siviglia*), or in sentimental pieces (*La gazza ladra*)—was a forced undertone that makes us sense a distinct brittleness beneath the elegant surface of the musicodramatic events. This undertone at all events explains how Antonio Amore, very much unlike Heine, could hear in Rossini's music the spirit not of the Restoration but of revolution (*Brevi cenni critici,* 1877). The jokes of opera buffa become eerie when they are taken to extremes, and Rossini's forcedness gave his comic operas a touch of the demonic strong enough to shock and repel an upright burgher such as Ludwig Spohr when he heard *L'italiana in Algeri* in 1816.

Rossini's aggressive and sometimes violent rhythms—his debt to French revolutionary opera—make us sense that opera buffa can come near to opera seria; conversely, he apparently thought nothing of transferring to the opera seria features associated with the comedy of opera buffa. It is as though he used the same colors to paint in different genres. Sometimes, in situations dominated by a mood of oppression or tragic pathos, particularly in the cabalettas, he strikes a note of tuneful, almost merry brio that seems oblivious of the characters and their plights.

On the surface, this switching of genres can look like a mindless confusion of styles. It becomes intelligible when, without undue psychologizing, we conceive of Rossini's music as an expression of its moment in history, including the history of the human psyche. Something in his comic operas conveys the impression of being forced and causes their buffoonery to turn for an instant (an instant is all it takes) into the demonic. And this factor is mysteriously one of a kind with the sugarcoated pathos of his serious operas, where the music unnervingly leaves us uncertain whether Rossini's ostentatious detachment derives from a spirit of musical smugness or from a surreptitious gloom that sees the cogs churning mechanically at the root of tragedy. In Rossini the extremes meet: the farcical takes on catastrophic proportions in the frenzy of the music; the tragic, in its moments of greatest despair, exposes the marionette strings from which the characters are dangling. For a skeptic like Rossini, whose cheerfulness is simply the obverse of a melancholy that afflicted not just himself but his entire age, these extremes prove to be complementary.

Opéra comique and German Opera

Opéra comique is a generic term whose "official" distinguishing feature is its use of spoken dialogue instead of the recitative of the *tragédie lyrique*. Yet this feature obviously does not take us very far in defining an operatic genre comparable to spoken drama as we have come to expect it. According to the terms set down in the monopoly on recitative at the Académie Royale, where the *tragédie lyrique* was performed, the original version of Cherubini's *Medée* (1797) had to be classified as an *opéra comique* because of its spoken dialogue, as happened later to Bizet's *Carmen* (1875). Only by adding recitatives ex post facto was it possible to rescue Cherubini's work for the institutions set aside for tragedy, the genre to which it belonged by dramaturgical criteria.

In France, then, unlike Italy, musical tragedy was inseparably associated with recitative, and comedy with dialogue. More precisely, *opéra comique* was simply the "leftover" works lacking one or both characteristics of a *tragédie lyrique*: a tragic subject from history or mythology and a through-composed score. However absurd this distinction may seem from an aesthetic standpoint, it became historically significant in that it caused heterogeneous works, or groups of works, to be lumped together collectively under the pejorative term *opéra comique*. This was more than a mere terminological blunder: it was a sign and expression of a current within musical theater that represented a further step toward the emancipation of the bourgeoisie. By juxtaposing heterogeneous types of drama, the *opéra comique* tended to "mix" styles. This fact was long decried as an aesthetic shortcoming, as a sign of historical "transition," of muddle-headedness and eclecticism, by historians whose mania for classification was stronger than their sense of history, and who saw nothing wrong in measuring postrevolutionary developments against the system of clearly delineated generic styles that predominated up to the 1780s. In fact, it is precisely this "aesthetic shortcoming" that points to the existence of a new aesthetic, and this "sign of historical transition" that documents a new age. The merging of stylistic levels, the alternation between elevated and low style (a practice derived in spoken theater from Shakespeare), became just as much a part of the history of musical theater as the tragic complications which, though still lacking tragic endings, were introduced at the same time. Originally, *opéra comique* had avoided tragic subjects in the same way that it had excluded highbrow musical devices associated with recitative opera. No longer did the bourgeoisie function in comic casts merely as the butt of jokes; it demanded, and received, its part in the dignity of tragedy. In the theater, this represented one of the decisive steps on the path to its emancipation, a step in which opera took part in the form of the revolutionary opera, the rescue opera, and the *Schreckensoper,* or opera of terror. (The conciliatory endings of rescue operas such as Cherubini's *Les deux journées* of 1800 or Beethoven's *Fidelio* in no way outweighed the tragic undertone of their plots; and as in Lessing's *Emilia Galotti,* the fact that some of their characters are aristocrats, though admittedly of lower standing, alters little or nothing of the fundamentally bourgeois character of these works.)

By the time of Boieldieu's and Auber's operas around 1820, tragic motives had disappeared altogether from the *opéra comique.* The reason for this can be found in the spirit of the Restoration, as is manifest in the librettos of Eugène Scribe. (The fact that a few years later this same Scribe could weave intimations of the July Revolution into the grand opera shows clearly what we mean by "zeitgeist.") As though nothing had happened in the meantime, *opéra comique* regressed to that mixture of comedy and sentimentality, of ingredients from farce and *comédie larmoyante,* which had originated before the Revolution. Admittedly, there is still a social aspect to the alternation of stylistic levels, the abrupt switches from low or middle to elevated style, in Boieldieu's *La dame blanche* (1825): it is the characters of high rank who present their monologues in cavatinas (No. 11) or arias (No. 14) in the grand Italian style. However, when *opéra comique* adopted this upper-class tone it did so with a view neither to parody (as in earlier *opéra comique*) nor to bourgeois tragedy (as in the rescue opera).

Rossini's influence on Boieldieu is easily detectable in certain details: in the appearance of rhapsodic or virtuoso vocal writing in the slow sections of his arias (No. 14, for instance), or in his manner of casting "third themes" as furious crescendos with motives relentlessly repeated (in the overture and in aria No. 2). However, the key musicodramatic features of *opéra comique* derive from the aesthetic of the dialogue opera. To avoid a disturbing jolt between the spoken dialogues, which formed a substantive part of the piece, and the musical numbers, the music had to function in a manner roughly akin to incidental music in a play: it either served a descriptive or picturesque function, assumed the character of a vocal insert (which might conceivably be sung in real life), or continued the dialogue with heightened means in the form of an ensemble. Whatever the case, unlike through-composed operas, where musical language is presupposed from the outset, music in the *opéra comique* had to be "motivated." (It is doubtful, though, whether this criterion is sufficient to distinguish "genuine" *opéra comique* from the "spurious" variety where spoken dialogue is incidental to the drama.)

During the Restoration period, *opéra comique* was dominated by a mixture of action ensembles, song forms, picturesque choruses, and descriptive orchestral music—or, to put it negatively, by a paucity of contemplative ensembles, pompous choral scenes, and large-scale arias composed of cantabile and cabaletta. All appearances of stylistic incongruity to the contrary, this mixture proved to be characteristic of dialogue opera and is thus thoroughly homogeneous in that it can be understood from a single dramaturgical principle. Action ensembles are dialogues put to music: the characters, speaking all the while, react with and against one another in order to further the dramatic action. This distinguishes the action ensemble from the contemplative ensemble, where the characters pursue their own thoughts in complete isolation, or the mood ensemble, where they depict conflicting or matching emotions as though frozen in time. The action ensemble coheres less in terms of its music than in its dramaturgy. It works with abrupt changes of compositional means: songlike strains sometimes stand unrelated alongside declamatory passages sustained by ostinato motives in the orchestra (Terzetto Finale, No. 7).

The picturesque choruses—the miners', peasants', and soldiers' songs—function as musical extensions of the stage decor. Yet even though they do not directly affect the plot, they are thoroughly consistent with the principles of a genre whose underlying dramaturgy lies in the momentum of its action and not, as in Italian opera, in a static situation giving rise to an "affect." Unlike affects, which fall into "types," action is "characteristic." It therefore gravitates toward the musical depiction of local color, adding finishing touches to the deliberately unusual and striking milieu of the plot setting. And however slight the role of these choruses in the actual stage action, they are indispensable for fleshing out the backdrop, which alone gives the plot that specific tinge so essential to dialogue opera.

The song forms, romances, ballads, and *couplets* of *opéra comique* can be envisioned as vocal interpolations in a spoken drama and hence seem to pose no problems with regard to their dramaturgical motivation. Either they function as a solo counterpart to the picturesque choruses (Romance No. 9 in *La dame blanche*) or they impinge on the plot (Ballade No. 5) by narrating some previous action. (The exposition ballad was one of the ever-recurring props of both *opéra comique* and German romantic opera. Considering that composers were not yet trying to avoid stereotypes in 1820, it is difficult to explain why Weber overlooked the obvious opportunity to add a "Ballad of the Ancestral Forester" to the first act of *Der Freischütz*.)

Auber, who to a certain extent superseded Boieldieu, would have to be called the "classic" *opéra comique* composer if the word were appropriate to the genre. Moreover, the nineteenth century regarded Auber's music as specifically French in the same way that it saw Weber's as specifically German. Terms like *élan* and *esprit* (German stereotypes for the French national character) virtually sprang to people's lips whenever they spoke of *Le maçon* (1825), *Fra Diavolo* (1830), or *Le domino noir* (1837).

The impact of these works could still be felt a century later, the main reason being, without a doubt, their rhythm. Snappy dotted notes and march rhythms—a holdover from the "revolutionary" strain of *opéra comique*—were regarded as the keystone of Auber's music, as was his penchant for stressing the beats of the time signature. Familiarity even seemed to enhance rather than dull their charm, the more so since Auber's musical idiom exactly matched Scribe's librettos. Yet, it is difficult to show, by musical analysis, how these features managed to keep Auber's music alive instead of quickly degenerating into insufferable clichés. The quotations from *Fra Diavolo* (Aria and Scena, No. 10, and Recitative and Aria, No. 12) obviously owe their effect in no small part to a mere presentation of the time signature per se, or more precisely to the accentuation of its beats (Ex. 4). We will have to bear this in mind if we want to sketch even a rough outline of Auber's musical language. (In extreme cases all Auber needed to do, without a trace of monotony, was to have a chorus or an ensemble scan the time signature in repeated chords.) Regardless of the tempo, Auber kept his beats short, terse, and dry—or, as Gustav Becking put it, "without reverberation"—as is shown by the rests. The only way that these disjunct beats can attain continuity, without which the rhythm would be lifeless and the music would evaporate altogether, is by a sense of rebound that makes us expect a second beat to follow the first, a third to follow the second, and so on. And it is apparently this alternation of stroke and rebound suggested by the rests that accounts for Auber's vaunted élan.

Example 4

Doubtless, it is historically significant that this primarily rhythmic "tone" became as characteristic of the *opéra comique* as it later became for the *opéra bouffe* of Offenbach and Lecocq. However, it is still not enough to warrant apostrophizing Auber's style as the national style of France. In the nineteenth century, the question of national style was linked with the notion of a national opera; and however characteristically French Auber's *La muette de Portici* (1828) may be, it is still not a national opera in the same sense as *Der Freischütz* (1821) or *The Bartered Bride* (1866). To the nineteenth century, a national style received its classic expression in a magnum opus, a national opera, which then seemed to stand above history. France simply sidestepped this process. The French national consciousness, then wholesome and intact, had no need of musical reinforcement; nor was *La muette de Portici* (which is set in Naples) or even *Fra Diavolo* a suitable object to reassure the French of their national identity. Strictly speaking, the question of national style has to do least of all with style. Only after a nation (or its educated classes) has decided, partly for extramusical reasons, to adopt a particular work as the musical expression of its being can an individual style, whether Weber's or Smetana's, be elevated to the style of the nation. (Without the passions surrounding the War of the Fourth Coalition there would have been no German national style in the strict sense, merely a narrow thread of German tradition in the ever-changing kaleidoscope of styles from which composers in Germany traditionally made their selection.) A style becomes a national style not so much on its own merits as by popular decree.

The history of German romantic opera spans three decades, from Hoffmann's *Undine* (1816) and Spohr's *Faust* (1816) to Schumann's *Genoveva* (1850) and Wagner's *Lohengrin* (1848). Even in works with spoken dialogue, which are more typical of the genre than through-composed operas, it seems to be separated from the contemporary *opéra comique* of Boieldieu and Auber by a barrier dividing not just the two genres but the two nations as well. All the same, it is by no means absurd, at least as far as the history of composition is concerned, to view the type of opera represented by Weber's *Der Freischütz* as a variant of *opéra comique*, even though this view is seemingly contradicted in intellectual history by the significance the work attained after it was elevated to the national romantic opera of Germany. (No historian who regards music as an aesthetic reality rather than simply as a printed text can afford to ensconce himself in the history of composition and discount intellectual history as an extraneous ideological additive.)

The notion that German romantic opera derived from the singspiel is not completely wrongheaded but merely askew. Terminologically, it is above reproach insofar as any German opera with spoken dialogue can be classified as a singspiel. However, it falls short historically, since neither the north German nor the Viennese singspiel represents an important step on the road to *Der Freischütz*. Nor was the Mozart tradition—or, more specifically, the tradition of *Die Zauberflöte* as represented in early-nineteenth-century German opera by Peter von Winter—of central importance to Weber. As seen from the history of genres, there was no line of development in German opera linking *Der Freischütz* with *Die Zauberflöte* and *Fidelio*. (*Die Zauberflöte* is a mixture of singspiel and opera semiseria, *Fidelio* a variant of *opéra comique* known as "rescue opera.")

The key compositional premises of *Der Freischütz* lie in early-nineteenth-century *opéra comique*. Besides its typical combination of song forms and ensemble movements—a combination in which the reminiscence motive played a mediating role—the *opéra comique* also provided, in embryonic form, those very features that were later regarded as characteristically romantic. We hear echoes of *opéra comique* not only in Ännchen's romance (No. 13), which obviously hearkens back to French forebears, but even in those pieces, such as the bridesmaids' and hunters' choruses, on which the whole notion of national romantic music hinges. The folklike spirit of the bridesmaids' chorus is clearly related to that of Chorus No. 11 in Cherubini's *Les deux journées,* even if their stylistic affinity cannot be localized in specific turns of melody. Similarly, Chorus No. 1 from Boieldieu's *La dame blanche* represents the same type of picturesque local color as Weber's chorus of hunters. (*La dame blanche* was composed over a seven-year period roughly at the same time as *Der Freischütz,* and any analogies we find in them do not reveal dependencies between these works so much as premises common to the genre.)

One might object that the national flavor evident in Weber is more crucial to the history of music than any basic similarities of style between German romantic opera with spoken dialogue and French *opéra comique.* However, once we turn from intellectual history to the history of composition, we note that the Germanic tint in *Der Freischütz* is merely a variant of a larger interest in ethnic coloration that Weber shared with several composers of *opéra comique,* an interest that led him not only to conjure up Spanish, Polish, or Russian associations but also to quote Arabic or Chinese melodies. (His fascination for distant lands and peoples seems to have been kindled by Abbé Vogler, the teacher not only of Weber but of Meyerbeer as well.) In this light, the national side of music is not so far removed from exoticism as politically motivated commentators would have us believe. We also find tendencies similar to Weber's in Boieldieu, whose *La dame blanche,* set in Scotland, incorporates a "Scottish national air" (Chorus No. 16) for the sake of local color, and includes in an ensemble movement (No. 3) a Scottish song that also appears as the first allegro theme of the overture in order to underscore its importance to the work. Now, it may be tempting to imagine that a profound gulf separates Boieldieu's Scottish tone and Weber's Germanicism, since the one composer quoted extraneous material whereas the other was working within his native national idiom. Yet, however much in accord with nineteenth-century modes of thought, this notion is virtually impossible to verify from the standpoint of compositional technique. (This is not to say that music cannot be tinted by its subsequent nationalistic reception, nor that this aesthetic phenomenon is unworthy of study in its own right.)

German romantic opera and French *opéra comique,* then, shared a complex of features that included not only an attraction to folk music but also a predilection for picturesque songs and choruses and a fondness for colorful timbres, tone painting, and descriptive orchestral music. As a whole—whether in Weber, Boieldieu, or revolutionary opera—this complex may be understood as a musical offshoot of an idea taken from aesthetics: the Characteristic. Around 1800 Friedrich Schlegel linked the notion of the Characteristic with romanticism in the same way that the idea of the Beautiful appeared central to a classical, or classicizing, aesthetic. And to the early-nineteenth-century mentality, "character-

Fig. 15   Carl Gropius: Stage design for *Der Freischütz,* Berlin, 1821. The room in the forester's house, conceived by Weber as a petty-bourgeois interior, was expanded by Gropius into a grand-bourgeois salon in which the dramaturgically indispensable prayer desk appears as an out-of-place stage prop, albeit one which conjures up the image of a Madonna with saints. The portrait of the forester, which falls from the wall in the opera, has become part of a grand ancestral gallery. (Berlin, Staatsbibliothek Preußischer Kulturbesitz.)

istic" meant idiosyncratic rather than general or typical, the exception rather than the rule, "interesting" and "striking" rather than "nobly simple," coloristic rather than statuesque.

Thus, on an aesthetic level, the inner coherence of the features that make up both German romantic opera and *opéra comique* is provided in part by the category of the Characteristic. On the compositional level, it is also determined by the technique of reminiscence motives as a means of bracketing separate musical numbers. Both Grétry's *Richard Coeur-de-Lion* (1784) and Cherubini's *Les deux journées* (1800), by using picturesque chanson melodies as reminiscence motives, blur the formal distinction between song and ensemble: the web of motivic relations spreads over the whole opera to include song and ensemble forms equally. On the other hand, in seemingly glaring contradiction to the technique of song quotation, Samiel's motive in *Der Freischütz* consists substantially of instrumental timbre: viola tremolo, low-register clarinet, and timpani. These extreme forms of the reminiscence motive—song quotation and timbral effect—

prove to be different ways of realizing the same idea. In both cases, under the banner of the Characteristic, an isolated, small-scale, self-contained, restricted entity—the vocal interpolation or momentary timbral effect—is turned into a unifying element extending beyond the confines of the individual numbers.

Now, aestheticians with classicist inclinations found the Characteristic suspect and pernicious when it meant tearing a melody apart and replacing it with an accumulation of momentary rhythmic and timbral effects. And there is no denying that Grillparzer was right when he referred, in his diary, to Weber's *Euryanthe* of 1823 as "mangled." Weber often sacrificed the seamless melodic continuity that dominated Italian opera, at least in its ideal form, for a drastically "characteristic" emphasis on rhythm as related to the events on stage. Nevertheless, the cut-and-paste technique so criticized by classicists like Grillparzer might be called a symptom of decline in a purely musical sense if it were not concealed and warranted by its context, which focuses more on dramaturgical than musical design. This applies above all to the ensembles that gradually came to supplant arias as the backbone of opera, or at least to dialogue ensembles if not to contemplative ones. A piece that threatens to fall apart musically may well cohere as an expression of stage dialogue. Even before composers had stopped dividing operas into separate and, originally, self-contained numbers, they had already begun to shift the emphasis from musical unity to a unity mediated by the events on stage. Moreover, once reminiscence motives had reached a certain density, they began to function as musicodramatic brackets, relieving the individual numbers of their aesthetic obligation to be musically self-sufficient and continuous. In this light, we find that we are dealing with a set of interrelated and mutually dependent features belonging both to romantic opera and to *opéra comique*: the use of timbral color for reminiscence motives, the dismantling of ensemble numbers into separate parts set in sharply contrasting rhythms and linked more by the stage action than by musical factors, and the use of reminiscence motives to impart musicodramatic coherence beyond the confines of individual numbers. These features form a technical counterpart to the aesthetic criteria associated in the early nineteenth century with the notion of the Characteristic: the striking momentary effect, local color, and, not least, the notion of a tight-knit web of relations in contrast to statuesque forms oriented on the idea of Beauty.

Weber gave his *Euryanthe* the subtitle "grand romantic opera." In 1823, the year of its Vienna premiere, this subtitle was a contradiction in terms: "grand" opera was through-composed and treated subjects from mythology and history rather than romantic themes, whereas "romantic" operas, such as Hoffmann's *Undine,* Spohr's *Faust,* and Weber's *Der Freischütz,* belonged to the tradition of singspiel or *opéra comique* with spoken dialogue. In *Euryanthe,* his failed magnum opus, Weber brought the concepts of national opera, grand opera, and romantic opera—at first merely labels for a choice of language, compositional technique, and subject matter—into a difficult relation with one another. Herein lies not only the significance of this work to the history of music, but also one of the grounds for its misfortune.

Composers wanted to see the idea of a national opera realized, not solely in the singspiel, where it quickly took root, but in grand opera as well. This ambition reaches back to the eighteenth century and recurred later, after Weber, in the relation between Smetana's *Bartered Bride* (1866) and *Dalibor* (1868). (Apart from the choice of language, it was not clear which features were supposed to constitute the "national" side of German national opera, since these features changed with time. It might reside in a subject taken from German history or Germanic mythology, or in recourse to ancient Greece as opposed to Rome, or to medieval romance as opposed to classical antiquity. No one seemed bothered by the fact that Germanic mythology was primarily Scandinavian and medieval romance largely French.) However, national opera faced a problem of style in grand opera. Since the compositional prerequisites for grand opera were not to be found in German singspiel, Ignaz Holzbauer had to decide between the French and Italian models of grand opera when he wrote his self-proclaimed national opera, *Günther von Schwarzburg* (1777). As it happened, he chose the Italian model. Weber, on the other hand, instead of drawing on the grand opera of Spontini, proceeded from the assumption that it must be possible to incorporate into the conception of grand opera the traditional bonds linking romantic subject matter and the musical techniques of singspiel and *opéra comique*. He realized this notion with a musicodramatic maneuver reminiscent of the principle of tragic irony. Vocal numbers such as Adolar's romance (No. 2), Euryanthe's cavatina (No. 5), Adolar's aria "Wehen mir Lüfte zu" (No. 12), or the duet "Hin nimm die Seele mein" (No. 13) are all romantic in spirit, and actually belong to the domain of singspiel or *opéra comique*. Yet Weber has integrated them into the framework of "grand" opera—meaning through-composed opera with a tragic plot—by casting a shadow of doom on the bucolic idyll they represent, a shadow recognized, or at least sensed, by the audience long before the characters on stage.

In order to forge a path to grand opera using the musical devices that he had mastered from *opéra comique*, Weber made do with a libretto whose weaknesses he must surely have suspected. In the event, his plan of creating an opera at once both romantic and grand, with the romantic aspect linked to the national, was a failure. The cause lay not so much in the confusions of the plot itself—it is no more garbled than *Nabucco* (1842) or *Il trovatore* (1853), which managed to be successful despite their plots—as in the confusion of musical genre. Weber, to put it bluntly, let traditional forms crumble into "musical instants," which take their meaning and coherence primarily from the dramatic characterization. By using reminiscence motives and joining numbers into scene complexes (Nos. 5 to 9), he created overarching units beyond the bounds of the individual numbers. Yet any piece that thrives for its effect on details of characterization and large-scale dramatic momentum, rather than on emotional postures in formally self-contained numbers, desperately needs a riveting dramatic dialectic in particular and a compelling logic to its plot in general lest it degenerate into an operatic pie-in-the-sky. (Wagner's dramaturgically motivated critique in *Oper und Drama*, though unjust to Rossini, was squarely on target with Weber.) Unlike the standard number opera, it was an invitation to disaster for an opera such as *Euryanthe*, written under the aegis of the Characteristic, to use a libretto that was dramatically weak both in its language and in its narrative design.

Weber left an indelible mark on the ideas that we associate with German national opera, so much so that we automatically place Marschner, who drew heavily on Weber, among the romantic composers. Yet we hesitate to do the same with Spohr, whose *Jessonda* was premiered in the same year as *Euryanthe*. *Jessonda*, Spohr's magnum opus, was through-composed like *Euryanthe* and is hence a "grand" opera. But even so it is not "romantic": the exoticism of its plot, which is set in India and turns on the practice of suttee, the self-immolation of widows, is no more romantic than Peter von Winter's *Das unterbrochene Opferfest* (1796) or Spontini's *Fernand Cortez*. Furthermore, Spohr's musical dramaturgy is different in kind from Weber's. There is little attempt at local color, and the predominant aesthetic category is not the Characteristic but the Beautiful, since the musical backbone of the work is formed of self-contained numbers: arias, duets, choruses, and finales. (Unlike Weber's ensembles, the duets are "contemplative" rather than "dialogue" movements, and elaborate a fixed emotion or state of mind in the same way as do the arias.) There is no hint of a tendency to polarize the work into picturesque song forms and formally disjunct ensembles primarily intended to characterize particular moments in the drama. Reminiscence motives are used in the manner of Méhul: less as a way of bracketing the disintegrating formal skeleton of the opera than as a musicodramatic ingredient added to the traditional motivic gestures of accompanied recitative. Basically, Spohr still considered an opera a succession of emotions *en tableau* (except for Chorus No. 26, the most progressive part of the work as far as form is concerned). Furthermore, the plot hinges on a stereotyped conflict from classical drama—love versus honor—and represents nothing more than a string of situations arranged according to the principle of alternating sentiments. In short, we have little cause to speak of *Jessonda* as a "romantic" opera, unless we let the "zeitgeist" hypothesis bully us into finding the same romantic spirit in all major works of the Restoration period.

In a letter of 1829 to Goethe, Zelter referred to Spohr's *Faust* as the work of a composer who was more of an "artist in notes" (*Tonkünstler*) than a "melodist": "Everything in it, down to the slightest detail, is executed with astonishing polish and craftsmanship to confound and surpass the most discerning ear. The finest lacework of Brabant is coarse by comparison." Marschner, on the other hand, even outdoes Weber in his penchant for exaggerated effect, and opera historians generally praise his effectiveness on stage at the same time that they bewail the coarseness of his music. However, we have no right to belittle Marschner for the variety and emotionality of the musical devices he chose to work with, as though they owed their theatrical effectiveness to musical negligence. In his successful works, particularly *Hans Heiling* (1833), the effect results not from the musical devices per se but from the function they serve; and this function—the "cause"

Fig. 16 Stürmer: Three figurines from *Der Freischütz*, 1821. However faintly the postures of these figurines project their respective characters (Max, "weak but no miscreant," is nothing more or less than a noble youth and Agathe a pious maid), they are revealing of a performance style far removed from modern stage productions, one that forced actors to seek refuge in stereotype gestures and attitudes. (Berlin, Staatsbibliothek Preußischer Kulturbesitz.)

of the "effect"—is based on dramaturgical calculation. Aria No. 3, for example
—in which Hans Heiling, the spirit-prince seeking redemption in mortality,
enjoins constancy from his bride—owes its emotional impact to a tragic dialectic:
Anna is repelled precisely by the fear-ridden urgency with which Heiling hopes
to ensnare her. Again, in the finale to Act 1 (No. 7), where Anna parts company
with Heiling during a ball, the waltz tempo remains to accompany his outburst
of despair, thereby generating a contrast between rhythmic pattern and melodic
idiom. This contrast brings his mental anguish more clearly to view than could
possibly have happened if the music had left the realm of the ballroom scene
and returned to accompanied recitative.

Nevertheless, it has always been the Prelude—Heiling's farewell to the
spirit-world—that music historians have considered the most significant part of
the score. Here, despite the recurring chorus of earth-spirits, a complex of open-
ended sections obtains coherence largely from the dramaturgy rather than from
purely musical factors. This music follows Weber's footsteps to the near proximity of *Der Fliegende Holländer* (1843). It is drastically "characteristic" music, which,
to serve the ends of the drama, does not shrink from changing mood so constantly as to leave the melody "mangled" by classicist criteria.

Beethoven: Myth and Reception

The nineteenth century was the age of historicism, a time when it still seemed
possible to find out "the way it really was." Yet, as a period of music history, it was
dominated by a myth which only began to pale in decades that thought of themselves as "modernist." This was the overpowering myth of Beethoven, which not
only forms part of music history but itself took part in making that history.

Ever since Antiquity men have disputed whether literature is a "lie" or
whether, as Aristotle maintained, it is superior to the truth of history. This dispute will never be settled; but no matter which side we take, it would be narrow-
minded to call the myth-making process that began during Beethoven's own
lifetime, in the writings of Bettina Brentano and E. T. A. Hoffmann, a mere
falsification of history, as though it could be refuted by documents. In the "romantic image of Beethoven"—as Arnold Schmitz called it in order to explode
it—the composer appears as a Promethean revolutionary, as a sorcerer, or as a
martyred saint. This image can neither be supported nor undercut by empirical
biography, where myth simply does not belong. When E. T. A. Hoffmann apos-
trophized the composer of the Fifth Symphony as the ruler of a realm of spirits,
or Richard Wagner saw in the C♯-minor Quartet, Op. 131, the musical expression of a day in the life of a martyred saint, this had nothing whatsoever to do
with Beethoven's personality as we might be able to reconstruct it from biographical documents. Of course, the anecdotes circulated by Bettina Brentano,
such as Beethoven's high-handed revolutionary posturings in Teplitz, muddle
the distinction between allegory and biographical truth. Still, this should not

blind us to the fact that pseudobiography is meant, not to explain "the way it really was," but rather to function as a language of cryptograms expressing insight into Beethoven's music. And the anecdotes that mask this insight must not be measured by the standards of biography.

Part of the legend, which has proved so intractable to questions of biographical truth or falsehood, is made up of a few standing formulas coined by Beethoven exegetes, among them his supposed "sufferings and triumph." This cliché is too close to the Prometheus myth—one of the models for the Beethoven myth—to be reducible to biographical proportions. Hans Heinrich Eggebrecht, in his *Zur Geschichte der Beethoven-Rezeption* (1972), could draw inferences about the factual content of Beethoven clichés from the stubbornness with which they have remained fixed in the popular imagination for a century and a half. Nevertheless, it is also true that they have resisted objections because myth belongs to a different dimension from written history, which is subject to a constant process of revision.

The Beethoven myth, then, is separated from empirical biography by a chasm that represents something more than a simple opposition of truth and falsehood. Still, it would be a gross simplification to claim that the myth of Beethoven is a direct imprint of his music. The mythical figure in the "romantic image of Beethoven," whether revolutionary, sorcerer, or saint, cannot be conveniently equated with the persona behind his works, however close the connection between them. Just as the aesthetic "subject" that we sense in Beethoven's music bears little relation to the man as we know him from his biography, it is no less foolish to try to identify this subject with the Beethoven of myth and legend. First of all, the works on which the Beethoven myth thrives represent a narrow selection from his complete output: *Fidelio* and the music to *Egmont;* the Third, Fifth, and Ninth Symphonies; and the *Pathétique* and *Appassionata* sonatas. It is not a fact in support of the Beethoven myth that these works are "representative," but rather one of the claims that make up the myth. To the same extent that the myth was abstracted from the music, the reception of the music was tempered by the myth. And if myth, once it impinges on biography, transforms anecdotes into allegorical ciphers, it also creates an order that separates symbolic works from nonsymbolic ones. Of course, there is little point in trying to argue that the *Pathétique* and *Appassionata* sonatas—it is no coincidence that these works have bynames—are "major" works against which "minor" works such as Op. 7 and Op. 90 pale by comparison. Yet, beyond a doubt, they belong to the symbolic works that sustain the Beethoven myth and that in turn owe their pride of place to that myth. (Popularity and symbolic function do not necessarily coincide, even though, especially later, a work's symbolic function may undergird its popularity. Some of the works most popular in Beethoven's own lifetime—the Septet, *Wellington's Victory*, or the second movement of the Eighth Symphony, which was often played without the rest of the work—were irrelevant to the formation of the myth.)

Fig. 17 Lyser: *Beethoven*. Despite slight exaggerations adding a touch of caricature to his features, Beethoven as drawn by Lyser fully conveys the "energetic and composed" personality that left an overpowering impression on Goethe, for all the great writer's opposition to his musical creed. Beethoven commanded the respect of his uncomprehending contemporaries to a degree never before granted to a composer. In spite of his obvious foibles, captured in countless anecdotes, Beethoven as an individual represented the claims that he raised for the cause of music with a vigor that marks a watershed in the history of music and culture. (Berlin, Staatsbibliothek Preußischer Kulturbesitz.)

The history of the changing accentuation of Beethoven's works during the nineteenth century has never been written, or even sketched. Without it, the historical platitude that the age stood in Beethoven's shadow before falling under Wagner's remains a vague and unsubstantiated claim supported by nothing more than the canonic status of his symphonies, string quartets, and piano sonatas.

We seldom think of how much we lost as the Beethoven tradition took root. His characteristic first-period works, which drew on the divertimento tradition, especially that of chamber music with wind instruments, vanished virtually without a trace from the late-nineteenth-century repertoire and sank into oblivion. Yet the verdict cast upon them by this process has never been sufficiently vindicated. Nor is there any hope of justifying it on aesthetic grounds. On the contrary, the reasons why this group of works has disappeared in its entirety are more likely to be found in the evolution of musical institutions, on the one hand, and the dead hand of the Beethoven myth on the other. Once the "grand concert" had crystallized into the "symphony concert" around the middle of the century, there was no longer any room for works of a divertimento character; and these works likewise slipped through the gaps of chamber music culture, which came to be dominated by string instruments and the piano. Moreover, being pieces with a social function, they did not fit the "romantic image of Beethoven," which increasingly determined the choice of repertoire. (There was in turn a close connection between the formation of a "classic" Beethoven canon, partly engineered by the Beethoven myth, and the emergence of the "symphony concert" and "chamber music recital" as institutions that resisted all change in instrumentation, apart from the soloists in the symphony concert, and any mixture of elevated, middle, and low styles.)

Thus, the divertimento tradition fell victim to a process that institutionalized Beethoven's "elevated" style as "genuine Beethoven." On the other hand, the subsequent history of the central genres—symphony, string quartet, and sonata—is likewise problematic, being split by a rift, or perhaps we should say a gaping abyss, between their roles in reception history and in the history of composition. However supreme Beethoven's symphonies and string quartets may have reigned in the concert repertoire, the later development of these eminently Beethovenian genres was, from the standpoint of composition, checkered and disjoint.

Mendelssohn's efforts to come to grips with Beethoven's late works shortly after their appearance left noticeable traces on his early string quartets Op. 12 and Op. 13, but in this respect he seems to be exceptional. Revealingly, it was precisely the nineteenth century's most "genuine" composers of chamber music, Schumann and Brahms, who were obviously wary of the string quartet and tended to avoid it in favor of chamber music with piano rather than confronting the overpowering legacy of Beethoven. Not until the modern music of our century was the history of the string quartet, which virtually seeped away in the nineteenth century, resumed in representative bodies of works by Schönberg, Bartók, and Hindemith. And in spite of the radically new musical idiom, or perhaps under its protection, these works unmistakably took Beethoven as their starting point.

Thus, we have little cause to speak of a continuous history of the string quartet after Beethoven and under his influence. The history of the symphony, on the other hand, looks almost like a history of the conclusions that composers were able to draw from Beethoven's various models of the symphonic principle: from the Third and Seventh Symphonies in the case of Berlioz, the Sixth in the case of Mendelssohn, and the Ninth in the case of Bruckner. Yet the line of development breaks off in mid-century. Mendelssohn and Berlioz strangely rub shoulders in the history of the symphony immediately after Beethoven, and from the 1870s to the early years of our century the symphony experienced a "second life." But the quarter of a century between these two periods is a yawning chasm with Gade, Raff, and Rubinstein as stopgaps. And it was during this "dry period" of the symphony that the "symphonic poem," which Liszt developed from the concert overture, emerged as the epoch-making genre of orchestral music in the grand style. Still, this break in continuity shows that in the history of the symphony, if less glaringly than in that of the string quartet, the aesthetic presence of an overpowering tradition in the concert repertoire could not only stimulate the historical evolution of a genre but also stifle it. The former took place at the end of the century, the latter in the middle.

Fig. 18 Beethoven monument. Bourgeois memorials suffer from an incongruity: they are forced to aspire to a monumentality fully out of keeping with bourgeois ideals. In the case of the Beethoven monument, this ambiguity is ameliorated by having Beethoven's bourgeois coat merge into the folds of a toga, and by seating him in a posture which, if not despotic, is at least contemplative rather than negligent. The paradox of modern monumental statuary is likewise reflected in the problems of a Beethoven legend which hovers inconclusively between anecdote and myth. (Vienna, Österreichische Nationalbibliothek.)

   In the nineteenth century, unlike the twentieth, the concept of a classical composer was still linked with the notion, taken from the theory of literature, of a *classicus auctor,* a writer whose works were exemplary for a particular genre. And doubtless one of the reasons why the vocal works, with the exception of *Fidelio,* fell into neglect was that Beethoven figured in the pantheon of composers as the classic of instrumental music in the elevated style—of the symphony, string quartet, and sonata. Indeed, the argument that Beethoven composed "against the voice" seems to be an ex post facto rationalization rather than an explanation. *Fidelio,* the *Missa solemnis* (1824), the song cycle *An die ferne Geliebte* (1816), even *Christus am Oelberge* (1803) were viewed with respect as outstanding pieces of music; but they scarcely affected the history of the genres they represented, and hence never achieved "classical" status as exemplary works in an aesthetic and historical sense, regardless of whether they established themselves in the repertoire (*Fidelio*) or not (*Christus am Oelberge*). The history of the oratorio was determined by Handel and Haydn, German opera by Mozart and Weber, and the lied by Schubert—not by Beethoven.

Beethoven's works have long been divided into three periods, a schema that has fallen into disrepute but has in no way vanished from the popular imagination. At all events, it garners support from the "new path" that Beethoven claimed he entered in 1802 and from the far-reaching hiatus around 1815, which we can regard as his period of silence. However, when we try to see the connection between Beethoven and romanticism, without resorting to catchwords, this schema proves to be an obstacle. It distorts our view of the nature and historical significance of the works from Op. 74 to Op. 97—works which, so to speak, represented Beethoven's "latest word" for Schubert when he started out as a composer.

Commentators have always felt that Beethoven's late works from Op. 102 on, although contemporary with Schubert's entire output, nevertheless do not belong to romantic music. And the isolation which gave rise to these works, and which they may be said to express, was given special emphasis in the Beethoven literature (and fleshed out with anecdotes) precisely because it was seen to allegorize the isolated position of Beethoven's late works within the history of music, a fact for which no explanation other than the biographical seemed to be forthcoming. Set against the backdrop of the Restoration, works such as the late string quartets and piano sonatas, the Diabelli Variations (1819–23), the *Missa solemnis,* and the Ninth Symphony stood out as "bizarre" phenomena in which contemporaries failed to detect any affinity with their age as they saw it. The late works proved strangely resistant to nonbiographical arguments that attempted to demonstrate their stylistic derivation from the aesthetic and compositional premises of the middle period. Nor could contemporaries do anything more than guess at the immediate impact these works were having on Schumann and Mendelssohn, an impact that projected their historical continuity into the future.

The works of the middle period prior to Op. 74—that is, the works from which the Beethoven myth was abstracted—dominated the nineteenth-century concert repertoire and fashioned our image of Beethoven as a classic composer, an image that took visible form in Max Klinger's sculpture. However, works like the Fifth Symphony and the *Appassionata* Sonata had, it seems, less of an impact on the history of composition than the pieces between Op. 74 and Op. 97, which they overshadowed in the history of musical performance and reception.

Aestheticizing biographers who clung to the three-period schema and found Op. 78 a "minor work" in comparison with the *Appassionata,* scarcely noticed that Beethoven had struck a "new tone" in the string Quartet Op. 74, the Piano Trio Op. 97, and the Op. 78 and Op. 90 piano sonatas. The romantic composers, however, realized that they could take these works as a starting point, as a stylistic phase which, unlike the fully rounded middle period, permitted a continuation and seemed to point toward new paths. The rigor and consistency of Beethoven's thematic and motivic manipulation relaxed, as it were, to make room for a lyricism that infringed against the spirit of sonata form by permeating whole movements rather than remaining confined to their second themes. Cantabile, a mere enclave in classical sonata form, became an underlying structural principle.

Now, it would be wrong to pin a "romantic" tag on this period from Beethoven's oeuvre—that is, to resolve the slightly threadbare dispute as to whether Beethoven was a classic or a romantic composer by wanly proposing that a classical phase in his work gave way to a romantic one. On the other hand, as mentioned above, Schubert obviously took his stylistic bearings from the works that Beethoven wrote around 1810. And to the extent that romantic music is a Schubert tradition—that the entire historical complex is tempered by the "tone" of a single composer—no one attempting to characterize romanticism can afford to overlook the fact that several preconditions of Schubert's "tone," and even his conception of form, derive from a series of Beethoven's works whose significance we distort when we view them entirely in the shadow of his classic middle-period works. The Beethoven of the "romantic image of Beethoven," devised under the impact of works like the Third and Fifth Symphonies, was not the Beethoven of romanticism as a period in the history of composition.

Beethoven's Late Style

Beethoven felt entitled to be treated not as a mere composer but as a *Tondichter*, or "tone poet." In the main, his claim was not an aesthetic and compositional program so much as a social demand, which he presented to a world that enjoyed listening to music but did not think highly of it. The term "tone poet" marks a stance in the battle between the arts; and no matter how much influence we attach to literary models in Beethoven's works, this term expresses the conviction that music is capable of being elevated to the level of literature. To use Herder's terms, music likewise serves the "education of humanity"; it, too, has its *classici auctores* whose works outlive their time rather than simply functioning as part of the latest fashion of entertainment. The earlier notion that music either moved the affections and touched the heart or was nothing but an "agreeable noise" was confronted around 1800 by a modern aesthetic which Beethoven held in common with Friedrich Schlegel: the idea that music, not unlike philosophical meditation, represents a train of thought.

According to Arnold Schindler, Beethoven "often used" the concept of the poetic idea. This concept has been subject to divergent and wildly contradictory interpretations, being at one extreme a literary program and at the other a purely musical concept for the "creation and production" (*poiein*) of a work. However, it is doubtful, indeed rather unlikely, that the controversy between absolute and program music which dominated the discussion from mid-century, after being unleashed by Hanslick's aesthetic theory and Liszt's compositions, is a suitable frame of reference for understanding Beethoven's notion of the poetic idea. The only way we can reconstruct what Beethoven meant by a poetic idea, if we can do so at all, is not by calculating the amount of "poetry" in the technique and expression of his music, but by trying to describe how technique and expression interact.

Speaking negatively, we might define the poetic factor that Beethoven reclaimed for music, in order to enhance its aesthetic and social dignity, as the "nonprosaic." However, the term "prosaic" applied equally to technique and expression: the tone-painting which Beethoven made fun of in Haydn's *Die Schöpfung* was no less "prosaic" than the ossified form of the fugue, which, as Beethoven remarked in conversation with Karl Holz, had to make room for "a truly poetic element" lest the form die out altogether. In other words, if we are to reach a more sophisticated understanding of Beethoven's notion of the Poetic, and not choose lopsidedly between a literary program on the one hand, and a purely musical conception on the other, we will have to search for a configuration that links the principle of nonschematic, individual form with a type of expression that rises above what Beethoven saw as the everyday banality of illustrating subjects, characters, or feelings.

In 1799, Ludwig Tieck, in his *Phantasien über die Kunst*, defined the "purely poetic" element of music, or more specifically of instrumental music, as virtually the opposite of the Characteristic and of the musical expression of emotion—namely, as a "world unto itself" inhabited by music alone. Of course it would be wrong simply to equate Beethoven's conception of the Poetic with the romantic metaphysic of instrumental music that was applied to Beethoven's works by E. T. A. Hoffmann. Still, there is no denying that subjects, characters, and feelings must be transformed aesthetically before they can belong to the realm that Beethoven had in mind when he spoke of the Poetic. What E. T. A. Hoffmann wrote of opera applies equally to a type of instrumental music that was not completely abstracted or divorced from elements of expressive content: "Every passion—love, hatred, anger, despair, etc.—given to us in opera, is clothed by music in the Tyrian purple of the romantic, and even those feelings we know from life lead us beyond life and into the realm of the Infinite." (Though Hoffmann postulated the existence of abstract instrumental music and found it realized in Beethoven, his discovery of it in Beethoven's Fifth Symphony represents a "romanticization" that does injustice to the importance of the "characteristic" in Beethoven's music.)

No one would wish to deny that Beethoven's conception of composition included the representation of subjects, characters, and feelings. However, it is unlikely that the representational side of his music was essentially what he meant by the Poetic. This would have contradicted the aesthetic claims to which he felt music was entitled: if music is to be a "loftier form of revelation" than literature, it must do more than merely illustrate literature in notes. Jean Paul, in his novel *Hesperus* (1795), counters the earlier view that music must accommodate and be subservient to language in order to become fluent, with the thesis that music is itself a language, moreover one that stands *above* the language of words. This view formulates in writing precisely what Beethoven was doing in composition and what later even entered the collective consciousness of the musical public as the popular aesthetic of the nineteenth century. However, any music that establishes its poetic legitimacy by appearing to be a transcendent form of literature parts company with an aesthetic theory that distinguishes clearly between poetic content and musical form, as though the one were the aim of expression and the other its means.

Subjects, characters, and feelings are not the "content" of Beethoven's music but merely its "material." And this material does not constitute the "Poetic," as Beethoven understood it, until it has been subjected to the strictures of musical form. However, if we interpret the Poetic to be an end result of the process of composition, rather than a substance that precedes the music as an extramusical premise to be paraphrased in notes, then our efforts to characterize Beethoven's late style will have to proceed from the compositional idiosyncrasies of his works, even if in the final analysis our goal is to find "poetic ideas." For these ideas are made up of formal processes which, in the late works, are based on somewhat different assumptions from those of the middle period, or from those of the "interim" period that Schubert took as his stylistic starting point.

In some of Beethoven's late works, the concept of "theme"—the main category of specifically instrumental music—is cast in an odd twilight in which its features begin to blur. In the first movements of both the Bb-major Quartet, Op. 130 (1825–26), and the A-minor Quartet, Op. 132 (1825), the main theme—if we can still call it that—consists of a combination of an adagio idea and an allegro idea; and the adagio part, although derived historically from the slow introduction, effectively counterbalances the allegro part in the overall thematic structure. Apart from the obvious contrast between adagio and allegro—a contrast that gives the work its rhapsodic character—the A-minor Quartet also has a four-note figure (g♯–a–f–e) that functions, latently, as the true germinal idea of the movement. This figure is quoted directly at the beginning of the adagio; in the allegro, though half-hidden, it inconspicuously permeates the entire motivic tissue. Nevertheless, we only become aware of the influence this figure exerts on the whole movement if we define this germinal idea, not in its initial form, but as a configuration of two (ascending or descending) half steps with a variable interval in between. This more inclusive definition leads us to realize that the germinal idea of the A-minor Quartet is not restricted to that work alone, but appears in modified form in some of the other late quartets as well—in the C♯-minor Quartet, Op. 131, the Bb-major Quartet, Op. 130, and the *Große Fuge,* Op. 133 (1825). It almost seems as though, secretly, the entire series is a cycle.

In the Bb-major Quartet, the second theme emerges from the motivic particles of the opening adagio (measures 1–2), namely, from the chromatic four-note figure bb–a–ab–g related to the germinal idea of the A-minor Quartet, and from the cantabile gesture g–eb′–d′–c′ (the chromaticism stands out more strongly in the recapitulation than in the exposition) (Ex. 5). The principle of "contrasting derivation" (Arnold Schmitz) that relates the adagio section of the main theme to the second theme is present from Beethoven's earliest essays in sonata form. What distinguishes the late style, however, is that the actual formal procedure is withdrawn from the domain of clear-cut themes and straightforward development into a "subthematic" realm. Here connections crisscross the entire form instead of being presented ostentatiously in a mighty sweep of rigorous logic and consistency, as in the middle-period works.

Example 5

This thumbnail analysis is enough to show that, in some of Beethoven's late works, the notion of theme operates on two levels: a thematic level and a subthematic level. We can see this dichotomy in the contradiction between the cracked and fissured exteriors of these works and their tightly knit internal structure. It is closely linked with the peculiarly detached expressive quality that has always been remarked upon as a feature of Beethoven's late style. The thematic structure is a mere façade: the actual musical idea, instead of being presented to view as a clearly defined theme, retreats into the interior of the music, half invisible, as a subtheme. This reduces the importance of thematic structure to the formal process, regardless of whether the sonata-form outline remains intact. The expressive character of the themes is kept, to a certain extent, at a distance, as though held under condition. Expression and structure mutually interact; and once the thematic structure becomes merely a surface phenomenon—even if to all appearances it satisfies the rules of formal design—the expression begins to take on a masklike aura. (No one alive to this music would claim that this undercuts the artistic integrity of its underlying pathos.)

In the popular mind, Beethoven's late works are excessively subjective. Theodor W. Adorno, on the other hand, saw a key to these works in their peculiar manner of "arresting" conventions that are in fact *not* "imbued and overpowered with subjectivity." His view coincides with the aforementioned division of the notion of theme into a surface structure and a deep structure. The conventionality evident in the forms of these works can be disregarded and left untouched because it merely represents a façade: the musical train of thought has been interiorized, and only partially resurfaces as thematic structure and development.

At first, these "arrested" conventions puzzle us; they contradict the radicality of musical thought which allowed Beethoven to return to the first principles of his forms in order to change them. Yet the contradiction is not unbridgeable. These two divergent tendencies have one trait in common, a trait that is characteristic of Beethoven's late works as a whole: the element of ever-increasing reflection. Nothing could be more wrong than to view the scraps of convention strewn throughout the late works as evidence of a second naiveté, of recaptured innocence. In fact, as in the Allegretto Scherzando of the Eighth Symphony, what we are dealing with is music about music. And the conventions that Beethoven chooses to quote are no less revealing of his inner detachment from tradition than those he breaks or casts aside.

Here music has reached the level of the Poetic by manifesting form as expression, and expression as form. Thus, any attempt to fathom the specific nature of the Poetic in Beethoven's late works, even as a first approximation, will have to proceed from the principle of reflection which governs both expression and structure alike.

Moderate cantabile and declamatory recitatives are basic forms of vocal expression. The fact that they come from long-standing vocal traditions causes their appearance in an instrumental work such as the Cavatina of the B♭-major Quartet, Op. 130, to take on the character of a quotation. However, this in no way results in a loss of expressivity: the phrase "adagio molto espressivo," given as an expression mark at the beginning of the Cavatina, is meant, not to conjure up an expressivity otherwise lacking in the piece, but merely to capture in words what is obviously already present in the score. The vocal models underlying the Cavatina are here assimilated into an instrumental idiom by means of motivic connection. In the cantabile section, the subordinate voice of measures 1 and 3 first enters the melody (m. 7) and ultimately supplants it (mm. 17–19) in the form of motivic development. And the melodic substance of the half-stifled recitative (m. 42) is transformed from a declamatory to an arioso style and integrated into the varied recapitulation of the cantabile (mm. 58–62). The levels of expression, then, though stylistically at odds with each other, are linked motivically. And it is this motivic element, a specific characteristic of instrumental music, that alters the originally vocal nature of the melodic substance.

We have seen how, beneath its simple *ABCA* outline, the real formal process of the Cavatina is the way it integrates vocal materials into an instrumental idiom. This is the "poetic idea" of the movement. The types of expression that result from this instrumental recasting of vocal styles remain strangely suspended between three poles: a stark realism, as is illustrated in the Recitative by the expression mark *beklemmt* ("agonized") at measure 42; a masklike aura pervading the vocal styles in their instrumental guises; and a spirit of reflection into whose coils Beethoven draws his quoted types of vocal expression by enveloping them in a web of specifically instrumental motivic relations.

Both the splitting of theme into a surface and a deep structure and the detachment of expression are manifestations of the principle of reflection. This principle is no less apparent in Beethoven's relation to the traditional canon of forms. In the late works, this relation became ambiguous. The view that Bee-

thoven's forms "shattered" under the force of expression is just as problematic as the opposite claim that, in the late works, the strictures of form are
satisfied in the same way as in the middle period, when Beethoven sought to
reconcile the general (i.e., predefined form) with the particular (the organic
internal structure). In fact, the late works derived from an effort to reduce traditional forms to their first principles, and from them to draw conclusions that
cause general and particular to merge. The forms that Beethoven chose as his
starting points—sonata, variations, fugue, and character piece—are by no
means left unchanged. They are subjected to striking transformations, striking
not just because of their radicality but because the meaning of one form seems to
emerge precisely from its transformation into another. (Friedrich Schlegel's
notion of a "progressive universal poesy" comes immediately to mind.) At all
events, we have little cause to speak of these forms as "shattered," since the
results of the transformations are no less tightly knit than the forms they supplant.

The Diabelli Variations (1819–23) are usually referred to as "character variations" in order to set them apart from tradition. Taken literally, this term
means that two genres, the variation cycle and the character piece, have fused.
The fusion may have started in the eighteenth century, in changes of tempo and
mode, but only in Beethoven did it reach a stage that makes it seem appropriate
to speak of a transformation.

Formally, the slow movement of the A-minor Quartet, Op. 132—the "Heili-
ger Dankgesang eines Genesenen an die Gottheit"—is a double set of variations.
Its sharply contrasting themes lead us to suspect the influence of sonata form, an
assumption all the more justified when we consider that the first movement seems
to take the opposite tack and adapt sonata form to the double variation. Its exposition, development, and recapitulation—the names hardly seem to apply—
merely state the main and secondary themes in different keys (A minor/F major,
E minor/C major, and A minor/A major). A thematic process does, in fact, take
place internally; but outwardly these sections merely stand as varied and transposed repetitions of each other.

In his late works, Beethoven incorporated elements of sonata technique in
the fugue, from the finale of the Cello Sonata, Op. 102, No. 2, to the *Große Fuge,*
Op. 133. Bach generally never tampered with the form of his fugue subjects, but
Beethoven's subjects tend to enter the process of thematic-motivic manipulation,
even at the cost of their integrity. Conversely, the introduction of the allegro
theme in the first movement of the B♭-major Quartet, Op. 130, takes the guise of
a fugal exposition with three entries (and obligato counterpoint). Here the
theme merely consists of a sequence on a two-bar motive, a strongly rhythmic
leap of a fourth. Yet, in essence, the theme is merely a development pattern, and
when "half" of it "splits off" in the development section we feel that it is being
reduced to its "basic form." In short, in a dialectic of formal principles, fugue
technique represents a way of creating a sonata exposition from a thematic idea
that is actually only fit to serve the needs of a development passage.

The relation between Beethoven's approach to form, with his interlocking formal principles, and that of the romantics is twisted and confused, particularly since the premises of the approach to form largely determine what we mean by "poetic idea," the central aesthetic category for the romantics and Beethoven alike. In any event, it is not enough simply to contrast closed and open-ended form in order to characterize the difference between Beethoven and a group of composers who saw themselves as representing the Beethoven tradition.

Musical form was strangely ambiguous in the romantic period. As a rough categorization, either it was schematic or it was disintegrated. Lyrical piano pieces preserved intact the simple, traditional form of the song (*ABA*) or the rondo (*ABACA*), whereas the complex layout of a symphonic poem, though making use of the principles of sonata-allegro form and sonata cycle, distorted them to such an extent that we can scarcely recognize their historical origins. Yet both forms are romantic in essence, and it would not be the worst criterion for judging an interpretation of romanticism to see how it accounts for this juxtaposition of extremes. A first step is to realize that both the schematic and the disintegrated forms are conditioned by their contents, by the stress they place on elements in their content which take musical form as themes and motives. (A "theme" is a topic, or subject, as well as a musical idea.) Either the form remains schematic because it is not the main issue, or it disintegrates in order to adapt at any instant to the subject that is meant to be given musical expression. In the first case, the "content" is likely to be a mood circumscribed by the continuous presence of a single musicopoetic motive; in the second, it is likely to be an epic or dramatic subject whose musical portrayal requires a change of themes. In both cases, however, the themes represent the overriding aesthetic arbiter, whereas the form is merely a medium for displaying the idea on which virtually the entire movement hinges. This idea, in turn, is "poetic" if it states a mood, a character, or a subject in such a way that we can sense its aesthetic presence from the very first moment. In a word, the crux of a lyrical piano piece lies in its opening measures.

The meaning of a piece of music does not "consist" in its extramusical substrate; rather it emerges from the relation between that extramusical substrate and its musical formulation. Nevertheless, in romantic music, it is not inappropriate to attach mottos, captions, or programs to the underlying moods, characters, or subjects—in a manner of speaking, naming them by name. This underscores the point that the elements of content are more essential to the music than is the case with Beethoven, and this for reasons which have to do with the relation between theme and form. In the romantic period, the individuality of a piece of music—which in turn established its status as art—was imparted primarily by the themes and motives as such rather than by the formal process they set in motion. And the fact that the paramount aesthetic factor is the musical idea per se means that the substrate of the contents is subject to less far-reaching transformations than is the case with Beethoven, where the "poetic idea" is focused in the formal process.

Beethoven's formal structures, unlike those of the romantic period, are neither schematic nor disintegrated but problematic. When we understand them in their own terms rather than simply classifying them as exceptions to imaginary rules, they turn out to be solutions to problems. Furthermore, each of these problems differs from the next, so that, in Beethoven's case, it is form that determines the individuality of a work and hence its status as art. However, a strong accent on form means a weaker one on theme.

In short, a sonata movement by Beethoven is far less beholden to the immediate "poetic" character of its themes, to the presence of the "Poetic" from its opening bars, than is a lyrical piano piece or symphonic poem of the romantic period. The decisive factor is not its thematic substance but rather the thematic process thus set in motion. Taken by themselves, Beethoven's themes may be terse or almost nonexistent without doing serious damage to the key issue, form. However, if the final arbiter for the aesthetic validity of a work or movement is to be found not in its thematic substrate but rather in its formal process, this likewise changes the function of the elements of content which are linked to the themes. A poetic idea may be associated with a theme or a complex of themes, or it may emerge from a formal process, which can prove significant despite its unassuming thematic material. And depending on where the poetic idea is focused, the influence of moods, characters, or subjects will increase or decrease accordingly.

The Metaphysic of Instrumental Music

Today, in the twentieth century, it seems trivial to think that music, like literature and philosophy, can manifest "mind" in the strong sense of the term as used in the age of Hegel. But when this notion arose in the eighteenth century, it must have been thought presumptuous and paradoxical. It is even possible to view the whole of nineteenth-century music aesthetics, for all its many contradictions, as an attempt to establish and justify the position of music in the hierarchy of human activities and experience. E. T. A. Hoffmann maintained of pure, autonomous instrumental music—the symphonies of Haydn, Mozart, and Beethoven—that it had extricated itself from extramusical ideas and was approaching a prevision of the Infinite and Absolute. By the same token, Liszt, in his symphonic poems, felt that he was enhancing the dignity of instrumental music by, as it were, projecting masterpieces of world literature and myth into the language of music. Yet these two wildly divergent aesthetic dogmas have one historically significant element in common: they both assume, as Eduard Hanslick put it, that music is capable of revealing "mind in intellectually tractable material." We can gauge the historical impact of this assumption by recalling that, in the eighteenth century, it was not just the—possibly unmusical—philosopher Kant who could speak of music as "doubtless more delectation than culture"; even a music enthusiast such as Charles Burney called music an "innocent luxury" in order to vindicate it aesthetically and morally in the Puritanical world of industrial and mercantile England. Nineteenth-century music aesthetics were colored by German romanticism, and the important thing about them was the new urgency they gave to thinking about music.

In the everyday speech of our century, the aesthetic of feeling is automatically called "romantic." However, this aesthetic is not characteristic of romanticism in the years around 1800 (which instead took their music aesthetic from the writings of Wackenroder, Tieck, and E. T. A. Hoffmann), but originated in the early years of the eighteenth century. The music aesthetic of the Enlightenment was by no means marked by the formalism that we hastily associate with rationalism; on the contrary, its main category was sensibility. Bourgeois audiences gradually came to self-awareness during the Enlightenment, and what they wanted from music was "feeling." (Aristocrats presented themselves musically with pompous dignity, the bourgeoisie with simplicity of sentiment.) Music that did not reach the heart, that was not intelligible as a reflection of inner emotion, was considered meaningless noise: however astonishing the virtuosity of the performance, it left the emotions untouched.

The musical creations that kindled the sensibilities were frequently extremely simple: a few notes, artlessly combined, were sometimes sufficient to reach the hearts of listeners whose imaginations were stirred by remembrances of the novels of Rousseau, Lawrence Sterne, or Jean Paul. The romantics, on the other hand, took their notion of art from the classicism of Schiller and Goethe and applied this notion to music. As a result they gravitated toward musical phenomena that manifested the notion of "grand design." Their ideal was no longer the simple song but the symphony—the genre which, as Haydn had demonstrated, was capable of creating a form spanning hundreds of measures using solely the logic of harmony and theme, without recourse to a text. In highbrow aesthetics—which thereby moved away from popular aesthetics—sensibility and the search for feeling gave way to a metaphysic based on Edmund Burke's and Immanuel Kant's theory of the Sublime in order to do justice to absolute instrumental music and to capture in words the aesthetic experience of the listener.

The metaphysical aesthetic of romanticism forms an antithesis to the psychological aesthetic of the Enlightenment. Anyone who expected music to touch the heart was using it as a means to an end. No matter whether the listener was giving free play to his own emotions in solitude or trying to establish bonds of sympathy with his fellow listeners, music was serving a psychological function rather than existing for its own sake. In contrast, Schopenhauer, to all appearances an adherent of the aesthetic of feeling, maintained that music expresses "not simply this or that individual and particular joy, this or that sorrow, or pain, or horror, or exaltation, or merriment, or moment of composure; but rather Joy, Sorrow, Pain, Horror, Exaltation, Merriment, Composure in and of themselves, one might say *in abstracto,* their inner essence devoid of accessories, by which I mean devoid of the motives thereto." Here Schopenhauer has to a certain extent transported the feelings of the listener into another realm. The emphasis has shifted from the aesthetic subject, intended to reveal itself through music, to the aesthetic object in whose meaning the listener is meant to become immersed. What Schopenhauer expects as appropriate behavior from audiences is no longer psychological reflection on themselves and their own feelings, but rather participation in a metaphysical quality within music itself. E. T. A. Hoffmann, in 1810, took a different tack:

> Beethoven's music sets in motion the mechanisms of dread, fear, horror, pain, and kindles that infinite longing that is the essence of romanticism. Beethoven is a purely romantic composer, and for that very reason a genuinely musical one; and this may explain why he is less successful in his vocal music—which does not admit indefinite longing but merely presents the affections given in the text as though experienced in the domain of the Infinite—and why his instrumental music seldom appeals to the masses.

Here Hoffmann is trying to express in words the overpowering impression left on him by Beethoven's Fifth Symphony. His starting point is the theory of the Sublime formulated in the late eighteenth century, by Burke and Kant, as a supplement to the traditional aesthetic, the theory of Beauty. On the other hand, Hoffmann clearly separates the metaphysic of instrumental music, which he borrows in outline from Tieck's *Phantasien über die Kunst,* from the aesthetic of feeling. The "domain of the Infinite" revealed by music is a world "that has nothing in common with the external world of the senses," a world that "surrounds" us and "in which we abandon all feelings that can be defined in words in order to submit to the Inexpressible." The sharply defined affections that, to the eighteenth-century mind, made up the substance of music, giving it meaning and a claim to artistic status in the first place, blur and dissolve in the "infinite longing" that constitutes the "essence of romanticism." By claiming that music, and instrumental music in particular, is capable of capturing the "Inexpressible" and "Unspeakable," Hoffmann elevated music to a language that, despite or perhaps because of its lack of concepts, is superior to and transcends the language of words. This claim is an enthusiasts's rejoinder to the skeptical eighteenth-century view that instrumental music is incapable of either "painting" or "touching"—or, to use the language of the theory of imitation, is incapable of imitating outer or inner nature—and hence is only inchoate and meaningless sound, prelinguistic stammering rather than articulate speech. Enlightenment aesthetics consigned instrumental music, with its lack of words and concepts, to an inferior status, condemning it as a mere shadow and deficient mode of vocal music. With romantic aesthetics—one of whose founding documents was Hoffmann's Beethoven review of 1810—it attained a virtually unbounded superiority: it was a language beyond language, capable of expressing the inexpressible and opening up profound depths that words cannot reach. Unlike instrumental music, vocal music remained bound to affections, which can be defined by means of concepts. But these, too, are apparently "experienced in the domain of the Infinite." Thus, for Hoffmann, vocal music partakes of the aesthetic dignity of instrumental music, the "pure expression and sole identifying source of the inmost essence of art," whereas in eighteenth-century theory instrumental music only attained meaning and artistic status by imitating vocal music and adopting its aesthetic criteria by attempting to "paint" or "touch." The primacy of instrumental music, the recourse to the theory of the Sublime, and the suppression of the psychological aesthetic for a metaphysical one—in Hoffmann's Beethoven review, which set the "tone" of musical discourse for an entire century, these are all different sides of the same issue.

Hoffmann's outline of a romantic aesthetic of music heralded a new era in the history of musical thought. It precedes a structural analysis of Beethoven's symphony which does not even shrink from a sober discussion of details. Nor would it be right to consider Hoffmann's aesthetic and technical interpretations as separate entities, since he obviously intended them to be interlinked. To understand music means, according to the romantic view that Hoffmann shared with Friedrich Schlegel, grasping the structure, the harmonic and thematic logic of a work, so as to be able to fathom its aesthetic meaning, a meaning that remains inaccessible to mere mindless enthusiasm. For Hoffmann, the element that makes music "cohere at its inmost center" is the same element that allows access to its metaphysical essence:

> Just as bookish aesthetes have often carped and caviled at the complete absence of true unity and inner cohesion in Shakespeare; and just as a tree, sprouting buds and leaves, blossoms and fruit from a single kernel, reveals its beauty only to the inquiring eye: so only a very deep examination of the inner structure of Beethoven's music will disclose the lofty circumspection of the master, a circumspection at once inseparable from true genius and nurtured by the continuous study of art.

Hoffmann's analysis of the first movement of the symphony deliberately counters the prejudiced view that sublimity tended to rhapsodic formlessness—to "beauteous confusion," as it was called in the eighteenth century. It reveals a close connection between the continuous interweaving of the parts and the expression of "nameless longing" that makes up the "character of the piece in its entirety." The unity of the technical and aesthetic dimensions is manifest in this close connection: unlike the verbally definable affections in which the eighteenth century sought to find the meaning of music, the metaphysical premonitions conveyed by the Fifth Symphony derive less from individual musical ideas, however expressive in themselves, than from the design of the whole—a design "sprouting from a single kernel." And this design, when subjected to ever-closer analysis (in principle a never-ending process), reveals an increasingly dense web of thematic and motivic, even submotivic relations. It would appear to be just this notion of a holistic entity, endlessly rich in relations and thereby directed toward something higher than the mere acoustic phenomenon, that Beethoven had in mind when he spoke of the "poetic idea" that guided him in the conception of a work of music. (Hoffmann, a thoroughly competent performing musician, must have been equally guided by this notion.)

The metaphysic of instrumental music elevated the Beethoven symphony into an *opus metaphysicum* in the first half of the nineteenth century, just as Nietzsche was to do with the Wagnerian music drama in the second. Granted that this metaphysic is the "genuine" musical aesthetic of romanticism, it is nevertheless unmistakable that the eighteenth-century aesthetic of feeling, a specifically bourgeois phenomenon, remained virtually intact as a popular aesthetic—and not merely as an aesthetic of popular music. Romanticism may have been the signature of the age as far as intellectual history is concerned, but from the standpoint of cultural history it is only part of the picture. On the one hand, we have esoteric romanticism: here, in the age of "art as religion," the quintessence of art was seen to reside in absolute instrumental music, divorced from texts, extramusical functions, and clearly defined emotions. On the other hand, in sharp contrast or in changing forms of transmission and assimilation, we have sensibility, or *Empfindsamkeit,* a holdover from the eighteenth century where, in Wackenroder's words, music was used as a means of collecting the stray feelings in life and allocating to them a position denied them in everyday existence. And when Eduard Hanslick, in his treatise *The Beautiful in Music* of 1854, railed against the "worm-eaten aesthetic of feeling," he basically added his voice to a battle started half a century earlier, by Ludwig Tieck in his *Phantasien über die Kunst,* against the aesthetic banality that the doctrine of sensibility had by then become. Hanslick provocatively advanced a doctrine of formalism in his paradoxical thesis that the "content" of music consisted solely in "forms of sound in motion." This doctrine is a sober version of the aesthetic of autonomy, robbed of its metaphysic but sharing with romantic aesthetics the crucial premise that music is, or ought to be, a "world unto itself"—not a means to a social or psychological end but an end in its own right. As formulated by Schopenhauer, this premise meant that music was by rights an object of aesthetic contemplation, in which the listener, heedless of himself and his surroundings, remains engrossed in the acoustic phenomenon, in the artistic creation. And this creation has nothing in common with functional nonart; instead, as Nietzsche later maintained, it is an object, not justified by human existence, but itself constituting the sole justification of that existence.

At first, the autonomy aesthetic was thoroughly esoteric; only gradually and with great effort did it overcome the irrepressible habit of associating images with instrumental music or immersing oneself in one's own inner feelings instead of in the aesthetic object. Its historical significance does not lie solely in the hold it took on early-nineteenth-century audiences in their patterns of perception and reaction, whether as a standard practice or as a widely held if sometimes disregarded postulate. The thesis that music exists to be listened to for its own sake may not have had an immediate and tangible impact on the history of musical reception. Nevertheless, in the history of ideas which altered reality instead of merely hovering above it, this thesis was a portentous phenomenon of far-

Fig. 19 Johann Carl Arnold: *Quartettabend bei Bettina von Arnim,* c. 1855. The early nineteenth century was at once an age of bourgeois revolution and an age of a romanticism that "immured itself from the world." Bettina von Arnim (1785–1859) could steadfastly assert her republican sentiments in Restoration Prussia and yet immerse herself in chamber music with an earnestness betokening the musical aesthetic of Wackenroder and Tieck. This is one sign of the inner breadth attained by the bourgeois spirit in the happiest hour of its history. The first violinist in the quartet is the young Joseph Joachim (1831–1907), who in the 1850s, as Bettina's daughter reports, "frequently traveled from Hanover to visit us in Berlin." In the background is a Goethe memorial designed by Bettina herself, whose published correspondence with Goethe is no less controversial than the three letters addressed to her by Beethoven. (Frankfurt am Main, Freies Deutsches Hochstift, Goethe Museum.)

reaching significance: as E. T. A. Hoffmann showed, it formed the aesthetic correlate to a development in the history of composition, namely, to the emergence of large-scale forms made up exclusively of their own internal musical logic. (Again borrowing Kant's terminology: aesthetics may be "empty" unless it is grounded in compositional technique, but compositional technique is "blind" unless it is grounded in aesthetics.) Beethoven's conception of form may have been clouded and confused by his contemporaries in their quest for secret programs hidden in the sonatas and symphonies; but in the late nineteenth and the early twentieth century it took an increasingly strong hold on the minds of his audiences—or at least on those who lay claim to musical culture. The cause of this was "musical analysis," a method that virtually came to form an "institution" of musical culture. We must not take it as a matter of course—indeed, adherents of the aesthetic of association or sentiment would hotly deny—that structural analysis is useful for a perception of music, that it turns perception into "understanding," or even that music exists to be "understood" at all. However, this only further underscores the truth of the fact that, in the century and a half that has passed since Hoffmann's Beethoven review, analysis has become one of the major and most profoundly influential instruments of communication in music culture, with a fundamental historical significance made all the more apparent by the violence with which its detractors rail against the "analysis racket." Modern twentieth-century music is inconceivable without the mode of aesthetic cognition which finds expression in analysis. Yet, in the early nineteenth century, the conviction that structural analysis could fulfill an aesthetic function instead of merely serving as an aid to theoreticians was still so shaky that Robert Schumann, in his essay on Berlioz's *Symphonie fantastique,* could practice analysis and find it suspect at the same time. The roots of this conviction are to be found in the autonomy aesthetic, whether in the romantic, metaphysical form of Ludwig Tieck and E. T. A. Hoffmann or the positivist, formalist version of Eduard Hanslick.

Thus, with aesthetic contemplation, the listener immerses himself in a work instead of circumambulating his own thoughts and feelings. Wackenroder, in his "Berlinger" novella *Herzergießungen eines kunstliebenden Klosterbruders* (1797), described aesthetic contemplation as a form of devotional exercise: "When Joseph was at a grand concert he seated himself in a corner, without so much as glancing at the brilliant assembly of listeners, and listened with precisely the same reverence as if he were in church—just as still and motionless, his eyes cast down to the floor. Not the slightest sound escaped his notice, and his keen attention left him in the end quite limp and exhausted." The "holy art of music" that sends Wackenroder-Berlinger into such religious transports is not church music but a symphony, and the location that causes him to feel "as if he were in church" is a concert hall. In other words, whereas music, in the form of church music, used to partake of religion as revealed in the "Word," it now, as autonomous music capable of conveying the "inexpressible," has become religion itself.

If Wackenroder spoke not just of music but specifically of pure instrumental music in the language of religious enthusiasm (Tieck went so far as to say: "For beyond a doubt music is the ultimate secret of faith; it is mysticism, religion fully revealed"), this does not mean that he ignored the aesthetic object in order to indulge in vague moods and sentiments. Rather, his devotional attitude toward music was the religious expression—and the religious roots—of strict concentration on the work as a self-contained musical process. For the late eighteenth century, in the decade that saw Haydn write his London symphonies, this form of concentration apparently represented a new development in the history of musical reception. (It took a long and arduous process before the mental retracing of musical logic—the aesthetic raison d'être of instrumental music—was able to gain ascendancy over other forms of perception, such as background listening, concentration on the text, self-absorption in one's own thoughts and moods, a feeling of camaraderie within a social circle, or the association of images and programs.) As Wackenroder wrote in a letter of 1792 to Tieck: "When I go to a concert, I find that I invariably enjoy the music in two different ways. Only one of these ways is the right one: it consists in alert observation of the notes and their progression, in fully surrendering my spirit to the welling torrent of sensations, in removing and disregarding every disturbing thought and all irrelevant impressions of my senses." (The "other way," which Wackenroder disparaged but could never keep entirely at bay, was associative listening.)

Thus, the "religion of art" proclaimed by Wackenroder was fully consistent with aesthetic concentration on the matter in question—on musical form as a process—rather than giving way to wild imaginings. It forms one of the historical prerequisites for that intense mode of perception that represents the subjective correlate to absolute instrumental music with its claims to artistic autonomy. We can assess the historical impact of these claims by taking Friedrich Schlegel at his word when he writes of the "affinity" between "pure instrumental music" and philosophy: "Is the theme of a purely instrumental piece not developed, confirmed, varied, and contrasted in the same manner as the object of meditation in a philosophical train of thought?" Structural hearing meant immersing oneself in the internal workings of a piece of music as though nothing else in the world existed. In its original form, it was accompanied by a metaphysic and a religion of art. Only in our century, in the name of that same structural hearing, were these mediating factors dismissed as extraneous additives to the acoustic phenomenon.

On the other hand, it would be misguided to see the religion of art as an offshoot of anticlericalism, and thus to think of it as an illegitimate attempt to deck out secular objects with a religious dignity that, in the end, proves to be nothing but empty metaphor. Any historian who forms his opinions without the aid of theological dogmatics will be able to see the nineteenth-century religion of art as a legitimate form of religious awareness, one that typified its age in the history of human piety. As Schleiermacher put it, it was a form of religion less beholden to the "Word" than to an adumbration of the "inexpressible," one that sought to grasp the essence of religion not in articles of faith but rather in "pious frames of mind." In *Die neue Kirche,* an anonymous pamphlet of 1815, the Berlin theologian Martin Leberecht de Wette expressed this as follows: "For the cultivated minds of our age, art and poetry are the most effective means of kindling religious sentiments. Faith finds its most direct expression in feeling, and religious feeling is best served by art." Most of all, it is music which, being a language beyond language, is capable of intimating the "inexpressible." As Karl Barth wrote in a survey of Schleiermacher's theology: "Of the three realms of language —the literary, the rhetorical, and the expository—the literary is supreme; and higher than and superior to all of them is music."

Lied Traditions

We habitually classify Schubert as a "romantic classic" composer, meaning that we can sense his historical proximity not only to Beethoven—especially to the works from Op. 74 to Op. 97—but also to Schumann. However, we also mean that Schubert is a "romantic" composer who has become the "classic" composer of the German lied. Strictly speaking, "the" lied is no more a genre than "the" piece of instrumental music. At one extreme, it is a musical type determined by Schubert, which is known in French as *le lied* and caused the Czech, English, or Norwegian composers who adopted it—whether Smetana, Stanford, or Grieg— to set poems in German. At the other extreme, it is a blanket term for a loose congery of genres ranging in their settings from solo to duet and quartet to chorus, and in their forms from simple strophic repetition to through-composed cavatinas or rondos to rhapsodic ode settings in the spirit of Klopstock. To grasp the historical character of the Schubert lied, as well as the European context from which it stood out, we will have to proceed from the wide array of lied traditions rather than the unity of the lied as an ideal. The lied type with which Schubert ushered in a new era is not the same as his entire output of lieder, and we spoil our chances of understanding its special nature if we elevate it prima facie to an ideal type against which the remaining types or genres degenerate into flawed subspecies instead of preserving their aesthetic independence. We have no right to measure an arietta, a cavatina, a romance, or an ode against a lied aesthetic derived from *Gretchen am Spinnrade* (1814) or *Wanderers Nachtlied* (1815). And any history which arrives at the conclusion, whether tacit or not, that an overwhelming majority of the various heterogeneous items falling under the heading of "lieder" are not "genuine" lieder at all is simply distorting the reality of history to fit an idealized construct. In fact, there were countless genres of song in existence at any one time.

Beethoven's *Lieder und Gesänge* are fully representative of the historical context of Schubert's lieder. No one who wishes to do them justice should let his sense of their aesthetic shortcomings as compared with Schubert, nor the fact that

Beethoven thought less highly of these works than other genres, mislead him into concluding that "the" lied was still "undeveloped" as far as Beethoven is concerned. The items included in a volume of Beethoven's collected lieder range from folklike songs such as *Das Blümchen Wunderhold,* Op. 52, No. 8 (before 1793), to a *scena ed aria* such as *Ah! Perfido,* Op. 65 (1796), with countless subcategories and variants in between. They form a continuum of formal types from *Ah! Perfido* to *An die Hoffnung* (1813) and *Der Wachtelschlag* (1803) all the way to *Mignon* (1809). For this reason we have no right to discount the extremes and no way of determining which genres Beethoven regarded as extraneous. In Beethoven's own words, his Metastasio settings Op. 82, written before 1800, are "ariettas," whether "buffa" or "seriosa." According to the definition given in Koch's *Musikalisches Lexikon* (1802), *La partenza* (1797–98), likewise to a text by Metastasio, is a cavatina, meaning "a short aria in which words are seldom repeated and melismatic extension of syllables seldom applied, and which in particular has no second section." *Die Himmel rühmen des Ewigen Ehre,* Op. 48, No. 4 (1802), is definable as a hymn, and *An die Hoffnung,* Op. 94 (1813), as an ode, provided we understand "ode" to mean the sophisticated dithyrambic type known in the eighteenth century as a "Pindaric ode." Finally, *Der Wachtelschlag,*

Fig. 20   Drawing of a bourgeois lieder gathering. Of all the lied genres in the nineteenth century the only one to survive in the modern concert hall and drawing room is the solo song. However, this should not obscure the fact that there also existed a rich duet, trio, and quartet literature, which has disappeared from music life and historical memory, not because of any aesthetic shortcomings on its part but for institutional reasons alone. Vocal ensemble music was better suited for convivial pursuits than as a "recital" and was thus unable to outlive a bourgeois culture in which music freely alternated with conversation and group readings. (Vienna, Österreichische Nationalbibliothek.)

although based on a strophic text, consists of two through-composed cavatinas separated by recitative, and might thus be classified as a miniaturized form of solo cantata, with its two parts held together by an ostinato motive. Moreover, despite the confused relation between the titles and contents of his Op. 52 and Op. 75 collections, Beethoven seems to have distinguished between *Lieder* and *Gesänge: Marmotte*, Op. 52, No. 7 (*circa* 1793), is a *Lied*, whereas the *Gesänge* include *Mignon*, Op. 75, No. 1, a varied strophic song with sharp contrasts within the strophes, and *Neue Liebe, neues Leben*, Op. 75, No. 2 (1809), a "sonata form" without development section.

In 1824 the *Allgemeine musikalische Zeitung* reported of Schubert: "Herr F. S. does not write lieder in the accepted sense, nor does he wish to. . . . Instead, he composes free songs [*Gesänge*], sometimes so free that we were better advised to call them capriccios or fantasias." In 1826 the same journal continued: "For lieder in the strict sense he seems less well appointed than for through-composed pieces." At that time, "lieder in the strict sense" meant unvaried strophic songs— a genre whose simplicity was vindicated in 1801 by Goethe, in his *Tag- und Jahresheften,* with the argument that it was the performer's task, not the composer's, to vary the expression from strophe to strophe. Referring to the actor and singer Wilhelm Ehlers, he wrote:

> He was tireless in his study of those peculiarities of expression that obtain when, in a single melody, a singer draws out the variegated meaning of the separate strophes, and thereby fulfills at a stroke the obligations of both the lyric and the epic artist. So possessed was he of this study that he gladly indulged me when I imposed upon him to spend several evening hours, even till deep in the night, in repeating one and the same song, expressing to a jot all of its many nuances; for his success in doing so convinced him how vain and futile is the so-called through-composition of songs, which nullifies lyric character in general, and induces and elicits a false participation in the individual poem.

Among Schubert's earliest songs we find strophic lieder such as *Der Jüngling am Bache* (1812) which fully conform to Goethe's lied aesthetic, as well as lyrical-dramatic scenes such as *Hagars Klage* (1811) which belong to a different genre and are hence not governed by Goethe's axioms. Nevertheless, the lied forms that Schubert was groping toward from 1814 on belong neither to the one extreme nor to the other. Rather, it seems as though Schubert envisaged a notion of lied which skirted the dangers, as he saw them, of incoherent through-composed "tone-painting," on the one hand, and servility to the principles of strophic song on the other—principles that made it difficult if not impossible to realize the claims he was raising for the lied as a musical form with pretensions to the status of a work of art.

To reduce the development of this genre to a simple formula, we might maintain that the initial sharp distinction between through-composed and strophic songs—a distinction grounded in the different traditions of these genres—gave way in 1814, with *Gretchen am Spinnrade,* Op. 2, to a combination of the two. This combination proved decisive to the history of nineteenth-century song. The result was a form as far removed from the simplicity of strophic song as it was from the disjointedness of tone-painting, a form suspended between cyclic design and varied strophic song. Broadly speaking, Schubert's song is in refrain form (*ABACADA*); yet sections *B, C,* and *D* are so closely interlinked, either being partly identical (mm. 14–17 and 43–50) or using analogous modulating sequences to build a crescendo (mm. 22–29, 55–62, and 85–92), that we can refer to the form as strophic variation.

However, it is not enough to construct a dialectical evolution culminating in "the" lied if we wish to do justice to an art that consists less in transformations of an ideal form—of what we might call the mid-point of the formal inventory—than in ever-different answers to a formal problem that will not admit a general, paradigmatic solution. True, in principle we could proceed from an ideal form suspended between varied strophic song and cyclic design, taking the through-composed and the strophic song as extreme, peripheral forms that are justifiable only under certain conditions. However, this would remain a superficial analytical approach to Schubert's songs, which are easier to understand as a configuration of forms rather than as proceeding from a single pattern. For the problem that Schubert faced was to find ever-new ways of striking a balance between criteria and postulates that sometimes complement one another, and yet at other times are mutually exclusive and contradictory. And only the success of the individual work stands as proof that a balance has indeed been struck.

For one thing, the music must seem to reflect both the outer and the inner form of the underlying poem, with the emphasis depending in part on the genre to which the lied belongs. For another, as Herder had already demanded of the lied as a poetic form, a lyric "tone" must be struck in the music as well:

> The essence of the lied is song, not painting; its perfection lies in tracing the course of passion or feeling in melody, a practice we might refer to with the ancient but fitting term "lay" [*Weise*]. Without it, a lied has no tone, no poetic modulation, no sustained motion or progression in its melody. No matter its form and imagery, no matter the composition and delicacy of its colors: it is no longer a lied.

We have seen how the lied was meant to attain the status of art by striking a balance between variety and integration in its musical structure. For this balance, to string together illustrative details into a rhapsodic potpourri was no less dangerous than the naiveté of the (unvaried) strophic song, whose sole justification—its "noble simplicity," where the pinnacle of art lay in a semblance of artlessness—had gradually devolved into an ideological *donnée.* Originally, the musical structure of the lied had served as a vehicle for reciting poems; now it was to become a "work" in the strong sense of the term. Moreover, Schubert was no different

Fig. 21   *Die schöne Müllerin.* This naive and unoffending illustration seems to have taken its inspiration more from the spirit of the times than from Schubert's work. Assuming that it attempts to do more than simply incorporate the title of the song cycle into a genre painting, ignoring the narrative entirely, the illustration apparently captures the scene of the sixth song, *Mein*: "Brooklet, leave thy murmurings . . . the maid of the mill is mine!" (Vienna, Gesellschaft der Musikfreunde.)

from Beethoven in distinguishing between various generic traditions which, though collectively lumped under the heading *Lieder und Gesänge,* could scarcely be regarded as offshoots of a single formal principle.

A lyric tone, as Herder called it, makes *Wanderers Nachtlied* ("Der du von dem Himmel bist") of 1815 almost a paradigm of the lied. However, this must not blind us to the fact that, as far as the historical origins of its form are concerned, it is a cavatina made up of an arioso opening, a suggestion of recitative (m. 5), and a cantabile ending, repeated. All of these features are characteristic of the cavatina. However, unlike Beethoven in his cavatina *La partenza,* Schubert is speaking in his own unmistakable voice rather than adopting a disguise. (By trying to set Metastasio's text to Italianate melodies Beethoven moved stylistically to the near proximity of Mozart.) Schubert's lyric tone is at the same time subjective, rather than being merely "sensitive" in a generalized sense; and this governs the impact of the lied to such an extent that its generic roots in the cavatina pale by comparison.

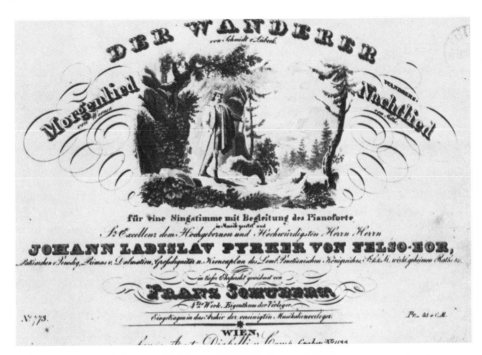

Fig. 22 *Der Wanderer*. The illustrator, who shows a wandering youth emerging from a mountain chasm into a sunbathed wooded landscape, may well have known nothing more of the poem than its first line ("From mountains high I come"), as there is not the slightest hint of the resignation that otherwise informs this song ("I wander silent, gone my cheer"). However, it is just possible that this illustration derives from that current in the reception of Schubert which transmuted his melancholy tone into the idyllic. (Vienna, Gesellschaft der Musikfreunde.)

Gruppe aus dem Tartarus (1816–17), to a poem by Schiller, is a lyric-epic scena, and hence belongs to a genre generally governed by the principle of "through-composition" rather than being a departure from strophic form. The three stanzas of the poem became four sections in the music since Schubert seized the opportunity to portray the contrast that splits the third stanza ("Fragen sich einander ängstlich leise"—"Ewigkeit schwingt über ihnen Kreise"). In the scena as a genre, the composer takes his bearings primarily from the internal form of the poem as dictated by its contents rather than from the external form. There is no "lyric tone" permeating the entire piece, which in this sense lacks the character of a lied. Its sections are juxtaposed in the manner of "images" and remain unintegrated on the surface of the music. However, without inner coherence the piece would not fully qualify as a work, and this inner coherence is provided by the obvious similarities of the chromatic sequences in the first, second, and third sections (mm. 1–9, 25–30, 32–39, 50–61). If the lyric-epic scena is endangered as a genre by a tendency to reduce the music to emphatic declamation and illustrative instrumental motives, Schubert achieves structural unity without forcing the melodic line into a cyclic mold, which would have been inconsistent with the inner form of the poem.

Halt, the third lied in *Die schöne Müllerin* (1823), is one of the few through-composed pieces in the cycle. Nonetheless, its lyric tone and simple scansion of the lines leave us in no doubt as to its character as a lied. It owes its coherence to a continuous, uninterrupted accompaniment figure, which is maintained despite irregularities in the meter (m. 31–36). Between the first and the final section (mm. 16–22 and 46–60) there exists an indistinct connection revealed by the melodic contour and by details in the harmony (Ex. 6). Syntactically, these related sections function as antecedent and consequent, even though separated by twenty-three measures. An open cadence on the fifth degree of the tonic (m. 22), is followed by a further open cadence on the fifth degree of the dominant (m. 30), generating a harmonic tension not entirely resolved by the full cadence at measure 45. This causes the concluding section to hover between the character of an appendix and that of a necessary cadence. Thus, in the context of the piece as a whole, the impression of consequence conveyed by measures 46–60—and the melodic association that gives rise to that impression—serve a formal function: they extend the cadential effect without completely dispelling our feeling that they form a coda. And it is precisely this ambiguity—our inability to hear these measures unequivocally as an appendix, a quasi reminiscence, or a complementary consequent phrase following a long gap—that makes the concluding section reflect the meaning of the text: the wanderer, struck by the sight of a mill, pauses, and his vision is transformed unawares into foreboding ("Ei Bächlein, liebes Bächlein, war es also gemeint?").

Example 6

It is no coincidence that Schubert was also one of the founders of the lyric piano piece, the instrumental pendant to the lied or *Gesang*. Both the vocal and the instrumental genre have certain peculiarities in common that make them characteristically romantic. (There is a similar parallelism in the lieder and piano pieces of Tomášek.)

A tiny number of works with unimpeachable claim to artistic status stand out against the vast output of nineteenth-century works which served an estimable social function but leave us under no compunction to include them in a history of music as art. The difference between these works and art music was not simply one of aesthetic degree, as though it were a question of separating the successes from the failures: these works differed in kind, in a way that simply did not occur in the symphony and the string quartet. Even the worst imaginable symphony still fell under a different category from what Benedetto Croce called "nonart," which made no effort to partake of "artistic status." Yet it is sometimes difficult in individual cases to draw a line of demarcation between the two which is not dictated by prejudice. Even if we are not insensible to the charm of Henry Bishop's *Home, Sweet Home,* we can still maintain of the English "domestic bal-

Fig. 23 William Alfred Nicholls: *Aufführung von Haydns "Schöpfung,"* 1843. When Haydn's *Creation* was performed in Vienna's Winter Riding Academy (temporarily transformed into a concert hall by installing platforms for chorus and orchestra) nearly a thousand musicians took part, even though the gargantuan forces scarcely seem warranted by the work itself. The great choral festivals of the early nineteenth century, patterned after the Handel Commemorations in eighteenth-century England, were musicopatriotic events with which bourgeois music culture (otherwise largely confined to the drawing room) aspired to monumental self-display. (Göttingen, Niedersächsische Staatsund Universitätsbibliothek.)

lad," particularly in its form as "Victorian ballad," that it remained fully as artless as its convivial function required. In contrast, the French *romance* has a history more complicated than would seem to be the case if we simply accept the general verdict, issued from the standpoint of the German lied, that it was nothing but salon music for voice. At the time of Rousseau's *Dictionnaire du musique* (1767) the *romance* may well have been a "folklike" narrative song in a "simple, touching" style with a "certain antique aura," but in the hands of Méhul and Boieldieu in the early nineteenth century it drew either on the cantabile of Italian canzonettas and cavatinas or on the declamatory melodic style of the German lied. True, before Berlioz there were no significant examples of the genre known as *romance dialoguée,* where the vocal part was held in balance by an illustrative piano accompaniment. Yet this does not alter the historical fact that the *romance,* like the German lied, existed in two variants: a "vernacular" form and an "artificial" one that likewise tended from lied-like simplicity (in the narrow sense of the term) to the complexity of the *Gesang.* It is also true that *lied* became a loan word in French for the sublime genre, whereas *Romanze* entered German as a term for the lesser, salon version of the French *romance.* But this should not blind us to the parallel evolution of these genres, which remains a fact of history despite the incomparable artistic stature of Schubert's lieder. Berlioz may have referred to his songs as *mélodies* to distinguish them from the by now threadbare *romance* (*mélodies* was the French term for Schubert's lieder), but they nonetheless belong as much to the history of the *romance* in the broad sense of the term as Schubert's *Gesänge* belong to the history of the lied.

Thus, in the case of lieder and piano pieces, the distinction between art music and utilitarian music was especially sharp, and for that reason especially hazardous, particularly since both genres derived from traditions with an ideal of simplicity that gradually came into conflict with their claim to artistic status. Yet these genres had a similar dialectic with regard to the problem of form. Like the strophic song, with its simple formal designs, the lyric piano piece also tended toward simplicity of form, as is shown by the frequency of the *ABA* pattern, which Adolf Bernhard Marx labeled "song form," although it more likely evolved from the dance. However, in those songs and piano pieces which owe their internal cohesion to a consistent use of motive, cyclical forms such as *ABA* or *ABACA* do not offer the composer a structural principle so much as a mere scaffold, which he is free to abandon without essentially changing the nature of his piece. Unlike the sonata, lyrical genres are left unaffected when a "disintegrated"—meaning through-composed—form is used in lieu of a schematic one: formal design is of minor importance when the main issue is how the composer elaborates his motivic material.

Ultimately, in the lied or *Gesang* no less than in the nineteenth-century piano piece, what distinguishes ballads from romances, rhapsodies from elegies, nocturnes from berceuses, and so forth, is not so much their formal design, which remains unpredefined, but rather the particular "tone" they strike. The fact that it was possible at all for composers to write narrative songs, "ballads," for instruments without resorting to preconceived programs, is ample proof that the various "tones" of the ballad, whether lyric, epic, or dramatic, had long figured among the fixed categories of musical language—proof, in other words, that the opening of Chopin's G-minor Ballade (1831–35) was immediately recognizable as a musical rendering of a "narrative posture." Even in vocal ballads, whether by Schubert or by Carl Loewe, the disputed problem of form—the urge toward formal unity that distinguishes Schubert's *Erlkönig* (1815) from discursive "renditions" of the text, such as *Die Bürgschaft* (1815)—is merely the outside surface of the crucial aesthetic postulate: the need to maintain a continuous "ballad tone," a sine qua non of the genre.

The "tone" that identifies a genre is closely connected to its "mode of presentation," its relation to the audience or listeners. This aspect cannot be ignored if we wish to understand the generic differences between ballad, lied (in the narrow sense of the term), and aria. A ballad (or romance) is a sung narrative; in its mode of presentation the author directly addresses his audience. The ballad singer is a reciter or bard who presents a story to a circle of listeners. The underlying notion of the genre is that the audience perceives the author as a musical narrator; to separate the composer from the singer is to modify but not to abandon this notion.

Arias differ from ballads in that the composer, in principle, remains hidden from his audience. It is not considered good aesthetic form for the composer of an opera or a solo cantata to speak "in the first person," as though it were he, and not his characters, who addresses the audience, or as though he were using his characters as his spokesmen. What distinguishes an aria from sung narrative is that it is invariably a "role poem" that evolves from the situation outlined by the introductory recitative or scena. Conversely, in a lied, it is the composer who is speaking, not as himself but as a "lyric ego" beyond the grasp of fact-hungry biographers. Unlike sung narrative, a lied is an utterance that is not directed ostentatiously at an audience but, in a manner of speaking, is overheard by the audience. Listeners are essential to the ballad, but incidental to the lied.

The Idea of Folk Song

Folk songs have been enthusiastically collected since the final decades of the eighteenth century. Yet these activities have gone hand in hand with controversies about the nature of folk song, controversies that bear the marks of virtually every intellectual current from the eighteenth to the twentieth century—from the Enlightenment and the *Sturm und Drang* to romanticism and neoromanticism to positivism and *Neue Sachlichkeit*. And however widely disseminated and influential were the fruits of this mania for collection, particularly in amateur music-making and music education, the idea of folk song itself was no less significant in its impact, not least of all because it was subject to endless disputes in which crucial tendencies of the times happened to clash. (It is often precisely the

least intelligible categories, the vaguest concepts, such as the classic-romantic antithesis or the notions of true church music or genuine folk song, that determine the course of music history in a cultural rather than a compositional sense.)

In his treatise *Über Reinheit der Tonkunst* (1825), a universal compendium of the spirit of the times (or rather of the bourgeois educated classes), the Heidelberg lawyer and music enthusiast Justus Thibaut distinguished between street songs, or *Gassenhauer,* which "have a brief life span," and folk songs, which "continue to flower among the common folk":

> In contrast, pure and bright as the soul of a child are those songs, generally, which proceeded from the Folk itself or, having been adopted by the Folk, were conserved therein for long periods of time. These songs almost always correspond to our image of strong, vibrant human beings untainted by culture, and attain a value all their own by partaking of the great attributes of a nation.

These few lines include virtually every motivation that gave rise in the early nineteenth century, the age of romanticism, to the fad for folk song, or for what people imagined was folk song. First of all, the conception of folk song was more normative than descriptive: the aesthetically or morally objectionable was expunged under the name of *Gassenhauer,* or what Lessing called "riffraff song" (*Pöbellied*), and only emphasized by detractors of the folk song in order to embarrass its enthusiasts. Moreover, unlike the later scholarly habit of distinguishing sharply between the theory of production and the theory of reception, little interest was apparently shown in whether a song "proceeded from the Folk itself" or was "adopted by the Folk": the national spirit so eagerly sought at the time was apparently just as likely to be found in songs produced by the populace as in those which it assimilated from other sources. Hence, the notion of folk song, with the word "folk" suspended between various meanings, even encompassed national anthems of the sort typified by *God Save the King* (1744)—songs, in other words, in which nations recognized their musical identity.

The romantic era shared this normative conception of folk song with the Enlightenment and the *Sturm und Drang.* Its basic assumption was the notion of the "purely human," which allegedly expressed itself musically and poetically in "genuine" folk song. At the root of this folk-song aesthetic was a utopian view of

Fig. 24 Eduard Jakob von Steinle: *Loreley.* During the Third Reich, Heinrich Heine's *Loreley* was declared the work of an "unknown poet." This provides unintentional proof that its folklike tone, "translated" into literature, was thoroughly capable of finding its way back to folk art, where its authorship became increasingly irrelevant as the work struck deeper into the popular imagination. The naive and the sentimental, spontaneity and ironic detachment, archetype and kitsch—none of these opposites are as distinct in the popular mind as in systems of aesthetics. Not infrequently it is precisely the aesthetically dubious aspects of a form or motif which take the firmest hold in our collective memory. (Munich, Bayerische Staatsgemäldesammlungen.)

man. The recurring claim that a *Gassenhauer* or *Pöbellied* is distinguished from a folk song by the brevity of its existence presupposes that the value of an object is revealed by the tenacity with which it outlives its own times. Yet this presupposition is just as dubious in folk music as in art music. Upon closer examination, the hypothesis that songs of lower origin, both aesthetically and morally, wear out faster than others proves to be wrong. The only way to rescue it is by the circular argument of appealing to what Eduard Baumstark called the "wholesome section of the populace," whose wholesomeness is in turn revealed by a liking for "genuine" folk song.

For Enlightenment thinkers, with their philanthropic leanings and never-ending attempts to intervene in the present, "noble simplicity" was to be found primarily in "folklike" songs that were written by composers and presented to the populace for the purpose of educating it. Not so the romantics, who were drawn to the past and felt that genuine folk song was to be discovered in songs which, it was thought, had emanated from the populace itself in a distant and eminently desirable bygone age.

Admittedly, in the early nineteenth century, songs that were sufficiently folklike even though produced by composers were not entirely discounted as folk songs, or at least not rigorously so. However, it is characteristic of the spirit of romanticism, which thought nothing of writing and composing new works from the substance of the folk heritage while clinging to the old and remote, that Wilhelm von Zuccalmaglio, unlike his eighteenth-century counterpart Johann Abraham Peter Schultz, disguised his "folklike" songs (some of which eventually became folk songs) as "ancient folk songs." To the nineteenth-century mentality, his urge to write, rather than collect, folk songs was just as legitimate as the romantic disposition that compelled him to hide his authorship.

In the late nineteenth and the twentieth century, the normative concept of folk song based on the notion of the "purely human" gradually fell victim to positivist ethnography, without however disappearing entirely. This tendency toward positivism was already apparent, as a penchant for straight description, in Ludwig Erk, a folk-song collector who, to Zuccalmaglio's annoyance, did not even balk at *Gassenhauer*. It found its purest expression when Hans Naumann abandoned Herder's thesis of the "productive spirit of a nation" and summed up folk art in the formula "deteriorated culture." In the provocatively level-headed reasoning with which Naumann, in 1925, rehabilitated the *Gassenhauer*, we can sense his pleasure in shattering high-flown ideals: "It falsifies our scientific picture of folk song when we simply discard the objectionable or ephemeral and classify it under the heading of *Gassenhauer*. On the contrary, *Gassenhauer*, 'street ditty,' is a fitting term for that widespread dissemination among the populace which, in the final analysis, is essential to the definition of folk song." Still, whether the normative element can disappear completely in description—or in a functional definition—is just as dubious in the case of folk song as with the concept of the Classical.

Besides Wilhelm Heinrich Riehl, Raphael Georg Kiesewetter, who was anything but a romantic, was among the few who distinguished clearly between "actual folk songs" originating in the populace, and "songs in a folklike spirit," which were written for the populace and represent nothing more than "folk songs in the illegitimate sense" (*Schicksale und Beschaffenheit des weltlichen Gesanges*, 1841).

However, once scholars dropped the "origin hypothesis" and considered it sufficient for a song, as Adolf Bernhard Marx put it, to "live among the Folk" and "become its property," it became exceedingly difficult to draw a line between a "folk song" and a "folklike song" adopted by the populace although originally the work of a composer. Claudius's poem *Der Mond ist aufgegangen,* for instance, found its way into Herder's collection *Stimmen der Völker in Liedern,* and Schulz's setting of it was praised by Reichardt as a genuine folk song.

This does not mean that commentators faintheartedly resigned themselves to a "reception theory" whereby everything that circulated among the populace had to be folk song. In order to exclude the *Gassenhauer,* which offended against the notion of the purely human, the functional concept of folk song based on the criteria of widespread dissemination and longevity was supplemented by a substantive concept, which permitted a distinction between "genuine" and "spurious" folk song, using other features than simply the song's origin. "Spurious" folk songs included not only the "low" but also the "artificial," those which bore the ineradicable signs of having originated in composed music. Not that composers were forever barred from taking the opposite path from composition to folk song. But any composer who tried to recapture the natural state of folk song "at one remove"—that is, by approaching it through art—had to conceal the exertions of his craft. Yet, by the classic aesthetic, the perfection of art lay precisely in this self-renunciation. Kant, in 1790, could maintain that art attains perfection by concealing itself and appearing as nature; and this dictum was echoed by Reichardt a year later when, referring to the "highly difficult task of writing a genuinely folklike song," he wrote that "for the artist the supreme art lies, not in ignorance of his art, but in its renunciation" (*Geist des Musikalischen Kunstmagazins,* 1791).

We have seen how the paradoxical notion of a "composed folk song" could be salvaged by interpreting it as "second nature" or "at one remove." Another fixed category of the functional concept of folk song, in addition to dissemination and longevity, was the practice of *Umsingen,* or the recasting of a song during a performance. *Umsingen* even authorized collectors to tamper with the surviving form of the song, to continue the work of writing and singing the songs in their findings. Clemens Brentano and Achim von Arnim felt compelled to retouch and add new lines to the texts in their folk-song collection *Des Knaben Wunderhorn* (1805–8), thereby provoking a polemical battle with Johann Heinrich Voss, but only the generously lenient comment from Goethe that even their "adulterations" should be "accepted with gratitude": "Who of us does not know what a song must put up with when it passes for a time through the mouth of the Folk, and not only its uneducated members! Why should he who ultimately writes down a song, and places it alongside others, not be entitled to do the same?"

The romantics clung to a divided notion of folk song. For the sake of the "purely human," which seemed extinct in their own day, they hunted for the venerable and unpretentious, and convinced themselves with sentimental longing for the unfamiliar that it was to be be found in things strange and remote from their own times, race, and social background. On the other hand, in contrast to the resignation of late-nineteenth-century romantics, they still sustained the hope that it was possible to "romanticize" and "poeticize" their own age, to assimilate from within the object of their longing, namely, the unfamiliar and remote. In other words, composers and recasters of folk songs proceeded alike on the assumption that they were participating in tradition as documented by the folk song, which they saw as the literary and musical expression of the productive spirit of their nation. As Ferdinand Hand wrote in his *Aesthetik der Tonkunst* (vol. 2, 1841): "Thus, for new folk songs to be effective, they must remain in the same vein as traditional tunes. In doing so they court no loss of originality; on the contrary, by taking traditional melodies as their starting point they preserve that peculiarity of spirit that continues to thrive inbred in the Folk until altered or spoilt by alien influences."

It was not the lower classes, the originators of folk song, but rather the bourgeoisie, the searchers after "noble simplicity," who rediscovered the folk song and restored their unearthed material to a "second life" in nineteenth-century music culture. However, at the same time that the bourgeoisie was smitten by its enthusiasm for folk song—or shortly thereafter—it was also possessed by the concept of nationhood. This concept soon petrified into nationalism—into the idea that, of all the many social groups that human beings belong to, the nation is the most crucial and formative, and that in situations of political conflict one therefore owed primary allegiance to one's nation rather than to one's class, religious creed, or dynasty.

National awareness was so deep-seated that it made palpable self-contradictions look like truisms. This had important consequences for the theory of folk song. Even as late as 1793, Heinrich Christoph Koch could still speak ingenuously of folk song as a product of the lower classes, "who had chosen, for the exercise of their professions, to cultivate not their intellectual faculties but their bodily nature." In the nineteenth century, however, the folk song became linked, or lumped together, with the national anthem, for which *God Save the King* (1744) and *Gott erhalte Franz, den Kaiser* (1797) were cited again and again as paradigms. The Folk no longer meant the lower classes but rather the Nation, the population of a state, even though it was not the lower classes but the bourgeoisie which sought its political identity in the idea of nationhood.

Thus, patriotic songs, although they usually came "from above," were categorized as folk songs. This fact reveals the mixture of adjacent meanings residing in the term "Folk"—a mixture which, however precarious in an objective sense, was all the more strongly motivated by considerations of politics and intellectual history. By the same token, Zuccalmaglio, in light of national anthems, spoke of folk songs "in the narrow sense of the term" as the "deepest expression of nationhood, of a population that recognizes its dignity in itself or in its prince." And Ferdinand Hand—an ideal specimen of the educated classes, the woolliness of whose thinking makes him a star witness for the zeitgeist—causes the "purely human" and the "national" to merge in his folk-song aesthetic with no thought that they might be separate entities.

No one seemed to notice that the spirit of nationhood had distorted the historical reality of the folk song. Instead of belonging to a nation, meaning a people with a common language, folk songs quite often bear traits from specific regions or professional classes; thanks to their dissemination by wandering minstrels, they could even be international. However, these facts were suppressed and sacrificed to the notion that a nation expresses itself musically, and reveals its nature, in the simple spiritual substance of folk song.

However, for folk song to appear as the musical expression of a nation, it was not only the nonnational features that had to be scuttled. The fact that it arose as the song of the lower classes—of peasants, artisans, and herdsmen—had to be, if not denied outright, at least historiologically prettified. Until now, the notion of the "purely human" had served to separate genuine folk song from both the "lowly" and the "artificial"—that is, to hold the *Gassenhauer* at bay and to pave the way for the "folklike song." Now this same notion enabled the bourgeoisie to detect a bit of the "Folk" in itself while it was busy appropriating its songs.

Just as the simplicity at the heart of folk song was sought in a distant and buried part of history, the notion of "Folk" as a purely human substance transcending class distinctions likewise had to be seen as an idea originating in a lost age. Franz Wilhelm Freiherr von Ditfurth, in his *Fränkische Volkslieder* (1855), was convinced that in the late Middle Ages up to the sixteenth century—the time when the "genuine folk songs" originated—culture was not yet rent by class distinctions. And, he continued, the spirit that permeated all parts of a nation expressed itself in folk songs, which represent a sort of communal literary and musical property. Whatever one hoped but did not expect to receive from the present was projected into a past that took on the flavor of a Golden Age—an age that also happened to be the age of folk song.

Bibliographic References

Abert, Anna Amalie. "Webers 'Euryanthe' und Spohrs 'Jessonda' als große Opern." In *Festschrift für Walter Wiora,* edited by Ludwig Finscher and Christoph-Hellmut Mahling. Kassel: Bärenreiter, 1967.

Adorno, Theodor Wiesengrund. "Spätstil Beethovens." In *Moments musicaux*. Frankfurt am Main: Suhrkamp, 1964.

Becking, Gustav. *Der musikalische Rhythmus als Erkenntnisquelle*. Augsburg: B. Filser, 1928.

Boettcher, Hans. *Beethoven als Liederkomponist*. Augsburg: B. Filser, 1928.

Burney, Charles. *The Present State of Music in Germany, the Netherlands and the United Provinces*. 2 vols. London: Becket, 1773.

Cooper, Martin. *Beethoven: The Last Decade*. London: Oxford University Press, 1970.

———. *Opéra comique*. New York: Chanticleer Press, 1949.

Croce, Benedetto. *Estetica come scienza dell'espressione e linguistica generale*. Palermo: Bari, 1902. Eng. trans. by Douglas Ainslie as *Aesthetic as Science of Expression and General Linguistic*. 2d ed. London: Macmillan, 1922.

Dahlhaus, Carl. *Musikästhetik*. Cologne: Hans Gerig, 1967. Eng. trans. by William W. Austin as *Esthetics of Music*. Cambridge: Cambridge University Press, 1982.

———. *Die Idee der absoluten Musik*. Kassel: Bärenreiter, 1978.

D'Amico, Fedele. *L'opera teatrale Gioacchino Rossini*. Rome: E. De Santis, 1968.

Eggebrecht, Hans Heinrich. *Zur Geschichte der Beethoven-Rezeption*. Wiesbaden: Verlag der Akademie der Wissenschaften und der Literatur, 1972.

Forbes, Elliot, ed. *Thayer's Life of Beethoven*. Princeton: Princeton University Press, 1964.

Georgiades, Thrasybulos. *Schubert: Musik und Lyrik*. Göttingen: Vandenhoeck & Ruprecht, 1967.

Goslich, Siegfried. *Die deutsche romantische Oper*. Tutzing: Hans Schneider, 1975.

Halm, August. *Beethoven*. Berlin: M. Hesse, 1927.

Hanslick, Eduard. *Vom Musikalisch-Schönen: Ein Beitrag zur Revision der Aesthetik der Tonkunst*. Leipzig: Weigel, 1854. Eng. trans. by Gustav Cohen as *The Beautiful in Music*. New York: Novello, Ewer & Co., 1891.

Kerman, Joseph. *The Beethoven Quartets*. New York and London: Oxford University Press, 1967.

Kirkendale, Warren. "The 'Great Fugue' Op. 133: Beethoven's 'Art of Fugue.' " In *Acta musicologica* 35 (1963): 14–25.

Klusen, Ernst. *Volkslied: Fund und Erfindung*. Cologne: Hans Gerig, 1969.

Koch, Heinrich Christoph. *Versuch einer Anleitung zur Komposition*. 3 vols. Leipzig and Rudolstadt: A. F. Böhme, 1782–93.

Marx, Adolf Bernhard. *Die Lehre von der musikalischen Komposition*. 4 vols. Leipzig: Breitkopf & Härtel, 1837–47.

Noske, Frits. *La mélodie française de Berlioz à Duparc*. Amsterdam: North Holland Publishing; Paris: Presses Universitaires de France, 1954. Eng. trans. by Rita Benton as *French Song from Berlioz to Duparc*. New York: Dover, 1970.

Pulikowski, Julian von. *Geschichte des Begriffes Volkslied im musikalischen Schrifttum*. Heidelberg: Carl Winter, 1933.

Radiciotti, Giusseppe. *Gioacchino Rossini: Vita documentata, opere ed influenza sull'arta*. 3 vols. Tivoli: Chicca, 1927–29.

Schäfke, Rudolf. *Geschichte der Musikaesthetik in Umrissen*. Berlin: M. Hesse, 1934.

Schenker, Heinrich. *Beethoven: Die letzten Sonaten*. 4 vols. Vienna: Universal, 1913–21.

Schmitz, Arnold. *Das romantische Beethoven-Bild*. Berlin and Bonn: F. Dümmler, 1927.

Schrade, Leo. *Beethoven in France: The Growth of an Idea*. New Haven: Yale University Press, 1942.

Schwab, Heinrich W. *Sangbarkeit, Popularität und Kunstlied: Studien zu Lied und Liedästhetik der mittleren Goethezeit*. Studien zur Musikgeschichte des 19. Jahrhunderts, vol. 3. Regensburg: G. Bosse, 1965.

Stephan, Rudolf. "Zu Beethovens letzten Quartetten." in *Die Musikforschung* 23 (1970): 245–56.

Stevens, Denis, ed. *A History of Song*. London: Hutchinson, 1960.

Warrack, John. *Carl Maria von Weber*. Cambridge: Cambridge University Press, 1968.

Wiora, Walter. *Das deutsche Lied*. Wolfenbüttel and Zurich: Möseler, 1971.

————. *Die rheinisch-bergischen Melodien bei Zuccalmaglio und Brahms*. Bad Godesberg: Voggenreiter, 1953.

CHAPTER THREE

1830-1848

A history of music which, following Wilhelm Pinder, adopts the notion of generation to demarcate a period bounded by the 1830 and 1848 revolutions could proceed from the fact that a number of prominent composers who had become "epoch-making" around 1830 had already completed their life's work by about 1848. Mendelssohn died in 1847, Donizetti in 1848, and Chopin in 1849; Schumann's output, some inconsequential works aside, was complete by 1851, while the decade and a half that remained to Meyerbeer after *Le prophète* (1848) was basically dead time, notwithstanding his completion in 1865 of *L'africaine* (abandoned in 1843) and an occasional minor work such as *Dinorah* (1859).

On the other hand, Verdi, Wagner, and Liszt—who belonged to the same generation as Mendelssohn, Schumann, and Chopin—all broke through into uncharted territory around 1848, and their breakthrough set the cornerstones of music history for the second half of the century. With *Rigoletto* (1851), and some critics would claim with *Luisa Miller* (1849), Verdi reached a level at which the "singers' opera" turned into a form of "musical drama" without abandoning its tradition. In Wagner's evolution, the years around mid-century—his period of exile following the suppression of the Dresden uprising of 1849—were a time of reflection; it was then that he wrote *Oper und Drama* (1851), a both forward- and backward-looking theory that bridged the gap between romantic opera (*Lohengrin*, 1848) and music drama (*Das Rheingold*, 1854). In 1847 Liszt withdrew from his triumphant career as a virtuoso and, in the provincial backwater of Weimar, founded a musical genre, the symphonic poem, which stood shoulder to shoulder with Wagner's music drama at the head of a "progressive party" in music, the manifestations of which in the 1850s and 1860s sparked the musico-aesthetic discussions that typified the age.

The years between 1830 and 1848 were the age of the "bourgeois king" Louis-Philippe, who, harried by royalists on one side and by republicans and Bonapartists on the other, saw his reign as a *juste milieu*. The catchword of the day was the concept of "zeitgeist," which mingled Hegel's spirit with that of the press, now risen to previously unforeseen importance. And what the "zeitgeist" demanded, whether in Parisian romantic circles or in Young Germany, was the fusion of art and politics. Accordingly, political repercussions and trends—the passion for freedom and the early, still liberal nationalism of the 1830 revolution

—left a strong imprint on certain operas of the time, such as Auber's *La muette de Portici* (1828), Rossini's *Guillaume Tell* (1829), or even Bellini's *Norma* (1832). Even so, we still have no call to speak generally, as Heine proclaimed in the spirit of Young Germany, of the "end of an age" in music. The traces of politics detectable in the works of Wagner, Liszt, Berlioz, Chopin, and Schumann—not to mention Mendelssohn—are so trifling that the "romantic" label applied to all composers up to the 1848 revolution hovers strangely between the French and German meanings of the term, with the former including an element of political involvement and the latter tending conversely to shun affairs of the day. With respect to music, we have even less call to speak of the demise of the strong notion of art—a legacy from the classic-romantic period whose death was announced by Heine. After all, Wagner's and Liszt's work can be viewed as an attempt to impose the rigorous strictures of art music on opera and expressive virtuoso improvisation, genres for which, up to then, the terms "work" and "art" did not entirely apply.

From the standpoint of social history, the "end of an age" thesis seems strangely feeble, considering that the thin "carrier stratum" that constituted the social foundation of music culture in the first half of the nineteenth century remained the same in Germany and Austria, if not in France. Even in Paris, the city touted by Heine as the "capital not just of France but of the entire civilized world" and the "focal point of its intellectual luminaries," the political repercussions that entered art, spelling the end of its autonomy, were indeed immediate and tangible, but not nearly as straightforward as we might expect from Victor Hugo's definition of French romanticism as "liberalism in literature." True, it is tempting to associate the style of grand opera—which, as Crosten has remarked, was both "an art and a business"—with the attitudes of a bourgeoisie which, having reached ascendancy in the world of finance in 1830, then sought ceremonial pomp in the world of culture. However, strictly speaking, there is no way of deciding whether the grandiloquent tone and flamboyant gestures that turned this amalgam of art and politics into a stage spectacle that passed for French romanticism were inspired by the spirit of Orleanism, Bonapartism, or republicanism (the genre was at all events not royalist). The heated musicopolitical concoction that Meyerbeer put on stage in *Les Huguenots* and *Le prophète* does not betray a political trend capable of being named by name.

On the other hand, the concept of commoner, or bourgeois, must first be refined before it can be a useful category for a social history of music that wishes to rise above platitude. (Notwithstanding the *Marseillaise* (1792), whose tone and rhythms echo throughout Meyerbeer's martial style even as parodied by Offenbach, no one would want to contend that the *citoyen* made music history.) In Germany and Austria, following the financial collapse of the Viennese nobility (on whom Beethoven, for all his bourgeois emancipation, was dependent until 1809), the legacy of classical and romantic music was borne by the "educated classes," one pillar of which was made up of the civil servants who emerged in Austria following the anticlerical measures of Emperor Joseph II and in Prus-

Fig. 25   Chopin monument in Warsaw. The Fryderyk Chopin captured here in a heroic pose, joined allegorically by a wind-blown tree, is the Chopin of the *Revolutionary Etude*, written in 1831 under the impress of the Russian occupation of Warsaw. The monument is apparently intended to commemorate not so much the composer as the failed Polish revolution, echoes of which were heard in Chopin's music by a Europe predisposed to republicanism. (Photograph by Antoni Buchner.)

sia after the legal reforms of Stein and Hardenberg. From the viewpoint of social history, however, the educated classes were a strangely "disembodied" stratum that remained virtually unscathed by the social turmoil of the century: the emergence of an industrial labor force, the displacement of populations, the confrontations of bourgeois capitalists with the landed nobility as well as with the "fourth estate," then haltingly becoming aware of its own existence and significance. As a result, we are at a loss to pinpoint any influence that the vicissitudes of social history may have exercised on music history. We notice immediately how weak, by sociological criteria, were the bourgeois foundations of music culture when we recall the large role played by "nonbourgeois" strata in the society and social fabric of the nineteenth century—in contrast to our own century with its masses of white-collar employees, its shrunken peasantry, and the bourgeois aspirations of its labor force.

Even journalism, an area of "bourgeois publicity" where the educated classes seemingly reigned uncontested, was transformed by developments in the Restoration period which quickly took hold in the years preceding the 1848 revolutions, at first in England and France. Thereafter, the educated classes felt cast to and fro between an urge to use the press as their vehicle and an insurmountable distrust bordering at times on revulsion (they have never escaped this unhappy dilemma). The invention of the high-speed press, coupled with the sale of separate issues (rather than annual subscriptions) and the printing of advertisements (with a resultant intermingling of editorial policy and the business of advertising), produced a type of newspaper which, if it did not supersede the older form of journalism, at least forced it into the background. The influence of this new type of newspaper on the evolution of music—an influence resulting primarily from the socioeconomic structure of the press and only secondarily from particular politicocultural "tendencies"—still awaits coherent scholarly investigation, although it doubtless figures among the basic prerequisites of modern musical culture, which might even be defined as music culture under the conditions of "bourgeois publicity."

Melodie lunghe: **Bellini and Donizetti**

In a letter of 1898, written three years before his death, Verdi remarked of Bellini: "Those are long, long, long melodies, melodies such as no one had written before him." Without exaggeration, we could even maintain that the melodic style of Bellini's arias, above all his slow cantabiles, was the quintessence of what the nineteenth century, with astounding unanimity, understood by melody in the strong sense of the term. Opera audiences dissolved in euphoric transports at the sound of *Casta diva, Ah! non credea mirarti,* or *Qui la voce sua soave.* Moreover, their enthusiasm was shared unquestioningly by composers as diverse as Chopin, whose nocturnes clearly betray the influence of Bellini, and Wagner, who had not forgotten his rapturous conversion to Bellini in 1834 when, a quarter of a century later, he wrote *Tristan und Isolde,* the music drama whose "endless melody" generates a sensuous and spiritual intoxication fundamentally akin to the effect of Bellini's melodies.

Ah! non credea mirarti, the Andante Cantabile from the final aria of *La sonnambula,* is one of those paradigms of Bellini's melodic style against which any attempt to discover one or another technical correlate to the aesthetic effect of his "long, long, long melodies" will have to prove its worth (Ex. 7). (However hopeless it may be for even a painstakingly detailed analysis to capture in words the full individuality and the aesthetic essence of a melody, our enthusiasm will ultimately devolve into sloganizing unless we take up the technical aspects of composition.) The first section of the aria is metrically irregular. This represents a departure from Bellini's standard practice, and paves the way in our search for the conditions of that long-breathed melody extolled by Verdi. Its subdivision into three two-bar units, followed by a two-and-a-half and a concluding two-bar unit, is linked with the transformation from downbeat to upbeat meter in measure 9. It also forms the metrical correlate to the irregularity of the melody: none of the phrases is repeated, either literally or varied. But it is the harmonic structure of this section which allows the composer continually to say new things without breaking the thread of his melody. The crucial feature of this harmonic structure is its precisely calculated manner of postponing the dominant–tonic cadence. The dominant appears in measure 1 of the melody as a quarter-note

Example 7

passing harmony, in measures 5 and 6 as a half note in the form of a dominant
seventh chord in third inversion, in measure 8 as a whole note in first inversion,
and finally in measure 10 as a dominant seventh in root position preceded by
a cadential six-four chord. While postponing the decisive dominant–tonic cadence, the melody constantly toys with temporary, half-cadential effects, thereby
giving the cantilena that "semblance of familiarity" and simplicity so indispensable to the nineteenth-century perception of melody. Further, this dialectic of
suggested and suspended cadences produces a delicate balance between simplicity in detail and grandness in the overall design. We might call this balance classical in that it precisely fulfills the requirements of "noble simplicity": Bellini attains an "elevated style" with the simplest of means rather than the most flamboyant—which, according to the rules of an earlier, preclassical aesthetic, belong to
the "lower style."

The second section of the aria is in the parallel key of C major, where, in defiance of the rule of unified tonality, it also ends. The major mode is intended, not to brighten the mood, but rather, as sometimes happens in Schubert and later in Mahler, to replace a mood of sadness and resignation with one verging on despair. The transition to the new key is accomplished in eight measures, during which Amina's cantilena is interrupted by interjections from Elvino. Though the modulation tends toward C major in Elvino's lines, it sinks back to A minor in Amina's, conveying an irresistible impression of resignation. However, this expressive use of harmony also has consequences for the form: the parallel key is ultimately attained only after two interpolated measures from the orchestra. Yet Bellini, always averse to discontinuity, was not content to leave this passage as an isolated phenomenon: the two measures, though merely an appendage to the meter, are related motivically to measures 3 and 4 of the eight-bar vocal period that follows. Though half concealed by the changes of rhythm, this motivic connection imparts continuity to the melody, a continuity that stands in contradiction to the periodic structure: measures 3 and 4 are related, not to measures 7 and 8, as convention demands, but rather to the "introductory measures" of the orchestra. (A similarly inconspicuous correspondence, concealed by the altered rhythm, exists between measures 1 and 5, which, together with the relation between half and full cadence, establish the periodic structure of this section.) Once again we see simplicity (the periodic design of the second section) and irregularity (the contradiction between motivic linkage and phrase articulation) held in delicate balance in order to give the melody that naturalness and breadth so admired by Verdi. In sum, the mood of resignation causes the modulation to be postponed, thereby compelling an orchestral interpolation, the metrical isolation of which occasions a motivic association that in turn upsets or complicates the periodic structure. It is this close interplay of expression, harmony, meter, and motive that constitutes the compositional stratagem, the touch of rational artifice, at the root of Bellini's melodic inspiration.

Ah! non credea mirarti is the slow section—the cantabile—of a *scena ed aria* that forms the finale of the opera. (In the 1830s, the aria-finale became a form that could hold its own against the ensemble-finale, just as fragments of ensemble writing penetrated aria form in the *aria con pertichini*.) In this scene Amina, walking in her sleep, gives way to melancholy memories, accompanied by reminiscences of earlier passages in the opera. (The Andante Sostenuto and the Andante originated in No. 3, and the Allegro Moderato Assai in No. 7; the Larghetto anticipates, if surreptitiously, the following cantabile.) In other words, in *La sonnambula*, as befits an opera whose turning point is brought about by reminiscences, the technique of reminiscence motives developed in *opéra comique* serves the formal function of equipping the scena section of a *scena ed aria* with the musical weight it requires to serve as a finale.

The change in the aria from *primo tempo* to *secondo tempo*, from Andante Cantabile to Allegro Brillante, or from *espressivo* to coloratura, is justified by a striking event on stage that brings about the solution of the drama's underlying conflict. It is no exaggeration to say of early-nineteenth-century opera seria that its dramaturgy was largely determined by the curious compulsion to motivate, again and again, a change from cantabile to cabaletta, as dictated by the conventions of the aria. Moreover, any librettist who knew his trade—which was a matter less of poetry than of stage technique—had to take into account the dramaturgically precarious fact that the main musical form of early-nineteenth-century opera was no longer the monologue aria (the exit aria of the eighteenth century) but rather the aria with supporting ensemble or chorus. This was the form that left audiences intoxicated with its melody, and at the same time with its sound. (The technique of changing from *primo tempo* to *secondo tempo* was associated with a fondness for the *aria con pertichini,* it being easier to motivate a dramatic turn of events in an ensemble than in a solo scene.) Of the fourteen numbers in *La sonnambula* no fewer than seven (Nos. 1, 2, 3, 4, 11, 12, and 14) are arias or duets with chorus or ensemble. Accordingly, Bellini's librettist, the distinguished playwright Felice Romani, faced the paradoxical challenge of creating and meaningfully relating situations whose basic character urged lyricism but whose events took place in public surroundings, thereby justifying the presence of a chorus. Strictly speaking, it is absurd to imagine the events of *Romeo and Juliet* taking place before a crowd of onlookers; yet this is exactly the imposition that Romani faced in Bellini's *I Capuleti ed i Montecchi* (1830). Before passing judgment on his libretto as compared with Shakespeare's tragedy we should recall the musicodramaturgical conditions that governed the writing of librettos at that time: apart from a single recitative (No. 5), the eleven numbers in the opera include two choruses (Nos. 1 and 7), a monologue aria (No. 4), a duet (No. 6), three arias with ensemble and chorus (Nos. 2, 3, and 9), two duets with chorus (Nos. 10 and 11), and a quintet with chorus (No. 8).

What is more, nineteenth-century audiences—who, as was mentioned earlier, no longer read along in the libretto during a performance, as did eighteenth-century audiences—considered it reasonable to expect the basic outline of the plot of a through-composed opera to be understandable in pantomime. Plots could no longer be so complex as to make an understanding of their events and "affects" dependent on details of the text. In particular, the text could no longer be heard intact in the form of recitative, since, as compositional technique evolved, composers tended to give an increasingly rich garb to accompanied recitative at the expense of *recitativo secco*. Considering that operatic convention included among its strictures that the librettist constantly motivate changes from *primo tempo* to *secondo tempo* and devise stage situations for the dramaturgically precarious form of *aria con pertichini,* all the while ensuring the comprehensibility of the plot in dumb show, it is not the "improbability" of many opera texts which is astonishing, so much as the fact that they did not turn out to be less "probable" than was in fact the case.

Italian librettists of the 1830s and 1840s vindicated the irrationality of their constructs by turning to subject matter that was regarded at the time as romantic. Here "romanticism" was a blanket term for all currents opposed to Classical art,

Fig. 26   Italian scene painting from the 1840s. Opera seria of the 1830s and 1840s, the opera of Bellini and Donizetti, is sometimes and not unjustifiably given the label of Italian romanticism. Contemporary audiences considered both its overheated passions (which Metastasio would have considered pathological excesses) and its recourse to medieval subject matter to be characteristically "romantic," but even more so its political pathos, neatly summed up by Victor Hugo in his quip that romanticism is liberalism in literature. Here the stage decor for *Norma,* an opera with patriotic implications, shows a Celtic temple whose cyclopean phantasmagoria make it as far removed as possible from the classicist settings which would have served any eighteenth-century Metastasian opera with a comparable plot. (Milan, Museo Teatrale alla Scala.)

by then reduced to classicism; it encompassed not only the plays of Victor Hugo but those of Shakespeare as well. Following Hugo's aforementioned characterization of romanticism as "liberalism in literature," the contemporaries of Bellini and Donizetti saw an intrinsic connection between the spirit of the *Risorgimento* and that of the Gothic novel. This was expressed in the fondness of librettists for settings in medieval Scotland or Sicily, which allowed them to add appropriately gruesome local color to "triangular" love stories compounded with political intrigue to create remorseless tragedies. As with every current marked by the pressure of censorship, it is difficult in historical retrospect to pin down a connection with political rebellion. Nevertheless, in the divided and oppressed Italy of 1830 and thereabouts, the spirit of the *Risorgimento* found expression less in political machinations than in a groundswell of desperation; and the crucial feature connecting romantic opera with this early *Risorgimento* spirit was apparently not the weak-kneed antiauthoritarianism of many libretti—where, for example, private antagonisms in a love tragedy might overlap with political antagonisms between a tyrant and a banished subject—as the extreme intensification of the emotions in general. When opera figures in politics at all, it does so not by virtue of its subject matter but because of the tone that it strikes.

Unlike the emotional detachment of Rossini, who seems almost to include passion in quotation marks, it is excessively overheated emotionalism that links the composers who upheld opera seria: Bellini and Donizetti, Pacini and Mercadante, and finally Verdi. For this reason, as Friedrich Lippmann showed in his *Vincenzo Bellini und die italienische Opera seria seiner Zeit* (1969), it is misleading or at least awry to view Bellini, despite what he once called his "melancholy muse," lopsidedly as noble and elegiac as opposed to the hyperemotional and grandstanding Donizetti. Bellini was in no way averse to outbursts of *agitato,* and Donizetti was thoroughly capable of striking a note of melancholy.

Although Donizetti wrote ceaselessly and, unlike Bellini, apparently effortlessly, he was by no means a headstrong, rough-and-tumble man of action like the young Verdi. On the contrary, the arias that conclude *Lucia di Lammermoor* (1835)—Lucia's mad scene and the death of Edgardo—give evidence of a rational cast of mind that succeeded in elevating the "solo number" into a "large-scale form" in which monumentality of design and sophistication of internal workings interact and mutually support each other.

The formal mold of Lucia's *scena ed aria* is a cantabile (*Alfin son tua,* larghetto) followed by a cabaletta (*Spargi d'amaro pianto,* moderato). However, the introductory scena, as well as the extended transitional piece between the cavatina and the cabaletta, consists of a string of arioso sections ranging in style over all gradations from recitative to "genuine" aria. The first Andante in the scena (*Il dolce suono*) is an orchestral cantabile, which the voice either joins or stands apart from by singing recitative. The Allegro Vivace (*Ohi mè*), following a quotation from the duet-finale to Act 1 (Allegretto), is an extreme outburst of passion, as suitable to an aria as to an accompanied recitative. The second Andante (*Ah! l'inno suona*) is a vocal number alternating between recitative and coloratura, with an incisive and pregnant motive in the orchestra. The Allegro following the cantabile (*S'avanza Enrico*) is a periodically structured passage of motivic elaboration, whereas the Allegro Mosso (*Ma ognor*) is a self-contained *agitato* melody, which differs from a standard cabaletta only in its abrupt ending and its transition, again motivically elaborated, to the "genuine" cabaletta.

If, in this scena, recitative takes the form of arioso, the boundary to cantabile is half hidden by the orchestra's anticipation of the Larghetto melody and a remnant of recitative in the vocal part. This is not to say that the division into scena, cantabile, and cabaletta has been obliterated, but merely that the listener must bear this schema in mind in order to understand the transmutations it has undergone in Donizetti's hands.

By adopting the arioso style, the scena came several steps closer to the musico-dramatic *Szene* then emerging in German romantic opera. Nevertheless, it would be wrong to measure the historical development of Italian opera against the yardstick of Wagner's music drama and its prototypes and to praise unstintingly the disappearance of the boundary between recitative and aria as "progress" in the direction of "endless melody." As seen from the history of form, the important point is not merely that, in Italian opera too, the trend toward more sophisticated dramatic characterization gradually caused the division into recitative and aria to be abandoned, or at least to blur, but rather the complementary fact that Donizetti was nonetheless able to establish the *scena ed aria* from within as a large-scale, self-contained form. And despite our involuntary fondness for viewing departures from norms as historical events (with history conceived as a string of innovations), we should not overlook that, in Lucia's mad scene, the cavatina–cabaletta schema, though obscured, is nevertheless distinct enough to warrant our listening to the piece with an ear to the original pattern. On the other hand, the various arioso sections are linked by a principle which we can already descry in the tempo relations: slow–fast–slow in the scena, and fast–slower–faster following the cantabile. Donizetti saw musical form as a balance among constituent sections. And if Wagner's *Szene* owes its internal coherence to being embedded in a web of leitmotivs, the unity of Donizetti's scena results from a sense of form that holds in poised balance the tempos and the various rhythmic moods they engender.

Edgardo's aria, the finale of the opera, also departs from convention in that its second section—the *secondo tempo* contrasting with the *primo tempo* (Larghetto) —is, in a manner of speaking, split in two. The initial Moderato (*Fur le nozze*) is offset by a second one (*Tu che a Dio*) in a different key and scoring, though with an identical tempo and rhythmic pattern. The first Moderato, justified dramaturgically as a recounting of Lucia's madness, is a chorus with solo interpolations; the second, motivated by the news of Lucia's death, is, conversely, a solo supported by the chorus. (Both Moderato sections are preceded by arioso passages.)

By doubling the cabaletta, Donizetti dangerously extended his aria, which, in view of its exposed position at the end of the opera, threatens to fall apart. To prevent this, he resorted to devices of "musical logic" which we would more likely expect to find in a symphony than in an opera seria. The second Moderato, the "genuine" cabaletta for solo singer, originates, so to speak, from a compositional dialectic. On the one hand, by modulating from D major to a cadence in F$\sharp$ minor and then back again to D major by means of the formula (V^7)–II–V^7–I, it mirrors the Larghetto. On the other hand, its rhythmic pattern comes from the first Moderato, where, however, the rhythm ♪. ♪ | ♩♩♩. ♪ | ♩♩ appears not in the first line but in the second, a variant of the first. The rhythm is then connected with a harmonic deflection from B major to D major, so that the central tonality of the aria (D major) functions as a secondary tonality within the context of the Moderato (B major). In other words, the rhythmic anticipation of the second Moderato forms the compositional correlate to a reminiscence of the central key of the piece.

Of course, it would be a gross exaggeration to point to the sophistication that Donizetti attained in Lucia's and Edgardo's arias as a norm indicative of the high level of form in opera seria of the 1830s and 1840s, instead of treating it as the exception that it was. Still, the exception was at any rate possible, and shows that the opera seria—which Wagner accused of melodic "narrowness" in order to set it up as a historical foil for his own "endless melody"—was thoroughly capable of elevating the solo number to a "large-scale form" in which the monumental tendencies of the age, apparent in broad outline, were balanced and held in check by a convoluted, almost "symphonic" logic in its internal harmonic and rhythmic structure.

The Dramaturgy of Grand Opera

Grand opera took form as a species around 1830 with Auber's *La muette de Portici,* Rossini's *Guillaume Tell,* and Meyerbeer's *Robert le diable.* Today, now that its

Fig. 27 Scene from *Guillaume Tell.* The Act 2 Terzetto from Rossini's *Guillaume Tell* (No. 11) shows Arnold von Melchthal, seconded by Wilhelm Tell and Walther Fürst, torn between his love for the Habsburg princess Mathilde and his urge to prove his worth as a Swiss patriot and as the avenger of his father's murder. The scene captured in this picture was felt to be the linchpin of the drama. This is characteristic in that the conflict between love and honor, rooted in French social history of the early seventeenth century, outlived its original social foundations by several centuries to become a basic theme of European drama, above all in opera. (Vienna, Österreichische Nationalbibliothek.)

theatrical career is finished, having lasted a good century, it is remembered first of all as a cultural document of the July Monarchy, just as Heine had characterized it, but also as the aesthetically dubious genre that prompted Wagner to coin his phrase "effect without cause." However, a species of opera that made Paris, as Walter Benjamin put it, the "capital of the nineteenth century" in music as well, cannot simply be explained away as a document on the spirit, or distemper, of the luxuriating bourgeois financial classes, as a spectacle devoid of any detectable dramaturgical principle. Nor should we be content with the concept of drama underlying Wagner's notion of "causes" that justify musical "effects."

Grand opera, at once one of the most fascinating and repellent phenomena of the nineteenth century, arose in the Paris of the *passages*, the panoramas, and the Eiffel Tower. In it, an age marked by the spirit of technology and industrial enterprise realized a unique and modern ideal of monumentality, independently of ancient models. And as William L. Crosten recognized in his *French Grand Opera: An Art and a Business* (1948), we must consider among the creators of this species not only Scribe, Meyerbeer, and Duponchel—the librettist, the composer, and the scene designer—but also Louis Véron, the impresario of the Académie Royale de Musique, with his astonishingly precise visions of the "Gesamtkunstwerk" whose spectacular success he calculated.

Originally, the term "grand opera" meant nothing more than a work that dealt with a serious subject and was through-composed with recitatives, as opposed to the *opéra comique,* where the musical numbers were separated by dialogue. By 1830, however, it had come to refer to an operatic genre that shifted the focus from arias to large choral and ensemble scenes and discarded stories from ancient history and mythology in favor of plots taken from "romantic" history—from the Middle Ages or the early modern period.

The principle of this species of opera was to switch abruptly between mass scenes and touching romances or prayers, between coloratura and outbursts of passion, between instrumental solos and violent orchestral devices. Schumann and other critics who had grown up in the classical tradition accused it of unbridled eclecticism, of shunning nothing that showed promise of generating an effect. Yet it is in this very semblance of a "style-less" musicotheatrical concoction that the modernity of the genre lies, as becomes apparent when we consider "tableau" and "shock" as legitimate dramaturgical categories instead of symptoms of decline.

Operas centering on large tableaux, instead of on arias or ensembles with a few protagonists, will have plots that hinge on scenes where the major characters act before or against a crowd. The crowd scenes in these plots betray the temperament of an age which still believed that major political decisions are made in the street. No doubt this accumulation of devices, the heaping up of solo, choral, and orchestral effects, also expresses a bourgeois aesthetic with a conception of art that included both a liking for breathtaking new technologies and a delight in the luxuries that reassured opera-goers of their status in society. However, we have no right to reproach grand opera for its "accumulation" technique until we have demonstrated that there is no dramaturgical idea behind the tableau. When Wagner criticized Meyerbeer in an attempt to prove his aesthetic illegitimacy, he proceeded from a concept of drama which is by no means universal. Wagner presupposed the dialogue principle—that is, the notion that the substance of a drama resides in a conflict that is carried out in exchanges of words. He also believed that operatic music had to be rooted in a drama of ideas and characters, and that this drama represented the "cause" of the musical "effects." Yet, by Wagner's criteria, grand opera is not the only instance of an "effect without a cause": eighteenth-century opera seria likewise fails to vindicate itself as a drama of ideas and characters, since its dramatic intrigues merely serve as vehicles to generate situations that spawn arias with different "affects." It is not obvious why a Scribean intrigue directed at tableaux should be less legitimate than a Metastasian intrigue that sets off a string of arias. Whatever the case, both species of opera differ from Wagner's music drama in that the mechanisms underlying the action do not form the substance of the work but are merely a device for setting in motion the actual dramaturgical categories—changes of situation and "affect" in the opera seria, tableau and shock in the grand opera.

In his memoirs, published in 1856–57, Louis Véron did not neglect to mention the sixty machinists occupied with the stage decor of the grand opera, nor the fact that the audience, being fully aware of the amount spent on stage machinery, had "correspondingly high expectations." However, Véron adds to this fondness for decorative spectacle—from the eruption of Vesuvius in *La muette de Portici* to the collapse of the palace in *Le prophète*—the by no means everyday insight that the dramaturgy of an opera centering on tableaux will tend of its own accord to pantomime. The dramatic events, Véron insists, must be comprehensible as visible action without regard for the text, just like the scenario of a ballet. It is not dialogue, which is virtually swallowed up by the music, but the striking, "speechlike" arrangement of the agents—among whom Véron also includes the chorus—that constitutes the primary expressive means of a dramatic technique as legitimate in the opera as it is inconceivable in spoken theater, except perhaps in melodrama, by which Scribe was doubtless influenced.

Crowd scenes leave scant room for the substance of dialogue, argument. Here, then, it is essential and indispensable to take one's bearings on the dramaturgy of pantomime. And it was in the crowd scenes that grand opera proved its worth as a spectacle for a cosmopolitan audience, one of whose formative, if by now subliminal, experiences was its encounters with thronging crowds that engulfed the individual.

On the other hand, the dramaturgy of configurations that underlies the tableau not merely permits a musical setting but virtually cries out for it. Unlike dramatic dialogue, which proceeds dialectically toward a goal, dramatic or theatrical configurations tend to be captured in *tableaux vivants*, in living pictures, whether static or mobile. (Hence, the decorative displays of splendor and pomp that represented the triumph of Duponchel's stage machinery were intimately connected with the dramaturgical core of a pictorial genre such as grand opera, and it betrays ignorance of the aesthetic of tableaux to speak of them as a shallow *bricolage* of effects.) Only music is capable of imparting to the isolated instant presented in the tableau, whether festive or stunned, that unreal duration it requires to become a "speechlike" configuration. This duration could never be attained in spoken theater, although even there, as Wagner showed in *Zukunftsmusik* (1860), pointing to the silence of St. Joan in Schiller's *Die Jungfrau von Orleans* (1801), there are moments at which dramatic time actually has to stand still. Far from merely paying lip service to musical form, which takes time to evolve, the principle of the dramatic moment frozen in time is not a makeshift but a thoroughly apt dramaturgical end for which music provides the means. In short, the frozen configuration is a theatrical category in its own right.

If the pictorial nature of the tableau becomes glaringly evident at moments when time stands still, whether from terror, expectancy, or exaltation, the law of motion governing the progress of the plot might be called the "shock" principle. The sudden outburst and the pause are opposite sides of the same coin. And if in grand opera, as was mentioned above, the isolated moments captured in tableaux are repeatedly either festive or stunned in their basic mood, the pattern underlying Scribe's "shock" dramaturgy is the sudden switch from one of these moods to the other. It is the éclat, the unforeseen event, breaking in like a thunderbolt, that drives the plot forward with a jolt and supplies the premises for the arrangement of the next tableau. And like the tableau, the shock is not a deficient dramaturgical species but a legitimate principle in its own right.

This tendency toward tableaux is linked with a fondness for "romantic" historical subject matter, which took hold around 1830 both at the Paris Opéra and in spoken theater. If *La muette de Portici* (1828) and *Guillaume Tell* (1829) were the works considered epoch-making at the Académie Royale de Musique, it was Alexandre Dumas's *Henri III et sa cour* (1829) that caused a breakthrough at the Théâtre Français, a breakthrough whose theory had been propounded in Victor Hugo's preface to *Cromwell* (1827). Grand opera may have been presaged by Spontini's *Ferdinand Cortez* (1809), but this does not alter the historical fact that it was the changes around 1830 that contemporaries regarded as a turning point in opera history, just as, in literature, it was Victor Hugo's noisy revolution in the theater, and not the quiet revolution of Chateaubriand's and Sénancour's novels around 1800, that contemporaries registered as "romanticism."

Ancient history, then, gave way to modern history as a source of operatic subject matter, though, as with Hegel, the term "modern," which was associated or even equated with "romantic," encompassed the Middle Ages and the early modern period. This formed the literary side of a stylistic transformation perceived at the time as a suppression of the "classical" tradition by a "romantic" revolution. Indeed, for Hugo, the term "romantic" stood for his cry that not merely the melodrama of the suburban stages but tragedy as well should present "pictures" rather than "descriptions," "scenes" in lieu of "narratives." Instead of the marmoreal pallor that seemed to infect dramatizations of ancient history and mythology, audiences called for local color of the kind they found in the historical novels of Walter Scott, and it seemed natural to turn to similar medieval or early modern material to achieve parallel effects in the theater. Local color, though primarily the task of the stage designer, is also a musical category; in fact, it is a central one, representing a confluence of characteristic nineteenth-century trends toward archaism, folklore, and exoticism. The monumental style of the grand opera, culminating in the tableau, was in no way inconsistent with musical landscape and genre painting as expressed in "picturesque" orchestral and choral numbers. On the contrary, the tableau, being essentially a grand ensemble and choral scene, integrated the picturesque into the background as surely as it placed a few solos from the protagonists in the foreground.

The concluding scene in Rossini's *Guillaume Tell* consists of a contemplative ensemble (comparable to the quartet in *Fidelio*), a *preghiera,* and a depiction of a storm and a sunrise (the finale effect might have served as a model for the end of *Das Rheingold*). If the ensemble is motivated by the unhoped-for rescue of Tell's son, and the *preghiera* by fears for Tell's life, the storm through which Tell steers Gessler's hijacked ship is at once a force of nature and a political allegory, and the Alpine sunrise a symbol of the liberty that dawns with Gessler's death. The scene, then, is composed of tableaux summoned forth by sudden events: the rescue of Tell's son, Tell's flight, Gessler's death. These tableaux freeze the action for a while into living pictures, no matter how unreal they may seem (in reality Tell's wife would be struck at once by gratitude for her son's rescue and fear for Tell's life instead of sensing these emotions at opposite ends of a lengthy ensemble). Recitative and dialogue are reduced to a meager residue, since there is little for words to do in a plot that unfolds graphically and unmisconstruably in stage images. Even the landscape, being allegorical, has been integrated into the events of the drama. Picturesque orchestral music, chorus of liberty, rural genre painting, contemplative ensemble of the protagonists—all join forces to create a finale that remains in the memory as an entity, namely, as a tableau.

From *Guillaume Tell* to Meyerbeer's *Le prophète,* grand opera was always political. Yet the picture is confused by the way political elements interweave with dramaturgical ones. However unmistakable the sympathy for oppressed peoples —for the Swiss in *Guillaume Tell,* the Neapolitans in *La muette de Portici,* the Protestants in *Les Huguenots,* the Jews in *La juive*—it is the unhappy love between adherents of conflicting parties (Fenella and Alfonso, Valencienne and Raoul, Rachel and Leopold) that forms the dramatic core of the plot and makes us sense the inherently destructive nature of political conflicts, no matter which side one takes. Nevertheless, it is characteristic of grand opera that, in the work as a whole, the "private" plot that motivates the arias and duets is overshadowed by the "public" plot manifested in tableaux.

Apart from Leopold's serenade (No. 3), which we can imagine being sung in a side alley, the first act of Halévy's *La juive* (1835) consists of a single choral and ensemble scene into which Cardinal de Brogni's cavatina (No. 2) has been integrated not only dramaturgically but also musically, as a solo with supporting ensemble. It was one of the conventions of early-nineteenth-century opera to

Fig. 28 Scene from Meyerbeer's *Le prophète*, Leipzig, 1850. The coronation scene in Münster Cathedral, the Act 4 finale of Meyerbeer's *Le prophète,* forms the turning point of the drama. Fides discovers to her horror that the Anabaptist messiah, whom she had previously abominated as a perpetrator of violence, is her own son, John of Leyden. Since, however, his charisma depends on the popular belief that he was "not born of woman," he forces her to deny his parentage. In grand opera the crowd pressing onto the stage had more than a decorative function to fulfil; indeed, it was crucial to the dramaturgy, its many changes of mood making it the hero's actual antagonist. (Berlin, Staatsbibliothek Preußischer Kulturbesitz.)

have the first cantabile number stand out against a lively ensemble, but here the cavatina goes beyond that to form part of the musical and theatrical configuration, a configuration that manifests the dramaturgical substance of the opera in a tableau. The compassion (subject to recall, as it turns out) of the mediating cardinal; the fanaticism of the crowd, whose excitement mingles holiday spirits with blood lust; the hatred of the oppressed Jew, Eleazar, a hatred that spills over into defiance—these are the premises behind the dramatic conflict, and they are present no less vividly in the inflections of the melody than in the images and gestures on stage.

The finale of Act 1 recapitulates the situation of the introduction, since the "public" conflict shown in the crowd scenes has now given rise to twin "private" subplots between Eleazar and De Brogni, on the one hand, and Rachel and Leopold on the other. It is precisely the rescue of Eleazar and Rachel from the crowd, owing to De Brogni's intervention and then to Leopold's, that sets loose a dramatic dialectic leading ultimately to inescapable tragic complications. The core of the drama—the gradual moral corruption of oppressed and oppressors alike—is made visible in the crowd scenes, which thus not only function as a decorative backdrop for the private action but, more important, capture its essence in an image, this essence being the political confusion of the participants. The fact that Leopold seems to "lack character" merely implies that he is the victim of a destiny that allows no room for moral fiber. Yet, the destiny into whose cogs he falls is a political and moral folly expressed musically and theatrically in the opera's tableaux, the large scenes for chorus and ensemble.

Musically, Halévy is a virtuoso in the technique of alternating, and even fusing, the splendorous and the sinister. The mere appearance of a Jew pushing his way into a crowd assembled before a church is sufficient to transform holiday joviality into a lust for persecution and murder. It almost seems as though the outbursts of excitement already contain in embryo a readiness to spill blood—as through Halévy, like Verdi in the Triumphal March from *Aïda* (1871), expected his audience to perceive the splendor of the music, even if subconsciously, from the perspective of both the jubilant crowd and the victims. Equally ambiguous is the state of mind expressed in the Andantino of the finale, a contemplative ensemble in which time stands still. Rachel's gratitude for being rescued from the angry mob mingles with speechless astonishment that Leopold, whom she had hitherto taken for a Jew, commands the power to intervene on her behalf. In the end, her astonishment gives way to fear of a tragedy whose inescapability she senses without as yet being fully conscious of it. Eleazar's feelings for Rachel (who is unaware that she is the Cardinal's daughter) and Rachel's for Eleazar are captured in the melody of the *stretta*. Its lightly chromaticized cabaletta tone expresses their feelings with an exuberance that sounds as if it were trying to drown out their forebodings of danger (Ex. 8). Here excitement, intended to give a sense of finality to the act, turns into latent hysteria. Yet this hysteria, being dramaturgically motivated, remains entirely within the bounds of "grand style" instead of degenerating into what Wagner, who utterly despised grand opera without ever managing to break away from it, called "effect without cause."

La juive is set during the Council of Constance (1414–18), and thus belongs, like Meyerbeer's *Les Huguenots* and *Le prophète,* to the genre of historical drama.

Example 8

To contemporary minds, this genre was not so different from the romantic genre represented by *Robert le diable* as claimed by the traditional, preromantic aesthetic, which drew a firm line between history—"the way it really was"—and the "supernatural." (One unresolved contradiction of Wagner's *Lohengrin* is that the work is both a romantic opera, with a fairy-tale vagueness of time and space, and a historical opera, whose plot can be clearly assigned to a particular location and date.) Scribe and Meyerbeer dominated the "zeitgeist" by subjecting themselves to it, and what the "zeitgeist" wanted from both theater and music was not "beauty" and "noble simplicity"—the idols of classicist aesthetics—but the "characteristic" and "striking." Classicist *grisaille* was to be replaced by local color, and it hardly mattered whether this local color was taken from spectacular events in recent history, from bygone days when history and phantasmagoria merged, or from myth and fairy tale.

The Middle Ages conjured up by *Robert le diable*—a Gothic novel transferred to the stage—was a period of history so distant that its contours had already begun to blur. It was also an age when, as people pretended to believe, the supernatural and the subterranean regularly intervened in earthly affairs. This fusion of historicism and romanticism—a hybrid form in the history of genres—was made to order for Duponchel's productions, which were not only fastidious in their attention to historical detail but inclined toward fantastic stage machinery; and it was equally made to order for the shock effects which, in Scribe's dramaturgy, formed the correlate to tableau technique. In *Robert le diable*, it is the collision between the natural and supernatural worlds that motivates the plot—a plot which, for all its absurdity as a narrative, is nothing short of ingenious as an arrangement of musicotheatrical tableaux.

There is a curious twist to the dramatic dialectic at the root of the Act 4 finale, the crux of the drama: Robert, having lost Isabelle according to earthly law, regains her by clemency; yet at the same time, in a confluence of extremes, he obtains this clemency by rejecting the magic powers which, till then, had seemed to him the only means to achieve his goal. The plot is driven forward by two "shocks": the incantation of the mystic branch, which casts a spell over the assembled guests, and the breaking of the branch, which lifts the spell and unleashes the tumult that engulfs him. These contrasting tableaux in the external plot, between the frozen and the tumultuous crowd, match the twisted dialectics of the internal action: Robert loses Isabelle when he tries to win her by force, and regains her when, by rejecting force, he seemingly loses her.

Robert and Isabelle find themselves in a situation dominated by violence and fear. This in turn makes possible a duet whose tone—an *élan terrible*—entered music during the French Revolution and was once again a topical issue in 1830 (Ex. 9). (Not the least criterion for judging an opera libretto is whether it provides dramaturgical motivation for the tone demanded by its age.) We can scarcely imagine a sharper contrast to the Allegro Agitato of the duet than Isabelle's cavatina *Robert! Robert! toi que j'aime,* a piece that moved audiences to tears for an entire century (Ex. 10). The sentiment is all the more irresistible for rep-

crains   ma fu - reur,   ne   me   re - pous - se   pas

Example 9

Ro - bert!   Ro - bert,   toi que j'ai   me!

Example 10

resenting the dramaturgical turning point of the drama. Robert's extreme alienation provokes Isabelle to confess her love for him, a confession that justifies psychologically the clemency granted almost as a ritual in the final act. Meyerbeer chose the simple device of beginning his cantilena with a turn to the parallel major—an obvious modulation, which, however, by coinciding with the entrance of the voice, is at once surprising and moving. Simple as it is, the device is extremely effective. Meyerbeer, who well knew how to put musical opulence on the stage, was no less adept at handling the opposite.

When Wagner, in *Oper und Drama,* polemicized against French "neoromanticism" so as to advance his own ideas, he put Berlioz in the same category as Meyerbeer. Nevertheless, and despite the fact that Berlioz's operatic masterpiece *Les troyens* (1856–59) is, formally, a grand opera, there is almost nothing about this work that recalls Meyerbeer or Halévy. Like the *St. Matthew Passion, Les troyens* had to wait a century for its discovery. It went against the conventions of grand opera, as dictated by Scribe, by drawing its subject matter from an ancient epic poem, Vergil's *Aeneid.* However, this point was not crucial, since Berlioz, a strict anticlassicist, had discovered a way to preserve the function of the "romantic" historical subjects he seemingly rejected, namely, by drawing musical local color from ancient myth.

From the excessive choral and ballet scenes to the aria and ensemble number, Berlioz turned the musical forms of grand opera into dramaturgical devices sharply opposed to Scribe's tableau and shock techniques. The real agent of the drama—strictly speaking a scenic epic—is not the protagonists and crowds that collide in Scribe's scenarios but an anonymous destiny, which decrees the fall of Troy and Aeneas's departure from Carthage to Italy. The unpitying force of the supernatural is so ubiquitous and overpowering that it nullifies the dramatic dialogue, the conflict of arguments or emotions among the characters: decisions are made not between the characters but over their heads. For this reason, it was

Fig. 29 Andreas Geiger: Scene from Meyerbeer's *Robert le diable*. Here, in the Act 3 finale of Meyerbeer's *Robert le diable*, Robert seizes the mystic branch to attain demonic powers. This is one of those notorious moments when grand opera seems to betray its essence as a cynical purveyor of cheap effects, not least because of the orgy of nuns, summoned from their graves and forced by their past sins to serve the cause of evil. However, if we apply the principle of pantomimic intelligibility (as formulated by Louis Véron, the director of the Grand Opéra), we notice that Robert's sorcery is made evident precisely by the nuns' ballet, where the change of costume captures in a single drastic image the ambivalence of saintliness and depravity that forms the underlying mood of the work. Here, at least, we have little right to speak of "effects without (dramaturgical) causes." (Vienna, Österreichische Nationalbibliothek.)

entirely natural for Berlioz to combine two plots—the story of Cassandra and the tragedy of Dido and Aeneas—which are insufficiently related according to the rules of dramatic theory. We sense the same destiny in both parts of his drama.

Without belittling the work's importance, *Les troyens* suffers musicodramaturgically from a difficulty that becomes apparent the moment we compare it with Wagner's *Der Ring des Nibelungen* (1854–74), not with regard to their musical styles but to the way they solve the problem imposed on musical drama by epic and mythological subject matter. In both works, the characters we call the "agents" of the drama are governed by an overarching destiny at times resembling a system of snares. Wagner renders this musically by weaving an ever-tighter web of leitmotivs, whereas in Berlioz's case the network of inescapable entanglements is expressed either in supernatural phenomena and voices or in fear and consternation left by forebodings of doom. We sense the core of the drama in those moving scenes where the supernatural tangibly intervenes in worldly affairs—when the shade of dead Hector speaks to Aeneas, for example, or when disembodied voices are heard during a storm scene to warn of the impending departure for Italy. Similarly gripping are those monologues where Dido and Aeneas submit to a destiny that is about to cast them into hopeless solitude—when Aeneas inwardly takes leave of Dido, and when Dido resolves to die. In contrast, the duet in which Aeneas tears himself from Dido is strangely insubstantial, as though Berlioz's powers of invention were lamed by the fact that the tumultuous dialectic of emotions is merely a façade for a process which emotions cannot hope to influence. Here the composer resorted to stock emotional gestures from Italo-French opera: to show feelings atrophying under the crush of destiny, Berlioz lacked a musical idiom like Wagner's leitmotivs with which to echo, from the innermost spirit of his characters, the doom being imposed upon them from without.

Virtuosity and Interpretation

One idea or myth that has captured the fancy of cultural historians is the thought that the traveling virtuosos of the eighteenth and nineteenth centuries were descended from wandering minstrels. However, it is not clear just how this connection is to be captured in sociohistorical categories that go beyond mere typological associations. It seems as though the actual task of the music historian, in describing the phenomenon of the virtuoso, lies not so much in advancing hypotheses about his semiobscure origins as in reconstructing the conditions under which virtuosity came to be part of the history of music *as art*. The fact that Paganini set cosmopolitan audiences ablaze in the years around 1830 has to be seen together with the odd fact that not just Liszt, but also Schumann and Brahms, attempted to transfer Paganini's virtuosity from the violin to the piano. Otherwise we cannot hope to understand the musicohistorical significance of the virtuosity that culminated in Paganini and Liszt, a significance at first cultural but which later affected the history of composition.

The emergence of the virtuoso violinist in the seventeenth and eighteenth centuries was conditioned by two features of composition, both of which mutually interacted with the achievements of instrument makers, as well as with the history of church music and the operatic entr'acte. The first feature was monodic cantabile, which permitted, indeed provoked, assimilation and adaptation by virtuoso instrumentalists. The second consisted in conceptions of form which allotted an essential, rather than merely ancillary, function to figuration, the "natural" element of improvisation. (Figuration forms the substance, and not a decorative adjunct, to the many modulating episodes in concertos around 1700.)

If, then, modern virtuoso violin-playing, which left its mark on the history of art music, originated in the seventeenth century, the forebears of virtuoso pianism, which achieved a similar significance, lay in the late-eighteenth-century *Sturm und Drang*. Besides the element of figuration, which was taken as a matter of course, a second constituent feature had to emerge for virtuosity to become a grand style of its own rather than a parasitic technique garnishing a composition. If seventeenth-century violin virtuosos thrived on monody, it was in the rhapsodic, expressive style of the *Sturm und Drang*—a style with free fantasy as its ideal form—that virtuoso pianists found the counterpart to passage work and figuration that they required in order to raise piano virtuosity to a compositional phenomenon of historic significance.

When Liszt heard Paganini play in Paris in 1831, he was swept into a state of frenzy and compulsive emulation which can probably only be explained by assuming that Paganini's example promised to solve a problem that, half-consciously, had tormented Liszt himself. Taking Paganini's violin technique as a paradigm, Liszt had a vision of piano technique that far outstripped anything even dimly imagined by his contemporaries Thalberg, Kalkbrenner, or Dreyschock. Yet, however incontestable this fact, we must see it in context. Although Liszt could write of Paganini "What a man! what a violin! what an artist!" his technique was not the decisive factor—though we must not underestimate Liszt's efforts in transferring it to the piano. The decisive factor was Liszt's fundamental insight that virtuosity, instead of remaining a peripheral and epigonal part of music, was capable in principle of participating in the "romantic revolution" which Berlioz, following the lead of Victor Hugo, had transferred from literature to music. Liszt's discovery of Paganini pointed a way out of the dilemma in which he found himself around 1830—namely, that as a virtuoso he was a prisoner of the *style brillant,* while as an "avant-garde" composer he was incapable of mastering the eruptive musical ideas then welling up within him, as is attested by his sketches of 1830 for a *Symphonie révolutionnaire*. Whatever the deficiencies of Paganini's own compositions, he evidently made Liszt aware of the potential of virtuosity for formally integrating "experimental" musical material, and conversely the potential of a radically modern musical idiom for giving virtuosity a substance lacking in the fashionable style in which he had grown up.

Liszt's *Après une lecture de Dante,* or "Dante Sonata," composed in 1837 and reworked in 1849, is a "fantasia quasi sonata" based on three themes, which we might label introductory theme, main theme, and secondary theme. The last-named proves, following Beethoven's principle of "contrasting derivation," to retain the melodic substance of the main theme while varying its rhythm (Ex. 11). Liszt's piece is at once a single sonata movement and a multimovement sonata cycle. Its material stands out from the music of the 1830s by its peculiar amalgam of modernity and primitivity, an amalgam that prompts us to think of

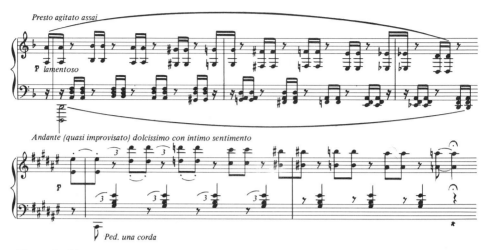

Example 11

Liszt as a musical *fauviste*. Its introductory idea derives from the tritone (Ex. 12),
its main theme from the chromatic scale. These motives provide ample evidence
of Liszt's intention to capture the "zeitgeist" in notes. Yet however "romantic"
and "revolutionary" they may be, the motives prove problematical as a basis for a
large-scale sonata. The dilemma seems inescapable; and yet, Liszt manages to
crack the problem of form in a thoroughly surprising and paradoxical fashion,
namely, by compounding the difficulties in order to solve them. The solution lay
in virtuoso variation: the main theme, hardly amenable to development "from
within," is presented in an ever-changing array of masks and guises. (The "character variations" of the thematic material reveal in outline, beneath the "fantasia"
surface, sections or entire movements of the "sonata" referred to by Liszt in the
work's subtitle: introduction, first theme and second theme in presto and andante versions, the first theme *scherzando,* a development section combining all
the themes, a varied recapitulation, and a *stretta* finale. Taken together, these
sections constitute a "large-scale form" rather than a mere string of transformations.) It is the virtually inexhaustible resources of virtuoso pianism, emulated
and transfigured from Paganini's violin technique, that make the rudimentary
motivic substance, here restricted to a tritone and the chromatic scale, capable of
sustaining large-scale form. Conversely, the convoluted modernity of the musical material provoked "excessive" harmonic effects, interspersed with unusual
dissonances and violent changes of key. This kept Liszt's virtuosity from devolving into mere "brilliance," the pianistic equivalent of the derivative, classicist
harmony and melody of the Thalbergs and Kalkbrenners. If, then, Liszt's virtuoso piano technique enabled "large-scale form" to evolve from "revolutionary
motives" that resisted formal integration, it is no less true that the peculiar modernity of his material prevented his virtuoso artifices from spinning idly in the
rut of convention.

Example 12

The fantasy was one of the nineteenth century's paradigmatic virtuoso forms, along with the set of variations and the rondo. The backbone of the latter two forms—a harmonic or melodic pattern in the case of variations, a ritornello in the case of the rondo—served as the necessary counterfoil to a virtuosity consisting of brilliant figuration and passage work unfolding in variants and episodes. In contrast, the fantasy, based on a late-eighteenth-century prototype from the *Sturm und Drang,* was dominated by expressive rhetorical gestures, played with a subjective verve that swept over the cracks and fissures inherent in rhapsodic form. Liszt's transition from fantasy to sonata in his musical commentary to Dante meant nothing less than that virtuoso pianism, at the pinnacle of its evolution, had seized the historical opportunity of going beyond the simple stolidness of concatenated forms such as the variation and rondo, as well as their negative counterpart, the formally loose-limbed fantasy, by assimilating the "logical form" of the sonata. However, in historical context, the fact that the fantasy took on sonata-form traits, and that virtuoso pianism served as a vehicle of "large-scale form," was in turn part of a larger process that ultimately caused the virtuoso principle to be supplanted by the interpretation of works. (Virtuosity, of course, did not simply vanish, but it ceased to be a central phenomenon in music history, one that spread from cultural history to the history of composition.)

The heyday of virtuosity began with Paganini's tours of the European capitals in the early 1830s and ended in September 1847 when Liszt abandoned his career as a pianist. In the evolution of compositional technique, these were years of ambiguity and dissension, a transitional period in which an earlier tradition based on "skeletal texture"—the firm bass and melody lines of *continuo* technique—was not yet extinct, but overlapped with a new instrumental tradition emphasizing themes as a mode of musical cognition. Because of the aesthetic assumptions associated with it, skeletal texture—that is, the variation of a melodic or bass pattern or a harmonic schema—challenged a musician's improvisational abilities, then considered a touchstone of instrumental virtuosity. Any formal principle whose essence lies in a dialectic between continuity and momentary effect—between a solid underlying framework and unexpected flashes of detail—will immediately accommodate a technique of virtuoso improvisation based on striking instantaneous effects. It is no coincidence that strings of variations became the paradigmatic form of a type of virtuosity that, even when set down in writing as a composition, never lost its close proximity to improvisation. Virtuosity, improvisation, the "skeletal texture" principle, and a focus on the aesthetic instant in its own right rather than as part of the functional nexus of musical form—all of these factors are mutually conditioned and interlinked.

By contrast, a mode of musical cognition centering on themes and thematic argument tended to produce "logical" forms, which, unlike the "skeletal" technique of improvisation, granted considerably more leeway to composers than to improvisers. The fact that improvisation, in the form of the free fantasy, nevertheless managed partially to adopt the principle of thematic manipulation—namely, in fragments whose lines of fracture were hidden by the expressive powers of the improviser—does not alter the fundamental differences between the two. In the same moment that improvisation reached its culmination as a part of cultural history, it was endangered from within by the march of compositional history. Once the dialectic of predefined continuity and improvised, or quasi-improvised, momentary effects gave way to thematic manipulation as the principal arbiter in the evolution of instrumental music, any form of virtuosity nourished on the legacy of improvisation was threatened in its very essence, regardless of whether it seemed to remain intact for decades as an institution. In other words, though Liszt's decision of September 1847 might seem on the surface to have been dictated psychologically by weariness and disgust, it in fact documented a historiological insight; and we may assume that it was this insight which prevented him from subsequently revoking his decision.

This compositional distinction between skeletal texture and thematic argument is closely linked to a distinction between, on the one hand, a mode of performance that tended to adapt or "arrange" pieces to the circumstances at hand, and on the other, a sense of "fidelity," which saw the spirit of a piece preserved in the letter of the original version, or *Urtext*. In eighteenth- and early-nineteenth-century concert halls, as in the opera, the virtuoso seemed to represent a musical culture that used musical texts as mere "scenarios" for performances that focused more on the player or singer than on the work being played or sung. The text was a function of the performance—its substrate or vehicle—rather than vice versa, the performance being a function of a text which it attempted to interpret.

The practice of "arrangement" scarcely left a single work untouched. Yet, appropriate as it may have seemed at a level of compositional evolution dominated technically by the skeletal variation and aesthetically by the dialectic between melody and idiomatic vocal or instrumental figuration, it was at loggerheads with a form of musical cognition based on the thematic process, a process in which every alteration infringed against the substance of the original. Paraphrases of melodic or bass patterns are by nature variable and subject to arrangement; the same cannot be said of a thematic argument whose meaning resides in its strictness and rigor. A melody may be embellished without damage; a thematic process, however, must be interpreted, its latent structures made audible, before it can be comprehended.

Around mid-century, the primacy of virtuosity was gradually undermined by the principle of interpretation, thus causing music critics, if haltingly at first,

Fig. 30　Eugène Delacroix: *Paganini*. Paganini's virtuosity was seen
by many of his contemporaries as
witchcraft, in a completely nonme-
taphorical sense of the term, and
wakened buried memories in an age
which otherwise regarded itself as
positivist. His fantastical excesses,
however, were precisely calculated in
advance, down to the homeliest
details of his appearance. It is therefore no accident that Delacroix's
drawing strikingly coincides with the
description of Paganini given by
Ludwig Weibarg in his *Paganini's
Leben und Charakter* (1830): "the
tall, gaunt figure dressed in old-
fashioned black coat-and-tails . . . his
right leg placed forward and bent at
the knee, nothing but spirit and bone
draped in a loosely flapping suit of
clothes." (Paris, Roger-Viollet.)

to judge virtuosity by the criteria of interpretation, rather than vice versa. This
development was apparently linked to a change in the intellectual climate of the
times, a change which, to use a catchphrase, we might refer to as the replacement
of nonhistorical thought by historical awareness. Yet however simple this formula, the process stands in a curiously twisted relation to several terminological
habits of our own time, thereby making it difficult to reconstruct.

At any rate, nothing would be more misleading than to proceed from the
premise, based on twentieth-century experiences, that there was a deep-seated
rift in the 1830s and 1840s between adherents of classicism and champions of
progress, a rift that made it necessary to side with one party or the other. On the
contrary, an understanding of classicism and modernity were two sides of the
same coin: it was not inconsistency but rather an awareness of history which led
both Schumann and Liszt to proclaim the imperishability of the works of Bach
and Beethoven and yet to herald the dawning of a "new poetic age." One's own
age was seen as a transition from the past, in which it originated, to the future,
which it brings about. The classical works kept alive in concert and opera repertoires were meant to serve as a foundation for what one then believed to be the
ineluctable march of progress. It was considered imperative to cherish and interpret the musical heritage of Bach and Beethoven lest this march into the future
mean a loss of vital substance.

Thus, to advocate the new and to cherish the old were complementary, not contradictory, stances; for Schumann and Liszt the one was as self-evident as the other. However, now that historical awareness has reigned virtually supreme for a century and a half, it is difficult to make the counterposition—contemptuously referred to by Schumann as the *juste milieu*—intelligible without automatically disparaging it by the vocabulary we choose.

To "salvage" this position we had best proceed from a category whose ill repute in the arts is matched only by its uncontested domination of adjacent fields: the concept of fashion. That opera repertoires and concert programs are governed by fashion is a fact that need not be mentioned with the aesthetician's customary note of disdain. Nowadays we have standing repertoires augmented by a few modern pieces, which, in the manner of an experiment, are given a chance to find their way into the repertoire after a certain lapse of time. In contrast, the *stagione* principle of the nineteenth century proceeds from the thoroughly unobjectionable premise that one season's hit, rather than being perpetuated, will be superseded by a new hit in the next.

If the repertoire principle is based on the dialectic between classicism as yesterday's modernity and modernity as tomorrow's classicism, the *stagione* principle embraces the no less tenable dialectic between convention and fashion. Still, convention was not recognized for what it is; instead, it was held to represent the "nature of things." In virtuoso instrumental music and opera, at least of the Italian variety, fashion dictated which direction the taste of the "opinion-making" strata would take, and rose above a secure foundation of established, seemingly axiomatic notions as to the parts that made up an opera or a virtuoso concert and the principles governing their disposition. (It was just as unthinkable to begin an opera with a cavatina instead of a tumultuous ensemble as it was presumptuous to end a virtuoso concert with a faithful rendering of a piece by Bach.)

As musical institutions continued to develop, the virtuoso concert gradually gave way to the symphony concert and to the recital, or *soirée*. In the latter, virtuoso pieces were long able to hold their own (in the end as encores) against the sonata, the work being "interpreted." The symphony concert, however, differed from the motley programs of early-nineteenth-century concerts by ultimately adopting a stereotyped three-part sequence of overture, concerto, and symphony. In its earlier form, deriving from the eighteenth century, the movements of the symphony were often rent asunder to serve as an introduction and a finale, as a setting for the solo instrumental or vocal works which the bulk of the audience had come to hear. In the new type, the "symphony concert" instilled with the spirit of the bourgeois educated classes, the symphony that gave this type of concert its name functioned as the crowning conclusion to a performance composed of three parts.

This transformation in the structure of the concert had a consequence for the history of genres, or rather, the above-mentioned institutional changes occasioned a correlate in the history of composition. By the 1840s the virtuoso piano concerto had begun to assimilate the symphonic style, producing a hybrid form to which Henry Litolff, around 1840, applied the term "symphonic concerto" in his *Concerto symphonique,* Op. 22. One obvious feature of the symphonic concerto —a feature adopted by Liszt in his E♭-major Concerto (1849) and later by Brahms in his B♭-major Concerto (1881)—was the insertion of a scherzo into the standard, century-old, three-movement design of allegro, slow movement, and finale. (Liszt's E♭-major Concerto, which was dedicated to Litolff, incorporates nothing less than a self-contained scherzo as the second section of the middle movement, the Allegretto Vivace.)

As developed by Liszt, the symphonic concerto emerged from a cross between virtuoso technique and his own notion of the symphony, a notion not derived from the Viennese Classic tradition. And as foolish as it would be to try to trace the new genre directly back to Beethoven's piano concertos, it is equally misleading, however tempting, to proclaim Schumann's A-minor Concerto—a historically unique, unreduplicatable special instance of the "romantic concerto" —as the prototype of the symphonic concerto.

Originally, in 1840, Schumann conceived the first movement of his concerto as a "fantasy in A minor for piano and orchestra" without the second and third movements, which were not written until 1845. This title expresses his inclination to dissolve sonata-allegro form from within while retaining its external contours. "I cannot compose a concerto for virtuosos," he wrote to Clara Wieck, "but must light on something different." Nevertheless, he stood apart not only from the virtuoso tradition but from the classical tradition as well. His "fantasy" is a piano piece with orchestral accompaniment, which, despite its unusually large dimensions, is lyrical in its tone and monothematic in its form. Its second group derives thematically from the first without triggering a symphonic dialectic from an internal contrast in the theme, as Haydn does on similar occasions. An andante version of the theme is interpolated as an episode before the development section, bringing to a halt the formal process and sequestering it in a momentary idyll. The central portion of the development section, which develops next to nothing, is occupied by a paraphrase of the theme, which, for all its outward similarity with Beethoven's thematic technique, dissolves in lyric effusion instead of being directed toward a dramatic climax. The movement is held together from within, not by symphonic dialectic, but by the unity of its lyric tone. The lack of contrast between or within its themes is matched by the weakness, except at the outset of the development, of the dialogue between soloist and orchestra, a sine qua non of the traditional concerto movement. In short, since the orchestra basically serves to enlarge and refine the timbres of an infinitely dilating piano piece, it would be an exaggeration to call Schumann's work "symphonic" in conception, an exaggeration that not only does an injustice to its historical position outside the main traditions, but seems more liable to obscure rather than illuminate that position.

In his E♭-major and A-major piano concertos (sketched in 1839–40 and completed in 1849), Liszt faced what might be called the problem of mediating between extremes: between the structure of the character piece and the technique of pianistic paraphrase, on the one hand—Liszt took these as his starting points—and, on the other, the concept of large-scale symphonic form which was meant to elevate the *concerto symphonique* above the virtuoso concerto. The solution that Liszt had in mind was to adapt variation technique, with its ample scope for virtuosity, to that perfect fusion of monumentality and sophisticated thematic logic, of grand gesture and ramified structure, which to the nineteenth-century mind constituted the essence of the symphony.

The E♭-major Concerto extends the principle of character variation—the creation of sharply focused character pieces with the devices of virtuoso variation technique—to truly monumental dimensions by expanding it into a quadruple variation. The finale as a whole is a transformation, in different tempos and rhythms, of the four themes of the Adagio and Scherzo that make up the middle movement.

Not by accident, the sequence of the themes remains the same. If their juxtaposition in the Adagio and Scherzo sections recalls an open-ended fantasy more readily than the closed form of the symphony, their confirmatory reappearance in the finale has the effect of granting them aesthetic legitimacy. Even though the themes of the middle movement—cantabile, recitative, pastorale, and *scherzando*—change profoundly in mood in the finale, being transformed into martial fustian, we nevertheless sense a rigor and logic in their succession, a logic none the less compelling for being independent of previous patterns. Moreover, the main theme of the first movement, being in fact the main theme of the work, helps bracket the form by reappearing as a transition between the middle movement and the finale and as a *stretta* in the finale. Here the transition is supplied by a development section with a hint of recapitulation, opening the way to the finale, and the *stretta* by a closing group clearly derived from the main theme. If, then, the goal of the thematic process is to bring about a merging of single-movement and multimovement forms, it is no less true that Liszt's happy amalgam of pianistic paraphrase, the character piece (a central tradition in piano music), thematic transformation (suggested by Schubert's *Wanderer* Fantasy), and monumental quadruple variation has formed a bridge between the virtuoso manner and the symphonic style. Herein lies the significance of the *concerto symphonique* for the history of genres.

Poetic Music

The idea of poetic music dominated early-nineteenth-century aesthetics, particularly the aesthetics of piano music. Yet it is one of those categories whose historical substance crumbles the moment we try to capture it in a definition. In a manner of speaking, the idea thrives on its own internal contradictions; and if we want this idea, the centerpiece of the aesthetic thought of the age, to shed light on musical reality, we must not make the mistake of trying to iron out its contradictions, but must let them remain as they are.

Wir sind beglückt! wir sind entzückt! die Lind hat uns den Kopf verrückt.

Fig. 31   The Hamburg audience at a Jenny Lind concert, 1845. This caricature is less a document on Jenny Lind, an important and by no means sensation-mongering singer and actress, than on her audience, here captured by the artist in a mass hysteria motivated by something more than music alone. The gentlemen's enthusiasm is not shared by the few ladies present, who tend to look indignant; the orchestral postlude is drowned in the outburst of applause, despite the conductor's vain pleas for mercy; and the winged boy lowering the laurel wreath looks more like Mozart's Cherubino than an angel. (The doggerel verse at the bottom reads: "We're delighted! We're held in thrall! / Jenny has turned the heads of us all.") (Museum für Hamburgische Geschichte.)

Generally speaking, the poetic is determined by its opposition to the prosaic—to the trivial and mechanical, in Jean Paul's curt formulation. Yet the changing hues in the apparent meaning of this category depend in part on the polemical or apologetical functions it is meant to serve.

Ludwig Tieck, in his *Phantasien über die Kunst* of 1799, praised instrumental music as the "supreme poetic language," one that "strikes out on its own path in disregard of text and underlying verse, composing and explicating its own poetry." In this way he expressed the challenging paradox that music, by liberating itself from poetry, itself becomes poetry. Poetry here means a renunciation of the doctrine of imitation, which demanded of instrumental music, lest it remain mere empty noise, that it be a mimesis of external or internal nature—in other words that it either paint pictures or render "affects." However, to his thesis that music can be "absolute" without sacrificing its status as art, Tieck added the insight that instrumental music, when liberated both from extramusical functions and from subjects and "affects," demands to be listened to for its own sake as an acoustic phenomenon, and that it vindicates itself aesthetically by taking on the structure of a thematic disquisition or argument—by "composing and explicating its own poetry," as Tieck put it.

In Tieck's theory, detachment from the traditional aesthetic of feeling was closely allied with an emphasis on theme as the central category of autonomous instrumental music. In contrast, Hegel, who clung to the primacy of vocal music, defined the "poetic dimension to music" as a "language of the soul" in which melody, not theme, provides the structural element that sustains music's aesthetic significance:

> This poetic dimension to music, this language of the soul which gives vent to our inner desires and pain, and in so doing alleviates and uplifts us above the natural force of emotion by turning our momentary inward feelings into self-perception and voluntary self-absorption, thereby liberating our spirit from the pressures of joy and sorrow—this free resounding of the soul in the realm of music is, first and foremost, melody.

In short, we have, on one side, an aesthetic of form, an emphasis on theme, and the primacy of instrumental music; on the other, an aesthetic of feeling, a focus on melody, and the preeminence of vocal music.

Another interpretation of the notion of "poetry in music" appeared in the works of Beethoven, who, on Schindler's evidence, "frequently used" the expression "poetic idea." Here the internal cohesion of music is vouchsafed in two ways: by rendering musical characters or moods—a view elaborated in the classical aesthetic of Christian Gottfried Körner (1795)—and by adopting a "thematic design." The latter, according to Heinrich Christoph Koch's treatise on composition (vol. 2, 1787), consists of the "main ideas of the music in mutual interrelation," ideas that "appear together in the mind of the composer as a perfect and complete entity." Thus, the "underlying idea" mentioned by Beethoven, according to an account by Louis Schlösser, is less likely to be an isolated musical thought than an "entity" of separate thoughts, joined together to represent a character or mood.

If the romantic era clung to the category of the Characteristic, elevating the character piece to a central form in piano music, the concept of "design," meaning a basic pattern of thematic ideas, was overshadowed by the notion of motive in the course of a historical movement which shifted emphasis from the sonata to the piano piece. Like "theme," "motive" is a dual category in a compositional and aesthetic sense: if "theme" ranges variously, and sometimes lopsidedly, from an emotion captured in notes to an acoustic pattern devoid of emotional significance, "motive" refers not only to the musical germ-cell that serves as the starting point of a piece of music, but also to what Wagner called the aesthetic raison d'être behind this cell.

Schumann, without retreating into the rigorism of absolute music, drew a distinction between "poetry in music," of the sort that he wrote about as a critic

and composed as a musician, and programmatic and virtuoso music. He praised
Mendelssohn's *Melusine Overture* (1833–35) for "invariably revealing a poetic
grasp" of its subject rather than spinning a "coarse historical fabric"—in short,
for suggesting a characterization rather than telling a story. Again, in a review of
two transcriptions, we read: "If Schumann's arrangement is designed to direct
our attention to the poetic side of the composition, Liszt, though without disregarding the poetic, stresses its virtuoso aspect." However, Schumann's distinctions presuppose that it is the minor differences between the two that matter,
and we should not misconstrue his remarks as polemical, or his distinction as a
gaping chasm. To Schumann, program music and virtuosity were not a priori
objectionable: after all, he enthusiastically championed Berlioz and even admired Liszt, though not without misgivings. However, he saw both styles as jeopardized by the danger of degenerating into the prosaic—program music by devolving into a fondness for realistic detail, which even Beethoven considered
petty and small-minded, and virtuosity by flaunting the opposite of the "poetic,"
namely, the "mechanical."

Virtuosity and program music form the aesthetic signature of a brand of
instrumental music conditioned by the spirit of the European capitals—meaning, in the final analysis, the spirit of the salons and concert halls of Paris. Both
Chopin and Liszt saw in Schumann's piano pieces—the work, they believed,
of a critic who dabbled in composition—a trait which they regarded, in Liszt's
phrase, as "Leipzigerian." Still, there is no reason for the historian, in retrospect,
to rush to Schumann's defense and deny the existence of his provincial tinge by
appealing to his historical significance. On the contrary, this gives us an opportunity to show the existence of provinciality of the highest order, as exemplified by
Schumann.

Schumann's character pieces have a poetry permeated by the spirit of Jean
Paul, a poetry of literary and even autobiographical allusions, of mottos and
eloquent titles that sometimes appear to mean more than they actually say. From
the standpoint of social history, we have no trouble categorizing this poetry as
the aesthetic of a narrowly circumscribed coterie of friends, one which even extended from reality into the imaginary in the form of his secret, anti-Philistine
society, the *Davidsbund*. The music in which Schumann wrapped himself until
about 1840, when he began to seek access to the symphonic tradition, was *Hausmusik* for cognoscenti.

Schumann's *Carnaval*, Op. 9 (1834–35), subtitled *Scènes mignonnes sur quatre
notes*, is based on a symbolic motive, or "cipher," referring to the town of Asch,
the birthplace of Ernestine von Fricken. One form of this cipher, A–E♭–C–B
(a–es–c–h in German notation), dominates the first half of the cycle, and another form, A♭–C–B (as–c–h in German), dominates the second. The connection between these two motives, though fundamental to the overall form (which
bears the same relation to a set of variations as the Fantasy, Op. 17, does to a
sonata), remains abstract and inaudible, residing solely in a "literal" dimension
with biographical overtones. Further, the "four notes" of the subtitle, which

Fig. 32 Constantin Hansen: *Hausmusik am Klavier,* c. 1840. This genre drawing provides a realistic picture of bourgeois music culture in Denmark, assembling virtually all the props of convivial domestic music-making in the *Biedermeier* period: the family atmosphere projected by the daughter seated at the piano; the connection with handicrafts, interrupted for a moment as the music transports the listener into a world of daydreams; the "poetry" of candlelight instead of the "prose" of the petroleum lamp; and the children, inhabitants of a "land" to which romantic piano music seemed ever to regress. (Copenhagen, Det kongelige Bibliotek.)

shrink to "three notes" for half of the piece, are more concealed than apparent in movements such as *Eusebius* (No. 5). This abstraction is an aesthetic consequence of the esoteric world which gives Schumann's piano music its sociohistorical character.

That this meager melodic substance could yield a web of motives spanning an entire cycle of twenty pieces is due to the aforementioned fact that the structure of the lyric piano piece, unlike the sonata, is determined by motives and not by themes. The hallmark of romantic piano music is the pregnant and telling motive; it is motive that sets in motion the musical development of this fundamentally lyrical art and, by remaining in the ear, imparts unity to a piece. Almost invariably, the motive has a distinctive rhythm while the pitch content remains open and variable. Thus the "four notes," instead of quickly cloying by frequent repetition and manipulation, merely serve as an initial impetus to the pieces. At the same time, the pitch content, by merely alluding to the opening of the movement, could be taken up again and again without courting monotony or "unpoetic" pedantry. Schumann's musical ciphers were effective aesthetically and structurally, and yet remained inconspicuous, being given ever-changing and extremely varied rhythmic guises that enabled the separate movements to appear as character pieces.

Schumann's portrait of Chopin in *Carnaval* (No. 12) has always been considered a self-portrait, even though certain tangible features such as its irregular metrical divisions, the roundabout harmonic path to the tonic, and the dichotomy between floating melodic line and urgent dynamics, are thoroughly reminiscent of Chopin's style. Yet, even though Schumann tried to disguise his voice, he still spoke with his own, as is most apparent in the intimate tone of the cadences in measures 6–7 and 13–14 (Ex. 13), a tone irreconcilable with Chopin's air of detachment. What Schumann wished to express in this tone is, to quote his own words, a "yearning for the true native land of art," a land which, he felt, was not to be found in the "salons of the rich and powerful" for whom Chopin wrote his music.

Example 13

Chopin once remarked to Liszt: "I am not fit to give concerts, as audiences unnerve me: I feel stifled by their breath, paralyzed by their inquiring gaze." Although he appeared once each year in the Salle Pleyel, Chopin felt best understood, both as pianist and composer, not in the concert halls where Liszt established his reputation, but rather in the aristocratic salons of Paris and London. We obscure the social character of Chopin's music when we feel an urge to defend it from the thoroughly appropriate term "salon music." Instead of clinging to a watered-down notion of this term, extracted from pieces that were intended to delude provincial middle-class audiences into a musical daydream of salons they were not allowed to enter, we should instead try to reconstruct the aesthetic of a musical genre imbued with the spirit of the authentic salon. (What is referred to nowadays as salon music is almost invariably pseudosalon music.)

In the first half of the nineteenth century, the salon was on a par with the opera house and the concert hall as a crucial venue for the history of music, one that bridged the preconditions of social history and the history of composition. At all events, we should not let the twentieth-century view that history is made less by events themselves than from their reflection in the media mislead us into concluding that, in the early nineteenth century, private concerts were inconsequential because they were not reviewed. On the contrary, private music could indeed be historically significant, as is amply proved by the example of Chopin. And any historian who speaks disparagingly of the salons and their music from the standpoint of cultural and compositional history is guilty of a double anachronism: first of all sociologically, by backdating the modern relation between public and private to early-nineteenth-century music culture, but also aesthetically, by continuing to take sides with Leipzig against Paris a full century and a half after the fact.

As music started to become (to stand Kant's dictum on its head) "more culture than delectation," it began to mirror the spirit of the philosophical and literary salon. This spirit was marked by essays and dialogues in a conversational tone, not by disquisitions and learned treatises. We need only take the classical sonata literally as a thematic disquisition, a meditation in notes, to understand why the sonata principle and salon music were mutually exclusive—though there is nothing to be gained by adding disparaging epithets to this historical dichotomy and speaking of shallow salon music or pedantic sonata mentality. (Schumann tended to do the first, Debussy the second.) Salon music's conversational tone in no way implied that the composer had studiously to avoid saying anything substantial lest he be accused of pedantry. (The deadly mixture of sentimental tunefulness and mechanical figuration and passage work that characterizes lesser examples of this genre is by no means stylistically representative of salon music as a whole.)

Chopin's Ballade in G minor, Op. 23, distantly recalls sonata form, being based on an underlying contrast of themes. The continuation of the second theme (m. 85) cites the opening gesture of the first (mm. 8–9), forming a belated clue that the two are latently related (the continuation motive, in paraphrase, links up with the opening of the second theme) (Ex. 14). This is fully in the spirit of the "contrasting derivation" principle found in Beethoven's sonata forms. However, it is not the first theme, with its narrative "ballad tone," but the cantabile second theme that forms the main idea of the work, an idea emphasized more and more strongly as the piece progresses. In this sense, Chopin's ballad stands well outside the sonata tradition: its lyric episode gradually becomes the focal point of the movement around which the musical events center.

Example 14

The piece presumably owes its title to its "change of tones," its alternation of the lyric, epic, and dramatic, and Chopin was faced with the problem of establishing a formal equilibrium between narrative ballad, lyric cantabile, and an urgent virtuosity that appears with the effect of an explosion. The means he chose are more sophisticated than they seem at first glance. In principle, all the parts or elements of his form may change function: virtuosity may serve as a transition or as a conclusion, and the first theme may either come to a close or erupt into lyric cantabile or even into virtuosity. The parts then, are recapitulated in substance but transformed in function; in this dialectic lies the structural and aesthetic point of the work, and no letter analysis will say anything revealing about the work's formal design, however adequate it might otherwise be for the simple forms of the lyric piano piece.

If sophistication and idiosyncrasy are hidden beneath the seemingly straightforward surface of this work, the genuine spirit of the salon demands not only that the music harbor an element of artifice but that this element be kept concealed. (Ever since the Renaissance, the aesthetic motto of aristocratic music culture was *nascondere l'arte*: art must be concealed. And nothing is more revealing of Chopin than his at once zealous and clandestine study of Bach, his latent assimilation of a tradition then held to be the quintessence of musical artifice.)

Besides Chopin's idiosyncratic form, which is closely connected to his inimitable "tone," another element that makes up the "poetic" dimension of his music —as Schumann recognized as early as Chopin's Op. 2—is his manner of transforming the functional and literary character of his genres, "character" being understood to mean the complex of features that define a ballad as a ballad, a nocturne as a nocturne, or a mazurka as a mazurka. Virtually the whole of Chopin's oeuvre thrives unmistakably on his practice of "interiorizing" the essential features of literary genres or functional music: the "change of tones" in the ballad; the serenade-like melodies of his nocturnes (which, incidentally, would seem to owe more to Bellini than to Field); or the rustic rhythmic and dynamic pattern of the mazurka, the rural counterpart to the aristocratic polonaise. As a result, his music exists in its own right as autonomous art, preserving the moods of the original literary or musical genres as reminiscences. The general and extrinsic has been subsumed in a "tone" that is Chopin's own.

Where Chopin transforms and assimilates the characters of different genres, Liszt draws on literary or pictorial subjects. Once we try to understand poetic piano music in its historical context instead of proceeding from abstract aesthetic criteria, it becomes patently more critical to grasp the similarities of conception between absolute and program music than to stress their opposition. As far as the history of composition is concerned, Liszt's "literarization" of music, which drew down upon him the reproaches of aesthetic purists, should be analyzed from the vantage point of structure: our task is to examine the significance of Liszt's conception as part of the general efforts of the time to establish, in opposition to mechanical virtuosity and classicist epigonism, a musical tradition that

offered an escape from the era of what Schumann called the *juste milieu* into the
"New Poetic Age." The crucial point about the piano pieces in Liszt's collection
Années de pèlerinage, of which the first *année* appeared in 1855 and the second in
1858, is not that the music is programmatic, and hence might rank alongside the
programmatic salon pieces of a Lefébure-Wély, but rather that Liszt, by taking
his subjects from the writings of Petrarch and Dante, the paintings of Raphael,
or landscapes tinged with reminiscences of early French romantic novels, gave
his music a claim to artistic stature of the loftiest and most ambitious kind imaginable. Insofar as he held good to this claim, his music attained a level that justifies the term "poetic" as used by Schumann to distinguish art in the strong
sense from nonart. It is not "literarization" per se which is "poetic," but rather
the substance that attaches to a work of music when the composer succeeds, as
it were, in picking up the thread of a major work of literature.

Liszt's *Sonetto 47 del Petrarca,* from the *Années de pèlerinage,* is based on formal elements unmistakably inspired by the poem whose essence he attempted to
capture in music: the chromatic harmonies of measure 1 by the image of the
phoenix, the "sigh" motive of measure 6 by the love pangs that sustain the sonnet, the cantilena of measure 14—half elegiac, half rapturous—by Petrarch's
unique tone, poised between ecstasy and lament. As in the poem, the aesthetic
crux of the music is the way image and emotion give rise to a structure conveying
both of these elements at once. And the most cursory analysis shows that this was
precisely Liszt's intention. The harmonization of the sigh motive mirrors the
chromatic harmonies of the opening measures (Ex. 15). The form as a whole is
made up largely of transpositions of the cantilena into a complex of distant, conflicting tonalities (D♭ major, G major, D major, E major, D♭ major) organized less
according to harmonic logic than in an effort to project a multicolored radiance,
as foreshadowed in embryo by the opening measures, the musical image of a
phoenix.

Example 15

Still, we sense throughout that the cantilena derives at root from the inflections of the sigh motive; nor would it be farfetched to recognize the final three
notes of the sigh motive (F–B♭–A♭) in the melodic contour of the first line of the
cantilena. However, the crucial point for the work's claim to rank as art is, to use
Hegel's words, that the melody—a "free resounding of the soul"—"uplifts" us

Fig. 33 Ludwig Richter: *Hausmusik,* 1855. The term *Hausmusik,* or domestic music-making, originally a counterfoil to *Salonmusik,* became no less popular through Ludwig Richter's drawing than through Wilhelm Heinrich Riehl's *Hausmusik: Fünfzig Lieder deutscher Dichter,* which appeared in the same year. Large-scale chamber music, inaccessible to amateur musicians at least since the time of Beethoven's Op. 59 string quartets, had been transplanted to the public concert, leaving private music-making to be dominated by opera arrangements, potpourris, and sentimental, pseudovirtuoso *pièces.* This type of subculture made use of provincial, petty-bourgeois *Salonmusik* in imitation of the Parisian salons of the grand bourgeoisie. It also served as the polemical target of Riehl's "simple, unadorned, and genuinely German" *Hausmusik,* a musical expression of the growing self-awareness of the lower middle classes. (Dresden, Staatliche Kunstsammlungen, Engraving Collection; photograph from the Deutsche Fotothek in Dresden.)

above the mere "natural force of emotion" as expressed in the sigh motive. And if, again to quote Hegel, the "poetic dimension of music" resides in giving melodic expression to the "language of the soul," we might say that the composer has, in a manner of speaking, retraced the process of "poeticization" in his music. The formal elements that immediately reflect the poem—the chromatic harmony and the sigh motive—convincingly motivate both the melody that makes up the piece and the principle of coloristic transposition by which it is developed.

The Symphony after Beethoven

To speak of the nineteenth-century symphony as the symphony after Beethoven is not to refer to a chronological truism but to point out a problem for the historian, a problem arising from the fact that later examples of the genre relate directly and immediately to models left by Beethoven, with intermediate stages playing only a minor role.

Even Beethoven's contemporaries realized that the *Eroica* had created a new era in the history of the genre, regardless of whether, like Prince Louis Ferdinand, they were overwhelmed by the power of the work or whether, like the author of the 1805 review in the *Allgemeine musikalische Zeitung*, they felt that its "very loose-limbed, bold, and unfettered fantasy" placed it outside the genre of the symphony as created by Haydn. Its novelty resided in a combination of monumental form and a "teleological," or goal-directed, structure that radically changed the traditional concept of theme. Yet however drastic this novelty appeared to early-nineteenth-century listeners, and however omnipresent Beethoven's example was to his successors, the genre did not simply evolve along pat dialectical lines, with problems calling forth solutions that in turn generated new problems. It is precisely because of its constant relation to Beethoven that the history of the symphony bears so little resemblance to the stereotype of a continuous chain, with each link joined to the next.

By and large, the task that composers faced in assimilating the Beethoven legacy had to do with a will to large-scale form. Beethoven had transformed the symphony into a monumental genre, just as his admired forebear Handel had done to the oratorio. Thereafter, a symphony manifested compositional ambitions of the highest order, the audience it addressed being no smaller than the whole of humanity. As the public concert became stylized into the symphony concert, it revealed aesthetic and social pretensions distantly but distinctly mirroring the ideal of the Roman Forum, whose imagery had exercised such a firm hold on the French Revolution. Even Mendelssohn, in his Reformation Symphony (1829–30) and the Second Symphony, or *Lobgesang* (1839–40), yielded to the urge toward monumentality. It was not until our century that the symphony gave way to the chamber symphony, in which each instrumental part is taken by a single player, this being the structural reflection of a new aesthetic.

The nineteenth-century symphony from Schubert to Mahler might be called "circumpolar" in the sense of the term used by Theodor Kroyer to describe German opera in the aftermath of Wagner. This label is meant to express, or suggest, that the history of the symphony did not proceed by evolution, with each step being the consequence of an earlier step and the prerequisite for a later one; instead, the major works cluster about a midpoint to which they are directly related, with no more than cursory connections to one another. True, Brahms may have owed some musical traits to Schumann (from whom he claimed to have learned nothing but how to play chess), but as a composer of symphonies he stands, like his contemporary Bruckner, in an immediate relation to Beethoven, whatever the historical distance separating them.

Still, to speak of "the" Beethoven symphony drawn upon by later composers is to distort our view of an important aspect of the history of reception. The range and variety of Beethoven's symphonies made it impossible to construct an ideal type of the sort that August Halm attempted for Bruckner, and turned these works separately into starting points and prerequisites for the conflicting trends within the nineteenth-century history of this genre. Schumann took his bearings on Beethoven's Fourth and Seventh Symphonies and Berlioz primarily on the *Eroica*, whereas Bruckner's works everywhere reflect the model of the Ninth. This led to profound differences in their respective symphonic styles, and their personal idioms appear indissolubly linked with an affinity for particular works by Beethoven, since a composer's choice of paradigms is as much the product of his personality as, conversely, his personality is partly conditioned by his choice of paradigms.

The disregard and contempt that befell the symphonies of Carl Czerny and Ferdinand Ries—works that attempt a Beethovenian tone without attaining the level of style associated with large-scale form—is one indication that, around 1820, workmanlike epigonism of the sort that still flourished in opera seria and oratorio had lost its aesthetic legitimacy in the symphony. To prove himself a worthy heir of Beethoven, a composer of a symphony had to avoid copying Beethoven's style, and yet maintain the same degree of reflection that Beethoven had reached in grappling with the problem of symphonic form.

In Schubert's own estimation, his *Unfinished Symphony* (1822) paved the way to large-scale symphonic form. In the first movement, he adopted one of Beethoven's structural principles only to apply it to a difficulty which, though nonexistent for Beethoven, exercised composers of romantic symphonies for decades: how to integrate contemplative lyricism, an indispensable ingredient of "poetic" music, into a symphony without causing the form to disintegrate or to function as a mere framework for a potpourri of melodies. It is no coincidence that the second theme of this movement, a complete and self-contained musical utterance, has entered the bourgeois stock of musical quotations. Yet even the first theme (m. 13), standing out like a lied melody over an accompaniment pattern that precedes it by four measures, strikes a lyric tone, a tone which invites the listener to dally and which is inconsistent in equal measure with both the dramatic and the monumental side of Beethoven's symphonic style. This first theme has no repercussions for the overall form, even if the descending fifth of measures 63–64 seemingly derives from it. Moreover, when a submotive from the second theme is isolated and manipulated in measure 73, this does not represent development—a revelation of the theme's potential—so much as a mere transition to a new version of the theme in close imitation (m. 94), a version with the function of increasing the theme's lyric urgency by presenting it, so to speak, as a cantilena in contrapuntal duplication. Thus, the sections in the first movement that fill the traditional sonata-form slots of exposition and recapitulation stand virtually at loggerheads with Beethoven's dramatic, goal-directed conception of the symphony, even in contemplative works like the first movement of the *Pastorale*. Nonetheless, Schubert attained a Beethovenian dialectic of monumentality and sophisticated thematic manipulation by basing the actual symphonic development on a theme which appears initially as a mere introductory figure (m. 1) and only later, in the development (m. 114) and coda (m. 328), proves to be a dominating idea of ever-larger proportions. This principle of evolving a monumental and "teleological" form from an inconspicuous motive, which does not even appear as a theme at first, but only attains the function of a theme gradually and unexpectedly by virtue of the consequences drawn from it, originated with Beethoven. Hence, it is no paradox to claim that Schubert has used Beethoven's devices to solve a problem that Beethoven himself never confronted—or, in other words, that Schubert, having "poeticized" his music in a way that tends ineluctably to the lyrical, drew on Beethoven to satisfy the axioms that Beethoven himself had posed for large-scale symphonic form. In this light, the formal problem that underlies and brings to life the first movement of the *Unfinished* is one manifestation of the historical status of the symphony "after Beethoven." For Schubert as an artistic persona (which is something different from Schubert as a biographical entity), this structural feature mirrors a thoroughly characteristic expressive compulsion to draw lyric urgency into an oppressive, and ultimately tragic, dialectical process.

It might seem absurd to mention Schubert and Berlioz in one breath, even though they belong to the same generation. But however grossly works such as the *Unfinished* and the *Symphonie fantastique* may differ in style, they nevertheless reveal, on closer analysis, comparable features resulting from the similarity of their positions in history. Contemporary phenomena may be noncontemporaneous in appearance, and ultimately it is the affinity between problems, however dissimilar their solutions, that documents the "zeitgeist."

"The author," we read in Berlioz's preface to the *Symphonie fantastique*, "flatters himself in the hope that his symphony may offer musical interest in and of itself, and apart from any dramatic intentions." And for all Schumann's skepticism toward program music, the formal outline that he sketched, in 1835, of the Allegro section of the first movement is intended to show that the musical "dream images," confusing as they may appear at first, fall into a straightforward design derived from sonata form:

First theme	Second theme	First theme	Second theme	First theme
C major	G major	G major	C major	C major

Since these "units" in the musical framework are separated by long "interim passages" that are crucial to the form as a process, it is idle to speculate whether the themes in the recapitulation appear in reverse order, or whether we are dealing with a relic of the Baroque suite—that is, a binary design with a sonata-like contrast of themes and an inverted modulation in its second section (G major to C major instead of vice versa). Instead, if we wish to analyze the problem of form in the "post-Beethovenian" symphony, we will have to proceed from the realization that Berlioz's *idée fixe*, unlike the musical ideas that sustain a Beethoven symphony, is not a concise theme but a long-breathed melody. And however faint the melodic similarities between Berlioz's aria and Schubert's lied, both composers faced parallel difficulties by discarding Beethoven's concept of theme. Admittedly, the *idée fixe*, whether in its entirety or in fragments, is part of a formal process and not, as with Schubert's first and second themes, part of a formal framework. The different guises taken by the *idée fixe*—whether as first theme (m. 72), as an opening to the second theme (m. 150), as a development pattern (m. 168), as a motive in the figuration of a harmonic sequence (m. 302), as a recapitulation with martial bombast (m. 412), or as a reminiscence in the coda (m. 453)—exactly parallel the formal functions it serves in sonata form. The "history" of this theme is conditioned by the formal process; and rather than dictating this process, the work's program is adapted to it. On the other hand, the *idée fixe*, being a melody with the function but not the appearance of a theme, is more the object than the subject of this formal process: it is drawn into the process without determining its course. This formal arrangement forms a correlate to the work's program, the "dream image" of the beloved vanishing in a flurry of hopes and fears. The true "motivating" element of the thematic process is a structure formed of a semitone and a chromatic sequence, a structure which is "thematic" without being a "theme." It is first heard in the continuation of the *idée fixe* at measure 87 (Ex. 16) and dominates all the development sections in various forms: as a chromatic sequence in counterpoint with a semitone motive (m. 168), as an augmentation of the semitone over a chromatic run (m. 200), or as a chromatic sequence with a semitone modulation from major to minor at each step (m. 372) (Ex. 17). This synthesis of diatonic melody and chromatic structure—a melody that appears on the surface to be a theme, and a structure that covertly motivates the thematic process—was foreshadowed in Beethoven's *Eroica*. In the first movement of the *Eroica*, the broken triad usually referred to as the "first theme" forms the actual thematic substance of the work not by itself but in relation to its chromatic continuation, which then influences the course of the movement at every "juncture." However, if Beethoven's "surface theme" is reduced to a musical rudiment, Berlioz's is extended to a melody spanning forty

Example 16

measures. Further, Beethoven's theme serves a "teleological" form in which the thematic rudiment only gradually, in the coda, achieves its full and proper shape, whereas Berlioz's theme functions within a "scenic" form, a series of musical images in which the *idée fixe* is not so much allowed to evolve as it is subjected to external intervention. Berlioz's formal conception reflects his programmatic ideal of a "dream image"; however remote it may otherwise be from Beethoven's, the two nevertheless have one notion in common: both relate a "surface theme" to a latent structure that motivates the formal process. As with Schubert, Berlioz has taken one of Beethoven's principles to solve a formal problem unknown to Beethoven—a principle, however, that would never have come into existence in the first place without the premise, accepted by Beethoven, that large-scale symphonic form emerges from the relation between monumentality and sophisticated thematic manipulation.

Example 17

Berlioz held to the demand for monumentality, even if he transformed it into the macabre. Mendelssohn, on the other hand, either abandoned this demand, as in the Scottish Symphony (1842) and the Italian Symphony (1832–33), or satisfied it by using means foreign to the symphonic tradition, as in the Reformation Symphony and the *Lobgesang*—an option also adopted by Berlioz, though not to the same degree. (To quote *Ein feste Burg* is more appropriate to an overture than to a symphony, which thereby turns into an oversized overture.) Thus, the verdict is likely to hold that, of Mendelssohn's works, the Scottish and Italian Symphonies belong to the history of the genre in the strong sense, a history that separates the substance of the past from the mere debris cast up by tradition. By avoiding a confrontation with Beethoven of the sort he had attempted in his early string quartets, Op. 12 and Op. 13, Mendelssohn was able to make the Scottish and Italian Symphonies the successful works that they have proved to be in the concert hall. For Mendelssohn, despite his affinity to the *Pastorale,* to establish oneself as a "post-Beethovenian" composer of symphonies meant stepping well out of the way of Beethoven's shadow.

The formal concept underlying the first movement of the Scottish Symphony stands outside all criteria abstracted from Beethoven, or even from Haydn. Both the first theme—an allegro version of the andante melody that opens and concludes the movement—and the second theme are "songs without words." (The fact that Mendelssohn half conceals the lied syntax of his first theme by starting with a more refined version, followed by the basic form as though it were a lesser variant, means merely that he was aware of the problems involved with this type of theme, not that he resolved them.) As a counterpart to his liedlike themes, Mendelssohn uses a technique of motivic linkage or association, a device which he evidently regarded as capable of giving a symphonic slant to the ballad tone he had struck. The opening of the first theme (m. 64) and a continuation motive (m. 76) are combined contrapuntally in E minor, the tonality of the second theme (m. 125), and the same melodies give rise to a cantabile theme (m. 182) that serves the function of a second theme even though its position in the form is that of a closing group (Ex. 18). For Mendelssohn, with his fondness for using counterpoint in development sections, the contrapuntal structure of the thematic complex that bridges the first and second themes (m. 125) makes it predestined to serve as a development figure (m. 239).

Example 18

Though seemingly self-contradictory, Mendelssohn's combination of lied melodies, counterpoint, and motivic association is thoroughly tenable on its own terms and served as a starting point for his attempt to establish and vindicate symphonic form in a different manner from Beethoven. It would be unfair to measure the results with Beethoven as our yardstick. Instead, we should marvel that Mendelssohn was successful at all in handling continuous lied melodies as though they were complex, intrinsically antithetical themes—that is, in dissecting these melodies and modifying and recombining the parts without making his technique look heavy-handed and extraneous. In any event, it is wrong to say that Mendelssohn simply filled in traditional symphonic form without tackling its

Fig. 34 Moritz von Schwind: *Die Symphonie* (detail), 1852. Beethoven's *Choral Fantasy,* Op. 80, for piano, chorus, and orchestra, formed an ideal motif for a fictitious suprahistorical symphony concert in that its unusual scoring allowed the performers to be placed in a decorative arrangement. In the background, beneath the bust of Beethoven, we recognize the conductor Franz Lachner; on the left, Schubert and the singer Vogl. (Munich, Bayerische Staatsgemäldesammlungen.)

problems. That Mendelssohn was able to solve the problem that brings this form to life, and to solve it so completely that we are hardly aware of its existence, should not blind us to the fact that its difficulties were virtually insurmountable and remained so for a full century. We need only recall what Schönberg called the "folkloristic symphonies," with their ill-conceived and unreconciled blend of national tunes and motivic manipulation, to appreciate how effortlessly Mendelssohn balanced the two in his Scottish Symphony.

We have seen how the problem of large-scale symphonic form lay in reconciling monumentality with subtlety of thematic elaboration. In the aesthetics of the nineteenth century, which took their bearings from Beethoven, not from Mendelssohn, the solution to this problem was to be found in the symphony. Beethoven's solution in the opening movements of his Fifth and Seventh Symphonies was to let the role of theme be taken by an ostinato rhythm whose prevalence conveyed an impression of sublime uniformity—also a feature of the "elevated style"—while allowing sufficient room for the melodic or "diastematic" elaboration without which the thematic process would soon come to a halt. Schumann, a confirmed "Beethovenian," unmistakably had this principle in mind when he tried, in the opening movement of his First Symphony (1841), to force the issue of large-scale symphonic form by clinging almost single-mindedly to a "thematic" rhythmic pattern. Unfortunately, whether accidentally or in a conscious effort to avoid epigonism, he transferred this principle to a lyric dimension that contradicts the original sense of this technique. Schumann's main motive, based on a line of verse ("Im Tale zieht der Frühling auf"), permeates virtually the entire movement; unlike Beethoven's similar motives, however, it remains fixed not only in rhythm but also in its sequence of pitches, apparently on the assumption that rhythm alone cannot do proper justice to the poetry of this romantically tinged line without the inflections of melody (Ex. 19). One wonders whether Schumann has deliberately translated into music the popular misconception that the initial, melodic version of the thematic rhythm in Beethoven's Fifth is its "theme." Deliberate or not, it is clear that both the lyric tone of Schumann's idea, which is more suitable to a character piece than to a symphony, and his lack of melodic variety work against the large-scale form he was seeking to create. The uniformity falls short of its vindicating sublimity, and the elaboration of the main motive lacks the sophistication and refinement necessary to save the thematic process from degenerating into mechanical development. Schumann himself seems to have sensed that his main motive, in its allegro form, was not going to manage its march to grandeur, and he tried to offset its shortcomings by prefacing the Allegro with an extended, solemn statement of the motive as a slow introduction, marked *andante un poco maestoso*. Then, in the recapitulation, the goal and culmination of the development section, he substituted this expanded version of the motive in place of the main theme, turning its reappearance into an apotheosis. By the same token, he softened the impression of empty, mechanical development—of uniformity without sublimity—by resorting to a formal idea taken from the first movement of Beethoven's Fourth Symphony (1806): the main motive appears as an accompanying melody to a cantilena (m. 150) that casts a poetic veil over the thematic process without rendering it inoperative. Taken by themselves, the conclusions that Schumann drew from his self-contradictory formal conception are thoroughly ingenious. Because it is the slow introductory version of the main theme that, as was mentioned above, appears in the recapitulation, Schumann can insert, in the middle of the development section, a false recapitulation in a remote key without courting the danger of tautology. This false recapitulation then becomes the goal of the first part of the development section (m. 178), just as the second part ends with the closing group of the exposition (m. 246). This closing group derives its rhythm from the main motive (Ex. 20). Having undergone endless sequences, the concluding group is

Example 19

Example 20

then appropriately omitted from the recapitulation and replaced by a *stretta* based on the main theme in its allegro form (m. 381), which, we may recall, is still available, having been suppressed at the opening of the recapitulation. Still, however shrewdly Schumann calculated the form of this movement, by substituting the motivic unity of the character piece for that of the Beethoven symphony he became embroiled in contradictions between lyricism and monumentality, contradictions that led not so much to a productive dialectic as to mutual paralysis of its various components.

Choral Music as a Form of Education

Of all the musical genres that brought forth any works of distinction at all, it is secular vocal music in the grand style whose future seems most in jeopardy. Vanished and nearly forgotten operas can sometimes be rescued in productions dictated by the rules of theater rather than written history. Moreover, their subsequent reception has in part been governed by the trivial fact that a visible opera plot is more readily grasped than an oratorio subject recounted in recitative or presupposed as general knowledge. Church music is sustained by institutions, provided that it fits into the liturgy, and texts such as the Mass and the Requiem belong to those linguistic creations that even a listener who cannot fully understand them accepts as a self-evident part of the culture in which he lives. Finally, simple songs have survived with no questions as to their age or provenance; any lines that may have become incomprehensible are simply ignored. Yet secular, nontheatrical vocal music in elevated style, from the late-sixteenth-century madrigal to the cantata of the seventeenth and the early eighteenth century to the secular oratorios and cantatas of the nineteenth, have always been preconditioned by notions of education, culture, and good breeding—in short, *Bildung*—that were neither as widespread and deeply engrained as the Christian tradition nor so amenable to vague appreciation, to ritualism rather than reflection. They were also supported by institutions—from the sixteenth- and seventeenth-century academies to the nineteenth-century oratorio societies—whose "lifespans" did not remotely approach those of ecclesiastical institutions. Since the history of institutions and education are intimately connected, and vocal music is less likely than instrumental music to survive transplantation to another social context, the decline of these institutions immediately affected their respective musical genres. (Vocal chamber music of the seventeenth century has fallen into oblivion, whereas its in no way aesthetically superior instrumental counterpart has been made available in countless editions.)

Fig. 35 Berlioz concert, 1846. This caricature, a Viennese copy with minor alterations of a drawing by Grandville, reflects the scornful Berlioz legend provoked by his "festival" of November 1, 1840 (comprising the *Requiem* and the *Grande symphonie funèbre et triomphale*), and propagated by the Parisian satirical press. The principal work on Berlioz's 1846 tour of Austria, the dramatic symphony *Roméo et Juliette*, is completely unsuited to the martial imagery employed by the German caricaturist on the example of his Parisian forebears. (Vienna, Österreichische Nationalbibliothek.)

To a large extent, if not exclusively, nineteenth-century secular vocal music in the elevated style, for chorus and orchestra with or without soloists, was sustained by amateur choirs. True, professional bodies, such as opera choruses (likewise made up in part by amateurs) or court chapels (who sang primarily in the church and only secondarily in the court opera), were willing to make use of the oratorio and cantata repertoires, but only on sporadic occasions; at all events, these groups were not indispensable to the genre. It was the choral societies, the *Singakademien* founded in the early nineteenth century in many cities following Fasch's Berlin prototype, and above all music festivals such as the Lower Rhine Festival (from 1817), that formed the institutional bedrock of the oratorio and the cantata.

Amateur choruses of the nineteenth century were divided clearly, if not rigorously, along social lines. Compositions for mixed chorus (with or without orchestra) and for men's chorus (without orchestra) were felt to be of different artistic stature, despite or even completely regardless of the existence of bad oratorios and good men's choruses. This reflects the social distinction made between a choral society (*Singakademie*) and a glee club (*Liederkranz*). (While it is true that Zelter's Berlin Liedertafel was originally, at the beginning of the century, intended to be an esoteric organization, the *Liedertafeln* as a whole were subject to interlocking artistic and social demands, and being men's choral groups they tended, socially and artistically, to the middle and lower stylistic rungs.) Even so, the thought that social status could be a decisive factor was studiously kept beyond the intellectual purlieus of the world of amateur choruses. These groups took their bearings on secondary rather than primary social criteria: the crucial factor was thought to be, not pedigree or property, but education; and though education was linked with pedigree and property, the link was incomplete and haphazard. (It was de rigueur in the nineteenth century to ignore the social preconditions of education, and remained so until the demise of the idealist legacy, which forbade equating education blatantly with social status.)

The educated classes extended from the lesser nobility—provided they had assimilated the spirit of the bourgeoisie—to academics and finally to those merchants who sat in offices rather than selling wares over a counter. One convention of this group was that the burgher put aside his inbred low opinion of the artist, and the artist his slowly emerging contempt for the burgher. Apparently this constellation was able to preserve its tight spiritual cohesion during the nineteenth century precisely because, as the events of 1848–49 showed, it was politically impotent. For the time being, it was spared the burdens of realpolitik, which would only have brought to light its conflicting interests rather than its common ideas. (As historians we have two options: either we conclude that, in the final analysis, it was social differences that placed the institutions of amateur choral singing and their resultant musical genres into opposing artistic realms, which had, at first, little basis in reality but which ultimately influenced compositional technique; or, alternatively, we can assume that ideas, rather than the interests behind them, left visible marks on the works.)

Any attempt to categorize the secular (or rather nonecclesiastical) vocal music of the nineteenth century into genres faces the difficulty that some of the criteria we proceed from are mutually contradictory. We cannot meaningfully call a genre part of music history until we have created a consistent and intelligible context for at least a few of the traits regarded in the nineteenth century as formative: subject matter and text, scoring and formal articulation, stylistic niveau and aesthetic character. Without this context, the genre is no more than a terminological mirage born of a compulsion to classify things *in abstracto*.

Like Handel's oratorios, the nineteenth-century oratorio, both sacred and secular, was concert music; there was no difference in function between the two. Sometimes style was affected by the choice of subject matter, an example being Mendelssohn's use, in *St. Paul,* of chorale melodies, which some critics regarded as out of place in the concert hall and hence as "lacking style." Nevertheless, it is doubtful whether distinctions of this sort justify dividing the oratorio into subspecies, particularly since the nineteenth century was fond of merging religious, ethical, patriotic, and historical categories, and it was precisely the blending of historical and sacred subjects, as illustrated by Georg Vierling's *Constantin* (1881) or Ludwig Meinardus's *Luther in Weimar* (1872), that was characteristic. True, it would not be absurd to divide the oratorio by choice of subject into, say, biblical, mythological, historical, and romantic oratorios; however, this would necessitate the further step of subdividing the romantic oratorio into medieval miracle plots (Liszt's *Die Legende der heiligen Elisabeth,* 1862), heroic romances (from passages of Ariosto's *Orlando furioso* or Tasso's *Gerusalemme liberata*), and exotic subjects (Schumann's *Das Paradies und die Peri,* 1841–43), thereby ultimately causing our classification scheme to disintegrate.

In the nineteenth century, the secular cantata was distinguished from the oratorio by its shorter duration, its less elevated style, and its tendency toward a lyric rather than an epic and dramatic character. However, the line between them was never hard and fast. Sometimes the collective term "cantata"—the definition of which nearly caused Heinrich Christoph Koch, in his *Musikalisches Lexikon* (1802), to throw up his hands in despair—was subdivided on the basis of the poetic form of its text. Hermann Kretzschmar, for instance, in his *Führer durch den Concertsaal* (1887–90), tried to distinguish the cantata from a genre which he called the choral ode and to which he assigned not only Beethoven's *Meeresstille und glückliche Fahrt* (after Goethe, 1814–15) and the Choral Fantasy, Op. 80 (1808), but also the large choral works of Brahms apart from the cantata *Rinaldo* of 1868—namely, the *Schicksalslied* (after Hölderlin, 1871), *Nänie* (after Schiller, 1881), *Gesang der Parzen* (after Goethe, 1882), and the *Triumphlied* (1871). Yet if we were to proceed systematically we would likewise have to distinguish the choral ode from a choral elegy such as *Nänie* and a choral hymn such as the *Triumphlied*. Altogether, literary classification schemes, including Kretzschmar's concept of the choral ode, offer a shaky foundation for classifying musical genres: first, because they in turn have historical subcategories (the Horatian Ode and the Pindaric Ode were distinct formal patterns in eighteenth- and nineteenth-century literature); second, because we would have a hard time trying to locate a continuous tradition that linked nineteenth-century choral odes and distinguished them from choral elegies. (There is no historical connection between Beethoven's *Meeresstille und glückliche Fahrt* and Félicien David's *Le désert* of 1844, which the composer himself called an *ode symphonique*.) Things begin to look different when we turn to the choral ballad, which, as practiced by Schumann and later by Max Bruch, established a tradition in which literary and musical elements combined to form a genre in the full sense of the word. In short, there is probably no avoiding the intellectually unsatisfactory but historically justified coexistence of a collective term, "secular cantata," and an independent subcategory denoting a clearly defined genre, "choral ballad."

Multimovement vocal works in the nineteenth century were unhesitatingly classified as cantatas whenever they included choral passages alternating with sections for solo voices. The genre of the text was considered secondary: no distinction was made between, for example, didactic lyricism, as exemplified by Romberg's setting of Schiller's *Die Glocke* (1808), and dramatic lyricism, such as Brahms's *Rinaldo* after Goethe. It was enough that the scoring matched the nineteenth-century notion of cantata, and that the work was not so short as to approach the lied or so long as to border on the oratorio. If the work called only for solo voices, or only for chorus, the nomenclature began to vacillate, and composers either did without a subtitle or chose a literary classification, which, as it turned out, had little effect in defining genre in nineteenth-century music.

The nineteenth century believed that there is a natural and self-evident connection between the length of a work and its stylistic niveau, and even if this connection fell into disrepute in the latter part of the century, being seen as a sign of philistinism, it was one of the criteria used to distinguish cantatas from oratorios. To put it simply, oratorio, cantata, and lied were thought to represent, in a sense adopted from literary theory, the high, middle, and low styles, just as Johannes Tinctoris had similarly maintained of the mass, motet, and chanson in the late fifteenth century. In Gustav Schilling's *Encyclopädie der gesamten musikalischen Wissenschaften* (1835–38) we read, in the entry "Cantata" by Gottfried Wilhelm Fink: "When the differences between the oratorio and the cantata came to be discussed, a special emphasis was placed on length and a more opulent style."

This theory of stylistic levels, derived from Antiquity, overlapped with an aesthetic of lyric, epic, and dramatic form whose basic tenets were formed in German classicism and romanticism. If music as a whole was considered lyric, attempts were nevertheless made to classify musical genres according to the varying proportion additionally taken up by the epic and the dramatic. The oratorio, it then followed, could be distinguished from the cantata by the fact that it throws greater emphasis on epic or dramatic traits. This classification was nevertheless ambiguous. On the one hand, it dealt with a tangible distinction, evident in the text, between narrative, plot, and contemplation—that is, whether events are depicted (epic), represented by dialogue (dramatic), or reflected by an outside observer (lyric). On the other hand, the terms referred to aesthetic qualities not clearly bound to modes of presentation: a narrative or a chorus reacting to external events may also take on a "dramatic" character, and contemplation, whether by soloists or the chorus, not infrequently alternates between a lyric and a didactic style. (In many aesthetic theories, didactic literature forms a fourth genre alongside the lyric, epic, and dramatic.)

The genres of nineteenth-century secular vocal music were so closely linked with the spirit and institutions of the public concert that a few changes in the inner constitution of concert life sufficed to cast the entire repertoire into oblivion, together with the ideas that sustained it.

We have already seen how the nineteenth century developed a religion of education and art, a religion that found architectural expression in a penchant for decking out concert halls with temple façades. However inclined we might be to reject this religion theologically, if we take it seriously from the point of view of history we will have to stop reproaching it for being a muddled, intellectually dishonest mixture of separate spheres. By judging the religion of education and art according to the criteria of twentieth-century dialectical theology, we block any chance of understanding an oratorio and cantata repertoire that merged history with religion, and vice versa, so as to have them culminate in art. Mendelssohn's *St. Paul* is chided with the argument that chorales are out of place in the concert hall; but this is unjust insofar as the nineteenth century saw the concert hall as a church, and the audience as a congregation, not merely in a metaphorical sense. Theologians may plead persuasively against this secularization of religion and the concomitant sanctification of the profane; as historians, however, we should be prepared to do justice to an age whose educated classes were firmly of the opinion that the substance of religion was sublated in art.

Besides being uncertain where to draw the line between sacred and secular, nonecclesiastical vocal music had other peculiarities which, in retrospect, make it difficult for us to understand it. These peculiarities are connected with the structure of concert life and the ideas that sustained it. It was a characteristic practice of the early nineteenth century to sandwich virtuoso concert pieces, arias, and entire scenes from operas and oratorios between symphonies or symphonic movements. However, it would be lopsided and unfair to dismiss this type of mixed program as a mere potpourri which later, in the second half of the century, gave way to three-part programs, composed of overture, concerto, and symphony and imbued with the spirit of education rather than mindless entertainment. Indeed, this mixture of vocal and instrumental music, of oratorio, opera, and symphony, may have expressed not merely a fondness for diversion but likewise an educational intent, one which drew, however, not on the metaphysic of absolute music but rather on the idea that music and literature merge. In the early nineteenth century, instrumental music, though no longer seen as a pale reflection of vocal music, was still placed in close proximity to vocal music, both aesthetically and hence institutionally: it was garnished with literary captions, mottos, or programs, whether in the score or in the listener's imagination, and placed alongside opera and oratorio scenes in the concert repertoire. The upshot of this practice of mixing vocal and instrumental pieces under the aegis of bourgeois education—and not simply of diversion—was works such as Mendelssohn's *Lobgesang* (1839–40) or Berlioz's *Roméo et Juliette* (1839), which straddled the symphony and the cantata, or incidental music intended primarily for the concert hall, such as the music Schumann wrote for Byron's *Manfred* (1852), or Mendelssohn for Racine's *Athalie* (1845). These works fall outside the classification system of musical genres, but their apparently hybrid form can be viewed as a "natural" consequence of the institutional and intellectual preconditions of concert life in the early nineteenth century.

Goethe's cantata texts *Die erste Walpurgisnacht,* which Mendelssohn set to music in 1831–32, and *Rinaldo,* set by Brahms in 1868, are poems that come close to music and yet preserve an ironic detachment from it. It is no easy matter to compose irony, and even though these texts appear superficially to be subjected to the strictures of music, it would seem that Goethe, who deliberately sought pride of place for poetry in the lied, and hence insisted on simple musical settings, likewise intended poetry to have the final word in the cantata.

Rinaldo is the more difficult of these two texts, and for that very reason the more suitable for revealing the peculiarities of the cantata as cultural and educational art. Goethe's text is literature at one remove: a poem about a poem, in which the original is not so much recast as given an added dimension. Goethe does not simply extract an episode from Tasso's *Gerusalemme liberata* in order to transform it into a cantata. Instead, he presupposes the audience's familiarity

Fig. 36 *Gesang der Geister über den Wassern.* Understandably, in order to capture Goethe's allegorical poem in an image at all the illustration clings to its title. The astonishing thing, however, is the figure of the bard, nowhere mentioned in the text, who evidently inspires the song. The artist seems to have taken Ossian, the mythical epic singer of the Celts, as the patron saint of romantic music. (Vienna, Gesellschaft der Musikfreunde.)

with the original and, in a manner of speaking, erects a lyric-dramatic poem on the foundation of Tasso's epic. At the same time this switch of literary genres inverts the psychology of the original by permitting its adaptation to musical forms. Herein, for Goethe, lay the attraction of his poem.

In Goethe's version, Rinaldo's departure from Armida is consigned to the past, a past that continues to haunt him; instead of epic immediacy, it is lyric recollection that sets the tone of the cantata. In recollection, however, Armida's magic, though dispelled in the epic, becomes virtually overwhelming. Goethe departs from Tasso by having Rinaldo escape from his ignoble liaison in utter despair ("to the quick destroy'd") after being freed by antimagic. A conflict then arises between him and the knights sent to fetch him back to his colors. This element of drama is not only a feature of the lyric-dramatic cantata as a genre but also the literary and psychological point of the work and the reason that Goethe wrote his poem in the first place. Rinaldo, now restored to heroism, is unable to return to his former self; it is his lapse into deceit and magic that has captured Goethe's sympathies. (As the ship disembarks Rinaldo joins the chorus in the lines "Das erfrischet, und verwischet das Vergangne," implying that the past has been obliterated from his memory. This adds an ambiguous note to the work's conclusion, a second ironic discontinuity as Rinaldo relativizes his feelings with sense impressions after already having relativized his heroism with feelings. Brahms evidently found this too contorted and marked Rinaldo's participation in the chorus *ad libitum*.)

Now, it is fully possible to view this scene simply as a dialogue between a chorus exhorting Rinaldo to his soldierly duties and a knight lamenting the magic of a lost moment. But only when we relate the cantata to the original epic from which it stands out in double discontinuity—as literature about literature —will we grasp its full essence, an essence whose psychological import is closely allied to the change in literary genre, to the introduction of lyrical and dramatic elements with an eye to musical form. We may find it hard to understand why a text that was intended for a musical setting should be made the scene of such literary convolutions, but this only underscores the degree to which the secular cantata as a genre had become bound up with cultural and educational presumptions. Not only was Brahms aware of the implications of Goethe's text, he also drew consequences from them for his music. Admittedly, though, these consequences are not easy to pinpoint. The aura of aria and cavatina in Rinaldo's music, in which Brahms reveals an untypical affinity for the Italian style, is strangely held in balance between gripping emotion and a gentle probing of generic limits, which, without blatantly violating Brahmsian good taste, was deliberately planned and calculated by the composer.

One extreme to which the conception of secular cantata as educational art could be driven is represented by Berlioz's *Lélio, ou Le retour à la vie* (1831). Berlioz intended his *monodrame lyrique* to be a sequel to the *Symphonie fantastique* and compiled it from unrelated pieces that he had composed between 1827 and 1830: *Le pêcheur*, a ballad after Goethe; a chorus of spirits taken from a *Cléopâtre* cantata and associated in *Lélio* with the appearance of the ghost in Shakespeare's *Hamlet*; a *Chanson de brigands,* which masks aesthetic rebellion as social rebellion; a *Chant du bonheur* from a cantata on the Orpheus legend; an orchestral sketch based on the Aeolian harp; and lastly a choral fantasy (with an Italian text) on Shakespeare's *The Tempest*. Taken together, they form a curious hodgepodge of movements with virtually no epic or dramatic logic to hold together the half-autobiographical (or pseudoautobiographical), half-philosophical musings of the Narrator, who has returned from the dream of *Symphonie fantastique* to a life consisting entirely of art. As absurd as this musical crazy quilt must seem to twentieth-century listeners, it was apparently not in the least puzzling to Parisian intellectuals of the time, who saw themselves reflected in a conception which, in retrospect, seems more like a private mythology. Recollections of Shakespeare and Goethe, of Byron (who introduced romantic brigandism to world literature) and Ossian (who inspired the image of "a lone Aeolian harp, suspended from the branches of an ancient oak beside a grave"), coalesce into a poetic vision whose internal coherence is as vague as the catchphrase "romantic" used around 1830 to describe it. In short, over and above the rambling and discursive poetic logic of the work, it is literary breeding—a factor that owes its internal cohesion to the "zeitgeist"—that forms the "cement" uniting the radically divergent movements of *Lélio*. These movements fall asunder the moment the educational preconditions that consolidated works of music in the 1830s begin to fade—namely, a knowledge of literature and an intuitive sense of homogeneity and coherence.

Nineteenth-century composers, then, whether Berlioz, Schumann, or Max Bruch, thought nothing of extracting episodes or scenes from world literature—from Homer's *Iliad* and *Odyssey*, Tasso's *Gerusalemme liberata*, or Goethe's *Faust*—and combining them to form cantata texts. In retrospect, this technique seems precarious, for it presupposes that the audience took pleasure in mentally supplying connections between the original poems. In the case of *Odysseus* (1873), a work that was equally successful in England and in Germany, the educational premises adopted by Max Bruch and his librettist Wilhelm Paul Graff evidently served to compensate for dramaturgical shortcomings that audiences either ignored or failed even to notice.

The cause of Odysseus's wanderings—Poseidon's anger—is never explained, as though it could be taken for granted that the educated audience for whom Bruch wrote his work would already be familiar with the story of the blinding of Polyphemus. The work is dedicated to the Bremen Singakademie, and if Bruch and Graff showed almost unlimited faith in the literary breeding of the choral societies, they also accommodated the wishes of these societies by selecting episodes from the *Odyssey* which are capable of being transformed, if violently at times, into choral scenes. In the oratorio, it is not Kalypso who is allowed to speak but the nymphs who sing her praises; the Hades scene focuses on the choruses of grieving children, maids, and youths, rather than on the prophesies of Tiresias and Odysseus's mother; even the depiction of the storm that casts Odysseus onto the shores of the Phaiakians is a choral fantasy in which it little matters that the chorus switches abruptly from the part of a Narrator recounting events from outside—though admittedly dramatizing them in the process—to the role of the Okeanides, who take part in the action. However threadbare the work may seem today, as a choral oratorio for the well-educated *Odysseus* remains an important document in cultural history. The gulf that separates the low opinion of the work in our century from the enthusiasm of the nineteenth is due less to a decline in our knowledge of Homer, thereby rendering the text incomprehensible, than to our reduced willingness to accept literary breeding as a substitute for dramaturgical logic.

Romanticism and *Biedermeier* Music

Biedermeier is a concept from cultural history which, when transferred to music history, at first brings to light more difficulties than insights. Nevertheless, it is by no means fruitless to try to continue this debate instead of abandoning it in fear of becoming mired in another conflict of labels. From a methodological standpoint, the efforts to define *Biedermeier* in musicohistorical terms simply form the other side of the question of what we mean by musical romanticism, a question which, after two centuries of use and abuse, is still not about to disappear.

In music history, it is obviously impossible to refer to the entire Restoration period from 1815 to 1848 as *Biedermeier,* as historians have attempted to do in German literature. Of course, we may find it tempting to view phenomena such as the convivial music-making of the Schubertiades, the tone of Mendelssohn's songs without words, or the introverted sentiment of Schumann's *Der Rose Pilger-fahrt* as expressions of the *Biedermeier* period. However, we have no cause to doubt the rightness of the term "romantic" that has been applied to Schubert and Weber, Schumann and Mendelssohn for a century and a half—or at least the term "classical romantic" (Schubert) or "romantic classicist" (Mendelssohn). The relation between romanticism and *Biedermeier* in music history will not be illuminated by applying that schema of successive historical styles which Ernst Bloch derided as "periods marching in single file."

On the other hand, it would be poor methodology to reserve the concept of musical *Biedermeier* as a portmanteau word for those composers whom we wish to exclude from a more rigorously defined concept of romanticism simply because they are of lesser stature than "genuine" romantics—that is, composers referred to by Walter Niemann as *Nebenromantiker,* or "subsidiary romantics," to show that despite their inferior stature they nevertheless belonged to the romantic period. Still, unless we wish to rob the category of its historical substance by reducing it to a mere label, there is no avoiding the difficulty that "romantic," like "classic," not only denotes a style but also functions as a mark of quality. As E. T. A. Hoffmann wrote in his review of Beethoven's Fifth Symphony: "Romantic taste is rare, romantic talent even more so. This explains why so few are capable of striking that lyre which opens up the wondrous portals of the Infinite." For Hoffmann, romanticism—the "pure expression of the inmost essence of art, found there and nowhere else"—is a recent evolutionary stage, one not attained until the instrumental music of the Viennese Classic period. (In Hoffmann's aesthetic nomenclature, the terms "classic" and "romantic," "exemplary" and "wondrous," are by no means mutually exclusive.) Like classicism, the concept of romanticism unites a notion from aesthetics (that romanticism manifests the true essence of art) with another from history (a stylistic period) and yet another from the philosophy of history (a point of culmination in the evolution of music). Descriptive and normative elements inextricably converge.

We involuntarily hesitate to classify Pleyel, Kozeluch, and Gyrowetz along-side Haydn and Mozart as Viennese Classic composers, even though they were active at the same time. This is because, like "romantic," the term "classic" in-cludes not only the notion of a stylistic period in which minor composers also took part, but also standards of quality which these minor composers never at-tained. Nevertheless, no one has yet proposed assigning a separate historical label to these "subsidiary classics" who, strictly speaking, were not "classic" at all. Thus, if we declare the "subsidiary romantics" of the Restoration period to be representatives of *Biedermeier* music, we must be in a position to show how, regardless of the quality of their music, their style differs from that of the "genuine romantics" and is not simply a lower rung of the same style. Alternatively, we have to demonstrate that *Biedermeier,* though not clearly distinguishable from a "romantic" style of composition, is nevertheless a tangible musicohistorical phenomenon that also played an important part in the history of composition. In other words, our arguments must prove that composers like Louis Spohr and Carl Loewe, Friedrich Schneider and Konradin Kreutzer, Robert Franz and Albert Lortzing, Friedrich von Flotow and Otto Nicolai, while having many features in common with the romantics, nevertheless merit more than the contemptuous tag "subsidiary romantics"; and that they deserve to be placed in a category of their own—the *Biedermeier*—in a way that does not apply to "subsidiary classics" such as Pleyel in relation to Haydn, or Peter von Winter in relation to Mozart.

Musical romanticism belongs to the history of composition *and* to the history of ideas. It was a holistic cultural phenomenon, which was formed almost as much by the aesthetic theories, or theoretical fragments, of Wackenroder and E. T. A. Hoffmann, who set the terms of discussion that an entire century used in order to capture musical impressions in words, as by the works of Schubert and Weber, works that gave "German lied" and "romantic opera" a historical impact whose traces have never fully disappeared from European musical awareness. This interaction between aesthetics and composition distinguishes romanticism fundamentally from Viennese classicism, which never brought forth an explicit aesthetic except in a few meager efforts, far away from Vienna, by Christian Gottfried Körner and Karl Philipp Moritz. (The aesthetic that was contemporary with the classical period was the romantic aesthetic.) Indeed, in Schumann's case, this interaction was so close that many contemporaries vacillated between calling him a journalist who wrote music and a composer who wrote journalism. On the other hand, the classical style was sustained by a virtually unbroken relationship to existing musical institutions. (The difficulties that Mozart encountered in the late 1780s were an isolated instance, and Beethoven's late works transcended the bounds of Viennese classicism, provided we understand this term to mean a historical "ideal type" and not simply the sum total of the works of Haydn, Mozart, and Beethoven.) In contrast, the relationship between musical romanticism and the institutions of musical culture was anything but straightforward and unproblematical, and it seems as though the pains which the romantics took to acquire an aesthetic, and to surround their music in a protective sheath of literature on music, simply mirrored the absence of a sufficient institutional bedrock.

The characteristic genres of romantic music—the lied, the lyric piano piece, and chamber music with piano—lagged behind the history of institutions and composition in that they had to produce the very institutions they required for their existence: the lieder recital, the piano recital, and the chamber music concert. This state of affairs is revealing of their ambiguous historical situation: music of quality (meaning romantic music), though it actually addressed a small circle of devotees, was forced by its technical difficulties to go outside the world of domestic music-making and into the bright glare of the public concert. This dilemma, neatly captured in the self-contradictory concept of a "public chamber music concert," has never been fully resolved. Even in our own century, music critics, particularly the serious ones, have paradoxically demanded of lied singers or pianists playing before audiences numbering in the hundreds, or even thousands, that they convey the aesthetic impression of performing in intimate private surroundings. Orchestral elements were no less to be shunned in "genuine" chamber music than was virtuoso display, even though the venue of the performance seemed to lend itself to precisely those features that aesthetic doctrine sought to keep at bay.

The alienation of the composer from his audience, the psychological impact of the complex relationship between romantic music and the conditions under which it was performed—these have been so emphatically and graphically described in literature, from Wackenroder's *Herzergießungen* (1797) to Thomas Mann's novel *Dr. Faustus* (1947), not to mention the mass of pulp literature and journalism, that any historian concerned with a just and balanced presentation feels compelled to offset them by making the gulf seem smaller in social reality than it appeared to be in an aesthetic theory now suspected of sentimentality and ideological bias. Doubtless, these corrective measures are necessary. Nevertheless, it is revealing that this legendary view of romanticism, with its mixture of fact and fiction, could arise at all in the nineteenth century. (Myths not only distort the intrinsic history of a subject, they also express and at times even make that history.) However little sociohistorical credence we need to pay to the doctrine of genius that continues to luxuriate in popular aesthetics, it would nonetheless be wrong to deny the existence of this perceived and therefore real sense of alienation.

We have seen how romanticism was marked by a troubled relationship between its most characteristic genres and the institutions of musical culture, and by hints of alienation between the composer and his audience as a whole. *Biedermeier,* on the other hand, can be seen as the very quintessence of a successful mediation—the last in music history, it would seem—between the history of composition and the history of institutions. Unlike romanticism, *Biedermeier* left little imprint on the history of ideas—the nearest candidate for a *Biedermeier* aesthetic would be Ferdinand Hand's *Aesthetik der Tonkunst* (1837–41)—but it was firmly anchored in the system of choral societies, *Liedertafeln,* and musical festivals. (It is no coincidence that a romantic composer like Schumann, by adapting to existing institutions in his oratorios, strayed dangerously close to the *Biedermeier.*) In sum, our methodological justification for distinguishing musical romanticism from the exactly contemporary *Biedermeier* music, rather than dispensing with it as "subsidiary romanticism," lies in the fact that, while both are part of the history of composition, musical romanticism is also definable primarily in terms of intellectual history, and *Biedermier* music in terms of the history of institutions. In the Restoration period, the "romantic" system of ideas parted

ways with the "nonromantic" system of institutions: the institutions were not vehicles for the dominant ideas, which thus inclined toward the esoteric, nor were the ideas a function of existing institutions, in which bourgeois society merely sought a musical mirror-image of itself.

Still, the musical societies and *Liedertafeln,* the choral groups and musical festivals of the Restoration period, cannot simply be labeled *Biedermeier* without further ado. The choral societies, or *Singakademien,* of Berlin, Leipzig, and Dresden all antedate the "epochal" year 1814, and the musical festivals, formed mainly for the performance of Handel's oratorios, drew on the model of London's "Handel Commemorations" around 1780. Moreover, the institutions of the Restoration period survived the year 1848 apparently unscathed. However, what characterized the *Biedermeier* period was the rapid spread of musical societies and the specifically and narrowly bourgeois nature of its system of institutions: it was primarily bourgeois societies, and not, as in our century, commercial agencies and state or public authorities, which—alongside that relic from the past, the court theater—sustained German musical culture during the Restoration period.

To be sure, composers were no longer dependent on patrons whose social and economic position enabled them to exercise an influence on the music. But neither were they yet confronted exclusively by an anonymous public which could be calculated "statistically" by applause or ticket sales or could have its reactions "translated" by the press into public opinion. On the contrary, the bourgeois institutions of the Restoration period still stood largely under the influence of local dignitaries and formed a historical link between the culture of the nobility (which sustained composers as recent as Beethoven, at least in the early decades of his career) and modern mass culture.

There is no question that the bourgeois system of musical societies both antedated and outlived the Restoration period: it arose under the aegis of the culture of the nobility and is still widespread in our century. But from the point of view of music history, it was only representative, in the narrow sense of the term, during the *Biedermeier* period. Compositionally, it set guidelines for works such as the oratorios of Spohr and Schneider, Loewe and Mendelssohn, who sought to mediate between technical simplicity and a high level of cultural breed-

Figs. 37 and 38   Leopold Kupelwieser: *Die Schubertianer auf dem Ausflug nach und in Atzenbrugg,* 1821. The Schubertiades, one of the earliest forms of musical bohemia, were by no means limited to drawing-room concerts but treated music as part of a convivial culture which included the *Biedermeier* fashion for *tableaux vivants.* The charade (*bottom*) observed by Schubert, who seems to have just interrupted his playing, represents the Garden of Eden: the serpent (Schober) twists around the tree of knowledge (Kupelwieser) while Adam (Jenger) receives the apple; a cherub raises a fiery sword, and Jehovah (Vogl) reigns above the scene. (Berlin, Staatsbibliothek Preußischer Kulturbesitz.)

ing. Socially, it served as a vehicle for a music culture of distinction, alongside the court theater and the virtuoso concert. Finally, from the point of view of intellectual history, it expressed in institutional form some of the predominant tendencies of the age, particularly patriotic republicanism, which flourished in cultural societies because it was forbidden to take the form of political parties.

The *Biedermeier* musical society was characterized by an intermingling of convivial culture, educational function, and bourgeois self-display. Conviviality was not kept separate and distinct from music, either as an adjunct or as its (tacit or confessed) principal function; on the contrary, it even held sway in the musical institutions themselves, whether openly in men's choral groups or less so in the "grand concert" (which had not yet reached the stage of a modern symphony concert). The mixed programs of these concerts, cobbled together from symphony movements, opera fragments, and virtuoso or sentimental solo pieces, predominated roughly until mid-century, revealing that education and entertainment had not yet become separate functions.

The element of self-display is unmistakable, if unobtrusive, in the musical culture of the Berlin grand bourgeoisie, or "middle-class aristocracy," which arranged private concerts such as the Sunday performances at the Mendelssohn home. For one happy moment in its history, the bourgeoisie apparently succeeded in maintaining a delicate balance between education as conviviality, conviviality as self-display, and self-display as sustained in turn by education.

A different but no less characteristic type of self-display was revealed in large music festivals, particularly by the Lower Rhine Festival, from 1817. In the minds of listeners and performers alike, the main pillars of these festivals—Handel's oratorios and Beethoven's symphonies—served the twin functions of communicating a different notion of the dignity and spiritual eminence of music from that expressed in Kant's scornful dictum "more delectation than culture," and of capturing in music a sense of solidarity which the German bourgeoisie of the Restoration period was otherwise forbidden to express in public.

From mid-century this combination of conviviality, education, and bourgeois self-display gradually began to wither as conviviality in the choral societies took a turn toward the trivial (dwindling enthusiasm for education), local dignitaries withdrew from music societies and the political element receded in importance (loss of ostentation and self-display), and concert audiences were transformed into an anonymous cosmopolitan public (decay of conviviality). Private and public music culture no longer overlapped as in the *Biedermeier* period but began more and more clearly to occupy separate realms.

We have seen how the intermingling of bourgeois self-display, conviviality, and educational zeal that characterized *Biedermeier* music life, giving it a specific aura of closeness and *Gemütlichkeit,* proved to be primarily a phenomenon in the history of musical institutions. However, *Biedermeier* would not merit the status of a musicohistorical category at all if it did not also have tangible repercussions for the history of composition. Even if there is no such thing as a *Biedermeier* "style," meaning a congery of features uniting Loewe with Spohr and Lortzing and distinguishing all three from Schumann, many works unmistakably strike a *Biedermeier* "tone," namely, those in which the "zeitgeist" comes particularly to the fore.

The most influential edition of Loewe's ballads ignores chronological order and opus number by opening with the ballad *Heinrich der Vogler* (1836). Obviously, Max Friedländer, the editor, saw in this work the combination of popularity and self-display which readers would expect of an opening piece. As a genre, the lyric poem is not actually directed at a body of listeners, even if its musical setting admits an audience. A ballad, on the other hand, is a narrative song that originates in, and furthers the cause of, conviviality. Moreover, the easy-going narrative tone of Loewe's piece, marked *andante commodo* and recalling singspiel, is fully in keeping with the tone of a ballad. (It narrows our notion of the ballad as a genre to derive its character exclusively, as is often done, from Herder's *Edward.*) This tone likewise provides a suitable musical rendering of the contents of the poem, in which reminiscences of a historical and patriotic slant are tinged with moods current at the time, moods that invite us to speak of a "pre-1848 political frame of mind." Henry the Fowler, as surprised as he is humbled by his nomination as German King, is nothing but a nineteenth-century daydream, projected into the Middle Ages, of a "bourgeois king" who both rules protectively over his subjects and nevertheless remains one of their number.

For all its simplicity, Loewe's setting of the ballad is anything but artless. In the Allegro section that follows the Andante Commodo, the otherwise rigidly four-square rhythm—the metrical correlate to the "noble simplicity" of the narrative tone—is broken and then immediately reconstituted at the words "Was sprengt denn dort herauf für eine Reiterschar?" ("What knightly host comes galloping at full charge?") (Ex. 21). The vocal line is telescoped from four measures to three, an expression of breathless haste equally as illustrative as the "charge" depicted by the varied imitation of measures 2 and 3 in the piano part. By a double deviation of compression and extension, the norm is reconstituted: in the end, the tone-painting caused by breaking the metrical pattern leads to the restitution of the pattern. Artifice is reintegrated into simplicity without being nullified in the process. Loewe escapes the simple-minded, ingratiating triviality that would have placed his song outside the nineteenth-century conception of art, but not for a moment does he leave the realm of the immediately intelligible. Educated music-lovers demanded of compositional sophistication that it be interpretable as a key to the work's expression, and Loewe has met these demands without sacrificing that convivial singspiel tone which, from the eighteenth century, had been the musical hearth and home of the German bourgeoisie.

Example 21

At the end of the ballad, the narrative melodic style is elevated to the realm of the church hymn (Ex. 22). Thus, in addition to the need for conviviality and education, appropriate musical expression is likewise given to bourgeois self-display, as provided in the text by superimposing current political sentiments onto historical and patriotic reminiscences. In a word, all the elements that make up *Biedermeier* music from an institutional standpoint are present in embryo in the compositional technique and aesthetic of Loewe's ballad.

Du gabst mir ei - nen gu - ten Fang. Herr Gott, wie dir's ge - fällt.

Example 22

Although it was never Lortzing's most popular comic opera, critics have always considered *Der Wildschütz* (1842) his most successful. Here the composer pillories the educational zeal of the epigonal, postclassical era in the form of a Countess who is constantly spouting malaprop quotations from Sophocles. Nonetheless, his parody remains "thoughtful" rather than malicious and is thus simply another way of partaking of a "zeitgeist" that characteristically outdid itself by turning education into a "religion."

A note of conviviality is apparent not only in the tunefulness that reigns over large sections of Lortzing's work, evidently with the intention of drawing the audience into the circle of like-minded protagonists on stage, but also in its formal design, dominated as it is by ensemble numbers—quartets, quintets, and sextets. We can even detect a bit of bourgeois self-display in this work, even if strangely fractured. The libretto, as is typical of the "bourgeois" singspiel tradition, is peopled with counts and countesses, barons and baronesses, with clear overtones of absolutist grandeur, whereas the middle-class characters merely staff the burlesque scenes. Yet this is just as typical of the social character of this genre as are the musical inflections used by Lortzing to implement his dramaturgy. From a simple reading of the text, we might conclude that the middle-class characters—the *parti buffe*—were being viewed from a perspective that exposed them to the laughter of the aristocrats—the *parti serie*. This would be thoroughly in keeping with the time-honored rules of social standing and levels of style. However, the folksy singspiel tone adopted by Lortzing even for his noble characters shows that aristocrats, from the moment they slip into an amorous intrigue, react in the same manner as the bourgeoisie. The music, then, breaks the rules of social standing which the libretto takes as its starting point. This very feature turns the dramaturgy of the piece into an expression of an age in which the bourgeoisie was coming to terms with the supremacy of the nobility by descrying common human traits at every turn—traits that were, however, in fact merely utopian generalizations of the bourgeois spirit.

Fig. 39 Moritz von Schwind: *Ständchen,* 1862. Schubert's male choruses, later one of the pillars of the *Liedertafel* and *Liederkranz* repertoire, were originally intended for solo quartet. Here Schubert himself and three friends (Lachner, Schwind, and Vogl), seconded by allegorical birdsong, present a musical serenade, disporting themselves like "children of nature" and revealing, with a touch of self-irony, how close the romanticism of the 1820s stood to *Biedermeier* the moment its esoteric music culture took on convivial trappings. (Vienna, Museen der Stadt.)

Of course, we must concede a certain degree of aesthetic and social raison d'être to musical works of lesser quality, but the exact degree varies in different ages and genres. The early nineteenth century was a time of ambiguity, as can be seen in the parallel existence of romantic and *Biedermeier* music, and it was still possible, though not for long, for a piece of music that laid little or no claims to originality to nevertheless claim status as a work of art.

When critics called Mahler's symphonies *Kapellmeistermusik* they used the word as a reproach to denigrate his music—whether justifiably, as was thought at first, or unjustifiably, as we have recognized in the meantime. To say the same thing of Spohr's music is to express a perfectly accurate assessment, which is in no way intended to disparage his music, at least on the part of historians. *Kapellmeistermusik,* a category that also encompassed Wagner's operas up to and including *Rienzi* (1842), was still an aesthetically legitimate genre in the early nineteenth century—not as commonplace as in the eighteenth century nor as unthinkable as in the twentieth.

The key feature of this genre is its eclecticism, an eclecticism that provokes our distrust precisely because of the perfection that it not infrequently attains. However, it is difficult to account for this distrust. In Spohr's Nonet, Op. 31 (1813), one of the composer's most successful works, the music strikes a divertimento tone prompted by its setting for five winds and four strings. On the other hand, the thematic and motivic manipulation is driven to such extremes—a single four-note motive permeates not only the Allegro but also the Adagio in a profusion of sequences, diminutions, and variants—that the work almost appears to be a schoolbook exercise in learned compositional devices. Consequently, we have as much call to speak of a "refinement" of the divertimento tradition as of a "decline" in a sense of style capable of distinguishing between techniques appropriate to the string quartet. Still, anyone who adopts this critical stance must try to show how Spohr's eclecticism, allegedly a shortcoming of his music, differs in kind from the "stylistic synthesis" that gave rise to the string quartets of Haydn.

Spohr's chromaticism is less well integrated into the formal design and more limited to local effects than Schubert's. All the same, it is unfair to treat Spohr as a Mozart epigone who discovered his "own style"—which more often than not turned into a mere "manner"—in a penchant for excessive chromaticism. This opinion contains an accusation of self-contradiction that applies least of all to Spohr. Spohr was a composer who practiced in his music what is generally considered a virtue in the world of ethics: evenhanded justice. His eclecticism ranged effortlessly and successfully from a Schumann-like romanticism (first movement of his Septet in A minor, Op. 147) to the *Biedermeier* inflections of a Friedrich Silcher (horn melody in the Larghetto of the same piece). And anyone who wishes to prove that his eclecticism is aesthetically ill-grounded and flawed will have little luck demonstrating that Spohr failed in his "synthesis," but will have to argue that he should never have attempted it in the first place.

Church Music and Bourgeois Spirit

The nineteenth century was less an age of church music than one of literature about church music, and the decline and regeneration of church music was a constant topic of discussion. Now, whenever this topic is discussed the arguments turn clumsily on a grouping of elements which, though connected, are sometimes linked so loosely that the degree of convergence or divergence between them can distinguish one age from another. The soundness or the frailty of the institutions that sustain church music may well be directly related to the presence or absence of religious sentiment behind this music; it may also be directly related to the degree to which composers accept or reject liturgical convention, although we can easily imagine strong religious ideals in an age of liturgical weakness. However, there is virtually no relation, at least in the nineteenth century, between the properties that made church music successful qua church music and the aesthetic stature it attained in its greatest or most representative works, or its role in the evolution of composition. It is one of the basic facts of this age that the aesthetic and liturgical aspects of church music were two separate issues, and any historian who aspires to be more than a mere archivist must try to explain this fact. Histories, whether Catholic or Protestant, that treat church music in isolation describe in great detail the destruction and rebuilding of its institutions, but these processes apparently have nothing to do with the creation of works that belong to music history in the strong sense of the term. A deep gulf separates general music histories, which habitually ignore such topics as the church hymn, the liturgy, and the restoration of choral music, and the specialist, hermetic, historical studies of church music which tend for their part to exclude from consideration the most significant works of the age because, although religiously inspired, they have become less at home in the church than in the concert hall. (What "church" means in the first place is left undiscussed as though there were no cause for disagreement.)

Any attempt to explain, in profane historical terms, the contradictions that rent church music in the nineteenth century will have to proceed from a trivial fact whose significance for music history has nevertheless passed more or less unnoticed—namely, that the period from the French Revolution to the First World War was a bourgeois age. However impossible it may be to characterize the church—the Catholic more so than the Protestant—as a bourgeois institution, the principles that undergirded the composition and reception of church music were formatively influenced by a bourgeois spirit so taken for granted at the time that it was not even recognized as bourgeois.

The central concept of the bourgeois attitude that took root in church music from the middle of the eighteenth century was "edification." Instead of being justified as singing God's praises, as was hitherto the case, church music was related primarily to the congregation with the object of instilling devotion. For the purposes of singing God's praises, church music had to meet only one stipulation: the musical offering had to be worthy of the recipient. As a means of kindling devout sentiments, whether humble or uplifting, church music had to take into account those members of the congregation with a limited understanding of music. To do so, church music of the edifying sort appropriated the aesthetic ideas of classicism (likewise an offshoot of the bourgeois spirit) which Winckelmann had formulated as "noble simplicity and silent grandeur." The musical pattern taken as the ideal of this edifying and classical brand of church music was a chordal setting of muted pathos above which hovered a melody vacillating between church hymn and sentimental song but always riding shy of exaltation. The principle of "noble simplicity," originally a vehicle for anti-Baroque and anticourt sentiments whose musical culmination was seen in Graun's *Der Tod Jesu* (1755), was by no means limited to the century from which it derived. Indeed, after joining forces with the romantic Palestrina renaissance, which added a touch of modality to the chordal settings, or being transferred to the *Biedermeier* tone, thereby altering its melody, it dominated the "middle style" of church music for the entire nineteenth century.

In Protestant states such as Prussia, Saxony and Württemberg, the bourgeois neo-humanist movements of the eighteenth and nineteenth centuries caused profound changes in the system of education, destroying in the process the institutional foundations that had sustained church music from the middle

Fig. 40   Carl Julius Milde: *Das erste Norddeutsche Musikfest in der Lübecker Marienkirche,* 1839. Protestant north Germany was no different from the Catholic south in considering the Palestrina style, along with the monumentality of Handel's oratorios, to be the quintessence of "genuine church music." The reason that the Handel style took hold, while the highly ramified counterpoint of Bach's cantatas did not, would seem in no small measure to reside in the spatial acoustics of the churches where this music was performed, acoustics which favored a spare, clear-cut style over refinement and sophistication. (Lübeck, Museum für Kunst und Kulturgeschichte.)

of the sixteenth century. The Gymnasium, which took the place of the Latin grammar school, was kept separate from the church; music was suppressed from the central position it had occupied for centuries in the grammar school curriculum; the cantor, a mediator between church and school and, within the school, between music and language instruction, lost his former function; and the musical offices provided at church by the Latin scholars—the *alumni*—were considered burdensome and time-consuming and were ultimately abandoned. (The Thomasschule in Leipzig and the Kreuzschule in Dresden remained as relics of the Latin grammar school of the type originally conceived by Melanchthon.)

The institutions of church music, then, declined as a result of a notion of education that enabled the politically impotent German burgher of the eighteenth and nineteenth centuries to cast an image of himself as a spiritual and intellectual being. These institutions were then rebuilt *ex nihilo* by elevating the status of the organist (a process that only began around 1900) and establishing church choirs, which were not only patterned after bourgeois oratorio societies but were frequently little more than oratorio societies in everything but name. (Nonetheless, with nineteenth-century notions of religion as our starting point, we might question the view that the church concert was nothing more than a concert housed in a church, as strict adherents of liturgy contend.)

The nineteenth century witnessed a revival of church music in the Palestrina renaissance (shared by Protestants and Catholics alike), the restoration of the chorale (whether Gregorian or Lutheran), the Protestant Awakening (with Prussian Agenda), and, on the Catholic side, the Cecilian movement, of which we should stress not the weakness of its music but rather its flair for organization. In all respects, this revival represented a return to "established truths" in which refuge was sought from the unwonted strangeness of the present.

This development is praised for restoring church music following a period of decline; however, it is equally suspected of being archaistic, of trying to breathe a "second life" into dead issues. A curiously ambiguous role was played by historical awareness, one of the century's most fundamental modes of bourgeois thought (bourgeois in that historicism stands in opposition to aristocratic traditionalism.). On the one hand, the Gregorian or Lutheran chorale could never have been restored, nor the works of Palestrina, Bach, and Schütz edited, without the philological methods of history worked out for the study of Antiquity. To a certain extent, the restoration was prevented by the rigors of historical method from becoming a style of its own, as it undoubtedly would have become in an earlier century for all its valiant efforts at "pure reconstruction." On the other hand, historical awareness left this reconstruction with a bad conscience: unlike other forms of historical memory, historicism of the nineteenth-century sort resides in an awareness that the final arbiter of history is not an extratemporal norm but the "spirit of one's own age," the "state of historical evolution." (It is possible to resuscitate a dead norm, but only at the price of the historical "authenticity" that a norm enjoys when it is in harmony with a progressive "zeitgeist.") The restoration of church music is beholden to historicism for the fact that it could take place at all, rather than becoming an amalgam of old and new. But that same historicism also cost the restoration its legitimacy.

The most effective part of Justus Thibaut's book *Über Reinheit der Tonkunst* (1825) was its title, but it gave the age a catchphrase for what it was looking for in church music. The concept of "pure" composition combined the notion of strict counterpoint and a cappella style, unsullied by instruments, with a sense of moral integrity and religious exaltation beyond the world of the profane. So closely were these thoughts united that we can understand how Raphael Kiesewetter, an otherwise eminently sober historian, could venture his notorious and risible dictum on the "moral impossibility" of parallel organum. The true, "holy" art of church music presupposes, according to Thibaut, "a deep, calm, introspective and pure cast of mind." It is music that encapsulates itself from the outside world.

This view clearly reflects the inspiration of Wackenroder's aesthetic and religious ideas, or at least the mood that underlay these ideas. Nevertheless, there is reason to doubt whether the romantic tinge to Thibaut's restoration represents its crucial element from the standpoint of history. For one, the Palestrina renaissance, with its enthusiasm for a "seraphic tone" in church music, is intimately connected with the ideas of "noble simplicity" and "edification" which historians studiously attribute to the Enlightenment. Furthermore, the romantic spirit, as we can see in Berlioz, was capable of producing church music exactly opposite in character, a music which, as Liszt put it, "unites theater and church in colossal proportions." Last, when historicism became productive toward the end of the nineteenth century (in the Cecilian compositions of Michael Haller), its underlying spirit was less romanticism than positivism: historicism is merely positivism as applied to history.

Thus, to apply the labels of cultural history to music is to obscure the continuity of its evolution from the Enlightenment to romanticism and finally to positivism. This makes it tempting to replace or supplement these labels with an interpretation starting from the premise that the age as a whole was bourgeois in character. The sociopsychological roots of an ideal of church music as an escape from the world can be seen in the bourgeois tendency to separate these two spheres and consign religion to a ghetto, thereby protecting it from "reality" and at the same time preventing it from interfering in that reality. In the nineteenth century, bourgeois religion was a religion of the inner psyche; hence, for music to prove its worth as church music it had to be "calm and introspective."

So firmly engrained was the notion of "noble simplicity" that cast the Palestrina style, along with edifying and tuneful chordal settings, as "true church music," that Protestant church music at first remained completely untouched by the enthusiasm that greeted the discovery in 1829 of Bach's *St. Matthew Passion,* an enthusiasm of a religious and patriotic character which invites us to compare the Bach renaissance to the completion of Cologne Cathedral. If the hall of the Berlin Singakademie, where Mendelssohn performed the *St. Matthew Passion,* seemed much like a church to an audience that felt much like a congregation, Carl von Winterfeld continued to imagine true Protestant church music solely in the "seraphic" Palestrina tone and found the "German Palestrina" in a second- or third-rate composer by the name of Johann Eccard. The calmness that the nineteenth century sought in church music was to be found not in the Bach style—a style that served as the target of the anti-Baroque, "noble simplicity" faction in its own time—but in the Palestrina style. Instead of singing Bach cantatas in church services, the nineteenth century equipped Palestrina and Lasso motets with German texts to make them acceptable to Protestant ears.

Toward the end of the century, Philipp Spitta, in his *Die Wiederbelebung protestantischer Kirchenmusik auf geschichtlicher Grundlage* (1882), advanced the thesis that Bach's chorale settings, organ chorales, and cantatas represented true Protestant church music. But he grounded his argument, without being aware of it, on an idea drawn not from the liturgy but from aesthetics—namely, musical classicism, an idea that had undergirded the musical culture of the educated classes ever since the crystallization of the concert and opera repertoire around mid-century. Bach became the *classicus auctor* of Protestant church music, a genre whose style he represented just as firmly as Palestrina represented Catholic church music, Handel the oratorio, and Beethoven the symphony. It was not by coincidence that Brahms drew on Palestrina for his Latin motets (Op. 37) and on Bach for his German motets (Op. 29); on the contrary, this expressed an awareness of the fact that a classical style worthy of emulation was not a universal style, but rather a conglomerate of different styles established for particular genres by "exemplary authors" from different periods. Nonetheless, the attempt to rescue Bach's cantatas for the liturgy failed; they remained in the church concert. And Rochus von Liliencron, the most influential liturgical specialist around the turn of the century, returned to Winterfeld's Palestrina ideal.

If, then, the nineteenth century consigned ecclesiastical matters to a circumscribed area resembling a nature reserve, it also extended immeasurably the category of the religious by proclaiming separate religions of art, culture, sentiment, and nature. However narrow the concept of "true church music," despite Spitta's objections, the ideas associated with religious music were all the more far-flung. In E. T. A. Hoffmann's essay "Alte und neue Kirchenmusik" (1814), the "holy art of music" that reigned supreme between Palestrina and Handel is treated as irretrievably lost. His adulation of Palestrina, though heartfelt, is not an open invitation to copy the Palestrina style, as was attempted later in the century by Eduard Grell and Michael Haller. Instead, Hoffmann realized that any attempt to reconstitute this music "from within" in a fundamentally non-Christian age would be doomed to failure:

> It is beyond peradventure a sheer impossibility for a composer of our day to write in the manner of Palestrina, Leo, and later Handel, among others. That age, when Christianity still shone in full glory, seems forever to have vanished from the earth, and with it the sacred ordination of the artist.

Still, if true church music belongs to a lost age, Hoffmann finds metaphysical substance—and for him that meant religious substance—in modern instrumental music, namely, in the Beethoven symphony, which speaks in notes of the "marvels of a distant realm":

> And yet, it is certain that a composer of today will take music to his heart only in the adornments of its present-day abundant richness and wealth. The splendor of its multifarious instruments, many of which resound so nobly in the high vaultings [of churches], abounds everywhere: and why should one shut one's eyes to the fact that it is the ever-drifting World Spirit itself that has cast this splendor onto the secret and magical art of our most recent age, an age whose aim is inner spiritualization?

Palestrina's "holy art of music" and Beethoven's "metaphysical" symphonies, then, are musical expressions of various stages in the evolution of a "World Spirit." Hoffmann, like Hegel, has conceived of this spirit in categories that merge historiology and the philosophy of religion: the "glory of Christianity" has given way to vague "previsions of the Infinite." However, we would misconstrue Hoffmann if we viewed this romantic form of religious expression as nothing but a deficient mode of the Christian faith. Indeed, granted the existence of a "religion of art," even Beethoven's symphonies become "religious" music, since

Fig. 41 Johan Christian Berger: *Jenny Lind bei einem Kirchenkonzert in Stockholm,* 1850. Always averse to the spectacular, Jenny Lind withdrew from the stage in 1849 at the age of twenty-nine to devote herself exclusively to concert appearances. On June 25, 1850, having been showered with official honors in Stockholm, she gave a farewell concert in the Church of St. Clara, singing "Then shall the righteous shine forth as the sun" from Mendelssohn's *Elijah.* It is the imagery of the oratorio text, not the concert itself, which the artist has attempted to capture in his drawing. (Stockholm, Musikmuseet.)

they represent an evolutionary stage at which the "ever-drifting World Spirit" has transmuted clearly defined Christian beliefs into previsions of the "marvels of a distant realm."

We have seen how Ludwig Tieck, with an exuberance that we should neither take literally nor dismiss as empty hyperbole, could refer to the symphony as "surely the final mystery of faith," as "mysticism, religion revealed." Faced with these claims, and with the fact that a composer of Protestant background, such as Robert Schumann, could write a Requiem for the concert hall as though the liturgical text were merely an elegiac poem, we might be tempted to speak of a confusion of concepts and emotions, of a secularization of the religious and a sanctification of the profane. Yet, by nineteenth-century criteria, it was virtually impossible to tell whether a composer of a concert mass had turned the concert hall into a church or the mass into a concert piece.

Brahms's *German Requiem* (1868) was one of those works in which the nineteenth century recognized its own identity. Here Brahms set out deliberately to attain what Schumann, it would seem, had previously reached by naiveté. In selecting his biblical passages, Brahms seems to have disregarded not only the liturgy but also the specifically Christian character of the occasion. This is not merely a sign of the composer's individual conception of religion—one in which a forlorn hope is made to substitute for faith—but also, it would seem, a conscious enactment of a process that had already taken place long before in the concert mass without creating a clear break in the history of nonecclesiastical sacred music. Namely, the articles of faith, rather than being captured in works of music, instead dissolved into a vague, if strong, feeling referred to by Schleiermacher, the most influential theologian of the nineteenth century, as the "feeling of utter and prostrate dependence."

If, then, religious music for the concert hall remained resolutely nonsectarian, it nevertheless was "confessional" music in the strong, subjective sense of the term. As long as ecclesiastical propriety could be taken for granted, it was possible for church music to be written with no questions asked about the composer's religious attitudes. However, in an age when ecclesiastical propriety was disintegrating and coming under pressure from an aesthetic that defined musical authenticity in terms of originality, sacred music required a subjective legitimation lest it raise suspicions of being "inauthentic." Thus, even in a work like the *German Requiem*, a note of individual confession is just as evident at the words "For here we have no continuing city" as in the sentiment of the soprano solo with choral accompaniment at "So will I comfort you"—a sentiment rescued aesthetically by the artifice of a canon in diminution.

Admittedly, this subjective slant in nineteenth-century religious music stands in curious contrast to the tendency at the time to regiment the Protestant service more strictly than even Luther himself had deemed necessary. Liturgical rigidity and extraecclesiastical subjectivity seemingly contradict each other. Both, however, can be viewed as characteristic traits of a bourgeois age in which religion became a "private affair" while the church was integrated into a system of state and societal administration based on the civil service. Apparently it was felt that the "liberty" of the Protestant church service, now being restricted, could only have emerged as an expression of a strong sense of community, of which little more than the institutional skeleton survived into the nineteenth century.

On the Catholic side, there also existed large-scale church music that made full use of the instrumental splendor forbidden by the Palestrina style. But apart from Bruckner's masses, these were invariably "occasional" pieces, written to celebrate events which encouraged a return to the Baroque view that no musical resources were too extravagant for the praise of God, even if praising God also meant praising the ruler who commissioned the work. Cherubini composed his C-minor Requiem (1816) for the funeral service in memory of Louis XVI in Saint Denis, Beethoven his *Missa solemnis* (1824) for the ascent of Archduke Rudolph to the archbishopric of Olmütz, Berlioz his *Grande messe des morts* (1837) for the burial of General Damremont in the Invalides, and Liszt a *Missa solemnis* (1856) to consecrate the cathedral in Gran, not to mention his *Hungarian Coronation Mass* (1867).

This is not to say that large-scale works of this sort, which tend to stand more outside than within the history of nineteenth-century church music, were "Baroque" in terms of their compositional techniques. Nevertheless, they drew on a notion of church music transplanted from an earlier period into an age whose liturgical church music was, in essence, governed by the bourgeois categories of edification and noble simplicity. Still, the royalist associations of the ceremonial mass could be transformed to republican purposes, as is exemplified by Berlioz's Requiem and by Verdi's, written to the memory of Alessandro Manzoni. Here the third estate used a special, uplifting occasion to adopt a form of display which it otherwise suspected of being mere posturing on the part of the first estate. It might even be argued that the idea of consecrating an uplifting event— an institutional prerequisite for large-scale church music in the nineteenth century—was consistent with bourgeois tendencies in that it was thoroughly in keeping with the bourgeois spirit to think of the church whenever an event proved too great to be handled by the resources of everyday secular reality.

Still, the fact that ostentatious ceremonial church music can be accounted for in terms of the history of ideas and institutions is not enough to explain why it arises in the first place. It also has to meet compositional prerequisites that enable works in the "grand style" to meet the expectations imposed by the aesthetic of the time on music that claims to rank as art. In other words, the institutional possibility of large-scale church music will remain unused if the compositional premises that make it possible are too weakly developed. In the nineteenth century, however, "grand style" meant the symphonic style of Beethoven, except in those works that drew anachronistically on Handel's oratorios. Thus, the question to ask is how the ceremonial mass came to be regenerated with the devices of the symphony, and to be justified in terms of the then current level of compositional evolution.

In Schubert's E♭-major Mass (1828), written a few months before the composer's death, the Credo is divided into a Moderato, an Andante ("Et incarnatus"), a recapitulation of the Moderato with its sections rearranged ("Et resurrexit"), and a concluding fugue ("Et vitam venturi"). By repeating the "Et incarnatus" and the "Crucifixus" sections according to an *ABAB* pattern, Schubert has altered the cohesion of the liturgical text to suit the formal design of his music. Moreover, if we examine his use of motivic variation in the Moderato section, we can clearly recognize the symphonic aspirations to which he felt challenged in writing a mass with full orchestra. The Credo theme recurs again and again in various guises, and the shapes it assumes are determined not only by the scansion of the text but also, and especially, by the various functions it serves in the form (Ex. 23). The first variant is a consequent phrase (mm. 13–19), the second an interlude (mm. 35–39) combining the opening measures of the theme in counterpoint with its closing measures (in a chromatic transformation, as in mm. 44–47). The third variant is a pseudoimitative passage presenting the opening of the theme intact in one voice and its closing measures in another (mm. 39–47). The fourth variant (mm. 83–91), a minor version of variant 3, can be viewed as an outcome of the opening of the theme as isolated and chromaticized in the preceding development passage (mm. 65–82). The text of the mass does not sufficiently account for the motivic unity that Schubert seeks, nor the type of

Example 23

variations that his theme is made to undergo. By the same token, the motivic technique shows all the more clearly that Schubert intended his work to meet symphonic standards. At this late stage of his life he was incapable, it seems, of imagining a large-scale work, even a vocal one, in any other terms.

Liszt's Festival Mass for Gran Cathedral shows an extreme form of the assimilation of symphonic techniques into the mass setting, its Credo being nothing less than a symphonic poem for solo voices, chorus, and orchestra. The movement follows the same formal principle as the B-minor Piano Sonata and several of his orchestral pieces: it is basically conceived as at once a sonata-form movement and a sonata cycle—that is, paradoxically, as a multimovement work consisting of a single movement, and a single movement consisting of a multimovement work. Roughly speaking, the Credo is divided into a main theme (m. 1), a second theme (m. 38, "Deum de Deo"), a slow movement (m. 71, "Qui propter nos homines"), a section of developmental character (m. 114, "Et homo factus est"), a recollection of the Gloria which serves to introduce the recapitulation (m. 172, "Et resurrexit"), a return to the main theme (m. 190, "sedet ad dexteram Patris") and to the second theme (m. 233, "Et in spiritum sanctum"), and finally a fugal finale (m. 273, "et unam sanctam"). These various parts form a sonata cycle of first movement, slow movement ("Andante con divozione"), and finale ("Allegro militante"), connected by the technique of thematic transformation which Liszt first developed in his *Ce qu'on entend sur la montagne* (1850). A single melody, or sequence of pitches, appears in different rhythms (mm. 1–5, 71–73, and 277–81), so that the moods of these movements are at the same time way stations in a process of thematic transformation (Ex. 24). Again, it is the symphonic principle which, in terms of nineteenth-century compositional technique, both underpins and vindicates the stylistic level of a festive mass. Moreover, this principle is apparent not only in the work's formal design but in its compositional details as well. It is revealing of Liszt's conception of a mass movement as a symphonic poem that the main theme, though it virtually pounds out the words "Credo in unum Deum," is introduced as an instrumental motive, which only receives a text much later when it is transformed into a fugue subject ("et unam sanctam"). The Credo theme permeates virtually the entire movement as an instrumental idea that captures in notes, if not in words, the articles of the Creed. In this way it represents a sort of symphonic transformation of the traditional principle of the Credo mass. And when the motive dominates the continuation of the second theme (m. 52 and especially m. 243) and the orchestral accompaniment to the "Et incarnatus" (m. 93), its "omnipresence" likewise expresses a religious attitude that keeps the word "Credo"—"I believe"—present musically at every utterance of the Creed.

Example 24

In Bruckner's *Te Deum* (1881–84), the technique of motivic transformation reaches a degree of sophistication so extreme that the work's symphonic status, though not abandoned, is less clearly underscored than in Liszt's mass. (In curious contrast to the highly ramified logic of its motivic development, the work attains large-scale form by means of a monumental style that perhaps comes closer to the ideal of "Baroque music" than any work of the seventeenth century.) Two sub-elements of the first *tutti* theme—a whole step, and a descending fourth followed by an ascending run of a third—combine to constitute the solo theme "Tibi omnes angeli" which immediately follows, thereby recasting the quasi-Gregorianic opening intonation in cantabile form (Ex. 25). At first the link between these two passages remains inconspicuous owing to their contrasting characters; however, when the *tutti* theme is repeated, they are varied in a manner that confirms and highlights this connection ("confitetur ecclesia"). Thus, the

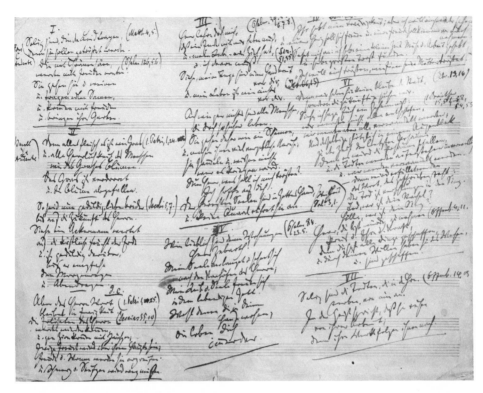

Fig. 42   Autograph text of Brahms's *German Requiem*. While writing out the biblical passages for the text to his *German Requiem* Brahms also jotted down the keys, time signatures, and tempos of the first and second movements, later replacing the Italian tempo marks with German equivalents. This provides ample evidence that he conceived large-scale relations between the movements when sketching a multimovement work. Despite some allusions to the *Dies irae* in its sixth movement, the *German Requiem* is separated from its Latin counterpart by the gulf that distinguishes liturgical from extraecclesiastical sacred texts. (Vienna, Österreichische Nationalbibliothek.)

opening themes have a common melodic substance. This same substance forms the basis of the concluding fugue ("In te, Domine, speravi") (Ex. 26). And if the pitch contour of the solo theme is given a different rhythmic form in the fugue, it is no less true that the rhythm of the fugue subject has already been anticipated, with different pitches, in the homophonic introduction to the closing section. The subject "In te, Domine, speravi" is in turn only one of two versions of the thematic idea within the fugue. This second version, "non confundar," differs from the first by beginning with an ascending run of a third, and thereby goes beyond the fugue to form the thematic material of the final grand crescendo (Ex. 27). The *Te Deum* is a musical "mountain range" whose motivic structure and sequences recall the Adagio of the Seventh Symphony, between whose first and second versions it was composed. If large-scale nineteenth-century church music was conceived symphonically, Bruckner expanded church music to incorporate elements from the symphony without thereby writing "esoteric program music," even if the melodic connection between the two is presumably semantic as well.

Example 25

Example 26

Example 27

Bibliographic References

Barblan, Guglielmo. *L'opera di Donizetti nell'età romantica.* Bergamo: Banca Mutua Populare, 1948.

Barzun, Jacques. *Berlioz and the Romantic Century.* 2 vols. Boston: Little, Brown, 1950.

Becker, Heinz. "Die historische Bedeutung der Grand Opéra." In *Beiträge zur Geschichte der Musikanschauung im 19. Jahrhundert.* Studien zur Musikgeschichte des 19. Jahrhunderts, vol. 2. Edited by Walter Salmen. Regensburg: G. Bosse, 1965.

Bekker, Paul. *Die Sinfonie von Beethoven bis Mahler.* Berlin: Schuster & Loeffler, 1918.

Benjamin, Walter. "Paris, Hauptstadt des neunzehnten Jahrhunderts." In *Schriften,* vol. 1. Frankfurt am Main: Suhrkamp, 1955.

Berlioz, Hector. *Oeuvres littéraires. Edition du centenaire.* Paris: Gründ, 1968–.

Blume, Friedrich. *Geschichte der evangelischen Kirchenmusik.* Kassel: Bärenreiter, 1965.

Celletti, Rodolfo. "Il vocalismo italiano da Rossini a Donizetti." In *Analecta musicologica* 5 (1968): 267–94, and 7 (1969): 214–47.

Crosten, William Loran. *French Grand Opera: An Art and a Business.* 2d ed. New York: Da Capo, 1972.

Dadelsen, Georg von. "Robert Schumann und die Musik Bachs." In *Archiv für Musikwissenschaft* 14 (1957): 46–59.

Dahlhaus, Carl, ed. *Das Problem Mendelssohn.* Studien zur Musikgeschichte des 19. Jahrhunderts, vol. 41. Regensburg: Bosse, 1974.

———. "Romantik und Biedermeier." In *Archiv für Musikwissenschaft* 31 (1974): 22–41.

Dömling, Wolfgang. "Die Symphonie fantastique und Berlioz' Auffassung von Programmusik." In *Die Musikforschung* 28 (1975): 260–83.

Egert, Paul. *Die Klaviersonate im Zeitalter der Romantik.* Berlin-Johannisthal: Egert, 1934.

Engel, Hans. *Die Entwicklung des deutschen Klavierkonzerts von Mozart bis Liszt.* Leipzig: Breitkopf & Härtel, 1927.

Fellerer, Karl Gustav. *Geschichte der katholischen Kirchenmusik.* Kassel: Bärenreiter, 1972–76.

Georgii, Walter. *Klaviermusik.* 4th ed. Berlin and Zurich: Atlantis, 1965.

Kahl, Willi. "Das lyrische Klavierstück Schuberts und seiner Vorgänger seit 1810." In *Archiv für Musikwissenschaft* 3 (1921): 54–82, 99–122.

Kiesewetter, Raphael Georg. *Geschichte der europäisch-abendländischen oder unserer heutigen Musik.* Leipzig: Breitkopf & Härtel, 1834.

Költzsch, Hans. *Franz Schubert in seinen Klaviersonaten.* Leipzig: Breitkopf & Härtel, 1927.

Lippman, Edward A. "Theory and Practice in Schumann's Aesthetics." In *Journal of the American Musicological Society* 17 (1964): 310–45.

Lissa, Zofia. "Die Chopinsche Harmonik aus der Perspektive der Klangtechnik des 20. Jahrhunderts." In *Deutsches Jahrbuch der Musikwissenschaft* 2 (1957): 68–84, and 3 (1958): 74–91.

Moser, Hans Joachim. *Die evangelische Kirchenmusik in Deutschland.* Berlin and Darmstadt: C. Merseburger, 1953.

Nef, Karl. *Geschichte der Sinfonie und Suite.* Leipzig: Breitkopf & Härtel, 1921.

Newman, William S. *The Sonata Since Beethoven.* Chapel Hill: University of North Carolina Press, 1969.

Pinder, Wilhelm. *Das Problem der Generationen in der Kunstgeschichte Europas.* Munich: Bruckmann, 1961.

Primmer, Brian. *The Berlioz Style.* 2d ed. London: Oxford University Press, 1975.

Puchelt, Gerhard. *Variationen für Klavier im 19. Jahrhundert.* Hildesheim: Olms, 1973.

Schumann, Robert. *Gesammelte Schriften über Musik und Musiker.* 5th ed. Edited by Martin Kreisig. Leipzig: Breitkopf & Härtel, 1914.

Söhngen, Oskar. *Theologie der Musik.* Kassel: Johannes Stauda, 1967.

Therstappen, Hans Joachim. *Die Entwicklung der Form bei Schubert.* Leipzig: Breitkopf & Härtel, 1931.

Weinstock, Herbert. *Donizetti and the World of Opera in Italy, Paris and Vienna in the First Half of the 19th Century.* New York: Pantheon, 1963.

CHAPTER FOUR

1848-1870

Seen from the perspective of industry and transportation, the post–1849 era has been called the first *Gründerzeit,* or, roughly, the "age of speculators." Nor would it be greatly exaggerated to claim that technology and economics took off on a firm tack of their own in virtual disregard of political constitutions and conflicts. It hardly mattered whether a revolution succeeded or failed, whether the republicans or the Bonapartists ruled France, whether German and Italian liberals clung to the principles of 1848 or fled to the governing party, whether a reform was inspired and sustained by the masses or whether, as Karl Marx put it in 1859, "the reaction carried out the program of the revolution." Whatever the case, the results were the same, for the simple reason that the "realpolitik" of the age broke free of the "attitudes" that had still represented a certain force in the early nineteenth century. Indeed, so complete was this break that it became impossible to distinguish between sobriety and cynicism. The stolid "captains of industry" had at least one thing in common with the confidence artists who flourished in a number reminiscent of the mid-eighteenth century: they were anything but idealists.

Similarly, for all their glaring extrinsic differences, the educated classes and the "Bohemian" subculture were likewise inherently related. There is little to choose, after all, between an attitude that isolates art from the purported drabness of everyday existence and Gautier's "art for art's sake" principle, one of Bohemia's characteristic mottos: both abandon the romantic dream of "poeticizing" reality.

Yet the era that appears in retrospect as the first "age of speculators" considered itself "positivist." And positivism, as proclaimed by Auguste Comte, entailed not only a rejection of metaphysics and an orientation on the natural sciences but also a tireless passion for accumulating objects and hard facts. (The nineteenth century was not philosophical enough to realize that materialism, too, is a metaphysic.)

Musical thought was beholden no less to the natural sciences than to the age's characteristic fondness for the grandiose, and to the increased pace of evolution that became noticeable in virtually all areas of culture. The only work that actually proved "epoch-making" in nineteenth-century music theory, influencing practically everyone from the philosopher pondering the problems of aesthetics to the humble musician teaching how to write chord progressions, was Hermann von Helmholtz's *Lehre von den Tonempfindungen* (1863). Yet, if the cornerstones of the industrial age were to be found in the natural sciences, its façade was marked by a passion for monumentality. Seen in this light, Wagner's *Ring* tetralogy and his proposed cycle of symphonic poems, as utopian as they must have appeared at first, were fully in keeping with an age that had to be sustained by superhuman feats of labor. (Wagner's ethic was, if nothing else, a work ethic, and the steadfastness with which he ultimately brought to fruition, and imposed on his contemporaries, the phantasmagoria crowding in his brain illustrates an aspect of the "zeitgeist" that deserves our admiration, even if posterity has inherited little more than the element of stress from this "achievement principle," which first emerged as a mass phenomenon in the mid-nineteenth century.) Finally, artistic currents alternated in ever more rapid succession, a feature of the industrial age which distinguishes it from absolutist-agrarian cultures, and one so patently evident that it became one of the critics' stock catchphrases.

Apart from a few connections extending as far afield as the world of anthropology, there was simply no such thing as a musical positivism serving as the style of the period. On the contrary, the age was characterized more by the detachment which music, unlike literature, increasingly bore to this particular "zeitgeist." The fact that the zeitgeist was "antimusical" and relegated music to an enclave means, in terms of intellectual and stylistic history, that no one expected music to participate in the realist tendencies of the time. (The *verismo* of the 1890s is basically traditional melodrama with a few added *frissons*, and Mussorgsky's realism falls outside the bounds of nineteenth-century compositional history precisely because it is genuine.) No small part of the music of this positivistically inclined age was considered at the time to be "neoromantic." This fact, and the fact that neoromanticism of distinction could exist at all, seems perplexing at first, since we are at a loss to find even a single tangible parallel in this extreme case of the "noncontemporaneity of the contemporaneous." However, the paradoxical aura disperses the moment we try to account for it with the unusual category of "negative explanation."

To begin with, there is no inner coherence to be detected in the music of the 1850s and 1860s. Wagner's music drama, Verdi's attempt to hybridize national opera with the universality of grand opera, Gounod's *drame lyrique*, Offenbach's *opéra bouffe*, the Lisztian species of symphonic poem, Brahms's chamber music—these key musical phenomena of the time diverge so sharply that any history that wishes to rise above the level of mythology is forced to abandon its search for a formula expressing the internal unity of the era and inquire instead into the conditions under which this divergence became possible in the first place (particularly in an age when composers in one place were fully aware of what others were doing elsewhere). It now seems as though the vast distance that separated music from the central technological and sociohistorical developments of the age

Fig. 43 Contemporary engraving of the 1848 revolution. Sometimes a failed revolution will leave deeper traces on the human consciousness and the subconscious than a successful one. The revolutions of 1848–49 (one of whose victims in Vienna was the music critic Alfred Becher) caused a clean break in the history of ideas: philosophy and humanistic culture, the basis on which the Frankfurt parliamentarians still attempted to make politics, were thereafter relegated by the German bourgeoisie to a "nature reserve" on the periphery of governmental, economic, and technological realpolitik. In the age of positivism, music seemed to be isolated from "genuine" reality, forming a world of its own. (Vienna, Österreichische Nationalbibliothek.)

favored the formation of "schisms" in musical language, conveying in retrospect the impression of mid-century "stylelessness." Not that the coexistence of contrasting and virtually unreconcilable musical languages is surprising in itself: the surprising thing is that each of these languages produced music of distinction, causing its representative works to take their place in music history (Offenbach no less than Brahms). And the reason that these musical languages could diverge so sharply with no a priori differences in their quality is probably to be found in the fact that the age of positivism could not boast of a "musically tractable" zeitgeist capable of proclaiming one style historically substantial and another insubstantial. In the post-1814 Restoration period a classicist such as Hummel had far less promising chances than a romantic such as Weber, regardless of their respective "talent" (which in any case is more or less inseparable from the "luck" of happening to agree with the zeitgeist), for reasons which can only be reconstructed by interweaving arguments from aesthetics and the philosophy of history. In the post-1849 "first age of speculators," however, there was no arbiter capable of deciding what was in tune with the times and what was not, thereby setting the aesthetic guideposts of the age.

The hallmark of this period was the principle of autonomy, which "sequestered" music into a realm of its own. Political and moralistic zealots have suspected this principle of ignoring social functions, which, when unmet, cause art to devolve into the abstract. (Ever since the years leading up to the 1848 revolutions, composers with delicate consciences have felt torn hither and thither between cries of art for art's sake and pronouncements on the social mission of art.) However, champions of political involvement forget that the ideal of nonalienated labor that they envisage as the goal of revolution (which, admittedly, must be a revolution in perpetuity) has found a refuge in art, specifically in autonomous art, and that without this refuge it would run the risk of vanishing from human consciousness, for human consciousness needs footholds of this sort for its ideals. When John Ruskin proclaimed his arts and crafts aesthetic, he could draw on the fact that, in the industrial age whose ugliness he so despised, it was art that preserved the original ideal of craftsmanship, of labor undivided from the initial design of an object to its completion.

Wagner's Conception of Musical Drama

Richard Wagner provoked the admiration and revulsion of a century which he, more than almost anyone else, may be said to represent. As Nietzsche remarked, with the gimlet eye of an apostate, he was a theatromaniac, a genius of the theater who forced upon an at first unwilling, then respectful, and ultimately enthusiastic public the idea that a theatrical event can be a work of art in the strong sense of the term. The crucial and significant point about his concept of a *Gesamtkunstwerk* (a pompous synonym for "theater") is not the truism that several different arts join forces and interact, nor the questionable thesis that these arts are equipped with equal rights and privileges, still less the historical myth that the *Gesamtkunstwerk* represents a culmination and sublation of the "special arts." On the contrary, its importance resides in the aesthetic and social demand we raise when we refer to theater as a "total work of art": the notion that theater, although more akin to an event than a work, nevertheless partakes of the ideal of art which was elevated to metaphysical dignity in the classical and romantic age. Wagner took a genre previously half ceremonial pomp, half entertainment, and declared it to be the ne plus ultra of art; this is the full import of the festival that he envisaged and attempted to realize in Bayreuth. And the astonishing thing is that Wagner succeeded in imposing on his age the "revolution of aesthetic values" and in raising for opera the same lofty claims that Beethoven had achieved for the symphony. In so doing, he transformed opera into music drama.

For various complementary, if heterogeneous, reasons, theater was considered a secondary art form occupying a lower rung in the aesthetic hierarchy. In the nineteenth century, actors and singers were still subjected to holdovers of the social prejudice that sedentary persons have borne toward wayfarers since time immemorial. Furthermore, any aesthetic which, in a Platonic spirit, presupposes a distinction between essence and appearance will necessarily subordinate the "reproductive" arts to the "productive" ones: like the performance of music, theater was viewed in terms of "work and rendition" rather than "sketch and realization." (To aesthetic purists, genres such as film and virtuoso music, in which "reproduction" in fact constitutes the actual artistic "production" and the emphasis thus shifts from the text to its presentation, are suspected of lacking "artistic substance.") Finally, the fact that theater, like music, is "transitory" and takes place in time makes it a less likely candidate for the category of *poiesis*—the production of works that bear up to observation—than for that of *praxis*. Kant and Hegel, as well as the educated classes guided by their philosophies, still found reason to doubt the artistic credentials of the genre.

Wagner, on the other hand, proposed that the theatrical event was not merely a means of presenting a work of art whose substance resides in a musico-literary text, but itself constituted the work of art, with literature and music serving as its handmaidens. This claim entailed nothing less than an aesthetic revolution that challenged not only the century's credence in texts but its social prejudices as well. Wagner was able to persuade an audience that took its cues from the cultured classes to identify drama—the highest species of art following the demise of the verse epic—with a transitory theatrical event, so that "appearance" was declared to be "essence." The impact of this historical process can scarcely be overestimated. (One of its upshots in our century is *Regietheater,* or "stage director's theater," even if the proponents of this principle show little awareness that it originated with Wagner.)

When Wagner, in *Oper und Drama,* spoke of music as a function of the drama, he by no means understood "drama" to mean the literary text—which likewise had to serve the drama. Rather, he was referring to the events on stage as a whole, including not only the stage action but also "melodized" speech (which as *parola scenica* also formed part of the action) and "verbalized" orchestral melody. In his Beethoven essay of 1870 he expressly states that "drama alone" is capable of "determining" the music, by which he meant "not the poem of the drama but rather the drama that actually unfolds in motion before our eyes." For Wagner, artistic status was to be found not in the "fixed letter" but in the "externalization of the poet's intentions for the sensory faculties," this externalization being the property of the music and the stage setting.

All the same, Wagner, viewing himself maniacally as the heir apparent and sole custodian of the classical legacy in both literature and music, as a "classic in his own time," attempted to ground the artistic status of the music drama in thematic and motivic manipulation, a technique and aesthetic ideal derived from the classical symphony. This would seem to stand in glaring and unresolved contradiction to the stress he placed on the drama as a theatrical event. However, the leitmotiv technique that distinguishes his "music dramas," beginning with *Das Rheingold,* from his "romantic operas" up to and including *Lohengrin,* can be viewed as a method intended to "sublate" the symphony into the music drama at the same time that it serves to "externalize the poet's intentions for the sensory faculties," this being in Wagner's view the dramaturgical function of music and stage setting. Unlike reminiscence motives, which were restricted to turning points in the plot, the leitmotivs in a music drama form a dense web spread over the whole of the orchestral setting, determining its structure at any given mo-

Fig. 44 Interior of the Coburg Theater, 1840–45. The theater in Coburg has one of those auditoriums in which the characteristic nineteenth-century intermingling of court and bourgeois opera has taken on architectonic expression. Though the prince's loge (from where the picture was drawn) is still directly opposite the stage, the bourgeois audience is not banished exclusively to the stalls, as hitherto, but also occupies the galleries, now no longer divided into boxes. (By gracious permission of Her Majesty Queen Elizabeth II.)

ment. Though Wagner worked on a different time scheme compared with that of Beethoven (his themes are primarily "reminiscences," whereas Beethoven's are "goal-directed"), this web has one fundamental feature in common with thematic manipulation as practiced by Beethoven: both establish a type of musical form that emerges from motivic logic rather than residing in a balance of melodic periods.

It is precisely because of the reminiscences associated with them that Wagner's leitmotivs fulfill the dramaturgical function of "externalizing the poet's intentions for the sensory faculties." However, their meaning only becomes recognizable once we have come to understand Wagner's notion of dramatic "present." For Wagner, the child of an age permeated with the philosophy of Hegel, the individual moment receives its meaning from the history accumulated within it, and the present, even as represented on stage, is virtually "inundated with the past." By contrast, in Italian opera seria (the antitype of the music drama), the preliminary events are fully contained and virtually forgotten in the momentary passion, or conflicting passions, in which they discharge their energy. For this reason, unlike opera seria, the narrative plot of a music drama is not so much a vehicle, a mere intrigue culminating in an emotion as its goal and ultimate purpose, as a system of relations and interweavings intended to be "externalized to the sensory faculties." Each moment on stage appears to be a point within the system, a point that sheds a particular color and perspective on the whole. In other words, each separate leitmotiv, besides expressing in music an instant within the drama, also forms a node within the web of leitmotivs. This makes it possible for us to sense what Wagner understood by "present": a point in time whose substance resides entirely in the fact that it serves to illuminate the meaning of part of the past.

Wagner outlined the theory of leitmotiv technique in 1851 in *Oper und Drama,* without, however, using the term itself, which was only introduced into the Wagner literature decades later by Hans von Wolzogen. The theory antedates its realization in *Der Ring des Nibelungen* by several years, a fact which Wagner, to avoid appearing speculative and utopian, attempted to conceal in his *Mitteilung an meine Freunde* (1852) by exaggerating the degree to which his forward-looking theory was rooted in his experience as a composer and consistent with his earlier practice from *Der Fliegende Holländer* to *Lohengrin.* The essay describes how, when writing *Der Fliegende Holländer,* he first "drafted Senta's ballad in the second act": "In this piece I unconsciously laid down the thematic germ-cell for all of the music in the opera. . . . When I finally came to execute the composition, this thematic image spread involuntarily before my eyes as a complete web covering the entire drama." (Here the words "unconsciously" and "involuntarily" are doubtless meant to dispel suspicions that the work was constructed or coerced by intellectual reflection.) Nevertheless, if we can avoid being led astray by Wagner's fondness for hyperbole, we note that there is no "complete web" of motives "covering the entire drama." Even a central scene, such as Senta's duet with the Dutchman—not to mention peripheral sections falling completely outside the motivic framework, such as the duets of Daland and the Dutchman or Erik and Senta—is connected with Senta's ballad solely by two quotations and incorporated in the "web" of recurring motives by nothing more than a sixteen-bar complex taken over from the Dutchman's monologue. In *Mitteilung an meine Freunde,* it would therefore appear, Wagner was describing not so much the music of *Der Fliegende Holländer,* written a decade earlier, as the compositional idea underlying his *Ring* tetralogy as it appeared to him in 1851, two years before he began to write it down. His vision of the future had superimposed itself unawares upon his recollection of the past. And another decade later, in his essay *Zukunftsmusik,* Wagner in retrospect actually characterized the theory developed in *Oper und Drama* as a correlate to his musicodramatic conception of the *Ring,* which in 1851 was pressing toward realization but had not yet taken on distinct contours:

Instead, it should be remarked that even my boldest conclusions regarding the po-
tentially realizable musicodramatic form were urged upon me by the fact that, at the
same time, I was occupied with the plan of my great Nibelung drama, which indeed
I had already partially completed in verse. I elaborated this plan in my mind in such
a fashion that my theory was almost nothing more than an abstract expression of the
process of artistic production then taking shape within me.

Up to *Lohengrin* Wagner had applied the technique, adopted from Weber, of
reminiscence motives, originally a product of French revolutionary opera. These
differed from the leitmotivs that he took up in *Das Rheingold,* with regard both to
their dramaturgical function and to their role in musical form. And the underlying principles of what Wagner called his "system"—among them the categories
of "leitmotiv," "musical prose," and "endless melody"—are connected in a manner that becomes most apparent when we compare the compositional criteria of
the "music drama" with those of "romantic opera," without, however, stylizing
the gap between *Lohengrin* and *Das Rheingold* into an evolutionary cleavage.

   Like *Tannhäuser* (1845), and unlike *Der Fliegende Holländer, Lohengrin* is not
merely a "romantic opera" but also a "grand opera." Here the regular periodic
phrase-structure that Wagner scorned as "compositional foursquareness" reigns
virtually supreme. Deviations from this syntactical rule can be viewed as exceptions—whether by extension, elision, or telescoping—to the norm, which at any
given instant is clearly in evidence as an underlying pattern. In contrast, from
Das Rheingold on, the four-measure group, however frequent, no longer functions as a pattern and frame of reference for the musical syntax, but is merely
one way of combining measures among many other ways, all of them with equal
rights and basically irreducible. "Foursquareness" tends to dissolve into "musical
prose." Moreover, this distinction between regular and irregular syntax—
between musical verse and prose—is closely linked to a formal and, indirectly, a
dramaturgical distinction between reminiscence motives and leitmotivs. A period is a form of syntactic subordination, or *hypotaxis*: it encompasses not only
phrases, half-phrases, and even phrase groups, but beats and measures as well,
all in accordance with the principle that any given unit must be counterbalanced
by a second unit. In the words of Eduard Hanslick, who praised Wagner's romantic operas and only turned to hostile skepticism with the music dramas, overall form is merely "rhythm in the large." Any composition that owes its internal
cohesion to the balance of its melodic passages can accommodate reminiscence
motives only as interpolations linking the stage action with earlier events: they
are motivated "from without" by the dramaturgy instead of having to establish
the musical structure "from within." What is more, the main category of opera
composition is the concept of melody (in the traditional sense of closed periods),
not motive. Accordingly, apart from a few musical props from the stage composer's stock-in-trade, the number of reminiscence motives in both *Lohengrin*
and *Tannhäuser* remains small. This is possible because it is not a "web" of motives but "rhythm in the large" that imparts formal continuity to the music.

Leitmotiv technique, on the other hand, is formally constitutive in a strong sense of the term. Irregular groupings of measures which will no longer bend to the law of "foursquareness" tend toward syntactic conjunction, or *parataxis,* where passages of melody are loosely juxtaposed instead of being bracketed by the subordinating principle of "rhythm in the large." The danger of formal disintegration must have specially tormented Wagner, who not only abhorred lack of cohesion but was prone to a compulsion for drawing relations. To confront this danger he attempted to use motivic logic to fill the void left by the demise of "foursquareness." The nexus of leitmotivs was intended to impart a continuity no longer vouchsafed by the syntax.

Admittedly, the claim that a congery of—seemingly—heterogeneous elements can establish internal cohesion must have sounded paradoxical at first, and was only intelligible at all in connection with Wagner's concept of melody. By the same token, the original meaning of the term "endless melody," soon worn to an empty catchphrase, can only be reconstructed in relation to the problem of how irregular groupings of measures, in syntactical conjunction, can produce self-contained form. The opposite of "endless melody" is the "mangled" melody of regular periodic phrases, which, Wagner maintained, seldom if ever managed to avoid meaningless formulae and stopgaps in order to fill out the "foursquareness" of its underlying musical thought. By dispensing with "unmelodic" additives, as Wagner urged, melody is reduced to its essence and periodic phrase-structure dissolves into musical prose. Musical continuity then resides in the fact that melody, having abandoned "rhythm in the large," is now "articulate" at any given instant, thereby becoming "melodic" in the strong sense of the term. Instead of being interrupted and clogged by meaningless padding, melody expands in "endless" continuity undisturbed by "nonmelodic" interpolations. Yet its "articulateness" is linked to the dramaturgical function which it serves in the music drama (and which, Wagner believed, was tacitly implied in Beethoven's symphonies). The motives become elements of a musical language by virtue of their meaning, a meaning that accrues to them from the overriding plot and from the contextual system which they establish among themselves. Describing the origins of the *Ring* tetralogy in his *Epilogischer Bericht,* Wagner observed that its panoply of leitmotivs derived from a few underlying germinal motives: "With *Rheingold* I immediately struck out on this new path, my task being first to find the plastic *Naturmotive* which, by becoming increasingly individualized, were to serve as the bearers of the emotional subcurrents within the broad-based plot and the moods expressed therein." This was not simply a whim or caprice on Wagner's part—one that exaggerates Thomas Mann's well-known dictum of Wagner's "wizardry of interrelationships" to the point of absurdity—but a prerequisite for the linguistic basis of his leitmotivs. The fact that the Valhalla motive in the first *Rheingold* interlude derives from the Ring motive is part of its semantic essence. By being derivable from each other, the leitmotivs fall into a configuration instead of merely accumulating, and are thus linked into a contextual system. Moreover, together with the plot, this contextual system in turn

Fig. 45 Swimming carriages for *Das Rheingold*. Richard Wagner, the despiser of grand opera, did not hesitate for a moment to appropriate its stage machinery, a holdover from Baroque traditions. The closing scene of *Das Rheingold* recalls Rossini's *Guillaume Tell*, that of *Götterdämmerung* Meyerbeer's *Le prophète*. These "swimming carriages," used to support the Rhinemaidens, resemble flying machines transported to another element. As a spectacle that gives the theater its full due, Wagner's *Bühnenfestspiel* or *Bühnenweihfestspiel* proves to be the heir of grand opera. (Bayreuth, Richard Wagner Museum.)

conditions the "linguistic" nature of the leitmotivs. It also serves as a prerequisite for the fact that we can sense musical logic in these motivic groupings, a logic that knits together the otherwise disjointed, proselike texture of the music.

Like the reminiscence motives of romantic opera, the leitmotivs of music drama speak of the past, though a past that forms part of the essence of the present. The reasons why, in the *Ring*, they form a "system" can be found not only in the musical form but in the work's dramaturgy as well, where present drama and past events characteristically merge.

The past also casts a shadow on the present in the romantic operas: it sends the Dutchman on his quest for redemption, forces Tannhäuser to conceal his past, enjoins Lohengrin to maintain his incognito by prohibiting questions. And it is the clash between past and present which, in the romantic operas, unleashes the tragic catastrophe, causing reminiscence motives to intervene decisively in the dramaturgy with the function of making musically sensible the link between the present action of the work and its prehistory. (In musical terms, the fact that the Dutchman seems to step out of Senta's fantasy, and Lohengrin out of Elsa's, means that the Dutchman and Lohengrin motives bear the coloration of the past from the very outset, without having previously been presented, like the Venusberg motives in *Tannhäuser*, in association with earlier events on stage.)

If, in the romantic operas, the conflict between past and present lies in plain view, the visible events in the *Ring* (apart from *Das Rheingold*, the "preliminary evening") are curiously independent of the past. Yet the past is constantly being invoked, and necessarily so, since it alone furnishes the overall context for the dramas that make up the tetralogy. Siegmund and Siegfried know nothing of the forces connecting their own misfortunes with the destinies of the world in which they are entangled. The tragedies that make up the reality of the *Ring* on stage are equally conceivable without the "world-historical" significance invested in them by the Ring myth. (Nothing in the plot of *Die Walküre,* with Wotan as Siegfried's protector and Fricka as the protectress of Hunding's marriage, would need to be altered if the Ring were to vanish altogether, and Siegfried's tragedy in *Götterdämmerung* would remain what it is even without the myth of the gods.) The Ring myth and the perceivable events that fill the foreground of the *Ring*— and in theater it is the foreground that matters—are not connected with each other as directly as are plot and preliminary history in the romantic operas. This made it necessary to construct scenes—such as Wotan's monologue in the presence of Brünnhilde, his riddling contest with Mime, the Norn scene, and Waltraute's scene—which fall outside the dramaturgical pale of the heroic tragedy but are indispensable for "externalizing" the overriding myth. It is no exaggeration to say that the origin of leitmotiv technique lies precisely in these "interpolated" scenes that tend toward epic form by narrating part of the preliminary history. It is these narrative, recapitulatory sections in which leitmotivs dealing with the past intrude most noticeably in the present. Moreover, they accompany the stage action as "orchestral melody" representing the "subconscious" of the visible plot. The reason for this is to be found in the curious configuration assumed in the *Ring* by heroic tragedy and the myth of the gods, with the former dominating the events on stage and the latter endowing them with significance. The Ring myth that brackets the separate dramas does not obviously direct and determine the course of events on stage. Precisely for this reason it forms the "deep structure" of the work as expressed in the system of leitmotivs, which allow the listener to sense connections unknown to the characters on stage, or at least to the main protagonists (except for Brünnhilde, who rejects her knowledge; Wotan, who traverses the plot as the Wanderer without actually being part of it; and Hagen, whose intrigue does no small damage to the tragedy by threatening to turn Siegfried into a marionette).

The practice of rigidly assigning identifying labels to Wagner's leitmotivs is as questionable as it is unavoidable: questionable in that they change meaning, and sometimes even musical form, in their various appearances within a work, almost undergoing stories of their own; and unavoidable because it is an illusion to imagine that we can understand the emotions without recourse to language. To grasp the ramified meanings of a motive we have to proceed from a fundamental meaning, realizing that it is temporary and questionable, and gradually make it more refined. The infinitely rich emotional understanding that Wagner wished to attain arises, not at first remove, but only at a second remove in which our reflections are subsumed and incorporated without obtruding as such.

By the same token, the confidence or uncertainty with which we can apply labels reveals part of the history of this very subject, namely, of leitmotivs and their functions within musical form and dramaturgy. It is no coincidence that attaching verbal labels to musical expression, as risky as it may be, proved more successful in the *Ring,* where the motives speak of past events that weigh upon the present, than in an introspective and timeless drama such as *Tristan und Isolde.* The motives in *Tristan,* rather than "having their own story," tend to circle around an obscure midpoint whose meaning, made perceivable by ever-changing combinations of longing for love and death, seems to be beyond the power of words to convey. Instead of undergoing an evolution in which their identity remains intact, no matter how modified they become in the process, they seem caught up in a maelstrom of meanings, which ultimately makes any verbally expressible distinctions between them futile and pointless.

In the *Ring,* then, the past extends into the present and is subjected to a process of recollection that links events with ideas, a process that gives the leitmotivs, for all their sensory impact, a certain air of abstraction which Wagner sought in vain to deny. In *Tristan,* by contrast, we confront an overpowering and boundless passion—the actual agent of the drama—a passion that turns love-longing into death-longing and back again, a whirlpool engulfing everything that chances under its sway, even the fates of the secondary characters. The appreciative listener is aware of the "meaning" of this music less in its separate motives than in the "tone" that permeates the work even in its remotest and least likely details, a tone which has compelled even dull-witted and pedantic exegetes to speak in paradoxes. Nor would it be farfetched to maintain that, in *Tristan,* Wagner unearthed for music one of the basic categories of modern poetry: ambiguity. As chary as we should otherwise be of historiological speculations based on dates, the temptation is well-nigh irresistible to see more than a mere coincidence in the fact that *Tristan* was written at the same time as Baudelaire's *Fleurs du mal* (1857), the *fons et origo* of the modern movement in poetry.

Tristan and Isolde—and with them the listener—feel transported into a timeless realm where the expressive motives are caused to merge, motives which harbor an overpowering experience in search of musical expression, and which in the end all say the "same thing." In sharp contrast, however, this timelessness encourages the creation of clearly etched allegorical figures, such as the Death Motive and Day Motive, labels which have never been questioned even though the meaning of the musical symbolism assumed in *Tristan* by "day" and "death" still remains beyond the power of words to convey. It is as though the emotion that forces the protagonists into "the world's driving whirlwind" has found a final foothold in an iconographical language which rescues it from utter silence. And if, as Wagner wrote in his essay *Zukunftsmusik,* the expressive leitmotivs have caused the "silence" that actually reigns between the characters to "resound," the allegorical motives cause language, being unequal to the ambiguity of the internal action, to collapse, as it were, into musical conundrums.

Fig. 46 Stage design for Richard Wagner's *Parsifal*. The stage set in which Gurnemanz escorts the "pure fool" Parsifal to the castle of Monsalvat is a curious amalgam of archaic architecture and wild, "Rousseauean" natural formations. It thus seems to be a scenic rendering of Wagner's idea, derived from classical aesthetics, that artifice must remain concealed and art must appear as nature. The escapist, insular, artificial world of the Knights of the Grail is meant to grow organically out of primeval nature instead of revealing its true character by standing out in sharp contrast. (Bayreuth, Richard Wagner Museum.)

Tristan, then, transports us into a mythical realm that we perceive as timeless, not as the "early Middle Ages." Thus, it is by no means anachronistic and contradictory for Wagner to interweave the archaic and the modern, which is one way of viewing the contrast between the drama's subject matter and the chromatic excesses of its music. *Die Meistersinger* (1868), however, being set in a clearly defined period of history, unmistakably bears the imprint of the past. This is true not only of its plot but also of its music, which, according to the metaphysic adopted by Wagner from Schopenhauer, expresses the "inner essence" of events and phenomena. (For the music to appear wafted to us from a bygone era, it is irrelevant that the events on stage belong to the sixteenth century, whereas the musical devices "archaized" by Wagner derive from the early eighteenth century.)

Being the "antitype" of *Tristan,* the *Meistersinger* likewise has a characteristic "tone" infusing the work down to its remotest details. One attribute of this "tone" is Wagner's return to diatonicism, in a spirit less of restoration than of reconstruction. The distinction between chromaticism and diatonicism, with *Tristan* being chromatic and *Meistersinger* diatonic, is so coarse that we hesitate to mention it at all. Even so, we must not allow this coarseness to obscure the fact that Wagner—despite his endless sophistication and his urge to relate everything to everything else—had a genius for simplification (and hence for the theater), and that he commanded a striking capacity to make abstract categories such as chromaticism and diatonicism "speak for themselves." Admittedly, the diatonicism that forms the musical "tone" of the *Meistersinger,* expressing a yearning, even nostalgic sense of remoteness, can be called a "second diatonicism" in Hegel's sense when he spoke of second nature or second immediacy. (Nowhere, not even in *Parsifal,* that troubled masterpiece of his old age, is Wagner's music more artificial than in the semblance of simplicity that surrounds it in the *Meistersinger.*) Modern chromaticism, though reduced and suppressed, is by no means obliterated wholesale: *Tristan* is cited in the *Meistersinger,* and functions as a tacit prerequisite for its style. It may seem that diatonicism has been restored with one regressive *coup de main* to its former prechromatic rights—the rights of a "natural" language of music—but this is mere deception. The banished chromaticism is ever-present, even if it usually remains implicit. At times we can even sense it explicitly: the second theme of the Overture, an E-major cantilena in anticipation of Walther's "Prize Song," shifts the chromaticism from the deliberately diatonic melody to the contrapuntal lines of its accompaniment. Here Wagner has "written out" what the listener is otherwise intended to "project."

The *Meistersinger* also resembles *Tristan* in that the sense of the music resides less in its separate motives and their identifiable meanings than in the "tone" imbuing the work as a whole. In terms of compositional technique, this implies that the leitmotivs may merge and overlap without detracting from our understanding of the work, which Wagner intended to be primarily an "emotional understanding" beyond language. For instance, in the Act 3 "baptismal scene," where the preliminary form of Walther's Prize Song, as notated by Sachs, is given the name "selige Morgentraumdeut-Weise," the leitmotivs, however varied and characteristic they may seem at first, are linked by common features and components manifesting the work's "tone" (Ex. 28). The "Art Motive" (b) is nothing but a fragment of the "Meistersinger Theme" (a) with a different continuation. Its ascending tetrachord recurs in the first line of the "Baptismal Chorale" (c), which, like the Meistersinger Theme, also opens with a descending fourth. Both of these elements—the descending fourth and the ascending tetrachord—appear in the second line of the chorale (d), a variant of the first line in inversion. Finally, the "Maiden Motive" (e) expands the fourth to a fifth while preserving the tetrachord.

These linkages and affinities among the motives do not imply that the words attached to them like name tags are merely superfluous labels, which we had best

Example 28

ignore in order to wallow mindlessly in "emotional understanding." On the contrary, this would then cease to be "understanding" at all. The "wizardry of inter-relationships" that casts its spell over Wagner's listeners should not—as hostile critics continually maintain of "endless melody"—be allowed to turn into a vague and undifferentiated "torrent." Wagner sought to strike a delicate balance among three factors: "emotional understanding," whose existence he presupposed; reflection on the rich and multifarious links between the motives; and concentration on the plot, which he conceived as a "scenic manifestation" of the music. In the final analysis, however, this balance turns into a primarily musical mode of perception which, as Wagner put it, "de-potentiates our sight" and allows music to emerge as the "inner essence" of the events on stage. If, as Wagner averred in his essay *Über die Benennung "Musikdrama"* (1872), plot is "musical event made visible," it is musical contemplation, described so penetratingly by Schopenhauer, that turns our perception of the music drama back to its origins. Or, as Nietzsche observed in his *Fragment über Musik und Sprache* (1871), the final word of Wagner the theatromaniac is "absolute music."

Opera as Drama: Verdi

Verdi was a popular composer before he became a significant one. The choruses from *Nabucco* (1842), *I Lombardi* (1843), and *Ernani* (1844) that established his fame—"Va pensiero sull'ali dorate," "O signore dal tetto natio," and "Si ridesti il Leon di Castiglio"—were received as musical symbols of the *Risorgimento* by a torn and disrupted nation whose political ardor flared up in opera as long as its republicanism remained more a matter of daydreams than deeds. Yet, as a dramatist, Verdi, a revolutionary who never broke with tradition, realized an individual conception of opera as drama. Only gradually did he emerge from the *compositore scritturato*, heaping one commissioned work upon another with varying success in the decade and a half of what he called his "years in the galleys." No one could have descried the composer of *Otello* (1887) and *Falstaff* (1893) in the rough-and-tumble genius that was the young Verdi. (In Germany, where the bearers of musical culture clung to a largely literary and philosophical notion of education, Verdi was a "hurdy-gurdy man" whose tunes ingratiated the ear but were devoid of artistic worth. It was not until the 1920s that Verdi's species of opera was discovered to be an antithesis to Wagner's *Gesamtkunstwerk* deserving of dramaturgical reflection rather than mindless enjoyment.)

Nevertheless, our appreciation of Verdi is distorted by our habit of pitting Italian "singers' opera" against Wagner's "music drama"—in other words, by our choice of terminology, which misleads us into reserving the term "drama" for Wagner's species of opera. This lopsidedness is little rectified by conceding to Verdi's works a "dramaticality" limited to the violence of their stage action. Italian opera cannot be grasped in trivial concepts such as "dramatic entrance." This is not to deny that one of the most popular of them all, *Il trovatore* (1853), invites us to seek the dramaturgical formula of Verdi's brand of opera in a combination of tumultuous (and, admittedly, largely incomprehensible) events, interspersed with moments of lyric or martial urgency when the plot freezes into a *tableau vivant*. But the actual drama of opera, even of the Italian variety, is not to be found in the turbulence of the plot.

It has long been a commonplace among music historians to view Verdi as progressing gradually from an opera composer, joining musical numbers on the principle of contrast and climax, to a "genuine" dramatist guided in his late works by the ideal of musicotheatrical "continuity." Yet this view, valid as it may be as a rough approximation, falls short as an aesthetic formula. True, it is plain to see that Verdi evolved, and that his works demarcate stages in this evolution. One of the paths he pursued most relentlessly was to blend recitative and aria, to abandon a sharp dichotomy between them in favor of countless hybrid forms in unpredictable alternation, thereby adapting his music to any instant in the drama. This path enables the historian to find, in the succession of works from his "breakthrough" in *Nabucco* to *Otello* and *Falstaff,* a logic or dialectic that gives this corner of opera history an appearance of teleological progression. Even so, it is false and misleading to presuppose an opposition between "opera" and "drama" when discussing the internal evolution of Verdi's species of opera. To posit a development from the "number" or "singers' " opera to the "musical drama" or "genuine musical drama" is to ignore, or at least obscure, the fact that the despised number opera is itself a species of "drama" which is perfectly capable of holding its own against other operatic forms sustained by different assumptions. (The term "singers' opera" merely turned disparagement into apology without affecting the actual core of the argument.) Wagner, who by no means understood his opponent as poorly as his egocentricity would make it seem, considered it absurd that opera should attempt to produce drama from music, instead of vice versa. Yet this absurdity, if neutralized into a characteristic attribute, proves to be a highly useful axiom for attempting to explain the aesthetic of Verdi's operas.

Starting with *Macbeth* (1847), and with an unrealized *Lear* project that he clung to for decades, Verdi attempted with impassioned and urgent tenacity to adapt Shakespearean drama to his own ends. On the other hand, and in glaring

Fig. 47 Verdi advertisement. With the triumph of *Rigoletto* (1851) and *Il trovatore* (1853) Verdi became Italy's leading opera composer following the death of Donizetti in 1848. Looking back with a transfigured gaze, contemporaries now idealized the failures of his "years in the galleys" (as Verdi called the 1840s) along with his successes. The medallion and the muse, stage props for a popularity now presentable as kitsch, are surrounded by vignettes from his operas, which bear a closer resemblance to *tableaux vivants* of the main characters than to actual stage scenes. So severely are they stylized that it is difficult to distinguish Luisa Miller from Lady Macbeth. (Milan, Museo Teatrale alla Scala.)

contradiction, the Schiller plays that he turned to no less frequently—from *Giovanna d'Arco* (1845) and *I masnadieri* (1847) to *Luisa Miller* (1849) and *Don Carlo* (1867)—seem merely to have served him as raw material to be handed over to the ministrations of his librettists without a moment's thought to the formal laws governing Schillerean drama. Salvatore Cammarano, using Schiller's *Kabale und Liebe* as a quarry for *Luisa Miller*, produced results that seem like a model libretto, a *pièce bien faite* of the musical theater: all motives in the play are shifted or interchanged while the main outline of the plot remains untouched. However, Cammarano was forced to sacrifice Schiller's dramaturgy in ways dictated by the so-called double aria, the bipartite form of cavatina and cabaletta in contrasting tempos. In the Introduction, unlike Schiller's play, Luisa's love for Rodolfo (Schiller's Ferdinand) is still innocent and uncomplicated, for she does not know that he is the son of Count Walter (the President), considering him instead to be one of her own kind. The two arioso sections, expressing expectant longing (Primo Tempo) and the joy of reunion (Cabaletta), function as a framework in the ensemble precisely because of their positions in formal scheme. In Scene 2, Miller, not wishing to tyrannize his daughter, rebuffs Wurm's marital designs on her (Cantabile), whereupon, to Miller's horror, Wurm betrays Rodolfo's identity (Cabaletta). Federica, intended by Walter as a wife for Rodolfo, is not, like Schiller's Lady Milford, the prince's mistress but a childhood friend of Rodolfo's. This enables Walter to express his paternal sentiments in an aria without appearing hypocritical (a quality inexpressible in music). Further, Rodolfo's conversation with Federica, in keeping with the premises of Cammarano's dramaturgical construct, falls neatly into sentimental reminiscences (Cantabile) and violent arguments following Rodolfo's confession of love for Luisa (Cabaletta). In short, whether or not we decry Cammarano's technique as a distortion of the play or praise it for its faultless craftsmanship, one thing remains certain: despite their similar plots, the opera, being based on unexpected turns of events to motivate a transformation from cantabile to cabaletta, represents a fundamentally different kind of drama from the play.

Opera, far from being a deficient dramatic mode, is drama on an equal if different footing from spoken theater. The reason for this, and the main difference between these genres, is revealed by the first finale of *Luisa Miller* with a vehemence that might be said to illuminate the aesthetic of Italian opera in one fell swoop. This scene, an extremely large-scale and demanding ensemble, is modeled on Act 2 of *Kabale und Liebe,* where Luisa refrains from adding a word to the dispute between Walter, Ferdinand, and Miller, a dispute of which she is both object and victim. Derided as a whore by Walter, she says nothing, stunned by an amazement for which no dialogue is conceivable that would rise above mute stuttering. Yet even silence, as no less a dramatist than Wagner well knew, can form the basis of a scene rich in dramatic potential.

Johanna's silence in Schiller's *Jungfrau von Orleans* is eminently "dramatic," forming in fact the pivot of the drama. Wagner used this scene to illustrate an aesthetic limitation of the spoken theater which can only be bridged by music ("silence made to resound"): what in spoken theater must remain a transitory if gripping instant can be expanded and elaborated in opera. Wagner, of course, had in mind the orchestral melody of opera. Once we cease regarding the texts of self-contained operatic numbers as "realistic" dialogues and monologues and think of them instead as images for the unsaid, it becomes obvious that the lyric effusions that make up the Italian librettist's stock-in-trade consist essentially of passions and emotional conflicts which "actually" remain unspoken, and whose silence only music can penetrate. Seen in this light, the text functions solely as a vehicle for the music, as an external condition for its existence.

The "contemplative ensemble" (the term is Richard Strauss's) is a type of operatic ensemble in which the characters, instead of speaking to each other, seek musical expression while remaining engrossed in their own thoughts. Contrary to the misconception that "drama" implies stage action, this type of ensemble serves a dramatic function, as "silence resounding." In the central, cantabile section of the first finale in *Luisa Miller*—the Andantino—each character is stunned in a different way. But all are rendered equally speechless, or at least incapable of realistic speech, by the situation in which they find themselves embroiled. The words they nevertheless manage to stammer merely serve as a vehicle for music harboring a wide variety of emotions, all of them inexpressible as dialogue. But the dialectic of emotions has no less claim to drama than that of rational argument. In spoken theater, the emotional conflict that motivates the characters tends to function less as the object of dialogue than as its tacit prerequisite. In opera, however, the reverse holds true: the dialogue incorporated in the recitative or scena merely provides a means of disclosing emotions, the essence of which, according to Schopenhauer's metaphysic, is only capable of finding expression through music. Conflicts represented by emotions against a background of dialogue are, however, no less dramatic than those worked out in dialogue against a background of emotions. We might even say that what is involved is the same drama viewed from different angles.

Still, the Andantino of the first finale differs in one important respect from the type of contemplative ensemble to be found in virtually every opera seria after Rossini: its characters are highly individualized. This gives evidence of Verdi's wish to depict character consistently rather than in isolated flashes. (As he wrote in 1850 in a letter to Marzari: "I can say quite frankly that my music, as beautiful or ugly as it may be, is never written by chance and is always intended to delineate character.") The cantabile, wandering from character to character, is melodically differentiated instead of forming a common musical denominator for the conflicting emotions. Nonetheless, the alternating phrases are covertly linked by what we might refer to as melodic association, even if we are unable to conclude whether their similarity (resulting from the recurrent pitches D–C♯–D–A) owes its existence to a conscious application of variation technique or to an involuntary self-restriction to a narrow circle of stock turns of melody (Ex. 29). In the finale, Verdi differentiates and individualizes the cantabile melody by adapting the structural principle of the opening scena—namely, by juxtaposing

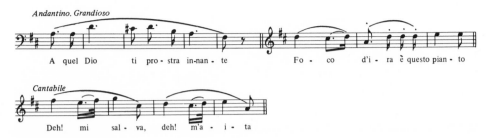

Example 29

periods that cohere internally through their characteristic motives but otherwise stand apart from each other. Recitative and cantabile sections no longer differ in being, respectively, "open-ended" or "closed" (as in the Italian tradition, which Verdi otherwise clung to elsewhere in this opera). Instead, the difference lies in whether they primarily use instrumental or vocal means in order to realize a common overriding technique—that is, to join together sections of contrasting music adapted to the situation on stage. To put it simply, the motive that imparts unity to these passages is an orchestral figure in the scena but a vocal phrase in the cantabile. Both styles, though, employ the same structural principle: dramatically motivated juxtaposition. Furthermore, while Verdi by no means abandoned the traditional operatic practice of recapitulating earlier sections to "close" his forms, he does so almost as seldom in the scena (where it consolidates a previously open-ended form) as in the cantabile (where it functions as the remains of a gradually disintegrating formal scaffolding).

Rigoletto, written in 1851, two years after *Luisa Miller,* catapulted Verdi from a *compositore scritturato* to world renown. Yet the qualitative leap separating this work from its predecessor is slighter than it once seemed to music historians who proceeded on the assumption that any work which ushers in a new era in a composer's reception history must a fortiori be a milestone in the history of composition. Without belittling the significance of *Rigoletto,* we can just as easily stress its proximity to the operas of the late 1840s instead of emphasizing its dissimilarities. One of the most prominent scenes in the history of the genre—the nightmarish dialogue between Rigoletto and Sparafucile in Act 1—is basically a scena. Yet the instrumental motivic work behind the setting attains a degree of musical eloquence, even cantabile (in the cello melody, with the double bass functioning as a *Verfremdungsaffekt*), that fully justifies Verdi's willingness to call this number a "duet." To put it in a different way, recitative and cantabile, formerly musical opposites, had been drawn together by Verdi (as is shown in Act 1 of *Luisa Miller*) in that both employ the structural principle of linking musicodramatic periods. This now enabled Verdi to transfer the technique of instrumental "phrase motives" from the scena to a dialogue, a dialogue which moreover merits the term "duet" insofar as its instrumental melody, in part if not throughout, is essentially vocal.

Fig. 48 Set design from Act 1 of the premiere of Verdi's *Otello* at La Scala, Milan, in 1887. The storm scene that opens Verdi's *Otello*, like Wagner's *Walküre*, serves the dramaturgical function of an overture in that the external tumult foreshadows the inner calamity about to befall the characters. This technique of "natural allegory" which Verdi shared with Wagner is far more crucial to opera, where a premium is placed on straightforward visibility, than in the more abstract spoken drama which unfolds in language: the storm, briefly mentioned in Shakespeare's original, becomes an overwhelming stage spectacle in Verdi's opera. (Berlin, Staatsbibliothek Preußischer Kulturbesitz.)

Thus, though with none of Wagner's rigor, a merging of opposites gradually became noticeable in the relation between Verdi's scena and arioso passages. Verdi pursued a similar path in his handling of the second fundamental category of nineteenth-century Italian opera: the cantabile-cabaletta dichotomy which, as we have seen in *Luisa Miller,* dictated the dramaturgy of opera librettos. In Rigoletto's duet with Gilda, the central scene of Act 1, this traditional distinction is "sublated" in Hegel's dialectical sense of the term, that is, it is at once preserved and superseded. If, with a certain license, we consign the first Allegro Vivo ("Figlia") to the introductory scena, and the second one ("Il nome vostro") to the transitional scena, we can then detect the conventional cantabile-cabaletta design, or a faint outline of it, in the contrasting tempos of the Andante ("Deh non parlare al misero") and the Allegro Moderato Assai ("Ah, veglia, o donna"). The essential point, however, is not the fact that these tempos contrast but the way Verdi mediates between them. The Allegro Vivo derives from a simultaneous contrast between lively motivic work in the instruments and sustained melody in the voices. This contrast can be viewed fully within the "singing allegro" tradition as a superimposition of two types of beat (half note and quarter note) and hence, strictly speaking, as an overlapping of two tempos (Ex. 30). This same phenomenon of double or split meter (quarter note vs. eighth note) recurs in the second period of the Andante ("Oh, quanto dolor"), making it abundantly clear that Verdi intended to cast the transition to the following Allegro ("Il nome vostro") not as an abrupt switch of tempo but rather as an internal shift of emphasis from one of the two superimposed meters to the other. In turn, the Allegro contains an interpolated cantabile in half notes ("Già da tre lune"), which functions as an andante without prescribing a change of tempo.

Example 30

The distance that Verdi, in *Rigoletto,* attained from conventional formal designs without breaking with tradition seems all the more astonishing when we consider that its source, Victor Hugo's tragedy *Le roi s'amuse* (1832), was capable of being reworked into a libretto with no changes required in its dramaturgical structure. Consequently, the drama that provided Verdi with his material offered him not the slightest incentive to tamper with operatic tradition. (As Louis Jouvet remarked, "Hugo, c'est de l'opéra.") Indeed, Hugo made it a practice to construct plots, heedless of aesthetic considerations, for the purpose of unleashing rhetorical lyricism (for which his appetite was insatiable) and motivating scenic tableaux in a histrionic confusion that left audiences bedazzled. This practice, however, in no way differs from the librettist's craft as far as its conception of drama and dramatic style is concerned. All the same, it would be unjust to deny the drama of affect (the goal of Hugo and opera librettists alike) its status as drama: it coherently and dialectically elaborates a tragic constellation, and we have no cause to accuse it of sensation-mongering, with the plot being nothing but an intrigue designed to motivate situations that collapse into isolated "numbers." Verdi, in a letter of 1853 to Antonio Somma, praised the plot of *Rigoletto* for turning convincingly on the mutual entanglements of its characters: "It has powerful situations, variety, excitement, pathos; all the vicissitudes arise from the frivolous, rakish personality of the Duke. Hence Rigoletto's fears, Gilda's passion, etc., etc., which make for many excellent dramatic moments, among others the scene of the quartet which as regards effect will remain one of the best our theater can boast." In drawing attention to the Act 4 Quartet as an "excellent dramatic moment" Verdi put his finger on the main crux of his musical drama,

Fig. 49 Stage design for final scene of *Falstaff*. The closing scene from *Falstaff* (1893) shows Sir John, gulled by the "merry wives of Windsor," in the mask of the "Black Huntsman," antlers and all, beneath the enchanted oak in Windsor Forest. Verdi's last opera, though justly famous, remains esoteric and demands tense concentration at madcap tempos from listeners who want to follow its more gestic than arioso music. Verdi, the "man of the theater," seems, at the end of his career, to have almost forgotten his audience in an effort to write a score that is genuinely theatrical. (Frankfurt am Main, Stadt- und Universitätsbibliothek, Music and Theater Collection.)

which he conceived as a drama of affects. The contrasting emotions appear simultaneously in the andante ("Bella figlia dell'amore"): the Duke's momentary infatuation, Maddalena's mockery, Gilda's desperation, and Rigoletto's outrage, now hardened into a lust for revenge. This causes the drama to culminate at a point where its substance is made manifest—a substance that resides in emotions presented not in isolated "numbers" but in dialectical combination. The Quartet sums up the structural principle of the opera in a single formula immediately accessible to the ear: the listener, rather than giving way entirely to the music of the moment, must constantly bear in mind the overall nexus of emotions with their tragic entanglements. Further, this nexus can be visualized as an interior drama emerging gradually from the exterior plot, more or less independently of the details of the intrigue whose coils run hither and thither between the scenes.

In *Rigoletto*, then, Verdi, for all his experimental daring in some of its scenes, was forced by his literary source to adhere to the dramaturgical laws that Hugo held in common with traditionally minded librettists. On the other hand, it is difficult to determine to what extent the spirit of Shakespeare's tragedy compelled Verdi to attempt "operatic realism" when, decades later, he came to write *Otello*. Obviously, Verdi intended to assimilate the substance of the drama in his opera, but it is no less undeniable that Boïto made far deeper changes in the structure of the original than Piave felt called upon to do in *Rigoletto*. Verdi's enthusiasm for Shakespeare did not prevent him from treating *Otello* much in the same way as *Kabale und Liebe*. By cutting Act 1, and thereby the events in

Venice, Verdi and Boïto created, as Dr. Johnson had foreseen, "a drama of the most exact and scrupulous regularity" (Joseph Kerman: *Opera as Drama*, 1956). Yet it is no less true that by transforming Shakespeare's drama into a *pièce bien faite* they also distorted the work's tragic dialectic. The roots of Othello's jealousy —the split in his personality between the commander to whom Venice entrusted its fleet and the blackamoor whom only magic could conceivably have empowered to win the love of Desdemona—is obscured in Boïto's text if not obliterated altogether. (As Kerman noted, "There is no reason for Otello to be black.") The foundations of the conflict which Othello himself later brought to fruition were laid in the Doge's Palace, a fact which Verdi and Boïto cast aside. The consequence was that Iago, who in the play brings to light a jealousy long preordained in Othello, appears in the opera as the instigator of that jealousy—hence his demonic characterization. In a word, Iago's Credo is a dramaturgical substitute for the Venice act.

Whatever the case, unlike the transformation of *Kabale und Liebe* into *Luisa Miller*, Boïto and Verdi did not take their sights entirely from the dramaturgy of Italian opera when they recast Shakespeare's tragedy into a libretto. The six operas that Verdi wrote between *La traviata* and *Otello* all bore the impress of his study of French grand opera. Ever since the triumph of his operatic trilogy *Rigoletto, Il trovatore,* and *La traviata,* Verdi had reigned uncontested as the leading light of Italian music. Thereafter he apparently sought confirmation from Paris, the "capital of the nineteenth century," that Italian opera was capable of attaining "large-scale form" as established by Meyerbeer, thereby becoming universal without having to abandon its national heritage. Traces of grand opera are still detectable in *Otello,* where they were mistaken for *wagnerismo* by critics enslaved by their attraction to or repulsion from Wagner.

The Storm Scene, many of whose passages recall the "Dies irae" from Verdi's *Requiem* (1874), functions as an overture followed by a chorus, "Fuoco di gioia," and the Brindisi, whose refrain ("Chi all'esca ha morso") climaxes in a frenzy worthy of a revolutionary chorus. Taken together, these three sections form an exposition which, as a musicotheatrical tableau, seems almost to be the fulfillment of a Meyerbeerean fantasy merely hinted at in the Introduction to *Robert le diable.* Yet Verdi, inspired by Boïto's text, revealed his genius for dramaturgy less in the tableau as such, overpowering as it is, than in the functions it serves. According to the rules governing the use of weather in drama and epic poetry, the Storm Scene is doubtless an allegorical rendering of the unrest fomented by Iago, which draws all of the characters in its wake, and of Otello's consternation a short while later. These tumultuous scenes—including the sword fight between Cassio, Rodrigo, and Montano, which likewise erupts like a force of nature—project the figures of the intriguer and the tragic hero into a world larger than life. (At Otello's first entrance it seems as though it is he who has quelled the storm.) At the same time, this outward chaos prefigures the inner chaos into which Otello is about to be precipitated. In short, the tragedy's sociopsychological motivation, grounded in Shakespeare's Venice act, has given way to a motivation from natural mythology, using the musical and stage techniques of grand opera, techniques which Verdi, however, has elevated to the level of "poetic truth." (This was the truth he had in mind when, in a letter of 1876, he spoke to Boïto of "inventing the true.") Moreover, the shadow cast by the tragedy gives Otello's entrances, with their swaggering expression of military glory and amorous bliss, a clarity of outline which would otherwise have been lacking in a nondialectical introduction devoid of dramatic tension. The tumult that Boïto and Verdi release on stage in Act 1 has several closely related functions: it sets forth the intrigue, prefigures Otello's tragic blindness, and serves as a foil for a display of grandeur which, in Aristotelian terms, allows us to measure the height from which the hero must fall.

This dramaturgical sophistication makes us sense how far Verdi has traveled within the grand opera tradition from its original schemata. It is matched by music which, in Otello's duet with Desdemona at the end of the act ("Già nella notte densa"), attains a degree of sophistication far beyond the powers of nineteenth-century music theory to convey. Only after confronting the modern music of our own century did analysts and historians realize that nineteenth-century composers had likewise dissolved time-honored relations between the "parameters" of composition.

The cantabile at the opening of the duet (Ex. 31) is followed by a contrasting narrative tone in its continuation ("Quando narravi"). Syntactically, however, and contrary to our involuntary expectations, the lyrical portion is "irregular" and the epic part "foursquare." The sixteen-measure cantabile, to all appearances a musical period, is composed internally of irregular groupings of measures: 4 (= 2 + 2) + 5 (= 2 + 3) + 2 + 5 (= 3 + 2). The first line (mm. 1–4) cadences on the dominant of the parallel minor; the second (mm. 5–9), seemingly a consequent to the first phrase because of their rhythmic similarity, ends on the dominant of the main key. The isolated two-measure group (mm. 10–11) forms an interpolation by virtue of its harmony, syntax, and recitative-like style. Not until the fourth line (mm. 12–16), melodically a fresh start, do we have a phrase that functions harmonically as a consequent by cadencing in the tonic. In other words, Verdi has extracted the "parameters" of meter and harmony, rhythmic and tonal correspondence, from the simple, venerable relations they enjoyed in the popular notion of "melody," and instead related them to each other "irregularly." A similar technique is used in the narrative section, where the recitative-like melody is offset by the "foursquare" syntax; here Verdi upsets the metrical simplicity by shifting the structural notes C–D–E–F in the second line by a quarter note. In Verdi's case this sophistication is anything but confused; indeed, far from obliterating the "melodic" character of the passage, it forms a prerequisite for *melodie lunghe* which—with devices other than Bellini's, but with the same aesthetic object in view—seem to expand into the measureless and unforeseeable.

Già nel-la not-te den-sa s'e-stin-gue ogni cla-mor. Già il mio cor fre-me-bon-do s'am-

man-sa in quest'am-ples-so e si ri-sen-sa. Tuo-ni la guer-ra e s'ina-

bis-si il mon-do se do-po l'i-ra im-men-sa vien questo immenso a-mor!

Example 31

The Idea of National Opera

National opera was one of the characteristic—and characteristically confused—ideas of the nineteenth century, and we stand little chance of capturing it in a single definition that applies to Weber and Glinka no less than to Moniuszko, Erkel, and Smetana. It only becomes intelligible once we visualize the preconditions, varying from country to country, under which a work was capable of being proclaimed a national opera at all. To keep our historical analysis from wandering aimlessly in circles, we apparently have to take, as our main starting point, not the music or musicodramatical substance of a work so much as this proclamation itself and the motives behind it. There is not the slightest similarity between Glinka's *A Life for the Czar* (1836) and Smetana's *Bartered Bride* (1866) with regard to their respective genres (rescue opera as opposed to village comedy) or their underlying stylistic concept (Glinka adopted folk song, or a folklike tone, while Smetana kept folk song doctrine at arm's length). And while it cannot be gainsaid that Glinka was the first composer to strike a Russian "tone" (and Smetana a Czech one) capable of founding a tradition, this does not answer the question of whether, and if so to what extent, Glinka and Smetana "discovered" the essence of "Russian" or "Czech" music or created it in the first place. There are other ways of explaining this phenomenon besides the notion, prevalent in the nineteenth century, that lying in the depths of the "national spirit" is a musical substance waiting to be unearthed by a major composer, who thereby becomes the "national composer" and who gives this substance artistic claims so compelling as to guarantee historical longevity both to the work in question and to its style. Indeed, the nineteenth century's fondness for cloaking nationalism in "national romanticism" might provoke a historian to maintain the opposite: that a national style in music only arises when the personal style of a major composer is welcomed as the style of a nation, and this at a moment in history when the carrier stratum of a musical culture is demanding a musical expression or reflection of its nationalist political sentiments. Seen in this light, the national side of music is to be found less in the music itself than in its political and sociopsychological function.

It is not obvious why the nineteenth century sought national style in the opera rather than in the symphony, but neither is it astonishing. In an age that drew its education primarily from literature, the principal guidelines were sought in classical poetics, which decreed that the supreme genre in art was the drama, or, more precisely, tragedy. (In Smetana's case, this aesthetic of genres led to a rare confusion: his national opera by proclamation, the *Bartered Bride,* stands alongside his national opera by design, *Dalibor,* whereas the "real" document of Czech national style is his cycle of symphonic poems, *Má vlast,* of 1879.) Further, in Paris, the "capital of the nineteenth century," whose revolutions inflamed nationalist sentiments in other countries, the musical genre that carried the greatest aesthetic weight, perhaps to the exclusion of all others, was opera. Opera owed its development as an institution in the eighteenth century to the needs of courts for "ostentatious public display" (Jürgen Habermas); the nineteenth-century bourgeoisie, forcing its way into the public eye, likewise viewed opera as the primary cultural means of flaunting its claims to social distinction. Instead of simply opposing court opera—part of a system of Italian opera embracing the whole of Europe from Naples to London and from Vienna to St. Petersburg—with the symphony concert, the nineteenth century posited the existence of a bourgeois national opera in the local vernacular. Finally, from a compositional standpoint, it was easier in an opera than in a symphony to realize the concept of national style, inasmuch as vernacular music was presupposed to reside in folk song. After all, folk melodies resist symphonic manipulation (it is rarely possible to break down the lines of a song into motivic particles capable of undergoing a Beethovenian process of development without seeming willful and heavy-handed), whereas they can easily be incorporated into an opera, where the resultant unavoidable fractures in style can be justified as fulfilling dramaturgical functions in the plot. (The sharp contrast of Russian songs and Polish dance tunes in Glinka's *A Life for the Czar* may sound naive—the Poles cling to their lightly chromaticized mazurka tone even in a state of fear and confusion—but it is at any rate aesthetically legitimate, unlike the internal contradictions of what Schönberg disparagingly called the "folkloristic symphonies.")

Some of the difficulties we face when analyzing the concept of national opera become clear the moment we try to explain why *A Life for the Czar,* and not *Ruslan and Lyudmila* (1842), is considered the Russian national opera. *A Life for the Czar* is a rescue opera in the tradition of Cherubini's *Les deux journées* and Beethoven's *Fidelio; Ruslan and Lyudmila* is a fairy-tale opera. The rescue opera as a genre was then at the end of a line of development that had originated in the French Revolution. (The material of *A Life for the Czar* had even been used in 1815, long before Glinka, for a Russian opera—albeit by an Italian, the court composer Catterino Cavos.) The fairy-tale opera, on the other hand, had a historical impact that gave rise to an unbroken tradition extending through Rimsky-Korsakov to Stravinsky. The fairy-tale tone struck by Glinka never vanished from Russian music, neither in the opera nor in the ballet or symphonic poem.

Late nineteenth-century Russian music, then, was influenced less by *A Life for the Czar* than by *Ruslan and Lyudmila*. This leads us to conclude that historical impact is not the key criterion for a national opera. But neither does the degree to which Glinka was able to liberate Russian opera from Italian models prove to be essential. The style of Bellini and Donizetti that Glinka adopted in the early 1830s during his Italian journey, when he first learned to "talk in music," left traces in both operas which only a fanatical nationalist could disavow. Antonida's rondo in *A Life for the Czar* (No. 2) is no less an Italian operatic piece in Russian garb than the quintet with chorus (Adagio) in the last-act finale of *Ruslan and Lyudmila* (No. 26). However, there is no denying that the Italian influence is more obvious and less well integrated in *A Life for the Czar,* just as the earlier work as a whole is, not surprisingly, more eclectic and stylistically less unified than the later one.

Thus, it was *A Life for the Czar,* and not *Ruslan and Lyudmila,* that the idea of national music seized upon in order to take tangible form. Yet the motives behind this choice on the audience's part do not fall into a clearcut line of argument. The mere fact that *A Life for the Czar* was the earlier of the two, being indeed Glinka's first opera at all, was crucial in that it was a typical nineteenth-century prejudice to believe that the essence of a strand of history is to be found in its origins. (While classicist historians stressed a *point de perfection,* attained after a long period of gestation, their romantic counterparts were forever groping back to first causes.) Moreover, in *A Life for the Czar,* the patriotism that instilled not only the plot, but also parts of the music so drastically that the final chorus could become a sort of second national anthem, took the form of a rescue opera—a form as acceptable to the rulers who acknowledge the sacrifice as to the ruled who offered it. If one ingredient that established a work as a national opera was its instantaneous or at least prompt success (as opposed to the decades that separated Mussorgsky's *Boris Godounov* and Janáček's *Jenůfa* from proper recognition), another firm foothold was a conciliatory attitude that made widespread approbation possible. (Political ambiguity was typical of the genre from its earliest prototype, Cherubini's *Les deux journées.*) Nor should we underestimate the psychological element in the reception history of opera: it is easy for audiences to identify with the main characters in the drama—with Susanin no less than Vanya and Sobinin—whereas the same cannot be said of *Ruslan and Lyudmila,* a jumbled fairy tale with a colorful plot (reminiscent of Ariosto) but bland characters. (Its text was written piecemeal by a whole team of librettists, all of them amateurs.)

In the nineteenth century, the age of nationalism, the idea of national opera was closely allied with the question of national identity, and in Russian music—unlike Polish, Hungarian, or Czech music—this question bore the hallmarks of cultural politics rather than problems of nationhood and social policies. Russians had neither resolved nor silenced the debate as to whether they should imitate, transform, or reject the Western culture imposed upon them since the time of Peter the Great. Nor had a clear, immutable connection arisen between cultural politics, on the one hand, and royalist, liberal, or democratic leanings on the other. It is against this background that the quest for a specifically Russian form of art music took place—that is, for a style which would elevate vernacular music, folk song, into art music without subjecting it to compositional techniques so patently derived from Italian or German models that the Russian "intonation" (to use Boris Asaf'ev's term), rather than being substantive, would merely function as a dash of local color.

Russian composers from Glinka to Rimsky-Korsakov and Stravinsky have placed special emphasis on orchestral timbre, creating a distinctly Russian brand of orchestral virtuosity independent of Berlioz and Wagner. This was doubtless related to their efforts to mediate intrinsically between folk song and art music rather than simply cobbling the two together—to avoid the twin perils of having composition degenerate into amateurism by clinging to a folk "intonation," or, conversely, sacrificing folk intonation to the artistic demands of composition. They found an escape in the "parameter" of orchestral timbre, by using harmony and counterpoint not infrequently as a function of tone color, rather than vice versa, as classical precepts prescribed. This can be viewed as part of their attempt to transfer, to the language of art music, the characteristically Russian aspects of folk melody and rhythm, capturing and preserving them without having their substance crushed by harmony and by that ne plus ultra of musical artifice, counterpoint. In other words, in order to make local color, the Russian tinge, essential rather than a mere additive, composers altered the traditional hierarchy of compositional parameters.

But rules of composition are not so unalterable as even a composer as recent as Beethoven believed, or claimed to believe. On the contrary, many chord progressions that would be out of place in strict harmonic writing may be permitted for the sake of their color. This realization forces us to rethink the allegations of dilettantism cast, in varying degrees, on almost every Russian composer of the nineteenth century (with the exception of Rubinstein, Tchaikovsky, and Rimsky-Korsakov in his late works), rather than judging them by textbook criteria. True, Glinka was not a professional musician but a gentleman farmer, even if he did study for a few months with Siegfried Dehn in Berlin. This was grist for the mill of historians who sought refuge in clichés from the confusions of reality, and the upshot was a view of history in which oppositions between Italian and Russian music, court opera and national opera, Western leanings and folklorist proclivities, professionalism and dilettantism, were lumped together into a rigid schema that invited mechanical associations. However, the most cursory analysis of a scene such as Ivan Susanin's entrance in *A Life for the Czar* (No. 3) suffices to show that the assimilation of folk song, or folk "tone," can be directly related to the art of unifying a dramatic scene by musical means. This is a far cry from dilettantism, even if the harmonies, without obvious "blunders," sometimes strike out on unwonted paths. The arioso opening of this scene, as Glinka reveals in his autobiography, is a folk song quotation (Ex. 32). The first line of the song, rhythmically varied, develops into the chorus that follows Susanin's arioso, while the

Example 32

third line gives rise to the balalaika melodies that form an instrumental counterpoint to the choral writing at the close of the scene (Ex. 33). Thus, the folk song substance permeating the whole of the music, whether directly or indirectly, and the half-submerged but effective musical links between sections of a scene spanning hundreds of measures, are opposite sides of the same coin. This scene successfully mediates between folk song intonation and a claim to rank as art—a claim which can be met in many other ways than by piously observing the rules of strict composition.

Example 33

The dramaturgy or poetics of nineteenth-century national opera—a dramaturgy that combines and intermingles political implications, ideas on opera as drama, and compositional assumptions—received virtually paradigmatic expression in Ferenc Erkel's *Bánk Bán*, the Hungarian representative of the genre. Despite its medieval provenance, the historical material (which also served as the basis of Grillparzer's tragedy *Ein treuer Diener seines Herrn* of 1828) must have seemed like a political parable in 1861. The Hungarian king, detained abroad in the wars; his foreign-born queen and her brother, who subjugate the country; the viceroy, Bánk Bán, who joins the rebellion from a sense of loyalty: all are symbolic figures in a political constellation relevant to the times. To an age which drew its popular notions of tragedy from Victor Hugo, however, *Bánk Bán* only became a drama by virtue of an intrigue hinging on that shopworn conflict of love versus honor that has prevailed throughout much of postmedieval drama. This conflict intrudes upon nineteenth-century literature like a fossil from the seventeenth; yet, as Verdi's reliance on Hugo showed, it was able, especially in opera, to survive the collapse of French romanticism in the 1840s. Even so, by presenting a national conflict, the plot of *Bánk Bán* fulfills the musicodramatic function of vindicating the stylistic compromise imposed upon Erkel by the state of compositional evolution in the 1850s. No observer with an appreciation of music unstifled by nationalist fervor would maintain that it was possible to write a through-composed piece with pretensions to "grand opera" using the devices of Hungarian music, namely, the rhythms and instrumental effects of the *verbunkos*. Accordingly, Erkel adopted the technique, already present in Glinka's *A Life for the Czar*, of characterizing the political parties by their national musics: Italo-French inflections, on the one hand, and a Hungarian coloration on the other. (That the *verbunkos*, or recruiting dance, originated in the eighteenth century and was more Gypsy than Hungarian in origin did not in the least trouble the adherents of national music, who fondly imagined this dance to be ancient and indigenous. The crucial issue with regard to national music is not its substance and origin so much as the function it served in the mid-nineteenth century's highly politicized musical awareness.) In its formal outline, Erkel's opera is unspecific without being conventional. At times, however, a nationalist slant seems to be intended: the tempos of Act 3, scene 1—the death scene of Bánk Bán's wife, driven to madness—can be derived not only from the Italian double aria (cantabile–cabaletta–*stretta*) but also from the *verbunkos* (slow–fast–faster). This very ambiguity is characteristic.

Bánk Bán, then, illuminates the political, dramaturgical, and compositional conditions of the national opera with a clarity more common to peripheral works of music history than to the central ones. By the same token, however, the fact that none of Erkel's subsequent works was acclaimed as a national opera only becomes fully intelligible when we see the dual motivation behind it. Understandably, Erkel refused to succumb to self-imitation by repeating the dramaturgy of the work that had made him Hungary's national composer. However, this psychological explanation must be complemented by a political one: with the founding of the Dual Monarchy, Hungary, or at least its aristocracy, switched roles from an oppressed people to the oppressors of other peoples. It would seem that a nation will cling to the idea of national opera as a means of finding its identity only when its nationalist spirit is in a stage of liberation rather than aggression. In Hungary, the hour of national opera had ended in the mid-1860s.

The Polish national opera, Stanislaw Moniuszko's *Halka,* is based on a text written by Wlodzimierz Wolski (less a librettist than a poet) under the impress of the 1846 peasant uprising in Galicia. (It was given a concert performance in 1848, mounted on stage in Vilna in 1854, and performed in an expanded version in Warsaw in 1858.) Its plot is patterned after bourgeois tragedy, a genre which had changed continuously since the eighteenth century but which still, in the mid-nineteenth century, retained its freshness in the opera, where it was slow to be adopted. Halka, a serf, is seduced by her master, Janusz. When he marries a woman of his own social station, she hastens to her death, torn to and fro between unsuppressed love and an impulse to set fire to the church. Despite its obviously "melodramatic" tendencies, this material is nevertheless consistent with the work's underlying revolutionary sentiments. Indeed, like the novels of Victor Hugo and Eugène Sue, it represents the literary guise adopted by social criticism in the mid-nineteenth century.

The specifically Polish tone that compelled Warsaw audiences of 1858 to proclaim *Halka* the national opera of Poland is evident in its songs and dances, which admittedly do not constitute the framework of the opera so much as its façade. Its musicodramaturgical brand of social criticism stands in a curiously tangled relation to the national character of its music, a relation that is virtually impossible to capture in a simple formula. If we proceed from the aesthetic of genres in our efforts to "decipher the music sociologically" (to use Adorno's phrase), it turns out that the decisive factor is neither the opposition between aristocratic polonaise and rustic *goralski,* nor the contrast between Halka's singspiel melodies and the operatic flavor of the aristocrats' Act 1 terzetto, where Halka's song intrudes from a distance. The crucial point is that Halka, in her duet with Janusz (dramaturgically the keystone of the exposition), partakes of the style of grand opera, attaining a tragic pathos reminiscent of a Meyerbeerean heroine. This is not simply a relapse into operatic convention following the "noble simplicity" of her initial folklike tunes. Rather, it expresses aesthetic and social claims which we are fully justified in calling revolutionary—namely, that even a serf like Halka can function as a tragic heroine, and that she too may appropriate the "elevated style" reserved in Aristotle's rules of social standing for "kings and potentates." The same applies to the contemplative ensemble in Act 4 (in E♭ major, Andante non troppo lento). This section captures a moment in which time stands still and all characters in the drama, confronted with the inexorable force of tragedy, give vent to their perplexity in mute self-absorption. It is precisely because the music eradicates any distinctions of social station that Halka reaches a stylistic level enabling her destiny to attain the dimensions of tragedy rather than misfortune. Drama reflects social reality not only directly, in its subject matter, but also "formally" with respect to the history of genres, and the actual revolution in *Halka* is its claim to rank as tragedy (in the aesthetic sense), even if the violence of its social conflicts is blunted in the process.

Czech national music originated in a different way from its Russian, Polish, or Hungarian counterparts, being preceded by a full century and a half of distinguished Czech composers. Bohemia was a major region in the European musical landscape. (One of the prejudices that distort our appreciation of Czech music is a mindless habit of associating national music with peripheral music cultures whose works we find attractive less for their artistic stature than for their exotic local color.) The emigration of Czech musicians in the eighteenth and the early nineteenth century was felt not only in Mannheim and Paris but in Berlin and Vienna as well, and was nearly equal in importance to the Italian emigration of the same time. All the same, we are at a loss to detect a Czech style, notwithstanding a few traces of folk music which eager ethnographers have claimed to dis-

Fig. 50 Stage design for *Nabucco*. *Nabucco* (1842) marked Verdi's "breakthrough" just as *Rienzi* did Wagner's. The enthusiasm of the audience was mingled with a patriotic fervor that turned the Prisoners' Chorus *Va pensiero, sull' ali dorate* ("Flee, O thought, on wings of gold") into a hymn of the *Risorgimento* and the work as a whole into a sort of Italian national opera. In the Act 2 finale Nabucco, or Nebuchadnezzar, struck by madness, curses the gods of Babylon and Israel and declares himself to be God, thereby provoking a lightning bolt, which strikes the crown from his head. This is only one of the musicodramatic "eruptions" in an opera whose uncommonly jumbled plot serves merely to provide slender motivation for moments when overheated emotions collide. (Berlin, Staatsbibliothek Preußischer Kulturbesitz.)

cover in Berlin and Viennese composers of Czech extraction. Similarly, Bedřich Smetana founded a music widely acclaimed as characteristically Czech, without making the slightest obeisance to the doctrine that a national musical idiom must thrive on folk song, a doctrine whose untenability had been demonstrated in 1826 by the ill-fortune that befell Škroup's folkloristic singspiel *The Tinker*. As Smetana put it: "Imitating the melodic turns and rhythms of our folk songs will not create a national style, still less an authentic drama, but at the most a shallow imitation of those very folk songs." In short, folkloristic proclivities are insufficient to explain why the Czechs found their national composer, not in Tomášek, a highly original fellow traveler of the Viennese Classics, but rather in Smetana, a stylistic adherent of the "New German" school. Both, after all, were equally remote from folk song. (It in no way contradicts Smetana's "New German" leanings that he first struck a national tone recognizable as such by the oppressed Czech people in a comic opera, *The Bartered Bride,* rather than a tragic one. Tragedy had been more or less commandeered by Wagner's towering oeuvre, and this prompted Liszt, around 1850 when Smetana was in Weimar, to advocate comic opera of the sort that Peter Cornelius essayed in "New German" circles with his *Der Barbier von Bagdad* of 1858.) Moreover, the "official magnum opus" and "genuine" programmatic national opera of Czechoslovakia is not so much *The Bartered Bride,* whose polkas, furiants, and galops make its national tinge obvious even to outsiders, but *Dalibor.* This complicates the problem of pinpointing the constitutive elements of national opera to such a degree as to make it appear insoluble.

To reach our goal, we must take a detour and begin our argument at a seemingly remote point: despite his affinity to the "New Germans," Smetana was not a "Wagnerian." (Admittedly, it is not clear what late-nineteenth-century critics meant in the first place when they reproached opera composers for being dependent on Wagner, since virtually none was able to escape him.) Even so, it is an unmistakable fact—which in turn links up with the problem of national opera —that *Dalibor* is rooted not only in *Fidelio* but in *Tristan* as well. True, the scenes between the captive Dalibor, Milada in her boyish disguise, and the jailer inevitably recall Beethoven's opera. But Milada's love for the slayer of her brother—a hopeless passion all the more consuming for being foredoomed—has its prototype in the entanglements between the love of Tristan and Isolde and the death of Morold. This parallelism is one indication that Smetana had obviously been moved by Wagner's precedent when he grounded his opera on an internalized plot with a seemingly motionless tragic dialectic. The courtroom, dungeon, and death scenes are external way stations in a drama consisting basically of a single situation: the moment when the entanglements are recognized as inescapable. Smetana, doubtless subconsciously, guided himself on *Tristan*'s bold contribution to opera dramaturgy: its plot simply inscribes circles around a dramatic constellation without moving it in the slightest. Similarly, Milada's monologue in Act 2, or Dalibor's in Act 3, has an eruptive force that maintains a note of relentless urgency over a time-span that seems to dilate into the infinite. This, too, is unthinkable without Wagner's precedent, even if we are hard pressed to detect specific "Wagnerisms." (The dramatic design of *Dalibor* is revealed in a single instant, at the end of the middle act. In consequence, however, the Dalibor-Milada plot suffers musically from an emotional factor extraneous to the events depicted on stage: Dalibor's lament for his slain friend Zdeněk, whose death he avenged by killing Milada's brother. This infringes against the basic rule of Italian opera—that the emotion represented in the music must correspond to a constellation visible on stage—and is probably one reason why the work has failed to establish itself in the repertoire outside Czechoslovakia despite the unquestionably high quality of its music.)

Dalibor, then, has both an interior and an exterior plot, the former paradoxically encircling a frozen dialectic, the latter forming a decorative façade. This dichotomy enabled Smetana to conceive of national opera as a festival—with processions, choruses, and conflicts resolved in public discourse (Acts 1 and 3)— and yet to portray, beneath the surface of events, a secret tragedy of an emotional force that virtually compelled him to adopt the most advanced compositional techniques of his day. In this way he avoided the grandiose style which, given the historical situation of the 1860s, would have consigned his work to a phantom existence of no significance to the history of composition. To put it another way, by imprisoning a symbolic national figurehead, the external plot vouchsafed the opera's national character to a people that considered itself oppressed (but was, nevertheless, since the Imperial Manifesto of 1860, free enough to complain about its oppression in public), while the internal plot allowed the work to attain its artistic stature. Without this stature *Dalibor* would merely have documented a will to national opera rather than becoming a national opera in its own right.

Opéra bouffe, Operetta, Savoy Opera

In ordinary parlance, "operetta" is clearly distinguished from opera as a genre of music theater—as though Auber's *opéra comique* (classified as "opera") were closer to Meyerbeer's grand opera or Gounod's *drame lyrique* than to an *opéra bouffe* by Offenbach (classified as "operetta"). To uproot this firmly engrained preconception by examining these terms would be simple but ultimately pointless: our task, after all, is not to correct but to understand a terminological usage which in turn made music history. Of course, no historian with a rational attitude toward his subject will want to argue that it was merely arbitrary and accidental that the term "opera" has been withheld from *opéra bouffe,* Viennese operetta, and Savoy opera, but extended to opera buffa and *opéra comique.* But neither will he want to abandon the concept of "opera" simply because there are no logically sound criteria for selecting from the untold number of musicotheatrical genres—from *vaudeville* and farce with interpolated songs to *opéra bouffe* and operetta and finally to *opéra comique* and opera buffa—a particular group to be classified as "opera." "Opera" is a historical category, and its meaning will not be grasped by a pigeonhole mentality. That *opéra bouffe* and Viennese operetta, unlike earlier analogous genres, were not included under the heading "opera" is a fact of reception history which in turn sheds light on the historical position and significance of *musiquette,* light music, in the latter part of the nineteenth century.

With *Orphée aux enfers* (1858), *La belle Hélène* (1864), *La vie parisienne* (1866), and *La Grande-Duchesse de Gérolstein* (1867), Offenbach turned *opéra bouffe* into a genre that established Paris, the city of international exhibitions, as the capital of Europe in music as well. Historically, this genre came from homely origins, emerging from one-acters of the sort presented by Hervé in the Folies Concertantes from 1854 and by Offenbach in the Bouffes Parisiennes from 1855. In other words, the "prehistory" of this genre differs not in the slightest from the developments that led from the intermezzo and *vaudeville* to, respectively, opera buffa and *opéra comique*. Like them, it was a *genre primitif et gai*, to use Offenbach's words, and not only made use of the song, dance, and march music of its day but also parodied forms and stylistic devices from "serious" music. Gradually its claims to artistic status elevated it beyond the purlieu of the town fair, suburban theater, and touring company, sometimes to the regret of actors and audience alike. (There is nothing left in an operetta theater like the Vienna Volksoper to recall the Variété.)

However, there was one respect in which the rise of the *opéra bouffe* and operetta in the late nineteenth century to aesthetic and social respectability differed from the superficially analogous process which, in the eighteenth century, caused the intermezzo to develop into opera buffa and the *vaudeville* into *opéra comique*—namely, their lack of importance to the history of composition. (This is not to say that they were irrelevant to the history of music. Music history encompasses not only composition but the performance, reception, and institutions of music, and however minor operetta's place in the annals of compositional history, it played an inestimable part in the everyday musical life of the public.) Opera buffa and *opéra comique* determined, to a large extent, the history of operatic form in the late eighteenth century: the aesthetic tumult unleashed by Gluck's reforms should not cause us to overlook the equivalent, if not greater, impact of the less conspicuous changes wrought by Mozart (and by Piccinni and Paisiello as well) in the musical structure and dramaturgy of the operatic ensemble. The history of these forms justifies our claim—and this is crucial to the use of the term "opera" as a historical category—that the intermezzo and *vaudeville*, as transformed into opera buffa and *opéra comique*, became "operas" by altering the history of operatic composition in mutual interplay with opera seria and *tragédie lyrique*. In contrast, apart from the waltzes in *Der Rosenkavalier* (1911) and hints of operetta in *Arabella* (1933), *opéra bouffe* and operetta seem to have had not the slightest historical impact beyond the confines of their own genre. From Wagner's *Meistersinger* (1868) and Wolf's *Der Corregidor* (1896) to Verdi's *Falstaff* (1893) and Strauss's *Der Rosenkavalier*, there is no trace of the musical structure and dramaturgy of operetta to be found in the historically significant comic operas of the late nineteenth and the early twentieth century, when in any case it was disadvantaged by the evolution of compositional technique. In the history of opera, operetta remained "extraterritorial." True, some works like Lehár's *Friederike* (1928) or *Paganini* (1925) aspired to the level of opera by their "seriousness," with a stylistic *coup de main* that revealed the parvenu. However, they did so not from within but by borrowing from "accepted" opera, from Massenet to Puccini, producing a pseudomorphic hybrid foredoomed to artistic failure.

Still, if operetta had little impact on the history of composition, where the present is made legitimate by bearing the seeds of the future, it was all the more closely bound to the social history of its day. Operetta arose under the conditions of its own age, dominating musical fashions just as it was dominated by them (an instance of the interaction between dictatorship and plebiscite). Offenbach's *opéra bouffe* was a musicotheatrical effigy of the Second Empire. Yet the socio-psychological relation between the two, however tangible, was nevertheless ambivalent. At all events, the notion that Offenbach was a "subversive" whose music harbors portents of "revolution" is, if not sheer myth, at least grossly naive. Indeed, in the Third Republic, which followed upon the catastrophe of 1870, political moralizers suspected Offenbach of being Louis Napoleon's "state musician," discovering in the concluding Galop of *Orphée aux enfers* or the waltz finale of *La belle Hélène* a sympathy with the corruption that *opéra bouffe* was ever at pains to expose. It is, in fact, striking that Offenbach, apart from minor annoyances occasioned by the censor, never encountered serious resistance from the grand luminaries and potentates of the Second Empire who joined his audience. Practically the only way to explain this is to assume that the political and financial tycoons who set the tone during Louis Napoleon's reign had one underlying attitude in common with their critic Offenbach, who, in the theater, exploded the decorum which scantily clad their corruption: they all shared a deep-seated sense of skepticism. Since the system's initiates believed in nothing, and since there was no need in a decade of economic prosperity to convince the public that the slogans being cast its way were true, Offenbach's mockeries, well-mannered and presented with a sort of perfidious good grace, could be taken with a grain of salt.

All the same, *La belle Hélène* of 1864 concludes with an announcement of the Trojan War, and the threat of imminent disaster darkens the musical euphoria which again and again resolves the tangles of the plot. At the end of Act 2 all characters on stage (except for Paris and Helen, who plan to flee) are drawn into the waltz melody—excluding not even the outraged Greek princes, stung by the scandal from their everyday corruption, nor the priest Kalchas, a patent scoundrel, nor the bon vivant Orestes. The waltz seems to capture the twisted dramaturgy in a single musical formula (Ex. 34). To this the Greek princes add the words "Un vil séducteur nous insulte et nous outrage," striking a tone that uninhibitedly conveys the very seduction that has left them so outraged. There is, to be sure, a touch of opera parody in this device (an ingredient to which Offenbach, feeling drawn to the opera, turned more frequently than other operetta composers): it mocks the convention, in ensemble finales, of using a single melody to express the conflicting emotions of characters in a concluding tableau. In this case, however, Offenbach's inversion of sentiment, with the music proceeding in disregard of the text, symbolizes a tacit acquiescence among swindlers and swindled alike—and here the two are indistinguishable. Namely, all consent to the corruption which holds them in thrall and which they collectively repress by fleeing into the euphoria of the waltz. Above all else, Offenbach knew full well

Example 34

that any music which owes its effect, and its inimitability, to a blend of melancholy and energetic verve will be most irresistible when it rises above tumultuous and seemingly insoluble conflicts with the triumphant indifference of Beauty.

In *opéra bouffe*, then, the plot dissolves in the orgiastic frenzy of a waltz or cancan finale. This effect originated in dance music, whose major proponents, Philippe Musard in Paris and Johann Strauss *père* and *fils* in Vienna, swept audiences into a state of giddiness which then received its glorified likeness in operetta. This orgiastic, euphoric aspect is the defining feature of a type of operetta whose musical dramaturgy does more than merely daub music on various combinations of elements from farce and the *comédie larmoyante*. Musard and the two Strausses represent a moment in history when the dance music of a monarchy jeopardized by democracy attained boundless popularity while still conveying a faint reflection of the splendor of court festivities. (In Vienna, court dance had lost its exclusivity to the waltz.) In art music, however, the waltz, notwithstanding its apotheosis in *Der Rosenkavalier* and echoes of it in Schönberg's dodecaphonic works, has never been integrated in the same sense as the allemande and courante in the Baroque or the minuet and contredanse in the Classic period. Unlike the contredanse, which a century earlier could serve as the rhythmic pattern for the last movement of a Haydn symphony, the waltz (not to mention the cancan), with its tendency toward the potpourri, stood outside the progression to "musical logic" that dominated the evolution of harmony and theme in the history of nineteenth-century compositional technique. As long as operetta clung to the principle of culminating in a dance—and to dispense with this principle is to abandon the genre altogether, as Lehár's "ambitious" operettas prove—it cut itself off from a movement in compositional history which had struck out on a path of increasingly sophisticated harmonic and thematic processes. This path later gave comic opera, in *Der Rosenkavalier*, an opportunity to explore a conversational melodic tone rooted in psychological orchestral counterpoint—a tone with which the waltz music, which seems to be quoted in passing, barely accords stylistically, no matter how justified it may be dramaturgically.

Still, it would be gross distortion of historical fact to view the frenzy of an Offenbach finale merely as the upshot of transplanting Musard's Variété to the theater of the Bouffes Parisiennes. This would misrepresent the dramaturgical context that makes a finale what it is. The waltz that holds spellbound the dramatic agents in *La belle Hélène*, and with them the audience, must be seen, not in isolation, but against the backdrop of the duet between Paris and Helen that immediately precedes it. In this duet, dream merges with reality and reality with dream, causing the contours of the plot to blur. Helen, cunning and superstitious, pretends to Paris that their adultery, inescapably preordained by Venus,

Fig. 51 Johann Strauss, the elder: *Der große Galopp*. During the 1830s and 1840s, in the ballrooms of Philippe Musard in Paris and Johann Strauss the elder in Vienna, the social dance was transformed into a phenomenon scarcely describable except in terms of mass psychology. The state of frenzy to which bourgeois society let itself be transported by a Musard quadrille or a Strauss galop was reproduced on stage in the latter half of the century—namely, in operetta, which culminated in the euphoria of a waltz finale or a cancan finale to resolve the tangles of the plot. (Vienna, Österreichische Nationalbibliothek.)

is taking place in a dream, and the dreamlike character of the scene is reinforced accordingly by the music. This casts these events into a twilight realm, enabling the transition to euphoria to take place without a break in continuity. The whirlwind that ultimately engulfs all the characters, bar none, seems to emerge almost naturally from a confusion of actions and feelings, a quid pro quo of appearance and reality, so turbulent as to upend the entire received system of values.

And yet, the tone of the duet is all the more moving for being fractured. Critics never tire of emphasizing Offenbach's narrow blend of sentimentality and aggressive satire—the sentimentality of the French *romance* and the satire of the *couplet*—portraying him as a musical Heinrich Heine. This explains why the irony in the duet from *La belle Hélène*, though unmistakable, is in no way at odds with sentimentality, even serving as its vehicle (Ex. 35). Conversely, the aggres-

Andante

C'est le   ciel   qui m'en voie.   Ce beau rêve   a-mou-reux   ce doux rêve   a- mou-reux.

Example 35

sion that surfaces in the orgiastic finales, above all in the cancan in *Orphée aux enfers,* is merely the obverse side of a nostalgia expressed most clearly by the song of Jean Styx, the erstwhile "Prince of Arcadia." In *La belle Hélène* this same nostalgia, if less prominent, is evident in the duet and in Paris's tale of Mount Ida.

The text of *Die Fledermaus* (1874) is the work of Offenbach's librettists Meilhac and Halévy, being merely revised and adapted to Viennese circumstances by Haffner and Genée. In its dramaturgical outline, and without detracting from its quality in the slightest, this "operetta to end all operettas" is actually an *opéra bouffe* in the style of *La vie parisienne.* Similarly, at a later stage in his development, in *Der Zigeunerbaron* (1885), Strauss ushered in the Viennese-Hungarian operetta of our century by removing the genre from the Variété and settling it in the Café Concertant. Musically, however, Strauss and Offenbach are leagues apart, as becomes apparent when we compare, for example, the Infernal Galop from *Orphée aux enfers* with the polka that pervades the entire plot of *Die Fledermaus* as a sort of musical emblem or leitmotiv for Falke's intrigue (Ex. 36). The difference in tempo between the Allegro Moderato of the Galop and that of the polka is slight (otherwise there would be no point in comparing the two). Nonetheless, Strauss's music, unlike Offenbach's, never seems precipitate or madcap, and thus lacks Offenbach's orgiastic tinge. The reason for this is to be found in their different rhythmic accentuation. Despite its quick tempo, Strauss's polka still maintains a metrical distinction among the four eighth notes of each measure, with 1 and 3 being heavier than 2 and 4, and 1 in turn heavier than 3. In this way, each measure forms a balanced system, a relatively self-contained unit. In contrast, Offenbach's Galop emphasizes successive quarter notes—and in some measures even eighth notes—with almost equal weight. Lacking metrical gradation, they drive the rhythmic motion irresistibly beyond the bar lines. Even at *allegro con brio* Strauss's rhythm seems to circumscribe a given state, whereas Offenbach's presses toward a goal.

Example 36

This difference in the way Offenbach and Strauss handle rhythm and meter goes beyond the distinction between these two dance types to include features of the composers' personal styles (it is no coincidence that Offenbach was a composer of galops and Strauss of waltzes and polkas). The same difference, for instance, is apparent in the way they handle waltz time: Strauss's two-measure units seem to be almost suspended in mid-air by the fact that each of the six beats differs from the five others, whereas Offenbach's more regular accentuation drives the music relentlessly forward. This musical distinction between suspended rhythm and driving rhythm is linked with a deep-seated variance in the dramaturgical outlooks of these two composers, in the way their music affects the plot. However, the exact connection eludes analysis. Even though—or all the more so because—the libretto of *Die Fledermaus* is close to *opéra bouffe,* the musical devices employed by Strauss and Offenbach to "stage" their euphoric finales contrast in the most glaring way imaginable. And it is in these devices, insofar as art lies in technique, that the spirit of operetta and *opéra bouffe* is made manifest. The Act 2 finale in *Die Fledermaus,* a waltz finale in which a busy intrigue gives way to a state of trance, is doubtless the most successful extended musicodramatic complex in the whole of Strauss's operettas, bearing comparison with the conclusion of Act 2 in *La belle Hélène.* Yet the two are significantly different. Offenbach takes the waltz, the musical expression of seduction, as his starting point for a situation in which dream and reality, divine decree and human frailty blur, and ultimately even the victims succumb to the orgiastic mood. Strauss, on the other hand, evokes a simple aura of camaraderie motivated by nothing more than champagne. The difference between the two resembles the difference between a well-chosen punch line that sums up its story and an ill-conceived one that misses the point. As a result, for all of its marvelous music, the *Fledermaus* finale is a dramaturgical letdown.

Thus, the waltz frenzy that seizes the characters in *Die Fledermaus,* leaving none untouched, completely nullifies the intrigue instead of culminating dramaturgically in the trance that follows, as in Offenbach. At least, however, it is clearly motivated and justified by appearing in the context of an all-night party. By comparison, the waltz in the Act 2 finale of *Der Zigeunerbaron*—or, more accurately, its excessive repetition following the "catastrophe"—is patently nonsensical. What functions in Offenbach as "absurd theater" (in the generic sense of the term) is merely a miscalculation in *Der Zigeunerbaron.* Here the waltz, a musical landmark for Vienna, captures the mood of setting out for the city, a feeling which, however, contradicts the situation on stage in the "tragic" Act 2 finale, where the lovers are separated so as to be reunited in a happy ending in Act 3. True, the text sung by Saffi and Barinkay offsets the mood of the waltz, but this is immaterial when measured against the overriding fact that they too take part in the waltz music. Strauss failed to take dramaturgical advantage of the insight that nothing is more heartrending in an inescapably sad situation than merry or festive music, provided the injured parties remain silent. In short, the interior plot bears no relation to the musically staged façade. Again and again we hear of

Strauss's disregard for his texts (usually with a quotation of the unspeakable words to "The Beautiful Blue Danube"), but in fact, in operetta, it is not so much literary as dramaturgical uncertainty that disturbs us the moment we stop submitting to the ravishes of the music and consider its function.

As a purely musical creation outside its theatrical context, the *Fledermaus* waltz deserves to be defended against the charge that it is merely a potpourri, that its dramaturgical weaknesses are matched by a want of formal continuity. The waltz, or waltz sections, preceding the ballet evince latent melodic similarities centering on the notes F−E−B♭, which momentarily recur at parallel passages in the form (Ex. 37). The waltz sections following the ballet are likewise related melodically—though it is impossible, indeed unnecessary, to determine whether and to what extent their affinities arose involuntarily or from a conscious application of variation technique. Subconsciously, we sense that these sections are held together not just by their arrangement but by an inner coherence, a coherence that can be localized analytically to a chromatic run of a fifth (Ex. 38).

wol-len al - le   wir sein, stimmt mit   mir   ein   dann ein Du,   Du,   Du,   im - mer-zu

Example 37

Example 38

Without its element of "absurd theater" operetta would degenerate into a form of entertainment that entertains nobody. In its characteristic English variant, the Savoy opera, this element was further refined to become not just a dramaturgical quality but a literary one as well. If Offenbach could not have become what he was without Halévy, Sullivan is as unthinkable without Gilbert as Gilbert is without Sullivan (Strauss's operetta music seems to stand above its texts, which

Fig. 52 Caricature of Offenbach. It did not cost the caricaturist any great effort to recapture Offenbach's parody of the beautiful Helen or the indecisive Orpheus, vacillating between dread of marriage and fear of public opinion. To caricature Jacques Offenbach himself (here shown astride his first instrument, the cello) was, on the other hand, almost impossible. Even a simple portrait already discloses traits mirroring the dramaturgy of *opéra bouffe*: a grotesqueness leading toward catastrophe but turning ultimately into festive tumult. (Frankfurt am Main, Stadt- und Universitätsbibliothek, Music and Theater Collection.)

have fallen into oblivion thanks to their own inadequacies). It is no coincidence that the Savoy opera is the only genre of music theater where librettist and composer are automatically mentioned in the same breath. If the success it merits by virtue of its artistic stature has remained confined to England and the United States, the reason is to be found in precisely that feature to which it owes its distinction: in the acerbity and satire of its texts, which resist translation no less completely than does the wit of Lear's nonsense verse.

Gilbert's librettos resemble experiments based on absurd premises: capital punishment for flirting in *The Mikado* (1885), or the conflicting legal codes for fairies and the peerage in *Iolanthe* (1882). His object was to provoke from Victorian society, which stumbled into these experiments like a trap, reactions that revealed it to be no less absurd itself. At times the fury beneath his satire touches on the foundations of a society which still felt at ease with the status quo and could therefore suffer mockery with nonchalance. The Procession of Peers in *Iolanthe* erupts into its refrain to the strains of a march as compelling as it is repulsive in its almost ideal-typical blend of pomp and brutality:

> Bow, bow, ye lower middle classes!
> Bow, bow, ye tradesmen, bow ye masses!
> Blow the trumpets, bang the brasses!
> Tantantara! Tzing! Boom!

The march puts its finger on the function of edifying music to intimidate and suppress, and does so with an unmitigated brashness that must have been shocking for the year 1882 (assuming that audiences did not prefer to evade Gilbert's

Fig. 53 Title page of *Wiener allge-meine Theaterzeitung,* 1842. In the first half of the century the prima donna was the center of a cult, an object both of importunate curiosity and of an ecstasy that found expression in unwieldy bouquets. In the second half, however, as Wagner and Verdi (in his later years) raised new artistic claims for opera, suppressing its functions of entertainment and public display, this cult found refuge in operetta. The honors showered upon Hortense Schneider as the Grand Duchess of Gérolstein (in Offenbach's operetta of 1867) brought this cult to a level that re-vealed what its true nature had been all along: a form of hero worship unwilling to distinguish between the diva as goddess and as courtesan. (Vienna, Österreichische National-bibliothek.)

aggression by declaring it to be humor). Generally, however, Gilbert's technique was intended to produce, not a shock effect, but a precisely calculated confusion of terms, a confusion of the sort that arises in a dialogue when the obvious fea-tures of daily life are gradually and subliminally transformed into monstrosities by adding a dash of absurdity and applying inexorable logic. These monstrosities took audiences by surprise, and Gilbert often blunted his points by undercutting them in a way which itself constituted a point—namely, by having his characters, like Alice in Wonderland, react to the most astonishing phenomena with utter nonchalance, as though they were everyday occurrences.

In opera aesthetics ever since the late seventeenth century it was assumed that, in the theater, the task of music was to justify the substitution of the super-natural for the mundane, or even to cause the supernatural to impinge on the mundane. It is thus fully in keeping with operatic tradition that one of the func-tions of music in the Savoy operas was to impart aesthetic plausibility to the ab-surd premises that Gilbert required for his dramaturgical experiments. The fairy music in *Iolanthe,* for example, is not simply a Mendelssohn parody, al-though it can certainly be appreciated on that level as well. Rather, its purpose is to suffuse a magical fairy-tale aura fractured but not smothered by irony, an aura without which Gilbert's daring dramaturgical construct would be nothing but a mechanism spinning idly in a void. There is no other way of motivating the confrontation between the "peers" and the "peris" except by music. (As with Raimund, the farce profits from the romanticism hidden in the premises of its plot.) Nonetheless, Sullivan's music is made up mainly of English song and march types, their Englishness being underscored with a thick application of syncopations and subdominants. (If Offenbach is a composer of *couplets* and galops, Sullivan is a writer of songs and marches.) And when, at the opening of *The Mikado,* the emperor's son, disguised as a minstrel, offers in succession a sentimental ballad, a bombastic patriotic anthem, and a sailor's shanty for no particular reason and with no relation to the dialogue, the scene is turned into a parody of Savoy opera itself, which thrives on stylistic quotation. Here the musical devices otherwise used to undergird a plot, as absurd as that plot may be, are divorced from any semblance of dramaturgical function.

The Symphonic Poem

Wagner proclaimed the death of the symphony, arguing that absolute music had reached the level of self-abrogation in the choral finale of Beethoven's Ninth Symphony and that the expressive means developed by Beethoven only found their true aesthetic vindication in the music drama, where they were "substantiated" by texts and plots. This claim was long contested by music historians who distrusted the influence of Wagner's thought (which became almost overpowering around 1900 in the wake of his music) and considered it egocentric presumption on his part to try to make history by misinterpreting the past. However, given the state of compositional evolution around 1850 as reflected in the historicomythological constructs of *Oper und Drama,* it was by no means absurd of Wagner to portray the symphony as empty and lifeless; indeed, it was almost prophetic. It was impossible then to foresee that a quarter of a century later, in the 1870s, a "second age of the symphony" would dawn. Historically, this rebirth comes as a surprise rather than a natural outgrowth that seems "ineluctable" in retrospect, and it should not keep us from recognizing in Wagner's dictum a prognosis which, after all, managed to be true for two decades. No one, except those who prefer statistics to "musicohistorical facts" grounded on aesthetic judgments, would claim that his prognosis was refuted by a few symphonies by Gade, Raff, and Rubinstein, works which at any rate were unable to escape entirely the trend toward "programs."

In 1851, then, the year of *Oper und Drama,* Wagner's hypothesis of the death of the symphony was part of an apology for the music drama as he envisioned it during his period of transition between *Lohengrin* and *Das Rheingold.* In 1857, however, in his open letter "Über Franz Liszts symphonische Dichtungen," he also included the symphonic poem, developed by Liszt from the concert overture, as an aesthetically legitimate outgrowth of the symphonic style, whose "end" had to be sought outside the symphony lest the "means" discovered by

Beethoven remain unused. Even so, for Wagner, "aesthetic legitimacy" meant that the means of musical expression are "substantiated" by the "object" which they represent. The question so hotly contested by later aestheticians—namely, whether a text or program, motto or caption, can uniquely denote the "formal motive" underlying the music—remains secondary. (A "formal motive" in Wagner's sense is an element that "motivates" the music and its reason for being. It may be a plot, as in the music drama, or even a dance of the sort still perceivable as a historical and aesthetic wellspring of the seemingly "absolute" music of Haydn and Mozart.) According to Wagner, the level of detail in the "literary" dimension appropriated by music is no criterion for determining whether a work does or does not have meaning. The sole criterion is the extent to which its "poetic intention" is intelligible to the listener and transcends mere "intention" by being "externalized for the sensory faculties" through music. For program music to be worth anything it must do more than just "illustrate," for the imagination, a text that functions as the literary "essence" of the musical "appearance." Rather, by "externalizing" the program for the listener, it captures in music the "truth" of things which lurks behind the verbally determinable "phenomena" of the world. At least this is the way Wagner saw it following his conversion in 1854 to the philosophy of Schopenhauer, a metaphysic of will and music alike. What Wagner praised in Liszt's symphonic poems was the "distinctness" of their expression and their "poetic" attitude, which never lost itself in trite, "prosaic" word-painting: "In this regard," he wrote, "I was surprised most of all by the grand and eloquent distinctness with which the object presented itself to me." The object Wagner had in mind, however, is not to be sought in empirically tangible entities, as Wagner attempted to do in 1851 when, in *Oper und Drama,* he denied instrumental music the capability of making objects intelligible: "This was, of course, no longer the object as denoted in words by the poet, but rather a completely different object beyond all description, an object whose ineffable quality makes it scarcely conceivable that it can likewise present itself clearly, distinctly, compactly, and unmistakably to our faculties." But what exactly is this "completely different object" which, when represented in music, imparts to the musical expression a distinctness otherwise denied to it—a distinctness which, according to Wagner, in turn depends on the clarity of the object represented? It seems as though Wagner was thinking of historically evolving images of mythical figures, such as Orpheus and Prometheus, or Faust and Hamlet, images that cannot be captured definitively in a single text. Furthermore, these images were not simply "portrayed" by Liszt in his music but "elaborated and magnified" in the same way that Wagner elaborated and magnified the legends of Siegfried and Tristan.

The symphonic poem that so startled Wagner in 1857, forcing him to modify his aesthetic, owes its existence to problems of an individual nature. In 1847, following a concert in Elizabethgrad, Liszt abandoned his virtuoso career and withdrew the following year to Weimar, a provincial town rich in memories.

Apparently, he sought solitude as a contrast to Paris in order to realize compositional plans and sketches, some of them already a decade and a half or two decades old, in a form equal to the aesthetic stature symbolized by his newfound home instead of remaining as semi-improvisations. The upshot was nothing less than the founding of a new musical genre, the symphonic poem, which held its own for half a century as a major form of instrumental music, not only in the concert hall but in the minds of the audience. Yet the essence of the symphonic poem is by no means restricted to its definition as a single-movement orchestral piece of symphonic dimensions with a program from literature or the beaux arts. We can see its essence most clearly by reconstructing the preconditions that gave rise to one of the key works in the genre, the *Bergsymphonie*, after Victor Hugo's ode *Ce qu'on entend sur la montagne* (1829). The idea for this work apparently dates back to the early 1830s, and its underlying motives were conceived in 1847. After being elaborated in 1848, a first version of the *Bergsymphonie* was performed in Weimar in 1850, followed by a second version in 1853 and a third and final version in 1857. The extraordinary length of the compositional process can be viewed as both a consequence and an indication of the difficulties which Liszt felt called upon to confront. His solution gave birth to a musical genre which apparently, unlike earlier genres, can be understood entirely in aesthetic and compositional terms, without regard for conditions of social history and the history of institutions. The idea of the symphonic poem is, it would seem, a generalized form of a conception that originally emerged from the special premises of a single work, the *Bergsymphonie*. To do justice to this work as a historical prototype, we must first probe the complex of questions which it is intended to answer.

Basically, the "poetics" of the symphonic poem came about as a solution to three interrelated problems. First, Liszt attempted to adopt the classical ideal of the symphony without yielding to a derivative dependence on its traditional formal scheme. Second, he wished to elevate program music, which he regarded, in Franz Brendel's phrase, as the "forefront of historical evolution," from a base, "picturesque" genre to poetic and philosophical sublimity. And finally, he was obsessed by the thought that it had to be possible to unite the expressive gestures of his earlier piano pieces, inspired by French romanticism, with the tradition of thematic and motivic manipulation. Rhetoric was supposed to be not dulled but consolidated by technical constructs, thereby turning from rhapsodic, improvisational "speech" into a "language" set down as a text.

As a single-movement piece for orchestra, the symphonic poem emerged from the overture, as is shown by the origins of *Tasso* (1849) and *Prometheus* (1850), the difference being that it raised aesthetic claims to the legacy of the symphony. Conversely, the symphonic tradition was meant to be rescued from what Liszt regarded as its "formalistic straitjacket" by programmatic tendencies deriving from the overture tradition. This programmatic aspect had been prefigured in the overture—even in the independent and self-contained species of concert overture—as had the orientation on sonata form which pitted it against the potpourri overture, particularly in the German tradition. The fact that the symphonic poem, as conceived by Liszt in the 1850s, could represent a new genre at all as compared with the concert overture is due to a reinterpretation of the programmatic aspect in close conjunction with a change in formal thinking. The sonata principle, though not abandoned, was modified to such a degree as to be unrecognizable at first glance. Liszt altered both the architecture of this musical form and its thematic and motivic logic by introducing two structural ideas: a relative application of formal categories and dimensions, and the technique of motivic transformation. In consequence, even today many analysts still have trouble detecting a sonata-form design (whether a sonata-allegro movement or a four-movement sonata cycle) in Liszt's symphonic poems, and misrepresent his very real formal experiments, which amply attest to an awareness of form, by wrongly accusing them of "formlessness" (as though "program music" consisted in pursuing a text or subject in blithe disregard of form).

Liszt applied identical principles to all different levels or dimensions of the symphony. In so doing he "relativized" its formal categories: first and second themes; exposition, development, and recapitulation; sonata allegro, slow movement, scherzo, and finale. The relation between themes or motivic groups recurs as it were in magnified proportion in the relations between sections or entire movements: tempos or moods became no less interchangeable than formal functions. The dimensions of sonata form and their defining features, though distinct and governed by different principles in the classical symphony, all merge together in Liszt's symphonic poems. At times it is virtually impossible to tell whether a passage is a second theme or a slow movement—that is, whether its order of magnitude is a section within a single movement or a movement within a four-movement cycle. This relativity of formal categories, however, seems to be at once the expression and the consequence of an idea that was meant to solve the problem posed by orchestral pieces that tend to form single movements because of their programmatic unity and yet press toward multimovement cycles because of their symphonic scale—namely, how to write a multimovement work in a single movement. The different types of symphonic movement—allegro, adagio, scherzo, and finale—are incorporated as contrasts of tempo and mood into a single-movement form based, however remotely, on the formal design of exposition, development, and recapitulation. By integrating the multimovement principle into the concert overture, now transformed into the symphonic poem, Liszt could provide formal justification for its aesthetic claim to rank alongside the symphony as a species of large-scale instrumental music. (Taken individually, the forms that resulted from Liszt's idea of "superimposing" sonata-allegro form on the four-movement sonata cycle—an idea that he took from Schubert's *Wanderer* Fantasy of 1822—are remarkably varied.)

The principle of writing multimovement works in a single movement proceeded from an assumption which gave it a foothold in musical tradition—namely, that audiences familiar with the formal aesthetic of the symphony were capable of associating expressive modes, such as the heroic, the elegiac, and the martial, with sections, such as first theme, second theme, and concluding theme, or even with entire movements, such as allegro, adagio, and finale. It was also possible, without sacrificing structural clarity, to associate the striking and sometimes glaring contrasts in tempo and mood with the programmatic tendencies that underlay symphonic poems. Indeed, this conception of form challenged audiences to account for these contrasts by seeking literary or pictorial subjects. However, any form that presents a configuration of themes and motives with no intention of reconciling them in a process of development, preferring instead to let them exist in their own right and impart meaning to the form as a sequence of contrasting moods, runs the risk of being misconstrued as a potpourri of momentary effects and expressive gestures. In other words, for the work to appear self-contained, it requires a principle to establish coherence from within. The device that Liszt used to combine the divergent sections of his forms was what Alfred Heuss called the technique of "motivic transformation": the practice of deriving opposing and seemingly unrelated themes and motives from common elementary structures of pitch and rhythm. Passages that seemed separate and distinct by virtue of their contrasting tempos and moods were all the more closely related internally. ("Motivic transformation" and "relativity of formal categories" are different sides of the same concept.)

As already mentioned, the *Bergsymphonie* derived its program from the ode *Ce qu'on entend sur la montagne*. Liszt summarized the "idea" of this ode in a prose sketch which he had printed in the score, not by itself but together with the poem:

> The poet hears two voices: the first immeasurable, splendorous, well-ordered, soaring heavenwards to the Lord in jubilant hymns of praise—the other dull, rent with pain, swollen with tears, blasphemy, and curses. The one cries "Nature!" the other, "Humanity!" The two voices grope ever closer to each other, crossing and fusing until, ultimately, they resolve and die away in pious contemplation.

The notion of voices "groping closer to each other, crossing and fusing" seems to have been the element that gave rise to and determined the musical conception. The resultant consequences for the musical structure were of a historical significance that went far beyond the work itself and the genre which it established, the symphonic poem. The technique of the *Bergsymphonie* differs radically from traditional thematic and motivic manipulation, which derived its substance from "concrete" themes and motives, that is, from themes and motives in which pitch, harmony, and rhythm "coalesce." Liszt based his work on "abstract" elements— on "elementary structures" of pitch and rhythm, which he then employed as through they were unrelated to each other. (A pitch structure is "abstract" in that it has no real existence without a rhythm of some sort.) Rhythms are transferred from one sequence of pitches to another, and pitch sequences from one rhythm to another; figures composed of pitch and rhythm are transplanted to wildly divergent tempos, upending their emotional character; striking intervals in the harmony are "horizontalized" into melody as through the dimensions of musical space were interchangeable, as later in dodecaphony. Even for listeners unversed in his method, Liszt's passion for weaving an increasingly dense web of relations in the structural "background" of his compositions conveys the impression that the themes and motives in the work's façade, as divergent as they may be, form a distinct if almost intangible unity. Clearly, Liszt derived his notion of a "submotivic network"—the voices that "grope toward each other, crossing and fusing"—from the literary impetus of Hugo's ode. No less clear is the possibility of generalizing this notion into a principle capable of serving, in the symphonic poem, as a counterfoil to the contrasts of tempo and mood which undergird the form in all of its dimensions. Moreover, the practice of starting primarily from abstract elements, from elementary structures of pitch and rhythm, rather than from themes and motives in which rhythm and pitch content "coalesce," is one of Liszt's ideas that made music history, if not in the nineteenth century, at least in our own.

The technique of motivic transformation, then, is indirectly connected with the programmatic content of the symphonic poem, being a counterfoil to the sharp contrasts of tempo and mood which invite programmic interpretation. But this connection is also direct. Liszt sought recourse in programs from a hybrid notion that music should inherit the legacy of world literature; this was part of his attempt to give music, conceived as a language, a distinctness lacking in absolute music with its vague intimations and allusions. Once we understand this, the level of detail which a program must assume depends on the degree to which it succeeds or fails, with other means, to attain that intelligibility of expression which Wagner saw fit to praise in Liszt's symphonic poems. One of these means is to weave a fabric of motivic relations: this seemingly formal technique must be understood as a linguistic technique as well.

Die Ideale (1857) takes its program from Schiller's poem, parts of which are printed in the score; the program of *Orpheus* (1854) is limited to allusions; and no program at all was formulated for *Hungaria* (1856). Yet Liszt always proceeded from the same aesthetic idea: that music is a language, one that can at times even dispense with commentary to say unmisconstruably what it is intended to say. As he wrote of Wagner's overture to *Tannhäuser*: "To maintain that an explanatory text is needed to understand this symphony is to imitate those of whom Shakespeare said that they would bleach the lily, paint the violet, and gild gold." It appears impossible to account for the significance of motivic transformation when it attempts to heighten the linguistic capacities of music, except by referring to the changing historical conditions under which music constitutes language at all. Thus, a short digression into linguistics seems unavoidable.

One of the commonplaces of linguistics is that a vocabulary becomes the more esoteric the harder one tries to attain the semantic precision of formal languages, and that ambiguity increases in proportion to the degree to which language is dependent on its context of utterance. In other words, comprehensibility can be attained either semantically, by introducing a rigor which causes language to become esoteric, or pragmatically by associating it with specific situations. The music of the seventeenth and the early eighteenth century—from Schütz's *Geistliche Konzerte* (1636–39) to Bach's cantatas—has an esoteric vocabulary codified in the doctrine of figures. Though semantically unambiguous, this vocabulary can be understood only by the initiated. At the same time, this music shows the beginnings of a musical "vernacular" that acquires intelligibility from the functions served by the music. Around the middle of the nineteenth century, however, when Liszt attempted to realize his principle of "musical speech," the fixed vocabulary of music, its supply of linguistic *topoi* that had arisen during the Baroque period under the ascendancy of musical rhetoric, had long disintegrated. What is more, art music had liberated itself to become an autonomous art, divorced from the functions that had sustained it in earlier periods. In other words, the technique of making musical language more precise by defining it pragmatically in reference to an external context had lost its influence.

However, the weakening of the external context and the depletion of musical *topoi* can both be compensated for by making the internal context, the infralinguistic relations, more sophisticated and refined. To put it another way, the more ambiguous a vocabulary, and the more indefinite the context of utterance, the more precise and comprehensive the syntactic nexus must be in order for language to remain intelligible. Liszt himself explicitly drew the conclusion that it is not so much musical themes and motives themselves as the transformations they undergo and the relations made to pertain between them that determine the "speechlike" aspect of instrumental music: "It is precisely in the unlimited alterations which a motive may undergo—in rhythm, key, tempo, accompaniment, instrumentation, transformation, and so forth—that make up the language which allows us to use this motive to express thoughts and, in a manner of speaking, dramatic action." A theme is made to speak by means of its history. Liszt's technique of motivic transformation—and his "submotivic network"—is not simply a formal principle intended to unite different musical moods. It is at the same time an attempt, by making the internal nexus more sophisticated and precise, to impart powers of speech to a program music whose programs occasionally collapse to a meager residue.

The demise of the symphonic poem can be seen (*pace* Respighi) in the works of Strauss and Sibelius, Debussy and Schönberg. Its evolution was only partly determined by the aesthetic and formal ideas that Liszt had presupposed when he founded the genre, as are most abundantly evident in Smetana's cycle *Má vlast*. Besides the "art work of ideas," as Liszt conceived the symphonic poem, composers such as Balakirev, Rimsky-Korsakov, and Dvořák took up fairy tales as characteristic of the genre. This is hardly surprising in view of the close relation between a fondness for fairy-tale materials and a tendency to musical tone-painting, a relation as apparent in late-nineteenth-century opera as it was in the symphonic poem. Sophistication of local color interacted with a relaxation of functional harmony to become one of the decisive evolutionary features of the age. Ultimately, around 1900, it led to a reformulation of the notion of timbre, one of the crucial features of fin-de-siècle musical modernism. This "emancipation of timbre," initiated by Berlioz, freed tone color from its subservient function of merely clarifying the melody, rhythm, harmony, and counterpoint of a piece, and gave it an aesthetic raison d'être and significance of its own. In retrospect, this seems to have been one of the symphonic poem's "anticipatory" traits, along with Liszt's idea of handling elementary structures of rhythm and pitch as though they were unrelated "parameters." The genre's claim to represent musical "progress" in the nineteenth century was, as we have seen, rooted in a historiologically inspired aesthetic of program music (Franz Brendel, the apostle of the "New German School," praised the programmatic side of Liszt's "art work of ideas" as an outgrowth of "intellect in music" and a triumph over the "standpoint of sensuality"). In the event, however, the weakest part of this generic idea turned out to be its aesthetic doctrine, whereas technical features such as the recourse to musical "parameters" and the "emancipation of timbre," originally nothing more than means to the end of depicting subjects, outlived their original purpose. Only in the modern music of our own century did they reach the historical stage at which, to use Ernst Bloch's phrase, they were "transmuted to recognizability."

We have seen how it was in the nature of the symphonic poem, the historical alternative to the more "abstract" symphony, to emphasize coloristic effects. Liszt's formal ideas, an aesthetic counterpart to his coloristic timbre, had their most obvious impact, as was already mentioned, on Smetana's cycle *Má vlast.* The first of its six sections, *Vyšehrad,* depicts a mythical crag, formerly the seat of Bohemian princes, together with the memories associated with it. It is marked by an idiosyncratic blend of formal simplicity and complexity. The "introductory" slow movement—a Lento with a harp solo to conjure up the image of a bard singing of olden times—returns at the end of the piece to establish a large-scale *ABA* form. At the same time it presents two themes or motives, *a* and *b,* which then form the substance of the entire work (Ex. 39). In short, this movement is at once introduction, ritornello, and exposition. In the Allegro section motive *a,* varied in pitch and meter, appears as the main theme while motive *b,* having come to the fore in the transition, accompanies the second theme. Initially, this second theme takes the form of a cantilena unrelated to previous motives only to take up motive *a* in one of its variants. Then comes a development section, a model of symphonic dialectic, to reconcile the conflict between motives *a* and *b.* This is

Example 39

followed by a return of motive *a* combined with part of the second theme, now in a triumphant apotheosis, to form a "recapitulation," even though, strictly speaking, all that is recapitulated is a fragment extracted from the middle of the second theme (Ex. 40).

Example 40

By adopting Liszt's technique of motivic transformation and weaving ever-new combinations of motives, Smetana arrived at a formal conception in which an initially inconspicuous motivic relation, magnified to monumental proportions, can take the place of the recapitulation. The "goal" of his development section is a combination of motives in triple *forte* which functions in the same way as a Beethoven recapitulation, namely, as an "exalted moment of form" (to use August Halm's term). On the other hand, by integrating his motives into a "network," Smetana combines or contaminates them instead of following the traditional path of reconstituting and reaffirming the themes "posited" at the outset of the movement. This is an apposite consequence of the notion that a development section is meant to produce a "result." In other words, a work like *Vyšehrad* "sublates" the formal tradition of the symphony in Hegel's dual sense of the term, preserving it and transforming it at the same time. Its departures from the schoolbook pattern evolve from and are vindicated by the distinctive features of motivic technique, and nothing could be more mistaken than to dismiss this type of sonata form by mindlessly accusing it of the "formlessness" allegedly typical of "program music." It was Beethoven's principle that the outline of a form must accord with the thematic process at work within it, and this principle remained a determining factor not merely in the late-nineteenth-century symphony but also in the symphonic poem, or at least in its few outstanding examples. The aesthetic stature of a genre is not independent of the formal tradition which it upholds with the dual aim of cultivating and exploiting it.

Music Criticism as Philosophy of History

Music criticism arose from tentative beginnings in the eighteenth century, the first era of journalism, to become an institution in the nineteenth. Any music that is primarily public and only secondarily private is now unthinkable without it. Music, whether of the artistic or the popular variety, is constantly surrounded by linguistic turns of phrase that influence our musical awareness in conjunction with, and sometimes no less significantly than, the acoustic phenomenon itself. Writings on music are part of music history in the same way as musical works, institutions, and performance practice, and the specific form they take in a given age belongs to that age's historical signature.

Two of the major categories that formed the pillars of nineteenth-century music criticism originated from the legacy of the eighteenth century: the concepts of rule and taste. The third, the notion of historicality, though traceable to the *querelle des anciens et des modernes* that erupted around 1688, did not noticeably influence music aesthetics and journalism until the nineteenth century, the age of Hegelianism. Even so, both the function and the tenor of these originally Enlightenment categories changed in an age that considered itself romantic.

The extent to which the nineteenth century took its bearings on the notion of musical rules should not be underestimated, and is by no means so slight as it might seem if we were to search for signs of the "zeitgeist" solely in slogans of the genius and originality aesthetics. That composers of the stature of Berlioz, Schumann, Liszt, Wagner, and Mussorgsky were subjected to accusations of dilettantism for one reason or another may have been nothing more than a scheme of the rear guard to ward off genius. Yet even composers themselves were aware that sensitive points of the composer's craft had become as uncertain as never before since the forgotten age of Monteverdi, and that each bold new step ran the risk of toppling into dilettantism. Unlike the modern music of our own century, it was a rare exception when composers such as Charles Alkan, Mussorgsky, or Liszt in his later years made themselves at ease in this uncertainty. Composers, and with them critics of distinction, were far more likely to vacillate between two extremes: an awareness that the rules of craftsmanship, while still in force, were becoming less and less valuable as an aesthetic "guarantee" for the claims of music to rank as art; and the hope of mastering one rule or another in order to lessen, at least, the unavoidable danger of failure (even if the rule, as Wagner put it in *Die Meistersinger,* had to be "self-imposed" in order then to be "followed"). Schubert, a few weeks before his death, sought counsel from Simon Sechter; Schumann, the composer of *Carnaval,* subjected himself to exercises in fugal style which he then published as works; Wagner, while writing *Tristan,* was seized in downhearted moments by pangs of envy for Mendelssohn's seemingly effortless mastery of the composer's craft; Bruckner inflicted upon himself an apprenticeship that lasted for decades; Rimsky-Korsakov "corrected" the works of Mussorgsky in order to "rescue" them. All these composers dreaded, in varying forms and degrees, the absence of rules. Their dread appears as a residue of a faith in rules so fully intact in the early part of the century that Beethoven could claim of figured bass, the touchstone of musical craftsmanship, that it stood above discussion for all ages to come. Even Arnold Schönberg, writing in his *Harmonielehre* (1911), was convinced that atonal composition had hidden rules that would be discovered within a few years or decades, leaving composers for the moment at the mercy of their intuition.

The appeal to rules often revealed a penchant for pedantry, one extreme being the quest for hidden parallel fifths and octaves. Conversely, the judgments of taste with which music critics attempted to hold in check the verdicts of compositional technique were open to accusations of arbitrariness. To be sure, it was a misconception characteristic of the century to suppose that taste, being, it was thought, individual, is therefore above discussion in accordance with the scholastic dictum *de gustibus non est disputandum*. Judgments of taste have always, even in the nineteenth century, been primarily and at times exclusively the province of a group, social stratum, class, or nation. (When German critics in the second half of the century spoke patronizingly of Verdi, as they invariably did, it was this deprecatory undertone rather than their preference for one work or another that revealed their judgment of taste, borne by national pride in the Viennese Classic tradition.) The concept of taste, formulated in the eighteenth century and surviving in such turns of phrase as "having" or "not having" taste, originally served an unambiguously social function: the function of helping a group to cohere from within and to insulate itself from without. The taste a person had, be it for *Opusmusik* or *Trivialmusik* (to use the pejorative catchphrases of their respective strata), associated him with "his own kind" and separated him from "others" (whether "above" or "below"). In spite of this, the nineteenth century was nevertheless capable of bringing forth the notion that taste is primarily individual. Perhaps the only explanation for this is that the educated bourgeoisie had no desire to proclaim as such the aesthetic it practiced, but simply regarded it as universal, and that it confused empathy with the individuality of a composer (the reception aesthetic's answer to the originality postulate of the production aesthetic) with the notion of taste, which actually belongs to a different system of categories. (The listener's "private" opinion of a Brahms symphony, whether it moves or bores him, is independent of the "public" judgment of taste—that is, whether it deserves to stand in a symphony concert alongside an overture by Weber and a Beethoven piano concerto.)

As the nineteenth century saw it, a person who makes a judgment of taste must vouch for it "subjectively." "Objective judgments" were sought seldom if ever in relation to group conventions (the "intersubjective" agreement that Kant meant by the term *sensus communis*), but rather by appealing to compositional norms or, alternatively, by forming hypotheses about the "course of history," which seemed to dictate over the heads of the participants whether the "time" of something had or had not arrived. As trust in the aesthetic import of compositional rules waned (it was still felt that damage would result from breaking them but that there was less and less aesthetic benefit to be gained from adhering to them), attempts redoubled to practice music criticism in anticipation of the "judgment of history." (One characteristic of classical works was their survival in the repertoire; now, conversely, works had the dignity of classicism bestowed upon them because they survived.) This historiological line of thought tacitly presupposed a curious mélange of classicism and a faith in progress, the two predominant if seemingly mutually exclusive tendencies of the age. As Stendhal put it, today's romanticism is tomorrow's classicism, and today's classicism is yesterday's romanticism. In the language of the twentieth century, this formula linked the idea of the "avant-garde" with that of the "imaginary museum." A work of music that marked what Franz Brendel called the "forefront of evolution" in history, conceived as a string of innovations, was by no means condemned, as it might seem at first blush, to fall prey after a few years to the "avenging angel of disappearance" invoked by Hegel. The work's novelty may well have formed part of its aesthetic and historiological substance, but this in no way implied that it had to yield its place in the repertoire when a fresh novelty pressed forward to the "forefront of evolution." Novelty was considered a condition of aesthetic authenticity, which remained forever denied to epigonism. Anything that used to be novel, even though loss of novelty ought to mean loss of substance, became the property of the classical, which accordingly was made up of past innovations (and not, as was formerly believed, of works that satisfied extratemporal norms). The century of revolutions was also the century of museums.

To inaugurate the 1835 volume of his *Neue Zeitschrift für Musik*, Schumann wrote:

> In the short span of our existence we have made a number of observations. Our attitude was fixed beforehand. It is simple, and runs as follows: to recall the past and its music with all the energy at our disposal, to draw attention to the ways in which new artistic beauties can find sustenance at a source so pure,—then to take up arms against the recent past as an age inimical to art, intent solely on extending the bounds of superficial virtuosity,—and finally to prepare for and help expedite the advent of a new poetic age.

The program sketched in these few lines of Schumann's draws on a historiological conception with three roots: a deep-seated experience of the past—the music of Bach—that determined the musical thought of Schumann, Mendelssohn, and Chopin as romantics; an acute and painful awareness of the present as "prosaic"; and an expectation of a "poetic" future already visible in outline in the present. Awareness of tradition, critique of one's own time, and faith in progress: all mutually interact with and complement one another.

Schumann speaks of the "recent past" as though Meyerbeer, the target of his polemics, were a living corpse long consigned to the past despite his seeming triumphs in the present. This present forms the antithesis in a three-pronged historiological construct, an unhappy middle between a long-lost "classic" period and a "romantic" one whose day has not yet arrived. The existing and predominant music which Schumann called "modern" proves to be garbled and hollow compared with that which used to be and that which is still to come.

In the same year, 1835, Schumann added a typology of composers to this historiological schema. His essay "Der Psychometer" speaks of "classicists," "juste-milieuists," and "romantics" as musical parties among which the composer must take sides. (It is apparently typical of the tendency to ground verdicts in the philosophy of history, rather than in compositional norms or criteria of taste,

Fig. 54 Caricature of Eduard Hanslick and Johannes Brahms, *Figaro,* 1890. It is no coincidence that Brahms's *Academic Festival Overture* (1880), written in gratitude for an honorary doctorate from the University of Breslau, is one of his weakest works, an unfortunate mixture of symphonic techniques and song quotations with a *maestoso* conclusion based on *Gaudeamus igitur.* The late nineteenth century was incapable of striking a note of secular solemnity. Although the caricature does injustice to Hanslick, who was by no means uncritical of Brahms, it at least underscores the danger of academicism that threatened Brahms's work as a whole: the acid pen of the caricaturist has drawn him back to confines beyond which he seldom ventured very far. (Vienna, Österreichische Nationalbibliothek.)

that these parties, though coexisting in the present, in fact represent different historical stages, thus implying that the verdict on them has already been pronounced, namely, by history.)

> The present is characterized by its parties. As with the political sort, one can divide these parties into liberal, middle-of-the-road, and reactionary, or into romantic, modern, and classic. On the right are the ancients, the contrapuntalists, the anti-chromaticists; on the left the striplings, the musical Jacobites, the rule breakers, the intrepid geniuses, among whom the Beethovenians stand out as a class apart. Young and old mix by turns in the *juste milieu.* It includes most of the products of the day, creations of the moment, which it brings forth only to destroy.

At first glance it may seem puzzling and provocative to equate "classics" and "reactionaries." Nevertheless, it need hardly be mentioned that this refers not to the *classici auctores* themselves but to their narrow-minded disciples and epigones who only have ears for the past. In contrast, the "romantics" or "liberals"— among whom, besides himself, Schumann included Chopin, Mendelssohn, and a few composers of lesser stature—stand opposed to and abhor the reactionary, but not the past. The longed-for "new poetic age" was not to be a mere replica of things past, but it was imperative that "new artistic beauties" find "sustenance" in the past and its music. Schumann revered the great composers of the past, even though he was fully aware of the historical distance that separated them from the present. What history hands down to the present is not an ageless model to be slavishly imitated, but neither is it dead prehistory. It is the harbinger of one's own age.

Finally, it was characteristic of the "moderns" whom Schumann so abhorred to lack coherence and internal unity and to mix heterogeneous materials. In his writings we can read of the "workaday and *juste milieu* overtures" which are "one-quarter Italian, one-quarter French, one-eighth Chinese, and three-eighths German, adding up to a sum total of zero."

As we have seen, historiologically based music criticism of the sort proclaimed by Schumann takes up sides for a party that claims to stand for the judgment of history. It was enough for Meyerbeer to represent the *juste milieu* to condemn him out of hand. Even Wagner, fulminating against Meyerbeer and Berlioz in *Oper und Drama* (1851), spoke less in his own name than in the name of history, which brooks no objections to its verdicts. He dismissed Berlioz as the "tragic victim" of a historical dialectic. (It should come as no surprise that this polemic, although formulated as the objective voice of history, was capable of being considered subjective and malicious. After all, as Balzac described in his *Illusions perdues* of 1837–44, one of the everyday perfidies of Parisian journalists was to mask personal spite as critique from the vantage point of the World Spirit.) On the one hand, opinions proffered as the verdict of history must guard against being dismissed as mere judgments of taste: Wagner claimed to see the *Symphonie fantastique* as evidence of an aesthetic blunder which, as it turned out, had positive repercussions on the course of music history. On the other hand—and this mitigates the verdict—the condemned work need not be cast aside as worthless; even if "refuted" by future developments, it can nevertheless remain an indispensable part of history in the strong sense rather than simply belonging to the debris cast up by the past.

According to Wagner, the evolution of the symphony after Beethoven was the "history of an artistic blunder." Beethoven, he argued, tried to use music, without text or plot, to say things that even the most sophisticated instrumental music is incapable of saying. (By abandoning its initial and, at first, formative origins in the dance without substituting the motivation of a text and dramatic plot, instrumental music fell unhappily between two stools, becoming "absolute music" cut off from its own extramusical roots.) However, the aesthetic blunder that beset Beethoven led to a new wealth of musical expression: "The boundless riches of music are now revealed to us by Beethoven's mighty blunder, which he did not redress until the finale of the Ninth Symphony."

Hence, Beethoven's "blunder" was rectified by the Ninth Symphony and thereby revealed as the mistake it was. Berlioz, casting Beethoven's musical testament to the winds, took this blunder to extremes. This, for Wagner, ensured the "failure" of the *Symphonie fantastique* but was in no sense a misfortune for music history. Even Berlioz, no less than Beethoven, is dragged into the dialectic of Wagner's historical mythology. Berlioz felt compelled to expand the orchestral apparatus precisely because he secretly sensed that instrumental music lacked "substantiation": meaning was to be forced upon music by multiplying its devices —by rhetoric. Nor was Wagner at all a despiser of Berlioz's discoveries. To accuse them of being the upshot of an "artistic blunder" is not to reject them wholesale; on the contrary, it is a call to restore them to artistic rectitude, to ground them in the drama, where even extreme musical devices receive their vindication. In this way Berlioz's works appear to be an "indispensable point of transition," indispensable in the sense that, in Wagner's view, it was precisely Berlioz's vain efforts to force "absolute music" to yield "content" from within that led to an explosion of musical devices which could then be put to use in his "art work of the future." There is great presumption in calling something "outdated" which one would like to dismiss but cannot call "bad," but Wagner seems to have been as little aware of this as the Hegelians of his day, who likewise grounded music criticism in the philosophy of history.

As Friedrich Nietzsche scornfully noted in *Der Fall Wagner* (1888): "The same kind of person who waxed enthusiastic over Hegel now waxes enthusiastic over Wagner; in his school one even writes in Hegelish." Apparently he had in mind Franz Brendel, the most eloquent spokesman for a brand of music criticism buoyed by historiological ambitions and inspired by Hegel. But the methods that music criticism chose to apply revealed which side it had taken among the conflicting musical currents of the day. For Eduard Hanslick, a critic inclined to conservatism (albeit a generous conservatism, which only became spiteful in the case of Bruckner), the starting point was the idea of absolute music as the quintessence of "genuine" music. The aesthetic which he sketched in 1854 in his essay *Vom Musikalisch-Schönen* is derived from hypotheses concerning the nature of music and of mankind. Brendel, on the other hand, the apologist of the "New German" composers (and, one might add, the inventor of the strange coupling of Wagner, Liszt, and Berlioz into a "New German School"), took as his authority the inexorable march of history when he proclaimed program music and the music drama to be musical progress. Nature and history, tradition and progress, absolute music and program music: these were the dichotomies that dominated musical thought in the 1850s and the decades beyond, forcing it to hew to party lines. It is no exaggeration to say of these dichotomies not only that they reflect part of music history but that they made history themselves. (Even at the outset of the twentieth century it was still no easy matter to untangle a knot of concepts such as absolute music, tradition, and the physical universe, as is clearly shown in the confusion occasioned by Arnold Schönberg when he chose "absolute" genres —the string quartet and the piano piece—for his fledgling efforts in atonality and referred to the "nature of music" to account for the "progress" he thereby achieved.)

In his *Grundzüge der Geschichte der Musik* of 1848, Brendel characterized Robert Schumann (whom he had succeeded as editor of the *Neue Zeitschrift für Musik*) as "decisively modern," unlike Mendelssohn who, "although quite modern in some ways, was less decisive in others and appears exclusively as a continuation of Beethoven, even joining the romantic current." In other words, as compared with Schumann's use of the terms, "romantic" and "modern" have switched historiological positions. Brendel does not use "modern" to refer to an interim period, one which Hegel would have called a stage of unhappy and fractured consciousness between past grandeur and a "new poetic" future. Instead, "modern" refers to that part of the present which bears within it the seeds of the future. The composers he had in mind were Liszt, Wagner, and Berlioz.

The "moderns" regarded themselves as sufficiently free of prejudice—as Brendel put it—"to recognize the demands of the times." Their self-confidence, however, strangely unlike their passionate faith in progress, was undercut by a recollection of Hegel's dictum regarding art's ineluctable loss of substantiality. As Hegel wrote in his *Ästhetik*:

> And above all else, the spirit of our world today, or more accurately the spirit of our religion and our rational education, seems to have transcended that stage at which art constitutes the highest means of apprising oneself of the absolute. . . . Whatever art inspires within us requires a still higher touchstone, a confirmation from another quarter. Thought and reflection have overtaken the beaux arts.

Brendel adopted Hegel's thesis in 1852 in his *Geschichte der Musik in Italien, Deutschland und Frankreich*: "In the decades of the modern period, art no longer forms the pinnacle of consciousness at all, as we observe in the halcyon days of ancient Greece." He drew from this thesis the surprising conclusion that progress in music, an ideal he clung to nonetheless, was transmitted in modern times through theory, criticism, and written history. He mentions the "large number of writings on music which have appeared in recent years," maintaining that "it is not saying too much to claim that the focus of the present day, as far as music is concerned, is to be found at least partly in this area." It was the French view, which ultimately took hold in Germany as well, that writings on literature belong, in essence, to literature itself, and here Brendel seems inclined by analogy, paradoxical as it may sound at first, to include the theory and criticism of music as part of music. Brendel thought that the threat, invoked by Hegel, of art's losing its substantiality was to be countered by radical reflection, not by rejecting thought altogether and attempting to rescue at least a semblance of the lost immediacy of art, if not that immediacy itself. "The essence of art today," he wrote in reference to Wagner's music drama and Liszt's symphonic poem, "lies above all in the fact that it no longer builds on received foundations in the old naturalistic way," by which he meant instinctively. "On the contrary, it consists in the fact that theory and criticism have stepped between past and present, that our art has theory and criticism within it as a condition of its existence."

Brendel also attributes to written history an importance similar to that of theory and criticism (his own interest as a historian was, in consequence, topical rather than antiquarian). Just as knowledge of world history and the history of culture "makes the educated man that which he is, so art history liberates the artist from a merely instinctive grasp of his tasks." The present thrives on the legacy from the past, but this does not mean that the past should be taken over as a matter of course, without reflection, as tradition. Instead, it should be steeped in historical awareness, which not only detaches one from the past but also brings to light unused possibilities.

Brendel's thesis of theory and criticism as mediators in the production of music was a challenging paradox in the nineteenth century which has become a platitude in our own. The earlier dogma, that theory always "lagged behind" practice, gave way in twentieth-century music to the realization that any art that lacks a basis in unreflected traditions will have to stand up for itself, and requires a theory in constant interaction with practice in order to confirm its own identity. In short, however distant the aesthetic of the music drama and the symphonic poem may be from an age that became "modern" (in the twentieth-century sense) precisely by turning away from "late romanticism" (as Brendel's nineteenth-century "modernity" came to be called), the belief that theory is a force capable of influencing the history of composition has bridged this historical gap and remained intact, with its aesthetic theories transformed into theories of structure.

Brahms and the Chamber Music Tradition

Johannes Brahms's fame was established in 1853 by Schumann's impassioned and prophetic essay "Neue Bahnen." It was consolidated in the 1860s, after an interim in which it seemed to fade, and entered public awareness in the music world no later than 1868 when the *German Requiem* was first performed in Bremen (the same year witnessed the triumphant premiere of *Die Meistersinger* in Munich). However, the esteem accorded to Brahms was linked with his unfortunate part in the dispute kindled by an 1860 manifesto in which a group of "serious-minded musicians" protested against the doings of the "New German School." This dispute split German music culture into two "camps" whose polemical zeal reduced aesthetic theories to jingoistic slogans. (Brahms, having been pressured into signing this manifesto, was thereafter powerless to prevent an unwanted confrontation with the "Wagner party.")

Musical "camps" had occasionally existed before the nineteenth century in genres such as opera and church music, but never before had they taken hold of a music culture as a whole. In this case, the partisan mentality was allied with a picture of Brahms as a composer primarily of chamber music, a picture drawn by historians attempting to establish his niche in music history, even though his presence in today's concert repertoire is secured not so much by his string quartets as by his symphonies and the *German Requiem*. By emphasizing his chamber music, historians could pit Brahms more squarely against the "New German School"—an opposition thought at the time to be a musicopolitical struggle between the conservative and progressive parties. Their stylistic differences were seen to be reinforced by a radically different choice of genres. As a composer of symphonies Brahms stood alongside Bruckner (categorized by shortsighted critics as a "Wagnerian"); as a composer of lieder he rubbed shoulders with Wolf. Chamber music, however, was an area generally spurned by the "New Germans": Wolf's string quartet is a youthful effort modeled on Beethoven's Op. 95, and the "orchestral" traits of Bruckner's string quintet infringe against the chamber music ideal. Moreover, the aesthetic and compositional techniques of chamber music were anathema to Wagner's music drama and Liszt's symphonic poem, the genres which, to the progressives, represented what Franz Brendel called the "forefront of historical evolution."

In Germany and Austria, the chamber music tradition where Brahms found his foothold was upheld by a social stratum whose decline in our century makes it difficult to form an unbiased opinion of the convivial music culture that arose from it in the nineteenth century. This stratum was the educated middle classes. As Arnold Schering remarked:

> Here, in the families of academics, of upper-echelon merchants and civil servants, of the prestigious artists of a community, for all their wonted liberalism in politics, there reigned a solid conservative spirit, a wholesome urge to preserve and transmit received culture and to make daily life as rich and variegated as possible by cultivating an idealist cast of mind. . . . The focus of their musical life was chamber music, performed in private domestic concerts by artists befriended of the family and attended by listeners who could be relied upon to possess discriminating taste in matters of literature and the spirit.

Admittedly, by about 1860, when Brahms entered this evolutionary current, it seemed as though chamber music, once a central genre of the Viennese Classics, had been shunted onto the sidelines of history, both in its influence and its quality. In the history of musical performance, chamber music was in the main a private affair, and its key works were largely esoteric. It was overshadowed by public music life: the opera, the virtuoso concert, and the "grand concert" with mixed program, which gradually gave rise to the symphony concert. Nor did it any longer seem particularly relevant aesthetically, as a means of reflecting on the evolution of musical language and technique. The decisions that affected the history of composition were made in the music drama and the symphonic poem, genres dominated by the "progressive party" of the "New Germans." Chamber music, in contrast, did not exist for Wagner, Liszt, or Berlioz. It was a nature reserve for conservatives too dazed by the new music to do anything but cling to the old.

Fig. 55 Max Klinger: *Brahms-Phantasie*. Klinger has not balked at combining his pictorial motifs into glaring paradoxes to underscore the meaning of his allegory all the more drastically. Here he has assembled virtually all of the props which the nineteenth century (less well equipped in this regard than the Baroque) had at its disposal to represent sublimity: the rugged landscape of snow-capped mountains, the cypress grove (recalling Arnold Böcklin's *Toteninsel*), the stormy sea with impending shipwreck, and a harp crowned with the mask of tragedy and played by nereids and tritons. Klinger was apparently struck most of all by the gloomy, harsh, tragic aspect of Brahms's music. From the standpoint of intellectual history, it is especially characteristic that a sober, positivistic age like the nineteenth century should have descried in music, an alternative world to its own, the tendency toward sublime style that Brahms shared with his musical opposite, Wagner. (Stuttgart, Alfred Kröner Verlag.)

Half a century later, around 1910, the tables were turned: chamber music became the field of innovations—the transition to atonality—and Schönberg could praise and draw on "Brahms the Progressive" in provocative defiance of the historians. This is a reversal truly deserving of the term dialectical, and one which no one around 1860 could have foreseen. To conservatives, chamber music was the supreme musical genre, a music par excellence for people of culture. Yet, while they may have been convinced of the eternal verity of the chamber music ideal, they by no means believed that they had the march of history on their side, history being for them not so much a court of appeal as a foreordained doom. They thought in terms of normative aesthetics rather than the philosophy of history, and conceded to their opponents the progress they so dreaded or despised. Around 1900, however, there was an abrupt turnabout in the impact of musical genres on the history of composition. The symphonic poem succumbed to a resistless process of trivialization following, if not in the hands of, Strauss and Sibelius. Schönberg, who bore the torch of musical progress after Strauss's conversion to traditionalism, was primarily a composer of chamber music: the advent of modern twentieth-century music is documented by a set of lyric piano pieces (Schönberg's Op. 11) and a movement for string quartet (the finale of Schönberg's Op. 10).

Brahms's contemporaries were hardly capable of grasping the historical dialectic inherent in his conservatism. With hindsight, however, we have little problem in reconstructing this dialectic, and the compositional devices it drew upon are plain to see. In the history of nineteenth-century music, the central category of musical conservatism was the concept of form. Further, we can distinguish in the sonata-allegro tradition between what Jacques Handschin called "architectonic" and "logical" form. Architectonic form is based on two properties: a balance between phrases, periods, and sets of periods—that is, the principle that each metrical unit is counterbalanced by a second unit at every hierarchical level—and a clearly focused, unambiguous scheme of chord progressions and tonalities. Logical form, on the other hand, resides in motivic connections, which hold a movement together from within, or, alternatively, in a thematic process, which gradually causes an at first inconspicuous turn of melody to become richer and richer in meaning as ever more conclusions are drawn from it. In the evolution of the sonata allegro from the late eighteenth century to the early twentieth, the focus shifted progressively from architecture to logic. This development is as clear as it is understandable: in an age dominated by the idea of progress there was a steady and seemingly ineluctable increase in the complexity of compositional devices, causing both periodic structure and tonal harmony to lose their capacity to function as the mainstays of musical form based on the principle of balance. Rhythmic structures that tend to dissolve into "musical prose," and harmony riddled with atonal fissures, are highly unlikely to establish musical form by setting up "rhythm in the large" (Eduard Hanslick) and a key scheme. The more sophisticated rhythm becomes, the more it ultimately tends to be limited to momentary effects rather than joining phrase to phrase and period to period in accordance with the antecedent-consequent principle. By the same token, the weaker the architecture, the greater the responsibility of musical logic to prevent the form from disintegrating into a potpourri—which even if relabeled as *Momentform* would not cease to be aesthetically substandard in nineteenth-century terms. The final stage in the evolution of the sonata allegro to logical form is represented by Schönberg's dodecaphonic works, where periodic structure and tonality have given way entirely to "musical prose" and "atonality," and motivic relations have become universal in the sense—and herein resides the full significance of the twelve-tone method—that they are incorporated in what Adorno called the "precomposition" of the material.

Schönberg used the term "developing variation" for the technique of drawing far-reaching conclusions from a limited base of material, in an extreme case from a single interval. This technique is an instance of the classical ideal of thematic and motivic manipulation and is thus thoroughly in line with tradition. However, where Haydn and Beethoven applied this technique primarily, if not exclusively, for purposes of development, Brahms used it as an underlying principle governing all the sections of entire movements, with a qualitative leap in consistency and rigor. Strangely enough, a similar change can be noted in the case of Wagner and Liszt, the "musical antipodes" of Brahms: in both the music drama and the symphonic poem, the technique of repeating patterns in "real" (that is, modulating) sequences is transformed from a development technique, as it was used by Beethoven, into a means of introducing thematic material (the *Tristan* Prelude is a prime example). For music history, the change of function of a technique can be just as important as its origin. Accordingly, it is no accident that thematic-motivic manipulation and sequential repetition shifted at the same time from the development section to the exposition. It merely implies that Brahms, on the one hand, and Wagner and Liszt, on the other, were attempting to solve the same problem by different means—namely, how to present the motivic material of a movement broadly and accessibly, rather than aphoristically in a few measures, at a time when both periodic structure (the "four-squareness" derided by Wagner) and cadential harmony (in interaction with the metrical scheme) were disintegrating. As composers found less and less support in the traditional metrical and harmonic edifice of Beethoven and Haydn, which made room for motivic material and passage work alike, the more difficult it became for them to find a cogent way to continue an initial musical idea consisting of two or three measures, or even a single interval.

Unlike Wagner and Liszt, who yielded almost blindly to sequence technique as an alternative to the disintegrating functional meter and harmony, Brahms occasionally tended to overdetermine his structures, as though neither architecture nor logic were by themselves sufficient to meet his need for musical solidity. The first ten measures of the G-minor Piano Quartet, Op. 25 (1861), still reveal the unmistakable outline of a musical period (Ex. 41). The antecedent phrase cadences on the dominant, the consequent in the tonic, and the extension of the consequent is clearly produced by interpolating sequences in measures 7 and 8. Here Brahms takes developing variation to an extreme which Schönberg, who arranged the piece for orchestra, must have found paradigmatic. Each measure is based on the same initially inconspicuous four-note idea, whether in ordinary motion (mm. 1 and 5), in inversion (mm. 2–3 and 6–8), in cancrizans (m. 9), or

Example 41

with its two middle notes "verticalized" (m. 4, where F♯–C♯–E–D = F–C–E♭–D).
The continuation of the theme likewise spans ten measures, though without
balancing the form, and has nothing in common with the metrical and harmonic
norms of classical syntax. (As Hugo Riemann pointed out, the term *Gang* used by
Adolf Bernhard Marx in reference to forward motion is a makeshift attempt to
provide an explanation where none exists.) In compensation, Brahms weaves an
even denser web of motivic relations. These ten measures consist of nothing
more than a descending second, which is imitated, inverted, and put into sequences (mm. 11–13). It constantly reappears in new rhythmic guises: in half
notes (mm. 11–13 and 20), dotted halves (mm. 17–18), eighth notes (mm. 13–
15), quarter notes (mm. 15–16), and dotted quarters (mm. 13–14 and 19). A
more rigorous economy of means is scarcely conceivable.

Developing variation is a compositional hallmark of chamber music, but in
Brahms's case the chamber music idea encompassed the lied as well, or at least
some of his lieder. (It might seem to contradict Brahms's lied aesthetic, based on
an ideal of simplicity adopted from Goethe, that he uses devices from the chamber music tradition to establish lieder as art music. This attempt to mediate between extremes is, however, a classical instance of a dialectic that keeps a form
alive by becoming at times less virulent without ever resolving entirely.) Even as
early as his Op. 3, No. 1, *Liebestreu,* the first Brahms lied to reach print (1854), we
sense an urge to motivic density so paradigmatic as to suggest a compositional
manifesto. A three-note motive forms the substance of both the melody and the
bass line, being imitated, expanded, and inverted; apart from the filler chords,
every note is thematically related (Ex. 42). (It is thoroughly typical of Brahms,
who drew contrapuntal conclusions from the increasing sophistication of harmony, to treat the bass as a motivically related part rather than merely as a supporting line.)

Example 42

The tone of Brahms's lieder reveals the proximity he sought to folk song
just as clearly as their motivic and contrapuntal techniques display the solidity of
his craftsmanship. This tone differs fundamentally from the romanticism of
Schumann's lieder; indeed, the notion that Brahms inherited Schumann's
musicohistorical legacy at all seems grounded more in biographical associations
than in compositional facts. When we try even approximately to pinpoint the

musical devices that make up the "poetic" element of a Schumann lied such as *Im wunderschönen Monat Mai*, Op. 48, No. 1 (1840), we discover that Schumann, like Brahms, sought to strike a balance between sophistication and simplicity, but that, unlike Brahms, he achieved subtlety by using shades of harmony rather than motivic connections. Schumann's lied is fully equal to the fractured, and for this very reason irresistible, sentimentality of Heine's verse. Its simplicity lies in its syntax, in the repetitive and sequential structure of the vocal part, while its complexity is to be found in the harmony, in the combination of melodic line and accompaniment. At first, the vocal part seems to be in A major, only to cadence unexpectedly in the subdominant, D major (which, being the goal of a harmonic sequence, has minimal cadential effect). The prelude, postlude, and interlude, however, clearly outline F♯ minor as the tonic, though in the form of a quasi-Phrygian cadence (IV⁶–V⁷). The conflict of keys remains unresolved; the cadences become progressively weaker instead of stronger (from the first and second lines of the poem and finally to the postlude); the piece is left open-ended. These techniques combine to produce a state of suspension perfectly expressive of the "longing and desire," the "Sehnen und Verlangen," which Heine's poem not only treats as a topic but embodies in words.

In Brahms's hands, not only the lied but its instrumental counterpart, the lyrical piano piece, underwent a process of ever-increasing sophistication in musical logic. Though not surprising, this is by no means self-evident, since Brahms, despite his fondness for dissolving or eliding periodic structure and cadential harmony, was inclined to take over formal patterns intact. Thus, the title of his *Capriccio*, Op. 116, No. 3 (1892), would suggest a nonschematic form (although Brahms, an avid student of history, may have been thinking of seventeenth-century music). In fact, however, it follows a simple formal design:

A		B		A	
a¹	a²	b¹	b²	a¹	a²

Yet, in its detail, the piece reveals Brahms's urge to cast musical form as an ever-denser web of motives without, however, flaunting his compositional prowess or displaying the "working parts" of his music. (For example, the superimposition of the original and augmented forms of a motive in measure 13 is omitted from the recapitulation in measure 83. This can be seen as a sign of tact on Brahms's part, a reluctance to repeat a contrapuntal point made once before.) Like Bach, whom he studied tirelessly, Brahms was a virtuoso in the practice of combining musical devices from different genres. The initial motive of the *Capriccio*, as it appears in measure 1, is augmented by a ratio of 2:1 in measures 13 and 14, and again by 4:1 in measures 29 to 31. It alternates with its inversion in measures 9 to 11, generating chromatic clashes that are exploited in a development section in measures 24 to 28. In short, even in his lyrical piano pieces, Brahms pursued the ideal of blending motivic counterpoint and developing variation, the legacy respectively of Bach's fugal and Beethoven's sonata style, to produce a hybrid cognitive pattern divorced from existing generic traditions.

If counterpoint reigns in the *A* section, the connection, by no means immediately apparent, between sections *A* and *B* is based on what Arnold Schmitz has referred to as the principle of "contrasting derivation." This principle was developed by Beethoven to link the conflicting themes in a sonata—or, seen the other way around, to move away from eighteenth-century monothematicism (without abandoning it entirely) toward the dialectical opposition of themes that he required to establish musical form as a process. If the connection between the repeated G's in measures 1 and 35 is a fleeting and perhaps unintentional association, the three-note triplet motive D–E♭–F in measure 35 derives unmistakably from measure 2 (Ex. 43). This motive, in its original and inverted forms, in imitation and sequence, pervades the entire *B* section, leaving not a single "nonthematic" measure. We cannot even discount the possibility, as we reconstruct the imaginative act of composition, that the F♯–G–A motive of measure 2 derives, through its simultaneous contrapuntal inversion E♭–D–C, from the submotive C–B♭–A in the opening figure of measure 1 that dominates the *A* section. (Admittedly, we risk going off on wild-goose chases when we apply analytic techniques honed on Schönberg and Webern in order to detect latent or half-submerged motivic relations in the works of Beethoven and Brahms. Nevertheless, it is no accident, but evidence of a connecting historical thread, that the quest for "substantive relationships," as Hans Mersmann called them, frequently produces plausible results with Beethoven and Brahms but not with Schubert or Bruckner. Nor need we speak of "projecting" Schönberg's categories onto works by Beethoven or Brahms: the history of musical analysis, like musical performance, is a never-ending process in which the current evolutionary stage of composition inspires us to discover facts of compositional technique that do not cease to be facts simply because they were unknown to the composer's contemporaries.)

Example 43

In the history of reception, the correlate to the nineteenth-century idea of chamber music is musical education, or *Bildung*. This concept, the centerpiece of Brahms's "poetics" and a mediating link between aesthetics and compositional technique, is extraordinarily difficult if not impossible to reconstruct, the more so since the notion of music for the educated, as understood in the nineteenth century, in no way coincides with the picture of music for experts conveyed by the findings of modern analysis. True, musical artifice is an element basic to chamber music, defining its character as a music for private rather than public performance; but it was supposed to remain half concealed, in accordance with the motto *nascondere l'arte*. This aesthetic axiom is constantly being violated by twentieth-century analytic methods with their injunctions to listen "intelligently," but was apparently respected by the nineteenth century educated classes. As a result, we are in virtually no position to decide whether, and to what extent, motivic relations of the sort propagated by Brahms in his Op. 116, No. 3, were heard at all, or whether, after being noted in passing, they were repressed so as not to endanger the "aesthetic mood." As a person of musical culture, the nineteenth-century bourgeois dilettante was the spiritual heir of the aristocratic dilettantes of the Baroque period (which in Austrian social history, as the reception of Beethoven's music shows, extended well into the nineteenth century). Nor was the late-eighteenth-century string quartet the earliest chamber music in the strong sense of the term, having been preceded by the sixteenth-century madrigal and the seventeenth-century sonata da camera. All the same, to reconstruct the aesthetic idea underlying chamber music, we must recall a few basic traits of the humanistic-aristocratic culture that arose in Italy during the *quattrocento*. Probably the decisive trait was its understanding of a notion of courtesy that enabled, indeed enjoined, aristocrats and bourgeois artists and intellectuals to ignore, for the duration of the learned entertainment, the social gap existing between them. The idea of chamber music, it seems, arose as a musical reflection of a humanistic-aristocratic culture primarily centered on conversation. The aesthetic of this genre may be derived from the constantly recurring comparison with educated discourse, a metaphor which by no means originated with Goethe but was already a cliché in the sixteenth century. It is characteristic of musical discourse that each party continuously shows regard for the other. In this way, the whole emerges from an interplay of voices sustained by an understanding of each participant for the overall context, and not as a jumbled amalgam of its parts, as in certain recent orchestral works. Another key consideration for the social character of chamber music is its informality. No matter how refined the writing in a sixteenth-century madrigal or late-eighteenth-century string quartet, musical erudition and ostentatious pedantry were prohibited. Aristocratic taste objected to an obtrusive use of strict counterpoint, regarding it as music that, to borrow Nietzsche's term, "sweats." The goal instead was an attitude of light-handed gentility, of *nobile sprezzatura*; the exertions of musical artifice, if unavoidable, were at least not to be flaunted. In sum, despite a widespread opinion to the contrary, chamber music was not originally a bourgeois concept. The fact that the bourgeoisie—or, more precisely, the educated classes of the nineteenth century—were able to adopt this category at all presupposes a large amount of leisure time occupied in convivial culture. Further, this leisure was regarded, not as an interruption of one's normal occupation, but rather—almost aristocratically—as its goal and true import. Education, as opposed to the "realm of necessity," was the realm of "freedom."

Bibliographic References

Adorno, Theodor Wiesengrund. *Philosophie der neuen Musik.* Tübingen: Mohr, 1949. Eng. trans. by Anne G. Mitchell and Wesley V. Blomster as *Philosophy of Modern Music.* New York: Seabury Press, 1973.

———. *Versuch über Wagner.* Frankfurt am Main: Suhrkamp, 1952.

Bekker, Paul. *Wagner: das Leben im Werke.* Stuttgart: Deutsche Verlagsanstalt, 1924. Eng. trans. by M. M. Bozman as *Richard Wagner: His Life in His Work.* New York: W. W. Norton, 1931.

Bengtsson, Ingmar. "Romantisch-nationale Strömungen in deutscher und skandinavischer Musik." In *Norddeutsche und nordeuropäische Musik.* Edited by Carl Dahlhaus and Walter Wiora. Kassel: Bärenreiter, 1965.

Brendel, Franz. *Geschichte der Musik in Italien, Deutschland und Frankreich von den christlichen Zeiten bis auf die Gegenwart. Zweiundzwanzig Vorlesungen gehalten zu Leipzig im Jahre 1850.* Leipzig: B. Hinze, 1852.

Budden, Julian. *The Operas of Verdi.* 3 vols. London: Cassell, 1973–81.

Cesari, Gaetano, and Luzio, Alessandro. *I coppialeterre di Giuseppe Verdi.* Milan: Tip. Stucchi Ceretti & C., 1913. 2d edition. Bologna: Forni, 1968.

Chantavoine, Jean. *Le poème symphonique.* Paris: Larousse, 1950.

Dahlhaus, Carl. *Wagners Konzeption des musikalischen Dramas.* Regensburg: G. Bosse, 1971.

———. *Richard Wagners Musikdramen.* Velber bei Hannover: Friedrich, 1971. Eng. trans. by Mary Whittal as *Richard Wagner's Music Dramas.* Cambridge and New York: Cambridge University Press, 1980.

Gerhartz, Leo Karl, *Die Auseinandersetzungen des jungen Giuseppe Verdi mit dem literarischen Drama.* Berlin: Merseburger, 1968.

Handschin, Jacques. *Musikgeschichte im Überblick.* Lucerne: Rüber, 1948.

Heuss, Alfred. "Eine motivisch-thematische Studie über Liszts sinfonische Dichtung 'Ce qu'on entend sur la montagne'." *Zeitschrift der Internationalen Musikgesellschaft* 13 (1911–12): 10–21.

Keller, Otto. *Die Operette in ihrer geschichtlichen Entwicklung.* Leipzig, Vienna, and New York: Stein-Verlag, 1926.

Kerman, Joseph. *Opera as Drama.* New York: Random House, 1956. New and revised edition, Berkeley and Los Angeles: University of California Press, 1988.

Kracauer, Siegfried. *Jacques Offenbach und das Paris seiner Zeit.* Amsterdam: A. de Lange, 1937. Eng. trans. by Gwenda David and Eric Mosbacher as *Offenbach and the Paris of His Time.* London: Constable, 1937.

Kropfinger, Klaus. *Wagner und Beethoven: Untersuchungen zur Beethoven-Rezeption Richard Wagners.* Studien zur Musikgeschichte des 19. Jahrhunderts, vol. 29. Regensburg: G. Bosse, 1975.

Mann, Thomas. "Leiden und Größe Richard Wagners." In *Leiden und Größe der Meister.* Berlin: S. Fischer, 1935. Eng. trans. by H. T. Lowe Porter in *Past Masters and Other Papers.* New York: A. Knopf, 1933.

Mayer, Hans. *Anmerkungen zu Wagner.* Frankfurt am Main: Suhrkamp, 1966.

Mila, Massimo. *Il melodramma di Verdi.* Bari: G. Laterza & Figli, 1933. 2d ed. Milan: Feltrinelli, 1960.

Miller, Norbert. "Musik als Sprache. Zur Vorgeschichte von Liszts Symphonischen Dichtungen." In *Beiträge zur musikalischen Hermeneutik.* Studien zur Musikgeschichte des 19. Jahrhunderts, vol. 43. Edited by Carl Dahlhaus. Regensburg: G. Bosse, 1975.

Newman, Ernest. *The Life of Richard Wagner.* 4 vols. Cambridge: Cambridge University Press, 1933–46.

Riemann, Hugo. *Große Kompositionslehre.* 3 vols. Berlin and Stuttgart: W. Spemann, 1902–13.

Schering, Arnold. "Aus der Geschichte der musikalischen Kritik in Deutschland," *Jahrbuch der Musikbibliothek Peters* 35 (1928): 9–23.

———. "Johannes Brahms und seine Stellung in der Musikgeschichte des 19. Jahrhunderts," *Jahrbuch der Musikbibliothek Peters* 39 (1932): 9–22.

Schmitt-Thomas, Reinhold. *Die Entwicklung der deutschen Konzertkritik im Spiegel der Leipziger Allgemeinen Musikalischen Zeitung (1798–1848).* Frankfurt am Main: Kettenhof, 1969.

Schmitz, Arnold. *Beethovens "Zwei Prinzipe": ihre Bedeutung für Themen und Satzbau.* Berlin and Bonn: F. Dümmlers Verlagsbuchhandlung, 1923.

Schüler, Winfried. *Der Bayreuther Kreis von seiner Entstehung bis zum Ausgang der wilhelminischen Ära.* Münster: Aschendorf, 1971.

Spitta, Philipp. "Johannes Brahms." In *Zur Musik.* Berlin: Gebrüder Paetel, 1892.

Szabolcsi, Bence. "Die Anfänge der nationalen Oper im 19. Jahrhundert." In *Bericht über den neunten internationalen Kongreß Salzburg 1964.* Edited by Franz Giegling. Kassel and Basle: Bärenreiter, 1964–66.

Wagner, Richard. *Sämtliche Schriften und Dichtungen.* 16 vols. Leipzig: Breitkopf & Härtel, 1912–14.

Werfel, Franz, and Stefan, Paul. *Giuseppe Verdi: Briefe.* Berlin: P. Zsolnay, 1926. Eng. trans. by Edward Downes as *Verdi: The Man in His Letters.* New York: L. B. Fischer, c. 1942.

Young, Percy M. *Sir Arthur Sullivan.* London: Dent, 1971.

CHAPTER FIVE

1870-1889

The French debacle of 1870–71 is of interest to historians of government primarily for the fall of Napoleon III, and to social historians for the collapse of the Paris Commune. Yet it was also one of the few profound breaks in political history which had clear repercussions on the history of music, repercussions which we can squarely put our finger on without having to construct vague and elaborate hypotheses. It was obviously the Prussian victory that inspired Wagner to implement his proposed festival (his dream since 1851) in the form of a national theater supported by the German Reichstag, just as it was the French defeat that prompted Saint-Saëns to proclaim his *ars gallica* in order to reassert France's unbroken cultural rights. (Considering Wagner's appropriation of the idea of the German Reich for the purposes of his music drama, and considering that the Bayreuth festival was originally intended to follow on the heels of a successful revolution, one is tempted to apply Karl Marx's dictum regarding Cavour: "The reaction carried out the program of the revolution.")

The Bayreuth institution was the work of a theatrical megalomaniac who claimed to embody the whole of culture. It has come to symbolize the *Gründerzeit,* or "age of speculators" (known in Vienna as the "*Ringstraße* period"), as though Wagner were a musical equivalent of Hans Makart. In reality Wagner's work, at least in part, refutes the widespread view of the age as insubstantial and vapid, as emptiness hiding behind monumental arrogance. Indeed, the nationalist pomp of Wagner's festivals was controversial and suspect to contemporaries who mistrusted the composer of *Tristan* no less than the former revolutionist now posing as "the Meister." (In spite of the triumph of *Die Meistersinger* in 1868, Wagner only became the idol of German nationalist culture after his death.)

If the nationalism which Wagner flaunted in 1871 was a means, momentarily tinged with political ardor, to the end of his music drama, the notion of an *ars gallica* in which Saint-Saëns sought refuge amidst the French catastrophe was almost insolubly ambiguous. In order to found a national symphonic and chamber music culture in opposition to their exclusive orientation on opera, French composers had to appropriate and recast a specifically German tradition— namely, Viennese classicism, a tradition upheld in Paris by Saint-Saëns himself. (The French bias toward opera had consequences for Berlioz for which the term "tragic dialectic" is none too inflated.)

Musical nationalism, whether in Wagner or Saint-Saëns, resembles at times a façade rent with cracks and fissures. This is apparently linked to a fact hotly denied by every nationalist but self-evident in retrospect: as liberal nationalism gradually gave way to the aggressive nationalism of the late nineteenth century the amount of idealism available to composers of clear aesthetic conscience was reduced accordingly. We do not even need to compare two unlikes such as Chopin's *Revolutionary Etude* (1832) and Wagner's *Kaisermarsch* (1871) in order to claim that the Polish debacle of 1830 was capable of inspiring musicians, whereas the Prussian victory of 1870 was not, neither for Brahms nor for Wagner.

In non-German literature, as represented by Tolstoy's *War and Peace* (1868–69) and *Anna Karenina* (1875–77), Dostoevsky's *The Idiot* (1868–69) and *The Brothers Karamazov* (1879–80), and Ibsen's *Peer Gynt* (1876) and *Ghosts* (1882), the *Gründerzeit* was an age of realism whose "Herculean epic burdens" (Thomas Mann) recall the work of Wagner. The *Ring* tetralogy, however, with its myth of disintegration and downfall permeating the music to its innermost structure, represents a current contrary to the predominant aesthetic and intellectual tendencies of the age.

In the case of Mussorgsky, Bizet, and Janáček (though less so in the case of *verismo,* which remained imprisoned in melodrama despite its occasional outbursts of naturalism), we are fully warranted to speak of musical realism. Nor do we need to justify our use of this term by seeking recourse in so tortured a theory of realism as the "double mimesis" theory, in which reality is reflected in feeling, and feeling in music. Musical realism of the late nineteenth century is plain to see and obviously links up with the literary realism then prevalent in Russia no less than in France. However, we should not let a misguided zeal to prove the unity of the age obscure the fact that music took little or no part in the historical dialectic that caused realism to give rise to impressionism, and naturalism to expressionism, in literature and painting, a dialectic emerging from the postulate that the aim of art is to expose and make manifest the "truths of reality."

Because of the constantly evolving and self-regenerating dialectic implicit in a concept such as "true" or "genuine reality," the "aesthetic of truth," propounded in avant-garde circles to offset the earlier "aesthetic of beauty" still predominant in popular philosophy, formed a motif that profoundly affected the history of art. Not even historians proceeding from social history and suspicious of intellectual history should make light of this motif. It made a difference whether one understood "reality" to be a summation of communicable and observable facts, as did Eugen Dühring, or agreed with Ernst Mach that "reality" is to be found in subjective feelings, a transient substance conditioned by categorical formation. It is no distortion, as intellectual historians have claimed of their opposite numbers in social history, to see in this distinction an epistemological correlate to the stylistic difference between realism and impressionism. As August Strindberg illustrates, naturalism can merge with or be transformed into expressionism when "genuine reality," as conditioned by the categories of milieu theory, turns out in fact to be a projection of an "interior world." In this case the language of description automatically and almost ineluctably gives way to a language of symbols. This dialectic, at once literary and epistemological, follows the same pattern that led from realism to impressionism.

The "aesthetic of truth," both in literature and in painting, evolved within currents that all left their mark on music between 1870 and 1914: realism in the case of Mussorgsky, Bizet, and Janáček, impressionism in Debussy, naturalism in Charpentier, Bruneau, and Schreker, expressionism in Schönberg and Berg. However, music history stands curiously aloof from the cultural and intellectual history of the age, and we have little cause to speak of parallel evolution as in the case of literature and painting, where changes of artistic approach were directly linked to changes of epistemological premises. Music participated only peripherally and sporadically in the paths struck by the literature and painting of the "aesthetic of truth." The fact that expressionism, unlike realism, naturalism, and impressionism, proved to be authentic rather than derivative as a musical style is explained by the legacy of romanticism and neoromanticism—the consequences of the *Tristan* style—rather than by the dialectic that caused naturalism to give birth to literary expressionism. Music, as in the age of positivism, was still "different."

The Second Age of the Symphony

Beethoven elevated the symphony from a genre that tolerated unconstrained mass production to a "grand form" in which composers tried with a few works to attain the utmost limits of their art. By the middle of the nineteenth century it had entered a crisis most clearly evidenced by the nearly two decades that separate Schumann's Third Symphony (1850), his final work in the genre, from any work of distinction that represented absolute rather than programmatic music. In *Oper und Drama* Wagner pronounced the death of the symphony, viewing the post-Beethovenian efforts as a mere epilogue with nothing substantially new to say. Instead of the symphony, it was the Lisztian symphonic poem that came to the fore in the 1850s and 1860s claiming to represent large-scale instrumental music. All the more striking, then, and all the more disconcerting for historians searching for an unbroken continuity in the history of the genre, that with the works of Bruckner and Brahms, Tchaikovsky and Borodin, Dvořák and Franck in the 1870s and 1880s, the symphony entered a "second age" whose legacy still continues to dominate a large part of the concert repertoire even today, a century later. The symphony had regained its apparently long-lost position in the minds of audiences and composers alike (a position, however, which it shared with the symphonic poem in the case of Tchaikovsky, Dvořák, and Franck). Granting Paul Bekker's thesis that the symphony is ideally directed to the mass audience of the entire bourgeoisie, we then want to ask how a monumental style could exist at all under the compositional preconditions of the late nineteenth century. If Nietzsche, not entirely without justification, could apostrophize even Wagner as a "musical miniaturist" who suffered endless torments to create his visions of large-scale form, how much more oppressive must these problems have been in instrumental music than in opera. Nietzsche had put his finger squarely on the problem with all the acumen of a philosopher plagued with similar problems of his own.

The difficulties that beset large-scale instrumental music under the premises of "late romanticism" are to be discovered not so much in Bruckner, who seems to have been born to monumentality and then transplanted to the alien and unsympathetic world of the nineteenth century, as in Tchaikovsky, whose irresistible rise as a symphonist should not obscure the fact that he was primarily a composer of operas and ballets. The stylistic pretensions raised by Tchaikovsky's Fourth Symphony in F minor, Op. 36 (1878), are announced clearly enough in the first movement by the horn and trumpet theme. The character and tempo (*andante sostenuto*) of this theme make it seem like an introduction even though it recurs at every "juncture" of the form—at the beginning of the development, recapitulation, and coda—and thus at least partially serves the function of a main theme. The "actual" main theme, however, with an urgent pathos curiously held in check by its meter ($\frac{9}{8}$) and tempo (*In movimento di Valse*), is hardly suitable, at least by Beethovenian standards, for establishing a symphonic movement spanning hundreds of measures. The fact that this theme reaches an ecstatic *fortissimo* in a development section emerging directly from the exposition (mm. 53–103) has little or no bearing on its weaknesses as the mainspring of a symphonic movement. These weaknesses become evident in the noticeable fact, inexplicable within the tradition of the form, that the development culminates in a quotation of the *andante* theme (mm. 253 and 263), thereby transferring this theme from an introductory to a formally constitutive role. We can put this another way. According to the rule established by Beethoven, the principal theme of a symphonic movement had a dual function: when broken down into particles, it served as material for the development section; when reconstituted, it served as the development's triumphant goal and destination. Tchaikovsky has spread this dual function over two different themes: an *andante* motive, which, though capable of serving as the climax of a development section, is not itself amenable to development, and a *moderato* motive, which can be drawn into a thematic process but is incapable of appearing as the main theme except at exposed locations protected by the *andante* motive. To put it bluntly, the grand style fundamental to the genre has been split into a monumentality that remains a decorative façade unsupported by the internal form of the movement, and an internal form that is lyrical in character and can be dramatized only by applying a thick layer of pathos.

The secondary theme (m. 116) is set apart from the main theme by its slower tempo (*quasi andante*). The continuation (m. 134) is made up of a (now indepen-

Fig. 56 Bilse concert in Warsaw. At first glance this picture conveys the impression of light music which is less entertaining in itself than a stimulus to entertainment. The programs which Benjamin Bilse (1816–1902) played on his tours were a combination of entertainment music and symphony concerts. The fact that the "grand concert" with mixed program had split around mid-century into the "symphony concert," upheld by the educated classes, and the popular concert, in no way implies that the earlier species had disappeared altogether. On the contrary, it formed one of the historical preconditions of the "popular symphony concert" that arose around 1900 under the motto of "art for the people." (Torun, Muzeum Nikolaja Kopernika, Biblioteka Główna.)

dent) cantabile countermelody to the secondary theme and a variant of the main theme, in an attempt to combine or mediate between them. By changing the articulation from *legato espressivo* to staccato the theme assumes a *scherzando* character. The concluding theme (m. 161) emerges from a crescendo to triple *forte* with a bombastically heroic motive in the tempo of the main theme.

In order to give his movement symphonic proportions Tchaikovsky turned to formal ideas that originated with Liszt. The extended development section between the main and secondary themes (mm. 53–103) and the change of tempo cause the boundary between a cantabile secondary theme and an interpolated slow movement to blur. By converting the main theme into a *scherzando* motive Tchaikovsky clearly made use of "thematic transformation," whose purpose was originally to preserve a substantive relation between contrasting passages, a device employed by Liszt to satisfy a program and at the same time to impart internal cohesion to his music. The moods of the themes recall the movements of a sonata cycle, with main theme, secondary theme, bridge, and closing theme governed respectively by passion, lyrical cantabile, *scherzando,* and triumphant apotheosis. Historically, this derives from Liszt's principle of composing multimovement works in single movements. Thus, in the "second age" of the symphony, separated from the first by the symphonic poem, large-scale form is partly vouchsafed by techniques derived from program music but divorced from the aesthetic premises originally associated with them. In this respect, the reconstitution of absolute music following its mid-century hiatus deserves to be called dialectical in that it emerged in part by abstracting features of its aesthetic opposite, program music. If the history of absolute music is a history of formal ideas requiring constant innovation lest it grind to a halt, then absolute music owes at least some aspects of its evolution to the symphonic poem, once chided for its formlessness.

In the aesthetic debates, mingled with cultural politics, that necessarily accompany the emergence of any national art still in its infancy, Tchaikovsky was considered a musical antipode to the "Mighty Handful." Nevertheless, the problem of how to create a symphonic form equal to the aesthetic claims of the genre and yet consistent with the historical situation of the 1870s was no different for Borodin than for Tchaikovsky. Moreover, a Lisztian approach was all the more natural for Borodin because of the biographical connections between the two composers. (Borodin's journey to Weimar, it is true, did not take place until 1877, the year in which his B-minor Symphony was completed, but it represents not the origin of their affinity so much as an expression and consequence of it.)

The first movement of the B-minor Symphony is conventional in form. However, it makes use of what we might call Liszt's "subthematic" chromaticism, which, by infusing different themes, links them internally so as to form a structure beneath the thematic level. Another Lisztian idea is its manner of putting the various sections of the exposition—main theme, secondary theme, and closing thematic group—in different tempos (*allegro, poco meno mosso,* and *animato assai*). Unlike Tchaikovsky, however, who handled tempo changes without difficulty, Borodin became mired in a contradiction which he leaves to the conductor to solve, although strictly speaking no solution is possible. Namely, when the themes are combined in the development, either the main theme has to be stretched beyond recognition or the secondary theme rushed at breakneck speed. This quandary on the performer's part can also be understood as an expression of the difficult historical predicament in which the symphony had landed by the 1870s: conventional traits, such as the combination of themes in the development section and the formal outline of the movement, were meant to preserve the continuity of the genre at the same time that modern formal conceptions, adopted from the symphonic poem, were required to create large-scale form. And this form would be scarcely conceivable without techniques such as changing tempo in order to mark sharp changes of thematic character.

We have seen that, for Tchaikovsky, the relation between lyricism and monumentality, so precarious to the symphonic style under "late romantic" conditions, became an open contradiction. To have expressive cantabile themes culminate in bombastic *fortissimo* was not to resolve the dilemma but to conceal an admission of failure. Brahms, on the other hand, tackled the analogous problem of combining the premises of chamber music with a will to large-scale form, a problem which he solved by going to the root of the matter: the thematic material.

The claim is constantly heard that Brahms, even in his symphonies, "actually" thought in terms of chamber music. The conclusions to be drawn from this contention have never been sufficiently examined. A psychological interpretation (which, however, can never be decisive in the final analysis) springs immediately to mind—namely, that Brahms's symphonies, though the heirs of Beethoven's, are in fact directed not at the bourgeois public as a whole but primarily at the individual listener, at the "subject" immersed in his feelings and thoughts, and are thus perceived, by aesthetic criteria, as though they were chamber music. This is undeniably true, and by no means utterly inconsistent with the historical fact that his symphonic oeuvre has found a more secure place in the repertoire and the popular imagination than his chamber music, for it is possible to think of this public as what David Riesman has called a "lonely crowd." A Brahms symphony is virtually a musical attestation of the fact that each member of a crowd, though fully aware of the surrounding crowd, is nevertheless entirely on his own.

Brahms's symphonic style circumscribes a paradox. We can pinpoint this paradox by analyzing the peculiar dual thematic structure underlying the first movement of his Third Symphony (1883). Here the main theme, a Schumann quotation, is, strictly speaking, a concluding idea: not until the diminuendo epilogues of the first and fourth movements does it reveal its true character, and the direction it then takes is one of introspection, where the subject immures itself to the world and turns ultimately to silence (Ex. 44). Basically, the symphonic development is borne by a single musical idea. We have difficulty in characterizing this idea as a theme or motive, motto or subject, precisely because its purpose resides in constantly changing its function (Ex. 45). The central idea, as it might be called, is heard as a motto prefixed to the main theme, giving the theme a foothold without which its exposition would be impossible. It then appears in coun-

Example 44

Example 45

terpoint with the main theme, holding together its various sections by ostinato repetition, and recurs in the transition as a motive in the literal sense of the term, "motivating" the musical process by providing melodic justification for a hasty modulation (F: I, D♭: V–I, followed by D♭: I, A: V–I). It then initiates a second transition, bringing about a by no means purely coloristic modulation from the A major of the secondary theme to the A minor of the concluding group (or third theme). Finally, it appears in the middle of the development section as a cantabile horn melody.

Scarcely less important than the function served by this central idea in the formal process is the aesthetic significance conferred upon it as a counterpart to the work's chamber music tendencies, to a logic so sophisticated as to court pedantry. One paradigmatic instance is the secondary theme, which evolves from a series of minute variations (Ex. 46). The substance of the theme appears in a single-measure motive (m. 36) into which a fourth is inserted at its repetition (m. 37). This fourth, together with a whole step transformed by a change of articulation from a dead interval (m. 37) to a motivic one (m. 38), then serves as a connecting motive (m. 39), which later takes on a prominent life of its own in the development section. In the same measure (m. 39) the cadential formula is expanded rhythmically and another note is added to its pitch structure. The resultant chromaticism then enters the counterpoint when the secondary theme is repeated (m. 41), and is highlighted as the main melody in the theme's epilogue: what began as an inconspicuous addition has attained motivic significance. A grace note added to the chromatic figure in measure 43 (C♯–B♯–C♯–B instead of C♯–B♯–B) in turn becomes the basis of a three-note motive (C♯–B♯–C♯ in m. 44) which later takes on an independent existence, forming a crucial component of the development section.

Despite this extreme sophistication, only perceivable with utmost concentration of the musical faculties, the grand gesture so indispensable to the symphonic style is never lost. The reason for this can be attributed to the ubiquitous central idea, which makes its presence felt everywhere but never courts monotony, since its formal significance and harmonic-tonal function constantly change. (It should be noted that the harmonies sometimes take their acerbity from the motive, thereby inverting the customary compositional hierarchy by making harmony

Example 46

derivative rather than formative.) The central idea, then, intrudes deep into the
formal process by the modulations it occasions or melodically sustains and by the
diverging compositional roles it variously serves. Yet, with its simple melodic
gesture and tenacious omnipresence, it also manifests that urge to monumentality without which the symphonic style cannot exist. This combination of simplicity and tenacity, which Brahms may have learned from Handel (a composer
greatly admired by Brahms and Beethoven alike), conveys a certain "gravity"
that is by no means sacrificed when coupled with extreme sophistication, a sophistication in which the central idea likewise directly participates with its changing harmonizations. On the contrary, simplicity and sophistication stem from the
same source, causing the monumentality to emerge from within rather than
functioning as a façade.

The anti-Bruckner polemics indulged in by the Brahms party in the 1880s
form one of the sorriest chapters in the history of music criticism, mainly because
they struck a man who, unlike Wagner, was largely unable to defend himself.
(The favor of the court hardly outweighed the ill will of the bourgeois public.)
However, it would be misguided, or at least inadequate, to think of these polemics as mere animosity, as an attack on genius by those who sense a greatness beyond their powers to comprehend. Rather, Bruckner's "symphonic boa constric-
tors," as Brahms called them, issued a challenge to learned musicians, who felt at
home in the Brahms camp, and who saw the basic axioms of musical thought
threatened, even more so than by Wagner. Moreover, the scandal occasioned by
Bruckner's music among the more learned of his detractors was matched all too
well by the ungainly appearance of the man himself, a prodigious organist and
tongue-tied simpleton from the provinces. (Nonetheless, it ill behooves an age of
rampant ignorance such as ours to pass judgment on the age of *Bildung* that did
such injustice to Bruckner.)

Categories of judgment combining elements from aesthetics and social psychology must, however, be mediated by compositional facts lest they remain in a
vacuum. And we have no trouble isolating those features of Bruckner's style that
dazed educated late-nineteenth century audiences weaned on the music of Bach

and Handel, the Viennese Classics, and the romanticism of Schumann and Mendelssohn. What apparently caused the most difficulty was the supreme nonchalance with which Bruckner presupposed symphonic monumentality while casually abandoning everything which the classical-romantic tradition, as represented by Brahms, understood to be musical logic. The opposition Bruckner faced was more than a matter of superficial mistrust, of trifles stylized into major nuisances; it was sustained by a feeling that radical partisanship was justified because the conflict itself was radical in its very nature.

Musical logic, the "developing variation" of musical ideas (as it was called by Schönberg, who admired Brahms and belittled Bruckner), rested on a premise considered so self-evident as to be beneath mention: that the central parameter of art music is its "diastematic," or pitch, structure. (Anyone trying to discover how a piece of music coheres internally will automatically look for what Hans Mersmann called a "relationship of substance" between its ostensibly divergent parts, where "substance" is almost invariably taken to mean pitch structures.) Bruckner's symphonic style, however, unlike that of Brahms's chamber music or Wagner's music dramas, is primarily rhythmic rather than diastematic, and thus seems to stand the usual hierarchy of tonal properties on its head.

The exposition of the first movement of Bruckner's Sixth Symphony in A major (1881) presents the first and second groups as opposing thematic blocks in a rhythm as rigorously unified internally as it contrasts externally. Both the first group and the second group cling stubbornly to a basic rhythmic pattern about fifty measures in length. And although both rhythms—the ♫♪ ♫♪ figure and the quarter-note triplets against a $\frac{4}{4}$ meter—can be explained as variants of the so-called Bruckner rhythm ♩ ♩ ♩♩♩ , the opposition between them is more striking than their similarities.

The ostinato rhythms constitute, as it were, the "ground level" of the music, forming a crucial aspect of the work's monumentality with their insistent repetition. However, there is a difference between this "formative rhythm" and the "motivic rhythm" in which the themes take shape. Motivic rhythm, to use the language of Gestalt psychology, stands out as a "figure" from the "ground" of the ostinato rhythm. The pitch structures that impart melody to the rhythms remain secondary, being merely different manifestations of a uniform rhythmic substance. Consequently, when Bruckner reduces melodic-rhythmic imitation to purely abstract rhythmic imitation, as in measures 25–28, he is not blurring the music but paring it down to essentials. And when a rhythmic structure exchanges one set of pitches for another (mm. 37–40 as compared with mm. 15–18), thereby retaining its melodic gesture while "compressing" its intervals, there is no need to search for an overriding thematic process to legitimize the change (Ex. 47). With Brahms it would be appropriate to view these deviations as part of a process of "developing variation" extending from measure 15 through measures 37 and 41 to measure 49; but not with Bruckner (Ex. 48). (The problem of any analysis with pretensions to do more than collect compositional bric-a-brac is not to discover possible constructions but to distinguish between those construc-

Example 47

Example 48

tions which are meaningful and those which are not.) True, pitch structure is crucial in many relations, such as the inversion of measure 4 in measure 10, but this should not blind us to the fact that Bruckner's method of motivic association resided in playing around with pitch structures as though intervals did not really count. Measures 53–54 and 61–62, for example, though located at analogous points in the secondary theme, reveal melodic and contrapuntal parallels as difficult to define as they are patent to the ear (Ex. 49). The countermelody, the vehicle of the rhythmic ground pattern, serves the same function in measures 61–62 as in measures 53–54, but it also incorporates a few elements from the melody line: the leap of a seventh with descending second (m. 61) replaces the leap of a ninth with descending second (m. 53), and the embellishment of the E♭ in measure 62 seems to echo that of the F♯ in measure 54. That the one version is able to substitute for the other means, aesthetically, that instead of developing variation, where each variant represents ("ideal-typically," to use Max Weber's term) a consequence of the preceding one and a prerequisite for the next one, Bruckner makes use of an analytically elusive but clearly perceivable similarity by association, which makes the later version seem like a written-out memory image of the earlier one. The logic of discourse, as conceived by Brahms, gives way to a system of approximate correspondences. This impression of a tight-knit web of relationships, spreading over the work with scant regard to accuracy of detail, forms the correlate to a conception of form based on rhythmically distinct

Example 49

"blocks." If the monumentality of Bruckner's technique is manifest in his use of "blocks," the associations covering the architectonic layers with a web of motivic relationships reaches a level of sophistication that enables monumentality to appear as grand style.

The growth of the symphony orchestra resulted from a confluence of currents in social history, aesthetics, and the history of composition. In the nineteenth century it was not simply a correlate to the emergence of an intrinsically self-sustaining monumental style; it also posed a challenge to composers, a challenge that proved difficult to confront and overcome because, contrary to popular notions of "late romanticism," an uncomplicated relation to musical gigantism of Bruckner's sort was more the exception than the rule. However, if we view the monumental style as the formal problem it undoubtedly was in an age characterized by conflicting penchants for lyricism and large orchestras, the cyclic ideal exemplified by César Franck's D-minor Symphony (1888) and elevated to a principle by Vincent d'Indy in the doctrine of the Schola Cantorum (his competing institution to the Paris Conservatoire) seems to be one of those precarious solutions whose semifailure illuminates the depth of the quandary faced by composers at the time. The plan of linking the movements of a symphony or a sonata by means of recurrent themes, thereby turning a group into a "cycle," had first been realized by Franck as early as the 1840s in a piece of chamber music, the Trio in F♯ minor, Op. 1, No. 1. However, this should not obscure the fact that, as a formal ideal, it only reached its true aesthetic potential by establishing monumentality in the symphony, turning loose-limbed form into large-scale form by gathering the parts about a thematic center. (It is not inconceivable that Liszt was influenced by Franck's Trio, with which, on Peter Cornelius's evidence, he was acquainted. However, the connection must remain uncertain for chronological reasons, because of the difficulty of retracing the evolution of Liszt's formal ideas.)

Obviously, to prevent the recurrence of a theme from sounding like an interpolated quotation it must be integrated into the musical context. This would go without saying if it were not accompanied by another difficulty: the moment its necessary connection to the other themes becomes all too clumsy and obvious the work runs the risk of monotony. To grasp the way Franck implemented his idea we have to distinguish between connections of substance and connections of form. When we do so, it turns out that, to avoid monotony, the partial intervallic correspondence in the main themes of all three movements (mm. 1, 17, and 7–8, respectively) is held in a state of suspension, as mere allusion, to an extent that makes us wonder whether the correspondence is aesthetically viable at all (Ex. 50). Unlike the integration of substance, Franck's formal integration, though

Example 50

Fig. 57 Bruckner monument in the Viennese Volksgarten. Stylistically the muse, arms histrionically uplifted toward the disdainful Bruckner, stands in almost grotesque contradiction to the realistic bust of the composer. Even more paradoxically, practically no nineteenth-century composer was less suited to antique symbolism than Bruckner. It almost seems as though Bruckner, decried throughout his lifetime in the "cultured" Brahms circles as "uncultured" and a prototype of the "idiot genius," was now to be posthumously awarded the emblems of neo-humanistic culture. What was formerly a "phenomenon of nature" became part of "cultural heritage." (Vienna, Österreichische Nationalbibliothek.)

clear, is by no means unproblematical, as is shown by the connection between the middle movement and the finale. The middle movement unites a slow movement and a scherzo, combining their conflicting themes, at first separately introduced and developed, at measure 184. This combination, which also superimposes two divergent meters (the first section has a quarter-note beat, the second an eighth-note beat), is all the more convincing, since the slow movement had been combining themes from the very outset: the opening chord sequence (m. 1) is joined by the theme (m. 17) and then by a cantabile countermelody (m. 25). (The principle of adding a striking cantabile countermelody was one of the characteristic structural ideas of the nineteenth century, even trickling down to the musical *souterrain* of march and dance music.)

The main theme of the middle movement carries the countermelodies associated with it as memory traces when it recurs in the finale. However, this "wizardry of relationships," effective as it is, should not obscure the fact that the attempted formal integration fails. The slow movement theme is out of place as a concluding group (or third theme) in the exposition of the finale (m. 124) in that the sequence of brass chorale (secondary theme) followed by lyric cantabile (concluding group) inverts the expectations we have inherited from the sonata-form tradition. Later, after being touched upon briefly in the development section (m. 224), the theme of the slow movement assumes the position of secondary theme by eliding with it in the recapitulation, so that melodic character and formal position coincide. On the other hand, this recurrence immediately initiates the coda, whose function consists in assembling all the themes of the cycle into a display of monumental unity, which, however, seems "staged."

We encounter a similar final effect in Dvořák's "New World" Symphony (1893), though there is no compelling need to assume that it arose directly under the influence of Franck's work. At the end of the last movement—in a "coda" undeserving of the name—Dvořák collects the main themes of all four movements, now in succession, now simultaneously, as though he wanted to reassure himself in retrospect of the work's unity. It seems as though the quotations scattered earlier in the work, establishing thematic associations beyond the confines of its movements, were nothing but a device to foreshadow and aesthetically legitimize the final effect. The flashback in the Largo to the main theme of the first movement is a brief reminiscence whose location, in the retransition to the recapitulation, at first merely foreshadows the ultimate purpose of Dvořák's quotation technique, namely, an associative conglomeration of the work's main themes. In the Scherzo, on the other hand, as a sort of partial anticipation of the final movement, the Scherzo theme combines with the main theme of the first movement to form a coda with a sense of arrival. In this combination of themes the Scherzo motive functions aesthetically as a reminiscence, conveying an impression (linked to the work's "internal program") that the themes have been wafted from the past to the present. Finally, the development section of the last movement—the last station on the way to the coda, the goal of the development —seems a suitable place to attempt a combination of the finale's theme (in diminution) with the principal themes of the second and first movements. Taken altogether, there is no denying that Dvořák, generally (and not without justification) regarded as a naive composer, was at least reflective enough to create a convincing fusion of quotation technique (the device used to evoke music from a remote time and place) and the formal symphonic process, a step-by-step elaboration of thematic material.

Drame lyrique and Operatic Realism

Categorizing literary genres according to the degree of their dependence on earlier models is by no means a vain occupation. Traditional subject matter and works are used more frequently in the drama than in the novel—and more freely, if more covertly, in comedy than in tragedy—and this in turn says important things about the nature of these genres. However, as little inclined as we are to excuse a novel for being woven according to a familiar pattern, we are all the more generous in allowing opera librettos to plunder literature without a qualm.

We may be perfectly within our rights to protest against eighteenth-century librettists in the name of Racine, or nineteenth-century librettists in the name of Shakespeare, but our efforts will prove useless in the end.

Nevertheless, it is noteworthy that the *drame lyrique* of the late nineteenth century, a genre that withdrew from the staged world history of Meyerbeer to interior tragedies, did not shrink for a moment from turning to materials such as *Hamlet* (1868) and *Mignon* (Ambroise Thomas, 1866), *Faust* (Charles Gounod, 1859), and *Werther* (Jules Massenet, 1892), all of them models that can scarcely be abstracted from their underlying philosophical spirit. The method that permitted *Kabale und Liebe* to be transformed into a libretto fully capable of standing on its own merits, and nowhere compelling listeners to think of Schiller, could not be applied to *Faust* or *Mignon*.

To German audiences, who found his artistic convictions as dubious as his melodies were irresistible, Gounod was the composer not only of *Faust* but of the *Ave Maria* (1853) as well, thus compounding desecration of Goethe with sacrilege to Bach. (In fact, however, Gounod was a church composer whose piety was as unimpeachable as the solidity of his musical craftsmanship.) It is absurd, or at least misguided, to accuse the libretto of *Faust* (shamefacedly renamed *Margarete* in Germany) of preserving little more than the plot outline and a few props from the original, which after all was well known in France through Gérard de Nerval's translation. The opera's greatest shortcoming, evincing not just a want of literary tact but a faulty dramaturgy as well, is not its remoteness from Goethe's play but its dependence on the play despite this remoteness. However tempting it may be to try to forget the play in order to enjoy the opera, this approach proves impossible the moment we take the libretto seriously as a theater piece instead of regarding it merely as a vehicle for vocal numbers such as Valentin's Prayer, Mephistopheles's Song of the Golden Calf, and Faust's Cavatina. For the moment we put Goethe's text out of mind we fail utterly to understand why all of Mephistopheles's magic tricks are necessary to generate the love between Faust and Marguérite that ultimately spells their doom. According to the rules of operatic dramaturgy, the sorcery that Mephistopheles applies at the beginning and the end of the Act 3 duet in order to turn Marguérite's fondness into love, and love into passion, is entirely superfluous: in light of Wagner's and Verdi's operas it seems almost to be a law of the genre that passion is visited upon the characters unawares. What Mephistopheles does could have been accomplished just as easily without him by the music. But if Mephistopheles's sorcery impairs the substance of the drama rather than deepening it, manipulating its psychological processes and turning the tragedy into a puppet show, it also represents the sole raison d'être for the existence of the Devil in a metaphysical tragedy reduced to the level of *drame lyrique*. For however domineering Mephistopheles's behavior may be on stage, with his *couplets,* macabre pranks, and shady intrigues, he is basically extraneous to the essentials of the plot. Since we cannot conceive why Faust, to function as the tenor of a *drame lyrique,* is at first an elderly man who then has to be transformed by sorcery into a younger one, we are forced to recall Goethe's play. Even though the libretto offends against the spirit of the play, it is nevertheless dependent on its structure. Literary reflection, though purportedly unnecessary, is constantly forced upon the listener.

What prevented Gounod from distancing himself even more from the play was presumably the church composer within him: *Faust* was composed not least of all for its opening and closing scenes—the choruses wafting into Faust's study and the transfiguration of Marguérite. If its relation to Goethe's play is contradictory, the reason is to be found less in the frivolity of which Gounod is accused by his German critics than in his piety. It is not the waltz that upsets the dramaturgical conception so much as the angelic chorus and its opposite, black magic.

Still, the *religioso* tone of the work—a tone to be heard not only in the final chorus or in Valentin's Prayer but also in Faust's Cavatina and the duet that quotes it—never left French nineteenth-century opera. Where Meyerbeer set religion against the backdrop of military history, the *drame lyrique,* having taken refuge in interior dramas, used religion as an ingredient in private affairs. And it is this dash of sanctimoniousness in works such as Gounod's *Faust* (1859) and Massenet's *Thaïs* (1894) which has given the *drame lyrique* its reputation as "bad nineteenth-century art" from our current perspective. The history of opera reception is just as inseparable from the emotional styles and fashions that distinguish one age from another as it is from the vicissitudes of musical taste (never an exclusively musical matter) or from changing notions as to what is theatrically effective and what is not. (It may seem puzzling to speak of "emotional fashions," which in turn are closely linked to the history of human piety, but it is by no means absurd. The notion that the innermost essence of a thing is also its most individual and characteristic is a preconception from the romantic legacy which we had best discard when we attempt to write reception history.)

We have no way of telling whether, and if so to what extent, Massenet and his librettist Georges Hartmann were aware of the religious slant to Goethe's *Werther* when they turned to it in 1886. (The text is filled with countless quotations and semiquotations from the New Testament, turning the love story, on careful reading, into a martyr's tragedy.) Whatever the case, when Max Kalbeck, for the 1892 Vienna premiere, translated the final line *tout est fini* with Christ's last words on the cross, he was not blaspheming but simply drawing attention to an element which, considering the history of the *drame lyrique,* probably attracted Massenet to this story in the first place, at least subconsciously or semiconsciously. Taken by itself, *Werther* would hardly have seemed a likely candidate for a libretto capable of succeeding as a stage piece (although earlier composers, among them Rodolphe Kreutzer, had also tried their hand at the material, without success). For Massenet, however, the composer of *Manon, Esclarmonde* (1889), and *Thaïs,* appropriating *Werther* as material for an opera meant recasting Werther's tragedy into a drama with Charlotte as its main character.

Werther's love is love at first sight. The fact that his exaltation turns into despair and back again alters nothing of his character, which remains the same in essence. Paradoxically, his aria *J'aurais sur ma poitrine*, famous outside the context of the opera as the *Désolation de Werther*, even unites and fuses the opposing moods between which Werther vacillates: depression and rapture become indistinguishable from each other. This is done by superimposing, as it were, an Italianate *agitato* onto Massenet's idiosyncratic tone of passion mingled, or at least tinged, with resignation, a tone more deserving of an *andante* or *allegretto* tempo (Ex. 51). Presupposing, with Walter Benjamin, that destiny and character are mutually exclusive, we might claim that unlike Werther, who is locked in his destiny, Charlotte is the protagonist of a drama of character. The very possibility of this claim points up the difference between the opera and the novel. If, in the novel, Lotte's liking for Werther remains an "inner sympathy" marked only for a single instant by a confusion of emotions, Massenet's Lotte is the victim of a love which she tries to hide from herself, a love which gradually takes on the proportions of tragedy by becoming all the more apparent as her situation becomes increasingly hopeless. In the novel Lotte is virtually a woman without a past ("so kind and yet so steadfast, her spirit at one with the true industry and activity of life"). Only by having her not merely unleash a tragedy but suffer it herself was it possible to create an opera which, apart from a few monologues and picturesque subplots, consists of nothing more than four duets, always between the same characters. Our analysis of the musical dramaturgy must therefore proceed from the work's underlying problem: the difficulty with which an internalized plot, fashioned into an opera libretto by making drastic changes in the novel, could become musically intelligible under the compositional conditions of the late nineteenth century.

Example 51

Like Puccini, Massenet had a genius for assimilating techniques without belying his own nature, and the leitmotiv technique he applies so openly, without thereby turning into a Wagnerian, sets up a close bond between the duets or dialogue scenes. Nonetheless, it fails to account for his success in transforming a situation play between two characters into an opera in which the music not merely illustrates the psychological processes but sustains them as well. True, in the final scene Lotte takes over a recurrent melody that seemed at first to belong to Werther as an expression of his amorous longing (Ex. 52). Still, though uncommonly moving, this artifice remains a momentary effect.

Apparently the crucial point is that, contrary to a popular misconception, Massenet, a professor at the Conservatoire, was not simply an "opera monger" but took musical forms to be "sedimented contents" (to use Adorno's term) and put them to dramaturgical use. In the first duet Charlotte's lines are character-

Lento, molto tranquillo e contemplativo

ben cantando e sostenuto, con sentimento penetrante

Example 52

ized by simple and clear-cut tunefulness (*C'est que l'image*); in the second, by a four-measure orchestral motive which threatens to develop into an expansive modulation only to return in the end to a simple reprise (*Werther! N'est-il donc pas d'autre femme*); in the third, by urgent sequences emerging from the stanzas of an Ossianic song (*N'achevez pas*); and in the fourth, by a passionate outburst based on a highly chromaticized orchestral version of the central leitmotiv (*Que ton âme et mon âme*). The four duets thus show an increasing complexity and intensification of form, beginning with simple song and progressing to motivic development with a hasty recapitulation, then to a widely modulating sequence, and finally to an excessively chromatic rendition of the opera's main motive. This formal differentiation mirrors and externalizes the changes of "tone" accompanying the progress of Charlotte's emotions, the work's interior plot. In this way, *Werther* takes its place among those operas by Massenet which turn on a female protagonist.

The *drame lyrique*, as established by Gounod, Thomas, and later by Massenet, is also linked to the central French opera of this period, Bizet's *Carmen* (1875), namely, in the character of Micaela, a dramaturgical expedient inserted into the plot by the librettists, Meilhac and Halévy. Micaela's sole function is to remind Don José in Act 1 and Act 3 of his origins, which contrast grossly with the milieu into which he has been dragged by Carmen. Unlike spoken drama, the only element of opera which is dramaturgically effective is not narrative but what we see on stage. Thus, it was natural to personify Don José's past, the height from which to measure his "tragic fall," in the form of a character who functions more as a symbol than as a dramatic agent. (In opera librettos, dramatic logic resides in the consistency of the visible plot, which must in principle be intelligible in pantomime. This is something quite different from the logic of narrative.)

Without Micaela's duet with Don José, and without her aria (whose prayer-like tone betrays the work's proximity to *drame lyrique*), the lyrical side of the opera would collapse to a meagre residue. All that would be left would be Don José's impassioned cantabile in the final duet and the so-called Flower Aria (not an aria at all, but rather part of a duet), whose lyric urgency has the opposite of its intended effect on Carmen, leaving her unmoved and turning her casual affection for Don José into a firm resolution to exploit his passion.

However, once we put aside the relics and leftover conventions of *drame lyrique* and attempt to uncover the musicodramaturgical individuality of *Carmen*, the work discloses its true identity as a paradigm or prototype of "operatic real-

Fig. 58   Caricature of Charles Gounod. The caricature exposes as mere ink the heart's blood that Gounod poured into his operas *Sappho, La nonne sanglante, Faust,* and *Roméo et Juliette.* More important, and contrary to the German view of the composer of *Faust* as the plunderer of a sacrosanct literary masterwork, the French caricaturist has emphasized the academic traits evident in Gounod, a composer with classicistic and religiously motivated aesthetic leanings. (Frankfurt am Main, Stadt- und Universitätsbibliothek, Music and Theater Collection.)

ism," as is underscored by its profound break with tradition. (In the history of art, in music no less than in literature and painting, realism is defined less by the reality it refers to than by the aesthetic challenge it poses to the artistic establishment.) But however revolutionary a historical innovation may seem, it is rarely a case of *creatio ex nihilo.* Far more often it results when a previously obscure part of tradition is unexpectedly put center stage. In a word, compared with the tradition of the *drame lyrique* (the foil for Bizet's operatic realism), *Carmen* inverts the relation between the lyrical and the picturesque. With Gounod and Massenet, genre painting, fleshed out musically with local color, is merely an additive to the main plot, which unfolds in lyrical-cantabile dialogues and monologues. With Bizet, on the other hand, the lyrical element, borne by an auxiliary figure in the drama, Micaela, is interpolated into a plot whose picturesque side (the Ibero-Gypsy milieu) is not incidental to the drama but part of its essence. The *Habañera* and the *Seguedilla,* far from being mere "inserts" (as they would be in a *drame lyrique*), are exactly those moments where music motivates the plot.

   In sum, Bizet's "realism" consists historically in a shift of emphasis: a peripheral element (musical genre painting) became central, and a central element (lyrical dialogue and monologue) became peripheral. This shift, it should be added, altered the essence of opera as a genre known in France as *tragédie lyrique* or *drame lyrique*. In its historical definition, however, realism was intimately connected with the choice of subject matter, which many contemporaries took to be indecent and suspect, both aesthetically and morally, by the standards of their day. As an opera heroine, Carmen is characterized basically by a negative trait: she is incapable of attaining lyric urgency. Carmen can parody lyricism, as in her duet with Don José, but cannot make it her own. (In one episode of the choral scene in the final tableau she manages to exchange a few words of heartfelt affection with Escamillo—*Si tu m'aimes*—but we are tempted to conclude that Bizet intended this strikingly conventional outburst of lyricism to show the hypocrisy or fickleness of her emotions.) True, Bizet's librettists, who as purveyors of operetta texts to Offenbach were by no means inclined to weak-kneed piety, idealized Mérimée's Carmen in order to make the figure presentable at all on the operatic stage. But this little alters the fact that in the 1870s Bizet's Carmen, compared with operatic convention (the yardstick of "operatic realism"), was almost shockingly realistic.

If we take the customary labels "realistic" and "romantic" literally, *Carmen* and Offenbach's *Les contes d'Hoffmann* (1881) seem to be poles apart. However, it is by no means historically irrelevant that both works treat subjects with a tragic dénouement in the external mould of *opéra comique,* drawing song and *couplet* forms into the domain of tragedy. And this similarity between them has aesthetic consequences that tempt us to analyze the one opera in order to illuminate the other.

Offenbach, like Bizet, stumbled upon a phenomenon whose discovery was anything but obvious in a decade dominated by Wagner: the sinister effect of musical banality. In the Act 3 terzetto (the Card Scene) Carmen, absorbed in gloomy forebodings, is confronted with a refrain sung by her two companions with a cheerful triviality recalling operetta. This glaring contrast, dispelling any semblance of pathos, makes Carmen's submission to her fate appear all the more hopeless and gives the refrain that macabre tinge associated with merriment in the presence of death. With all emotion smothered, Carmen's doom takes on the appearance of meaningless coincidence, an implacable and irreconcilable brute fact.

For Bizet, the operetta tone, now turned sinister, was a passing inspiration. For Offenbach, it was the legacy that he imported from the *opéra bouffe* into "genuine" opera (to which, like all operetta composers, he always felt a secret attraction). The Barcarole and Dapertutto's aria in *Les contes d'Hoffmann,* both central pieces of the Venice act, are tunes that cannot for an instant delude the listener into trusting their euphony. Consonance, generally condemned as poverty of expression according to compositional standards of the 1870s, proves to be two-faced and deceptive. It is as though we sense the odor of organic dissolution rising from cracks hidden in the music's smooth, diaphanous exterior.

In its vocal stanzas the Barcarole is as physically present to the listener as music is capable of being. At the same time, the instrumental introduction projects it into a realm so remote as to make the music seem like a mirage. Beneath the music we hear, there seems to be a second musical level descending into the abyss. Offenbach, like Bizet, was able to take simple consonance, seemingly consigned to the banality of operetta by Wagner's technique of dissonance and chromatic alteration, and extract from it an effect with dramaturgical applications that remained fresh even as late as Berg's *Wozzeck* (1925) and Weill's *Die Dreigroschenoper* (1928). In terms of compositional technique, this accomplishment alone deserves to mark a break in the history of music.

Ars gallica

On February 25, 1871, a few days before the Prussian army marched down the Champs Elysées, Camille Saint-Saëns and some friends of his founded the Société Nationale de Musique. Its motto, *ars gallica,* expressed a cultural self-confidence to counteract France's setbacks on the political and military fronts. Yet however simple the motives for founding this institution, the musicohistorical situation it attempted to change was tortuous and complex.

One of the goals of the Société Nationale was to elevate orchestral and chamber music, hitherto overshadowed in Paris by opera, to that place in the bourgeois consciousness that was their due, given their importance to the history of compositional technique. In Germany, unlike France, they had long occupied this place, so much so, in fact, that it was generally forgotten just how strange was the expectation that music should be accepted on its own as an aesthetic object—as "form moving in sound"—without an accompanying text or program and without a purpose or function.

This is not to say that instrumental music had been neglected in the Paris of the 1850s and 1860s to the same extent as under the July Monarchy. Pasdeloup's Concerts Populaires de Musique Classique had been in existence since 1861, the Société des Derniers Quatuors de Beethoven since 1851, and Lamoureux's Séances Populaires de Musique de Chambre also since 1851. Parisians had not entirely forgotten Habeneck's Conservatoire concerts, where Beethoven's symphonies had been presented to an astonished circle of devotees, eliciting mixed feelings of enthusiasm and stupefaction. Nor had they forgotten Berlioz's musical extravaganzas, which, sporadic as they had been, at least remained in memory as a reminder that French orchestral music of distinction did exist. French chamber music, however, was an unknown category, César Franck notwithstanding. On the whole, the efforts of the Société Nationale were novel and formative in that they were designed to offset the musical public's automatic tendency to associate the term "instrumental music" with Viennese classicism, and to advance the notion that instrumental music, just like opera, requires the support of permanent institutions lest it remain a pipe dream. Instead of representing a musical state of emergency, as happened to Berlioz's concerts (for reasons both in-

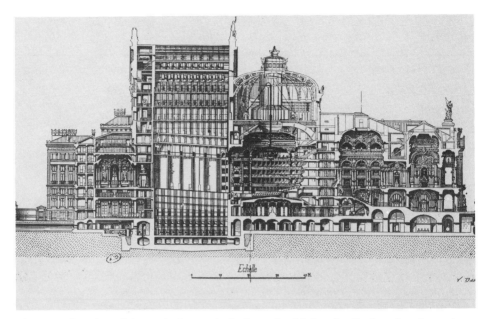

Fig. 59 Elevation of the Paris Opéra. As is shown by this longitudinal section through the central axis, the constant height of the tiers of boxes has served as a basic unit for the division and arrangement of spaces. The same unit also applies to the superimposed foyers adjoining the stage, but not to the administrative wing, vestibule, or basement. The auditorium is partitioned from and at the same time linked to the stairwell by seven superimposed connecting passages which, except for those on the ground floor and the fourth tier, are circumjacent to the galleries.

The silhouette reveals that the entrance wing has been subordinated to the central dome of the auditorium. The stage and backstage area is both higher and deeper than the rest of the building, its gigantic dimensions dominating the entire structure. It is adjoined by the foyers and the self-contained administrative wing. The principal rooms in the Pavillon des Abonnés—the carriage entrance on the ground floor, the restaurant at the level of the first tier, and the library situated above the fourth tier and beneath the dome—are connected by low galleries with the Salle d'Attente or the connecting passages. The Pavillon de l'Empereur is clearly set off from the auditorium. (Paris, Roger-Viollet.)

trinsic and extrinsic), instrumental music was to be allowed to evolve in unbroken historical continuity, disseminating not only the classics (this was the purpose of the institutions of the 1850s and 1860s) but also modern styles in which French composers were to participate with works that were specifically French. The patriotism of the Société Nationale's motto, then, resided primarily in its intention to let French instrumental music speak for itself in a language of its own.

On the other hand, the composers who upheld the Société Nationale had an ambivalent attitude to opera, a mixture of fascination and revulsion. This ambiguity in turn reflects the dire state of Parisian opera at the time. In the 1850s and 1860s neither the Grand Opéra nor the Opéra Comique was able to maintain the prestige accorded them by the successes of Meyerbeer and Auber; Gounod's works from *Faust* (1859) and *Mireille* (1864) to *Roméo et Juliette* (1867), for example, were premiered at the Théâtre Lyrique. Even so, this in no way hindered either Wagner or Verdi from attempting a "breakthrough" in Paris in order to expand their national reputations, acquired in the 1840s and 1850s, to a European scale. (The apparent miscarriage of *Tannhäuser* in 1861 was, as Gounod recognized with the shrewd eye of a colleague, in reality a triumph.) Berlioz's failure with *Les troyens* was the crucial factor for the bitterness that befell him in the 1860s. And Saint-Saëns, who sometimes drew comparisons with Brahms as a champion of instrumental music with classicizing tendencies, wrote a not inconsiderable number of operas with which he at first either sought refuge abroad (*Samson et Dalila* was premiered at Weimar in 1877) or was torn to and fro among the Parisian theaters—the Grand Opéra, the Opéra Comique, and the Théâtre Lyrique (*Timbre d'argent,* 1877)—before finally establishing himself in the Grand Opéra (*Henri VIII,* 1883, and *Ascanio,* 1890). Even César Franck, at the end of his life, felt called upon to take up opera composition (*Hulda,* 1895, and the unfinished *Ghisèle* of 1896), a fact hardly less dumbfounding than if Anton Bruckner had succumbed to a temptation to mingle with theater people.

It was in the French tradition to gravitate toward opera and to equate music history with operatic history. This bias was connected with the French emphasis on literature (ever since 1700 opera had again and again served as a target for literary diatribe, and was thus granted a degree of publicity which in turn determined its image in history). All the same, in the 1870s and above all in the 1880s, Wagner's influence made itself felt even in circles whose motto, *ars gallica,* could hardly be said to imply the sympathy obviously felt for Wagner as a composer and dramatist, if not for his politics and cultural philosophy.

However, the phenomenon of French Wagnerianism only partly belongs to music history, just as Wagner as a whole exercised a greater extramusical influence than any other composer in history. The *Rèvue Wagnérienne,* founded by Edouard Dujardin in 1884, was a journal for poets and *littérateurs,* not for composers and music critics. The names that strike our eye are not those of Saint-Saëns, d'Indy, Chabrier, or Lalo, but rather Mallarmé, Verlaine, Huysmans, and Villiers de l'Isle-Adam. Still, it would be wrong to claim of the *Révue Wagnérienne* that it was based less on Wagner's works than on the theories he used to package them. Unlike the *Bayreuther Blätter,* in which Hans von Wolzogen and Houston Stewart Chamberlain cobbled together Wagnerian ideas into a conservative philosophy of culture as vague in substance as it was fatal in its aftereffects, the Wagnerianism of the *Révue Wagnérienne* was a collective term for any and all efforts to meet Baudelaire's demand for unflinching modernity, regardless of their divergent assumptions and implications. The philosophy of Schopenhauer and Nietzsche was received in France in the name of Wagner. Wagner's "orchestral

Fig. 60 Grand Staircase in the Paris Opéra. Thanks to Baron Haussmann, the urban designer entrusted with the replanning of Paris under Napoleon III, the Opéra became the *centre de luxe*. In 1860 a competition was announced for its reconstruction, with three designs being mandatory: a ground plan, a longitudinal section, and a façade elevation. Of the 171 proposals submitted, the jury chose five architects for the final round. In the end, however, none of them was entrusted with the project, and a new competition was announced for these five. Charles Garnier was commissioned with the project in March 1861. The key item in the design of the staircase is the element of surprise occasioned by the contrasts among the variously proportioned spaces, a *système des oppositions* typical of

melody," which in Schopenhauerean terms intimated the metaphysical essence beneath the appearances of the real world, was thought to be inherently related to symbolist poetry. (This term, coined by Moréas, was misleading in that Mallarmé's approach to poetry consisted precisely in gradually extracting words from their relation to objects and ideas and letting them become ciphers of the Absolute.) And if Wagner was proclaimed in Germany as the prophet of aggressive Teutonism (even though the *Ring* myth is a story of decline, originally conceived by Wagner in a Feuerbachean "demythologizing" spirit), in France he was seen, conversely, as the idol of *décadence.* We do not have to decide whether, and if so to what extent, leitmotiv technique in literature was dependent on its musical counterpart, whether Wagner influenced the emergence of free verse, or whether the link thought by Dujardin to exist between "endless melody" and "interior monologue" is a fact or a construct. Whatever the case, literary Wagnerianism, however unrelated to Wagnerianism as practiced by composers, was a conglomeration of efforts and currents based not on Wagner's theories but on his works. Or, more precisely, these currents were inspired by the phenomenon of Wagner—by the dynamism of a man who could assert radical artistic claims in opera, the most intractable institution in the whole of music culture—to attempt a brand of modernity capable of making good Nietzsche's maxim that the sole justification of life is art.

As different as they were otherwise, literary and musical Wagnerianism shared a common detachment from Wagner's philosophy of culture. (This is not to exclude the possibility that Debussy's convoluted Wagnerianism, unlike that of other composers, will become more intelligible when it is understood as partly literary in essence.) The composers of the Société Nationale de Musique made pilgrimages to Bayreuth (Saint-Saëns and d'Indy in 1876, Chabrier and Duparc in 1879, and Fauré in 1883) to experience at first hand the modernity of his works, meaning not their philosophy but their musical workmanship. They felt thoroughly repulsed by the German Wagnerians, whose blind enthusiasm Saint-Saëns described as hysteria.

It is extraordinarily difficult to do aesthetic and historical justice to operas such as Chabrier's *Gwendoline* (1886), Lalo's *Le roi d'Ys* (1888), and d'Indy's *Fervaal* (1897) and *L'étranger* (1903), which were written under the direct influence of Wagner, not just with regard to their technique but also in their choice of

---

the structure as a whole. Another key consideration for the intended *aspect étrange* is the relation between staircase and stairwell. Garnier took as his models the stairwells in French and north Italian palaces of the seventeenth and eighteenth centuries, as well as theater stairwells, being influenced in particular by Giuseppe Galli-Bibiena's *Architetture e prospettive dedicate alla Maestà de Carlo Sesto* and the Carceri etchings of Piranesi. (Paris, Roger-Viollet.)

Fig. 61 Salle du Grand Opéra, Paris. Not only do the conductor and the auditorium reveal that the work being performed is an opera, so also does the blocking of the characters on stage. Two protagonists emerge from the warring groups in swords and halberds, indicating that, besides a political conflict, jealousy is also at work. This scene directly illustrates, in pantomime, the conglomeration of motives governing the actions of the characters. (Paris, Roger-Viollet.)

subject matter and their fondness for symbolically heightening the stage action. Though clearly modern by the standards of 1890, even going several steps beyond Wagner (barely detectable in retrospect from the standpoint of contemporary music), they were more or less deflated by Debussy's soft-spoken radicality. On the other hand, the French Wagnerian adepts were by no means epigones in the aesthetically pejorative sense of the term, and their failures demonstrate how puzzling are the conditions under which Wagner's leitmotiv technique, chromatic alterations, and orchestration can provide a musical groundwork for theatrically effective drama.

The enthusiasm for Wagner which reigned in the Société Nationale de Musique, even among composers whose work betrays virtually none of his influence, stands in glaring contrast to the indifference or disparagement cast upon Brahms. An impartial observer has no trouble in seeing parallels between Brahms's orchestral and chamber music and the attempts of the Société Nationale to meet the historical demands of the moment without abandoning the classicist premises of instrumental music. Even as late as 1901 Romain Rolland, a first-rate music historian whom no one can accuse of national prejudice or want of a sense of justice, spoke of the "German pedantry" that virtually "luxuriated" in the music of Brahms.

Conversely, Saint-Saëns is known in Germany merely as a virtuoso of the composer's trade, capable of assimilating any style because he possessed none of his own. (Like Brahms and Glazunov, Saint-Saëns had minimal international impact, a fact that tempts us to reach an initially dubious-sounding but by no means absurd conclusion—namely, that unlike opera and the symphonic poem, what the French called *musique savante*, meaning classicistic, "abstract" instrumental music, remained national in its influence precisely because it lacked any obvious national tinges.)

Saint-Saëns, whether as composer, performer, or writer, declared himself squarely on the side of Liszt. This is apparent not just in his symphonic poems of the 1870s but also in his symphonies, of which the third, the Symphony in C minor with organ, Op. 78 (1886), stands out as his "official magnum opus." Their aesthetic pretensions are raised not only intrinsically, in their sophisticated musical logic, but also extrinsically in an acoustical façade which does not even shrink from displays of musical violence. What is complicated, however, is the relation between these intrinsic and extrinsic aspects, between the work's logic and its architecture. Saint-Saëns became enmeshed in a technical contradiction that points to an aesthetic problem related in turn to his moment in history. If Brahms was a "pedant" to his French detractors (and insofar as Liszt was a French composer, a nationalist element entered the conflict between the Brahms faction and what was unjustifiably known as the "New German School"), Saint-Saëns faced accusations of "eclecticism," of technical perfection applied to a stylistic patchwork. Instead of countering these accusations with useless rebuttals, we should try to understand what constitutes high-quality eclecticism in the first place and how it was possible historically.

The last movement of Saint-Saëns's C-minor Symphony (the second movement of part 2) is divided into a Maestoso and an Allegro section, following a transition leading from the Scherzo to the Finale and belonging to both movements. The second theme of the Maestoso and the first of the Allegro are variants or transformations of a central idea heard in every movement of the work, from the first theme of the Allegro Moderato through the middle section of the Adagio to the second theme of the Scherzo. The remaining themes are likewise joined by a tight-knit skein of associations. The first theme of the Maestoso, for example, is presented (or anticipated) in the transition from the Scherzo to the Finale, where it is joined contrapuntally by the theme from the middle section of the Scherzo. It then appears in augmented form in the "development" section of the Finale, where it fuses with the latter's main theme to form a "double idea" encapsulating the substance of the entire movement. (It makes perfect sense to repeat the "development" section after the "recapitulation" of the augmented main theme and second theme because the combination of themes is less a transition than a goal.)

The technique that Saint-Saëns uses to mutually derive his themes is none other than the method of thematic transformation developed by Liszt in his *Ce qu'on entend sur la montagne* in reference to its underlying program. One and the same melody, turned into major or minor, is presented in ever-new rhythmic guises, sometimes contrasting so wildly that an untutored listener is at a loss to recognize their common source (Ex. 53). The fact that Saint-Saëns transferred a technique from program music to absolute music is one indication of the problems that beset his notion of a classically grounded and yet modern instrumental music. Doubtless he sought to avoid the "pedantic" Brahmsian approach of exposing the interior of the musical structure by belaboring its thematic-motivic processes. However, while thematic transformation is fully warranted in Liszt, where the abrupt rhythmic contrasts are harnessed in support of a program, it appears strangely wan and disembodied in Saint-Saëns, as though robbed of its raison d'être. And being weakly motivated, it is for that very reason difficult to perceive. At all events, the orchestral pomp that Saint-Saëns flaunts as a decorative façade to the Finale of his C-minor Symphony stands in curious contrast to the fastidiousness of his motivic technique. There is a rift between the architecture and the logic of this work, a rift that seems symptomatic of the failure to which, in the final analysis, any eclecticism is condemned that seeks to unite the decorative monumentality of grand opera with a classicistic formal design and a transformation technique abstracted from program music. The urge to large-scale form, as evidenced by Saint-Saëns's extravagant display of resources, winds up sounding theatrical, since the internal coherence that prevents monumentality from remaining empty gesture is not allowed to come to the surface. Conversely, the musical logic concealed behind this façade does indeed turn ultimately into an exercise in *musique savante*, confirming the existing suspicions of a

Example 53

musical culture already accustomed to refer to straightforward displays of musical thought processes as "pedantry" and to hidden displays as "algebra in notes."

As measured against the German yardstick (which may or may not have been historically legitimate), French chamber music almost invariably represented a compromise. The composers of the Société Nationale, Saint-Saëns no less than Fauré or even Franck, were suspected by purist critics of secretly gravitating toward salon music. As absurd as this suspicion proves to be when we compare the champions of *ars gallica* with a real salon composer like Lefébure-Wély (who nevertheless preceded Saint-Saëns as organist at the Madeleine), we can still regard it as a sign of the contradictory relation then obtaining between the chamber music tradition and the stylistic devices which, from the retrospective vantage point of twentieth-century music, were branded as "late romantic."

Now, no one who can read music would dare gainsay the contrapuntal expertise of Saint-Saëns, Fauré, and Franck. To these composers a canon was not simply an exercise but a mode of thought, which they mastered without sacrificing an iota of the character, color, and cantabile of melody. Nor did advanced nineteenth-century harmony, whether the excessively chromatic variety exemplified in Wagner's *Tristan* or the modernized modal harmony, pose problems for Fauré and Franck: both composers commanded it at will, Fauré discreetly and Franck all the more blatantly. (The nineteenth century based its music theory primarily on the principles of harmony and measured musical progress accordingly.) The solidity of their craftsmanship was no less in evidence than the modernity of their styles. If, then, the idea could nevertheless arise that they were secretly close to the salon, the reason must be sought in a contradictory relation between the genres of music and the modes of musical perception.

Fauré's fame as a composer of chamber music rests on his A-major Violin Sonata, Op. 13 (1876), and on his piano quartets in C minor, Op. 15 (1879), and G minor, Op. 45 (1886). Both quartets emphasize their first movements, which are marked by an almost opulent cantabile and extreme refinement of texture. The easy manner in which Fauré, like Schubert, seems to "squander" his music upon us may in fact imply much hard work; at all events, it requires a certain effort of conscious listening to recognize that his melody is a consequence of the compositional setting, and vice versa. If we simply yield passively and mindlessly to his cantabile, the sophistication of Fauré's harmony and rhythm—his subtle manner of avoiding or concealing "rhythmic foursquareness" (unlike Franck, who tends to emphasize it)—turns into mere vagueness combined with coloristic effects that might well be tolerable in orchestral music but which are inconsistent with the stylistic principles of chamber music. Confronted with the rigorous aesthetic strictures of chamber music, these pieces convey, on casual hearing, the impression that they are near to salon music, a music composed of cantabile phrases over a backdrop of diffuse, kaleidoscopic sonorities.

It was no easy matter to balance simplicity and lucidity of form (the legacy of classicism) with the harmonic complexities that even composers with conservative instincts felt compelled by the zeitgeist to adopt. Just how difficult this could

Fig. 62 Autograph of Edouard Lalo. In answer to an admirer who had apparently asked for a longish autograph, Edouard Lalo, prevented by illness from continuing his work, sent a quotation from his ballet *Namouna* (1882), a work that became famous as an orchestral suite. This leaf gives ample proof that autographs, normally left behind as relics after a composer's death, could be produced as secular devotionalia during his lifetime. (Vienna, Österreichische Nationalbibliothek.)

be is illustrated by Franck's D-major String Quartet (1889) with a clarity characteristic of major works of art, part of whose nature it is to make problems manifest rather than concealing them in artifices, a sure sign of mediocrity. The first movement, is, strictly speaking, a double movement: the Lento section (no fewer than eighty measures long) is not simply an introduction to the Allegro but itself outlines a sonata form, with first and second themes appearing in the tonic and dominant and being recapitulated in the tonic. The development section, a fugato on the first theme, is inserted into the Allegro section, and the return of the Lento at the end of the movement is not just a reminiscence but a full-fledged recapitulation. If, then, the design of the Lento forms the premise for the fugato, it can also be shown that the fugato, as in Liszt's symphonic poem *Prometheus,* offers a way out of the difficulty of how to write a development section when developmental techniques (chromatic modulation and sequential patterns) already predominate in the exposition. The themes in the Allegro section are presented ambiguously: at first, we have no idea which of the thoughts Franck spreads before us is meant to be the second theme. This is another indication of the formal problem that a string quartet movement had to solve, given the historical situation around 1880: how to integrate "late-romantic" harmony, the yardstick of musical progress, without abandoning the key schemes of sonata-allegro form, to all appearances a defining feature of the genre. F major, the opposing key to the tonic D minor, is not reached until the end of the exposition, by which time the F-major section consists thematically of a "closing group." By melodic criteria, on the other hand, the actual second theme seems to be an idea that modulates from D minor through E♭ major to A♭ minor. (The second measure of this theme is related by inversion to the first measure of the main theme, and both are combined in a sequence in the development section.) Thus, however much Franck wished to preserve the simple key scheme dictated by the classicist theory of sonata form, he was no less unwilling than Liszt (the source of his approach to form) to dispense with the effect of "wandering tonality," even when presenting his themes. (The technique, adopted for the first theme, of repeating the opening of the theme in D minor with divagations to remote keys, could not have been applied to the second theme without courting structural monotony.)

The path that Brahms took in an effort to preserve sonata form from disintegrating under the relentlessly increasing complexity of harmony seems to have been closed to the composers of the *ars gallica*. It would apparently have smacked of "pedantry" to shift the emphasis from the key scheme to thematic manipulation, an approach which led ultimately, in Schönberg's third and fourth string quartets (1927 and 1936), to the extreme case of an atonal sonata form. The composers of the Société Nationale pursued a fata morgana, imagining a form as tightly knit as a Haydn quartet and, paradoxically, as luxuriant as a score by Wagner. Here, too, the life of compositional history is to be found less in its actual results than in its problems and utopias.

Russian Music: Epic Opera

Russian music was split into two camps that marked their respective boundaries by bandying slogans of mutual contempt. On the one hand were the nationalist musicians, the "Mighty Handful" assembled around Balakirev (with Stasov as their ideologist); on the other, the cosmopolitans, thought to be represented by Tchaikovsky and Anton Rubinstein. Now, this split is one of those all too evident antitheses whose simplicity may at first seem tantalizing to historians caught in the confusions of historical reality. Yet its importance in cultural history does not automatically imply an equivalent significance in compositional history, and its scope is by no means so firmly established that the dichotomy merits acceptance as the measure of and precondition for any historical account of the era. The split belongs to the material of written history, not to its methodological assumptions. And it is at all events legitimate, when attempting a comprehensive account of Russian opera, the central genre of Russian music at this time, to proceed from a problem faced no less by Tchaikovsky and, later, Rimsky-Korsakov than by Mussorgsky or Borodin: how to handle a dramaturgy that tended clearly, even radically, to the epic.

Mussorgsky's *Boris Godounov* (1869) and Borodin's *Prince Igor* (1890) are historical operas, Tchaikovsky's *Eugene Onegin* (1879) a *drame lyrique,* or musical novel, and Rimsky-Korsakov's *Le coq d'or* (1908) a satirical fairy tale with a hint of parable. However different the genres of these representative late-nineteenth-century Russian operas, and however individual the personalities of their composers (an individuality already apparent in their choice of genre, and made operatically viable in interaction with the respective generic norms), all of these works have one trait in common above and beyond their stylistic divergences: they plainly and deliberately avoid the "closed" dramatic form imposed upon opera by European theater of the modern age.

As Aristotle wrote in his *Poetics*: "One should also . . . not write a tragedy on an epic body of incident (i.e., one with a plurality of stories in it) by attempting to dramatize, for instance, the entire story of the *Iliad*." Aristotle's demand became a platitude of academic poetics under the catchword "unity of plot." Of course, European aestheticians of the modern period were aware that this demand did not apply to the genre of history plays, as amply demonstrated by Shakespeare's histories, the typical, if inimitable, examples of the genre. However, the historical drama, as distinguished from tragedies based on historical occurrences, had only recently been introduced to opera. (A few early attempts in the Baroque period found no successors.) Despite Meyerbeer's *Les Huguenots* and *Le prophète, Boris Godounov* and *Prince Igor* mark a watershed in the history of opera.

Meyerbeer's operas represent an ambiguous hybrid genre somewhere between the history play and the tragedy based on historical material, a genre from which the Russian works clearly stand out by their insistence on being histories. On the one hand, *Les Huguenots* and *Le prophète* refer to historical reality outside the theater, not merely in their subject matter but as works in themselves. History does not serve them merely as a quarry, as raw material for a self-contained tragic plot proceeding seamlessly from its own internal postulates. On the contrary, an interest in and recollection of history as past reality form an important element in the work's aesthetic posture. Even so, in *Les Huguenots*, history, in order to be presentable as opera, forms the surroundings of a plot which takes on an independent existence as a drama of emotions, retaining its links to historical events but standing apart from them. (If Meyerbeer had not been so concerned with crowd scenes and historical "local color" he might easily have extracted the "actual" plot from the history in accordance with the rules of historically based tragedy, thereby converting history into a mere backdrop. In *Le prophète,* admittedly, the drama of emotions interlocks more tightly with the political intrigue.) In *Boris Godounov,* on the other hand, the "Poland act" (a later addition to the "original version" of 1869) is a bit of conventional opera which stands out all too glaringly from the parts composed earlier, regardless of whether the stylistic break can be explained as a dramaturgical ploy in the Glinka tradition. From the standpoint of opera history, however, the decisive factor is that the drama of emotions (or, as Marina sees it, the comedy of emotions) is a means to the end of political tragedy, and not vice versa. Historical reality has been transformed from a backdrop into the true object of the plot, and the drama of emotions has turned from a constructive principle, determining the shape of the dramaturgy, into a mere adjunct, which might even be scrapped entirely if its absence would not entail a danger of monotony.

Boris Godounov is a "multiplot" drama with parallel or intersecting stories: the story of the Czar, the story of the Pretender, the story of the People. Of these, only the Boris plot comes to a conclusion in that his death marks a stopping point; everything else remains open-ended, pointing toward the future. Even the Revolution Scene in Act 4—to all appearances a key scene that throws unexpected emphasis on the People and the Pretender—is a later addition to the 1869 version. The fact that its absence was not considered a shortcoming sheds light on the principles of epic dramaturgy, which tends to flesh out images of static states of affairs. The level of sophistication of these images increases or diminishes by adding or omitting detail, but they nevertheless remain intelligible as images, whereas similar changes made to a self-contained tragedy would reduce the piece to, or expose it as, a patchwork. (The fragmentation technique permitted in a history would, if applied to tragedy, cause the resultant scenes to resemble gears spinning idly in a machine.) Unlike tragedy, however, a history need not generate a beginning or an end from its own axioms, and is more likely to break off than to reach a goal. Instead, it refers to a historical reality outside the drama, a reality which the observer must keep in mind as the work's context.

This form, characteristic of the history, is clearly tied to the fact that the plot, at least in its key features, takes shape less in dialogues where opposing interests and viewpoints collide than in tableaux, narratives, and monologues. Tragedy, even if based on history, is a closed form, and the conflict of characters is carried out in a dialectic of statement and response, virtually the only medium in which the drama can unfold as a continuous and self-sustaining process. In the history, on the other hand, it is possible but by no means absolutely necessary to include dramatic dialogue, which compels characters to make decisions, thereby keeping the goal-directed plot afloat. One of the most conspicuous and dramaturgically revealing peculiarities of *Boris Godounov* is that its dramatic agents, strictly speaking, scarcely speak to one another except to dissimulate. Gregory's decision to take on the role of the Pretender Dmitri, though motivated by Pimen's account of the death of the Czarevitch, is not uttered explicitly nor is it traceable to a particular moment in time. In Gregory's duet with Marina, the conclusion of the Poland act, the lyric urgency (sounding like a stylistic quotation) merely puts a thin veneer on the irreparable "cleavage" between the two characters, the unbridgeable gulf separating Marina's ambition (hypocritically masquerading as love) and Gregory's self-alienation in his role as usurper, a self-alienation from which he seeks escape in love but which can only be overcome by sacrificing his usurper's role. Thus, in a tragic reversal, it is precisely Gregory's attempt at inward salvation that drives him to perdition. All the stations in the

Boris plot, from the Coronation Scene to the Death Scene, are marked by monologues. These monologues may take the form of a prayer before the assembled populace or a confession before his son and future successor, but in reality they are nothing more than interior conversations of a lone figure "walled in" by his oppressive sense of guilt. In epic opera—which, unlike self-sufficient tragedy, has no need for dialogue as a structural principle, being anchored instead in historical reality—the juxtaposition of plots is the counterpart of a juxtaposition of characters. Mussorgsky is a tragic poet of loneliness.

The internal plot of the drama, then, is manifest in the Czar's monologues. These differ so radically in their underlying structural principles as to silence any suspicion that Mussorgsky, as a musical realist, simply took the text as his guide, setting momentary speech inflections in blithe disregard of musical form. It is no accident that the Death Scene, following Pimen's narrative, offers a tight-knit skein of leitmotivs. True, the choice of motives seems dictated by the dramatic situation: the motive of the Czar's distraction, the Czarevitch's motive (in various versions), and the Czaritza's motive all appear "on cue." But beyond that, leitmotiv technique is by its very nature appropriate to a scene that attempts to capture in music a recollection of the past. Leitmotivs are essentially musical reminiscences whose function, even for Wagner, lies in linking the present with the past. Thus, the technique that Mussorgsky adopted in the final scene, without elevating it into a universal principle, is dramaturgically functional in and of itself, independently of the "contents" of the motives.

If a patchwork of dissimilar leitmotivs is legitimate in a monologue made up of recollected images, Mussorgsky revealed in the "Boris aria," the centerpiece of Act 2, that he was perfectly capable of writing music of long-breathed continuity when the dramatic situation required it. This explodes the error, resulting from insufficient analysis, of accusing Mussorgsky of amateurism, of imagining that his patent genius for inventing momentary effects was offset by an inability to apply form consciously. The adagio section of the "aria" (in C♭ minor) is based on a refrain form, which we are perfectly at liberty, in a context where formal repetition is the exception rather than the rule, to interpret as representing the obsessive thoughts crowding in Boris's brain.

A^1	A^2	B^1	A^1	B^2	C	A^1	A^3	D
4	4	7	4	6	11	4	4	10

Most instructive, however, for our picture of Mussorgsky as a composer are the more covert artifices intended to establish subtle but musically effective bonds between the sections. The *B* section varies a motive from beyond the confines of the "aria" itself. This motive appeared in the preceding "recitative" as an orchestral melody and is subsequently repeated in the Act 4 Death Scene (as in the Act 2 "aria") in two versions, one slightly expanded and one compressed (Ex. 54). At the same time, however, the "aria" itself is a self-contained form aiming at

Example 54

continuity, and its *B* motive is linked with section *A* by two common features: the harmonic progression II–V–I and what Heinrich Schenker would call a melodic *Terzzug* (from the sixth degree of the scale through the seventh to the octave). As indistinct as the association may be, it cannot be dismissed as coincidence, since the method shows tendencies of being systematically applied. The chord C♭–E♭–F–A♭, which distinguishes section *B*² from *B*¹ (at a syntactically analogous and therefore conspicuous moment), also forms the starting point and main substance of section *C*, whose second characteristic chord, an augmented triad, in turn anticipates section *D*, the motive of the Czar's distraction. It may be too much to call this device a "system," but there should be no doubt that Mussorgsky, contrary to a widely held opinion, did not simply display a genius for detail but followed a sound intuition for establishing internal coherence, no matter how conscious or unconscious this intuition may have been.

Prince Igor, Alexander Borodin's magnum opus, was conceived in 1869 and left unfinished when the composer died in 1887, thus inviting comparisons with *Siegfried* and *Les troyens* with regard to the length of its gestation. Like *Boris Godounov*, it is a historical drama, and it illuminates the problems of the genre (a proclivity to a random disposition of scenes) all the more glaringly in that its dramaturgical construct suffers from an irremediable weakness. When Stasov proposed the medieval Igor poem as subject matter for an opera (specifically mentioning the epic breadth of the material, its national tinge, the variety of its characters and emotions, and its oriental setting) he revealed a sound awareness of Borodin's temperament as a composer but overlooked an important fact. The main theme of the poem—the internal conflict between Igor's promise not to flee captivity under the Tatars, his heroic arrogance that forbade him from concluding peace (and thereby made flight the only possible way for him to return home), and his duties as a ruler, which call for quick action to allay the decaying situation in his native land—forms a paradigmatic instance, indeed almost the extreme case, of an operatically "nonviable" motif utterly incapable of clear presentation in music. The loose sequence of scenes in *Prince Igor* is incomprehensible as a coherent plot unless we constantly refer back to the dialectic of heroic honor outlined above. (The first act, seemingly nothing more than a genre painting, serves a dramaturgical function for Igor's internal conflict by depicting the social decay in Putivl.) Thus, the dramatic core being more or less impervious to musical treatment, the work takes on the appearance of an operatic picture book that offers variegated and even garish local color in lieu of dramatic motivation.

Fig. 63 Caricature of *Boris Godounov*. To claim that Mussorgsky's *Boris Godounov* is an opera "in which woman is . . . of no importance whatever" seems puzzling at first in view of the Marina episode. In fact, however, it betrays the caricaturists's awareness of the stylistic incongruity of the Poland act, both musically and dramaturgically. Unlike Meyerbeer's *Les Huguenots, Boris Godounov* is an authentic "history" in the same sense as Shakespeare's histories, and not merely a private drama with historical backdrops. (Frankfurt am Main, Stadt- und Universitätsbibliothek, Music and Theater Collection.)

As we have seen, when Stasov detected in the Igor legend an opera subject suited to Borodin's cast of mind, he drew attention both to its nationalist Russian tinge and to its Tatar orientalisms. As was only natural in an age that tended on all sides to musical exoticism and folklore, the ethnic conflict in the plot of *Prince Igor* left a deep impress on its music (Prince Galitsky's song, No. 2, is as typically Russian as Konchakovna's cavatina, No. 9, is notably oriental). Even so, it is equally obvious that Borodin lacked complete confidence in the principle of stylistic discontinuity of the sort that Mussorgsky applied unflinchingly in *Boris Godounov* and Glinka in *A Life for the Tsar*. We can sense the infinite pains he took to keep the stylistic contrasts demanded by the opera's subject matter from splintering his work aesthetically into unrelated parts.

Some of the features that add local color to the Chorus of Polovtsian Maidens (No. 7), such as the raised seconds in the melody, its pedal points and drones, and its structural chromaticism, are taken from the repertoire of musical orientalism, a collective category that rode roughshod over ethnic distinctions so that Arabic, Tatar, and Indian musics all appeared interchangeable. (The term "structural chromaticism" refers to the technique of basing a composition on a chromatic run as a structural framework.) The riches of authentic oriental music necessarily collapsed to a meager residue so as to be integratable at all into the European tonal system. As a result, it is not astonishing that the same oriental-isms, albeit in characteristic variants, recur in the Dance of the Polovtsian Maidens (No. 8) and in Konchakovna's cavatina (No. 9), where the structural chromaticism functions both as a framework and as a melody line. Even so, in Act 2, structural chromaticism, sometimes combined with drones, is a noteworthy feature of those numbers that emphasize a Russian tinge or a cosmopolitan operatic tone: Vladimir's cavatina (No. 11), his duet with Konchakovna (No. 12), and Igor's aria (No. 13). True, we have little difficulty identifying the different ethnic milieus, which by and large are characterized by distinctive rhythms (one exception is No. 25, the lament of Yaroslavna—Igor's Penelope—who slips from Russian *espressivo* into an oriental ambience with no apparent dramatic motivation). But Borodin's drones and structural chromaticism, especially when combined, are overriding devices that prevent the changes of local color (a sine qua non for an epic opera pieced together from images) from causing a discontinuity of styles that would jeopardize the unity of his work.

In Rimsky-Korsakov's *Le coq d'or* orientalism, an heirloom of Russian music, forms a sub-element in a musical dramaturgy that combines reckless simplicity with a complexity verging on the experimental. This mixture is as revealing of the character of a late work bordering on modern twentieth-century music as it is of a composer who from the very outset thrived less on spontaneity than on studied reflection. At the end of his career Rimsky-Korsakov no longer adopted a pose of second immediacy but openly showed his true colors in an opera which is at once a fairy tale, a political satire, and a virtually insoluble parable.

Pushkin's tale, the basis of the libretto, is a modern-day fairy tale with an ironically ambiguous tone. It resists dramatization in that it is designed to climax in a final moral whose significance remains obscure, however indelibly the image of a rooster hacking at the King's skull—an image with an unsettling if indecipherable meaning—remains in our memory. A denouement that poses a riddle, even if it seems to sum up the otherwise disjunct or at best loosely connected events, is unlikely to favor the construction of a goal-directed, dialectical plot in which each step is a consequence of its predecessors and a springboard for its successors. Dodon, a king as muddle-headed and lethargic as he is tyrannical, falls prey to an intrigue of the phantom realm, an intrigue that weaves invisible strands to and fro between the Astrologer (the source of the Golden Cockerel, which warns the King of impending danger) and the Fairy Queen, who seduces the King after destroying his army. The fable, though obscure, is thoroughly effective. Poor as it may be in dramatic substance, and as little opportunity as it gives for presenting conflicts in the medium of dialogue, it nonetheless offers a rich array of occasions for colorful tone painting, being essentially an epic sequence of episodes.

To separate the realm of the King from that of the Fairy Queen, the banality of the Western world from the wonders of the Orient, Rimsky-Korsakov resorted to a contrast between diatonicism and chromaticism. By the outset of the twentieth century, sixty years after Wagner's *Tannhäuser,* this device had become an operatic convention, and Rimsky-Korsakov vindicated its simplicity aesthetically by cloaking it in a tone of ironic ambiguity adopted from Pushkin's narrative. (Rimsky-Korsakov, who sympathized with the 1905 Revolution, put an added emphasis on the element of political satire, which is merely hinted at in Pushkin's original.) Still, the contrast is applied with sufficient clarity (and with a heavy-handedness warranted by the parodistic bent of the fairy tale) to form a solid foundation for those sophistications and interconnections which, in the hands of a composer like Rimsky-Korsakov, who left nothing unreflected, tended to fall into a musicodramaturgical system.

The opening of Act 2, the battlefield scene, is based on the whole-tone scale, a symbol for the world of the demonic in Russian music, in Glinka's *Ruslan and Lyudmila* (1842) no less than in that musical gospel of the "Mighty Handful," Dargomyzhsky's *The Stone Guest* (1872). Besides motives derived from the whole-tone scale, however, Rimsky-Korsakov also presents a theme which divides the octave into a series of alternating half steps and augmented whole steps (A♭–G–E–E♭–C–B–A♭). This anticipates the orientalesque melodies of the Fairy Queen, who is characterized by a half step and an augmented second. For the moment, however, the theme remains integrated within the sphere of the augmented triad, the "basic chord" of the whole-tone scale. The funeral march in the same scene is based on the "gypsy scale" (F–G–A♭–B–C–D♭–E–F), functioning as a distorted minor mode. Here the intervallic structure, albeit a "submotivic" element rather than a proper motive, may allude to the fact that the army was brought to ruin by the Fairy Queen, who is symbolized musically by this scale. By the same token, when the triads underlying the "gypsy scale" in the Fairy Queen's aria are shifted chromatically from B minor to B♭ major (Ex. 55), a latent affinity is disclosed to the realm of the Astrologer, whose motive is based on triads at half-step intervals: E major–F major–C major–D♭ major–A♭ major–A major. (When rearranged, the Astrologer's chords as a whole form a variant of the aforementioned sequence of alternating half steps and augmented whole steps: F–E–D♭–C–A–A♭.) And when the Fairy Queen, in her duet with Dodon, indulges in effusions on her native realm, another chord sequence associated with the Astrologer (E major–A major $\frac{4}{3}$–E major) is quoted in passing (Ex. 56). This progression clearly functions as a motive because of its startling

Example 55

Example 56

novelty, a paradoxical result of the simplicity of the chords when taken by themselves and their complexity when combined.

If *Le coq d'or* draws on the epic of fairy tale, and *Boris Godounov* and *Prince Igor* on the epic of historical drama, Tchaikovsky's *Eugene Onegin* (1879) confronts the epic of the novel. Novel-like opera had already become a sort of tradition in the *drame lyrique*, but this should not obscure a basic distinction: whereas in *Manon Lescaut* and *Werther* Massenet's librettists subjected the epic material of the novel to the strictures of the *pièce bien faite*, Tchaikovsky did not make the slightest effort to alter significantly the epic structure of Pushkin's narrative poem, its juxtaposition of episodic plots. The original title of the opera, referring to "lyric scenes," frankly declares its allegiance to the technique of juxtaposition, and hence to its disregard (characteristic of Russian theater and opera) for classical poetics, which posited a distinction between drama and epic in order to keep writers from selecting inappropriate material.

It is no coincidence that the musical core of the opera—the place where the leitmotivs suffusing the whole of the work appear, as it were, in a single package —is a monologue, Tatyana's "Letter Aria" (No. 9). Further, the scene between Tatyana and Eugene that sets the course of the drama is presented not as a duet but rather as an aria by Onegin (No. 12), a carefully formulated and woundingly rational speech that leaves Tatyana stunned into silence. However realistic its conception, and however appropriate to the rules of spoken theater, this aria flies in the face of an operatic tradition which was able to hold its own even in Massenet's *drames lyriques*—namely, it is precisely in moments of deepest affliction that music is capable of attaining an expression that Wagner (speaking of the orchestral melody of his music dramas, but inadvertently characterizing the vocal melody of standard opera as well) referred to as "silence resounding."

Proceeding from the subtitle of *Eugene Onegin*, "lyric scenes," we can draw a distinction between lyrical moments and "scenes." That the closing scene between Tatyana and Onegin is a duet in the grand style (No. 22) does little to alter our overall impression of a work whose substance resides less in pathetic duets, with dialogue as the proper medium for modern-day drama, than in lyrical or contemplative monologues (Nos. 3, 9, 17, 20, and 21), picturesque interpolations (Nos. 1, 2, 11, and 19), and in "scenes" that either staunchly maintain a conversational tone or represent a burgeoning conflict in quick-tempo arioso recitative rather than enacting it in the form of emotion-laden duets. It is inconceivable that Massenet, in scenes Nos. 6 and 16, would have foregone duets between Olga and Lenski. And a comparison between the two composers, prompted by their common association with the *drame lyrique,* reveals that Tchaikovsky, for all his fondness for lyric pathos, partook of the realistic tendencies of the time, tendencies that were characteristic of late-nineteenth-century Russian opera as a whole.

Exoticism, Folklorism, Archaism

Musical exoticism is the attempt to add a musical dimension to a depiction, on stage or in literature, of a remote and alien milieu. In the end, it proved to be a characteristic trend of the nineteenth century. Owing to the lack of a clear-cut definition of the phenomenon, its origins are indeterminable, but they clearly extend far into the past. The monotonously repeated "Allahs" that Lully wrote for the Turkish scene of Molière's *Le bourgeois gentilhomme* (1670) differ from those in Félicien David's ode-symphony, *Le désert* (1844), only in that Lully thought nothing of repeating a triad verbatim two dozen times, whereas David attempts to relieve the monotony of his choral declamation by varying the orchestral harmonies. Both works are otherwise full-fledged instances of musical exoticism: both incorporate exoticism into the context of European composition (even though they violate one of its cardinal rules, namely, that repetition ad infinitum is not art); and both recall, in conjunction with a text or set design, a non-European musical device (even if the original meaning of that device is half-submerged in counterpoint or harmony). In any case, it is wrong to judge exoticism by the criteria of descriptive anthropology. (This did not, however, prevent nineteenth-century criticism of music, costume, and set design from furiously disputing the purported "authenticity" of exotic local color, an authenticity that exists solely in the imagination of the perceiver.) The crucial point is not the degree to which exoticism is "genuine," but rather the function it serves as a legitimate departure from the aesthetic and compositional norms of European music in the context of an opera or a symphonic poem. It is not so much the original context as the new, artificial context which we should examine if we want our analysis to be historical—that is, to pursue the aesthetic and compositional significance of the phenomenon in the nineteenth century. To do otherwise is to lose ourselves in comparative anthropology, which can do nothing more than establish various degrees of corruption in the music or style quoted. In a word, musical exoticism is a question of function, not of substance.

"In the age of Louis XIV one was a Hellenist, today one is an Orientalist. . . . The entire continent is leaning toward the Orient." Thus, in 1829, wrote Victor Hugo in the preface to his *Les orientales.* Unlike the *chinoiseries* of the rococo period or the China ideal of the Enlightenment, nineteenth-century orientalism was aimed first at the Middle East and only later at the Far East. It was a century-

Fig. 64 Contemporary engraving from the Paris International Exhibition of 1878. Here a Tunisian ensemble is playing on original instruments in the reconstructed environment of an oriental coffee house. In its impact, however, this genuine, imported exoticism was no different from the imaginary exoticism then fashionable in opera. For the European public, music that it did not understand merely functioned as audible local color. Even as received by Debussy and Ravel, it was not the structural principles of oriental music that composers adopted so much as melodic details, which, when transplanted to a different compositional context, turned into picturesque allurements. (Copenhagen, Det kongelige Bibliotek.)

long fashion, a phenomenon of cultural history which luxuriated in post-Delacroix painting no less than in post-Hugoean literature. Music, it seems, merely added to this phenomenon with works such as David's *Le désert*. Nevertheless, extramusical explanations are never sufficient by themselves in music history, and here we must supplement them by looking at the history of compositional technique. Oriental subjects virtually mushroomed in the operas and concert pieces of the late nineteenth century: one need only think of operas such as David's *Lalla Roukh* (1862), Gounod's *Le reine de Saba* (1862) and *Le tribut de Za-*

mora (1881), Verdi's *Aïda* (1871), Bizet's *Djamileh* (1875), Goldmark's *Die Königin von Saba* (1875), Massenet's *Le roi de Lahore* (1877) and *Thaïs* (1894), Delibes's *Lakmé* (1883), and Rubinstein's *Sulamith* (1883). These works do not simply mirror literary fashion; they are also an expression and consequence of the state of composition at the time.

The Turkish opera of the eighteenth and the early nineteenth century (from Mozart through Weber, Rossini, and Boieldieu to Peter Cornelius) was a species of comic opera which used exoticisms, such as monotone declamation or the then unusual instrumentation of Janissary music (bass drum, cymbals, and triangle), to parodistic effect. Aesthetic and compositional norms were broken to create comedy as measured against the rationality of European classical music; indeed, ethnic peculiarities as a whole were regarded as accidental deviations, occasioned by untoward circumstances, from the inherent rationality of the human mind. But in the nineteenth century, as exoticism entered serious opera and symphonic concert music, Arabs, Indians, and Chinese had the dignity of tragedy conferred upon them, just as had happened to the bourgeoisie (hitherto likewise the butt of comedy) in eighteenth-century bourgeois tragedy. This fact was apparently allied with the emergence of a sense of justice (inherited by ethnology from written history) which was known to its detractors as "relativism." It seems also to be linked with the declining belief in a general and uniform rationality (the term fondly applied by Westerners to their own ethnic norms) and the slowly growing conviction that even remote regions, as Ranke maintained of remote ages, "stood directly in God's grace."

Furthermore, once the medieval romanticism of Scott and Hugo had lost its novelty, exoticism offered nineteenth-century opera librettists an untapped reservoir of material that virtually cried out for exploitation, especially in view of the endless stream of oriental literature in France following Napoleon's Egyptian campaign. (As seen from the history of ideas, the nineteenth-century fashion for exoticism was partly motivated by the fact that colonialism, formerly an entirely commercial affair, became a national ideology with obvious implications for literature.) However, the crucial factor in the spread of exoticism among serious-minded musicians was a development in compositional technique: just as functional meter disintegrated into "musical prose," functional harmony began to give way to coloristic harmony.

Any attempt to get to the root of exoticism and grasp the phenomenon at a point where it motivated compositional history, rather than merely reflecting intellectual history, will stumble upon an initially surprising but ultimately obvious fact—namely, that exoticism is closely allied with folklorism, or at least more closely than those observers would have us believe who imagine that a gaping chasm separates the musical expression of their own "national spirit" from a picturesque rendering of a foreign milieu. Nineteenth-century folklorism was linked with the idea of a national style, turning national styles into artistic species of folk music and, conversely, folk musics into national styles in embryo. The connection between the two, however, is not self-evident; indeed, it proves to be a hypothesis rooted less in the physical universe than in the nineteenth-century mind. For a folk-music tradition consists to no small degree of elements, melodies, and structures that were local and regional in origin, but also of others that "migrated" throughout the whole of Europe. In short, a folk-music tradition never represents one nation and one nation only. Moreover, any peasant music of local or regional origin (or flavor) which has been transferred to the urban bourgeois milieu where national styles are concocted will, when extracted from its evocative theatrical or literary context in an opera or a symphonic poem, be essentially no less "exotic" than an orientalism made congenial and familiar by being adapted to the key schemes and instrumental timbres of European art music.

Both exoticism and folklorism thrive on stylistic quotations interpolated into a polyphonic setting governed by the principles of art music. At the same time they flourish on an aesthetic illusion that arises when the defining features of music, painting, and literature intermingle: without a picture to pinpoint a milieu, or a caption to suggest a country of origin, the ethnic elements inserted into a European art composition are seldom distinctive enough to be pinned down to a particular locale, except perhaps in the case of certain dances. (This illusory aspect, as in the novel, is not a shortcoming of the genre but rather its aesthetic raison d'être: whether ethnic styles in an opera or a symphonic poem are genuine or spurious is just as immaterial as whether the fragments of reality in a novel are historically documented or freely invented. The fact that opera and the novel belong to the realm of the fictitious is one of their aesthetic premises, and the semblance of "authenticity" conveyed by a stylistic quotation in an opera, or a bit of newspaper reportage in a novel, is an effect whose legitimacy does not depend on whether or not it is anthropologically or historically "genuine." The Spanish character and aesthetic import of the Habañera from Bizet's *Carmen* is completely untouched by the dispute as to whether the piece is an invention of Bizet's, a Spanish folk song, or an adaptation of the song *El Arreglito* by Sebastián Yyradier.)

Exoticism and folklorism, then, have analogous aesthetic functions, manifested musically in the notably stereotype devices they use to represent both local and alien milieus. (Composers such as Weber and Glinka took inspiration both from their hereditary folk song, thereby turning themselves into national composers, and from Spanish or oriental music, alternating freely between the two as though there were no real difference between expressing one's own "national spirit" and quoting someone else's. However poorly this fact fits into the ideological context of the nineteenth century, it is comprehensible from a purely compositional standpoint.)

There is no tangible difference between the double bourdon of open fifths in the Chorus of Bayadères from David's *Lalla Roukh*, intended to depict an Indian subject, and the ones that paint a Jewish milieu in Gounod's *Le reine de Saba*, a Moorish backdrop in Saint-Saën's *Suite algérienne* (1881), or a Russian setting in Balakirev's folk-song arrangements. Nor can we raise the obvious rejoinder that musical elements only take on a distinctive national character in context, not in isolation. After all, it is no easy matter to see a definitive distinction between the combination of double bourdon, Lydian fourth, and chromatic coloration in the Jumping Dance of Grieg's purportedly Scandinavian *Nordic Dances and Folk Tunes*, Op. 17 (1870), and the similar stereotype combination used as an orientalism in the dance *L'Almée* from Bizet's *Djamileh* (Ex. 57). In neither case can the local color be localized in purely musical terms without a scenic or linguistic tag. Regardless of the milieu being depicted, exoticism and folklorism almost invariably make do with the same technical devices: pentatonicism, the Dorian sixth and Mixolydian seventh, the raised second and augmented fourth, nonfunctional chromatic coloration, and finally bass drones, ostinatos, and pedal points as central axes.

Example 57

In sum, we can speak of exoticism and folklorism per se without having to specify the folk tradition or exotic land involved. This indicates that the key issue is not the original ethnic substance of these phenomena so much as the fact that they differ from European art music, and the function they serve as deviations from the European norm. As categories governed by the principle of integratable irregularity, however, exoticism and folklorism were linked in nineteenth-century music with a tradition that likewise runs against the mainstream of compositional evolution: musical landscape painting. Familiarity has made this connection so close that we seldom realize just how unusual and unnatural the association of folk music and musical landscape painting actually is. (The term "picturesque" does not explain the matter but merely attaches a label to it.)

Whether for Weber or Glinka, Smetana or Grieg, the musical landscape is among the permanent components of a national musical style, even if we have even more difficulty and uncertainty in identifying the landscape than in determining the ethnic origin of double bourdons and raised seconds and fourths. To keep our analysis on firm ground we should proceed from the function this phenomenon served in the context of European art music, and not from aesthetic impressions of an ideological stamp. As far as compositional technique is concerned, almost all the outstanding musical renditions of nature—the Forest Murmurs from *Siegfried,* the Nile scene from *Aïda,* or the riverbank scene from Gounod's *Mireille*—follow a principle that was driven to extremes in modern art music, even serving as the basis for entire works: the sound-sheet, or *Klangfläche,* outwardly static but inwardly in constant motion. Regardless of whether the scene is a bucolic idyll or a thunderstorm (like the Prelude to Act 1 of *Die Walküre*), the music remains riveted to the spot motivically and harmonically, no matter how gentle or violent its rhythmic motion. To put it another way, a musical depiction of nature is almost always defined negatively, by being excluded from the imperative of organic development which, at least in the mainstream of compositional history, dominated the thematic and motivic structure of nineteenth-century music as well as its harmonic schemes. The *Klangfläche* conveys a landscape because it is exempted both from the principle of teleological progression and from the rule of musical texture which nineteenth-century musical theorists referred to, by no means simply metaphorically, as "thematic-motivic manipulation," taking Beethoven's development sections as their *locus classicus.* As Hegel would have put it, musical landscapes arise less from direct tone-painting than from "definite negation" of the character of musical form as a process. Nor do we have to plunge into abstruse speculations regarding the way economic, sociopsychological, aesthetic, and compositional categories interlock in order to see in this fact a starting point for our attempts to "socially decipher" aesthetic phenomena, in the sense demanded by Adorno. (Beethoven himself recognized the possibility of applying "definite negation" to his own formal principles and did so in the first movement of the Pastoral Symphony, where the *Klangflächen* of the development section depict Nature as an idyll and a place of refuge.)

Without their internal motion, the *Klangflächen* would not stand in dialectical contradiction to the temporal structure of the music but would merely sound dull and lifeless. This internal motion, however, derives not only from the rhythmic patterns underlying the arpeggiated chords but also from a device connected with the handling of dissonance: the unresolved nonharmonic tone. The horn calls that evoke a landscape in the opening scene of Act 2 in *Tristan* do so not simply because hunting scenes are associated with nature, but also because the superimposition of fifths and octaves (f–c'–f' and c'–g'–c"), a device originating in the finale of Beethoven's Pastoral Symphony, forms a constant sonority of unresolved dissonance suggesting that processual cognition has been suspended. The call of the forest bird, in the Forest Murmurs from *Siegfried,* sounds like an evocation of nature not merely because it is a melodic rendering of actual

Fig. 65 Stage design for Antonín Dvořák's *Rusalka*. As an opera composer—which, to an age that clung to opera as the representative genre of musical nationalism, meant the same thing as "national composer"—Dvořák was overshadowed by Smetana. However, his fairy-tale opera *Rusalka,* based on a variant of the Undine legend, gave him a subject that allowed him to make telling musicodramatic use of his native lyricism and his ability to transform a landscape by simple means into a fairy-tale world. Dvořák's work treats the unhappy love of a prince for a nymph whose father, a merman, directs the dramatic action at will. Like the subjects of Russian fairy-tale operas since the time of Glinka, this tale is an international "migratory motif," which nevertheless takes on a distinctively national-romantic flavor. (Prague, Muzeum Antonína Dvořáka, Národní Muzeum.)

birdcalls but, in almost equal measure, for the negative reason that its unresolved added sixth stands outside the harmonic logic, just as its fluid rhythms stand outside the meter. Schönberg, in 1911, objected to the term "nonharmonic tone," arguing that there is (or ought to be) no such thing as a dissonance that does not influence harmonic progression. Yet it is this very lack of influence which forms the defining feature of dissonances that evoke nature (as opposed to society) in a *Klangfläche*. In music, nature is the negation of the musical logic so ardently championed by Schönberg.

Fig. 66 Stage design for Antonín Dvořák's *Rusalka*. These stage photographs of the Prague premiere (1901), with Ružena Maturová as Rusalka and Václav Kliment as the Spirit of the Lake, illustrate a production style characteristic of fin-de-siècle neoromanticism in that it attempts to convey an overall romantic impression by means of realistic details. If stage techniques of the time seem to anticipate the cinema, two decades later they were "disembarrassed" of their realistic trappings by the film and forced back into stylization. (Prague, Museum Antonína Dvořáka, Národní Muzeum.)

So obvious is the technical parallel between a *Klangfläche* with unresolved nonharmonic tones, and a double bourdon supporting melodies with raised seconds and fourths, that the nineteenth century's fondness for linking musical landscapes with exoticisms and folklorisms seems to be rooted in the material of music itself rather than being explainable aesthetically with reference to the category of the picturesque. The combination of a "static" acoustic backdrop and a nonfunctional, coloristic additive, whether a dissonance or a chromatic note, is a structural principle that links musical landscape painting with exoticism and folklorism, placing both of them outside the classical-romantic norm of harmony as consisting of chord progressions set in motion and directed toward a goal by dissonance and chromaticism.

Nevertheless, it is not enough to analyze musical exoticisms and folklorisms exclusively as integratable deviations from compositional norms if we wish to do historical justice to this ambivalent phenomenon. Instead of contradicting the nineteenth-century processual mentality, recourse to folklore was also capable of furthering the evolution of tonal harmony, an evolution premised on the idea that any increase in harmonic sophistication had to be held in check by increasingly tight-knit integration. (To alter a chord chromatically was, at least ideal-typically, to complicate its structure and at the same time to strengthen its function as a dominant.) Even so, the practice of using modal touches as a means of harmonic sophistication—that is, resorting to archaisms in order to underscore a work's modernity—not infrequently brought harmonic complexity to the verge of disintegration. In a passage from No. 4 of Edvard Grieg's *Norske fjeldmelodier*, written before 1875, harmony functions less as a foundation for the melody than vice versa (Ex. 58). The simplicity of the upper voice serves as a foothold without which the harmonic progression, from the secondary subdominant to the Neapolitan seventh, would remain dangling in mid-air. In this case, however, harmonic sophistication, brought about by tonally integratable dissonances, comes close to splitting the piece into unrelated "layers," creating a bitonal dichotomy between late-romantic chromaticism and modal folk melody.

Example 58

The rift between melody and harmony, a musical fait accompli in the afore-mentioned passage from the *Fjeldmelodier,* is part of an ongoing process in the fourth of Grieg's *Norwegian Folk Tunes,* Op. 66 (1896) (Ex. 59). If the opening measure and a half still permits a functional interpretation (with G–D–A as a root progression), the parallel chords in the accompaniment gradually form a structural element in their own right as the simple G-minor melody increasingly comes into conflict with the chromatic harmony. Grieg has notated the passage so as to maintain a semblance of functional tonality, but this merely proves to be a façade behind which can be seen a harmonic mechanism bursting the bonds of tonality. Melodic pitches so straightforward as to have ineradicable tonal implications are forced into almost bizarre nonfunctional roles in the harmony. This collision between harmonic alteration, a byword for late-nineteenth-century modernity, and folk melody, an element of archaic provenance, gives rise to techniques, such as bitonality and chord streams, that anticipate modern music of our own century. Hence, it is no exaggeration to see a historical dialectic between them.

Still, that archaism and modernity could overlap should not blind us to the fact that, in nineteenth-century music, archaism usually meant a picturesque

Example 59

deviation from the norm, a variant adding a touch of color to the tonal-harmonic setting without seriously affecting its structure. And the dialectic of any restoration—the fact that past things change meaning when transposed to the present—is nowhere more apparent than in the attempt to reinstate sixteenth-century modal harmony, as advocated and propagandized by Carl von Winterfeld in his book *Gabrieli und sein Zeitalter* (1834). In the nineteenth century, ecclesiastical modes were not perceived as they once were; instead, they represented enticing modifications of major and minor. The very terms applied to them betray how they were misunderstood: concepts such as the "Dorian sixth," "Lydian fourth," or "Mixolydian seventh" were unknown in the sixteenth century, since, in the original Dorian mode, the third or seventh degrees were no less characteristic than the sixth. These terms were merely labels for those degrees that distinguished the modes from major or minor keys, to which they were automatically related rather than standing on their own. The nature of the past conjured up by an archaism is to be found not in an earlier historical reality but in its distance from the present.

Trivial Music

The "trivial" music of the nineteenth century, the repertoire of its dance halls and promenade concerts, salons and *variétés*, is as familiar as it is unknown. The very fact that we all know roughly what to expect from works entitled *Alpenglühn, Les cloches du monastère,* or *A Maiden's Prayer* seems to have obstructed serious thought on the nature and curious popularity of these creations. Even the sheer volume and monotony of musical banality leaves us awestruck. However colorful and enticing is an area ranging from the vulgar *Gassenhauer* to the affected salon piece, from the disciplined march to the anarchical cancan, we are soon disenchanted when we discover the narrowness of its musical devices. (Hans Mersmann once defined musical banality as music for which technical analysis is pointless.)

The word "trivial" implies an aesthetic judgment. This may seem suspect to a historian or a sociologist: the principle of impartiality suggests that we adopt a more neutral term, of which there is no shortage of candidates. Labels such as light music, popular music, entertainment music, or functional music are far more widespread than "trivial music," but none of them, though less marked by intellectual arrogance, seems to capture the phenomenon we have in mind. Eighteenth-century divertimentos were also designed to entertain, but no one would wish to place them alongside a nineteenth-century Viennese coffeehouse *pièce.* "Functional music," though aesthetically neutral, is too inclusive and unspecific: it embraces the whole of church music insofar as the liturgical element predominates. It would seem more appropriate to speak of "light music" if the term did not convey a carefree attitude not common to all the products of this genre, in which sentimentality was no less important than merriment. Finally, it need hardly be mentioned that the term "popular music" is too vague. Not only are works of unspeakable banality "popular," but many works of art music as well, or at least sections of them. Conversely, most of the rubbish produced is just as unsuccessful as the majority of works written under the banner of art music.

The term "trivial music," then, expresses not only a difference in kind but a difference in quality from art music. This may disturb logicians who insist on a sharp distinction between normative and descriptive terms, but it is fully in accord with the nature of the subject under description. The music which Heinrich Besseler (drawing on Heidegger's opposition of the "ready-to-hand" and the "ready-at-hand") referred to as "vernacular" to distinguish it from autonomous art, from music designed to be listened to for its own sake, tended ineluctably toward banality in the century of artistic autonomy. No one denies that even salon pieces, marches, *couplets,* and *Gassenhauer* have specific qualities which distinguish a tiny number of successful works from the mass of failures. (Advertising, still underdeveloped in nineteenth-century musical culture, is seldom sufficient by itself to impose a piece on the public.) Still, it is uncertain whether, and if so to what extent, the surprisingly elusive qualities that determine a "hit" deserve to be called aesthetic at all. If the nature of the subject and the effect it has on us force us to switch from aesthetic to psychological criteria, this unavoidable change of methodology merely confirms that there is a categorical distinction between these two realms, a distinction that implies a difference of quality in every aesthetic judgment we make. It is not unwarranted to apply aesthetic criteria insofar as the composers and public of trivial music, unlike the sociologists who analyze the phenomenon, insist on the aesthetic rather than the exclusively psychological quality of their musical stimulant: a hit, in Kantian terms, should be considered "beautiful" and not simply "pleasant." Furthermore, regardless of which perspective we choose, this categorical cum qualitative distinction is a well-attested sociopsychological and hence historical fact: whether lowbrow music is dismissed as bad ("trivial music"), or highbrow music as pretentious ("opus music"), the important point is the common belief that music falls into lowbrow and highbrow types in the first place. Both opinions presuppose a separation and a qualitative difference between the two areas, which in turn has left its mark on concert programs and musical perception.

Lowbrow music has existed in various forms throughout the ages. However, the earlier stages in its evolution are divided from its nineteenth-century variety by a qualitative leap. Pseudomusical considerations, now mass phenomena of stifling proportions, have transformed lowbrow music, by sociological as well as music-historical criteria, into a hitherto nonexistent genre. The sociohistorical preconditions of this genre are to be found, not just in a misapplication of eighteenth-century philanthropic tendencies, but also in the economic progress of an age marked by industrialization on a scale so vast as to be called a revolution at the time, a revolution from which hardly any area of culture remained unscathed.

Fig. 67 Dejonghe: *Une mélodie de Schubert,* 1880. The young lady at the piano, no doubt playing Schubert's *Ave Maria* as though it were Gounod's, seems almost an illustration of the thesis that kitsch resides less in art itself than in the listener's relation to art. Almost anything can be transformed into kitsch by a distorted mode of perception, by falling into sentimental self-absorption instead of focusing on the object at hand. Still, many works probably invite being treated as kitsch, or indeed would be meaningless otherwise. Nor is the aesthetic injustice perpetrated upon serious-minded music by trivialization seldom entirely unmerited. (Paris, Collection Viollet; photograph from Bärenreiter Bildarchiv, Kassel.)

In popular education as prescribed by Pestalozzi, unlike the Latin schools of the sixteenth through eighteenth centuries, music was bound neither socially to a privileged class nor functionally to the church service. Instead, it became a potential means for educating all levels of the population, namely, by cultivating sensitivity. As the detailed and elaborate program of eighteenth-century philanthropical education became coarse reality in the nineteenth century the result was a mass acquisition of music and an emphasis on the emotional effects of acoustic phenomena, even those of minimal or dubious artistic qualities. What

Pestalozzi had in mind was not education in music as an art, but education with humanity as its goal and music as its vehicle. Nineteenth-century music education was given another particular slant by the fact that, in the popular imagination, piano and voice lessons were de rigueur in the education of any young woman of station, and of those who aspired to this station. Domestic music culture, then, was determined by notions which a patriarchal age had of the female character. "A woman should not excel, but touch and gladden the heart." Thus the author of an essay, published in the *Allgemeine musikalische Zeitung* (1806), on the degree of musical education desirable in women. And it is scarcely possible to define the function of trivial music more accurately than by the words "touch" and "gladden."

The philanthropical tendencies of the eighteenth century, however, could not be perverted into preconditions for trivial music until they had been victimized, in the nineteenth century, by a process of commercialization or industrialization which took hold in virtually all areas of society as a compulsion to mass-produce and distribute commodities. From the perspective of social history, the production of trivial music can be regarded as an industry that undertook to achieve the enlightened educational end of cultivating ("touching" and "gladdening") the spirit in all levels of society with the means of mass production, whereby the means eventually overshadowed their own end. Still, the industrialization of musical culture—or at least of that part of musical culture which, as trivial music, forms the musical signature of the industrial age—would not have been possible without the profound social upheavals resulting from the mass migration from the countryside to the city. Unlike folk song, defined by Béla Bartók as peasant music, trivial music was originally, and "ideal-typically," an urban phenomenon, even if it has long since become universal.

Here on the outskirts of music (or, as Benedetto Croce would say, of music as nonart), the mode of reception becomes a crucial factor. Trivial music can virtually be defined as encouraging trivial, or trivializing, listening. True, this mode of perception is equally applicable to works with an impeccable claim to rank as art, but these works neither encourage such an approach, nor were they intended for it. (The fact that art music can likewise fall victim to trivializing listening keeps the definition from being tautological.)

Trivial music is a special form of lowbrow music and, as such, a historically delimited phenomenon. It belongs to the age dominated by the classical-romantic notion of art, an age whose reception history is still very much alive today, as our opera and concert repertoires show. (In our century the actual opposite of trivial music, determining its role in our awareness, is not "modern" but "classical" music.) Unlike the norms of art music, however, trivializing listening ignores or violates one of the major theoretical premises of classical-romantic art: the principle of self-absorption in the work as an aesthetic object. It does this by sidestepping the dialectic of form and content in music, extracting from it a topic or subject matter (mistaken for the work's "contents") and withdrawing from the acoustic phenomenon into the listener's own frame of mind. In this way the mu-

Fig. 68 *Moderne Liebes-Walzer.* One peculiarity of popular music, both in the nineteenth and the twentieth century, is its blend of sentimentality and cynicism: the feelings evoked are accompanied by the scorn they engender when viewed from the outside. We are often at a loss to decide whether sentimentality is a vehicle for irony, or vice versa. Listeners may have been moved to tears by the music, but at the same time, as children of an age that praised its "sense of reality," they distanced themselves from their own sentiment. (The doggerel verse at the bottom reads: "How quickly hearts and hands unite / When pops counts up his fortunes bright.") (London, British Library.)

sic, instead of constituting an aesthetic object, degenerates into a vehicle for associations and for edifying or melancholy self-indulgence. Still, trivial music, or music that invites trivializing listening, has to meet certain technical prerequisites without which neither false objectification nor false subjectification could succeed: it must be simple enough to permit easy listening, but not so clichéd as to discourage hearers from listening at all.

In Lefébure-Wély's *Les cloches du monastère,* one of the most famous salon pieces of the nineteenth century, the alternation of dominant and tonic at one-measure intervals is no less stereotypical than the succession of functional tones in the melody (E–D–E–D / D–C–D–C / C–B–A–B / C–D–E), made more monotonous still by their repetition in measures 1 and 2 (Ex. 60). The dash of "interest" which banal music requires to become effective is provided by the appoggiatura relationship between melody and harmony, and by the repeated octave G's (intended as an imitation of monastery bells) that wrap the structural melody, as it were, in a sheath of sound. If the piece is sufficiently "characteristic" to be perceived at all (and selected from the vast oversupply of "musical commodities"), its harmony, rhythm, and melody nevertheless remain so simple that it poses not the slightest obstacle to a mode of listening that glides across the musical structure and loses itself in an imaginary vision of monastic quietude, or in melancholy self-indulgence in the listener's own need for repose.

If, then, contrary to widespread methodological objections, triviality in music can be pinpointed analytically in the pieces themselves and not just in their

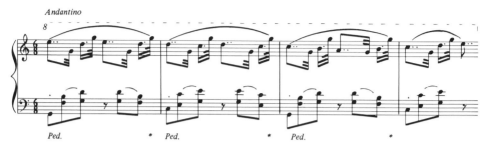

Andantino

Example 60

effect on the listener, there is nevertheless a qualitative leap separating the trivial music of the nineteenth century from lowbrow music of earlier epochs, a leap whose sociohistorical premises we have already outlined. It appears most clearly in the way this genre was received, in the reasons given for ostracizing it. Even as late as the early eighteenth century there were basically three motivations for polemicizing against the practices of the musical *souterrain,* of buskers and beer-hall fiddlers: musically, they broke the rules; morally, they were shady and disreputable; and socially, they belonged to a lower order deserving of contempt. The privileged musician was outraged by the disenfranchised, the sedentary musician by the peripatetic, the guild artisan by the outsider suspected of shoddy workmanship, however patent his virtuosity. (A remnant of the combined fascination and disdain felt for the itinerant musician can still be detected in nineteenth-century criticism of virtuosos.)

Today, centuries later, we can raise our doubts about the justice of these opinions of lower, unprivileged music. However, in one respect these criteria compare favorably with those of the nineteenth century: they were easy to grasp and (relatively) unequivocal. Rules of craftsmanship, judgments of morality, and distinctions of social class are unsophisticated but safe and clear-cut arguments. Under the banner of the aesthetic views that gradually took hold from the late eighteenth century, however, these judgments threatened to become vague and intangible. As was already mentioned, the classical-romantic concept of art was taken as the final arbiter, and this concept excluded, in principle, not only lowbrow music but functional music as well, down to liturgically motivated church music. And any functional music held in disdain will automatically tend to become as bad as it is assumed to be (hence the paralysis that seemed to befall liturgical music in the age of romanticism). It was accused no longer of breaking the rules but of being derivative or prosaic. (The concept that joined functional and lowbrow music in the age of aestheticism was precisely the notion of the trivial.)

Stylistically, as we have seen from our analysis of *Les cloches du monastère,* trivial music presupposed two phenomena, which arose independently only to merge later: sentimentality (the reverse side of the Enlightenment) and the discovery that the modern compositional technique that emerged around 1740 could be mechanically applied at lower levels. Music, as Johann Mattheson wrote in his *Vollkommener Capellmeister* of 1739, is the art that "pleases the sense of hearing dwelling in the soul, using the ears as its tools, and firmly moves and touches the heart or emotions." "Touching," a word combining sensual and emotional properties, was the catchword of popular music aesthetics. At the same time, however, for the use of ambitious dilettantes, recipes were published for composing dances, tables indicating how to piece together polonaises and menuets from prefabricated motives. These mechanical practices, naive as they may be, nevertheless point out an element characteristic of eighteenth-century compositional technique as a whole: the temptation to regress to a second primitivity. Melodies are often nothing more than paraphrases of chords reduced to two harmonies, tonic and dominant.

Trivial music, then, emerged as a paradoxical cross between sentimentality and mechanization, this being the aesthetic reflection of a sociohistorical clash between a philanthropical tradition and a drive toward commercialization and industrialization. It is deliberately bland, but with the pretense of being emotional. It wishes to be direct and intelligible to all, and for this reason remains within the narrowest confines of convention at the same time that it tries to appear as a spontaneous outpouring of feeling. It is banality masquerading as poetry, if only in the form of its title, for the simple reason that the nineteenth century discovered the effect of the poetical in a world that was becoming more and more prosaic.

Still, any interpretation of trivial music as mere deception would fall short of the mark. The mechanics behind its power to "touch," though half-submerged, are nevertheless half-visible. The listener is permitted at once to enjoy and despise it. He is spared the exertions of immersing himself in the work, as required of him by great art. The cynicism of the popular-music industry, which converts sentimentality into capital, is answered by a sentimentality which threatens at any moment to turn into cynicism and is not about to stand any nonsense.

We have seen how the romantic notion of art was contradicted not so much by rule-breaking as by tawdriness and banality. It is not manifest compositional blunders so much as aesthetic deficiencies that raise the hackles of art lovers. Triviality offends against taste, the aesthetic counterpart to social tact, whose verdicts brook no court of appeal. It is less a matter of compositional workmanship than of aesthetic reflection, which admittedly must be converted into high-quality workmanship lest it remain vain and futile.

Robert Schumann was apparently among the first to recognize the aesthetic problem posed by the existence and spread of a kind of music that is neither poorly written (in any obvious sense) nor capable of ranking as art. His distinction between "poesy" and "prose," two fundamental concepts in his aesthetics, expresses this state of affairs in the language of Jean Paul. When Schumann labeled the tune *Schier dreißig Jahre bist du alt* "prosaic" he equated musical prose with trivial music. And, as he wrote in his *Neue Zeitschrift für Musik*, the decade

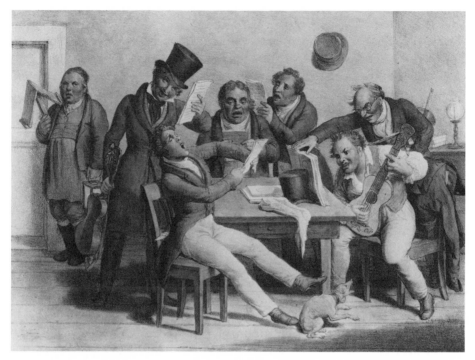

Fig. 69 Contemporary caricature of tavern music-making. One noticeable trait of this tavern scene (at first glance more bellowed than sung) is the fact that, uninhibited as they may be, the singers are reading from sheet music. The use of the printing press to disseminate popular music is one of the key factors separating the "trivial music" of the nineteenth century from vernacular musics of earlier times. The broadside ballad and *Gassenhauer* were industrialized as soon as the ability to read music had spread, thanks to a Pestalozzian program of mass education. (Vienna, Österreichische Nationalbibliothek.)

between 1820 and 1830 was a time "when half of the musical world pondered over Beethoven while the other half lived for the moment." Music split into two realms, into art and nonart.

All the same, music that is nothing else but unabashedly prosaic and disarmingly banal, no matter how annoying its existence and popularity, poses no problems that might seriously trouble aestheticians. The actual stumbling block is music that involuntarily draws upon itself the condemnation of being "sham poetry," a dubious verdict in that the aspect of simulation and pretense in art (unlike ethics) cannot be dismissed without further ado as reprehensible. Anyone who suspects the "poetic" character of *Les cloches du monastère* of being "inauthentic" has, it would seem, switched from aesthetic to moral criteria, for his verdict basically reads "aesthetic hypocrisy." The argument ultimately vacillates between the accusation that the piece was deliberately tailored to the sentimentality of the public, rather than emerging from an inner emotional compulsion of the composer, and the claim that it is poorly composed. This first objection, however, is naive: ever since Poe's *Principles of Composition* theorists of poetry have agreed that calculation and artistic character are by no means mutually exclusive. The second is unspecific, for music with a claim to rank as art is not simply turned into trivial music by having technical shortcomings. (A piece such as *Les cloches du monastère* is not a weaker example of the same genre as Chopin's nocturnes but represents a different sphere of music altogether.)

The question, then, is what distinguishes the originality essential to the artistic character of poetic music (according to the principles of the classical-romantic aesthetic) from the titillations that a trivial composer has to deal with in order to turn unprepossessing and ineffectual musical banality into a piece of trivial music striking enough to lift it out of the mass of its failed competitors. Since aesthetic aspects are dependent on compositional correlates to be perceivable at all, the answer to this question must be sought in the technique of composition, even though the pieces whose "shams" are meant to be hunted down by analysis were not composed against the rules in any obvious sense of the term. The best way to determine the aesthetic shortcomings of a piece such as *Les cloches du monastère* is to examine internal contradictions, such as the lack of proportion between its pretentious opening, with an appoggiatura sixth leading to a dominant seventh chord, and the shopworn simplicity of its harmonic-metrical scheme. (This is not to say that the whole truth about the triviality of these pieces lies in their compositional technique.) The grandeur implied by its opening measure remains unfulfilled, and herein lies the "sham." It is technical rather than psychological insufficiency that, at least in part, distinguishes Lefébure-Wély's musical "poetry" from that of a Chopin or a Schumann. To use Schumann's terms, the poetry degenerates into its opposite, prose.

Pseudopoetic music, then, is the characteristic nonart of the romantic age, partaking of its aesthetic criteria but failing to satisfy them. Yet it was also the trivial music of an industrial age, competing with art music as a musical text printed in prodigious quantities. For centuries lowbrow music had been handed down without notation. Only around 1750, starting in England, did it begin to be disseminated in print. By the nineteenth century this dissemination had reached the proportions of an industry, triggering the mechanism of alternating increases in demand and production. Economic and sociopsychological motives merged in the mass manufacture of printed songs and romances, salon pieces and opera arrangements. As was already mentioned, by about 1800 piano playing and singing had become status symbols which soon took hold of the middle and even the petty bourgeoisie. (One of the father's expectations, in Goethe's *Hermann und Dorothea*, of an acceptable daughter-in-law was that she should play the piano.) Admittedly, it is difficult to attempt a more precise sociohistorical description, to assign different types of music to particular classes or strata. We find ourselves in a quandary the moment we try to rephrase, as we ought, plausi-

ble-sounding conjectures into empirically verifiable hypotheses. In an outline of
the sociology of literature Matthew Arnold, not without ill will, defined upper-
class culture as conspicuous consumption, middle-class culture as trivial, and
lower-class culture as rubbish. It is questionable, indeed unlikely, that the audience that helped Chopin's music on its path to success represented a different
stratum from the consumers of banal salon pieces.

Trivial music is bound to the present and its changing fashions. This is
widely held to distinguish it from folk music, one of whose features is its survival,
the tenacity with which its melodies are handed down over decades or even centuries. However, this picture is too coarse: it is not difficult to find countless exceptions. It might be that the difference lies in the mind of the age rather than
the actual longevity of melodies. Seen from a distance, folk music is not without
its history, but in continuous traditions it seems to be perceived as timeless. The
fact that folk music is old thus means not that it bears the impress of the past, but
rather that it is taken as a matter of course, which in turn encourages the belief
that it was no different then from what it is now. In contrast, it is the raison d'être
of trivial music, even if written a decade or even a century ago, to appear current
and up-to-date to its listeners—or, to use a phrase from the world of fashion, to
be "this year's model." As soon as it ages it is recognized and rejected as trivial,
not least of all by last year's enthusiasts (nothing is more ridiculous than yesterday's fashions). The trivial reveals its essence the moment it loses its mode of
existence by becoming out-of-date.

Historicism

Musical historicism, whether of the nineteenth or the twentieth century, has
always been a paradox. Any attempt to reach a historical understanding of the
evolutionary stage it had attained in the nineteenth century, rather than treating
it simply as the prehistory of our own time, will have to do more than trace the
slow growth of historical thought and performance from their rudimentary
beginnings: it will also have to do justice to the resistance that historicism encountered.

The combination of historical awareness and conservative practice that
characterizes the musical culture of our century is a self-contradiction. To believe that music is "historical through and through," that to grasp the essence of
a piece we have to reconstruct its origins and historical context, is not to uphold
traditionalism so much as to contradict our firmly engrained habit of filling our
concert and opera repertoires with works from the eighteenth and nineteenth
centuries. By unearthing the historical preconditions of a piece, historical
thought puts the music at a distance from its present-day performance. The
greater our understanding of historical conditions governing the past, the more
difficult it becomes to reconstruct that past aesthetically, to turn a work from a
historical relic and document into an aesthetic object.

Fig. 70 Michael Neder: *Musik im Weinkeller,* 1866. The man seated at the table is playing a zither, a folk (i.e., peasant) instrument which, like folk song, was adopted by the bourgeoisie and practiced as a picturesque musical fashion. Not until middle-class sentiments became associated with this item from peasant culture was it permissible to use the instrument in a painting that depicted a rural milieu for the benefit of a bourgeois clientele. (Vienna, Niederösterreichisches Landesmuseum.)

On the other hand, the ease with which Bach and Schönberg, Mozart and Weber, are made to stand cheek by jowl in our concert and opera repertoires is a clear sign, not of historical awareness, but of its very absence. Our imaginary musical museum is made up of heterogeneous works perceived as though they stand outside history. Their past is not so much "sublated" (in Hegel's sense) in their aesthetic presence as simply forgotten. This nonhistorical mode of reception is matched by performances whose standards of pianistic or violinistic perfection are not influenced or troubled in the slightest by historical thought.

For the moment, the efforts toward "historically authentic" performances are directed exclusively toward so-called early music, meaning music that antedates the end of the Baroque around 1740. This music is separated by a break in tradition from the classical-romantic legacy, whose standards of reception and performance have continued unabated to the present day. As a result, Beethoven's symphonies are still, a century and a half later, not considered "early music," as were Bach's cantatas a mere decade and a half after their composition. Admittedly, historicizing performance practice runs the risk of transforming aesthetic perception into antiquarianism: the listener may be aware of the work less as an aesthetic object than as a document on the zeitgeist or the stage of compositional evolution in a past era. (On the other hand, the temporal remoteness emphasized in these performances can in turn become a source of aesthetic pleasure.)

If we understand by historicism the tendency to take the historical basis of music not simply as a condition of its origin and reception but as a fundamental substance which must guide performers and listeners alike, we can then distinguish two separate issues: the fact of music's historicality (no one would wish to deny that music bears the marks of history), and the by no means obvious, indeed hotly disputed, historicist thesis that these marks of history constitute the essence of each individual work. As readily as the nineteenth century conceded the historicality of music's origins, historicism as an interpretive scheme encountered fierce, and understandable, resistance both in music theory and in aesthetics.

It was a firm nineteenth-century conviction, despite the century's untiring efforts to amass historical and ethnographic material, that the key preconditions of European music—its tonal system, its metric rhythm, the distinction between stable consonances and unstable dissonances requiring resolution, and the principles of functional harmony—were not at all "historical through and through" but were grounded in the nature of the physical universe. (The historical and ethnological conditions of non-European musical norms were viewed not as roots of equivalent systems but as obstacles to the evolution of a general and uniform logic of music. History was construed as the summation of accidents which either favored, as in Europe, or hindered, as outside Europe, the development of a rationality preordained by the nature of the universe and the human species.) The theorems employed to grasp the nature of music changed, it is true, but no one doubted their existence. Antiquity had handed down the proposition that the proportions underlying musical intervals are not simply measurements but active principles, that the simplicity of ratios such as 1:2 and 2:3 is by no means accidental but actually causes these intervals to sound consonant. This mathematical foundation was exchanged by Jean-Philippe Rameau in the eighteenth century for a physical foundation (using the partial overtone series) and by Moritz Hauptmann in the nineteenth for a dialectical one (in which intervals, chords, and keys became manifestations of an all-pervasive spirit beholden to the law of thesis, antithesis, and synthesis). But in neither case did these changing interpretations touch the validity of the dogma that the nature of music is immutable. The sole historicist among nineteenth-century music theorists, Hermann von Helmholtz, a distinguished physicist and physiologist, knew the rules of rigorous scientific explanation far better than his theorizing musical colleagues, who naively turned to physics in order to create a basis for music theory that would enable it, too, to partake of the dignity and inviolability of the natural sciences. In 1863, a half century before composers were to abandon tonality, Helmholtz in his *Lehre von den Tonempfindungen* boldly proposed that "the system of scales, keys, and their connecting harmonies does not rest on immutable natural laws, but is the consequence of aesthetic principles which have been, and will continue to be, subject to change during the continuing march of human evolution." (This thesis made such a strong impression on Lautréamont, who had little knowledge of the subject but an unerring sense for destructive trends undercutting the foundations of the century, that he quoted it in his *Maldoror* of 1869 without mentioning Helmholtz's name.)

Still, despite Hauptmann and Helmholtz, nineteenth-century music theory remained steadfastly "physicalistic," and the notion that music is grounded in a scientifically intelligible universe stood in the way of historicism. In aesthetics, on the other hand, which in turn influenced written history, it was the idea of the classical that posed an obstacle to viewing music as "historical through and through." True, one way of conserving the past is by piously elevating a tradition in retrospect into a classic style. However, this should not obscure the fact that classicism, by extracting works of music from history in order to assemble them in that imaginary museum known as the concert hall, rubs against the grain of historicism, or at least against that form of historicism which sees the substance of a work as residing in its moment in history and considers it the task of performers and audiences not only to reconstruct part of the past but to make us sense our distance from it. (Strictly speaking, a naive mode of perception, with the listener dreamily projecting himself into the past, is not "historical through and through." This quality only arises with a reflected mode of perception, one ever aware of the distance separating past and present in any attempted reconstruction. In this mode of perception, one's notions of the way things used to be overlap with a realization that the past is alien to the present, thereby creating a sense of ambiguity that can be enjoyed aesthetically in its own right.)

Moreover, the classic ideal did not always mean the same thing in the various genres whose aesthetics it influenced. Palestrina was the classic composer of liturgically functional masses and motets, but not in the same sense that Beethoven was the classic composer of symphonies, string quartets, and piano sonatas. In music intended for the church service, whether Catholic or Protestant, the Palestrina style was a model to be taken as a guide lest the composer stray from the path of "true church music" (or what Thibaut called the "holy art of music"). The point was not the composer's individuality and originality, which is inimitable, but a codifiable style that can and ought to be imitated. The Palestrina style, though historical in origin, was extrapolated from his work and placed outside history. Combining textual intelligibility, a "pure texture," and a "seraphic tone," it was an ideal that burst the bonds of history, standing lofty and immutable ever since it was sanctioned by the Council of Trent. Michael Haller, a nineteenth-century imitator of Palestrina, or rather of the Palestrina style, considered himself, not an epigone restoring part of the past, but the standard bearer of a musical verity that would remain true regardless of when it happened to be uttered.

Beethoven, on the other hand, became a *classicus auctor* in the nineteenth century by setting aesthetic and technical standards for the symphony and sonata. To imitate his works, unlike the case of Palestrina, would be to violate the principle for which he stood: that the only way to gain a place in posterity is by being original, even at the price of immediate failure. The notion of *imitatio* (to use the language of classical aesthetics around 1800) gave way to *æmulatio*. The place where operas or symphonies manifest themselves as classical works inviting emulation—or, as Stendhal put it, the place where romanticism confronted established classicism in order to give rise to a classicism of the future—was the repertoire, which did not become a permanent fixture until the nineteenth century. If Palestrina was an exemplary composer mainly by virtue of a compositional technique extracted from his works and associated with his name, Beethoven was exemplary because of the works themselves, which stimulated the emergence of a repertoire precisely because they were strikingly individual and thus inimitable. (The fact that there also arose a standing repertoire of "true church music" embracing not only Palestrina and Lasso but Haller and Grell is a secondary process unrelated to the formation of the concert repertoire.)

With some exaggeration we can maintain that Monteverdi's distinction between *prima prattica* and *seconda prattica*—between an earlier style, preserved in church music, and a modern style—survived clandestinely in the nineteenth-century consciousness. The typical genres of the *prima prattica*—mass, motet, and choral anthem—were considered authentic only insofar as their extramusical function was consistent with their musical devices. They were viewed as outgrowths of a codex of compositional rules capable by themselves of establishing vocal polyphony as "classical," regardless of the individual works involved. On the other hand, the genres of the *seconda prattica*—opera and instrumental music—represented an autonomous art divorced from functions and subject to the aesthetic postulate of innovation. These genres became "classical" by maintaining themselves in the standing repertoire in the form of individual works, discouraging imitation and inviting emulation.

It is a misnomer to refer to the preponderance of past music in the repertoire that gradually emerged in the nineteenth century, and became the norm in the twentieth, as "historical." After all, the thesis that music is "historical through and through" encourages us to think of the past as dead and gone since its spirit (or "zeitgeist") is bound to its moment in history, whereas the founding and handing-down of a repertoire presupposes that classical music stands outside history. Even so, to restore a piece of "early music" antedating the historical divide of 1740 does constitute an act of "historicism" insofar as the performance tries to be "historically authentic," and thereby to convey a sense that the piece is foreign to us and bears the marks of a past age.

Fig. 71 Fritz von Uhde: *Das Familienkonzert,* 1881. Here the seventeenth and nineteenth centuries merge in an Old Masters scene intended to depict a domestic concert around 1880, with clarinet and mandolin. The very stylization conveys something of the spirit of nineteenth-century *Hausmusik,* which transported inhabitants of the Industrial Age back to an imaginary milieu for which seventeenth-century Dutch genre painting provided ready-made backdrops. (Cologne, Rheinisches Bildarchiv.)

Any attempted reconstitution of a historical practice will present pieces of "early music" not primarily as unique, individual creations in their own right but as representatives of a style. As in the church music of the Cecilian movement, the works are, in effect, interchangeable. This is not an aesthetic reproach, however, since the basis of the reproach, the ideal of originality, belongs to a domain contrary to that of "early music."

Music histories in the nineteenth century were as closely intertwined with the classic aesthetic as they were with the formation of the repertoire; historicism was merely an added hue, coloring the fabric without affecting its basic pattern. Whereas music historians from Burney, Hawkins, and Forkel down to Kiesewetter, Fétis, and Ambros concentrated their learning in universal histories, the representative genre of ambitious music historiography in the latter half of the nineteenth century was biography, as is attested by such monumental works as

Jahn's *Mozart* (1856–59), Thayer's *Beethoven* (1866–79), Chrysander's *Händel* (1858–67), and Spitta's *Bach* (1873–80). The transition from universal history to biography was doubtless methodologically motivated as historians exchanged a historiological for a positivist approach: the broad historical outline, whose "truth" resided in the plausibility of an evolutionary pattern for which facts merely provided illustrations, gave way to narrower fields in which authenticity could be vouchsafed by source criticism. This change of historiographical objective, however, also implied that music history was seen no longer as the totality of techniques, with composers figuring primarily as "inventors," but as the totality of works, of creations owing their essence to the individuality of their composers, which biography was then meant to illuminate.

Yet neither universal history nor biography was historicist in the sense that the essence of music was seen to reside in its historicality. Indeed, historicism remained rudimentary in the age of written history (as the period from the late eighteenth to the early twentieth century appears in retrospect), whereas in our own time, now that the principles of historicism are taken for granted, music historiography has come to a standstill. Considering this at first puzzling fact—that historical awareness fails to coincide with an urge to write history—it seems more than likely that important motives for writing music history will be found in ideas antithetical to historicism.

Johann Nikolaus Forkel, one of the earliest universal historians of music (along with Hawkins and Burney), expressly resisted viewing the unexpected existence of alternative tonal systems among "backward peoples" as evidence that the European tonal system had not, after all, emerged from the nature of the physical universe. Yet, at the same time, he revered Bach as a *classicus auctor* whose work represented a *point de perfection* in the history of music. Indeed, the urge to write universal history seems almost to have been motivated by a belief that it must be possible to reconcile music's basis in the physical universe and its historical progress to a zenith in the present or immediate past. The classical in music was to be revealed as the culmination of its origins in nature, and its origins in turn as the foundation of the classical. (This same impetus lies behind attempts to discover "folk-song intonations" in the music of the Viennese classics.) Regardless of whether the alleged goal of music history was the Palestrina style, Bach's harmonically motivated counterpoint, or Haydn's instrumental style with its combination of "logical" and "architectonic" form, it was always the intention of broad-based music histories to discover the foundations of musical classicism in the nature of music itself, which gradually came to light, either favored or hindered by ethnic and historical conditions, in the musics of preceding centuries. Compared with this basic thought, that the continuity of history is rooted in the connection between natural origins and classic culmination, it was immaterial whether the *point de perfection* was sought in the past, the present, or the future. In any event, music historiography was precisely not motivated by the notion of a *beau relatif* that emerged in the early eighteenth century as a palliative to the *querelle des anciens et des modernes*. (Not even August Wilhelm Ambros, a

Fig. 72 Anselm Feuerbach: *Das Konzert.* Renaissance music was a subdued, reclusive art in an era of political strife, an aural alternative to reality. As far as the history of ideas is concerned, however, it is astonishing that a nineteenth-century artist inspired by the painting of the Renaissance, rather than by its music, could intuit this vanished musical culture long before musicians so much as dreamed of restoring sixteenth-century violin and lute music. (East Berlin, Staatliche Museen, National Gallery.)

disciple of Jacob Burckhardt and Karl Schnaase, shared Ranke's conviction that "every age stands directly in God's grace." For all his evident concern for impartiality, he drew a distinction between the "classical" vocal polyphony of Palestrina, in which he saw the "spirit of the Renaissance," and medieval speculative art, which, he maintained, lost itself in vagaries.)

If universal history thus seems intent on mediating between the notions of origin and progress, it is patently obvious that biography proceeds from the notion of the classical composer. Nevertheless, this still does not entirely account for the urgency with which late-nineteenth-century scholars turned from collecting memoirs to writing historical-critical studies. The care with which Friedrich Chrysander did his research into Handel's youth was motivated not only by the philological spirit that had reigned preeminent in biography ever since Otto

Jahn's *Mozart,* but also by patriotism, by an attempt to present Handel as a German rather than an Italian or an English composer. Similarly, Philipp Spitta's Bach biography is sustained by the thesis that Bach—and not Johann Eccard, the "Prussian Palestrina" proclaimed by Carl von Winterfeld—realized the ideal of Protestant church music, a music founded on the chorale, which assumed the dimensions of art in the organ chorale and the chorale cantata. That Spitta, a first-rate musical archivist, could view Bach's chorale cantatas as late works, despite obvious evidence to the contrary, is revealing of the hidden motivation behind music histories that could not rest content until they had presented the essence of their subject—in Spitta's case Protestant church music—as the culmination and ultimate rung in a process of historical evolution. If we were to search for a motto for nineteenth-century music historiography, we could do far worse than quote Karl Kraus: "Origin is the goal."

Bibliographic References

Abraham, Gerald. *Studies in Russian Music.* London: W. Reeves, 1935. 2d ed. Freeport, N.Y.: Books for Libraries Press, 1968.

——. *Slavonic and Romantic Music.* London: Faber, 1968.

Becker, Heinz, ed. *Die "Couleur locale" in der Oper des 19. Jahrhunderts.* Studien zur Musikgeschichte des 19. Jahrhunderts, vol. 42. Regensburg: G. Bosse, 1976.

Bekker, Paul. *Die Sinfonie von Beethoven bis Mahler.* Berlin: Schuster & Loeffler, 1918.

Benjamin, Walter. "Schicksal und Charakter." *Schriften,* vol. 1. Frankfurt am Main: Suhrkamp, 1955.

Besseler, Heinrich. "Grundfragen des musikalischen Hörens." *Jahrbuch der Musikbibliothek Peters* 32 (1925): 35–52.

Cooper, Martin. *Bizet: Carmen.* London: Boosey & Hawkes, 1947.

——. *French Music from the Death of Berlioz to the Death of Fauré.* London: Oxford University Press, 1951. 2d ed. London: Oxford University Press, 1969.

Dahlhaus, Carl. *Grundlagen der Musikgeschichte.* Cologne: Gerig, 1977. Eng. translation by J. Bradford Robinson as *Foundations of Music History.* Cambridge: Cambridge University Press, 1983.

——. *Studien zur Trivialmusik des 19. Jahrhunderts.* Studien zur Musikgeschichte des 19. Jahrhunderts, vol. 8. Regensburg: G. Bosse, 1967.

Doflein, Erich. "Historismus und Historisierung in der Musik." *Festschrift Walter Wiora,* edited by Ludwig Finscher and Christoph-Hellmuth Mahling. Kassel: Bärenreiter, 1967.

Fischer, Kurt von. *Griegs Harmonik und die nordländische Folklore.* Berne: Haupt, 1938.

Forkel, Johann Nikolaus. *Allgemeine Geschichte der Musik.* 2 vols. Leipzig: Schwikertscher Verlag, 1788–1801.

Halm, August. *Die Symphonie Anton Bruckners.* Munich: G. Müller, 1913. 2d ed. Munich: G. Müller, 1923.

Handschin, Jacques. *Camille Saint-Saëns.* Zurich: Orell Füssli, 1930.

Harding, James. *Gounod.* London and New York: Allen & Unwin, 1973.

——. *Massenet.* London: Dent, 1970.

Hauptmann, Moritz. *Die Natur der Harmonik und der Metrik*. Leipzig: Breitkopf & Härtel, 1853.

Hohenemser, Richard. *Welche Einflüsse hatte die Wiederbelebung der älteren Musik im 19. Jahrhundert auf die deutschen Komponisten?* Leipzig: Breitkopf & Härtel, 1900.

Istel, Edgar. *Bizet und "Carmen": Der Künstler und sein Werk*. Stuttgart: J. Engelhorns Nachf., 1927.

Keldany-Mohr, Irmgard. *"Unterhaltungsmusik" als soziokulturelles Phänomen des 19. Jahrhunderts*. Studien zur Musikgeschichte des 19. Jahrhunderts, vol. 47. Regensburg: G. Bosse, 1977.

Korte, Werner F. *Bruckner und Brahms: Die spätromantische Lösung der autonomen Konzeption*. Tutzing: Hans Schneider, 1963.

Kümmel, Werner Friedrich. *Geschichte und Musikgeschichte: Die Musik der Neuzeit in Geschichtsschreibung und Geschichtsauffassung des deutschen Kulturbereichs von der Aufklärung bis zu J. G. Droysen und Jacob Burckhardt*. Marburg: Görig & Weiershäuser, 1967.

Kurth, Ernst. *Bruckner*. 2 vols. Berlin: M. Hesse, 1925.

Mersmann, Hans. *Angewandte Musikaesthetik*. Berlin: M. Hesse, 1926.

Riesman, David. *The Lonely Crowd*. New Haven: Yale University Press, 1964.

Ringer, Alexander L. "On the Question of 'Exoticism' in 19th Century Music." *Studia Musicologica* 7 (1965): 115–23.

Rolland, Romain. *Musiciens d'aujourd'hui*. Paris: Hachette, 1908. Eng. trans. by Mary Blaiklock as *Musicians of To-Day*. New York: Holt, 1915.

Schenker, Heinrich. *Der freie Satz*. Neue musikalische Theorien und Phantasien, vol. 3. Vienna: Universal, 1935. 2d ed., edited by Oswald Jonas. Vienna: Universal, 1956.

Wiora, Walter, ed. *Die Ausbreitung des Historismus über die Musik*. Studien zur Musikgeschichte des 19. Jahrhunderts, vol. 14. Regensburg: G. Bosse, 1969.

CHAPTER SIX

1889-1914

In terms of political events, the years around 1890 were marked by the fall of Bismarck, the repeal of the anti-Socialist laws, the beginning of an aggressive German maritime policy, and signs of an impending Franco-Russian entente. For political historians with "structuralist" leanings, these years constitute a hiatus which is even thought by many, among them Geoffrey Barraclough, to lay bare the basic features that distinguish the "contemporary history" of our own day from "modern" postmedieval history belonging to the past.

For the music historian, no matter how much or how little significance he attaches to chronological simultaneity, the year 1889, by witnessing such works as Mahler's First Symphony and Strauss's *Don Juan,* stands out from the continuum of history as the dawning of "musical modernism." This alone is enough to justify our singling out the quarter century between 1889 and 1914 as a self-contained period in music history as well, without having to advance hypothetical connections between music and politics. (These connections, insofar as they exist at all, are extremely obscure at present. Not even the links between, say, musical culture and the educational reforms around 1890 have been examined in any depth.)

The years around 1890 saw a rapid accumulation of profound changes in politics: the consolidation of nationalism and imperialism, the shift from Eurocentrism to world politics (as was already anticipated in the late eighteenth century by the Seven Years War), and the headlong rush to industrialization and the transition to mass democracy. This "statistical" fact further justifies our positing a historical hiatus at this time. Yet, at first, none of these factors impinged significantly on music history, neither in its reception nor in its compositional technique. (No one could seriously maintain that the growth of the labor movement left traces in the music of Schönberg or Webern. True, a music historian with a sense of daring might wish to link the decline of European hegemony, a fact gradually recognized from 1890, with the emergence of ragtime in the 1880s, and thereby abandon the Eurocentrism of music historiography at the transition to modernist music. Yet the decisive musical events in the United States did not occur until our own century, in the age of contemporary music. It would be instructive, though, to pursue the impact on European musical thought of the discovery that non-European musics are based on fundamentally different musical concepts and tonal systems, a discovery rooted in the musical impressions of the Paris International Exhibition of 1889 and in the bewildering insights propagated by Alexander Ellis in his *Tonometrical Observations on Existing Non-Harmonic Scales* of 1884. This essay, which sounded the death knell of the alleged "physical basis" of tonality, made Ellis the founder of musical ethnography in the form of "comparative musicology.")

Despite Debussy's Maeterlinck opera, and despite the fact that cultural historians automatically think of Bergson's élan vital when they hear the opening bars of that musical symbol of fin-de-siècle modernism, Strauss's *Don Juan,* it is by no means clear how the musical events of 1889 tie in with developments in literature: the emergence of Strindberg and Hamsun, Hauptmann and Wedekind, Bergson and Maeterlinck. Even so, the fact that we are dealing with a "watershed year" in both fields is obvious enough, even if for the moment this fact must remain "dead" and uninterpretable.

The crucial link, allowing us to speak of the 1890s as a relatively self-contained period in cultural and intellectual history, only becomes evident when we turn from the history of artistic production to the history of reception. The "zeitgeist" does not become intelligible until we relate the European reception of Nietzsche, beginning with Georg Brandes's lectures in Copenhagen, to the Wagner vogue, which reached epidemic proportions in the 1890s. The mutual recriminations exchanged between their respective camp-followers should not blind us to the fact that, taken together, Nietzsche and Wagner stood for that "epochal" tendency referred to by Ernst Troeltsch in 1913 as "end-of-the-century cultural critique," a tendency that arose in protest at what he called the "democratic-capitalist-imperialist-technological century." This sense of a fin de siècle, this critique of the waning nineteenth century, formed the obverse of modernism, which saw Wagner's and Nietzsche's works as standing at loggerheads with their own age. (Music, meaning *Parsifal* rather than church music, provided necessary footholds not only for the "quest for religion" that erupted around 1890, but also for the urge to flee industrial mass democracy by seeking refuge in the esoteric "preciosities" of art nouveau, or to escape the culturally all-pervasive rationality which Max Weber took to be the guiding principle of modern European history.)

It was precisely because music, as presented by Wagner, was "different" that it became of immediate cultural import in the age of positivism. In general, we fail to recognize its significance and historical impact for the simple reason that we now take for granted the music culture established at the time: the mass propagation of the classical-romantic legacy, a phenomenon which has no musical counterpart in the nineteenth century and no literary counterpart in the twentieth. (The key aspect of Stefan George's animosity toward music, or more accurately toward Wagner's music, is a tacit presupposition, unthinkable in the seventeenth or the eighteenth century, that profound cultural-historical issues can be decided by polemicizing against music.)

The emergence of a mass musical culture nourished on the classical-romantic legacy is all the more curious considering that there were no similar developments in literature and the fine arts. In our century, the music of the classics has become common aesthetic property to the same extent that literary classics have vanished from our reading habits. (Today we listen to Mozart just as naturally as we avoid reading Goethe.) This is doubtless only partly accounted for by the mass media, which favor music over literature. Hence, it is tempting to venture a sociopsychological explanation: music reveals that, in an age of perpetual revolutions affecting even our day-to-day lives, we seek tranquility in music that is openly expressive and yet harbors a rationality whose existence we can at least sense subliminally, even if we need not trouble ourselves to pursue it at every instant.

Modernism as a Period in Music History

In order to characterize turn-of-the-century music in terms of intellectual or stylistic history, journalists have been eager (scholars less so) to appropriate concepts from literature and the fine arts. Consequently, these concepts are suspected of regressing to a methodological approach supposedly long dead and obsolete: the mutual "illumination of the arts," which was thought fifty years ago to reveal a "zeitgeist" pervading all realms of human existence. However justified we may be in speaking of naturalism, impressionism, symbolism, and *Jugendstil* in music, these terms only touch on partial aspects of the works in question. True, there is a distinct if virtually ineffable tie between *Jugendstil* and the Viennese Secession, on the one hand, and many works by Mahler, Schönberg, Zemlinsky, and Schreker on the other, but we cannot pinpoint it technically without doing interpretive injustice to these pieces. As a result, the term *Jugendstil*, though serviceable for characterizing some traits, proves worthless as a means of capturing in a nutshell the newness of music around 1900. No matter how we bend the terms, it is hard to imagine a category linking the primacy of "sonority" (meaning the fusion of harmony and instrumentation) in fin-de-siècle music and the bold outlines of *Jugendstil*.

Moreover, these stylistic terms are all the more inappropriate to music, where the trends against which symbolism and *Jugendstil* wielded their polemical slings were weak and undeveloped, or at least not sufficiently developed to unleash contrary tendencies strong enough to establish a style. Symbolism was directed against naturalism, and *Jugendstil*, a self-proclaimed style in the strong sense of the term, is unthinkable except in opposition to historicism, then considered "style-less." (Admittedly, the will to style in *Jugendstil* is itself historicist, forming what we might call an "ideal" historicism as opposed to the "practical" historicism of nineteenth-century architecture. By deliberately attempting to embrace all areas of human existence, *Jugendstil* sought to convert into artistic

Fig. 73 Two drawings of Max Reger. The changes wrought in music culture from the mid-nineteenth century by the modern European system of transportation still await thorough investigation. Max Reger spent a large part of his later years traveling as a conductor and pianist "to further his own cause." The fact that he nonetheless left behind a voluminous oeuvre documents the spirit of an age that practiced a work ethic for its own sake. (Frankfurt am Main, Stadt- und Universitätsbibliothek, Music and Theater Collection.)

reality the alleged but by no means indisputable stylistic unity thought to exist in earlier and more fortunate times. Artists took their bearings on an image they made of the past, a past antedating their own benighted age of historicist "style-lessness.")

Gustave Charpentier and Alfred Bruneau attempted to found musical naturalism by drawing from Zola their idea of the *roman musical* in opposition to Massenet's *drame lyrique*. However, not only did the "musical novel" remain a peripheral phenomenon, it is also unsuitable as a historical foil to symbolist music, the proclaimed counterstyle of the age, since it is exactly contemporary with the traces of symbolism detectable in Debussy. Nor could music lay claim to a historicism of the sort revealed by nineteenth-century architecture, where the entire legacy of history served as a treasure trove for eclectics in search of styles appropriate to museums (Egyptian), theaters (Greek), and municipal or court churches (Gothic and Renaissance). Or, if music did share this historicism, it did so only in weak and isolated instances rather than as a current dominating the entire century (even if Mendelssohn and Brahms were not averse to drawing on Handel for their oratorios, Palestrina for their Latin motets, and Bach for their German motets).

Nevertheless, it is noteworthy that no matter how divergent the terms from stylistic or intellectual history bandied about by music historians, they all seem to hover about the year 1890, which lends itself as an obvious point of historical discontinuity even if disagreement still reigns as to the spirit governing the resultant period. The "breakthrough" of Mahler, Strauss, and Debussy implies a profound historical transformation regardless of the vacillating nomenclature used to capture its novelty in a single formula.

If we were to search for a name to convey the breakaway mood of the 1890s (a mood symbolized musically by the opening bars of Strauss's *Don Juan*) but without imposing a fictitious unity of style on the age, we could do worse than revert to Hermann Bahr's term "modernism" and speak of a stylistically open-ended "modernist music" extending (with some latitude) from 1890 to the beginnings of our own twentieth-century modern music in 1910. (The fact that a term originated in the age it names, instead of being devised after the fact or discovered in the terminologically chaotic vocabulary of the time, is one indication that the age had historicist leanings, viewed itself in terms of history, and produced journalism that anticipated future historiography.) The phrase *fin-de-siècle* is another which, though harmlessly chronological in one sense, has distinct connotations of decadence, which in turn invite comparisons with the decline of Rome. These connotations, it is true, may have left their mark on music or its subject matter, from *Pelléas et Mélisande* (1902) to *Salome* (1905), but they merely represent details in the overall picture of the age. Finally, the label "late romanticism" applied by apologists of contemporary music (and now firmly established even among its opponents) is a terminological blunder of the first order and ought to be abandoned forthwith. It is absurd to yoke Strauss, Mahler, and the young Schönberg, composers who represented modernism in the minds of their turn-of-the-century contemporaries, with the self-proclaimed antimodernist Pfitzner, calling them all "late romantics" in order to supply a veneer of internal unity to an age fraught with stylistic contradictions and conflicts. This veneer has nothing to do with reality but is merely the logical upshot of a methodology fixated on a notion from intellectual history: the "zeitgeist." Moreover, "late romanticism" is a pejorative and polemically loaded term used in the 1920s by adherents of neo-classicism and the *Neue Sachlichkeit* to separate themselves from the immediate past and condemn that past as a holdover from the "bad nineteenth century." Turn-of-the-century modernism, as the term *Jugendstil* implies, saw itself as a fresh start in a new direction. It was the next generation that turned it into a historical denouement, a dead legacy, using terminology as a means to commit, as it were, historiological patricide.

The claim that "genuine" modern music did not begin until the 1920s obviously aims a polemical barb at the Schönberg school, consigning its expressionist phase to the nineteenth century. This fact was lamented with bitter irony by Schönberg himself, who saw himself catapulted by his adversaries' critiques in a single bound from the future to the past, skipping the present entirely. However, this should not prevent us from feeling that it might be historiographically useful to posit the existence of a period of "modernist music" (rather than "late romanticism") extending to the sudden demise of expressionism in 1924, which collapsed at the end of the hyperinflation like an overnight bankruptcy. Our decision depends not on how we weigh the facts but on how we weigh our criteria. There is no denying the significance of the historical discontinuity of 1907, a discontinuity associated with compositional features such as the emancipation of dissonance and the transition to atonality. Still, by extending modernist music beyond this date we can demonstrate the interaction of the Schönberg school with Mahler and composers such as Zemlinsky and Schreker, who did not take full part in the march to atonality but nonetheless continued even later to represent modernism (or more accurately the spirit of the Secession). We should also consider the fact that it was not until 1920 that the topography of European art shifted from Vienna and St. Petersburg to Berlin and Paris. A historian unafraid of simplification might maintain that a revolution in musical technique around 1910 was succeeded by a profound transformation of aesthetic outlook around 1920, just as after the Second World War serialism was influenced technically by Schönberg and Webern but aesthetically by Stravinsky.

Thus, difficult as it may be to conclude whether the "nineteenth century" in European music history ended in 1889, 1908, or 1924 (i.e., whether the deciding factor was the advent of modernism, the transition to atonality, or the collapse of expressionism), it ought nevertheless to be patently clear that any music historian who wishes to do more than squeeze works into historical periods, and attempts instead to locate the historical aspect to these works (and to the problems they solved), should examine the dialectic between aesthetics and compositional technique. Here he will find a useful point of departure, enabling him to portray music history as a process unfolding before our eyes in its own acoustical creations.

It is more often the exception than the rule that musical events seen by posterity to represent far-reaching historical discontinuities are viewed and appraised in this same light by the agents of history. Still, the historical impact of the transition to atonality around 1908 was apparently recognized not only by Schönberg himself (who, like Sigmund Freud when founding psychoanalysis, was frightened to make the final leap) but also by such composers as Strauss and Reger, who felt compelled to make decisions that led to the disintegration of musical modernism. Both composers made a *volte-face* after 1908, the year of Strauss's *Elektra* and Reger's *Symphonischer Prolog zu einer Tragödie*. Like Schönberg when he abandoned modernism in the direction of contemporary music, Strauss and Reger were forced by their historical predicament to choose between one path or the other. And any music history unbeholden to the doctrine that innovation alone matters in history and art will have to explore the causes of this "reaction" no less than those of the "revolution." Reger's String Quartet Op. 74 still bears comparison with Schönberg's Op. 7, and *Elektra* with *Erwartung* (1909). This enables us to speak of a musical modernism represented at the outset of the century not only by Schönberg but by Strauss and Reger as well. Yet only a few years later there was a seemingly unbridgeable gap separating the Strauss of *Der Rosenkavalier* (1911) and the Reger of the *Mozart Variations* (1914) from the

Schönberg of *Pierrot lunaire* (1912). In a word, modernism had split into modern music and classicism.

Strauss's and Reger's rejection of modernism—their presumably painful renunciation of a place at the "forefront of evolution," as the phrase went at the time—was obviously influenced if not directly occasioned by the shock of Schönberg's earliest atonal compositions. Schönberg, a Strauss protégé until 1908, encountered the elder composer's bewilderment in 1909 with his *Five Pieces for Orchestra,* Op. 16: "However, your pieces are such bold experiments, with regard both to their contents and to their sonorities, that for the moment I dare not present them to a more than conservative Berlin public." A few years later Strauss, speaking privately without the restraints of courtesy, put the matter in words so blunt that we can regard them as a sure sign of his perplexity in the face of the disintegration of modernism into avant-garde and regression. Strauss recommended Schönberg for a grant, "since one never knows what posterity will think about it," but went on to say, "I believe he would be better off shoveling snow than scribbling on manuscript paper."

A similar bewilderment can be sensed in Reger when, in 1910, he wrote the following lines in a letter to the pianist August Stradal: "I am acquainted with Schönberg's three piano pieces. I myself can't make heads or tails of them; I have no idea whether this sort of thing can still be called 'music.' My brain really is too old for this stuff! Now we'll have to put up with poor misunderstood Strauss and all that drivel. It's enough to turn a man conservative." It need hardly be added that it took more than Schönberg's bold break with tradition to "turn a man conservative": he had, after all, written the *Gurre-Lieder* (1901–3) and could not simply be dismissed out of hand as a cultist or worse. This break must be seen in conjunction with one of the less familiar aesthetic preconditions of the age in order to account for the split of the "progressive party" around 1910, a split that signaled the end of musical modernism.

This precondition was the notion of a "magnum opus," a monumental piece of music in the "sublime style." Musical genres stood in a hierarchy in which grand opera, oratorio, and the symphony were generally placed on a higher rung than the cantata and the string quartet, and far above the lied and the piano piece. In musical modernism around 1900, unlike contemporary music, this notion reigned virtually uncontested, an aesthetic heirloom of the nineteenth century which composers accepted as a matter of course. (Even Schönberg, unlike Webern, clung tenaciously to the notion of a magnum opus, remaining in this respect a representative of modernism. The proclaimed object of his twelve-tone method was nothing less than to revive the possibility of "large-scale form," whose internal coherence had been undercut by atonality.) Reger aspired relentlessly to the oratorio and the symphony in the "grand style" as his goals, even if, like Brahms, he repeatedly lost heart and left his projects unfinished.

By Reger's aesthetic premises, his works of 1908, the *Symphonischer Prolog zu einer Tragödie* and his setting of Psalm 100, indicate a penultimate evolutionary stage which, however, was never followed by an ultimate one. Given the problem

Reger was trying to solve, we have no trouble in understanding why, faced with Schönberg's atonality, he should turn his back in consternation on the musical progressivism he had till then helped to sustain. He realized that grandiose works of the sort he envisioned could never be written using the devices of atonality; on the contrary, that musical progressivism, as driven to extremes by Schönberg, tended in the opposite direction, namely, to aphorisms (or to text-related musical designs). A similar motive presumably guided Strauss, at least as a subcurrent in his historical reflection (which no composer of the nineteenth or the twentieth century could afford to do without, even if his only concern was the artistic success of his works). Contrary to histories that proceed from the subsequent fame of a work rather than from the historical situation at the time of its writing, Strauss's actual turnabout came, not with *Der Rosenkavalier* (1911), a comic opera that might have remained a stylistic intermezzo, but with *Die Frau ohne Schatten* (1919), his "official magnum opus," which stands to *Die Zauberflöte* (1791) in Strauss-Hofmannsthal's historical mythology as *Der Rosenkavalier* does to *Figaro* (1786). There is little doubt that his decision to write a "grand opera" in *Die Frau ohne Schatten* was influenced by Hofmannsthal: to judge from its subject matter, the Semiramis opera that Strauss planned (but Hofmannsthal assiduously avoided) could easily have continued along the same path as *Salome* and *Elektra*. With *Die Frau ohne Schatten*, however, Strauss irrevocably parted company with the musical modernism which he, along with Mahler and Debussy, Reger and Schönberg, had represented for two decades.

Fig. 74 Caricature of Richard Strauss. In Strauss's *Elektra* the size of the orchestra reached an extreme from which the composer himself recoiled in *Ariadne auf Naxos* by returning to a chamber music setting. Its growth was a perennial target for caricatures denouncing monumentality as noise, even to the grotesque extent of associating *Elektra* with the electric chair. Yet this expansion of the orchestral apparatus served not merely to generate mass effects but also to make instrumentation more refined and subtle, a fact studiously ignored by critics who clung to the obvious. (Frankfurt am Main, Stadt- und Universitätsbibliothek, Music and Theater Collection.)

The transition, shunned by Strauss, from musical modernism to contemporary music was tied to a shift of emphasis in the system of musical genres, a shift which, with perverse logic, turned apparently backward-looking genres into bearers of progressive tendencies. Around 1900 progressive composers still felt most at ease in the music drama and the symphonic poem, just as they had a few decades earlier when Franz Brendel construed the friendship between Wagner and Liszt into a "New German School." (Symphony and lied, as represented on the one hand by Bruckner and Mahler and on the other by Brahms, formed more or less neutral genres in late-nineteenth polemics.) Chamber music, however, was considered a genre attractive above all to the progressives' adversaries, who, it should be added, thought of themselves not as conservatives but simply as "solid musicians."

To audiences with fixed ideas as to which styles belonged to which genres, it must have been doubly perplexing that Schönberg dared to wage his "emancipation of dissonance" not only in the lied and piano piece but, of all places, in chamber music as well. Indeed, when we consider the aesthetics of reception, it is at first hard to see why the unresolved dissonances that scandalized the "solid musicians" and their more learned adherents were presented in string quartets and piano pieces instead of in music dramas and symphonic poems, which at least have texts and programs to justify their musical acerbities. (That opera requires direct, unreflected acceptance on the part of the audience is no reason to avoid using advanced musical devices. Opera permits an aesthetic "double standard": the composer can write for the initiated and at the same time for audiences who perceive difficult passages in the same spirit as film music, as musical illustrations of visual events that are riveting in themselves. This exonerates the listener from having to take the music at its full value.)

With chamber music, however, there are only two options: the listener either understands the music or knows that he does not. He cannot cling to a text or a program, nor can he wallow mindlessly in music whose continuity is vouchsafed by regular syntax and undisturbed functional harmony. Instead, he is forced to pursue the motivic-thematic logic to its nethermost ramifications lest the music appear as nonsense. Following the demise of tonality and the disintegration of "foursquare meter" into "musical prose," virtually the only factor that gave tangible meaning to music was the "developing variation" of motives. In other words, when Schönberg moved to atonality he took the chamber music aesthetic—the precedence of thematic-motivic manipulation over harmonic-metrical patterns of cadences and periods—so seriously that the listener was left with no alternative but to do the same. Modern music forced him to honor demands that originated in the legacy of chamber music.

This emphasis on the dialectic of genres, however, also causes us to revise our historical verdict of Reger's chamber works: they did not single-mindedly follow in the Brahms tradition but confronted problems arising from the historical predicament of turn-of-the-century modernism. Reger, as his biographer Max Hehemann observed, likewise tended toward "musical prose," and despite his apprenticeship with Hugo Riemann, he too undermined (but never abandoned) tonality. With Reger, tonality is no longer used to underpin a motivic-contrapuntal texture; on the contrary, his chord formations are justified by the melody on which they are, in a manner of speaking, "strung out." By dissolving traditional syntax at the same time that he shifted the emphasis from harmonic to motivic logic, Reger, as Rudolf Stephan has shown, clearly reveals intrinsic affinities to the beginnings or immediate forebears of contemporary music, affinities which he admittedly scuttled after 1908 but which form part of the historical and therefore the aesthetic substance of works such as his C-minor Piano Quartet, Op. 64 (1902), or the D-minor String Quartet, Op. 74 (1903–4).

Still, before motivic logic can yield "large-scale forms" instead of remaining trapped in musical aphorisms, it must be augmented by a device that we also encounter in symphonies and symphonic poems at the turn of the century: the technique, derived from sonata-allegro form, of presenting thematic contrasts in different orders of magnitude. The opening movement of Reger's D-minor String Quartet, Op. 74, a movement of truly symphonic proportions, illustrates how categories such as first and second theme, thematic contrast and manipulation, and exposition and development can still be viable even when the tonality is weak. The first thematic group presents a sharp internal contrast (m. 1 as opposed to m. 6), which in turn invites developmental treatment (m. 17) with the aim of returning to the opening idea (m. 29). The bridge is substantially an independent contrasting theme (m. 34); the fact that it gives rise to a passage resembling a development section and harking back to the two contrasting motives of the first group (m. 49) implies nothing less than that Reger has repeated a basic sonata-form pattern (thematic contrast followed by development, likewise the pattern of the first theme) in a larger order of magnitude. The second theme (m. 82), for its part, is related to the concluding group (m. 140)—a fourth theme following the first theme, "bridge," and second theme—as the first theme is to the bridge. The internal contrasts in the secondary theme (mm. 84 vs. 92) provoke a developmental passage (m. 117) whose destination is the first theme, and which forms a contrast to the concluding theme, a contrast that also motivates a development-like section (m. 161). Yet, at the same time, the first theme, plus bridge, and the second theme, plus concluding group, form, in a third order of magnitude, a conflict which then gives rise to the development section proper (m. 179). In sum, sonata-form categories pervade the entire movement from its structural details to its overall outline, and it would be wrong to view Reger's design, although virtually divorced from tonality, as symptomatic of formal decay.

Post-Wagnerian Opera

Richard Wagner's impact on the late nineteenth and the twentieth century was always mediated through his music but seldom limited to musical aspects alone (except in the case of Bruckner, a composer whom Brahms derided as "uncultured"). Indeed, his music became the vehicle for an extramusical influence of a force exerted by no other composer before or since, not even by Beethoven.

Yet there is a peculiar dialectic to Wagner's aesthetic: in *Oper und Drama* he justifies music solely as a means with drama as its end, whereas two decades later he concluded that drama must be viewed as "musical deed made visible." And this same dialectic has clearly been recapitulated in the subsequent history of his works, whether in the realm of politics or in music (to mention only the two extremes).

It is not enough to accuse the dyed-in-the-wool Bayreuth devotees—who cherished volume 10 of Wagner's collected writings as gospel truth and were less concerned with his music than with their own cultic hodgepodge of anti-Semitism, vegetarianism, and antivivisectionism—of using or abusing Wagner's music as a means with their *Weltanschauung* as its end. Rather, the crucial point is that even in political Wagnerianism, as in Wagner's aesthetic itself, a variant of Schopenhauer's metaphysic of music was ultimately able to gain the upper hand. The worst damage that Wagnerianism did to politics is to be found, not in any of the dogmas it propagated, not even in its anti-Semitism (with its specious physiological "arguments"), but rather in a far-reaching aestheticization of the political conscious or subconscious, a process we can see at work in, say, the development of Gabriele d'Annunzio. Its fateful consequence was to glorify violence with a euphoria deriving from the spirit of music. Music could no more rise above politics than vice versa: politics cast its shadow on music, and was infected by music's emotionally charged irrationality in return.

In the final analysis, then, it was the music and its elevation (as decreed by Schopenhauer and "enacted" by Wagner) to the realm of metaphysics which carried Wagnerianism into extramusical precincts and turned it into a force in its own right. This doubtless goes some way to explain why, alongside the one extreme of Wagnerian politics, it was also possible for an opposite extreme of Wagnerian absolute music to arise and gain influence even though Wagner rejected absolute music in theory. Aestheticization, though disastrous in politics, favored an attitude in the arts which could tolerate (against Wagner's intentions) the proliferation not only of absolute music but also of *poésie pure,* whose supporters in France were, not accidentally, Wagnerians such as Mallarmé and Verlaine.

Wagner's impact, then, was almost equally as strong in the symphony and symphonic poem, in chamber music and lied (genres thought in Bayreuth to be secondary if not extraneous), as in the musical stage, where, it was thought, he had brought the entire history of art to its appointed goal and destination. And in one respect Wagnerianism in late-nineteenth-century opera is fully comparable to Wagnerianism in nonoperatic genres as represented by Bruckner and Hugo Wolf (a Wagnerianism denied by their apologists in our century because of its polemical motivation in the nineteenth). Namely, the farther opera departed from the mythological music drama central to Wagner, the more likely it was to achieve aesthetic authenticity. Pfitzner's *Der arme Heinrich* (1893) is a romantic opera harking back behind the level reached in *Das Rheingold* (1854); Wolf's *Der Corregidor* (1896) is a comic opera, and Humperdinck's *Hänsel und Gretel* (1893) a fairy-tale opera. Of course there are obvious ties with individual facets of Wagner's oeuvre—from, respectively, *Tannhäuser* (1845), *Die Meister-singer* (1868), and *Siegfried* (1876), where myth crosses with the fairy tale *Von einem, der auszog, das Fürchten zu lernen*. To put it paradoxically, the path around Wagner led through Wagner. However, this little alters the fact that, even in the official Bayreuth view (assuming the Bayreutheans did not consider writing and composing superfluous altogether after Wagner), legitimate Wagnerianism lay in departing from mythological tragedy, in avoiding the overwhelming presence of Wagner's legacy by seeking refuge in musicotheatrical genres considered peripheral by Wagner himself.

Besides his operas and incidental music, Hans Pfitzner also wrote orchestral works, chamber music, choral pieces, and lieder, none of which can be dismissed as marginalia. In this respect he revealed a universality that was unusual for 1900 (unlike 1800), and which he shared with only one of his illustrious contemporaries, his bête noir and opposite number, Arnold Schönberg. Even so, although his universality is rooted equally in his personal style and in the style of the genres he cultivated, and is thus authentic rather than fabricated, this did not prevent him from emphasizing some genres over others. If we can characterize Schönberg as a chamber music composer even though his work is spread almost equally over all areas of music, Pfitzner's oeuvre centers on the lied—though this is not to contest the claim of his opera *Palestrina* (1915) to figure as his magnum opus.

Pfitzner apologists, while not denying that *Der arme Heinrich* (1893) is beholden to Wagner, attempted to construe its partial stylistic self-sufficiency as a historical step beyond Wagner. They also discovered in Pfitzner a proclivity toward "absolute music," toward the supremacy of music in drama, which caused him to avoid stage effects of the sort that not even Wagner spurned. This proclivity, they felt, proved an obstacle to the success of his operas with audiences so jaded that they took no less pleasure in *Carmen* (1875) and even *Cavalleria rusticana* (1890) than in *Tristan und Isolde* (1865). However, Wagner's dictum that drama is "musical deed made visible" implies nothing less than that, in the *Gesamtkunstwerk*, it is music, a prefiguration of "the inmost essence of the world" (as Schopenhauer would say), which has the final and decisive word. It was the common belief of all turn-of-the-century Wagnerian composers who adopted Schopenhauer's metaphysic—from Mahler and Strauss to Schönberg and Pfitzner—that music, whether in music drama, symphonic poem, or lied, articulates the meaning of the text, rather than vice versa.

The crucial difference between Pfitzner's and Wagner's musical dramaturgies lies not in their perfectly natural emphasis on the music but rather in the relation of music to the stage action and the text. Pfitzner, a self-consciously German composer, shared one preconception which distinguished the German aesthetic of opera not only from its Italian and French counterparts but from

Wagner's aesthetic as well: that the main complement to music in musical drama is the written word rather than the stage events, or "pantomime." German operatic theory proceeded from the "word-note relationship" rather than from the theatrical function of music, and in Pfitzner's case this led to operas that saw language, rather than stage configurations, as the primary medium for communicating his "poetic idea." However, the aesthetic associated with the "word-note relationship" is that of a lieder composer in the Schumann tradition. This is not to say that Pfitzner, an authoritative conductor and producer of opera, was "untheatrical" in any obvious sense of the term. He was, however, and greatly to his disadvantage, one of those Wagnerians who took Wagner too seriously as a poet, a writer of words, and not seriously enough as a dramatist, an arranger of scenarios. (Wagner's actual "poetry" lies not in his texts but in his images.)

Act 2 of *Der arme Heinrich* consists of a single situation: Agnes attempting to convince her parents that she has been ordained to cure the knight Heinrich of his illness by sacrificing her life. She senses this mission as a religious experience, as an opportunity to partake of the image of Christ, and her mother's abrupt switch from desperate remonstration to ecstatic acquiesence is meant to be understood as enlightenment. Thus, unlike Gerhart Hauptmann, whose stage version concentrates the psychology of Hartmann's epic, Pfitzner treats the material as a legend pure and simple, but a legend which can nevertheless hold its own as a modern drama, since the miracle, the crux of the plot, can be made credible from the spirit of the music. The crucial moment, however, the inner transformation of the mother, seems curiously lifeless and vague, since Pfitzner was loathe to adopt the key element in Wagner's musicotheatrical "strategy": his paradoxical combination of an "art of transition" (or anticipation) and the shock effect. True, the orchestral motives underlying the melodic declamation (A–B–G and B♭–D♭–G♭) previously appeared as leitmotivs (the Agnes motive and the Doctor motive), and thus convey a past history. But they are so nondescript and unassuming that they meet none of the conditions Wagner would have posed in the same situation. (Unless we want to do Pfitzner a grave disservice, we had better not apply a paradigm of "strategic motives" as represented by the dramaturgy of the Sword Motive in Act 1 of *Die Walküre*.) These two motives fail to conjure up memories linking the present to the past in a long backward glance, nor do they have the force of a sudden reversal, illuminating the dramatic moment musically as a point of arrival in an interior plot. Instead, Pfitzner, like a true lieder composer, places his trust in the written word (of dubious poetic value in the case of James Grun's libretto), rendering it audible by dint of his musical asceticism, but without, as Wagner demanded, "externalizing it for the sensory faculties" in the music and on stage.

To compare Pfitzner's romantic legend with Engelbert Humperdinck's almost contemporaneous fairy-tale opera *Hänsel und Gretel* (1893) is as natural as it is problematical. In the first place, both are post-Wagnerian works that struck out on byways to avoid mythological tragedy; moreover, the educated classes, shocked and disoriented by the triumph of *Cavalleria rusticana*, considered the "neoromanticism" that appeared at the end of the century (in literature as well) an alternative to *verismo*. Yet it is by no means clear in what sense a work such as *Hänsel und Gretel*—whose worldwide success was acknowledged with equal satisfaction by Brahms and the Bayreuth clique, but which established itself as a Christmas opera for children and was yoked for decades with a musical nonentity like Josef Bayer's ballet *Die Puppenfee* (1888)—is deserving at all of a place in the history of musical composition, as opposed to the social or reception history of music.

Humperdinck's amalgam of Wagnerian style and folk song quotations or imitations made his fairy-tale opera easy prey for the critics, who applied the category of stylistic inconsistency as though stage music deserves to be judged by the same criteria as chamber music. On the other hand, this same amalgam has ensured its survival in the repertoire, something that would never have happened to a singspiel draped with nursery rhymes, or to a through-composed fairy-tale opera in the *Siegfried* or *Meistersinger* vein but without folk song allusions. To stylistic and generic purists, the first of these two opposing forms would have miscarried because of its spoken dialogue, the second because of the contradiction between its low genre and its lofty style, between fairy tale and pathos. (This is not to deny that Humperdinck strikes a successful balance between simplicity and sophistication in the Witch scene, where he adopts a *Siegfried*-esque combination of triadic melody, seventh and ninth chords, and chromatic modulation.) However, the heterogeneity that "saves" this work is the result less of conscious deliberation than of the accident of its birth: the piece originated as a few songs interpolated into a children's play, and then passed through the stage of singspiel with lied and ensemble numbers and spoken dialogue before becoming a through-composed opera. By incorporating the singspiel version, finished and complete in 1890, into the through-composed opera, however, Humperdinck was not completely able to patch over and obliterate the cracks and fissures resulting from the discrepancy between "closed" and "open-ended" form, between the operatic "number" and the "scene." This contradiction, apparent throughout the work, appears most glaringly in just those places where it is supposed to be reconciled, in passages where nursery rhyme lines such as "Suse, liebe Suse" are subjected to the technique of motivic manipulation with modulating sequences.

The success of *Hänsel und Gretel,* then, rested on two unforeseeable preconditions: on the willingness of the educated classes, unsettled by *verismo,* to accept a fairy-tale opera with folksong quotations and imitations as a work of art and a musicohistorical event (instead of dismissing it as children's theater), and on an aesthetically useful stylistic dichotomy that no highly trained and well-versed Wagner adept such as Humperdinck would have deliberately planned, but which nonetheless crept into his work through the vicissitudes of its genesis. Any criticism of the work which, like Rudolf Louis's (*Die deutsche Musik der Gegenwart,* 1912), clings to its "deficient sense of style" is as irrefutable as it is inappropriate. Opera and autonomous music obey different rules, and there is little sense in concocting style-critical arguments to inveigh against the historical good fortune that happened to befall a piece of musical theater.

In the 1850s Liszt, then in Weimar, promulgated comic opera as an alternative to mythological tragedy. From that time on it was a standing *donnée* of music criticism that, in addition to fairy-tale opera (as represented by Alexander Ritter before Humperdinck), comic opera also offered composers a chance to escape Wagner's shadow without committing themselves to *verismo,* which in Germany was held in bad odor aesthetically. Yet, except for *Die Meistersinger,* the high-quality German comic operas written in the late nineteenth century—Peter Cornelius's *Der Barbier von Bagdad* (1858), Hermann Goetz's *Der Widerspenstigen Zähmung* (1874), and Hugo Wolf's *Der Corregidor* (1896)—were unable to take hold in the repertoire, despite their initial success, and have become objects of periodic attempts at exhumation. Critics have attributed this fact to the weaknesses of their librettos (librettists invariably serve as the whipping boys of opera history, which is seen as the history of a monstrous waste of music). However, it would be not sophistry but an expression of a sense of justice to invert our historical perspective and proceed from the argument that, at a time when compositional technique made it difficult if not impossible to produce "authentic" comic opera (as opposed to "inauthentic" comic opera, meaning operetta), a few works were "saved by chance" through the lucky stroke of their librettos: *Die Meistersinger, Falstaff,* and *Der Rosenkavalier.* In other words, what we have to explain is not why an opera failed but why it succeeded.

Strictly speaking, the history of Italian opera buffa had reached its end with Rossini's *Il barbiere di Siviglia* of 1816. Verdi's *Falstaff* (1893) and, long before that, Donizetti's *Don Pasquale* (1843) are as it were posthumous works in the history of this genre, exceptions to the rule that nineteenth-century Italian opera was all but taken up with opera seria.

French *opéra comique* as represented by Boieldieu and Auber (and in turn by Donizetti) gave way shortly after mid-century to Offenbach's *opéra bouffe.* With this, comic opera passed out of compositional history in the narrow sense of the term, meaning a history interpretable or reconstructable as the continuing evolution of musical material. Throughout music history, comic opera has always been more a special late-eighteenth-century phenomenon than a permanent option, and in the nineteenth century, as in the seventeenth, it became precarious. Thus, we are not astonished to discover that it flourished hardly at all in Germany, where the Mozart tradition, Germany's sole national species of comic opera, was gradually overwhelmed by Wagner.

Originally, Hugo Wolf's *Der Corregidor* bore the subtitle "comic opera," a term he later discarded for "opera." After originally rejecting Rosa Mayreder's libretto, he ultimately accepted it without a single reservation, a change of heart that has long puzzled his biographers. Apparently he realized that, given the historical situation of "post-Wagnerian" opera, his sole hope of success lay not in a continuous buffo tone, nor in a mixture of parody and sentimentality, but rather in a combination of the tragic and the burlesque. The style of the times

Die musikalische Knusperhexe
(ENGELBERT HUMPERDINCK)

Fig. 75 Caricature of Engelbert Humperdinck. Humperdinck is here caricatured as the Witch in his own *Hänsel und Gretel*, apparently in allusion to the fact that this part, like the witch in *Faust*, can be cast for male voice. But the caricature is also meant to portray Humperdinck, with his attempted mixture of fairy-tale tone and Wagnerian style, as a musical corrupter of youth lurking behind nursery rhymes in order to entice the young into the perdition of Wagnerianism. (Frankfurt am Main, Stadt- und Universitätsbibliothek, Music and Theater Collection.)

tended to extremes in both directions, but not in the direction of simple merriment. (Beckmesser lurks behind the Corregidor, Hans Sachs behind Tio Lukas.) Dramaturgically, too, a farce is always a latent tragedy, and a tragedy a latent farce. Tio Lukas's jealousy monologue, where the cloak-and-dagger comedy threatens to turn tragic, has always been regarded as the most successful part of the work. The weakness of the final act, sealing the doom of the work as a whole, is not only to be found in the dramaturgical blunder of having the characters narrate events long known to the audience. It also, and above all, lies in the absence of a central ensemble number in which Frasquita, like Tio Lukas before her, could be brought musically to the brink of tragedy, though this time in a contemplative ensemble rather than a monologue (for the sake of structural variety). Wolf's artistic conscience forced him to adopt an elevated style, as is evident in the work's rapid harmonic rhythm, the dense fabric of its leitmotivs, and its thick orchestral counterpoint. Since this pointed him in the direction of serious opera anyway, the best way of dramaturgically saving *Der Corregidor* (which Wolf rightly recognized as an opera subject appropriate to the state of music in the 1890s) would have been to show more courage and resolution in pointing up the dialectic of burlesque and tragedy than he and his librettist were able to muster.

The choice of libretto was particularly problematical in comic opera, since, to put it simply, comedy is almost invariably more closely linked than tragedy to topical subjects and events, which in turn clash with musical form. The problem, in other words, lay in fashioning a text suitable for a musical setting but rising above sentimental effects. In the late nineteenth and the twentieth century, however, this same problem reared its head in serious opera, where librettos became at once more urgent and more difficult to write. When the operatic number gave way to the scena, libretto writing ceased to be a workaday matter of hewing to a set of more or less fixed rules. No longer did librettists simply squeeze subjects such as *Kabale und Liebe* into separate numbers and motivate transitions from cantabile to cabaletta, a process whose result was to a certain extent predictable in advance. To turn *Othello* into an opera made up dramaturgically of sung dialogue was a task without standards or precedents. Moreover, the *Gesamtkunstwerk,* at least in Wagner's original theory (subsequently modified by his reading of Schopenhauer but never retracted), had proclaimed the visible plot to be the actual "drama," with music and text subordinated to it as means to an end. This turned the mise-en-scène, the "realization" on stage of the "poet's intentions," from a peripheral to a central category of opera aesthetics. The increased importance of the director (leading after World War II to the phenomenon of *Regietheater,* or "director's theater") in turn placed additional demands on the libretto. (Wagner's stage writings may have been criticized for their poetic language, but this did not prevent the transition from "libretto" to "operatic poem," which he claimed to have brought about with *Der Fliegende Holländer* of 1843, from being generally accepted as an evolutionary leap which writers of opera texts could little afford to ignore.) Lastly, at least since Wagner's *Tristan* there had been a relentless and ultimately headlong increase in the sophistication and individualization of musical language, a process which a composer could escape only by sacrificing the historical "authenticity" of his work. This development harbored the danger of alienating audiences from post-1890 modernism (and later from twentieth-century contemporary music), a danger thought to be avoided most easily in opera by shifting the emphasis from the music to the libretto, which then ceased to function as a libretto at all. In extreme cases the music was demoted to an acoustical backdrop, at times illustrating the text, at times adding a dimension of depth psychology, but in any event evading structural perception, the sine qua non of any understanding of music as a language. (The discovery that audiences who detest Schönberg's music in the concert hall will accept it without a murmur as background film music is as fundamental as it is depressing.)

Thus, turn-of-the-century librettists were caught in a dilemma resulting from the disintegration of their craft, their need to employ compensatory poetic and theatrical devices in order to counteract the increasing unintelligibility of musical language, and the ascendancy of the director. One obvious way out of this dilemma lay in *Literaturoper*, the notion (anticipated by Mussorgsky in 1868 in *The Marriage*, his unfinished opera after Gogol) of adopting a spoken play unchanged, if abbreviated, as an opera text. The notion was taken up by Debussy in *Pelléas et Mélisande* (after Maeterlinck, 1902), Strauss in *Salome* (after Wilde, 1905), and again Strauss in *Elektra* (after Hofmannsthal, 1909) as a solution to the problem of the "post-Wagnerian" libretto. Eventually the *Literaturoper* proved as characteristic of our own century as it was unthinkable in previous eras of opera history. It was this problematical relation between the dramaturgy of *Literaturoper* and the language of musical modernism that provoked Strauss and Debussy, at the turn of the century, to write operas, and that drove Strauss in *Elektra* to the most extreme consequences available to him before he more or less lost heart in *Der Rosenkavalier* (1911).

Elektra is at once an esoteric and a popular work, an opera both for cognoscenti and for the specific audience which is, by its own criteria, more discriminating and, by objective criteria, less discriminating than that of spoken theater. This aesthetic duality, probably calculated in advance by Strauss, is symptomatic of a moment in history that was pressing forward to the *Literaturoper*. Hofmannsthal's text is made up of dialogues which, though appreciable as literature (where every detail is essential), we can also perceive directly as stage configurations without understanding a single word. Provided we know the outline of the story, Clytemnestra's confrontation with Electra and the recognition scene between Orestes and Electra are so heavily underscored in tableau or pantomime that not even performances that drown out the voices in orchestral polyphony are capable of distorting the work to the point of absurdity. Like the text, the musical setting can be appreciated in either of two ways, and to choose the coarser of the two is not necessarily to do aesthetic injustice to the work.

The orchestral accompaniment takes the form of a dense tissue of leitmotivs. Yet we would do the work more harm than good to assign pedantic labels to them. For however pointedly the Agamemnon motive declaims the name of the king, and however clearly the Aegisthus motive illustrates the regicide's hypocritical posturings, a motive only acquires its full meaning gradually in changing musical and literary contexts, and conversely its meaning in turn sheds light on its surroundings. Any interpretation of leitmotivs deserving of the name must therefore be more than an annotated table of themes: it must undertake the hermeneutical task of examining the intellectual content of the motives in the various transformations they are made to undergo. The difficulties faced by an adequate motivic analysis of this work (as yet hardly attempted) show the amount of esotericism inherent to *Elektra*, a piece which Strauss considered to mark an extreme which a composer may only attempt once before turning back.

On the other hand, the structure of the orchestral accompaniment in *Elektra* also permits a mode of perception unconcerned with the exact meaning of its

Fig. 76 Stage design for Richard Strauss's *Elektra*, Scene 1. For Strauss, given the historical predicament of post-Wagnerian opera, Hofmansthal's play *Elektra* was a veritable *trouvaille*. As a libretto it drove the Wagnerian confrontation between the archaic and the modern, between mythical detachment and a decadence rooted in psychoanalysis, to an extreme that enabled Strauss to take the music drama one step beyond Wagner. Its prehistoric setting, here represented by cyclopean masonry to symbolize the prison enclosing the dramatic agents, is the scene of a psychological drama expressed in sophisticated orchestral counterpoint with no noticeable break in continuity between interior and exterior, music and stage. (Frankfurt am Main, Stadt- und Universitätsbibliothek, Music and Theater Collection.)

musical and literary details. Namely, the listener can cling to the stage action and at the same time submit to the "wizardry of relationships" among the leitmotivs, not with an eye to their meaning but in a vague sense that they cohere on some unutterably sophisticated level. This gives the music the function of a psychological or psychoanalytical commentary to the images on stage, a commentary as riveting as it is difficult to capture in words.

All the same, even a motivic analysis that successfully advances from codification to interpretation will remain incomplete unless it is accompanied by a formal analysis to explode the misconception that, in music drama, the composer simply lets his pen be guided by the text in disregard of the principles of form.

Electra's monologue is divided along the lines of Wagner's scenas into "musico-literary periods" both linked to and separated from each other by characteristic motives or motivic constellations. These periods are generally sixteen to twenty measures long, with so few deviations that the listener can take his bearings on the music's periodic structure, expecting points of articulation to occur at regular intervals. These subdivisions, however, in turn condition the way we perceive the links that Strauss (again following Wagner's example) used to demonstrate an "art of transition" so sophisticated that it dissolves into an amorphous flux if we fail to perceive the periodic structure. For example, period IV (rehearsal number 42) takes a characteristic chord from period III, changing its triplets into syncopations. A few measures later these syncopations prove to be an accompaniment figure to the period's central motive, sometimes called the "motive of Agamemnon's shadow." This motive is in turn transferred from the fourth period, a dynamic crescendo, to the fifth (rehearsal number 44), the goal and climax of the crescendo, where it is combined with the Agamemnon motive, which now dominates the vocal part. And if period V is apparently a varied recapitulation of period II (five measures after rehearsal number 36), period VI presents a cantabile second theme (six measures after rehearsal number 46) that merges into a section resembling a development. In short, the division into "musicoliterary periods" interlocks with relics from the sonata-allegro tradition to impart formal solidity to the orchestral accompaniment, which would otherwise be a shapeless motley of leitmotivs with poetic associations.

Being a tragedy based on a mythological plot and a fabric of leitmotivs, *Elektra* is obviously a music drama—though this is not to say that Strauss's choice of genre (not expressly mentioned in his score) is necessarily a measure of his dependence on Wagner. It would be misleading, however, to call *Pelléas et Mélisande* a *drame lyrique*, if only to underscore its distance (staunchly insisted upon by French critics) from Wagner, or more precisely from its latent models *Tristan* and *Parsifal*. Except in a few passages of stylistic weakness and complacency, Debussy is leagues apart from Massenet. It is not fortuitous that Debussy preferred the company of writers to that of musicians, and his sole opera, composed between 1892 and 1902, seems accordingly to owe its conception less to the *drame lyrique* than to its literary namesake, the lyric drama.

As was already mentioned, Debussy adopted Maurice Maeterlinck's play unchanged, if somewhat abbreviated (by cutting the servant scenes he made his opera even more abstract and historically intangible than the original play). As a lyric drama Maeterlinck's play, like Hofmannsthal's, belonged to a genre that emerged not so much from a continuous, century-long formal tradition like tragedy and comedy as from the state of fin-de-siècle literature, from the difficulties faced by the drama around 1900, whether symbolist or naturalist. Lyric drama apparently sought an escape from a crisis in dramatic literature as a whole, a crisis which might best be understood historically as a problem of dialogue, of interpersonal conflicts enacted in statements and rejoinders. For centuries postmedieval European drama had taken shape in the medium of dialogue; with Maeterlinck, however, the dialogue is constantly in danger of asphyxiating in the silence that surrounds it (this is evidenced most strikingly in a piece like *Les aveugles* of 1891, where the characters would not speak at all if not forced by their blindness to exchange a few scraps of language). In *Pelléas et Mélisande* language is nothing but a thin veil covering the silence that reigns between the characters, less agents in the plot than objects of an inscrutable destiny. The key moments in the drama are those of a sudden hush, when we sense the abyss separating the characters. *Pelléas et Mélisande*, like turn-of-the-century lyric drama as a whole, is a play about anxiety and death wishes (one decisive moment in the play, the scene in the subterranean vaults, hints between the lines at a murder that narrowly escapes taking place).

In *Pelléas et Mélisande* the lyricism that gives the lyric drama its name resembles a poetic arabesque, which, as Wagner would have put it, causes "silence to resound." And if, in Debussy, the lyric drama sought fulfillment in music, it might never have come into existence in the first place were it not for the influence of the music drama, whose "orchestral melody" had been characterized by Wagner as "silence resounding." After all, the lyric drama was itself the product of decades of French literature marching under the banner of Wagnerianism. In this sense, *Pelléas et Mélisande* would be a "post-Wagnerian opera" for literary reasons alone, reasons which in turn had consequences for music.

Debussy used speech to capture the essence of melody in the guise of recitative. From the very outset, even among otherwise hostile critics, his handling of speech was lauded as an exemplary musical rendering of French prosody. Yet, as important as a precise understanding of the words may be in the lyric drama, which thrives on poetic detail, it is obvious that the dramatic focus will fall on the orchestral setting in musicotheatrical scenes where the dialogue, instead of reaching a conclusion, repeatedly turns into silence, making us sense the frailty and remoteness of the characters. Still, and despite its leitmotiv technique (which Debussy scorned but nevertheless appropriated from Wagner), the "orchestral melody" of *Pelléas* is so radically different from Wagner's that we hesitate to apply the Wagnerian terminology to them both, thereby implying that they are intrinsically related. The motives referring to characters (Golaud, Mélisande, and Pelléas) and those symbolizing objects ("Golaud's ring") or meaningful surroundings ("in the woods") are leitmotivs in the sense that they recur in ever-new contexts instead of being restricted to the scene of their first appearance. Yet they differ from their Wagnerian models or counterparts in that they seldom if ever undergo a development capable of being called symphonic, except in a few interludes added later where deadline pressure forced Debussy to resort to traditional Wagnerian devices, resources whose traces he otherwise studiously expunged from his works. With Wagner, however, symphonic development predominates to such an extent that the visible drama seems to do little more than mirror on stage the drama of the leitmotivs. Debussy despised thematic-motivic manipulation as blatant pedantry (thereby incurring the wrath of d'Indy) and tended during the course of a scene to dissolve rather than elaborate the motives that emerge as symbols from the orchestral background. To put it another way, he is a composer who retracts rather than expands. In psychological and music-dramaturgical terms, this means that he confronted Wagner's technique of escalation, expressed in an almost insatiable lust for sequences, with a technique of reduction that ultimately leads the music into silence. It is his tendency to retract, not his use of musical symbols, that reveals his proximity to the literary current unjustly, or at least confusingly, known as "symbolism." If the lyrical process in Mallarmé's poems consists in "retracting" the meaning of the words until they stand as ciphers for the unutterable, a similar process takes place in Debussy's music as the nominal meanings attached to his leitmotivs gradually fade so as to make way for premonitions arising from anxiety, the psychic core of fin-de-siècle lyric drama.

Melodrama and *Verismo*

One of the historian's most basic discoveries is that events which coincide chronologically may seem to belong to different eras. In part, this "noncontemporaneity of the contemporaneous" is accounted for by the different speeds at which change takes place in parallel historical traditions. Thus, the hiatus marked in Germany around 1890 by works such as Strauss's *Don Juan* and Mahler's First Symphony, works heralding the transition to (or "dawn" of) modernism, is matched in Italy by Pietro Mascagni's *Cavalleria rusticana*. In view of this, we are tempted to conclude that "evolution" in Italian opera and in German instrumental music or music drama must be measured with different yardsticks, and that basically, apart from stylistic differences between romanticism and *verismo*, opera as Italian composers imagined it was virtually impervious to radical change. (Naturally, those differences that do occur will seem less significant to an outsider than to an observer who has grown up in the Italian tradition. This fact, a source of distortion in one direction or another, must in turn be made the object of historical reflection, alerting us to hidden premises so as to minimize their influence.)

The libretto of *Cavalleria rusticana* is based on a play by Giovanni Verga that represented *verismo,* an Italian variant of naturalism. However, this by no means implies that musical *verismo* is a genuine analogue of its literary counterpart. Indeed, as Eugen Voss has shown, the differences between them are so glaring that one can doubt whether, and if so to what extent, it is meaningful at all to speak of *verismo* in opera, or to take this terminology at its aesthetic face value instead of using it as a quick guide for orientation. Mascagni sacrificed one of the basic preconditions of Verga's plot, social criticism in the Zola mold, to a dramaturgy deriving from the opera seria tradition as founded by Rossini. Without this Rossinian prop, the changes he advanced would have turned into experiments ensuring the work's failure.

In Verga's play Lola abandons Turiddu because he is a poor peasant and Alfio a rich teamster. Turiddu's feigned love for Santuzza is merely a ruse to provoke Lola, who has wounded his self-esteem. Conversely, Santuzza's treachery, which brings about the work's climax, the murder of Turiddu by Alfio, is her way of exacting revenge on Turiddu for abusing her feelings to his own ends. With Mascagni, on the other hand, the plot is largely a drama of emotions based on love and jealousy in the abstract and divorced from any particular place and time. Verga's social motivation vanished when the play was recast into a libretto. Instead of functioning as a major factor, the milieu merely serves as a picturesque backdrop, even if it governs the musical form for long stretches at a time.

Mascagni's musical dramaturgy, then, follows the rules of melodrama rather than of realism. This is demonstrated at a crucial moment, in the duet between Santuzza and Turiddu (No. 8), when the end of the cantabile section (Andante Appassionato) casually turns into a forced unisono (Maestoso) even though the two characters, for all their melodic unanimity, are motivated by completely contradictory emotions. The interior catastrophe, the duet's ultimate goal, is postponed to an appendix to the number itself. We are even tempted to maintain that the formal principle of Mascagni's "verismo" lies in leaving the basic outline of Italian opera intact and adding a few dashes of naturalism as picturesque elements to enhance interest without endangering convention. As the Goncourt brothers had predicted, naturalism reverts to aestheticism. (Moreover, the numbers that have given this work its virtually undimmable popularity, despite all aesthetic objections to the contrary, are precisely those that paint the work's locale rather than undergirding its plot: the opening chorus, No. 1; the prayer, No. 2; the *Intermezzo sinfonico*, No. 10; and the brindisi, No. 11.)

Mascagni's only nod toward naturalism, implying a break with operatic convention, is his omission of a finale to assemble the dying characters into a musical tableau with the survivors. Turiddu's murder takes place offstage, and the denouement is marked by nothing but the cries of his mother and Santuzza, confronted with the catastrophe. Still, this is not to say that Turiddu, the tenor, is denied the privilege of a concluding aria. The only problem is that this aria, a farewell to his mother, precedes the climax instead of echoing it lyrically as tradition demanded (thereby conveying a false reconciliation rooted in the musical form alone and not in the substance of the drama). This abrupt switch to naturalism—a mere appendix in the duet, where it was outweighed by the cantabile—receives added dramaturgical emphasis at the end of the opera simply by demarcating its end.

Musical *verismo*, then, differs from its literary counterpart by being melodramatic at the price of a crucial element of naturalism, social criticism. The notion of operatic *verismo* is thus something of a contradiction in terms, prompting a historian less to ask whether, or to what extent, the concept is tenable than to wonder how the term arose in the first place. Apparently it was precisely melodrama, the aesthetic opposite of realism or naturalism, that provoked contemporaries to refer to turn-of-the-century Italian opera as *verismo,* namely, because it drove this melodrama to such extremes.

As a category of art history realism means, not the presentation of one reality or another, but an attempt to elevate a part of reality previously considered "unworthy of art" into an object presentable in painting, literature, or music. In turn-of-the-century popular aesthetics (which a historian has to take seriously, no matter how low his opinion of them as philosophy), naturalism was viewed, not without a shudder, as an art that wallowed in coarse, filthy, and repulsive subjects. Seen in this light, it was doubtless the brutal aspects of *Tosca* (1900), *Madame Butterfly* (1904), and *La fanciulla del West* (1910) that caused Puccini to be ranked among the musical *veristi.* Another, more trivial reason was that he abandoned the customary historical costume for modern dress, a break in operatic tradition which, though picturesque in its own right, made the crudities of the plot more palpable to the audience than could have been possible in a Renaissance setting.

In short, a historian who examines terminology for insight into the ideas used by an age to articulate its own identity will come face to face with a bewildering fact: the excessive melodrama considered a mark of "romanticism" in the age of Scribe, Dumas, and Hugo was declared to be "verismo" half a century later.

Yet this naturalism versus melodrama perplex was not simply a matter for aesthetic lucubration; it was also a problem of musical dramaturgy reaching deep into the inner makeup of the works themselves. *Madame Butterfly* was conceived by Puccini as a "monodrama" in which the antagonists—Pinkerton and Sharpless, Yamadori and Suzuki—are simply adjuncts supplying dramaturgical machinery to an interior drama within Cho-Cho-San, her metamorphosis from a life as a geisha to an inextricable and hopeless passion and finally to an acceptance of death. Yet the great duet at the end of Act 1, a duet whose melodic urgency and sophistication Puccini was never to surpass, looms so large in the musical dramaturgy that we refuse to see Pinkerton as nothing but an arrogant and deplorable Yankee whose cowardly bravado and lack of imagination are the causes of Butterfly's misfortune. He is drawn into the cantilena by Cho-Cho-San as though he were functioning as Puccini's musical mouthpiece, as though the artist had momentarily lost his detachment to his own heroine. So irresistible is the cantilena that audiences actually imagine this trivial if durable plot to be a story of love and happiness betrayed. In the true, realistically conceived plot, Pinkerton is too mediocre, too much a prisoner of his racial prejudices to help Butterfly, a victim of her passion, to the higher right which she deserves by virtue of that very passion. In short, the realistic stage events which Puccini's librettists adopted from Belasco's play are disfigured beyond recognition by an overlay of melodrama that transmutes Pinkerton's uneasy conscience, plagued with misconceptions, into a clear one. This melodrama demonstrates once again that, in opera, the dramatic intention can be dramaturgically weaker than the music.

Local color, or milieu painting, was one of the key features of nineteenth-century opera, where it served a dual function. First, it allowed composers to add songs, choruses, dances, and illustrative instrumental pieces to the numbers that make up the structure of the drama, thereby enriching the music without complicating the plot. (Complex intrigues, a prerequisite for adding dramaturgically relevant scenes, were appropriate for eighteenth-century librettos, which turned again and again to the same subjects, but not for those of the nineteenth century, which sought fresh material. Novel plots tend toward simplicity so as to remain intelligible.) This fondness for local color, for the exotic, folkloristic, or archaic, enlarged the musical palette and kept stylistic devices from becoming stale, but without puzzling audiences by parting with tradition. It also offered an escape from a dilemma that plagued opera composers during the period of musical modernism, in the movement that led from Wagner's *Tristan* (1865) to Berg's *Wozzeck* (1925) and *Lulu* (1937): either they jeopardized theatrical effectiveness by using a modernist style, or they sacrificed stylistic modernity to theatrical effectiveness and thereby lost all claim to historical "authenticity." Local color, however, which seemed "new" and yet was immediately accessible, offered a refuge to opera composers who felt unequal to the aesthetic problems imposed upon their genre by modernism.

If the 1870s and 1880s, both in opera and in instrumental music, were dominated by an exoticism conjuring up a musical phantasmagoria of the Near East, a few decades later Puccini discovered the Far East (*Madame Butterfly*, 1904, and *Turandot*, 1926) and Paris of the recent past (*La Bohème*, 1896) as milieus with tantalizing and unusual colors but as amenable as the Renaissance or the late Middle Ages to melodramatic treatment, the mainspring of Italian opera. Although *verismo* adopted a realist or naturalist pose by choosing subjects from normal life and the present day, from the standpoint of intellectual history it can be viewed as a variant of exoticism, the appeal of the faraway and remote. In opera, after all, nineteenth-century Paris was a milieu fully as unusual, and therefore as picturesque, as China and Japan.

Local color had the dramaturgical function of painting the background of the plot, but this function was by no means fixed and immutable. True, scene 3 of *La Bohème*, the street scene (in which Puccini depicts the snow flurries as realistically as the frozen cityscape), functions as an introduction to Mimi's duet with Marcel and to the Terzetto, the turning point in the drama. Yet in scene 2, stylistically the most advanced in the opera, the Quartier Latin does more than provide a setting where the bohemians can mingle with street vendors and *flaneurs*. Indeed, it serves as the actual subject matter. The climax of this scene, Musette's Waltz, is a self-presentation not only of Musette as a character but of the entire milieu. In *verismo*, milieu moves center stage as a musicodramatic "agent."

A comparison with scene 2 from Gustave Charpentier's *Louise* (1900), a street scene at the foot of Montmartre, reveals that this tendency to use milieu as a dramatic agent, as evidenced in *La Bohème*, was still undeveloped. In Puccini's

Fig. 77   Stage design for Giacomo Puccini's *La Bohème*, Act 2. Here we have a Parisian streetcorner transplanted to the theater in the way the twentieth century viewed the "capital of the nineteenth century," namely, with the eyes of Utrillo. On the opera stage this scene was scarcely less exotic than the Far East or the Golden West. Italian *verismo* sought unusual, picturesque settings—Japanese or Chinese, Californian or rural Sicilian—revealing unmistakably that the naturalistic vein in opera, besides being merely an adjunct to melodrama, represented a form of aestheticism even more glaring than the novels of the Goncourt brothers. (Milan, Archivio Fotografico G. Ricordi.)

work the cries of the street urchins and vendors merge seamlessly with scraps of conversation from the café customers and passersby. Even if its parallel triads sound somewhat recherché, the resultant ensemble as a whole is a compact and formally self-contained vocal and instrumental number whose ingredients are developed according to the strictures of motivic-harmonic logic. (Puccini was always willing to learn from the avant-garde in order to add unusual touches to his basically conventional musical dramaturgy.) Even the "naturalisms" in the cantabile sections differ in degree but not in kind from the countermelodies of the traditional *aria con pertichini*.

Charpentier, on the other hand, a composer with a deficient sense of form but sound dramaturgical instincts, uses characteristic musical details ("picturesque" instrumental motives and striking vocal phrases) so freely and disjointedly that the musical texture disintegrates, or at least shows cracks and fissures. Leitmotiv technique, the orchestral counterpart to "realistic" declamation, serves merely as a device for creating a musical patchwork devoid of compelling musical logic. The harmony, likewise oblivious to large-scale coherence, forms daring passages of "wandering," "floating," or "free" tonality of the sort more familiarly associated with Arnold Schönberg a decade later. Unlike Puccini, Charpentier does not impart musicotheatrical coherence by means of formal unity (which, in *La Bohème*, relates to the picturesque details as a solid architectural skeleton relates to an exotically decorated façade). Instead, the profusion of apparently unrelated fragments gives rise to a unity of mood, and it is precisely by ignoring the constraints of musical logic that the details contribute to the work as a whole, a work whose underlying principle is the accumulation of heterogeneous parts.

Charpentier's portrait of Paris, as a chaotic (but not meaningless) jumble exuding an irresistible allure, is the core of the plot, not simply an additive. The duet between Louise and Julien at the end of scene 2 is not the dramaturgical crux of the scene, with the milieu merely functioning as a backdrop, but rather an explicit rendering in dialogue of an event whose principal agent is Paris itself, magnified (as in Zola's novels) from a realistic setting into a myth. In this event Louise flees the confines of her parental home in order to yield to the temptations of the city, the true protagonist of a work classified by Charpentier himself as a "musical novel." Here, as in Utrillo's paintings, Parisian audiences recognized their own natural environment. (In view of the mythical aura enshrouding the "capital of the nineteenth century," it is hardly surprising that the work also met with success outside Paris, though to a lesser extent.)

It was thoroughly typical of Zolaesque naturalism, as represented by Charpentier's "musical novel," that *verismo* should ultimately turn into mythology by casting the background milieu as the principal dramatic agent. For an eclectic composer such as Franz Schreker, however, the historical situation at the outset of the century provided an opportunity to adopt Wagner's notion of a drama "borne of the spirit of music" (i.e., the legacy of the "grand style") without thereby abandoning naturalism, the "sign of the times."

Schreker's *Der ferne Klang* (1910) was barred access to court theaters because of its naturalistic traits, which can best be understood aesthetically as violating the classicist codex of stylistic levels. It was not its depiction of brutality and drunkenness per se that caused offense but rather the fact that they were presented without the mitigating detachment of stylization in comedy or opera buffa, being instead motifs in a tragic plot which struck audiences a bit too close to home. In his essay "Wie entsteht eine Oper?" of 1930 Schreker describes how he "decided on the spur of the moment to part company with Wagner imitation" by "placing on stage simple, bourgeois, everyday people with their sometimes vulgar habits of speech—a daring undertaking." Admittedly, it would be going too far to call this social criticism, for the vulgarity that Schreker counterposed to the sublime was primarily motivated by aesthetic (or even aestheticist) considerations and must therefore be seen in the context of trends that made up the contradictory picture of turn-of-the-century modernism.

Der ferne Klang is by no means dominated throughout by naturalism: Paul Bekker wrote of its "penchant toward symbolism," which then took the upper hand in Schreker's second opera, *Das Spielwerk und die Prinzessin* (1913). The final scene of Act 1, a *Waldzauber* in the Wagnerian mold, abruptly transforms Grete's mood from despair to vague expectation, causing her to yield to a myth of "life" which, in reality, merely holds out the misery of prostitution as the sole alternative to oppressive small-town bigotry. Dramaturgically the *Waldzauber* is "borne of the spirit of music": it represents a mythical power which, as in Maeterlinck's symbolist dramas, directs the actions of the characters and cannot be reduced to a poetic symbol for intelligible psychic processes. To observers versed in classical dramatic theory, this abrupt change, this "total transmutation of the character's psyche" noted by Bekker, must be a sign of faulty construction. Yet the inconsistency is all the more revealing of the modernist, nonclassical dramaturgy assimilated (if only partially, as we shall see) by Schreker in *Der ferne Klang*.

To repeat, the conception of a musical drama "borne of the spirit of music" was a legacy from Wagner, which Schreker adopted in a nonimitative spirit. It also coincided at the turn of the century with a literary style, symbolism, which unexpectedly gave Wagner's aesthetic principle, that opera plots are "musical deeds made visible," an opportunity to be modernist in more than a merely musical sense. However remote Schreker may be from twentieth-century modern music (whose adherents branded him a "late romantic"), he is fully representative, along with Strauss and Schönberg, of musical modernism at the outset of the century.

Admittedly, it would be foolish to maintain of *Der ferne Klang* that its dramaturgical conception is unified and self-contained and to deny the work's eclecticism. When Fritz, in search of the "distant sound," strikes out on a path that only takes him farther away from his goal, and when in Act 2 he turns his back on Grete for becoming what he himself has unwittingly forced her to become, he is in both cases behaving in accordance with a time-honored tradition of classical drama: tragic irony. For this very reason he fails to find the path leading to himself and to his work. (As so often happens in bourgeois tragedy, narrow-minded morality is both a motivating factor and a condition without which the tragic mechanism would grind to a halt. The entire genre might be summed up in Hebbel's line "Darüber kommt kein Mann hinweg"—"No man can rise above it.")

Yet the music of *Der ferne Klang* raises its voice in protest, as it were, against the dramaturgy of bourgeois tragedy and its moral implications, expressing an interior drama to counteract the ostensible plot. Act 2 recapitulates the key situation of Act 1: Fritz, more in his imagination than in reality, again hears the Distant Sound, which he feared never to hear again, and once again he turns away from Grete without realizing that she and the Distant Sound he seeks are one and the same. What appears on the dramaturgical surface of the work to be Grete's fall from grace proves in the musical dramaturgy (Schreker took up Karl

Kraus's apology for the prostitute, as Berg later did in *Lulu*) to be the exact opposite: the overwhelming presence of the Distant Sound.

Schreker's eclecticism is an expression of a stage in music history as obscure to its contemporaries as it is confusing to the present-day historian, and opinions as to what is or is not connected with what diverge to an unusual degree. We hear as many claims as denials that Leoš Janáček's operatic realism, as expressed in his choice of subject matter and his handling of language, is a Moravian species of *verismo*—that is, that his *Jenůfa* of 1904 (revised in 1908 and again in 1916) is a counterpart to *Cavalleria rusticana* (1890), a work he held in inordinately high esteem. Yet neither the thesis of a "zeitgeist" transcending national boundaries, nor the antithesis of the primacy of the Czech national character or of a specifically Slavic realism represented by Mussorgsky and Janáček, can account for the work's unique mixture of old and new. Stylistically, *Jenůfa* marks a transition to twentieth-century modern music; indeed, Janáček's works have been heard in this spirit ever since the 1920s. At the same time, however, the narrowness and backwardness of the opera's rustic setting seems to be a dramaturgical precondition that enabled Janáček to reconstitute the bourgeois tragedy, a species of drama which, given the state of literature and social history at the turn of the century, actually belonged to the past. (The plot of the libretto, adopted by Janáček from a play by Gabriela Preissová, recalls Hebbel's *Maria Magdalene* of 1846, though the similarities may result from generic stereotypes rather than a direct influence.)

Yet nothing could be more wrong than to construe an abstract contradiction between the archaic premises of Jenůfa's tragic entanglement with the Kostelnička and the modernist style which Janáček, living in provincial isolation, evolved step by tentative step with astonishing singleness of purpose. For Janáček's evident proximity to twentieth-century modern music is closely related to the folkloristic trends that he pursued—and that musically vindicate his choice of a tragedy "from Moravian peasant life." *Jenůfa*'s stylistic ambiguity, the merging (or transmutation) of archaism into modernism, serves a dramaturgical function in its own right, a function detectable even in the work's details.

In the first act of the opera Jenůfa's relation to Števa, the man by whom she is pregnant (and to whom, according to village morality, she is totally beholden), is broken off the moment she upbraids him for again being drunk. This does not have to be expressed in words in order to be perfectly clear as a stage gesture. The remainder of the scene proceeds in a mood of tortured futility, which is given a tragic aspect by the choral song (intended to be heard from Jenůfa's perspective rather than enjoyed as a folkloristic interpolation) and by the high-spirited dance which Jenůfa is reluctantly persuaded by Števa to join. The "wildness" of the dance, specifically mentioned in the score, is at once a sign of exuberance in the exterior plot (a rustic tableau) and an expression of desperation in the interior drama taking place within Jenůfa. Janáček, a dramaturgically motivated rather than an abstract composer, has incorporated the conflicting elements of this scene into his music: the (for Jenůfa) heartrending levity of the

Fig. 78 Leopoldo Metlecovitz: Poster for Giacomo Puccini's *Madame Butterfly.* Unlike most Italian operas, which remain in the audience's memory as a conglomeration of tumultuous scenas in heightened arioso, *Madame Butterfly,* notwithstanding the great duet at the end of Act 1, is recalled largely by the image of the waiting Butterfly, now a modern myth. The effectiveness of this work remains undiminished by criticism of its sentimentality, and probably resides not least in the fact that its key scene, though devoid of action, has entered the stock of archetypal images on which the human imagination thrives. (Milan, Museo Teatrale alla Scala.)

chorus, seemingly a folk-song quotation; the ambiguously uninhibited dance; and the orgiastic conclusion, resembling a force of nature. He does this by progressing from a major tonality in the chorus to a folklike modality and finally to a bitonality hovering at the brink of twentieth-century modern music. Retaining the same motives, the music replaces E major with G♯ Phrygian (in a strange Phrygian harmonization), which in turn gives way to a juxtaposition of A♭ minor and F♯ minor (Ex. 61). Nor are we being unjust to the work by interpreting these changes of tonality as symptomatic of a musical dramaturgy that took full advantage of the ambiguity inherent in its moment in music history.

Example 61

Program Music and the Art Work of Ideas

For all its seeming continuity, the debate over program music which raged from the eighteenth to the twentieth century was conducted with changing premises and directed at changing objects. At the turn of the century it was waged under the banner of an aesthetic as natural and self-evident to composers of the time (from Strauss and Pfitzner to Mahler and Schönberg) as it was consigned to the ash heap of history by their successors: the aesthetic of Schopenhauer, elevated on Wagner's authority to a metaphysic of music in an age of positivism. In the decades of "musical modernism" absolute music and program music, symphony and symphonic poem, were linked in a manner that flies in the face of popular aesthetic clichés about the "formalism" of the one and the "formlessness" of the other. But this link will remain incomprehensible unless we consider the assumptions that underlay large-scale orchestral music in the minds of the composers who determined the course of historical evolution.

Schopenhauer believed that "the true essence of things" is to be discovered in feelings and emotions. These, he felt, are expressed by music in accordance with their "form" but "without content"—that is, they are devoid of object and motive. However, it is precisely by being divorced from their accustomed nexus of empirical conditions that feelings manifest their true essence in music:

> All conceivable exertions, excitations, and externalizations of the Will, all of those processes of the human psyche which Reason places under that broad negative concept, Feeling, are expressible by means of the infinite number of conceivable melodies. But they are only expressible in the generality of their form alone, without content; only in accordance with the thing-in-itself, not its appearance; only the innermost spirit, as it were, not the body.

In other words, Schopenhauer inverts the customary notion that, in vocal pieces, the text gives the work its intelligible "meaning," which is then decked out with "emotive reflections" by the music. Instead, he proposes that the feelings reflected in music represent the work's actual "meaning," any additional literary text or stage event remaining purely secondary. "This intimate relation between music and the true essence of things," he continues, "also accounts for the fact that whenever a scene, plot, event, or setting is given a fitting musical accompaniment, the music seems to unlock its innermost meaning." For Schopenhauer, there are no hard and fast boundaries between images associated with instrumental music, the programs of program music, and the texts of vocal music: all, in relation to the essence of the music, fall under the negative heading of accidental properties. "This explains why music can be assigned a poem to produce song, a visual representation to produce pantomime, or both to produce opera. These separate images of human existence, when assigned to the general language of music, are never connected to it with universal necessity, nor are they equivalent to it. Rather, they stand to it in the relation of an arbitrary example to a general concept."

When Wagner adopted Schopenhauer's aesthetic he gave a curious twist to the thesis that theatrical or linguistic dimensions merely function as interchangeable commentaries, which can be used to elucidate the music. In Wagner's view, extramusical elements can be helpful or even indispensable as stimuli and points of departure, but remain secondary in the resultant acoustic creation, the object of aesthetic contemplation. As he wrote in his "open letter" of 1857, *Über Franz Liszts Symphonische Dichtungen*: "On this point we are therefore in agreement, and grant that, in this human world, divine music must be given a binding—even, as we have seen, a conditioning—dimension in order that its manifestation be possible." In Wagner's view, the elements that condition the possibility of music are language, dance, or stage action: music requires a "formal motive," a reason for its existence, in order to come into being and manifest its potential. However, like a true Schopenhauerean, he distinguishes the metaphysical (or "divine," as he calls it) essence of music from its empirical trappings, the conditions of its origin "in this human world." That music cannot come into being, or take shape in the composer's imagination, without an extramusical "formal motive" does not preclude the possibility that a sensitive listener can penetrate from the "appearance" and conditionality of music to its "essence," to a vision of the "Will" which, according to Schopenhauer, constitutes the substance of music. "Formal motives" may be part of the genesis of music, but they are not the essential factor in its claims to aesthetic validity.

The consequences of this view for the theory of program music were strange enough. Roughly, Schopenhauer adepts felt that it was permissible to resort to programs as "formal motives" or hermeneutic vehicles when writing or listening to music because they left the substance of music untouched. The only argument against program music which struck a nerve in the Schopenhauer-Wagnerian camp was the proposition that a work needed its literary props because its internal musical coherence was flawed. Music, an image of the "innermost essence of the world," had to be self-consistent rather than dependent on the structure of—interchangeable—"appearances" that might help to elucidate it. Thus, if Otto Klauwell, in his *Geschichte der Programmusik* (1910), defined program music as "sidestepping the laws of musical form and adapting the norms of its development to extramusical factors at every step of the way," we can easily understand why Richard Strauss abandonded the term, saying: "What these people call program music doesn't exist. It is a nasty epithet from the lips of those with no ideas of their own." New forms beyond the comprehension of an Otto Klauwell, who therefore denies their status as art, are ascribed to the unwholesome influence of "extramusical" ideas or circumstances. Strauss, on the other hand, insists that it is sheer bigotry to dismiss nonschematic forms as "formless" instead of investigating their individual formal principles, and that neither the existence nor the nonexistence of a program has the slightest bearing

Fig. 79 Emil Orlik: *Gustav Mahler,* charcoal drawing, 1902. Orlik portrays Mahler not in a histrionic conductor's pose but in a posture that exudes composure and self-possession, thereby heightening all the more the impression of impassioned suffering in his facial features. Mahler's personality and music have always called for clear-cut reactions, both during his lifetime and posthumously, and scarcely leave a middle path between enthusiasm and revulsion. (Vienna, Österreichische Nationalbibliothek.)

on whether a work does or does not have an internal musical logic: "A poetic program can inspire a composer to new formal conceptions, but wherever music fails to develop logically on its own—in other words, wherever the program is meant to function as a substitute—the result will be *Literaturmusik.*" In sum, regardless of whether it was or was not inspired by a program, a good piece of music has a self-contained musical logic with no need of extramusical props. For a musical form to be "essential" (with the program being a reflection of the music in the world of appearances) rather than "accidental" (with the program serving as the music's substance), it must stand on its own merits.

The poem by Alexander Ritter which Strauss had printed in the score of his tone poem *Tod und Verklärung* (1890) was written after the event as a poetic reflection of the completed work. We can view it as a commentary on Strauss's work rather than its program, or insist that when Strauss printed it in his score he incorporated it into his work as an aesthetic object. In either case, however, the musical form of Strauss's symphonic poem is, without a doubt, contrary to Klauwell's verdict, comprehensible in and of itself, although it is not enough to squeeze the piece into the Procrustean bed of sonata-allegro form and to laud its compatibility with leitmotiv technique (now transferred from the music drama to the concert hall) as a "synthesis."

If we divide *Tod und Verklärung* into sections of roughly equal duration (and any analysis that ignores temporal proportions will remain abstract), the vocabulary we feel obliged to adopt from the traditional doctrine of form proves to be little more than a makeshift. Terms such as "introduction" (page 5 of the Eulenberg score), "exposition" (p. 17), "development with truncated recapitulation" (p. 52), and "coda" (p. 95) may seem well-nigh unavoidable in a work of symphonic dimensions inviting comparison with sonata form. They are, however, if not wrongheaded, at best inadequate. The "recapitulation," restricted to a few bars from the introduction (p. 88) and main theme (p. 90), and the "coda," which seems to expand into the infinite (p. 95), stand in such glaring disproportion to each other that we are forced to abandon or at least augment these categories. For the "coda" is, in fact, also a final movement at the same time that it recapitulates not only the second theme, but also a third theme, which was appended to the first theme in the exposition (p. 41) and grew to become the culmination of the development section (p. 76). The second theme, in other words, functions as a transition to the final movement, and the third theme as its principal musical idea. As in the work's Lisztian prototypes, Strauss has fused a sonata-allegro movement with a multimovement sonata form, and the second theme is likewise a slow movement (p. 44) with a scherzo as its central section (p. 47). In sum, the concept of recapitulation, though not undermined entirely, has been profoundly modified. The change of function and shift of emphasis given to the themes in the finale are indications that this formal section is in a state of arrested metamorphosis into a separate movement. The "history" of the third theme—from rudimentary allusions in the slow introduction through its appearance as an appendix to the exposition and finally to its triumphant culmination in the development and its "transfiguration" in the coda—can be viewed as a thematic consequence of writing a multimovement work in a single movement. This implies nothing less than that, regardless of the work's program, its deviations from the sonata pattern represent a specific solution to a general formal problem posed most forcefully by Liszt.

In *Tod und Verklärung,* the technique of applying sonata-form categories in different orders of magnitude led to a form that is nonschematic without being arbitrary. If the first section as a whole is a slow introduction (of such exploded dimensions that the term only seems applicable at all because of the clearly anticipatory character of the themes), the second, the exposition, begins with a small-scale introduction of its own (p. 17). The continuation of the main theme (p. 23) forms a contrapuntal complex of motives with all the earmarks of a development section (p. 25). The varied return of the main theme (p. 37) then seems to function as a recapitulation, and it comes as no surprise that this varied version later represents the main theme during the large-scale recapitulation (p. 90).

This device of applying analogous structures at different orders of magnitude can also be regarded as a substitute for, or counterpart of, the classical principle referred to by Eduard Hanslick as "rhythm in the large." Haydn and Mozart could still counterpoise an initial musical unit with a second one, applying this technique in ever-increasing orders of magnitude, from beats and measures to phrases, periods, and groups of periods. However, following the disintegration of metrical-syntactic "foursquareness" (Wagner's term for this magnified antecedent-consequent principle), "rhythm in the large" gave way to a "multidimensional" use of sonata-form categories. Liszt's notion of a multimovement work in a single movement proved to be part of a larger technique extending from minute details to the overall formal design. This technique made it possible to write large-scale instrumental music even after periodic structure had crumbled into "musical prose." Hence, as far as the technical assumptions of the monumental style were concerned, at the stage of compositional evolution around 1900 there was little or no difference between the symphony and the symphonic poem.

The first movement of Mahler's Seventh Symphony (1904–5) drives symphonic dimensions to an extreme, but there is neither a program nor a motto or title to guide the listener through its labyrinth of themes and thematic metamorphoses. Though Mahler's symphonies, the late ones no less than the earlier ones, are clear instances of *Weltanschauungsmusik,* of the "art work of ideas," it is not only possible but appropriate to interpret them as self-sustaining formal-logical nexuses. Mahler's notion of form was typical of his era as a whole, and its substantive elements are the same as those employed in *Tod und Verklärung* to produce an idiosyncratic formal design which, however, does not risk unintelligibility by breaking radically with tradition. These elements are the ambiguity of many passages and a "multidimensional" use of sonata-form categories. The opening movement of his Seventh Symphony fuses exposition and development in such a way that, as Paul Bekker has suggested, the large-scale varied repeat of the exposition (three measures after rehearsal number 18) can also be interpreted as the first section of the development. Moreover, the entire exposition shows signs of "multidimensionality." The subsidiary idea (four measures after rehearsal number 10) that supersedes the main theme (rehearsal number 6) originated in the slow introduction but is closely linked rhythmically to the main theme. Thus, though relatively self-sufficient as a small-scale "second theme" because of its ties to the introduction, it never entirely loses its character as a continuation of the main theme. In a word, motivic association and formal function, both means for creating broad-based connections, are different sides of the same coin. Further, the existence of this small-scale "second theme" is sufficient to give the actual second theme, additionally distinguished from the main theme by a change of tempo, the character of a slow movement in the midst of the Allegro (four measures before rehearsal number 15). Thus, the notion of a multimovement work in a single movement, a notion deriving from the symphonic poem, is at work in this symphony as well. The concluding group of the exposition (two measures before rehearsal number 17) then takes on the character of a final movement by dint of its march rhythms. (This same group emerges from a motive in the slow introduction, two measures before rehearsal number 2, and is later transformed in the development section into a chorale, one measure after rehearsal number 32. This is yet another indication of the degree to which Mahler independently varies and develops his compositional parameters, whether rhythm or pitch.)

All Mahler analyses that proceed from the notion of formal integration are at once unavoidable and suspect. They are unavoidable in that we can hardly imagine any other way of explaining how movements spanning hundreds of measures can cohere and be heard as an irresistible progression with a force so compelling as to go far beyond a mere unity of "tone," no matter how evident that unity has been to Mahler's audiences. But they are also suspect, since any attempt to deny rather than comprehend the stylistic discontinuities in Mahler's works would be an abstract and pointless exercise in special pleading. This rift between formal coherence and discontinuous style (a rift that is less a shortcoming than one of those problems that breathe life into works of music) has implications which left their mark on the debates kindled by Mahler's seemingly casual attitude to banal and trite material. Schönberg insisted that Mahler's banalities, as clumsily as they intrude into the symphonic context, in fact merge seamlessly with the logic of his thematic and motivic work. Adorno, on the other hand, argued that it is precisely Mahler's stylistic discontinuities that make up the aesthetic essence of his works: they are the scars left by his attempt to salvage "lowbrow music" (long left behind by the intellectualization of "highbrow music") for symphonies which claimed, as Mahler himself put it, to do nothing less than "erect a universe."

Thus formal integration, stylistic discontinuity, and unity of "tone"—three categories difficult to interrelate—must be combined in any analysis that wishes to come to grips with the aesthetics of Mahler's works as well as their historical significance. The moment we isolate one of these factors from the others it becomes incomprehensible. Yet we even have trouble finding terms appropriate to the central category, Mahler's specific "tone," which from the very outset left audiences practically with no option between the extremes of addiction and revulsion. At the most we can warn against basic misconceptions. Important as this tone is to the effect of Mahler's works on a great many listeners, it would be wrong to yield to the temptations of popular aesthetics and explain it from the standpoint of Mahler the man. Biographical curiosity is not an aesthetic concept, and we must be wary of false subjectification, of demeaning a symphony into "musical autobiography" (i.e., of seeing Mahler's music as a function of his life, rather than vice versa). However, this danger is matched by the equivalent danger of false objectification, of reclaiming Mahler's earlier symphonies for program music and thereby conjuring up a nonexistent aesthetic gulf between the Fourth (1899–1901) and the Fifth (1901–2). The historical break purportedly separating the *Wunderhorn* symphonies from his purely instrumental works is a myth which will not withstand a few moments' deliberation on turn-of-the-century aesthetics. To do justice to Mahler's "art work of ideas" we must again recall Schopenhauer's philosophy of music, which, to the modernist composers, was not simply a *Künstlermetaphysik* adding ideological decor to the drabness of their everyday practice but a full-fledged aesthetic, implemented in music and translated into acoustic reality.

When Mahler, in his letters to Max Marschalk, reflected on the meaning of programs or proposed titles for his First (1889) and his Second Symphony (1894), he distinguished between "exterior" and "interior" programs. The former can serve as a stimulus for the work's conception or as a guide to the listener. As Mahler remarked of the Marcia Funebre to his First Symphony:

> Admittedly, I took my external stimulus from the well-known children's painting [*Des Jägers Leichenbegräbnis*]. What the movement depicts, however, is irrelevant; the point is the mood it is trying to express. So it is at all events advisable at first, while my art still occasions confusion, for the listener to be given a few [programmatic] signposts and milestones on his journey . . . but that is the most this sort of explanation can offer.

The "signposts" serve as a means of attaining a purely musical understanding of the work, and that only temporarily. However, if (as Mahler explicitly maintains) the exterior program leaves the essence of the music untouched when used as a listener's guide, then, according to Schopenhauer's premises, it is in the final analysis likewise aesthetically irrelevant when used as a stimulus for composition. True, it functions as what Wagner would call a "formal motive," but it is not part of the "thing-in-itself," being no more than a scaffolding to be torn down as soon as the edifice it helped to erect is finished.

If the exterior program appears as a series of images, the interior program is, as Mahler put it, a "succession of feelings" (*Empfindungsgang*), albeit one that escapes empirical-psychological categories: "My need to express myself in a symphony only begins at that point where *dark* feelings hold sway: at the gateway leading to the 'other world,' the world in which things are beyond classification into time and place." Writing about the Second Symphony, he added: "I have called the first movement '*Totenfeier*,' and if you want to know, it is the hero of my D-major Symphony whom I am carrying to the grave, and whose life I capture, from a higher vantage point, in a crystalline mirror." This "hero," however, is neither Jean Paul's "Titan," cited in the program to the First Symphony, nor Mahler himself, but rather the aesthetic subject of the music, a figure belonging to the aesthetic substance of the work itself in the same way as does the "narrator" in a novel or the "lyric ego" in a poem. This figure must not be identified with the hero in a literary source, nor with the composer as a person: the external stimulus of the one is just as much sublimated in the musical form as are the accumulated experiences of the other. The interior program is to be found, not in a meaning capturable in biographical documents (indeed, its meaning belongs to the material consumed by the musical form), but rather in a "succession of feelings" in the abstract: "dark feelings."

The turn-of-the-century modernists, a group represented not only by Strauss and Mahler but by Debussy, Schönberg, and Scriabin as well, have been split into a late phase of romanticism and a preliminary or early history of contemporary music by historians who failed to take seriously enough the age's sense of its own identity. Nor were historians aware to what extent this split gave rise to judgments that could easily turn into false preconceptions. Composers such as Jean Sibelius and Ferruccio Busoni doubtless belonged to the modernists, as they were understood at the time, yet hesitated to take the final step to contemporary music. For critics incapable of making aesthetic judgments without first establishing a figure's historical "import," these composers fell into an aesthetic no-man's-land by failing to conform to historiographical formulae.

In his Fourth Symphony of 1911 Sibelius reached a "state of musical material" (to borrow a phrase from his detractor, Adorno) which he was never to surpass, not even in his Seventh Symphony (1924). His biographers, seeking to decipher his works as documents, related this fact to difficulties and anxieties that racked the composer in the years preceding the First World War—as though advanced compositional techniques could be rendered more intelligible by rationalizing them as expressions of impending doom.

Sibelius faced the problem of how to consolidate a style tending toward the rhapsodic by means of structures lying "beneath" the level of motivic-thematic processes. This problem was all the more significant in that it related to trends that motivated modernism as a whole, meaning the phase of compositional evolution between Liszt's symphonic poems and Schönberg's twelve-tone method.

As the Sibelius literature sufficiently informs us, the first movement of his Fourth Symphony in A-minor, Op. 63, is developed from a motivic "germ-cell," C–D–F♯–E, with the tritone as its characteristic interval. Thus, to choose the most obvious example, the second theme (two measures after B) is nothing but a rhythmic variant of the opening idea. Historically more significant (and less obvious) than its thematic transformation is, however, the transition in the Fourth Symphony from motivic to "structural" thought, a compositional feature that places the work squarely within the pale of musical modernism in the strong sense of the term. The keys C and F♯ are related as early as the passage for solo cello in the main theme, a combination of compound thirds (A–C–E–G) over an F♯ pedal point. Similarly, the tritone is plain to hear in the characteristic phrase which gives the broken triads of the theme their unique flavor (one measure after A and four before D) (Ex. 62). In other words, the "germ-cell" functions as

Example 62

the basis of a chord progression which itself attains thematic significance. Conversely, by neutralizing the characteristic interval (i.e., by lowering the tritone to a fourth), Sibelius derives from the main theme a number of motives that later form a concluding passage (four measures after D) (Ex. 63). Different aspects of a single musical idea—the tritone and the melodic contour—are abstracted from the motive and developed separately. The same holds true of the relation between pitch and rhythm. The beginning of the second theme is based on the intervals of the main theme, but the continuation derives from its syncopations. Thus, the parameters of the main theme are spread over different sections of the derived theme.

Example 63

Rhythmic pattern, melodic contour, pitch content: in the traditional notion of theme or motive these three factors "coalesce." Sibelius, however, "abstracts" them from one another, isolating them from their context. This urge toward abstraction was a quality which Sibelius, ostensibly a rhapsodist, took up in a deliberately modernist spirit. It is also one of the key features of the "structural" thought that took possession of music in the twentieth century, under the aegis of that process of rationalization diagnosed by Max Weber. Thus, however slight Sibelius's connection with modern twentieth-century music, it would be wrong to call a work like his Fourth Symphony a late-romantic relic in need of special geographical pleading to justify it aesthetically in the midst of musical modernism.

Linguistic Character and the Disintegration of Tonality

Musical logic, a term coined in 1788 by Johann Nikolaus Forkel, a Bach admirer in the age of *Sturm und Drang,* was understood in the nineteenth century to mean both harmonic and motivic logic. In the aesthetic of the age, the raison d'être of music resided in its linguistic character, and musical logic formed a counterpart to the accents and inflections of emotionally charged speech, declared by Rousseau and Herder to be the essential quality of musical expression. The debate between Rousseau and Rameau as to whether melody takes precedence over harmony, or vice versa, actually hinged on the problem of whether musical expressivity was based primarily on the adoption of speech inflections or on tonal relations governed by harmonic and motivic logic. In nineteenth-century aesthetics (less prone to confrontation and antithesis), this debate was resolved by assuming that musical expression resided in the combination of "inflection" and "logic," elements one-sided when taken by themselves. (Not until a melodic rendering of the "accents of speech" is made part of a harmonic-motivic frame of reference is it transformed from an extramusical substrate to musical material.)

The nineteenth century, though with various emphases, almost always maintained a balance between speech intonation and harmonic-motivic logic, a balance which formed the central precondition for musical expression. At the end of the century, however, this balance was plunged into a state of crisis by the disintegration of tonality, an extreme consequence drawn a fortiori from the *Tristan* chromaticism by an age that equated musical evolution with rigorous compositional logic. This crisis made it necessary to formulate and join the subelements of musical structure differently from the classical-romantic tradition so that they could again form a meaningful whole.

One genre particularly susceptible to disruptions in the musicolinguistic frame of reference was the lied. Its history, especially in the evolutionary step (or leap) from Hugo Wolf to Arnold Schönberg, reveals with paradigmatic clarity the problems adumbrated in the catchphrases "disintegration of tonality" and "linguistic character."

Wolf's three Michelangelo settings, written in March of 1897, are the final instances of lieder thriving in equal measure on the legacies of Schubert and Wagner. Yet even here Wolf, a contemporary of composers who dared to take the step into musical modernism, never touched the foundations of harmonic-motivic logic that sustained nineteenth-century music. The first setting, *Wohl denk' ich oft*, should probably be classified more accurately as a *Gesang* rather than a *Lied*, since its vocal part is so near to the rhythms and melodies of speech as to recall recitative (Ex. 64). In compensation, the instrumental part (long since elevated beyond the status of accompaniment) reveals a dense tissue of motives. Yet, rather than maintaining an abstract conflict between declamation and motivic development, Wolf partially integrates the vocal melody into the motivic nexus of the piano part, and it is the fusion of these two that constitutes the linguistic character of the music. The vocal phrase in measure 3 (B♭–A–F♯–G) is

Example 64

obviously related to the instrumental motive of measure 1 (C♯–D–B♭–A), almost as its inversion. In measures 1 and 2, a chromatic progression in the bass contrapuntally offsets the repeated B♭–A figure, and we hear the same progression echoed in measure 4 if we telescope the vocal and instrumental parts, as seems natural in light of what happens at the parallel passage in measure 8. The chromaticism, openly displayed as vocal melody in measure 8, is anticipated in inversion by the instrumental bass line. On the other hand, unlike measure 4, it is tonally "colored": the pitch C♯, under the influence of an E♭ in the piano, is enharmonically changed to D♭, though without losing or endangering its motivic identity. This enharmonic change produces an E♭⁷ chord fully within the tonal context of G minor, where it functions as a dominant to the Neapolitan six. By filling out scale steps IV, VI, and V, Wolf achieves in measures 8 and 9 a tontal sophistication in which we sense a barely integratable remoteness from the tonic. Furthermore, this tonal sophistication, together with a melody whose chromaticism betrays a melancholy aptly captured in Wolf's tempo mark, *ziemlich getragen, schwermütig* ("solemnly and mournfully"), in turn expresses the text, a lamentation on the sense of isolation felt by the poem's persona ("What mortal then did think of me or mind me? / Was not each day in life lost, void of love?").

The web of motives, then, spreads over the seemingly declamatory vocal melody, thereby enabling it to become musical language in the strong sense. But it also extends beyond the bounds of the piece. Both the opening motive (C♯–D–B♭–A) and the compressed version of it recur in the second lied (Ex. 65). Finally, the third lied develops, in several variants, the chromatic progression presented in the first, where it was extracted from the piano introduction. Thus we are fully justified in viewing these lieder as a cycle held together by motivic association.

Example 65

The exact boundaries of tonality are not fixed: the theories that supply our terms of definition tend to inflate its scope to music per se instead of presenting it systematically (and usefully) as a historically delimited phenomenon. Even so, Max Reger, like Hugo Wolf, never willingly overstepped these boundaries with the thought that the nineteenth-century legacy was depleted. Yet even the works of this composer, who was capable of accounting theoretically for every note of them, provide ample evidence of the irresistible decline of functional harmony; indeed, we are tempted to adopt the historiological thesis that, in many ages, revolutionary upheaval and conservative retrenchment both move in the same direction.

In measures 3 to 7 of Reger's lied *Dein Bild*, Op. 70, No. 12 (1902–3), the vocal part reveals an unmistakable motivic structure, with measure 4 containing a sequence to measure 3, and measure 7 a sequence to measure 6 (Ex. 66). Yet Reger, who thought primarily in instrumental rather than vocal terms, seems curiously unconcerned about the flatness of his declamation (note his scansion of the word "Namen"), the crucial issue in turn-of-the-century vocal style, which tended to abandon verse meters for prosody. Further, the relation between these vocal motives and the piano part is precarious in that he deliberately avoids giving similar harmonizations to parallel passages. This brings him dangerously close to the point at which variety of context turns into want of cohesion, and want of cohesion into anarchy, into disintegration of the musical texture.

Example 66

Typically for Reger, it is precisely in the area where he felt most at home, in enharmonic modulation, that he tended to the labyrinthine (as though he wished to vindicate retroactively Moritz Hauptmann's conservative and narrow-minded antienharmonic diatribes of 1853). In measure 5 of the vocal part the rewriting of Ab–Fb as G♯–E is unavoidable, but to write B–D♯ as Cb–Eb is unnecessary: indeed, it does violence to the context, causing a rift between the voice part and the piano, where a "Neapolitan" connection between F major and Cb major is mandatory, or at least plausible. What is more, the remaining enharmonic changes in the piano part (measure 5, beat 2: D♯–F♯ to Eb–Gb; measure 9, beat

2: G♯ to A♭) are ignored orthographically in the vocal part, which they leave unaffected. Strictly speaking, then, measure 5 is in E major in the vocal part and B♭ major in the piano, and measure 6 in A minor in the vocal part and F major in the piano. This bitonality, however, does not come openly to the fore but remains submerged in Reger's chordal technique. True, the structure of each chord and the function of each progression are evident, but the tonal context attains a degree of complexity in such a short span of time that the listener ultimately loses the thread, and ambiguity (Reger's handhold on the fin-de-siècle style) turns into incoherence. Even if we otherwise adhere to the proposition that a work of art is only as sophisticated as the most elaborate interpretation it permits, we stand precious little chance of hearing the enharmonic contradictions spun by Reger in measures 5 and 6 of *Dein Bild* as musicolinguistic refinements imparting an undertone of desperation and paradox to the vocal part (as the text of the poem demands). Instead, we are left with an impression of randomly juxtaposed chords, linked by threads which, though not severed, are so tangled that it is hardly worth trying to unravel them. Refinement, a daily exercise for Reger, turns into coarseness.

The music around 1900, as we have seen, though labeled "late romanticism" as a precautionary measure twenty years after the fact, was sensed by its participants as a breakthrough into modernism. Stravinsky adherents conferred upon it the reproach that it was self-contradictory and dichotomous, since it tended at one and the same time to extreme sophistication of harmony and to shapeless viscosity in its rhythm. In fact, the shock unleashed by Stravinsky's music has dulled our awareness of turn-of-the-century rhythm, turning its differentiation into shapelessness. But this should not blind historians to the fact that composers at the outset of the century were fully aware of the problematical relationship between harmony and rhythm, and that they set out to find solutions, as even a comparison of Webern (his orchestral pieces) and Reger (the *Hiller Variations*) will show.

One of the pieces that tried most clearly to mediate between the two was Karol Szymanowski's lied *Geheimnis*, Op. 17, No. 2 (1907). This lied, a setting of a poem by Dehmel, is dominated structurally by its piano part and follows a pattern (subject–sequence–development–optional recapitulation) that governed large expanses of Wagner's musical forms no less than those of the turn-of-the-

Fig. 80 Pablo Picasso: *Old Man Playing a Guitar*, 1903. The guitar has become a prop of modern art symbolizing Picasso's Spanish heritage. Like Chagall's fiddles, it conflicts with the spirit of modern music which ran parallel to painting in the history of ideas. In our century, affinities between these two arts are revealed not by the musical motifs in many modern paintings but by the analogous techniques and aesthetics apparent in the work of Kandinsky and Schönberg, or Klee and Webern. (Courtesy of the Art Institute of Chicago.)

century modernists still working partly in Wagner's shadow. (The technique of putting a subject through sequences or transpositions, and then isolating its motives and elaborating them separately, was a developmental device in the classic period, but served Wagner and Liszt as a means of exposition, at times even determining the form as a whole.) In Szymanowski's lied, the sequence (mm. 5 to 7) is limited to three measures of the four-measure subject, and the development section (mm. 8 to 13) concentrates on a single motive, a half step in dotted rhythm. The conclusion (mm. 14 to 16) returns to the opening of the development passage, but nevertheless conveys a sense of recapitulation. This is because measure 8 (and hence measure 14 as well) recapitulates measure 1, and also because the restitution of the main idea in measure 14 (unlike measure 8) conspicuously denotes a return following the long elaboration of the dotted submotive.

In the exposition, the measures are progressively truncated. Szymanowski, if in rudimentary form, seems almost to anticipate the technique of "variable meters": $\frac{6}{8}$ collapses to $\frac{5}{8}$, to $\frac{4}{8}$, and finally to $\frac{3}{8}$ by gradually deleting particles of the main idea, starting with its initial note and then the first group (Ex. 67). One might even regard the entire development section as an extreme consequence of this process of reduction, the notated $\frac{3}{4}$ measure consisting in reality of $\frac{2}{8}$ measures based on a residual motive from the main idea, the half step in dotted rhythm.

Example 67

Measure 12 traces the melodic contour of measure 11 in "rhythmic inversion," with the short notes turning into long ones and vice versa (Ex. 68). The rhythm of measure 12, however, mirrors the rhythmic shape of the main idea, and thus prepares for the recapitulation in measure 14. This recapitulation, compared with measure 12, seems to add fresh pitch content to a recurrent rhythmic pattern, just as measure 12, related to measure 11, rhythmically inverts a recurrent pitch set. Considering the rigor with which Szymanowski, in Op. 17, No. 2, not merely presents but systematically elaborates a complex rhythm, we are forced to conclude that he struck a balance between harmonic and rhythmic sophistication. At all events, its rhythm is anything but amorphous or monotonous.

Example 68

To explain the structure of this lied as the result of "developing variation" is not the only possible interpretation. Indeed, if we are prepared to take an interpretative risk, we might even descry the beginnings of a "matrix rhythm" analogous to Scriabin's "matrix sonority." And since Scriabin was one of Szymanowski's exemplars at the outset of the century, it is not farfetched to presume that the notion of a "matrix rhythm" was inspired by the "matrix sonority" which Scriabin was groping toward from about 1903.

The "matrix rhythm," notable as ♪ ♪. ♪ ♪, is a tacit or at least a half-hidden structure that remains in the background as a frame of reference rather than taking the form of a motive. Its separate components—♪ ♪., ♪. ♪, and ♪ ♪—are assigned to particular intervals: a descending fourth, an ascending half step, and an ascending minor third. (The tritone forms a point of articulation without a fixed rhythm of its own.) Like the harmonic and melodic shapes derived by Scriabin from his "matrix sonorities," the actual rhythms of the piece are based on a varied selection from this abstract and unstated "matrix rhythm." In other words, the exposition of this piece is based on an everchanging selection from a set of rhythms functioning as a frame of reference.

Still, Szymanowski (unlike Scriabin) gives us no cause to speak of a formal law pursued to ultimate conclusions. His approach remained in embryo and devoid of immediate historical consequences.

Mahler never seemed to cast doubt on tonality, not even in his most advanced works, such as *In diesem Wetter,* the last of the *Kindertotenlieder* (1901–4). Tonality remained for him an unchallenged prerequisite, though it is unclear just how far it was crucial to the internal makeup of his music. (It is doctrinaire to assume that tonality must necessarily predominate wherever it happens to appear.) And as exaggerated as it would be to claim that he undermined tonality by ignoring its relevance, it is equally clear from the music of Alban Berg that a continuation of the Mahler tradition was also possible under the conditions of atonality. Mahler thought primarily in terms of counterpoint, a fact which established, or decisively contributed to, his individual style in an age virtually held in thrall to the harmonic consequences of *Tristan.* (We are not obligated to pursue the unfortunate question, first circulated by Ernst Kurth, as to whether harmony is the foundation or the result of counterpoint in order to do analytic justice to the relation between the two.)

Measures 54 to 60 of *In diesem Wetter* are a variant of measures 35 to 41 on the same line of text. Yet the relation between these parallel passages cannot be described with the terminology developed for variation technique and thematic-motivic manipulation (Ex. 69). The differences in tonality between these passages are too far-reaching to be solely a matter of harmonic variation. Yet the melodies are almost repeated verbatim: their pitches change tonal meaning without endangering their melodic identity (or formal coherence) in the slightest. Something more than reharmonization is involved. True, it is possible and by no means absurd to isolate the subtonalities in these two passages (D minor, C minor, B♭ major, F major) and then search for an overriding tonal formula to encompass them all, but this would not bring us any closer to the underlying structure of the work. The harmony is secondary, and the crucial difference between these parallel passages proves to be melodic and contrapuntal in nature—namely, that measures 35 to 41 are based on a descending chromatic progression in the upper voice (D–C♯–C and B–B♭–A–A♭–G–G♭), whereas measures 54 to 60 use an ascending chromatic progression in the bass (F–G♭–G–A♭–A–B♭–B–C–C♯–D). Thus, the bass line changes while the melody remains the same: this accounts for the harmonies of measures 54 to 60, the enharmonic respelling of measure 54 as compared with measure 35, and the transposition of the middle voice in measure 57 as compared with measure 38. (However, this observation is not meant to propound or support a general thesis about harmony emerging from counterpoint.)

Example 69

Mahler's lied captures a death-wail in notes, and the chromatic progression from which its harmonies derive is "thematic" in both a musical and a literary sense. Namely, it follows in the tradition of the "lamento" bass pattern, a chromatic tetrachord that belonged to the musical clichés of the Baroque. This chromatic progression is thus an allegorical formula, which Mahler incorporated into the musical iconography of modernism as easily as he adopted folk song inflections. By giving this cliché the function of determining the harmony "from without" (and thereby undermining its coherence "from within"), he revitalized the expressive potential of this allegorical formula under the historical preconditions of fin-de-siècle modernism.

Teleological histories are suspected of squeezing the past into schemata that distort almost beyond recognition the rich panoply of causal connections and accidents of which history is actually made up. Nevertheless, it is hard to resist the temptation to see some of Schönberg's lieder of 1907 and thereabouts as the goal of an evolutionary process. Here the disintegration of tonality (with disintegration being a process rather than a result) unleashed a power of expression that opened to music a hitherto virtually inaccessible realm of lyric sentiment.

Schönberg's Op. 14, No. 1, a lied written in December 1907 to a poem by Stefan George, documents his transition to atonality, a transition made not in a spirit of revolutionary fervor but in full awareness of the risks involved. The text is a lyric poem of self-denial, sustained by emotions of detachment and withdrawal (its first line translates roughly as "I durst not grateful on thy breast recline"). Schönberg's choice of text is not fortuitous; on the contrary, its renunciatory spirit is one of the reasons that, given the stage of musical evolution around 1907, it was George rather than Dehmel or Rilke whose lyric tone was to guide Schönberg in his search for a musical equivalent.

The lied opens with a harsh discord of compound fourths "resolving" into a gentler one (Ex. 70). This is a casebook example of that initial lyrical sonority which Schönberg, in his essay, "Das Verhältnis zum Text" (1911), described as the pivotal factor in lied composition:

> Even more crucial for me was the fact that in many cases I was intoxicated by the sound of the poem's opening words and finished the piece without bothering in the slightest about how the poem continued, indeed not even registering it in the heat of composition. Not until days later did I inquire into the actual poetic contents of my lied. Then, to my boundless surprise, I discovered that I never did greater justice to the poet than when, guided by my first immediate contact with the initial sonority, I intuited everything that was evidently predestined to follow.

The lied bears a key signature of two sharps (as though it were just barely tonal), and ends somewhat puzzlingly in measure 30 with a resolution of the first quarter harmony into a B-minor triad. And if we base our analysis on Schönberg's principle that a work of music is an accumulation of tensions which only reach a point of stasis in the final measure, we might view measures 1 to 5 in the following musical example as a suspension or withholding of B minor. The basic chord, modified to B major, is hinted at in measure 3, but thwarted by a forward-moving motive in the bass, which follows up an idea from measure 1 (and is hence at once a conclusion and a premise). The characteristic half step of the bass motive (m. 1) is taken up by the upper part (m. 2), which is in turn imitated in the vocal part (m. 3). The piano's melodic gesture in measures 2 to 3 (E♯–F♯–D♯–G–F♯) is expanded in measures 4 to 5 (A♯–B–F♯–E–D♯), where its middle intervals now outline or paraphrase a quartal harmony (F♯–B–E), thus anticipating the return of the initial chords, transposed, in measure 5. The two quartal chords constantly recur in the course of the piece (mm. 9–10, 10, 12, 13, 14, 15, 16–17, 19, 24, 25) and harbor in embryo the resolution to B minor (the "hidden goal") that actually takes place at the end of the lied. Yet they have become autonomous to such a degree that we are warranted in saying the dissonance has been "emancipated," that its need to resolve has been suspended (or rather abol-

Example 70

ished, since it is highly unlikely that an expectation of B minor, withheld in measure 3, can be sustained all the way to measure 30). However, if we understand meaning in music to be a system of relationships between notes, then once dissonance had been emancipated and divorced from harmonic progressions it lacks justification, and therefore requires a new legitimacy in lieu of tonality lest it remain an isolated and hence meaningless phenomenon. And in Op. 14, No. 1, this legitimacy is to be found in Schönberg's manner of treating chords as motives. This principle had been prefigured by Wagner in the *Tristan* chord or the "mystic chord" in *Parsifal*, but not until Schönberg was it elevated to a formal idea offering a convincing escape from a dilemma posed by the state of compositional evolution. Yet at the same time this combination of two quartal chords, the lied's "harmonic leitmotiv," functions as an expressive or symbolic entity, a musical metaphor, in the same way as do Wagner's leitmotivs. The sense of renunciation conveyed by the words and inflections of George's poem finds its musical equivalent in an elementary harmonic formula, which, though fully capable of standing on its own as emancipated dissonance, still retains a residuum of the need to resolve to B minor, as eventually happens. And this residuum is just enough to make the brittle harmonies of the opening chords seem to "withhold" their resolution. In this way, the harmonic leitmotiv of Schönberg's Op. 14, No.

1, "articulates" the tonal and atonal implications that express its moment in history, an unreduplicatable instant in the evolution of compositional technique and the history of ideas.

Emancipation of Dissonance

The history of nineteenth-century harmony is marked by a dialectic that makes the disintegration of tonality at the end of the age seem to be an extreme consequence of premises originating as far back as the beginnings of tonality in the seventeenth and eighteenth centuries. Sophistication must be held in check by clear-cut attempts at integration lest it dissolve altogether, and once we bear this in mind, the most cursory analysis will suffice to show that, in the nineteenth century, the increasing complexity of harmony (the measure of musical progress at that time) tended to become an end in itself. The autonomy of art manifested itself in an autonomy of artistic devices, as though composers had drawn technical implications from an aesthetic premise. These trends toward sophistication were foreordained in the structural principles of tonal harmony—that is, in compound tertial chords, chromatic alteration, nonharmonic tones, and the construction of tonicized nonscalar degrees. In the nineteenth century they overpowered the integrative devices that were still capable in the eighteenth century of striking a balance. (Principles such as compound tertial harmony and chromatic alteration harbor an innate tendency to expand, causing them ultimately to self-destruct.)

This is not to say that composers ignored or neglected the need to save harmony from destruction, from dissolving into momentary effects vindicated aesthetically by the romantic category (coined by Friedrich Schlegel) of the interesting and striking. Nor was it ignored by music theorists, whose role in the history of musical thought has been more than merely to echo ideas thought up by composers. On the contrary, the evolution of harmonic theory, from Jean-Philippe Rameau through Moritz Hauptmann and Hugo Riemann to Arnold Schönberg and Heinrich Schenker, is noteworthy for its efforts to make ever more complicated and remote chord progressions intelligible as tonal, self-contained, functionally unified relations. The terrain thought to belong to a single tonality was extended to include secondary dominants, tonal deviations (instead of modulations), and tonicized nonscalar degrees; in extreme cases theorists even disavowed the possibility of key changes altogether. A similar tendency to present the increasing wealth of harmonic devices as the obverse of an ever more tightly knit integration was evident in the details of chord analysis: unusual harmonies were made plausible by being interpreted and rationalized as intensified forms of functional tonality. The nineteenth century was insatiable in its drive to complexity, in its lust for fresh compounds of thirds, nonharmonic tones, and chromaticizations. These were viewed as clear evidence of a further strengthening of the dominant and subdominant, thought at the time to constitute the true import of harmonic phenomena behind their coloristic façade, just as in philosophy the essence of things was thought to lie behind their appearance.

In the first analysis, it was entirely apt to argue that sophistication and integration were mutually conditioned, and that this in turn made it possible for the material of harmony to expand without sacrificing its functionality. Generally, as is exemplified paradigmatically by the Rhinegold motive, a ninth chord does indeed have a stronger dominant effect than a seventh chord; and chromatic alteration, besides being a coloristic effect, is also one way of making more compelling the innate tendency of chords to resolve and form progressions (what Schönberg referred to as their "inner drives"). Raising or lowering the fifth in a dominant seventh chord progressing to the tonic (i.e., substituting G♭ or G♯ for the G in C–E–G–B♭) in no way lessens its dominant effect; on the contrary, the effect is heightened. In short, the coloristic aspect of chromatic harmony is also functional: sophistication and integration were two sides of the same coin, at least for the time being. Even nonharmonic tones—passing tones, appoggiaturas, cambiatas, and anticipations—provide a means for linking chords: they are all dictated by a need to resolve, and thus make the second chord seem a consequence of the first. (Schönberg, who understood "harmony" to mean chord progressions rather than chord types, rejected the term "nonharmonic," since the tones thus named, though foreign to tertial harmony, nevertheless play a role in joining chords.)

However, there is a certain point (sometimes impossible to determine theoretically without arbitrariness) where sophistication, till now offset by integration, becomes neutralized. This caused functional harmony to atrophy, a fact denied in the nineteenth century but nonetheless one of the crucial phenomena of the age. To illustrate this process with a crude example acceptable even to reluctant theorists, the doubly altered dominant ninth chord (C–E–G♭–G♯–B♭–D) with the ninth transposed down an octave turns into the whole-tone scale (C–D–E–F♯–G♯–B♭–C), one of those extratonal additives of which nineteenth-century music was never in short supply. It is no coincidence that theory prohibited this transposition. Nor is it clear to what extent the basic form of this chord, without the transposed ninth, still remains a tonal harmony with a stronger if not magnified dominant function, or has become an extratonal whole-tone complex with lingering traces of tonality. Whatever the case, the distinction is not as clear as those theorists believed who tried to counteract the loss of integration in musical reality by reconstructing it all the more single-mindedly in their theories. Instead, it depends entirely on the context and instrumentation of the chord and on the listener's willingness to listen functionally rather than coloristically. In the words of the leading music psychologist of the age, Carl Stumpf, the limits of tonality, like tonality itself, are "a matter of point of view and referential cognition."

Given our difficulties in pinpointing precisely when, in the nineteenth century, tonal integration began to disintegrate, we can either cling to the findings of modern experimental psychology (though it is unclear how far its verdicts

Fig. 81 Arnold Schönberg: *Der Kritiker*. Schönberg's style of painting, being expressionist, accentuates the harsh and exaggerated regardless of its subject, but even this cannot hide the hatred in the critic's features. For decades Schönberg was the victim of hostile criticism. Thanks to the triumphant reception of his *Gurre-Lieder* (1911), however, he became a perennial target for minutely detailed polemical diatribe rather than being dismissed in a subordinate clause as a cult figure or subjected to the malicious silence of a boycott. (Los Angeles, Arnold Schoenberg Institute.)

apply to the past) or try to determine the extent to which tonal integration was central to a composer at all for the structural nexus he had in mind. If a fabric of motives or counterpoint suffices to hold a piece together from within, it is, strictly speaking, superfluous to advocate seamless tonal integration as insistently and obdurately as did the harmony manuals of the nineteenth and the early twentieth centuries, especially those with scholarly pretensions (as though music theory could prove its worth only by explicating each and every phenomenon of harmony, no matter how obscure). After all, tonal integration, though effortlessly reconstructable on paper, is often almost impossible to follow in the reality of musical perception. In short, the real question is whether a complex tonal configuration was "composed" at all, in the sense that the piece would fall apart structurally without it.

However, it is methodologically no easy matter to determine just what was "composed." Psychological experiments, which run the risk of extrapolating unalterable laws of musical perception from the mediocrity of their test subjects, almost always lag behind musical "reality," behind that which was "composed." Structural analysis, on the other hand, is accused of doing just the opposite, of driving to extremes its externally imposed esotericism and constructing relations far in advance of musical "reality" (though we have yet to establish just where this "reality" is situated at all). The problem faced by music historians—a problem they are as yet unable to solve—does not reside, therefore, in the menial and easily accomplished task of defending the works of Wagner, Liszt, Mahler, or Schönberg against accusations of structural disintegration by applying modern analytical techniques derived from contemporary music. Rather, the problem is that it is impossible to decide convincingly just what constitutes musical "reality" at a given point in history. The composer's intention, even when documented, merely represents material for our investigation, not its result; only rarely can we reconstruct the level of awareness of competent contemporary observers; the findings of experimental psychology, as was already mentioned, tend toward the least common denominator; the methods of structural analysis harbor a propensity to exaggeration and unrestrained system-spinning. In short, none of these factors will suffice as a reliable final arbiter. All we can do, it seems, when describing the phenomena that mark the transition from tonality to atonality, and hence the end of the "nineteenth century," is to rely on our intuition, but to hold it in check by constantly bearing in mind the dangers lurking in the methods of biography, reception history, experimental psychology, and structural analysis. (Methodological eclecticism, however objectionable in theory, is indispensable in scholarly practice, at least in its negative function as a monitoring device.)

Alexander Scriabin revived the formally constitutive function of harmony, then jeopardized by the transition to atonality, by means of a device which might be called a musical *coup de main* if this metaphor did not flatly contradict the composer's lyric temperament. Scriabin, who was born in 1872, two years before Schönberg, parted company with tonality at almost exactly the same time as Schönberg, around 1910. Hence, his later works (from Op. 58 on) can be considered documents of twentieth-century modern music. Nevertheless—and unlike Schönberg, who favored a melodic-contrapuntal texture—Scriabin clung tenaciously to the primacy of harmony at the same time that he abandoned chord relations based on fifths, the principle that had underlain chord progressions from the seventeenth to the nineteenth century. As a result, he was confronted with a dilemma: he understood music primarily as a series of chords, but found the traditional means of connecting them insufferably threadbare and obsolete. To escape this dilemma he devised a method known as the "matrix sonority," or *Klangzentrum* technique, using a complex of six or seven pitches from which different chords could be quarried, as it were, by selecting various combinations. The chords are then related to each other by their common origin in a matrix sonority rather than in cadences of subdominant, dominant, and tonic. In contrast to tonality, Scriabin's chords interact not as players in an ensemble but as parts of a whole, parts that differ by pitch choice and transposition.

A basic form of the matrix sonority, used by Scriabin with slight modifications in many of his works, is a chord made up of five intervals of a fourth, two of them augmented, one diminished, and two pure (C–F♯–B♭–E–A–D). His apotheosization of this altered quartal harmony into a "mystic chord" is merely a theosophical additive of scant interest to listeners not initiated into his "mysteries" (purportedly of Indian provenance). Equally extraneous are the programs underlying many of these works, programs which Scriabin maintained should be ignored at first, preferring his listeners "at the outset to confront the music itself."

Scriabin sought a justification for his matrix sonority in the natural sciences, with results of such minimal explanatory value that they in turn require an explanation of their own. The "mystic chord" comprises the pitches C–D–E–F♯–A–B♭, which, when presented as a scale (and ignoring some discrepancies in intonation), correspond to the eighth to eleventh, thirteenth, and fourteenth partials in the natural overtone series based on the fundamental C. Scriabin was apparently convinced that the derivation of this chord from the natural overtone series was sufficient to ensure its intelligibility and musical meaning. Yet, however typical the belief in the physical basis of music may have been for the turn of the century, Scriabin's underlying argument is fatally flawed. The intervals in the natural overtone series from the first to the twentieth partial range from the octave to the quarter-tone, including some that are useful and others that are useless for musical purposes. In a word, the natural overtone series justifies everything, and therefore nothing. Hence, the true origin of the matrix sonority is to be found not in nature but in the history of harmony. Scriabin's quartal harmony is nothing but a dominant ninth chord with a lowered fifth (C–E–G♭–B♭–D) to which has been added a major sixth, A, a "nonharmonic" tone originating in the so-called Chopin chord (C–B♭–E–A).

Scriabin's altered quartal harmony, then, is a historically conditioned entity rather than one given by nature. This is of crucial importance for its expressive content, for the relation between expression and technique in Scriabin's music. Musical expression is imparted by deviations from the norm, from customary and well-worn patterns. However, for a deviation to be perceived as such, it presupposes an awareness or sense of the norm from which it departs. If, then, the altered quartal harmony is to be expressive, the listener must not lose sight of its origins in the dominant ninth chord. On the other hand, Scriabin wished his chord to function as an independent and self-sustaining sonority, standing on its own instead of resolving, as does the traditional dominant ninth chord. To ask whether Scriabin's matrix sonority is an altered dominant ninth with an added "nonharmonic" tone (i.e., is still tonal), or whether it represents an atonal entity, is to mistake the meaning of a chord that forms a transition between the two.

Yet, when transferred from the lyrical piano piece (where Scriabin's method originated) to the piano sonata, the matrix sonority automatically gives rise to the formal device of "contrasting derivation." The main theme of his Ninth Piano Sonata, Op. 68 (1913), combines two sharply conflicting ideas, which, however, rather than being unrelated, form an authentic contrast by being grounded in a common substance: the first (m. 1) presents the matrix sonority C♯–G–B–F–B♭–D (or, more precisely, a selection of tones from it) over the pitches C♯ and B, while the second (mm. 8 and 9) does the same over A and C♯ (Ex. 71). The transpositions of the matrix sonority seemingly form the "inside" of sequences, here used in the manner of Liszt and Wagner—that is, in the exposition rather than the development section. To put it the other way round, since the only means of

Example 71

variation and development permitted by the matrix sonority technique (besides pitch selection and octave displacement) is transposition, Scriabin gave a new lease on life to the "real" sequence, a technique long worn out a full fifty years after Wagner's *Tristan*.

The contrasting characters of the motives, capable of triggering a dialectical sonata-form process, form the obverse of a structural cohesion imparted by the matrix sonority. Nonetheless, once we leave its technical aspects aside and consider Scriabin's sonata aesthetically, it invites the reproach that its formal façade —motivic contrast and the accumulation of sequences—is at odds with its interior structure, the one being as conventional as the other is progressive.

Scriabin, to repeat, attempted to legitimatize the contrasts between his themes and his use of sequences as a method of exposition by deriving his themes from a common substance and the sequences from transpositions of the matrix sonority. Yet his attempt was a failure in that the listener fails to grasp the connection between the almost intangible matrix sonority and the obtrusive features of sonata form. All that remains is a "dead" contradiction between a Lisztian exterior and an atonal interior.

The musical revolution captured in Schönberg's dictum "emancipation of dissonance" was carried out by mystics who crossed the bounds of tonality at roughly the same time, around 1900, apparently without knowing of each other's existence. If Scriabin felt drawn to theosophy, Erik Satie embraced Rosicrucianism, becoming its staff composer from 1890 to 1892. Satie, more a musical inventor and discoverer than a composer, had a genius for anticipating the future. In 1891, twenty years before Schönberg's *Harmonielehre*, which outlines a theory of quartal harmony in an appendix, Satie wrote chains of quartal chords in the Prelude to Act 1 of his *Le fils des étoiles*, a "Chaldaic pastorale" by Joséphin Péladan, who reestablished the Rosicrucian Order. These chords stand out glaringly from their historical context, portending future developments that Satie anticipated even if he himself failed to bring them about (Ex. 72). The advanced chord structure, consisting of four superimposed pure fourths and a tritone, stands in sharp contrast to the rudimentary melody (a three-note motive repeated ad infinitum throughout the movement) and to the simplistic form, a crazy quilt of repetitions, sequences, transpositions, and diminutions jumbled together in stubborn and provocative defiance of any semblance of develop-

Example 72

ment. It is as though the music were frozen to the spot instead of coming into flux. This immobility and lack of development, this concentration on the musical moment, accounts in turn for Satie's use of quartal harmonies: by emancipating dissonance, by suspending the age-old need for dissonant chords to resolve and form progressions, Satie isolated the individual sonority, thereby extracting it as an acoustic phenomenon from the temporal progress of the music. His "advanced" chord structures, in glaring contradiction to his rudimentary form, thus have the same underlying meaning as his "backward" and primitive formal design with its deliberate lack of development: both arose under the banner of a mysticism that sought to obliterate any sense of the passage of time. Insofar as Satie's forward-looking harmonies were "programmatic," being part of Rosicrucian mysticism, they could be safely abandoned following his break with Péladan and exchanged for completely different principles, whether tone-painting (sometimes stretched to the brink of absurdity) or an affinity with cabaret and music hall. Satie's emancipation of dissonance was the experiment of an outsider who either disdained or was unable to draw compositional consequences from his technical discoveries. As such, it remained an "ahistorical" fact of little or no impact on the progress of history, where problems give rise to solutions that in turn engender further problems.

Another outsider of modern music was Charles Ives. His output, written largely at the start of the century, became in a manner of speaking his musical estate during his own lifetime, only being discovered long after the historical hour had passed in which it might have impinged directly on musical evolution. (This is not to deny the existence of an underground tradition, as it were, extending from Ives through Henry Cowell to John Cage.) Ives was the musical spokesman of an America expressed in philosophy by Emerson and in poetry by Walt Whitman, but this realization was slow to take hold in a country seemingly incapable of believing that it could achieve a musical identity, and thus all the less willing to accept the fact that this identity already existed.

Ives's *Concord Sonata* (1909–15) is a work of four movements—*Emerson, Hawthorne, The Alcotts,* and *Thoreau*—of which the first three were written in the years 1909–10. It attempts a musical recreation of "transcendentalism," a philosophy whose emotional substance (the rest is of little interest to art) can be reduced to the rough formula that all things, from the most inconsequential to the most sublime, are permeated and moved by one and the same spirit. From this Ives drew the conclusion that it is not a sign of stylistic disunity but an expression of a philosophical creed to create a jumble of mismatched musical ingredients: reminiscences of church hymns, scraps of melodies by Stephen Foster, ragtime rhythms, Beethoven quotations, and accumulations of dissonance that can only have seemed anarchic to his contemporaries. Yet this conclusion, though convincing when we proceed (as Schönberg demanded) from the notion of "idea" rather than "style," fails to explain how Ives was able to achieve an emancipation of dissonance independently of European models, and this not tentatively but with almost reckless bravado.

Measures 7 to 9 from the first movement of this sonata use a motive of two ascending seconds followed by a descending fifth, an *idée fixe* recurring in all movements of the work (Ex. 73). Behind the mask of strict part-writing (Ives had received a thorough grounding in the composer's craft from Horatio Parker at Yale) lies an acerbity of dissonance that serves the counterpoint not as a means but as its ultimate end (a view Schönberg maintained, if incorrectly, of Bach. It is pointless to try to discover principles—partial transposition, bitonal superimposition, harmonic alteration, and the like—capable of being reversed in order to reconstruct an unassuming "basic form" behind this façade of randomly colliding voices. For Ives, dissonance was primary and irreducible. He seems to have viewed it as a musical expression of the energy dwelling, he felt, in everything that exists. And a historian undaunted by grandiose historiological constructs might maintain that, in an age obsessed with the concept of élan vital, Ives reversed the millennia-old notion of the music of the spheres (hitherto always bound to the axiom that music is a system of consonances) and adopted in its stead an equally metaphysical but opposite notion: that accumulations of dissonance offer a musical simulacrum of the vital spirit that "suffuses the inmost essence of the universe."

Example 73

If random accumulation of dissonance is characteristic of Ives, Arnold Schönberg's writing, though at first almost impenetrable by analysis, conveys a sense of rigorous logic, a logic that works in parallel with what Schönberg called the "urge to expression" rather than thwarting it. This applies even to so explosive a work as his piano piece Op. 11, No. 3, perhaps the most forthright example from the early years of atonality (Ex. 74). Though Schönberg placed absolute trust in his formal intuition, he did not preclude the possibility that laws for his music might be discovered in the future. We are thus perfectly at liberty to search for underlying principles. Measure 1 unmistakably demonstrates his use of added half steps to "alienate" major thirds, a technique applied in measures 2 and 3 to augmented triads, that is, to two major thirds superimposed. On a melodic level, these harmonic "additives" form motives governed by the principle of "developing variation": the sixteenth-note C♯–D♯–F♯–G♯–D–C♯ in measure 1 is transformed by omission and alteration to C♯–D♯– D–C, shifted to G–A–E–D, and finally truncated again to C♯–G–F.

Example 74

Not only melody but harmony too takes on "motivic" significance: the quartal harmony A–D♯–G♯ recurs unchanged in measures 1, 2, and 3 like a sort of harmonic leitmotiv, with a remnant of this motive (D♯–A) functioning as a "cadence" at the end of the section. All the same, our attempt to discover musical logic in every corner of this piece reaches a limit beyond which analysis, albeit possible, is of doubtful value. It may or may not be meaningful to explain the lower voice in measure 2 (E–G♯–A♯) as a diastematic and rhythmic cancrizans of the middle voice (E♭–D♭–A). If we accept this derivation, however, measure 2 falls effortlessly into a scheme of augmented triads, added seconds, developing variation, harmonic leitmotiv, and retrograde counterpoint. Whatever the case, we have little cause to speak of "random sonorities."

The work's rigorous texture complements rather than contradicts its emancipated dissonance. Similarly, it was in the strict metrical and rhyme schemes of the George poem that served for the final movement of his String Quartet, Op. 10, that Schönberg sensed the "air from another planet" which he involuntarily associated with the liberation of dissonance. As he wrote in retrospect:

> The thing that distinguishes dissonances from consonances is not their greater or lesser degree of beauty but their greater or lesser degree of intelligibility. . . . To say that dissonance has been "emancipated" means that it has been made equally as intelligible as consonance. A style based on this assumption will treat dissonances like consonances and dispense with a tonal center.

Schönberg's thesis of the intelligibility of dissonance implies nothing less than that even complex sonorities can, with sufficient effort, be seen as clear and self-contained entities that do not require derivation from another chord. Yet it is uncertain whether intelligibility is enough. True, the quartal harmony C–F–Bb–Eb is immediately understandable as a complex of tonal relations; indeed, according to the norms of the Pythagorean system, it is even simpler than a second-inversion dominant C–F–A–Eb, which requires resolution in a tonal composition. But an emancipated dissonance, unlike its unemancipated forebears, is an event without consequences, an isolated sonority. The chord has been robbed, not of its intelligibility, but of its implications. For Schönberg, who thought of music in terms of musical logic, this was an aesthetic flaw, insufferable even in a piece with the explosive emotional force of Op. 11, No. 3. Harmonic leitmotiv, complementary harmony, chains of intervals or chords with added seconds, and the motivic vindication of these harmonic additives by developing variation: all of these principles offset the emancipation of dissonance, weaving the individual sonorities into a network of relationships (and thereby justifying them aesthetically) just at the point where they threaten to become isolated. In the earliest documents of contemporary music—documents that likewise mark the end of nineteenth-century compositional history—expressivity and logic, rigor and emancipation appear as different facets of the same thing.

Bibliographic References

Adorno, Theodor Wiesengrund. *Mahler: Eine musikalische Physiognomik*. Frankfurt am Main: Suhrkamp, 1960.

Bekker, Paul. *Gustav Mahlers Sinfonien*. Berlin: Schuster & Loeffler, 1921.

Busoni, Ferruccio. *Von der Einheit der Musik, von Dritteltönen und junger Klassizität, von Bühnen und Bauten und anschließenden Bezirken*. Berlin: M. Hesse, 1922.

Carner, Mosco. *Puccini: A Critical Biography*. London: Duckworth, 1958.

Cowell, Henry and Sidney. *Charles Ives and His Music*. New York: Oxford University Press, 1955. 2d rev. ed. New York: Oxford University Press, 1969.

Dahlhaus, Carl. *Schönberg und andere: Gesammelte Aufsätze zur Neuen Musik*. Mainz: Schott, 1978.

Danuser, Hermann. *Musikalische Prosa*. Studien zur Musikgeschichte des 19. Jahrhunderts, vol. 46. Regensburg: G. Bosse, 1975.

———. "Der Orchestergesang des Fin de siècle." *Die Musikforschung* 30 (1977): 425–52.

Eberle, Gottfried. *Zwischen Tonalität und Atonalität: Studien zur Harmonik Alexander Skrjabins*. Munich: Katzbichler, 1978.

Forchert, Arno. "Zur Auflösung traditioneller Formkategorien in der Musik um 1900." *Archiv für Musikwissenschaft* 32 (1975): 85–98.

Gerlach, Reinhard. *Don Juan und Rosenkavalier: Studie zur Idee und Gestalt einer tonalen Evolution im Werk Richard Strauss'*. Berne: Haupt, 1966.

Hehemann, Max. *Max Reger: Eine Studie über moderne Musik*. Munich: R. Piper, 1911. 2d ed. Munich: R. Piper, 1917.

Istel, Edgar. *Die moderne Oper vom Tode Wagners bis zum Weltkrieg*. Leipzig: Teubner, 1915. 2d rev. ed. Leipzig: Teubner, 1923.

Klein, J. W. "Verdi's Italian Contemporaries and Successors." *Music and Letters* 15 (1934): 37–45.

Kolleritsch, Otto, ed. *Gustav Mahler: Sinfonie und Wirklichkeit*. Vienna: Universal, 1977.

Lockspeiser, Edward. "Mussorgsky and Debussy." *Musical Quarterly* 23 (1937): 421–27.

Louis, Rudolf. *Die deutsche Musik der Gegenwart*. Munich: G. Müller, 1909.

Mahler, Gustav. *Briefe 1879–1911*, edited by Alma Maria Mahler. Berlin: Zsolnay, 1924. Rev. and enlarged by Herta Blaukopf. Vienna: Zsolnay, 1982.

Mersmann, Hans. *Die moderne Musik seit der Romantik*. Wildpark-Potsdam: Akademische Verlagsanstalt Athenaion, 1929.

Mitchell, Donald. *Gustav Mahler: The Early Years*. London: Rockliff, 1958. 2d rev. ed., edited by Paul Banks and David Matthews. London: Faber & Faber, 1980.

———. *Gustav Mahler: The Wunderhorn Years*. London: Faber & Faber, 1975.

———. *Gustav Mahler: Songs and Symphonies of Life and Death*. London: Faber & Faber, 1985.

Pfitzner, Hans. *Gesammelte Schriften*. 3 vols. Augsburg: B. Filser, 1926.

Schuh, Willi. *Über Opern von Richard Strauss*. Zurich: Atlantis, 1947.

Stephan, Rudolf. "Max Reger und die Anfänge der Neuen Musik." *Neue Zeitschrift für Musik* 134 (1973): 339–46.

Strauss, Richard. *Briefwechsel mit Hugo von Hofmannsthal*, edited by Franz Strauss. Vienna: Zsolnay, 1926. 4th ed., edited by Willi Schuh. Zurich: Atlantis, 1970. Eng. trans. by Hans Hammelmann and Ewald Osers as *A Working Friendship: The Correspondence Between Richard Strauss and Hugo von Hofmannsthal*. London: Collins, 1961.

Stumpf, Carl. *Die Anfänge der Musik*. Leipzig: J. A. Barth, 1911.

Tawaststjerna, Erik. *Sibelius*. Stockholm: Bonnier, 1965ff. Eng. trans. by Robert Layton as *Sibelius*. London: Faber & Faber, 1976–.

Troeltsch, Ernst. "Das neunzehnte Jahrhundert." In *Die moderne Welt*. Leipzig: 1913.

Voss, Egon. "Verismo in der Oper." *Die Musikforschung* 31 (1978): 303–13.

Weber, Max. *Die rationalen und soziologischen Grundlagen der Musik*. Munich: Drei Masken Verlag, 1921. Eng. trans. by Don Martindale, Johannes Riedel, and Gertrude Neuwirth as *The Rational and Social Foundations of Music*. Carbondale: Southern Illinois University Press, 1958.

Wörner, Karl Heinz. *Die Musik in der Geistesgeschichte: Studien zur Situation der Jahre um 1910*. Bonn: Bouvier, 1970.

CHAPTER SEVEN

End of an Era

Our history of nineteenth-century music ends with the transition to atonality, depicting the end of this era as a process of disintegration. In so doing it unwittingly risks being accused of substituting a history of decline for a history of progress (the way the age itself interpreted the course of events) and thus of standing the underlying historiology of the era of romanticism and realism squarely on its head. Yet it is not the task of the historian to denigrate the past, our own prehistory, as the "bad nineteenth century," a jingoistic catchphrase common among avant-gardists around 1920. But neither should he adopt wholeheartedly the mindless enthusiasms of today's concert and opera audiences (for whom eighteenth- and nineteenth-century music history consists of an imaginary museum of great masters) and turn music historiography into a pantheon of famous names by interpreting music as biography (less a methodology than an aesthetic misconception). This is not to say that our goal should have been a "music history without names," analogous to Heinrich Wölfflin's unrealized notion of an "art history without names," a goal unattainable in an age that emphasized the concept of individuality as never before or since. But every name mentioned in this history is meant to stand, not for a biography, but for works that manifest the person as author. Psychology—an "effrontery," as Gottfried Benn once put it— is secondary in art. The nineteenth century, it is true, was so well endowed with individual personalities that the temptations of biographical narrative or even anecdote sometimes become overwhelming. But individuals should never be allowed to overshadow the generic traditions that sustained the history of musical works by allowing them both to break from and to adhere to those traditions. It is precisely in musical genres that we find history in the strong sense of the term: continuity and evolution, the setting and breaking of norms. And as the aesthetic theory of the Russian formalists tell us, it is the breaking of norms that enables structures to become perceivable at all by deviating from the customary and worn-out.

We have little cause to expect the beginning and the end of a music history to cohere as convincingly as in a novel (the tacit model for nineteenth-century historiography), even less so considering that the boundaries of the "nineteenth century" are still an object of controversy with an unforeseeable outcome. Nor can we dismiss this controversy as a pointless debate on where to mark breaks in the historical continuum. The criteria we choose to demarcate the beginning and end of an age automatically influence the way we describe the events themselves, provided we are talking about a historical presentation at all, with claims to reveal connections rather than simply list dates and facts.

We have chosen to end our history of "nineteenth-century" music in 1907, the watershed year of Schönberg's transition to atonality and Richard Strauss's about-face from modernism following *Elektra* (having represented modernism for two decades). This choice, if taken literally, implies the by no means obvious proposition that the genuine protagonist of twentieth-century modern music was Schönberg and not Stravinsky, a proposition ascribed to by practically no one at the high noon of neoclassicism around 1930 but by almost the whole of the avant-garde when the twelve-tone row came universally into the ascendant around 1950. By the same token, those historians who heard remnants of "romanticism" or "late romanticism"—in short, of the "nineteenth century"—in Schönberg's modernist works, and who found no musical trends in keeping with a twentieth-century spirit until the neoclassicism and *Neue Sachlichkeit* of the 1920s, were forced to choose as their watershed year not 1908 but 1924, the year of the collapse of expressionism. In other words, the limits of the "nineteenth century" as a period in music history depend, among other things, on what phenomena we see as constituting the "genuine" modern music of our own century.

The beginnings of the era referred to roughly as the "nineteenth century" (without meaning to confer historiological dignity on abstract chronology) are as controversial as its end. Music historians who, like Friedrich Blume in *Die Musik in Geschichte und Gegenwart,* presuppose the inner unity and unbroken continuity of the "classical-romantic age," an age extending from the mid-eighteenth century to the beginning of the twentieth, make a decision which, by ignoring the watershed year of 1814, has consequences detectable in the nethermost assumptions of their historiographical method. To ignore the hiatus around 1814 when dividing music history into periods is to accept, tacitly, a methodological premise —namely, that any empirical history of music should take its bearings on profound changes in compositional technique of the sort that appeared around 1740 and 1910 but not, or less so, around 1814. Yet no one would wish to maintain that the aesthetic reality of music was influenced more by the history of musical technique than by the less tangible changes in intellectual history. The romantic music aesthetic of Wackenroder and E. T. A. Hoffmann marks a dividing line that influenced the way music was heard for a full century. Equally significant were the changes in the history of genres where, in response to the new modes of musical thought and perception introduced by romanticism, the lied and the lyrical piano piece were elevated to forms with the loftiest claims to rank as art. There is, of course, no denying that the decline of thorough-bass as the foundation of composition (rather than as a mode of performance), the emancipation of instrumental music, the rise of tonality, and the emergence of modern concepts of theme and form were processes that made the mid-eighteenth century, in the words of a contemporary observer, a "time of catastrophe" in the

Fig. 82 *Schubert im Himmel.* The procession of well-wishers, headed by Mozart and Beethoven with Bruckner bringing up the rear (and Liszt third from the end), is intended to show that Schubert, by the end of the century, had unquestionably entered the Pantheon of classics in the minds of the educated classes. Though Schubert was famous early in his career as a lied composer, it took decades for his symphonies to be accorded a place in the repertoire, and his operas have never been successful. The touch of irony implicit in the inappropriate instruments wielded by the cupids may, or may not, be intended as a timid criticism of Schubert's *Biedermeier* stylization in the popular imagination. (Vienna, Museen der Stadt.)

history of music. But we can accept this and nevertheless maintain that the end of the Napoleonic period left a deep mark not only on political history but on music history as well, without at the same time implying that music was merely echoing politics.

Still, despite the break in continuity that allowed Bach to be "rediscovered," it was precisely the composers of the nineteenth century who refused to see in the end of the Baroque age a historical cleavage as profound as later historians have maintained in retrospect. One of the basic ideas tempering the awareness of the past in the educated classes of nineteenth-century Germany was a notion which we can refer to as the "idea of German music" as opposed to Italian opera and the Parisian *juste milieu* (to borrow Robert Schumann's term for this Franco-

Italo-Germanic congery of styles). Both Schönberg and Strauss, the musical antipodes of the twentieth century, were surprisingly in agreement that the German
music tradition as founded by Bach (i.e., before the 1740 hiatus) was the only
one that seriously mattered as far as artistic stature and compositional technique
were concerned. Despite their divergent presuppositions, Bach's Passion settings
and keyboard works, Mozart's comic operas, Beethoven's symphonies and sonatas, and Wagner's music dramas all fused, in minds predisposed to historical
myth-making, into a self-contained complex that gave nationalistically-minded
Germans a foothold lacking in politics until 1870. The emphasis fell lopsidedly
on instrumental music, whether in the case of Bach (whom the nineteenth century saw primarily as an instrumental composer and the *fons et origo* of "absolute
music"), Beethoven, or even Wagner, whose music drama was advertised as opera in the spirit of Beethoven's symphonies. Instrumental music became "German home territory" as opposed to Italian singers' opera and Parisian cosmopolitanism. "German music" meant symphonies and symphonically conceived vocal
works with claims to rank as metaphysics, claims raised by Wackenroder and
E. T. A. Hoffmann for absolute music (in their eyes the only "genuine" music)
and passed down through Schopenhauer, Wagner, and Nietzsche to Schönberg,
for whom these claims were as patently valid as they were for Mahler or Strauss.

The curious difficulties that beset any historian who refuses to subscribe to
the spirit of the age he is studying are nowhere more apparent than in his deal-
ings with nineteenth-century nationalism, which forms the context for the "idea
of German music." The age of bourgeois musical culture took it as a matter of
course that national character, or at least a national flavor, formed the substance
of any music with claims to aesthetic authenticity. Equally unquestioned was the
dogma that music must be new in order to be valid. The "national spirit" hypothesis and the notion of originality interlocked in a manner that would prove to be
precarious if we thought about it deeply enough. Taken together, they determined the aesthetic of the age, not just as codified in theory but as put into actual
practice.

In contrast, any historian who sets out in the belief that nineteenth-century
nationalism is less a principle of historiography than part of its material is confronted with a problem similar to that posed by a "music history without names"
in an age dominated by the idea of individuality. Namely, he has to attach or
impute a basic structure to an age that knew, and wanted to know, nothing about
it. Still, there is apparently some profit to be gained from assuming that any history of nineteenth-century music which seeks to convey a coherent picture of its
subject rather than listing the holdings of an imaginary museum, and yet treats
music as art rather than as a document on extramusical occurrences, might proceed primarily from the evolution of musical genres. It was here that aesthetic
and compositional principles intermingled with conditions from intellectual and
social history, so that a history of musical genres outlines a structural history
relating the various facets of music-historical processes. Admittedly, this premise
contradicts the notions of the age we wish to characterize, an age which saw

Fig. 83 Small Auditorium in the Copenhagen Concert Palais, c. 1904. The prevailing doctrine of nineteenth-century music aesthetics—the idea of "absolute" music, divorced from purposes and causes, subjects and clear-cut emotions—gave rise again and again, from the outset of the era, to the demand for an "invisible orchestra" concealing the mundane origins of transcendental music. What Wagner was able to institute in Bayreuth was also, around 1900, attempted in the concert hall. Admittedly, when the screen hiding the musicians is covered with paintings, as here in the Copenhagen Concert Palais, the end of a purely abstract conception of music is thwarted by the means. (Kiel, Musikwissenschaftliches Institut der Universität.)

works of music as the products of mutually incompatible individuals, each contesting the other's right to exist. But any history that aspires to be more than a compilation of dead facts, and yet shuns the historiographically comfortable path offered by aesthetic misconceptions such as viewing music as biography in notes, or as the expression of a national spirit emerging from the depths of the collective unconscious, can hardly afford to do otherwise.

Glossary

The definitions given here are not intended to be complete in a lexicographical sense. Instead, they are limited to matters which the reader needs to know in order to understand this book.

a cappella   Vocal writing without instruments, particularly in the sixteenth-century style. It survived in church music from the seventeenth century on as the "old style" (*stile antico*).

allemande (Ger. "Deutscher Tanz")   Dance in duple meter ($\frac{4}{4}$) and moderate tempo. It was frequently used in the seventeenth and eighteenth centuries as the opening movement of a suite.

altered harmony   The alteration of chords by raising or lowering individual pitches (G–B–D♯ or G–B–D♭ for G–B–D). In the nineteenth century harmonic alteration led to an intensification and ultimately, through frequent application, to a dissolution of functional tonality.

appoggiatura   Use of a lower or an upper neighbor note to postpone the occurrence of a chordal tone.

aria   In nineteenth-century opera, a large-scale, multisectional type of solo song, frequently divided into an initial section in slow tempo (cantabile), a second in faster tempo (cabaletta), and a still faster *stretta*.

aria con pertichini   Aria with interpolations or accompaniment parts for one or more supporting characters or the chorus.

arietta   In late eighteenth- and early nineteenth-century *opéra comique*, a simple piece for solo voice, distinguished from the aria by its brevity and folklike tone.

arioso   A cross between recitative, from which it derives its open-ended form, and the aria, the source of its melodic style.

atonality   The dissociation of chords from a tonal center. Arnold Schönberg's transition to atonality around 1907 marked the onset of modern music in our century.

augmentation   An increase in the duration of the notes in a theme or motive, usually in the proportion 1:2.

ballad   Narrative song, frequently treating subjects from legend or myth. In the nineteenth century it was both a genre in its own right (Schubert's *Erlkönig*) and part of an opera (Senta's ballad in Wagner's *Der Fliegende Holländer*). Robert Schumann took the solo ballad as a basis for developing the choral ballad.

bass pattern   Stereotype bass line used as a foundation for varying the upper voices.

bel canto   Italian ideal of "beautiful singing." *Bel canto* includes fixed characteristics, such as *messa di voce* (i.e., varying the dynamics of a sustained pitch), as well as historically mutable elements, such as ornamentation in the eighteenth century or, in the nineteenth, the incorporation of cantabile and emphatic declamation.

berceuse   Lullaby, frequently in $\frac{6}{8}$ meter; a type of nineteenth-century character piece.

Biedermeier   Style of the Restoration period from 1814 to 1848. Unlike romantic music of the time, it was noted for its fondness for simplicity and a strict dependence on bourgeois institutions: domestic music-making, choral groups (*Liedertafeln*), oratorio societies (*Singakademien*).

bourdon   Sustained drone or pedal point in the low register.

cabaletta   In nineteenth-century Italian opera, the second, fast-paced section of an aria, occasioned by a change in the situation on stage.

cadence   A concluding sequence of chords, consisting of dominant and tonic, subdominant and tonic, or subdominant, dominant, and tonic.

cadenza   In concert music, an improvisation by the soloist which begins with a tonic six-four chord and draws out the tension of a final cadence.

cancrizans   In canon and fugue technique, the playing of a theme in retrograde motion; also applied to the twelve-tone series in dodecaphonic technique.

cantabile (It. "singable")   A term associated since the eighteenth century with simple, sustained, expressive melody, frequently characterized by the alteration of passionate declamatory sections and expansive endings.

cantata   A seventeenth-century genre for solo voice with a multisectional form made up of recitatives and arias. In the early eighteenth century cantata form was transferred to the Protestant "church piece." Thereafter the term came to refer primarily to multimovement sacred works made up of choruses and solo numbers, and secondarily to similarly constituted secular works.

cantilena   Singing of a markedly lyrical and cantabile character.

canzonetta   Short, songlike piece for voice.

cavatina   In late eighteenth- and nineteenth-century opera, a form for solo voice which was simpler in character and less extended than the aria.

chamber music   Term used from the sixteenth to the early eighteenth century to refer to vocal or instrumental music intended for "private" performance, unlike the "public" music of church and theater. Since the late eighteenth century chamber music has been a collective term for instrumental music with one instrument per part, in contrast to orchestral music.

character piece   Instrumental piece, particularly for piano, either self-contained or part of a cycle. In the nineteenth century it drew on the concept of "poetic" music, which it was able to realize by depicting a program, adopting a literary genre (rhapsody), or evoking a type of functional music (nocturne).

chord progression   A succession of chords linked by the movement of their bass voices, as opposed to their relation to a tonic center.

chromaticism "Coloring" (altering) a pitch by raising or lowering it by a half step (e.g., D to D♭ or D to D♯).

coda Concluding section of a movement in sonata form. In the nineteenth century the coda was frequently expanded into a second development section.

comédie larmoyante (Fr. "tearful comedy") The sentimental play of the eighteenth century, in which the bourgeoisie was presented in serious roles rather than as the butt of comedy. It entered music theater as *opera semiseria*.

contredanse (Eng. "country dance") In the eighteenth century, a duple-meter dance in quick tempo. It served as the model for Haydn's symphony finales in $\frac{4}{8}$ meter.

couplet A strophic song with trenchant refrain, used in *opéra comique* and operetta and as an interpolated vocal number in stage plays and cabaret.

courante Originally a fast, later a moderate dance in triple meter, frequently with a change from $\frac{6}{4}$ to $\frac{3}{2}$ rhythm. In the seventeenth and eighteenth centuries it was often the second movement in a suite.

development The middle section of sonata-allegro form, in which the thematic material of the exposition is broken down into submotives and incorporated into modulating sequences and passages of counterpoint, thereby causing, in the words of August Halm, the reconstitution of the original themes in the recapitulation to become an "event."

diastematic Pertaining to the pitch structure of a melody.

diatonic The division of the octave into five whole steps and two half steps (D–E–F–G–A–B–C, with half steps E–F and B–C). It is derived from the circle of fifths (F–C–G–D–A–E–B).

diminution Shortening the duration of the notes in a theme, either proportionately (2:1 or 4:1) or by dividing a larger value into two or more smaller ones (two quarter notes for one half note).

dodecaphony Twelve-tone technique, i.e., the derivation of a piece or passage from a fixed sequence of the twelve notes of the chromatic scale.

Dorian sixth Raised sixth degree of the scale (B instead of B♭ over D) which distinguishes the Dorian mode on D from D minor.

drame lyrique French operatic genre of the second half of the nineteenth century, generally performed at the Théâtre Lyrique in Paris. It differs from *opéra comique* by the seriousness of its subject matter, and from grand opera by its lyric character.

duet In nineteenth-century opera, a vocal form involving two characters. It differs from musical dialogue, as represented by Wagner and Mussorgsky, in its regular periodic structure, repetition of sections, and its use of two voices singing simultaneously.

elegy Literary genre, defined in Antiquity by its form (the metrical structure of the distich) and in the Renaissance by its content (a tone of plaintive longing). In nineteenth-century music the elegy was used as a poetic model for instrumental character pieces.

enharmonic In seventeenth- to nineteenth-century harmony, a term designating identical pitches that differ in function (G♯ and A♭). It also refers to the technique of introducing a pitch with one function and continuing with another.

entr'acte   Music between the acts of an opera or play.

espressivo (It. "expressive")   Term used in nineteenth-century scores to indicate the imitation of emotional speech or a heightened form of *bel canto*.

étude   A technical study. In nineteenth-century piano music the étude was elevated into a character piece suitable for concert performance.

exposition   In sonata-allegro form, the opening section which introduces the themes or thematic material. It is subdivided into a first theme or group in the tonic and a second one in the dominant (or in the parallel major if the work is in a minor key).

fantasy   A form of instrumental music which evolved in the late eighteenth century from improvisation and which, even when notated, attempted to preserve the flavor of extempore playing by adopting a rhapsodic structure.

fifth

    bagpipe fifths   Sustained open fifths (double bourdon or drone) used as a foundation for a freely unfolding melody line.

    doubly altered fifth   Simultaneous raising and lowering of the fifth degree in a seventh or ninth chord (C–E–Gb–G♯–Bb–D instead of C–E–G–Bb–D).

    descending fifth   A drop of a fifth (invertible to a leap of a fourth) in the roots of a chord progression. In tonal harmony from the seventeenth to the nineteenth century, this was the most effective way of connecting chords.

figured bass (thorough-bass, *basso continuo*)   In seventeenth- and eighteenth-century music, a bass part used for improvising a chordal accompaniment. Together with the upper voice it formed the skeletal texture of the composition.

finale   Final movement of a multimovement instrumental composition, or a number concluding an act of an opera. The opera finale evolved into a multipartite ensemble movement in late eighteenth-century opera buffa and into a large-scale ensemble and choral scene in nineteenth-century opera seria and grand opera.

forms of drama   In literary parlance, the "closed" drama of Racine, which entered music history in the Metastasian opera of the eighteenth century, is distinguished from the "open-ended" drama of Shakespeare, which influenced nineteenth-century librettists.

fugato   Passage of fugal writing within a larger piece or movement—e.g., as interpolated into the development section of a sonata.

fugue   Contrapuntal elaboration, in two or more independent voices, of a theme in two tonally complementary parts (subject and countersubject).

gigue   Quick dance, usually in $\frac{6}{8}$ meter. In the seventeenth and eighteenth centuries it was frequently the final movement of a suite.

hymn   Song of praise with religious or cultic overtones. In nineteenth-century music the hymn appeared in ecclesiastical and patriotic contexts ("anthem") and was also important to lied composers as a literary genre derived from traditions of Antiquity.

impresario   Theatrical entrepreneur. In nineteenth-century Italian opera based on the *stagione* principle, the impresario also commissioned works to be performed in succession during the winter, spring, and fall seasons (*stagioni*).

improvisation Extempore creation of music, often based on patterns or formulae that offer support to the improviser. In the nineteenth century it was commonly practiced by singers (ornamentations, however, tended from Rossini's time to be written out), pianists (who improvised on themes submitted by concert-hall audiences), and organists.

intermezzo A theatrical or instrumental interlude. The theatrical form—a burlesque scene interpolated between the acts of an opera—was a historical forerunner of opera buffa. The instrumental version became an independent genre in the nineteenth century as a character piece for use in the concert hall.

introduction (It. *introduzione*) In the late eighteenth and the nineteenth century, a term for the opening number of an opera, frequently cast as an ensemble movement or as a large-scale scene for chorus and ensemble.

inversion Changing the direction of a sequence of pitches (G–A–F instead of G–F–A) or moving one of the upper notes of a chord to the bass (e–c′–g′ instead of c′–e′–g′).

leitmotiv In music drama, a recurring musical theme or motive which is associated with a particular character, idea, or object, but whose meaning is expanded and modified by the various contexts in which it appears.

libretto (It. "little book") The text of an opera, singspiel, or oratorio.

lied In the nineteenth century, a collective term for songs based on texts ranging from simple strophic forms to rhapsodies and from the sonnet to the elegy; more specifically, a genre characterized by a strophic form or a lyrical tone or both.

lieto fine (It. "happy ending") A convention of eighteenth-century opera seria which, however, did not countermand the genre's claim to rank as musical tragedy.

local color In nineteenth-century opera (more beholden aesthetically to the Characteristic than the Beautiful), the exotic, folklike, or archaic aura of the music in close interaction with the stage decor.

Lydian fourth Raised fourth degree of the scale (B instead of B♭ above F) which distinguishes the Lydian ecclesiastical mode on F from F major.

madrigal In the sixteenth century, a literary genre without a fixed number of lines or a rhyme pattern, usually consisting of lines of seven or eleven syllables each. In music, a collective term for polyphonic settings of Italian poems (including sonnets and canzonas).

mass As used by music historians, a polyphonic setting of the five sections of the Ordinary, i.e., those sections of the Catholic service which recur unchanged (Kyrie, Gloria, Credo, Sanctus, Agnus Dei).

mazurka Polish dance in quick $\frac{3}{4}$ meter, frequently with irregular accents on the weak beats of the measure.

melodrama Stage play, section within a stage play, or piece for concert performance, in which spoken lines are underscored and illustrated by instrumental music.

menuet French dance in moderate $\frac{3}{4}$ meter, used at court in Versailles from the mid-seventeenth century and fashionable throughout Europe in the eighteenth century. In stylized form it was incorporated in the symphony as a third movement.

mise-en-scène Stage production; a blanket term for direction, sets, and costumes.

Mixolydian seventh Lowered seventh degree of the scale (B♭ instead of B over C) which distinguishes the Mixolydian mode on C from C major.

modern music Collective term for the twentieth-century avant-garde styles deriving from Arnold Schönberg and Igor Stravinsky. Formerly a term denoting the music of the immediate present, it later crystallized into the name of a period (as opposed to the romantic and classic periods).

modulation Transition from one key to another.

monody "Song for one voice." In the seventeenth century it denoted the new type of solo song which, unlike polyphonic song, was accompanied by a figured bass and sought a precise rendering of the text and the presentation of specific emotions.

monodrama Stage play with only one character speaking and acting.

motet Since the fifteenth century, a polyphonic setting of a sacred or sometimes a eulogistic secular text, usually in prose (Latin in Catholic regions but also vernacular in Protestant ones). From the seventeenth century the motet was a vehicle for the older polyphonic style, as opposed to the cantata.

music drama Wagner's species of opera beginning with *Das Rheingold* (1854). It was characterized by "musical prose" (the disintegration of regular period structure), "endless melody" (the abandonment of self-contained musical numbers and the recitative-aria distinction in favor of a through-composed texture), and a web of leitmotivs pervading virtually the entire structure of the music.

musique savante (Fr. "learned music") A term referring to German instrumental music, which was regarded in France as strange and forbidding.

musiquette Light music.

natural overtone series The overtones or partials of a vibration perceived as a single pitch. The first six partials form a major triad (C–c–g–c′–e′–g′), and were hence regarded by "physicalist" theoreticians of the eighteenth and nineteenth centuries as a basis in nature for tonal harmony.

Neapolitan sixth An altered subdominant chord—e.g., D–F–B♭ in A major or minor.

neoromanticism Term variously used to distinguish any later romantic period (e.g., those around 1830, 1850, or 1900) from an earlier one. It has remained in the parlance of music historians particularly in reference to the romanticism of the second half of the nineteenth century, a romanticism centered on Wagner and set in an age of positivism.

ninth chord Five-note chord compounded of thirds. In the nineteenth century it occurred most commonly as a dominant ninth (G–B–D–F–A in C major).

nocturne (Fr. "night piece") A species of character piece in nineteenth-century piano music.

ode Term used since the Renaissance for singable strophic poetry. In the eighteenth century it was also used for the Pindaric eulogy as revived by Klopstock.

opera

    grand opera Large-scale, through-composed opera (with recitatives instead of spoken dialogue) on serious or tragic subject matter. In particular, grand opera denotes the species represented by Meyerbeer, culminating in mammoth ensemble and choral scenes, which dominated the period of the July Monarchy.

number opera   An opera made up of self-contained vocal pieces numbered consecutively in the score, in contrast to the "endless melody" of the music drama.

opéra bouffe   Name originally given to Offenbach's brand of operetta.

opera buffa   Collective term coined ex post facto for all Italian opera of the late eighteenth and nineteenth centuries on burlesque or comic subjects.

opéra comique   An opera with spoken dialogue (instead of recitative) on a comic subject, as opposed to the *tragédie lyrique* of the eighteenth century and the grand opera of the nineteenth. Since the term focuses mainly, for institutional reasons, on the feature of spoken dialogue, it was possible from the late eighteenth century for an *opéra comique* to be based on serious subject matter.

opera semiseria   Musicohistorical term for a variant of opera buffa deriving from the "sentimental play," the *comédie larmoyante*.

opera seria   Species of eighteenth- and nineteenth-century Italian opera seria, "purged" of the burlesque scenes found in Baroque opera.

rescue opera   Species of opera characteristic of the Revolutionary period and represented by Cherubini's *Les deux journées* and Beethoven's *Fidelio*. It developed from the *opéra comique* and used plots depicting a rescue from danger of a political sort.

romantic opera   Species of German opera cultivated in the early nineteenth century (from E. T. A. Hoffmann's *Undine* of 1816 and Weber's *Der Freischütz* of 1821 to Wagner's *Lohengrin* of 1850). It emerged from singspiel and the *opéra comique*, but with a tendency toward through-composed forms. Its texts were characterized by subjects from folklore and myth, its music by a combination of number opera with reminiscence motives and a bent toward large scenic complexes.

Savoy opera   English species of operetta as developed by W. S. Gilbert and Arthur Sullivan. It took its name from London's Savoy Theatre, the site of most of the premiere performances.

oratorio   A musical rendering of a plot on a sacred or sometimes secular subject. It was intended for use outside the theater and liturgy and combined epic, dramatic, and lyrical elements.

ostinato   The "obstinate" repetition of a theme, especially a bass pattern.

Palestrina counterpoint   The compositional technique of the late sixteenth century, governed by strict rules. It was codified into academic counterpoint, particularly in Johann Joseph Fux's textbook of 1725, which remained authoritative for centuries and in which Pierluigi da Palestrina figures as the foremost representative of the style.

parallel organum   Early form (or prototype) of polyphony, documented in the ninth century. It was produced by doubling a Gregorian plainchant at the interval of a fifth or a fourth.

passing note   A nonharmonic note that moves on an unaccented beat between two notes belonging to the harmony—e.g., the note D between E and C in a C-major triad.

pentatonic scale   Five-note series consisting of three whole steps (C–D, F–G, G–A) and two minor thirds (D–F, A–C) and based on a circle of fifths (F–C–G–D–A).

Phrygian second   Lowered second degree of the scale (B♭ instead of B over A) which distinguishes the Phrygian mode on A from A minor.

polonaise   Polish dance in moderate $\frac{3}{4}$ meter, characterized since the eighteenth century by the division of its second eighth note into two sixteenths.

polyphony   As used in the nineteenth century, a work or passage consisting of independent voices, as opposed to homophony, the "ideal type" of which is a melody with chordal accompaniment.

postserial   Collective or makeshift term for avant-garde currents following the demise of the serial method of composition around 1960.

potpourri   In the nineteenth century, a colorful series of selected opera and operetta tunes arranged for instruments.

preghiera (It. "prayer")   In nineteenth-century opera, a fixed type of solo aria; sometimes also a number for ensemble and chorus.

prelude   An overture or introduction; in nineteenth-century piano music a species of character piece.

prima prattica   The earlier sixteenth-century polyphonic style handed down in church music, as opposed to the *seconda prattica,* the modern, monodic style which dominated seventeenth-century secular music.

ragtime   A piano technique developed in the southern United States during the late nineteenth century in imitation of banjo playing; a forerunner of jazz.

realism   As a style in the history of art, music, or literature, a tendency to give artistic treatment to areas or aspects of reality which were previously, in classicism or romanticism, excluded from the realm of art.

recital   Term used since the nineteenth century for a solo concert.

recitative   Speechlike singing with instrumental accompaniment. Since the mid-eighteenth century recitative has been categorized into two types: *recitativo secco,* or "dry" recitative in *parlando,* or "talking," style, with spare accompanying chords in the harpsichord (used primarily in opera buffa); and *recitativo accompagnato,* or "accompanied" recitative, which tended toward arioso in the melody line and a motivically elaborate orchestral texture in the accompaniment.

reminiscence motive   The technique, used in opera since the eighteenth century, of relating separate numbers musically and dramatically by means of a striking motive.

rhapsody   Since the late eighteenth century a vocal or instrumental composition of indistinct form. The rhapsody derives from the literary model of the epic poem, which in Antiquity was declaimed by a rhapsodist.

ritornello   In the rondo, the late Baroque concerto, and the eighteenth-century da capo aria, an instrumental theme presented at the outset of a movement and recurring in the middle and again at the end of the movement.

romance   French term used since the late eighteenth century to refer to simple strophic song. The German *Romanze* is a loan word from Spanish indicating a narrative song similar to the *romance,* though generally with "Latin" rather than "Nordic" subject matter.

rondo (*rondeau*)   Musical form made up of a recurring ritornello (refrain) and alternating episodes (couplets); e.g., in an *ABACA* or *ABACABA* pattern.

sarabande   Spanish dance in slow $\frac{3}{2}$ or $\frac{3}{4}$ meter with a dotted second beat as its characteristic rhythm. It frequently formed the third movement in the seventeenth- and eighteenth-century suite.

scena   A *recitativo accompagnato* in the manner of a monologue, with arioso melodies and striking orchestral motives.

scherzo (*scherzando*)   Instrumental piece in quick $\frac{3}{4}$ meter, characterized by sharp rhythms and accents. It was frequently used by Haydn and Beethoven as a substitute for the minuet movement in sonata cycles (symphonies, string quartets).

sequence   Repetition of a series of notes or chords on a different degree of the scale. It can either be modified to remain within a key (tonal sequence) or left unchanged, thereby going outside the key (real sequence, modulating sequence).

serial technique   Extension of row technique from pitch (dodecaphony, twelve-tone technique) to the remaining parameters of duration, dynamics, and attack. The English use of the term includes ordinary dodecaphony, which in German is limited to pitch.

singspiel   German counterpart of the French *opéra comique* of the late eighteenth and nineteenth centuries, dealing with comic or sentimental subject matter and made up of self-contained musical numbers and spoken dialogue.

sixte ajoutée   Additional sixth (D) appended to a triad on the fourth degree of the scale (F–A–C in C major), which nevertheless retains its subdominant function.

skeletal texture   Texture in which a bass pattern or chord sequence serves as a framework sustaining the motion of the remaining voices.

sonata-allegro form   Form of the first movement in a sonata cycle. It is divided into an exposition which presents the first theme in the tonic and the second theme in the dominant; a development section where the themes are manipulated by fragmentation and modulation; and a recapitulation, where the entire thematic material is repeated in the tonic.

stagione   In Italy, the season when operas are performed, at first during Carnival, then in spring, and finally in autumn as well.

string quartet   Since the late eighteenth century (Joseph Haydn), a cycle of movements for two violins, viola, and cello. The first movement is generally in sonata-allegro form and, in works of high aesthetic standards, has a texture in which the lower parts also participate in the motivic fabric ("obligato accompaniment").

stretta   In nineteenth-century opera, the concluding section of a multipartite vocal number in a quick, sometimes recklessly fast tempo.

symphonic poem (Ger. "symphonische Dichtung")   An orchestral genre that was developed in the 1850s by Liszt from the concert overture and differs from the symphony by using a program and being in a single movement.

symphony   Multimovement composition for orchestra, whose first movement is generally in sonata-allegro form.

syncopation   Upsetting the metrical sequence of accents by tying a note from a light beat to the following heavy beat.

tableau   In nineteenth-century grand opera, a scene for ensemble and chorus in which the plot "freezes," forming an image that remains intelligible as a stage configuration even without the text, which is smothered by the multivoice texture.

tetrachord   Four scalar degrees occupying the interval of a fourth. Besides two whole steps, it also includes a half step whose location determines the type of tetrachord involved.

theory of imitation   Aesthetic doctrine of the sixteenth to the eighteenth century which required of music that it imitate external nature or internal nature (i.e., human sentiments) lest it remain an empty, if agreeable, noise.

tonality   Grouping of notes or chords around a center (tonic) to which they are related in a manner that determines their function (subdominant or dominant). As a principle of tonal coherence, tonality produces a system of pitches and intervals known as a key.

tragédie lyrique   The French serious opera of the late seventeenth and eighteenth centuries, which drew its rendition of recitative from the rhetoric of classic seventeenth-century tragedy.

tritone   Combination of three whole steps (F–G–A–B) or the interval they outline, an augmented fourth (F–B instead of F–B♭). The tritone was prohibited in strict, or "Palestrina," counterpoint.

variation   Changing the motivic elaboration of a fixed melodic outline, bass pattern, or harmonic-metric schema.

vaudeville   Songs interpolated into French comedies of the seventeenth and eighteenth centuries; a historical forebear of *opéra comique*.

verismo   Stylistic current in Italian opera around 1900. By adopting naturalistic traits only to subject them to traditional melodrama, *verismo* ignored the social criticism inherent in literary naturalism.

Index

Page numbers in boldface type refer to detailed discussions of particular pieces. Items in the Glossary are not included here.